Ethical Practices and Implications in Distance Learning

Ugur Demiray
Anadolu University, Turkey

Ramesh C. Sharma
Indira Gandhi National Open University, India

INFORMATION SCIENCE REFERENCE

Hershey · New York

Director of Editorial Content: Kristin Klinger
Managing Development Editor: Kristin M. Roth
Senior Managing Editor: Jennifer Neidig
Managing Editor: Jamie Snavely
Assistant Managing Editor: Carole Coulson
Copy Editor: Lanette Ehrhardt
Typesetter: Amanda Appicello
Cover Design: Lisa Tosheff
Printed at: Yurchak Printing Inc.

Published in the United States of America by
        Information Science Reference (an imprint of IGI Global)
        701 E. Chocolate Avenue, Suite 200
        Hershey PA 17033
        Tel: 717-533-8845
        Fax: 717-533-8661
        E-mail: cust@igi-global.com
        Web site: http://www.igi-global.com

and in the United Kingdom by
        Information Science Reference (an imprint of IGI Global)
        3 Henrietta Street
        Covent Garden
        London WC2E 8LU
        Tel: 44 20 7240 0856
        Fax: 44 20 7379 0609
        Web site: http://www.eurospanbookstore.com

Product or company names used in this set are for identification purposes only. Inclusion of the names of the products or companies does not indicate a claim of ownership by IGI Global of the trademark or registered trademark.

Library of Congress Cataloging-in-Publication Data

Ethical practices and implications in distance learning / Ugur Demiray and Ramesh C. Sharma, editor.

    p. cm.

  Includes bibliographical references and index.

  Summary: "This book provides ethical insight into the world of e-learning through case studies that elucidate the issues through real-world examples"--Provided by publisher.

 ISBN 978-1-59904-867-3 (hardcover) -- ISBN 978-1-59904-868-0 (ebook)

  1. Distance learning--Moral and ethical aspects. I. Demiray, Ugur. II. Sharma, Ramesh C.

 LC5800.E84 2009

 371.35--dc22

                        2008009103

British Cataloguing in Publication Data
A Cataloguing in Publication record for this book is available from the British Library.

All work contributed to this book set is original material. The views expressed in this book are those of the authors, but not necessarily of the publisher.

If a library purchased a print copy of this publication, please go to http://www.igi-global.com/agreement for information on activating the library's complimentary electronic access to this publication.

Editorial Advisory Board

Table of Contents

Chapter I

Ugur Demiray, Anadolu University, Turkey
Ramesh C. Sharma, Indira Gandhi National Open University, India

Section I
Contextual-Based

Chapter II
Michael F. Beaudoin, University of New England, UK

Chapter III
Paul Kawachi, Open Education Network, Japan

Chapter IV
J. S. Dorothy, Indira Gandhi National Open University, India
Ugur Demiray, Anadolu University, Turkey
Ramesh C. Sharma, Indira Gandhi National Open University, India
Ashwini Kumar, Indira Gandhi National Open University, India

Chapter V
Dele Braimoh, University of South Africa, South Africa
Jonathan Ohiorenuan Osiki, National University of Lesotho, Southern Africa

Section II
Technology-Based

Section III
Case-Based

Detailed Table of Contents

Chapter I
Ethical Practices and Implications in Distance Education: An Introduction 1
    Ugur Demiray, Anadolu University, Turkey
    Ramesh C. Sharma, Indira Gandhi National Open University, India

This chapter sets the stage for discussion on ethical issues in the context of distance education. The editors highlight the significance of ethics in and for distance education. This chapter further traces ethical dimensions of research. The editors have also discussed the stand international bodies and other organizations on ethics.

Section I
Contextual-Based

Chapter II
Ethical Conundrums in Distance Education Partnerships 12
    Michael F. Beaudoin, University of New England, UK

Michael F. Beaudoin, besides tracing the mysteries behind the launch of online courses' full programs of study offered at a distance by novices in the field, also describes how the modus operandi of the international distance education partnerships, Organizational Culture of the Partners, and leadership patterns in the partner institutions in the distance education field, affect the extent of responsibility and accountability for effective service to the students.

Chapter III
Ethics in Interactions in Distance Education 25
    Paul Kawachi, Open Education Network, Japan

Paul Kawachi based on his personal experience as a Teacher and the Learner in the ODL system, presents the desirable interactions involved in teaching and learning at a distance. Linking to the various theories of teaching-learning, Paul explains of how one's own learner autonomy is reduced, both to facilitate others and oneself, to learn in both cooperative group learning and in collaborative group learning in distance education. The author, after defining ethics as those pro-active interactions that induce the motivation to lifelong learning in all the students, has also focused on good and bad practices in terms of human conduct.

Chapter IV

     J. S. Dorothy, Indira Gandhi National Open University, India
     Ugur Demiray, Anadolu University, Turkey
     Ramesh C. Sharma, Indira Gandhi National Open University, India
     Ashwini Kumar, Indira Gandhi National Open University, India

In this chapter, the authors have identified eight spheres of concern, including student support services, collaboration, credibility, duplication of efforts, provision of intersystem transfer, and expertise. The aspects which fall under each gamut of concern for ethics in distance education have also been depicted. The authors have enumerated the advantages and disadvantages of facilitating ethics in distance education, besides giving a brief about the future of distance education on the basis of ethics.

Chapter V

     Dele Braimoh, University of South Africa, South Africa
     Jonathan Ohiorenuan Osiki, National University of Lesotho, Southern Africa

This chapter delves into such unethical practices which are not only found among students of both conventional and the virtual learning institutions, but also which extend to parents and tutors who cannot be exonerated, as they are equally guilty perpetrators of this immoral behaviour. The authors express their concern to the devastating consequences of unethical practices in the education industry, because of its pivotal role as a potent tool for achieving national socio-economic development in any society. They make some pragmatic recommendations for further debate at all levels in finding a lasting solution to this endemic problem as it may invalidate the virtues of distance education in the long run, if not quickly arrested!

Section II
Technology-Based

Chapter VI

     Glenn Russell, Monash University, Australia

This chapter highlights the concerns of ODL practitioner and puts forth how globalization remains a challenge for ODL designers and teachers to concentrate on cognitive tasks and market-driven aspects of open and distance learning, as it emphasizes instrumental aims (instead of social aims) of education.

The author expresses his displeasure of how the ODL functions at the expense of the social harmony and is unable to implement an appropriate pedagogy which satisfies both aims.

Chapter VII

Deb Gearhart, based on the research findings, documents how the students, in spite of being accustomed to the use of technology such as computer chats, instant messaging, and text messaging, are either ill-prepared for using technology or use technology unethically. The author also lays emphasis on the importance of nurturing ethics at a young age, as instilling ethical values is difficult at a later stage. Deb stress the importance of institutional/contextual/attitudes/personal factors related to academic integrity/academic dishonesty.

Chapter VIII

In this chapter, Rocci Luppicini renders an overview of the key concepts and strategies underlying Conversation Ethics besides identifying key elements of Conversation Ethics for online learning communities. The author also offers practical suggestions for influencing online learning communities, mainly through increased attention to conversation ethics, so that social interactions are optimized.

Chapter IX

Terry D. Anderson and Heather Kanuka, besides tracing the differences of the network enabled education and the conventional mode in terms of culture and principles, have also highlighted how the network enabled education is both the means and a institution. Light is also thrown on the misuse of Internet-based research.

Chapter X

Here, Michael Sankey and Rod St Hill investigate the changing nature of distance education in the context of higher education. The authors, drawing from four case studies, suggest a two-phased ethical approach to developing courses, which highlight integration of multimodal learning/teaching strategies and availability of opportunity for the students to discover their preferred approach to learning. "Massification" and delivering technology-enhanced courses to an increasingly diverse student body are discussed after being viewed as questions in relation to the ethics of quantity reach.

Chapter XI

In this chapter, Shalin Hai-Jew, after reviewing some relevant research literature findings, has highlighted how subject matter experts, instructional designers, faculty, teaching assistants, global online learners and others affect cultural sensitivity and localization in global e-learning, which is relevant in terms of educational ethics, and examines the importance of cultural sensitivity and localization in the delivery of global e-learning. The author has also appended a tool, "Cultural Sensitivities and Localizations Course Analysis (CSLCA)," which covers the course the four arenas of a global e-learning course, namely ecology, curricular content, planned and unplanned interactivity and instructional strategies.

Section III
Case-Based

Chapter XII

In this chapter, Ormond Simpson, attributing multiculturalism as the causative factor to studying ethical dimensions in higher education in the UK, stresses the need to review ethical issues in the light of recent developments like the increasing use of e-learning. Osmond, laying emphasis on the need for formulation of models by practitioners to judge ethical issues in distance and open learning instead of adapting from the medical fields, poses as a challenge that the research, theory and practice should be focused to have optimum ethics in the field of distance education.

Chapter XIII

In this chapter, Chi Lo Lim discusses the problem of persistent academic dishonesty in the United States. The author, besides offering cases of ODLS misconducts at an American University, enumerates the procedures involved to curb this evil and the causative factors for the students to cheat. The author stresses that the academic integrity is both the responsibility of the institution and the faculty.

Chapter XIV

Patrick J. Fahy, in this chapter, has mainly concentrated in the sphere of Canada, starting with the *Tri-Council Policy Statement* that governs research ethics in Canada, to reviewing the ethics of research involving humans. The author covers the factors that facilitate distance researchers and highlights the things to be known by all the three kinds of researchers, namely well-informed experienced (published) internationally known distance researchers, nonpublishing practitioners and nonresearchers.

Judy Nagy, discusses how, in the era of globalisation of education, a rise in academic cheating is more prominent. Citing the ready availability of technologies to the higher education students as the causative factor for rendering challenges and opportunities for exhibiting cheating behaviours, the author has discussed the scenario in the Australian higher education system in the context of cheating as a case study.

Lesley S. Farmer reports how case studies can serve as a way to teach ethical behavior. The author, taking the case of Teachers of the Library Media, highlights how a case study serve as a tool to reflect both the instructor's and students' knowledge base.

Peter Bemski and Tina J. Parscal ponder how ethical principles for online facilitation are integrated into an online training course. The authors recommend that ethical principals must be deeply integrated into online courses and be a guiding force for the teacher and the taught.

Chapter XVIII

In this chapter, the authors describe the work on computer education ethics in Turkey, starting from conceptual framework of computer ethics, to unethical computer using behaviors prevalent in undergraduate students, to the provision of the implications of ethical practices for distance education. The authors also lay emphasis on the prevention of unethical behavior in all forms, because computer science has a crucial place in distance education.

In their chapter, Harper and Luck explored the effects of online learning using a sample of 60 students from Northern Ireland and England and investigated ethical issues such as individual integrity and rights affecting online students who were Early Years Managers. The authors have focused on describing and analyzing ethical dimensions of relationships between tutor and student, and student and student on-line, in the context of the pedagogical approach of the subject/institution. The authors have used Pelz's framework, which attempts to identify best practices in online learning to examine the ethical issues as perceived by students, and found that no major ethical concerns emerged regarding students' individual integrity and rights. The authors also highlight from the findings that optimum social interaction existed when students preferred the opportunity to share and learn from their colleagues and when there was no contradiction between working in their professional context (an ethical environment) and studying online.

Chapter XX

Carmel McNaught and David M. Kennedy begin tracing their experience of how their papers were translated into a different language without due acknowledgements. Tracing academic theft under the head of translation to facilitate reach to the potential group, the authors opine that copied work can never be hidden and most of the time plagiarized work in a different language is being identified by the original authors themselves especially by the presence of graphics. After enumerating four factors, namely, language competence, personal advancement, institutional advancement and ease of detection, as drivers for and against bilingual plagiarism, the authors call for integrity in the individuals of the academic fraternity in all forms.

Chapter XXI

This chapter discusses briefly the issues which have emerged out of the discussions under various themes.

Foreword

I am very pleased to be asked to write a Foreword to this volume on such an important subject. It is interesting to reflect on why the ethical issues in distance learning are currently becoming more of a priority in the eyes of practitioners, as evidenced in this volume and elsewhere (e.g., in the special issue of the journal *Open Learning* that appeared in 2007).

There is, of course, the general issue of the rise of ethical concerns in business and indeed in public life, with some well known scandals at the highest levels in both. This gives us our first clue as to why those who work in the field of distance learning are taking time at present to stand back and ask about the ethical bases of their own and their organisations' practice. Distance learning had a stance in its first modern phase—say in the 1970s and 1980s—of challenging power. Despite the fact that the major institutions at that time were the state established open universities in one form or another, the ethos was of challenging a conventional higher education system that was inadequate in its capacity and in its thinking to want to expand opportunity to those who were marginalised and excluded, and hostile to innovation in technology supported learning. These institutions were accompanied in this endeavour by some NGOs and a wider range of institutions that took on the dual mode identity and practice, as for example, in Australia. At the heart of the endeavour from an ethical point of view lay what we would now call social justice. This term has a wide variety of meanings from the soft end of simply opening up opportunity (and that is no bad thing, of course), to more radical notions of challenging power structures and elites. At its heart lies the notion that all in our societies are full citizens, with the same needs, rights, expectations and obligations.

Since that period the world has changed very substantially, and more neo-liberal policies have driven competition into an international educational landscape, and have also adopted the human capacity theories that demonstrate the core role of an educated and skilled population in international economic survival. The distances within and between our populations, in terms of economic and social well being, have become greater. How we balance livelihoods, personal preferences and sustainability in the environment have come to be overwhelmingly important questions, the failure to resolve which threatens the survival of humanity in very large parts of the world. And how we do this through democratic participation and consent when wealth has accumulated in major international corporations to the extent that many of them run larger budgets than small nations has become more of a challenge than ever before.

Distance learning has through the 1990s been widely adopted as a means of institutional expansion in a competitive institutional landscape, and comprehensively supported by governments as a means of improving the skills of the population at scale to manage in an internationally competitive environment. It is in this context I suggest that practitioners in distance learning who find themselves serving rather than opposing dominant ideologies of the day find the need to stand back and examine the practices they work within. Some do this from the perspective of the "golden age:" They observe that change has taken place, regret it, and wish for the past to come back. This does not of course help, and the task which has been taken up so ably by the contributors to this volume is to examine the ethical challenges of practice for distance learning in a contemporary world.

There is, however, a continuity that I suggest is both possible and desirable. And that is to attempt to steer by the core notion of social justice, which while by no means a precise term does, demand the explicit making account of how distance learning seeks to include the excluded, challenge the elites, and seek through the "open" concept that is so often associated with distance learning to regard all of society as full citizens. Core questions for consideration in this context would include:

- How do we ensure that the needs for organisational survival in a competitive landscape do not obscure but can be brought to serve the ethos of social justice?
- How do we respond to the need for curriculum to serve a population that has to find a sustainable livelihood in a competitive world?
- How do we place sustainability and environmental concern at the heart of our educational practices?
- How do we examine what openness and inclusion means in our varied societies, and how do we articulate explicitly our understandings of this?

Distance learning through its flexibility and its commitment to innovation has the potential to engage with these core ethical issues effectively in my view, which revolve at heart around the issues of sustainable livelihoods for us all. In particular, in the higher education sector where so much of distance learning still takes place, we need to ensure that organisational purposes framed within ethical understandings are not suborned by the interests of those who work in them: a danger of course in all organisations.

I commend this volume to readers as an important contribution to maintaining the core activity of reflecting on why and how we do things. That remains an obligation for us all.

Alan Tait
Professor of Distance Education and Development, and Pro-Vice-Chancellor,
Open University UK

Preface

INTRODUCTION

Ethical values are deemed to have a positive effect on the day-to-day conduct in the lives of the people. More so, when ethical values are less held in the priority list, still caliber coupled with high morale has been the most adorable theme for many. Achievement and progress without any moral character seem to be more criticized than being acknowledged. And distance education/open learning discipline is no exception to confiscate this issue of ethics in its practice. Above all, ethics should be highly regarded amid nuclear deals, space growth, blue/green/white revolutions and to make this a practice, every human being irrespective of origin, education and monetary status have to join hands together right from the entrance to the exit of life in this world. For those who ask why a book on ethics in distance education, our answer simply will be, "Why not?"

OBJECTIVES

The objective of this book is to present the experiences of teachers, administrators and researchers toward the implementation of ethical practices in the distance education setting. The field of open and distance education has witnessed much transformation from simple print-based communication to the WEB 2.0 strategies. With the increasing use of new communication technologies, adoption of distance education by traditional educational institutes, and owing to growing demand on the part of learners, it becomes more important to discuss the ethical issues. UNESCO has advocated ethics in its educational programmes and has initiated deep instilling of the ethical values based on the cultural, legal, philosophical and religious heritage of the various human communities. Keeping in tune with the rapid growth in the area of scientific knowledge and technology, the General Conference of UNESCO in 1997 approved the formation of a World Commission on the Ethics of Scientific Knowledge and Technology (COMEST) which is consultative in nature. Ethics in education in general and distance education in specific has its manifestations in various forms like those pertaining to pupil-teacher relationships, research ethics, cheating on examinations, information and Internet ethics, and so forth. The main objective of this book is to bring out the experiences pertaining to such domains.

OVERVIEW OF THE BOOK

The book contains 21 chapters that cater to the theme of ethics. All these chapters have been organized under three sections: contextual, technology-based and case-based. The contextual section sets the background for the ethical field and comprises four chapters.

The chapter "*Ethical Conundrums in Distance Education Partnerships*," by Michael F. Beaudoin, traces the mysteries behind the launch of online courses' full programs of study offered at a distance by novice in the field, and describes how the modus operandi of the International Distance Education Partnerships, Organizational Culture of the Partners, and leadership patterns in the partner institutions in distance education field, affect the extent of responsibility and accountability for effective service to the students. After recalling the ICDE Dusseldorf 2001 Conference, where the dire need for the establishment and monitoring of a set of standards for ethical practice in distance education was felt initially, the author feels sad that even now there is no recognized body that ensures the adoption or enforcement of a code of ethics for distance education. While condemning this effort as an narrow-minded activity intended for profit mainly by academic institutions partnering with for-profit corporate organizations, the author presents mini-case studies and emphasizes on ethical dilemmas both at the philosophical and practical realm for those who enter into distance education partnerships so as to ensure promotion of the "right" values and fostering of ethical behavior.

Paul Kawachi, in his chapter entitled "*Ethics in Interactions in Distance Education*," presents the desirable interactions involved in teaching and learning at a distance, based on his personal experience as a teacher and the learner. He describes, by linking to various theories of teaching-learning, how one's own learner autonomy is reduced both to facilitate others and oneself to learn in both cooperative group learning and in collaborative group learning in distance education where student interactions with other students constitute a major part of the education process. Kawachi has recalled the four-stage model of learning (which illustrates the cyclic iterative process through Stages 1 to 4 to equip and bring the student to go onto independent learning in a further new cycle, starting at Stage 1 in a new learning venture) and at the three dimensions of structure, dialogue, and autonomy of transactional distance theory that can describe distance education. He defines ethics as those pro-active interactions that induce the motivation to lifelong learning in all the students, which should override individualist autonomy as a goal in education. However, the author had focused on only that human conduct that is good practice, and not on that which is bad.

In their chapter "*Ethics in the Ambit of Distance Education*," J. S. Dorothy, Ugur Demiray, Ramesh C. Sharma and Ashwini Kumar have encircled the various aspects in the realm of distance education. After a brief about the factors that made the Distance Teaching Institution (irrespective of the type) a fair option to many, the authors define ethics and state the reasons for adoption of ethics in distance education. The authors have identified eight spheres of concern for ethics in distance education, namely, student support services (administration, admission, eligibility criteria/calibre, academic counseling, medium of instruction); collaboration (learner support centre, how, why they are selected); credibility (employability vs. continuing education); duplication of efforts (material production, launch of programmes, course writing); provision of intersystem transfer (lack for interface to aim transfer); and expertise (academic activity, administrative activity, resources, research, who does, how it is done). In each sphere, the authors have also depicted the aspects which fall under each gamut of concern. The authors have also enumerated the advantages and limitations of facilitating ethics in distance education besides giving a brief about the future of distance education on the basis of ethics.

Dele Braimoh and Jonathan Ohiorenuan Osiki in their chapter, "*Creating a Firewall against Unethical Behaviours in Open and Distance Education Practice*," highlight those grey areas which should be of great concern to many stakeholders in distance education practice globally, including those of quality control, policy formulation and ethical issues. This chapter has contextualized ethics and ethical practice in open and distance learning against the operational philosophy and belief of what is a morally right or wrong behaviour in the education sector of the society. This unethical practice is not only found among students of both conventional and the virtual learning institutions, but it also extends to parents and tutors who, unfortunately, collaborate with the learners. The reasons why this is the case is conjectural. For a worthwhile education, therefore, and in particular, for a lasting premium on professional behaviour and academic credibility of distance education and, or the open distance learning to be highly regarded, clear and definitive proviso should be put in place to mitigate on multiple interpretation of academic standards.

The next section deals with ethics in the context of technology, and thus is named as technology-based.

The first chapter in this section "*Ethical Concerns with Open and Distance Learning*," by Glenn Russell, highlights the ODL Practitioner, while the chapter "*Preparing Students for Ethical Use of Technology: A Case Study for Distance Education*," by Deb Gearhart, concentrates on the learner. The note from the editorial desk suggests to the reader that these two chapters should be read together. Glenn put forths that because globalization emphasizes instrumental aims (instead of social aims) of education, it remains a challenge for ODL designers and teachers to concentrate on cognitive tasks and market-driven aspects of open and distance learning at the expense of the social harmony instead of implementing an appropriate pedagogy which satisfies both aims. Glenn also outlines certain pedagogies which highlight the prevalence of human touch for use by the ODL practitioners, and also expresses deep concern about how the pedagogy should be seen in association with deep rooted social and cultural contexts.

"*Preparing Students for Ethical Use of Technology: A Case Study for Distance Education*," by Deb Gearhart, is based on the research of how the students, in spite of being accustomed to the use of technology such as computer chats, instant messaging, and text messaging, are either ill-prepared for using technology or use technology unethically. Gearhart, with so much concern, warns educationalists that ethics, if not nurtured in school and higher education levels, is sure to mar the societal ethics in the end. In essence, Deb traces how computing technology intended for educational purposes are misused by the learners during the study process. Deb also acknowledges that the challenge to instill ethical values in students or to have students understand the issues of social responsibility leading to ethical behavior is very hard to achieve during the learning process by the teachers. Deb stress the importance of institutional/contextual/attitudes/personal factors related to academic integrity/academic dishonesty, and suggests that review of institution's policies, a work environment comprising of faculty who assist in developing and maintaining an ethically sound distance learning atmosphere, and constant upgrading of policy to be remedied to maintain ethics in computing technology courses offered through distance education.

Luppicini, in "*Conversation Ethics for Online Learning Communities*" after rendering an overview of the key concepts and strategies underlying conversation ethics, identifies key elements of conversation ethics for online learning communities and progressed to offer practical suggestions for influencing online learning communities through increased attention to conversation ethics to optimize social interactions. Highlighting technoethics, the author concludes that research in key areas of technoethics has the potential to revolutionize social practices and institutions (including distance education) relying on technology use for social benefit.

Terry D. Anderson and Heather Kanuka, in their chapter "*Ethical Conflicts in Research on Computer Mediated Conferencing for Education Purposes*," have traced how the culture and principles of the network enabled education is different from that of the conventional mode. The authors have also complimented the network enabled education for serving the dual role of being a means (by ways of networked mediated activities) and also an institution at the same time. Concentrating on the Internet-based research, the authors highlight how they are vulnerable of misuse by wicked researchers, who not only degrade the research but also the participants. The authors hold the view that ethical behavior is a conscious act aimed at social good and are more person specific than cultivated by rules and regulations. The authors also opine how the application and adoption of tools in the Internet are the key factors governing the moral values of e-research. The authors also stress the importance of free and voluntary consent, authenticity, privacy, confidentiality, and anonymity in e-research. They also discuss the various online forums, namely privately-public, publicly-private or semi-public, which are widely used in e-research. The chapter ends with the conclusion that interaction between the members of Internet communities, research participants, and the research community is the best possible way to maintain ethics in e-research.

The chapter "*The Ethics of Designing for Multimodality: Empowering Nontraditional Learners,*" by Michael Sankey and Rod St Hill, after investigating the changing nature of distance education in the context of higher education, suggests a two-phased ethical approach to develop courses, namely (1) integrating a range of multimodal learning and teaching strategies and (2) giving students the opportunity to discover their preferred approach to learning, which were drawn from four case studies. Questions in relation to the ethics of quantity reach, "massification" and delivering technology enhanced courses to an increasingly diverse student body, are discussed. A coherent way of adherence by academics to the policies set by the institutions is still a dream. The major recommendation of the authors are to have an array of different learning modalities, namely "multimodal course materials along with the additional multimedia components," so as to fulfill the needs of the multiliterate, culturally diverse and dispersed student groups.

As the chapter titled "*Why 'Cultural Sensitivities' and 'Localizations' in Global Elearning?*" suggests to the reader, Shalin Hai-Jew examines the importance of cultural sensitivity and localization in the delivery of global e-learning. She had traced the intersection at which global e-learning lies, namely cultural boundary crossing and "brain drain" in terms of economy, besides being a means to "study abroad." After reviewing some relevant research literature findings, she had highlighted how subject matter experts, instructional designers, faculty, teaching assistants, global online learners and others affect cultural sensitivity and localization in global e-learning, which is relevant in terms of educational ethics. The author had also given some helpful principles and strategies for promoting cultural sensitivity in global e-learning. The author had also appended a tool "Cultural Sensitivities and Localizations Course Analysis (CSLCA)," which covers the four arenas of a global e-learning course, namely ecology, curricular content, planned and unplanned interactivity and instructional strategies.

The third section deals with specific cases which are country specific or group specific, or based on individual experiences. This section brings out some unique examples of how the practice of ethics is followed in different countries like the United Kingdom, the United States, Australia, Turkey, and Hong Kong.

The chapter "*Open to People, Open With People: Ethical Issues in Open Learning,*" by Ormond Simpson, attributes multiculturalism as the causative factor to studying ethical dimensions in higher education in the UK. Simpson also stresses the need to review ethical issues in the light of recent developments, namely the increasing use of e-learning, which excludes the educationally disadvantaged people, and the high dropout rates, which poses the question of whether the distance education has catered to yield optimum results and done the optimum to retain vulnerable students, and the development of methods of predicting student success, which targets the means to convey the information to the student from time to time. He also highlights the need for formulation of models by practitioners to judge ethical is-sues in distance and open learning instead of adapting from the medical fields. This chapter puts forth the challenge that research, theory and practice should be unanimously targeted to have advanced state of maturity in terms of ethics in the field of distance education.

In the chapter, "*An American Perspective of Ethical Misconduct in ODLS: Who's to Blame?*" Chi Lo Lim discusses using three specific cases in the American institution, and the problem of persistent academic dishonesty in the United States. The author besides offering cases of ODLS misconducts at an American university, also documents the process that faculty members took to document academic dishonesty, the appeals process used by students, and the consequences of dishonesty, and provides insights from faculty faced with dishonesty. Besides enumerating the causative factors for the students to cheat, she also suggests what administrators should do to support their faculty in curbing dishonesty in their institutions. Concluding, the author stress that the academic integrity is both the responsibility of the institution and the faculty.

Patrick J. Fahy in "*Ethics Review Issues Faced by Distance Researchers*" explains the *Tri-Council Policy Statement* that governs research ethics in Canada, and then reviews the ethics of research involving humans intended to protect human dignity by balancing harms and benefits. He also opines that distance researchers should be facilitated by psychological, geographical, temporal, and other distances existing between researchers and online subjects to have desirable attributes of research like candor, reflection, thoughtfulness, and objectivity. The author places stress on the need of the nonpublishing practitioners and nonresearchers to be well-informed about the policies under which distance research must be con-ducted. Dr. Fahy also covers the issues related to "internationalization" and "localization" often faced by well-informed experienced (published) internationally known distance researchers. He concludes by placing importance for independence and autonomy to be prevalent in all types of researchers, which seems to be the need of the hour for all around the globe.

Judy Nagy, in the chapter "*Market Forces in Higher Education: Cheating and the Student-Centred Learning Paradigm,*" discusses how in the era of globalisation of education, a rise in academic cheating is more prominent, mainly because the higher education students are prone to challenges and opportunities for exhibiting cheating behaviours due to the ready availability of technologies. Dr. Nagy has discussed the scenario in the Australian higher education system, which is a complex mix of competing ideolo-gies and constraints, which places pressures on academics and supporting infrastructures, and the ways adapted to prevent cheating as a case study. The author also describes how the positive outcomes of the case study were used to support a plan to offer the increasingly diverse students more than one learning pathway, that is, diversity in teaching paradigms. After categorising the contributing factors to be either traditional or due to recent developments, the chapter traces the existence of academic dishonesty and plagiarism, besides highlighting the use of software to detect students who exhibit such cheating, by means of cutting and pasting from the Internet. The author, through the case study, also culminate that academics have little influence on the reasons for cheating.

Lesley S. Farmer, in the chapter "*Using Real Case Studies to Teach Ethics Collaboratively to Library Media Teachers*" has reported how case studies can serve as a way to teach ethical behavior. The author, focusing on Teachers of the Library Media, highlights how a case study serve as a tool to reflect both the instructor's and students' knowledge base. The author's choice of targeting the Teachers of the Library Media, is being mentioned in the first line of the chapter, wherein it is written that "As professionals, librarians are expected to behave ethically." The author has also explained how Bloom's 1973 affective domain taxonomy can serve as a viewpoint to examine how preservice library media teachers (LMT) become ethically competent. In addition, this chapter examines how using case studies can facilitate professional ethical behavior. The author has also traced how ethics-based case studies assist practice and pave the way to improve the day-to-day life. In the closing paragraph, Dr. Farmer has given cues for further research about the potential use of case studies, especially with the increased use of digital communication.

Tina J. Parscal and Peter Bemski, in "*Preparing Faculty to Integrate Ethics into Online Facilitation,*" explore through a qualitative case study in Regis, a Jesuit university, how ethical principles for online facilitation are integrated into an online training course for 18 randomly selected faculty members who are preparing to teach online. In this case study, for each assigned ethical principle, the participants were asked to frame two engaging discussion questions that support two different cognitive levels of learning followed by providing feedback to their partner's questions. The authors conclude that ethical principles can and should be built into online courses, and must also be modeled and proactively made a part of the course by faculty as the need for the ethical principles has been felt by both the teacher and the taught.

As evident from the title, "*Computer Ethics: Scenes from a Computer Education Department in Turkey,*" Yavuz Akbulut, H. Ferhan Odabasi, and Abdullah Kuzu in their chapter take the reader to the work on computer education ethics in Turkey. Starting with the conceptual framework of computer ethics, the authors identify five categories of unethical computer using behaviors of undergraduate students, which were classified as intellectual property, social impact, safety and quality, net integrity and information integrity, and move on to summarize the applications of the research conducted in the department on the departments' courses. However, the grand finale of the authors is the provision of the implications of ethical practices for distance education, which urge the professionals to keep themselves abreast about the concepts and practices regarding integrity. The authors also lay emphasis that, because computer science has a crucial place in distance education, necessary precautions for the framing of the base level policies and implementation of the instructional processes should be well laid to prevent unethical behavior in all forms.

In the chapter "*Ethical Practice and Online learning—a Contradiction?: A Case Study,*" Donna Harper and Petra Luck have explored the effects of online learning using a sample of 60 students from Northern Ireland and England, and investigated ethical issues such as individual integrity and rights affecting online students who were Early Years Managers. The authors have focused on describing and analyzing ethical dimensions of the relationships between the tutor and student and between student and student in online, in the context of the pedagogical approach of the subject/institution. The authors have used Pelz's framework, which attempts to identify best practice in online learning to examine the ethical issues as perceived by students and found that no major ethical concerns emerged as regard to students' individual integrity and rights. The authors also highlight from the findings that there was optimum social interaction where students preferred the opportunity to share and learn from their colleagues and above all, there was no contradiction between working in their professional context (an ethical environment) and studying online.

In the chapter "*Bilingual Plagiarism in the Academic World,*" Carmel McNaught and David M Kennedy begin tracing from their experience of how their papers were translated into a different language without due acknowledgements. Multilinguistic professionalism is an asset in the era of globalization, but has serious negative effects in that plagiarized work can be found in other languages. The authors, while acknowledging the fact that the ownership of knowledge varies with the culture, challenges the academic community not to do academic theft under the head of translation to facilitate reach to the potential group. As borders cross over for mutual benefit in this shrinking universe, the authors state that copied work can never be hidden and most of the time plagiarized work in the different language is being identified by the original authors themselves. The authors have highlighted that they were able to identify bilingual plagiarism of their original work, because of the presence of the diagrams in their work. The authors have enumerated four factors, namely language competence, personal advancement, institutional advancement and ease of detection as drivers for and against bilingual plagiarism. Finally, the authors call for integrity in the individuals of the academic fraternity and encourage academic cooperation not only to cultivate the habit of honoring the original work, but also to prevent misusing them by any means.

CONCLUSION

To conclude, it can be said that even though this book covers various topics ranging from general administration-based to case-study context-based to technology-based, it would claim to have a wide coverage, when the discussion on subjects like ethics governing editorial board in writing of the distance education (be it course materials or papers or books), ethics related to ghost writers, outsourced writers and hired writers and ethics related to coauthoring, and vetting and refining as a second person also gains priority. However, it is the sincere hope of the editors that a Volume II on the same topic be released to cover the aspects which have significant implications for the open and distance learning practices.

Ugur Demiray
Ramesh C. Sharma

Acknowledgment

The work of this magnitude and significance is not possible without the support, efforts and time of many persons. At the outset, as the editors, we would like to thank all of the authors for their excellent contributions. Through your efforts, we have been able to produce this valuable resource. It has been an exciting experience working with colleagues from across the world. We take this opportunity to thank those colleagues who devoted time in developing and submitting their proposals but later on could not join our team. Thanks goes to those authors also who submitted their papers but could not be accommodated being not suitable to the theme of this volume.

We express our gratitude to Professor Alan Tait for the foreword. He has been very kind to support us on a very short notice.

The IGI Global has been kind enough to accept our proposal to publish this work. The staff at IGI-Global has been wonderful, fully cooperative and provided all the help whenever needed by us. Special thanks goes to Dr. Mehdi Khosrow-Pour, D.B.A. and Ms. Kristin Roth, Development Editor. We are also deeply grateful to Ms. Michelle Potter, Acquisitions/ Development Editor; Corrina Chandler, Assistant Business Manager; Jessica Thompson, Assistant Managing Development Editor; Heather A. Probst, Editorial Assistant, Ross Miller, Editorial Assistant; and Megan B. Custer, Sales and Marketing Assistant. Jessica and Heather have been in regular touch with us, keeping a track of the progress of the book on every stage of development and replying to our queries.

Any quality work is not possible without a strong reviewer base. We have been fortunate enough to have received full support of our authors who acted as peer-reviewers. In addition, we requested other friends and colleagues to do the reviews of the chapters submitted. We place on records our sincere thanks for the positive, constructive and critical comments through which we were able to improve upon the quality of the submissions. We feel extremely grateful to Kinshuk, School of Computing and Information Systems, Athabasca University, Canada; Sanjaya Mishra, Indira Gandhi National Open University, India; Jack Fei yang, Hsing-Kao University, Taiwan, R.O.C; Bethany Bovard, New Mexico State University, USA; Carmel McNaught, The Chinese University of Hong Kong, Hong Kong; Chris Groeneboer, Simon Fraser University, British Columbia, Canada; Donna L. Russell, University of Missouri-Kansas City, Kansas City, USA; Douglass Capogrossi, President of Akamai University, Hawaii, USA; Elspeth McKay, RMIT University - School of Business IT, Australia; Glenn Russell, Monash University, Australia; John Beaumont-Kerridge, University of Luton Business School, England; Julia Parra, New Mexico State University, USA; Katia Tannous, State University of Campinas, Brazil; Lesley S. Farmer, California State University, USA; Michael Sankey, University of Southern Queensland, Australia; Ormond Simpson, Institute of Educational Technology, Open University, United Kingdom; Patrick J. Fahy, Athabasca, Alberta, Canada; Paul Kawachi, Shin-Ai Women's College, Japan; Petra Luck, Liverpool Hope University, United Kingdom; Raffaella Sette, Università di Bologna, Italy; Rocci Luppicini, University of Ottawa, Ottawa, Canada; R. Subramaniam, Nanyang Technological University, Singapore; Sharon Radcliff, Saint Mary's College, USA; and Yan Hanbing, East China Normal University, Shanghai, China.

The proactive support received from Martine Vidal, Chargée de mission recherche - Cned, Direction générale, Rédactrice en chef Distances et saviors; Wanda Jackson, Educational Technology Services, UNSW @ ADFA, Australia; Wilhelmina C. Savenye, Arizona State University, Tempe, AZ; Madhumita Bhattacharya, Athabasca University, Canada; Brent Muirhead, University of Phoenix, Atlanta; Nick Bowskill, ElearningConsultancy.com & President, World Association of Online Education; Colette Wanless-Sobel, University of Minnesota / Inver Hills Community College, USA; K.C. Chu, Department of Engineering, IVE (Tsing Yi), Hong Kong; and Jarkko Suhonen, Department of Computer Science, University of Joensuu, Finland is most heartily accepted and acknowledged. Thanks a lot to all of you.

Ramesh Sharma would like to thank his employer, the Indira Gandhi National Open University, and its staff members for providing support and encouragement to bring out this quality work. He has a special thanks to his friends Veer Sain Batra, Hapag-Lloyd (America) Inc., Piscataway NJ and Dr Sanjaya Mishra, Reader in Distance Education, Indira Gandhi National Open University. Thank you Veer and Sanjaya, for being there, always. Ramesh further expresses his wholehearted thanks to his wife, Madhu Sharma, and kids (Aakanksha and Apoorv) for the support and understanding when he has been busy in bringing out this book.

It is also worthwhile to mention here that all the software and Trademarks mentioned in the book chapters or referenced therein, are the property and Trademarks of their respective owners.

We take this opportunity once again to thank from the core of our heart all our contributing authors for their excellent chapters. Initially this book was thought to be published as an e-book. Then it was decided to get it published through a reputed publisher. Thus this project took more time to completion. Our thanks goes to all the authors for their understanding. We have been demanding much information from them every now and then, they have been very gracious in accommodating us on every step. Due to their efforts and willingness, we were able to bring this book within the schedule.

Ugur Demiray
Ramesh C. Sharma

Chapter I
Ethical Practices and Implications in Distance Education:
An Introduction

Ugur Demiray
Anadolu University, Turkey

Ramesh C. Sharma
Indira Gandhi National Open University, India

ABSTRACT

Education is intimately connected with ethics, because holistically speaking education is more than simply passing examinations and acquiring degrees. Education is character building and life long learning. Savants and philosophers throughout the history of humankind have borne testimony to this aspect of education. Today there is a great deal of emphasis on continuous and life long learning which implies that education is a continual learning process and not merely relegated to certification. Our experience in the field of distance education indicates that the profile of distance learners varies, cutting across barriers of gender, class and caste. The distance learner may be suffering from a sense of isolation as he/she makes a return to study after a gap of time or while working. It is there that the distance educator makes a positive, ethical and interventionist role by helping the student to learn beyond the stereotypical classroom situation and can act effectively as the friend, philosopher and guide of the learner. Thus practicing what you preach is the moto of ethics in distance. This chapter deals with ethics in general, its role in distance education and its significance to educational agencies.

INTRODUCTION

Knowledge is growing exponentially. The subjects or disciplines of knowledge are being specialized. Nowadays, it is not necessary to go to schools or colleges or universities to be literate in the traditional sense to become acquainted with information, adding to the knowledge we already possess. Modern means of information and communication technology are serving as information providers. But there is a dark side to this glowing picture, in that there can be such a huge inflow of information, blinding people's consciousness that they may sometimes fail to discriminate between what is right or wrong. The phenomenon of globalization and liberalization has added problems of their own to the social, economical or spiritual lives of people. In the modern world, if we carefully delve into the struggles most human beings make to achieve worldly success in wealth, power or fame, one can easily spot that human beings have become selfish and self-centered. They wish to achieve what they want to and at any cost. This greed on the part of either individuals or groups (business firms, politicians, sports persons or whoever) takes them to a level where the thirst for more and more is not satisfied. As a result, the atmosphere of unhealthy competition, raising unethical, illegal and even criminal behaviors, is created. The field of education is not insulated from this darkness. Due to lack of wisdom, the students, teachers or administrators cannot make right decisions. Accordingly, we should strive to enrich our education with principles and values that contribute to the development of personality and creates such an environment in educational institutions that they become ideal places for learning about the diversity and wealth of cultural identities and respect of others. The education plans and policies should be a tool to promote understanding, knowledge, values and attitudes among all. There is an urgent need to establish a synergy between formal educational systems and different sectors, or nonformal education, includ-ing open and distance education, in conformity with the aims of "Education for All."

Over the last few decades, the world of open and distance education has changed dramatically. It has come a long way, starting from simple print-based instructional delivery to media-based to satellites to Web-based and mobile learning and Web 2.0 technologies. As with any other new phenomenon, Web-based instruction and communication systems for education have brought a new set of emotional, physical and psychological issues. The teaching and learning through this new medium exposed the learning community to such experiences where the teacher and students normally do not see face to face. The electronic communication occurs through synchronous and asynchronous means like e-mail, discussion forums, list-serves, electronic chat, bulletin board systems, Web-based, Internet-based, and so forth. Thus, the virtual classroom faces issues like humanizing, roles, norms, ethics, privacy and socio-psychological. The ethical issues become significant, and we keep reading in magazines and newspapers about misuse of Internet and e-mail. The university administrators, teachers and students are often faced with such issues where the commercial use of institutional resources, illegal use of Internet facilities and invasion of privacy are reported. Sexual issues are perhaps the most common breaches of this medium.

ETHICS

The most striking feature of IT in education is to open the doors of global education to the student at his desktop. What is critical to the success of this mode of education is to have ethics in place; this is a world which is based on mutual trust and respect. These ethical concerns have been carried on from the traditional education to the online education, and thus form a very significant base for the future of online education. Ethics has become a buzz word as each discipline of work, say, engineering, medicine, or education, is trying to create standards of its own, thereby aiming to keep an edge over the competitors and peers. One is aware of various jargons like situational ethics, business ethics, business to customer ethics, management ethics, engineering ethics, medical ethics, and educational ethics to name a few. The simplest meaning of "ethics" is "moral principles." The word "ethics" is derived from the Greek "ethos" which implies "custom or character." The Oxford English Dictionary explains ethics as the moral philosophy or (set of) moral principles. It pertains to what and what not to do of behaviour by an individual in a right and righteous manner. An individual is expected to conduct himself in a manner so as not to be looked down upon by society.

The Greek philosophers, particularly Plato and Aristotle, have been very instrumental in pondering deeply into the ethics. Plato argued that people try to be good and seek happiness, and the only dilemma was how to make people aware of how to bring that goodness in them. In case exhibition of any undesirable behavior, the reasons would be epistemological and not behavioral. Plato pointed out four virtues: wisdom, courage, justice and temperance. Aristotle added other virtues like generosity, truthfulness, friendliness and prudence. Barnes (1979, p. 16) defined ethical factors as those which arise when we try to decide between one course of action and another, not in terms of expediency, but by reference to standards of what is morally right or wrong.

RELEVANCE OF ETHICS

The education of the 21st century is facing some challenges. Overall, world population is increasing. New means of information and communications are being developed due to innovations of science and technology. The unemployment rate is increasing among educated youth. Politicalisation of education can be noticed in various spheres of the educational arena. The students are under great pressure to achieve excellence and expertise. The teachers are under pressure to meet the demands of students. It is high time that moral and ethical values be put in proper place in the education to make it character-oriented, instead of information-oriented. The Daler's Commission report, while advocating four pillars of learning: (1) learning to know, (2) learning to do, (3) learning to live together, and (4) learning to be, identified some challenges which create tension, anxiety, frustration and depression in a person. Other threats to the educational system are due to knowledge and technological advancements, attitudinal changes in the society, and the changing nature of social institutions, like the family system.

In the technology driven world, where each human is considered as a mere number and an object filling this planet earth, the significance of ethics is felt especially in the field where the value of the individual has to be highlighted, and reaching out to the differently challenged and underprivileged is the sole motto. The education sector is a service sector in which the ethics should be intertwined in every aspect, and the newly evolved distance education system is no exception.

After the four decades of experimentation and utilization of the distance education system in the world, the moral principles are more highlighted as globalisation and business types of management and implementation of the policies in the distance education system seem to creep up. Ethics is what individuals do, irrespective of whether or not they are a part, without succumbing to peer/monetary/superior/family pressure. The demand for the distance education system is enormous as it has no boundaries and its potential for growth is without any limit. Peters (1966, p. 91) indicated that all educational are ethically driven to some extent. The problem arises when there is a conflict between two principles. What becomes important here is to see how one overcomes those conflicting situations by making decisions about the best alternative. Garrard (2006) examined ethics from the society point of view that ethics is what a society thinks morally right and wrong, acceptable and unacceptable, permissible and impermissible. One of the repercussions of this would be that ethical values may differ from culture to culture and even what is wrong or right may change with passage of time, due to social changes or needs of society.

ETHICS AND DISTANCE EDUCATION

Whether it is ethics in distance education or ethics of distance education, there is interlink between the two, and coexistence prevails among these two in standardized situations. If quality has to go hand in hand with the increasing quantum of work, then ethics has to be maintained right from recruitment of students and staff, to conferring degrees, to generation of reports. Concurrent results can be obtained in all activities, only if ethical standards are first standardized. Amid the various reforms committee which say what has to be done in the educational sector, the integrity of the individual sitting in the chair responsible for making the decision matters a lot in the distance education sector, as it deals with the molding of the character and personality of the individual who may either have a positive or negative impact on the day-to-day activities in the society. A detailed analysis of the moral controversies and the social responsibilities will help to set standards in ethics, which in turn will become a milestone in education. Macfarlane (2004) suggests instituting an ethical relationship between the learner, instructor and institution in distance education. He recommends building professional virtues like moral character, duty to learner and critical self-reflection. Similar kinds of sentiments were echoed by Starratt (2004). He reflects that intellectualism and morality be accorded priority by the educational leadership. According to him,

the work of leadership should be humanly fulfilling and socially responsible wherein the human, professional and civic concerns are blended.

Gourley (2007) has pertinently identified the timely need of ethical practices in distance education. Keeping in view the exponential growth of ODL during the last 4 decades, certain concerns like equality of access, digital divide, equality of services and resource provisions, quality control, ownership of courses and material need to be taken seriously. Owing to the distinct nature of distance education where isolation of the learner is unique, effective student support forms the basis of the success of the ODL. To overcome the barrier of isolation in distance education, the learner needs to be provided adequate experiences of interaction with the instructor and institution. The ODL systems can overcome the barriers of geography, society and economics, and broaden participation by generating their own dilemmas (Kelly & Mills, 2007). Kelly and Mills (2007) had experiences where when some decisions were taken (either by individuals or through institutional committees), issues related to equity, fairness or responsible behaviour were raised, leading to the nonachievement of goals by staff or students.

Building support services around ethics has a direct relevance to this success. One such support to the learner is through library services. Needham and Johnson (2007, p. 119) proposed 10 ethical principles for providing library services to the distance learners:

1. Ensure that each originating institution takes responsibility for providing library support to its own distance learners;
2. Provide distance learners with access to equivalent levels of library services, resources and support as students at campus-based universities;
3. Treat all information users equitably: all users receive the highest quality service possible;

4. Acknowledge the reality that distance learners may need library services that are more personalized than those for on-campus students;
5. Respect and provide for user diversity;
6. promote awareness of distance library services and resources;
7. Respect confidentiality, privacy and dignity;
8. Defend intellectual freedom, and avoid bias;
9. Respect the integrity of information and intellectual property; and
10. Ensure that professional development of distance education librarians is an ongoing process.

ETHICS AND UNESCO

Realizing the significance of ethics, the United Nations Educational, Scientific and Cultural Organization (UNESCO) in 2002 designated ethics as one of the five priority areas. The establishment of the World Commission on the Ethics of Scientific Knowledge and Technology (COMEST) was another significant development which has an advisory role in areas like ethics and space technology, ethics and energy, and ethical issues related to water use. Another milestone was achieved in December 2005 with the launch of the Global Ethics Observatory (GEObs) to deal with emerging ethical challenges in science and technology (http://www.unesco.org/shs/ethics/geobs).

GEObs comprises of three databases. The first database contains details on experts in various areas of ethics in the form of "Who's who in ethics?" The second database includes data of institutions such as ethics committees (at local, national, regional, and international levels); departments and centers in the area of ethics; and associations and societies in ethics. This database covers all areas of applied ethics: bioethics, nursing

ethics, law and ethics, social sciences and ethics, science ethics, environmental ethics, engineering ethics, and so forth. The third database possesses information of ethics teaching programs.

ETHICS DIMENSIONS OF RESEARCH

Every research has some ethical implications. Ethical issues can significantly affect any stage of research. Oates (2006, 2007) commented, "*it is possible to do research that is legal but not ethical*" (p. 55). Out of the 6Ps of research (*purpose, products, process, participants, paradigm* and *presentation*) defined by Oates (p. 11), he gives due importance to *participants.* Participants include the respondents who would be interviewed or observed; the researcher; and a member of an academic community or the people affected by the products of research. It is very important that everyone who is involved in research (directly or indirectly) be treated fairly and with honesty (p. 54). Therefore, the ethical issues must be set outrightly while designing the research, in terms of any ethical clearance either from the institution or parents of respondents/participants and so forth. The participants need to be informed of their rights like they have the right not to participate in the research, the right to withdraw, the right to give informed consent, the right to anonymity, the right to confidentiality, and so forth. Oates (p. 60) describes the responsibilities of an ethical researcher, such as he should not intrude unnecessarily into the activities of the participants, he must be open and honest in recording the facts, he must follow appropriate professional code of conduct, he must not resort to plagiarism and he must review the research work of others ethically.

Frankfort-Nachmias and Nachmias (1996, p. 77) identified situations where ethical issues may arise.

- The research problem (e.g., determinants of intelligence or child sexual abuse)
- Settings in which research would take place (e.g., school, hospital or prison)
- Research design (e.g., an experimental research design affecting its subjects psychologically)
- Methods of data collection (e.g., secret means of data gathering)
- Sample of the study (e.g., the participants or respondents would be children, or homeless people or mentally retarded)
- Nature of data collected (e.g., personal or private information about respondents)
- Publication of research findings (would there be any attempt to withhold any or all part of research findings that do not conform to the policies or practices or objectives of the funding agency?)
- Influence exerted by some external source on the research participants (e.g., pressure by the employer or government)
- Misrepresentation of other's experiences (may be due to cultural differences or wrong interpretation of data)

While studying human behavior, there may be some inherent ethical dilemmas. Such dilemma pertains to consent, privacy, consequentiality, harm, confidentiality and anonymity of the research respondent. Burgess (1984, p. 185) raised the following ethical questions.

- What would be the risk and benefit of research for the participants?
- The state may like to take some gains from the findings and thus produce such findings suited to its political needs. How can this influence be controlled?
- What information should be given to participants about the conduct of social research?
- Is secret research justifiable?
- How should the finding be disseminated?

- What protection would be extended to the participants?

Barnes (1979) found that much of the concern for ethics in social research has recently been shown due to a shift in the balance of power from the research establishment toward ordinary citizens. It has only been after the civil rights gained momentum that social research was viewed from ethical and legal angles. Prior to this, ordinary citizens had little say in what should be investigated, by whom and how. Deployment of computer technology has changed the way the data is collected and analyses are done. As a result, the scope and the potential of social research has widened. Punch (1998) cites three developments in the research field that have strengthened the ethical dimensions of social research.

- Scholarship arising due to influence of feminist methodology (based on trust, openness and nonexploitative relationships);
- shift from "subjects" of research to "participants" or "respondents;"
- signing of an agreement based on ethical standards by the researchers who get their research funding by the public bodies.

ETHICAL CODE OF CONDUCT

Ethical code of conduct is often discussed across disciplines like physical sciences, medical sciences, social sciences, anthropology and so forth. While a physical scientist undertakes his work in closed laboratory, for a social scientist it is the open society itself. It has been argued in favour of physical scientists that the results of their experiments may bring solace for mankind (e.g., cure for pain or a disease), but such immediate results in case of social sciences are not easily available. This makes ethical dilemma predominant here. Unlike physical scientists, social researchers establish personal contact with their subject, which takes on a more ethical relevance. But whatever the field of research it be, and whatever life form be it (lower level organism, or animals or human beings), they deserve to be treated ethically and with dignity. This makes a fit case for following the ethical code of practice. Literature shows that "Nuremberg Trials" (popularly called The Doctors Trial) have been the earlier cases for the ethical code of practice. The actions of Karl Brandt (personal physician of Adolf Hitler) and other doctors caused psychological and physical harm to many people and even death when they performed experiments on human beings for the Nazis during the Second World War. The *Nuremberg Code* (a 10-point code) was laid down to guide involvement of human beings in medical research. The key areas of this code relate to informed consent of the participant, results for the benefit of the society at large, conducting research in a manner as to not let physical or mental suffering happen, freedom of participants to terminate their involvement at any point of time and even provision of termination of research by the researcher at any time the ethical concerns arise. Although the Nuremberg Code was put in place, some cases of unethical practices on humans were still reported, such as infecting Willowbrook School in New York with hepatitis between 1963 to 1966 as a part of a medical research. Katz (1972) reported of an experiment where the patients (at the Chronic Disease Hospital in New York) were not informed and were injected with live human cancer cells. The World Medical Association, by taking strong objections to such cases, came out with the Declaration of Helsinki in 1964 which is still in modified form. There also has been some criticism of such ethical codes of practice (Douglas, 1976; Punch, 1998). They argue that such codes are sometimes used to protect the powerful and do not serve the purpose.

Some of the organizations having codes of conduct can be found at the following locations:

- Association for Computing Machinery, www.acm.org
- Association on Internet Researchers, www.aoir.org
- Association for Information Systems, www.aisnet.org
- American Psychological Association, www.apa.org
- American Medical Association (AMA), http://www.ama-assn.org/
- American Sociological Association, www.asanet.org
- British Computer Society, www.bcs.org.uk
- British Psychological Society, www.bps.org.uk
- British Sociological Association, www.britsoc.co.uk
- Center for the Study of Ethics in the Professions at IIT, http://ethics.iit.edu/codes/coe.html
- Institute of Electrical and Electronics Engineers, www.ieee.org
- International Center for Information Ethics (ICIE), www.capurro.de/icie-index.html
- The Journal of International Business Studies (JIBS) code of ethics for authors, editors and reviewers, http://www.palgrave-journals.com/jibs/jibs_ethics_code.html
- Market Research Society, www.market-research.org.uk
- National Association of Social Workers, http://www.socialworkers.org/pubs/code/code.asp
- National Education Association, http://www.nea.org/aboutnea/code.html
- New Zealand's Teachers Council, http://www.teacherscouncil.govt.nz/pdf/codeofethics.pdf
- Political Studies Association, www.psa.ac.uk
- School of Professional Hypnosis, http://www.hypnosisschool.org/hypnosis-school-code-of-ethics.php

- Social Research Association, www.the-sra. org.uk/ethics03.pdf
- World Psychiatric Association (WPA), http://www.wpanet.org/

ETHICAL DIMENSIONS OF INTERNET RESEARCH

The emergence of the Internet, (then called as ARPANET) in 1969 enabled researchers and academicians to collaborate and share research findings. Since then, the Internet has changed the way online research is conducted. Researchers have a whole range of different medium to conduct research like through e-mail, chatrooms, Web sites, blogs, social networking Web sites, instant messengers, online journals, multi-user environments and so forth. Web 2.0 technologies have added another dimension to Internet research. While the Internet has been a boon to researchers, it has brought legal and ethical problems too (Oates, 2006, 2007). "Some of the ethical difficulties in Internet research arise from not being clear about whether people in the on-line world are the subjects of research, as in, for example, medical research in the off-line world, or authors of works (e-mails, Web sites, etc.) which they have knowingly put into the public domain for information and comment" (p. 65). He explains that because the Internet is a global phenomenon, hence it cannot be bounded by the code of law of any single country. What can be a legal activity in one country may be illegal in another. Some countries have censor policies put in place to control the Internet. Capurro and Pingel (2002) argue that online research faces some serious epistemological and methodological questions. Some of the key ethical issues of online communication research are online identity, online language, online consent and online confidentiality (AOIR, 2001, 2002). Capurro and Pingel argued that instead of dichotomy, the tension between face-to-face and interface communication must be the basis of ethics in online research. They point out that a person may lie in a face-to-face situation, whereas they speak the truth in a chat room, or vice versa.

MAINTENANCE OF ETHICS

Who is responsible for maintaining ethics? Is it a collective venture or an individual commitment? Can it be reinforced by rules and regulations? What is the extent to which it can be violated? These are the frequently asked questions on this subject. Generalizing the fact that ethics has to be established at every sphere of the life of the human being, one can say that each organisation/institution should have a mandate of ethical values to be practiced like their mission statement. It is the collective responsibility to be ethical in all the dealings. However, because individuals make the organisation/institution, the ultimate onus lies on each and every individual.

CONCLUSION

The ethical or moral values must be inculcated since infancy so that it becomes a part of the behavior of an individual and when re-introduced or re-inforced at the higher education level, it is carried over all along as a philosophy of life. Owing to their role in the society, the universities must act like "ethical beacons" (Watson, 2006, p. 2). Ethics may seem to be in the agenda of a philosophical individual, but in reality, it deserves to be made a component of each and every activity of every individual, be it in dealing with others or dealing with oneself. For example, smoking is not only injurious to one's health, but also to others.

REFERENCES

Barnes, J. (1979). *Who should know what? Social science, privacy and ethics.* Harmondsworth: Penguin.

Burgess, R. G. (1984). *In the field: An introduction to field research.* London: Routledge.

Capurro, R., & Pingel, C. (2002). Ethical issues of online communication research. *Ethics and Information Technology, 4*(3), 189-194.

Douglas, J. (1976). *Investigative social research: Individual and team research.* London: Sage.

Frankfort-Nachmias, C., & Nachmias, D. (1996). *Research methods in the social sciences* (5th ed.). New York: St Martin's Press.

Garrard, D. J. (2002). *A question of ethics.* Retrieved April 15, 2008, from http://www.watton.org/ethics/subject/ethics/index.html

Gourley, B. (2007). Foreword. *Open Learning, 22*(2), 105.

Katz, J. (1972). *Experimentation with human beings.* New York: Sage.

Kelly, P., & Mills, R. (2007). The ethical dimensions of learner support. *Open Learning, 22*(2), 149-157.

Macfarlane, B. (2004). *Teaching with integrity. The ethics of higher education practice.* London: RoutledgeFalmer.

Needham, G., & Johnson, K. (2007). Ethical issues in providing library services to distance learners. *Open Learning, 22*(2), 117-128.

Oates, B. J. (2006, 2007). *Researching information systems and computing.* New Delhi: Sage.

Peters, R. S. (1966). *Ethics and education.* London: George Allen and Unwin.

Punch. M. (1998). Politics and ethics in qualitative research. In N. Denzin & Y. Lincoln (Eds.), *The landscape of qualitative research: Theories and issues* (pp. 156-184). London: Sage.

Starratt, R. J. (2004). *Ethical leadership.* San Francisco: Jossey-Bass.

Watson, D. (2006). The university and civic engagement. *Ad-lib: Journal for Continuing Liberal Adult Education, 31,* 2-6. University of Cambridge Institute of Continuing Education, Cambridge.

ADDITIONAL READING

AOIR. (2001). *Ethics working committee—a preliminary report.* Retreived April 15, 2008, from http://aoir.org/reports/ethics.html

Baird, R. M., Ramsower, R., & Rosenbaum, S. E. (Eds.). (2000). *Cyberethics: Social and moral issues in the computer age.* Amherst, NY: Prometheus Books.

Bell, F., & Adam, A. (2004). Information systems ethics. In B. Kaplan, D. Truex, D. Wastell, T. Wood-Harper, & J. DeGross (Eds.), *Information systems research. Relevant theory and informed practice* (pp. 159-174). Boston: Kluwer.

Capurro, R. (2000). Ethical challenges of the information society in the 21st century. *The International Information & Library Review, 32*(3/4), 257-276.

Ess, C., & The AoIR Ethics Working Committee. (2002). *Ethical decision-making and Internet research: Recommendations from the AoIR ethics working committee.* Retrieved April 15, 2008, from www.aoir.org/reprts/ethics.pdf

Floridi, L. (2000). *Information ethics: On the philosophical foundation of computer ethics.* Retrieved April 15, 2008, from http://www.wolfson.ox.ac.uk/~floridi/ie.htm

Johnson, D. (2001). *Computer ethics* (3rd ed.). Upper Saddle River, NJ: Prentice Hall.

Mauthner, M., Birch, M., Jessop, J., & Miller, T. (Eds.). (2002). *Ethics in qualitative research.* London: Sage.

Oliver, P. (2003). *The student's guide to research ethics.* Maidenhead: Open University Press.

Radoykov, B. (Ed.). (2007). *Ethical implications of emerging technologies: A survey.* Paris: UNESCO, Information Society Division, Communication and Information Sector.

Ryen, A. (2004). Ethical issues. In C. Seale, G. Gobo, J. F. Gubrium, & D. Silverman (Eds.), *Qualitative research practice* (pp. 230-247). London: Sage.

Tavani, H. T. (2003). *Ethics in an age of information and communication technology.* Chichester: Wiley.

Section I
Contextual–Based

Chapter II
Ethical Conundrums in Distance Education Partnerships

Michael F. Beaudoin
University of New England, UK

ABSTRACT

Launching and sustaining innovative new academic programs is typically a complex enterprise, especially distance education projects, and more particularly, such initiatives attempted by individual institutions with little or no prior experience in this arena. Inherently parochial, colleges and universities usually experiment with online courses on their own, but increasingly, as institutions engage in more ambitious efforts to develop full programs of study offered at a distance, they are recognizing, enthusiastically or reluctantly, that collaborative arrangements may make the difference between success and failure, especially for those with little expertise and few start-up resources. Partnerships are being forged between two or more higher education entities, and even more remarkably, there is growing evidence of academic institutions partnering with for-profit corporate organizations. Unfortunately, these unions too often result in more collisions than collaborations, especially when there are differing values among the parties involved. Through the presentation of selected mini-case studies representing several actual higher education-corporate partnerships, this chapter identifies and analyzes a number of ethical dilemmas, some philosophical and others practical, which should be considered by those who enter into distance education partnerships.

INTRODUCTION

The relatively sparse body of literature on the topic of ethics in distance education is now finally being augmented, as evidenced in this volume, as well as a few other selected publishing and presentation venues. To date, most work on this subject has taken a microview, focusing primarily on ethical issues that may arise with individual faculty and students, or within teacher-student relationships in the distance environment. Another approach has been the interest in so-called values education or character education, in hopes that education can promote the "right" values and foster ethical behavior. Less common is attention to the macroview of distance education ethics, that is, at the organizational level. It is this author's working assumption that academic quality and ethical integrity of any distance education course depends approximately 50% on the individual faculty responsible for that offering (microlevel), and 50% on other academic officers who plan, manage and evaluate distance education programs and courses (macrolevel). This author leaves it to fellow contributors in this volume to further address critical forces at the microlevel; he here attempt to extend the discussion by examining related questions regarding ethical dilemmas from a broader macro perspective.

In an era, that seems to amplify a decline in public morality, corporate scandals, and global conflict, these well-publicized events are assumed to influence attitudes about individual ethical behavior, especially among the younger citizenry who witness their elders engaged in chronic misdeeds. There is evidence that as many as three-quarters of students today admit to some form of academic fraud, most commonly in the form of cheating on exams and plagiarism. This has caused considerable concern among faculty, especially those who teach at a distance, that students enrolled in such courses and programs are particularly vulnerable to unethical behaviors, and at the very least, to uncivil behavior in online discourse. As a result, institutions and instructors have taken great pains in recent years, as distance education offerings have proliferated, to address ethics related to computer usage, and formulate policies that provide guidelines for students. Virtually every institution has established a set of well-promulgated regulations for students to follow, designed to ensure some semblance of ethical behavior in classrooms and cyberspace.

Curiously, despite this heightened attention to ethical practice, directed primarily at consumers of distance education, those who plan, manage and evaluate distance education activities seem to give little attention to ethical practice as providers. This is not to suggest that unethical behavior is noticeably rampant in the distance education arena, but rather to note that the telecommunications revolution in academe has provided significant opportunity for new initiatives, growth and income and, with this development, there are also situations in which individuals and organizations can easily overlook, or perhaps ignore, areas in which their own ethics may, at times, be compromised.

Should the establishment and monitoring of a set of standards for ethical practice in distance education be the responsibility of a government, an NGO, a national association of providers, institutional providers, or self-regulating by individual faculty (ICDE Dusseldorf 2001 Conference)? Who is to blame, and what is the degree of liability when students become victims of poor quality in distance education? At present, there is no recognized body that ensures the adoption or enforcement of a code of ethics for distance education. In their rush to capitalize on the burgeoning distance education market, many institutions, in addition to having little resident expertise in technology-aided pedagogy, certainly have little awareness of potential ethical considerations in this arena.

DISTANCE EDUCATION PARTNERSHIPS

Organizational arrangements in which partners with differing attitudes and values enter into collaborative agreements to design and deliver new academic programs are increasingly common. Long known for their parochial approach in the knowledge industry, colleges and universities are suddenly being challenged by new educational providers able to compete with them, often utilizing a for-profit mode as a strong incentive to encroach into a domain in which institutions have enjoyed a monopoly for so long. The "forced marriages" that now occur with some frequency between these unlikely partners exacerbates the danger of having two or more players with disparate goals and distinct means of achieving them.

While there are certainly many examples of viable partnerships that function compatibly, achieve shared goals, and deliver quality products and services to students, and do so in an entirely honorable manner, it is certain that there are also less noble ways in which an opportunist mentality gets in the way of one or more partners that inevitably clouds ethical standards of the enterprise. One party may be insistent that academic quality, however it may be defined, must be paramount in all decisions and actions, while the other, though equally convinced that it too adheres to these same principles, appears nonetheless intent on pushing enrollment numbers, regardless of how this is to be accomplished.

The growth of online courses and degree programs, virtual institutions, corporate universities, for-profit providers of instructional software and, as a consequence, the exponential increase in online registrations, is surely one of the most dramatic developments in the education and training sectors worldwide, in terms of scope and speed. On the surface, this remarkable phenomenon should be seen as a great equalizer, driven by the availability and use of technology by greater numbers of learners. But many see a dark side to this, identifying technology as "a new engine of inequality" (Gladieux & Swail 1999). Those that use technology regularly, whether at home, work, or school, gain significant advantages that magnify further opportunities, thus creating the specter of a "digital divide" on a world-wide basis. Certainly, minimizing the adverse impact of this

trend, whether it is real or imagined, ought to be an ethical responsibility of distance educators.

There are practices in distance education that are generally recognized as "Best Practices," yet there are no widely accepted ethical principles that can be touted as standard operating procedure. While there are surely many practices in distance education that could be called into question, both in terms of efficacy and acceptability, there is generally an air of benign tolerance of these, in the absence of any widely promulgated and adopted criteria. While certain standards of performance are expected, much latitude is provided to allow for differing styles, especially in the online environment, to avoid reducing such teaching to a mechanistic process. So-called "Best Practices" usually reflect a prevalent school of thought adopted by a program or institution; likewise, ethical approaches to teaching and learning generally reflect an explicit or implicit ethos by the provider.

Ethical issues may encompass a wide variety of beliefs and behaviors including, for example, what is or is not taught, how it is taught, and what constitutes effective teaching and satisfactory learning. In this regard, distance educators bear significant responsibility, now and in the future, for defining and practicing what constitutes ethical acts, whether on the part of individuals or institutions engaged in distance education. This is especially so because any unethical act potentially creates conditions that invite others to act likewise (ICDE 2001 Dussledorf Conference). And the advent of "diploma mills" utilizing electronic resources puts even greater demands on legitimate providers to actively address ethical practices.

Those who facilitate others' learning must be guided by ethical concerns and moral values. Universal access to education may be considered by many as an ethical priority, and instructional technology is recognized as a means to facilitate this goal. Yet, the increasing dominance of technology can also foster unethical behavior, without adequate safeguards and the clear presence of an ethical culture. Educational administrators and teachers, whether in classroom or online courses, regularly face ethical issues, to a greater or lesser degree, without any training whatsoever in dealing with such matters (Beck & Murphy, 1994). Personal and professional and institutional principles designed to guide day-to-day practice may exist in some fashion, but ultimately, individuals must create an atmosphere of honesty and fairness in dealing with peers and others affected by their behaviors.

Added to this phenomenon is the emergence of the student-centered approach to pedagogy, which increasingly removes the instructor from a historically authoritative role, and recognizes the learner's prior knowledge base, current learning styles, and so forth. This trend can allow for significant student control and greater detachment on the part of the instructor, resulting in less social presence and greater psychological distance. In these settings, it is possible that ethical dilemmas faced by either teachers or students are further exacerbated by a more equitable balance of power and lessened authority of the teacher? In short, ethical issues may take on additional meanings in the distance education arena, and perhaps be more difficult to monitor and appropriately address. Still, educators must model the behaviors they expect of students, despite the distance factor. This may be done by articulating and exhibiting ethical teaching and research standards and practices.

There are likely those in academe who view differing positions on ethical questions, especially if these situations involve a connection between an academic institution and a for-profit organization, as an existential struggle between capitalism and democracy. Most academic types are determined that any program or course they are associated with must remain pristine and immune to any nefarious motives, especially if these seem to

have monetary consequences favoring a for-profit partner or are adverse to students' interests. This author proposes that such variances in how individuals and organizations interpret and resolve ethical challenges are typically more modest in scope and significance While one or both parties in disagreement regarding how best to proceed in resolving an issue may be tempted to claim the moral high ground, it is probably more likely that their discord revolves around relatively mundane matters of a more practical nature.

ORGANIZATIONAL CULTURE

Every organization has a culture, with values and expectations that may be implicit with each entity, but are seldom explicit between two partners hoping to work in tandem. Goodwill may be easily outflanked by desire for success that is defined differently by each party. For example, one side sees the need for students who receive satisfactory services; the other sees the highest possible number of recruits converted to registrations as the goal. In short, the more entrepreneurial partner values tangible results; the other values meaningfulness of purpose. This dichotomy might also be characterized, in some instances, as a distinction between servant leadership and entrepreneurial leadership. Neither side is more obviously professional than the other; rather, each has a particular perspective on what it values most (e.g., short term gains-admissions and retention), or perhaps long-term goals (e.g., reputation and legacy).

Ethical dilemmas are often exacerbated by two different but interactive parties, each having to make choices based on what each sees as the "right" values. And if getting it done is viewed as more important than getting it right, tough issues may not benefit from much, if any, self-reflection before action is taken. Too often, a wrong decision can seem temporarily right, and attempts at intervention to correct the situation may come too late. Complicating collaborative decision-making between two groups, each anchored by its respective core values, is that the situation may well constitute a dilemma for one party, yet the other remains oblivious to any conflicting issue to be resolved before action is taken. As Kidder (1995) points out, one's moral imperative could be another's moral dilemma, or even another's moral outrage. Yet, seldom do contractual partners agree in advance to a set of principles for problem solving and decision-making.

Organizations should systematically engage in values clarification at the start of a relationship to define the rules of engagement and to identify parameters of mutually acceptable behavior. Kidder further suggests that nobody can claim exclusive hold on moral discernment, and that 21st century choices demand a "morality of mindfulness." Clinging stubbornly to one value at the exclusion of others leads to thoughtless moralizing rather than moral thinking.

Thomas Sergiovanni (1992) suggests that congeniality should not be a substitute for collegiality, nor apparent cooperation for true commitment. Collegiality relies on norms and values agreed to by like-minded people, based on a common commitment, with shared identity and goals, and thus feel obligated to work together for the common good. This strong dedication to a set of ideas and values leads to a firm course of action, even to the point of creating an artificial reality that compels the players to stay the course. Such cohesion within a single organization is difficult enough to achieve and sustain, but to establish and maintain it between two ambitious partners can be even more elusive.

Sergiovanni argues that, ideally, decisions should transform the environment for the better, and thus constitutes the highest form of "rightness." But instead, decisions typically produce results, followed by a reaction, often one that is unanticipated and not necessarily shared by both affected parties. Kidder also notes that if the setting in which two parties are engaged in complex planning and processes represents a new, exciting accelerated situation for opportunity, one side may be more daring and more nimble, and less constrained by a need to examine the moral landscape before taking a gamble on what happens next.

ETHICAL RELATIVISM?

Is one moral stance as good as another? Is **ethical relativism** a legitimate principle to follow? Do certain situations justify altered ethics and actions? Is it reasonable to adopt a code of situational ethics, wherein one does what is contextually appropriate? Thinkers from Plato to C.P. Snow have written of two cultures and the clashes that ensue; ultimately this dichotomy is what Kidder refers to as a "dilemma paradigm." He offers, as an example, gender-based differences, with men valuing justice, rights, and equality, and women valuing nonviolence, relationships, and caring. It is quite possible that in certain types of organizations, senior leadership is in the hands of a female team, while its partner is dominated by men with an entirely different ethos and decision-making approach largely determined by certain gender-based values and priorities.

Ethical conundrums involving two partnering entities are more public than moral dilemmas being sorted out between individuals. They typically involve individuals who represent their organization's position, and this sometimes requires discussion among various stakeholders who then become more aware of issues under consideration at the organizational level. At this stage, both individual and organizational values may enter into the arena of discussion and disagreement, with the former watching to see what the organization will ultimately say or do, and if it truly represents a collective position compatible with their own values, or with those the organization officially espouses.

Kidder reminds us that Socrates opined that only the individual can remain truly principled, and that a more public life demands compromises that make true morality impossible. Thoreau, likewise, argued that his public/political obligation would compel him to act against his own conscience. But Hobbes contended that those in public positions are subject to a public morality, not a private set of values. Today, in a different environment of media scrutiny and religious activism, the public demands that one's public and private life must reflect a moral consistency

In an era of burgeoning distance education programs, precipitated by the advent of the Internet, quite a number of small, faith-based institutions with declining enrollments explored distance education delivery modes as a means of increasing enrollments to a viable level for growth and, in not a few instances, for survival. Some were enticed to enter into agreements with for-profit entities that promised attractive numbers for a substantial share of tuition revenues. For many of these, it became a financially attractive arrangement. But this particular category of distance education partnership also created especially challenging dilemmas for institutions that operated on the basis of strong religious convictions that guided their instruction and services to students, as well as their business practices. Ethical stances founded on creed may present somewhat inflexible postures that can quickly clash with a partner more inclined to adapt to the situation at hand and promote a culture governed more on what might be labeled ethical relativism.

INTERNATIONAL PARTNERSHIPS

International distance education partnerships have the potential to be both especially satisfying, as well as particularly challenging, to execute effectively. Once educational programs cross national borders, any number of social and cultural issues may arise, along with all the same issues that can plague partnership programs offered within the same country. Tony Bates (1999) has written about such partnerships, and distinguishes between franchise arrangements and joint programs. Franchises are typically designed by one institution but delivered by another under a license or contract agreement. Despite a number of advantages to such arrangements, there are also inherent difficulties; there is often not equity between the two partners, especially if there is an assumption that one has greater academic expertise than the other. On the other hand, as Bates notes, the "weaker" partner may still have some competitive advantage over other peer institutions in their setting who don't have the benefits a partner can provide. Joint programs create the prospect for more equality among two or more partners who may engage in programming together, each contributing more or less equal resources. In this case, each partner is likely to have some academic leverage to safeguard its own interests.

What motivates institutions to enter into such international partnerships? Obviously, the potential for revenues is key, because online courses might be offered to foreign students at a premium rate. Although one could argue that this raises some ethical issues (e.g., only more privileged students can gain access to required technology; tuition dollars are leaving impoverished countries), another view is that the partnership allows access to education not otherwise available and thus contributes to increased individual and national prosperity. And it can be argued that the increased availability of technology via relatively inexpensive, public Internet cafes does, in fact, make technology readily available to those seeking education delivered online. International partnerships can also enable a poorer or less experienced institution in a developing country to more quickly acquire distance education expertise and enhance its prestige and fortunes (Bates, 1999).

At another level, one partner may advocate a teaching/learning philosophy that its partner finds inappropriate for the population it serves.

For example, a "Western" institution will likely promote discussion, critical thinking, and group work as essential to learning, while the partner finds the notion of students discoursing with, or challenging the teacher's views to be culturally, socially and politically incorrect. And what about language-driven issues between partners with differing notions regarding the appropriate language of instruction? Should the "Western" institution insist that all instruction be in English, even if students have limited ability in English, while the partner requests that all or at least some instruction be in the native language? These issues may be complicated even further if a primary motive of some students is to be exposed to new approaches to learning, so that they might become more competitive for admission to advanced studies in other countries later (Bates, 1999).

Then there is the matter of ensuring equal services at the same level of quality for different consumers. Bates asks the provocative question: Is it realistic to expect that students studying through a partner institution in another country will receive the same resources as counterparts registered at the sponsoring institution? Who is responsible for assuring integrity of content, delivery and assessment for all? How much latitude, if any, should be allowed to accommodate cultural differences that could make a program relevant and viable for diverse learners?

LEADERSHIP

In any distance education partnership, similar to the situations described in this discussion, or any number of permutations thereof, is it realistic to expect distance education faculty and administrators to become ethical leaders? Wilcox and Ebb (1992, p. 27) define an ethical leader as "serving the common good, … by working within a framework of shared beliefs concerning standards of acceptable behavior." This seems to

be a reasonable and doable proposition, but what if those leaders in a partnership do not hold and value shared beliefs that guide their approach in problem solving and decision-making?

Ethical dilemmas are often compounded by issues of power. Someone with more resources has more power and so can manifest that power imbalance by making decisions that impact someone in a more dependent situation (e.g., professor over student). But power can also result in "nondecisions" wherein the person with power can prevent consideration and resolution of issues. Another variation of power distribution is evident in the situation where key players each hold a certain degree of power, but mainly in their respective spheres of influence, thereby possibly canceling out one another's authority to influence or act where their spheres intersect.

Leadership within each organizational body is guided by a selective moral authority, with shared values that define the group; these are not easily changed within the group, nor are they likely interchangeable between two groups. In fact, a tribe mentality often sets in and is reinforced by mutually antagonistic positions that are fueled by that moral authority. If such differences are not expressed and negotiated in good faith, partnerships can become flawed, and not likely to ultimately succeed; indeed, the relationship may deteriorate to the point where no resolution is possible. This condition may exist even while both parties pretend their working relationship is civil and productive.

Partnerships require careful stewardship from each party, and this is not necessarily always located at the top. In many instances, it is a second-tier manager, program director or other mid-level leader who is critical in guiding a collaborative relationship with the least amount of miscues and misunderstanding among partners with disparate positions on key issues. But what happens if the top leader is unenthusiastic about the partnership and so forces the liaison to give his or her counterpart mixed messages? And what happens if an organization is in transition, or if there is a change in leadership, with possible difference in style and substance? Or the partnership principals each bring a distinct style to the engagement, one with a transactional style, wherein the most effort goes into maintaining a cordial relationships, while his/her counterpart is a transformative leader who sees the partnership as an opportunity for organizational innovation and growth? A stable and comfortable partnership can be disrupted and even sabotaged by any one or more of these seemingly small and often subtle differences.

CASE STUDIES

The selected **cases** presented here are intended to illustrate the dynamics involved between partners in distance education situations. These are composite sketches of varied circumstances reflecting several different partnerships with which the author is familiar with, rather than scenarios exclusively representing any actual single partnership. Do these cases represent a clash of ethical positions? Perhaps not ostensibly, but they can be viewed as examples of situations where differences in academic philosophy, as well as opposing business considerations, gradually begin to compromise a previously viable partnership. Facile resolution of the myriad dilemmas summarized in these cases are not proposed here. Each situation requires careful diagnosis, thoughtful problem solving, and strategic action enabled by those empowered to act in each unique time and place.

Case #1: International Partnership

A small, growing U.S. university launches its first international program for health professionals in a Middle East nation. To do so, it establishes a contractual relationship with an in-country organization that has arranged several successful partnerships with a select few other U.S. institutions. An effective working affiliation quickly evolves, due in large part to a solid relationship between the key contact persons in leadership roles representing each entity. The in-country partner is able to recruit a critical mass of degree-completion candidates to make the program quite cost-effective at a relatively early stage of development. The two academic departments involved are enthusiastic, as it is an expedient means of increasing student numbers, and also offers faculty an opportunity for cross-cultural teaching experience abroad. In the fall and spring terms, some university faculty are sent overseas to teach, and their host-nation counterparts are hired to teach in-country. Students also attend a summer residency on the U.S. campus.

However, costs for travel, compensation, housing and per diem escalate, and due to security issues, it becomes increasingly difficult to lure U.S. faculty to teach abroad. Some university personnel overseeing the program come to recognize that this program is an ideal candidate for offering some courses via distance delivery, as a significant reduction in operating expenses would likely be realized. But as this option is explored, it becomes quite apparent that the partner has serious reservations regarding the prospect of converting a number of courses to an online format. They contend that students are unaccustomed to this approach, and that the National Council of Higher Education in their country would likely not approve moving in this direction.

Here, we have a situation in which the two partners come to have a serious difference of opinion, with one side concerned about reducing costs and the other concerned about losing income due to possibly lowered enrolments as a result of any changes in a program that seems to be running well. To complicate matters, the partner is also able to use the argument that a third party will make life difficult for all if distance education is introduced. The U.S. partner is uncertain if the resistance to distance education is real or imagined, but in either case, it emerges as an impediment to program changes that it feels are vital to continued success.

Case #2: Short vs. Long-Term Gain

A campus-centric university enters the distance education arena by offering a new master's degree in education, working with a west coast for-profit organization that is establishing partnerships with several other small institutions just getting started in this delivery mode. Agreements are easily reached regarding an appropriate division of labor between the two partners, with the clear understanding that the university plays the lead role in all academic matters. The nonacademic partner is to receive a substantial portion of tuition revenues for product development, materials distribution and marketing. Approvals for this new program are secured within the institution, and the for-profit partner designs an aggressive marketing campaign. But almost immediately, once basic operating procedures are agreed upon, several issues surface, making it quite obvious that there are significant differences of opinion on how to actually implement the program. These issues involve a complicated mix of business considerations and academic principles.

First, there is the question of marketing and how recruiters for the for-profit arm are to be compensated; salaried or on a per-enrollee basis? The for-profit wants the latter, as a motivator to generate numbers. What is the appropriate number of credits for a master's degree? The nonprofit argues for the minimum acceptable number in order to facilitate the "sale" of the degree program. What tuition should be charged? The nonprofit contends that a discounted tuition will be attractive and result in a critical mass of students early in the life of the program. Should there be a residency requirement? The nonprofit prefers there not be one, as this would result in

higher costs and less convenience for students, and so make the program less attractive. And how flexible should policies be? The nonprofit encourages very student-friendly policies (e.g., leniency regarding extensions for course completion). As might be expected, the educational institution assumes exactly the opposite stance on each of these questions.

As with the first case, one party interjects a third party into the equation to bolster its position, when the university insists that unless the dispute is resolved in its favor, the regional accrediting body may find fault with the program. Similarly, the for-profit group strengthens its position by reminding its academic partner that the other peer institutions also implementing a similar program have no difficulty at all complying with the recommendations proposed by the for-profit partner.

Case #3: Service vs. Cost-Effectiveness

A college creates its first fully online degree program, a certificate of advanced graduate study, and contracts with a for-profit company to provide technical support in setting up courses, training faculty, and offering ongoing online support as requested to faculty and students. The organization also provides the instructional platform, as well as the server for course delivery. As is the usual arrangement, the for-profit partner is to receive a percentage of each course registration as payment for these various nonacademic services. The institution chooses to market the program, having developed a strong curriculum with little apparent regional competition, having successfully sought all necessary academic approvals, and having created a curriculum that will certify students in the field in all states, and thus is confident there will be a strong market demand for such a program of study.

However, inadequate attention is given in the first year of the program to aggressively market it;

as a result, enrollment numbers are discouragingly low, and neither partner realizes any significant new net revenue from the venture. Despite low numbers of both students and faculty, the institution understandably still wants its partner to provide adequate tech support, training and course set-ups, but the original contractual arrangements were sufficiently vague that the for-profit group is able to gradually reduce its battery of services, so that it can realize some cost-savings and avoid having to terminate the contract at the next renewal point. Contact between the two partners lessens, enrolments fall, and the program is barely self-sustaining as it enters its second year of operation, with no clear direction or intervention from the college administration to address problems.

The **cases** described above also raises the specter of dissolution, as already precarious relations between partners can become even more fragile and quickly unravel. Much of this discussion has focused on issues to be attentive in establishing distance education partnerships, but ethical conundrums can be at least as vexing at the exit point of such relationships. As with marital separation, organizational partners are unlikely to decide at precisely the same moment that the arrangement ought to be terminated. Despite termination clauses and other written agreements, things happen and circumstances may change unexpectedly for one or both parties. A financial exigency for one, justifying a breach of contract, can be seen by the other as an egregious ethical lapse.

SUMMARY

Are there viable models for ethical decision-making in partnership arrangements? Partners need, at the very least, to identify and articulate their respective assumptions and values to determine how disparate these may be, and if these are likely to encumber further collaboration. Participants must respect one another's multiple and differing responsibilities, loyalties and obligations to various constituencies; then some attempt to define the dilemma may be useful; followed by sharing options; realistically assessing consequences of each choice; exploring possible compromise positions; and finally, coming to agreement on the most suitable response to the situation.

All parties must be clear regarding their respective motivation for moving into any joint international distance arrangement. Each should acknowledge the benefits it envisions for itself and its constituents. Letters of agreement are important to clearly define goals, expectations, responsibilities, timeframes for planning, deliverables, financial arrangements, and so forth, before any actual activities are launched. All key players, planners, course developers, instructors, and so forth, should be sensitized to any potentially volatile issues before any products or services are offered. The rush into online courses and full programs delivered within or across national boundaries ought not to be undertaken unless participants benefit from lessons previously learned by others.

Kidder suggests three principles that could effectively guide decision-making at the organizational level, though these are unlikely to be actively acknowledged, especially by both sides.

- Do whatever produces the greatest good for the greatest number;
- Act only as you would want all others to act; and
- Do to others what you would want done to you.

In the final analysis, no detailed formula is readily available, nor are any presented here, for guiding appropriate action in partnership situations, whether in the realm of distance education, or any other field of endeavor. Making ethical decisions depends on many variables, and such dilemmas are not easily resolved, even among fairly compatible partners. Kidder argues that "noble compromise" is necessary in most cases, oftentimes requiring that a third option be reached that is not the first choice of either party, but is nonetheless an acceptable one. Kidder also suggests that by successfully making a tough choice on one issue, the partners can clarify their respective positions, and thus guide them toward subsequent satisfactory resolutions on tough issues in the future.

The ambitious work to be accomplished in the distance education arena is often too complex to be effectively accomplished without a partner, and the outcomes are too important for the benefits of such partnerships to be squandered. The difference between success and failure in these enterprises ultimately depends on adequate attention and commitment to maintaining the highest ethical standards individuals and organizations can possibly achieve together.

DIRECTIONS FOR FUTURE RESEARCH

Ethical relativism holds that morality is relative to the norms of one's culture. The belief related to what is right or wrong differs across cultures and individuals. Due of this difference of opinion about the morality, cultural relativism and subjectivism, it becomes difficult to arrive at a common agreement on moral values. Thus, research efforts must be directed toward planning, designing, developing and marketing educational products for distance learners. Further research needs to be focused on how the culture would shape the learners, faculty and administrators' ethically appropriate behavior. More studies are needed to investigate misconduct of different stakeholders in the area of education. Research studies are recommended to examine the pressure the academics face during ethical decision-making. There are situations selecting between two rights. How this situation of conflict is tackled involves ethical dilemma.

Corporate social responsibility is gaining momentum. International partnerships and increasing use of technology to the cause of education are renewing emphasis on corporate ethics. Organizations and institutions are investing in ethical trainings and programs. We need to focus our attention on the impact of such training and programs that would provide an insight into the relationship between formal programs and workplace culture and ethical behavior. Suitable investigations to understand the ethical elements of organizational culture, the relationship of organizational values and organizational behavior, and how the behavior is controlled by organizational culture would provide measures to promote ethical conduct. Further important issues seeking attention relate to examining the impact of various leadership styles on ethical dilemma, culture, effect of punishment and reward systems, degree of involving employees in culture change, ways of crisis management, and how an ethics program impacts organizational leadership and culture. Research studies may be oriented to assess the effectiveness of national, regional, racial, gender, economic, and political culture on the culture and values of an organization.

REFERENCES

Bates, T. (1999). *Cultural and ethical issues in international distance education*. Vancouver, Canada: University of British Columbia/CREAD Conference.

Beck, L.G., & Murphy, J. (1994). *Ethics in educational leadership programs: An expanding role*. Thousand Oaks, CA: Corwin Press.

Gearhart, D. (2001, Spring). Ethics in distance education: Developing ethical policies. *Online Administration*. Retrieved April 15, 2008, from http://www.*Journal of Distance Learning* westga. edu/~ojdla/spring41

Gladieux, L.E., & Swail, W.S. (1999). *The virtual university and educational opportunities*. Washington, DC: The College Board.

Kidder, R. (1995). *How good people make tough choices*. New York: Fireside.

Sergiovanni, T. (1992). *Moral leadership—getting the most of school improvement*. San Francisco: Jossey-Bass.

Wilcox, J.R., & Ebbs, S.L. (1992). The leadership compass: Values and ethics in higher education. *ASHE-ERIC Higher Education Report* (No. 1). Washington, DC: George Washington University.

ADDITIONAL READING

Aaron, R. M. (1992). Student academic dishonesty: Are collegiate institutions addressing the issue? *NASPA Journal, 29*(2), 107-113.

Angeles, P. A. (1992). *Dictionary of philosophy* (2nd ed.). New York: Harper Collins.

Ashworth, P., & Bannister, P. (1997). Guilty in whose eyes? University students' perceptions of cheating and plagiarism in academic work and assessment. *Studies in Higher Education, 22*(2), 187-203.

Baggaley, J., & Spencer, B. (2005). The mind of a plagiarist. *Learning, Media and Technology, 30*(1), 55-62.

Beck, L. G., & Murphy, J. (1994). *Ethics in educational leadership programs: An expanding role*. Thousand Oaks, CA: Corwin Press.

Born, A. D. (2003). How to reduce plagiarism. *Journal of Information Systems Education, 14*(3), 223.

Bull, J., Collins, C., Coughlin, E., & Sharp, D. (2001). *Technical review of plagiarism detection software report*. Retrieved April 15, 2008, from http://www.jiscpas.ac.uk/images/bin/luton.pdf#search=%22technical%20review%20of%20plagiarism%20detection%20software%20report%22

Capurro, R. (2005). Privacy: An intercultural perspective. *Ethics and Information Technology, 7*(1), 37-47.

Cavalier, R. (Ed.). (2005). *The Internet and our moral lives*. Albany, NY: State University of New York Press.

Council of Writing Program Administrators. (2003). Defining and avoiding plagiarism: The WPA statement on best practices. Retrieved April 15, 2008, from http://www.wpacouncil.org/positions/WPAplagiarism.pdf

Crown, D. F., & Spiller, M. S. (1998). Learning from the literature on collegiate cheating: A review of empirical research. *Journal of Business Ethics, 17*, 683-700.

Galus, P. (2002). Detecting and preventing plagiarism. *The Science Teacher, 69*(8), 35-37.

Gaskell, G., Thompson P. B., & Allum, N. (2002). Worlds apart? Public opinion in Europe and the USA. In M. W. Bauer & G. Gaskell (Eds.), *Biotechnology: The making of a global controversy* (pp. 351-375). UK: Cambridge University Press.

Gibelman, M., Gelman, S. R., & Fast, J. (1999). The downside of cyberspace: Cheating made easy. *Journal of Social Work Education, 35*(3), 67-76.

Gitanjali, B. (2004). Academic dishonesty in Indian medical colleges. *Journal of Postgraduate Medicine, 50*(4), 281-284.

Harris, R. A. (2001). *The plagiarism handbook: Strategies for preventing, detecting and dealing with plagiarism*. Los Angeles, CA: Pyrczak.

Heberling, M. (2002). Maintaining academic integrity in online education. *Online Journal of Distance Learning Administration, 5*(1). Retrieved April 15, 2008, from http://www.westga.edu/~distance/ojdla/spring51/heberling51.html

Kidder, R. M. (1995). *How good people make tough choices*. New York: William Morrow.

Kirby, P. C., Pardise, L. V., & Protti, R. (1990, April). The ethical reasoning of school administrators: The principled principal. In *Paper presented at the Annual Meeting of the American Educational Research Association*, Boston. ED 320 253.

MacKay, E., & O'Neill, P. (1992). What creates the dilemma in ethical dilemmas? Examples from psychological practice. *Ethics & Behavior, 2*, 227-244.

Martin, D. F. (2005). Plagiarism and technology: A tool for coping with plagiarism. *Journal of Education for Business, 80*(3), 149-153.

McCabe, D. L., Treviño, L. K., & Butterfield, K. D. (2001). Cheating in academic institutions: A decade of research. *Ethics & Behavior, 11*(3), 219-232.

Olt, M. R. (2002). Ethics and distance education: Strategies for minimizing academic dishonesty in online assessment. *Online Journal of Distance Learning Administration,* (5), 3. Retrieved April 15, 2008, from http://www.westga.edu/~distance/ojdla/fall53/olt53.html

O'Neill, P. (1998). Communities, collectivities, and the ethics of research. *Canadian Journal of Community Mental health, 17*, 67-78.

O'Neill, P. (1999). Ethical issues in working with communities in crisis. In R. Gist & B. Lubin (Eds.), *Response to disaster: Psychosocial, community, and ecological approaches*. Philadelphia, PA: Taylor & Francis.

O'Neill, P. (2002). Good intentions and awkward outcomes: Ethical issues for qualitative research-

ers. In W. C. van den Hoonaard (Ed.), *Good intentions and awkward outcomes: Issues for qualitative researchers*. Canada: University of Toronto Press.

Rowe, N. C. (2004). Cheating in online student assessment: Beyond plagiarism. *Journal of Distance Learning Administration, 7*(2). Retrieved April 15, 2008, from http://www.westga.edu/~distance/ojdla/summer72/rowe72.html

Seitz, J., & O'Neill, P. (1996). Ethical decision making and the code of ethics of the Canadian Psychological Association. *Canadian Psychology, 37*, 23-30.

Sichel, B. A. (1993). Ethics committees and teacher ethics. In K. Strike & P. L. Ternasky (Eds.), *Ethics for professionals in education: Perspectives for preparation and practice* (pp. 162-75). New York: Teachers College Press.

Starratt, R. J. (1991). Building an ethical school: A theory for practice in educational leadership. *Educational Administration Quarterly, 27*(2), 185-202.

Tavani, H. T. (2004). *Ethics and technology: Ethical issues in an age of information and communication technology*. Hoboken, NJ: John Wiley and Sons.

Thompson, P. B. (2007). *Food biotechnology in ethical perspective* (2nd ed.). Dordrecht, NL: Springer-Verlag.

Trevino, L. K., Hartman, L. P., & Brown, M. (2000). Moral person and moral manager: How executives develop a reputation for ethical leadership. *California Management Review, 42*(4), 128-142.

Whitley, B. E. (1998). Factors associated with cheating among college students: A review. *Research in Higher Education, 39*(3), 235-274.

Chapter III
Ethics in Interactions in Distance Education

Paul Kawachi
Open Education Network, Japan

ABSTRACT

This chapter presents the desirable interactions involved in teaching and learning at a distance. In these interactions, there are considerable ethical issues–notably that one's own learner autonomy should be reduced at times in order to help others learn, to achieve the learning task, and at the same time help oneself to learn. Accordingly, learner autonomy is not an overarching goal of education. This is controversial, and this chapter deals with this issue in detail to explain that learner autonomy at best is a rough guideline, and ethically based on reasoning that autonomy should be interpreted as flexibly applied. The maxim that learner autonomy must be flexibly applied is particularly true in both cooperative group learning and in collaborative group learning in distance education where student interactions with other students constitute a major part of the education process. The ethics in interaction in distance education are extended to cover all possible interactions, especially the important interaction by the teacher to each student followed by the interactions by the student with the learning process, that can initiate the aesthetic social intrinsic motivation to lifelong learning and thus to one's own emancipation. Accordingly, ethics are defined here as those pro-active interactions that induce the motivation to lifelong learning in all the students. Such ethics should override individualist autonomy as a goal in education.

INTRODUCTION

This chapter aims to define what is meant by ethics in interactions in distance education and presents the 2007 current state of the art with respect to such ethics. At first it is best to define and frame what is meant by ethics. Here, ethics covers what human conduct is right or wrong based on reasoning, whereas morals can be interpreted as that conduct based on social custom. This chapter will focus on only that human conduct that is good practice, and not on that which is bad. Therefore, bad practices such as copyright infringement, plagiarism, and intellectual property theft are not discussed, mainly because they are generally covered by relevant local law.

It is also important to explain what is covered by interactions in distance education. There are at least five types of interaction reported in the literature: student-teacher, student-student, student-content, student-technology, and vicarious interaction. The fifth one of vicarious interaction was suggested by Sutton (2001) to occur when a student observes interactions between or among others, but in a carefully controlled study, Kawachi (2003a) found that no educational advantage was attributable to such vicarious interaction, likely due to those active participants who were interacting also deploying similar attention so no significant difference was found. Because some poorer quality of learning was seen in those not participating, then vicarious interaction was concluded to be disadvantageous and that active participation was to be emphasized for learning. The fourth, student-technology interaction, was suggested by Hillman, Willis and Gunawardena (1994) mainly in terms of there being a human-computer interface barrier to learning for some students with weak computer and technological literacy. Both these are not discussed any further here. This chapter will focus on the other three interactions.

Distance education may need clarification, and here the definition is drawn from the transactional distance theory of Moore (1993). Transactional distance may be interpreted as the psychological gap between what the student already knows and the content about to be learned. In particular, this theory describes transactional distance in terms of the three dimensions of structure, dialogue, and autonomy. Based on this theory, a four-stage model of learning has been proposed and validated by Kawachi (2003b, 2005), notably in open and distance education in 15 regions throughout Asia. How to interact optimally and therefore ethically through applying this model will be one of the two

key points presented in this chapter. The other key point will be that autonomy must be moderated by some affective motivations in the student in order to interact optimally to learn.

METHODS

Transactional distance theory postulates four categories of distance education according to the amount of structure (S+) imposed by the institution, and the amount of educative dialogue (D+) between the student and other persons. The most distant category has no dialogue and no structure (D- S-), the next closer has added structure (D- S+), the third has then added dialogue (D+ S+), and the fourth category of minimal transactional distance has dialogue and freedom (no imposed structure) (D+ S-). It should be kept in mind here that dialogue (D+) means being with educative intent. Accordingly, it should be mentioned somewhere here that young distant students often want student-teacher interaction such as face-to-face tutorial time to get their money's worth, and at the other end of the scale, older distant students want student-student interaction for socialization purposes, but because other students may be much younger, then they choose student-teacher interaction. Both these can be moved aside as not being ideally educative in purpose or intent.

Based on these categories, a model of learning in distance education has been designed and tested out as effective by Kawachi (2004) with four stages that constitute the learning process, bringing the student from furthest transactional distance to closest; in other words, bridging the gap between not knowing and knowing. The first Stage 1 (D- S-) is characterized by cooperative brainstorming and eliciting the student's prior knowledge and ideas; the second Stage 2 (D- S+) is characterized by vertical thinking to discern collaboratively the theory underlying the student's knowledge; Stage 3 (D+ S+) is characterized by collaborative hypotheses testing, problem solving or disjunctive horizontal thinking to consider all other possible solutions and ideas, and find a potentially better way forward; and then Stage 4 (D+ S-) is characterized by experiential learning cooperatively to test out this potential new way to socially construct new personal meaning, as detailed in Kawachi (2003c). These four stages constitute one cycle, and new learning then proceeds iteratively.

Worldwide, validation has found that students have difficulty in the collaborative theorizing of Stage 2 and in collaboratively performing disjunctive reasoning in Stage 3. Generally, students successfully completed the four-stage cycle and achieved deep quality learning if they were in small groups of 4-8 students, if they had high prior knowledge, or if they received close tutor monitoring and guidance. When in large classes, with low or mixed prior knowledge, and when given normal tutor care, then students were unable to move into and through Stage 3. Similar findings have been reported by Perry (1970), who found college students in large classes could not acquire critical thinking skills. Piaget (1977) has also acknowledged that many people do not reach the Stage 3 level of formal operations involving hypotheses-generating and testing even in adulthood. Similarly, Renner (1976) has reported that only 81% of final-year law students, and McKinnon (1976) that only 50% of college students overall at seven different colleges, could acquire critical thinking skills, expressed here as the goals in Stages 3 and 4. In their analysis of computer-mediated conferencing, Gunawardena, Lowe and Anderson (1997) found that participants did not proceed beyond the discovery and sharing of ideas, concepts and statements of Stage 1, and did not reach any collaborative phase of negotiation and co-construction of new knowledge. The participants in their study were relative experts in the use of distance education being (likely) graduate students and university-level teachers participating in ICDE95-Online virtual preconference of the International Council on Distance

Education. In a following study, Gunawardena, Plass and Salisbury (2001, p. 39) found that the "intended collaboration and sharing of ideas and issues simply did not happen."

In cooperative group learning in which one participant already knows the content to be learned by the others, the ethics of the cooperative interactions by the knower—either the teacher or an expert student—have been reported by Lewis (1995, p. 27) as being limited to the four following educative purposes: (1) summative to explain a grade, discuss and link the student's work to the institutional criteria; (2) formative to further the student's learning; (3) summarising what has been done; and (4) comment to help the student plan future learning. The ethics of all other cooperative interactions need to be weighed carefully according to whether the interaction is performed synchronously or asynchronously. In synchronous media, other participants may not have adequate time to read or listen to long utterances. Being overly verbose in synchronous mode may be deemed unethical by others in the group. In asynchronous mode, files can be transferred and read more easily. Cooperative lengthy exposition is unethical during the collaborative learning stages, Stage 2 and Stage 3, and should be put aside into a Virtual Coffee Shop or other chat forum for the explicit purpose of keeping the collaborative forum uncluttered. It is, however, in the collaborative stages that all the participants (the teacher here is equally as unknowing as the students) need to understand and follow some right conduct based on reasoning, in other words, abide by some ethics in the interactions they engage in, for learning together.

Scaffolding has been suggested (Kawachi, 2003b) to guide students through collaborative group learning, particularly the disjunctive reasoning and group interactions of Stage 3 (D+ S+) for hypotheses testing and co-construction of new nonfoundational knowledge. Scaffolding may be cooperative between a participant (such as the teacher) who knows the content and the student who does not, where according to Wood, Bruner and Ross (1976, p. 89) "an adult or expert helps somebody who is less adult or less expert … a situation in which one member knows the answer and the other does not," while Vygotsky (1978, p. 86) indicates that cooperative scaffolding can be from a "more capable" student to a less capable student. The ethics of teacher to student interaction in Stage 1 involve the teacher making explicit to the student the aims and objectives of the task so the student can indeed comprehend these, noting that if the teacher fails here, then any later teacher feedback and error correction become merely vehicles for imitation and copying (which in turn may be described as student unethical conduct). The difficulty actually lies in scaffolding the collaborative interactions, and ethics here can pre-empt needless "flaming" and irrelevant argumentation in countering views from others.

Zimmer (1995) has proposed the collaborative scaffolding, involving three functional turn-taking steps ABA between two persons A and B, which when repeated as BAB give both participants the opportunities each to give opinions and receive counter-opinions empathically, as follows.

(A) (Hello) Affirm + Elicitation
(B) Opinion + Request understanding
(A) Confirm + Counter-opinion
(B) Affirm + Elicitation
(A) Opinion + Request understanding
(B) Confirm + Counter-opinion

The scaffolding of the ethical interactions necessary is reproduced here from Zimmer (1995, p. 142) as a three-leaf pattern in Figure 1.

In Figure 1, the ethical expressions are as follows: (1) warm affirmation "you're okay by me;" (2) inviting open disclosure in response "please tell me what you want to do here, so that I can see your point of view;" (3) open disclosure "here's my own experience and what I want to do …;" (4) inviting empathic comprehension in response "I'd

welcome knowing what you think I mean, to be sure my feelings are accepted" or "I'd like your sense of what I mean;" (5) empathic comprehension "what I think you mean in essence is …;" and (6) "my own view differs …" or "I'd like you to hear my own view" inviting warm affirmation in response.

The phrases in the above paragraph for use in the interactions are reproduced almost verbatim from Zimmer (1995, p. 142 and p. 144). Zimmer suggests that these interactions (p. 143) "dissolve competitive opposition, by inviting open disclosure, warm affirmation and empathic comprehension in direct response to perceived dogmatism, disparagement and invalidation." It can be noticed for ethics that the interactions (3), (4) and (6) on the left side deal only with one's own learning, and the interactions (1), (2) and (5) on the right side deal altruistically with the learning in the other student. Moreover, I suggest that any participant(s) may be behind either voice, so the scaffold could be effective for more than two persons at the same time. In the distance education virtual classroom in a collaborative group task, the author can confirm that prior awareness of this template by (at least) one participant can successfully scaffold the interactions to reach the task goal.

Figure 1. Ethical interactions in collaborative distance education

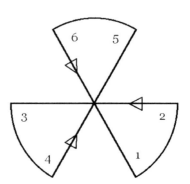

Now a literature search has found (only) one other scaffolding model, suggested by Probst (1987) as transactional theory for literature. From reading his work, I have drawn the ethical interactions for collaborative learning in literature and art, in which the interactions are not aimed at hypotheses-testing characterised by counter-opinion, but rather aimed at achieving a new insight built on critical reflection that while shared may be personalised in each individual. In literature, learning is not cooperative: There is no "knower," the teacher or expert student does not guide the less able student to some preset conclusion of the meaning of the text. In literature, the teacher or any expert student (A) elicits opinion to initiate the three functional turn-taking steps BAB, and then followed by ABA, as follows.

(A) (Hello) Affirm + Elicitation

(B) Opinion/Analysis + Request understanding
(A) Affirm + Elicitation of Evidence
(B) Reflect + Elicit other opinions/Analyses

(A) Opinion/Analysis + Request understanding
(B) Affirm + Elicitation of Evidence
(A) Reflect + Elicit other opinions/Analyses

This scaffolding model involves reflective analysis followed by articulation, bringing in ideas from one's own prior reading or ideas elicited from other students, then repeating the reflective analysis with accommodation to construct a new personal insight. As in Zimmer's model, I suggest any participant may be behind each voice, so any number of participants can be collaboratively involved.

RESULTS

These two models each illustrate and scaffold the desirable ethical interactions which are essential for achieving one's own collaborative learning and ethically helping others to learn. The interactions can be performed either synchronously in a virtual classroom or asynchronously through e-mail or discussion board. In each model, the scaffolding clearly and explicitly indicates what content should optimally be included in an utterance (and therefore what should not be included), and specifies in what serial order to progress toward achieving discovery and co-construction of new understanding and new knowledge. It should also be noted that the use of a framework also implies some timeliness in replies. The system would not function if turn-taking were violated or not forthcoming. Participants need to take responsibility for the group succeeding by actively providing ethically what is required and when it is required. In this way, some pacing is inevitable if the group is to move toward achieving its goal. To some large extent, nonresponse in an asynchronous environment can be overcome by others offering up the required content in time. This is often the case in synchronous free discussions. However, group cohesiveness depends on the active participation of all members of the group. If a student does not participate, the group is fragmented and not functioning as a whole. Prior to the task, coping strategies should be acquired, agreed upon, and then used when required, such as pre-arranging the time interval allowed within which a student should contribute, pairing up students to provide back-up in case one is at a loss, or behind-the-scenes coaxing and elicitation by the moderator.

DISCUSSION

Ethics in interactions in distance education can be determined as those that are appropriate to achieving emancipation and learning for one's self, and to helping altruistically learning in others. Such help may be at one's own expense in money, time and effort, and are not just with kind intentions but constituting educationally effective help. There is an old Indian proverb that is relevant here concerning these ethics: "Help your friend's boat cross the raging river, and lo you will find that you yourself have crossed the river."

Here then, the ethically good interactions are identified. And it is noted en passant that student-student interaction such as only commenting "Great work!" on another student's Web-log does not ethically qualify as fulfilling a course requirement for interaction.

The above discussion has looked at the two dimensions of structure (S+) and dialogue (D+) in distance education. There is the third dimension of autonomy to be discussed now. Autonomy was defined by Moore (1990, p. 13) as "the extent to which the learner determines objectives, implementation procedures, and resources and evaluation." Generally, definitions of autonomy in learning have in common an emphasis on the capacity to think rationally, reflect, analyse evidence, and make judgements; to know oneself and be free to form and express one's own opinions; and finally, to be able to act in the world, according to Tennant and Pogson (1995). These qualities characterise the collaborative thought processes of Stage 3, and also the experiential aspect of Stage 4. Stage 1 has maximal transactional distance, and for a student to succeed here in independent learning Moore (1993, p. 27) points out that the student would need maximum autonomy. Autonomy is thus seen as a highly powerful and desirable quality for independent learners. Not all students bring this high level of autonomy with them initially into their studies, and so the teacher must bring the student around to acquire this autonomy. The four-stage model of learning illustrates the cyclic iterative process through Stages 1 to 4 to equip and bring the student to go onto independent learning in a further new cycle starting at Stage 1 in a new learning venture. Autonomy has also been related to recognizing one's interdependence on others (Boud, 1988). Interdependence relates to understanding the need to learn together with others either in cooperative mode or at other times in collaborative mode. Interdependence is a maturity characterising an adult student, and is acquired through awareness and prior experience of the critical thinking process. Toward the end of Stage 4, the student can have acquired this sense of interdependence. So in entering a new Stage 1 iteration, the student may be interdependent (post-Stage 4) and once more newly independent (starting a fresh Stage 1). These attributes of independence and interdependence have already been found to be separate, orthogonal, and coexisting in mature students at the end their course (Chen & Willits, 1999). While autonomy is defined as an attribute of the student, different distance education programmes and the different stages in the model relate to different levels of autonomy for the student to be a successful learner. In a programme at Stage 2, the deployed structure means that the student is charged with thinking rationally but vertically rather than horizontally, and is analysing already given evidence, rather than finding new evidence, so the quality of autonomy is somewhat measured to fit the limited freedom given to the student. At Stage 3, different qualities of autonomy for hypotheses testing are needed for success, including a mature openness to new ideas that might be in conflict with one's previous and present conceived view of the world. The student needs to exercise the freedom to formulate or reformulate one's own conceptions. While in Stage 4, the quality of autonomy should include the willingness and ability to act to test out these newly constructed ideas to see experientially how they operate in practice. The amount of autonomy in each stage or different programme varies according to the task and nature of the course. The ethics involved in the interactions then in distance education govern the conduct of autonomy at some times requiring certain qualities to be forthcoming and at other times different qualities in order to achieve learning. It is difficult therefore and moreover unhelpful to assign an integrated level of autonomy to each stage in the model of learning. The student should utilize measured amounts of the various qualities that constitute autonomy during each stage to support learning.

Clearly, ethics are needed in interactions in distance education to achieve efficiently one's own learning, and also to help others to learn cooperatively and collaborative in a group, as detailed in the four-stage model of learning.

Finally, in this chapter it may be useful to consider the various lines of interaction between the student and content, student and teacher, and between the student and other students, and the affective motivations that drive these interactions and consequently moderate the level of autonomy. Here "modulating" the level of autonomy may be a more appropriate term, because autonomy must be varied and at times be consciously reduced, and such variation and occasional reduction is ethics in the interaction: One does not single-mindedly pursue ever-increasing autonomy; rather, some aspects are relaxed or reduced while other aspects are increased to achieve one's own learning goals and, more importantly for ethics, to help others learn. This chapter has so far considered aspects in three of the four known dimensions of learning: the cognitive, metacognitive, and the environment. The fourth dimension is the affective domain, involving the will and motivations that drive learning, detailed in Kawachi (2006). A comprehensive categorization of the motivations to learn was discovered and drawn by Taylor (1983) with the vocational, academic, personal, and social motivations, and later divided by Gibbs, Morgan and Taylor (1984, p. 170) into their subcategories of extrinsic and intrinsic. Of interest here is the social intrinsic motivation to learn, that acts along the lines of the interactions in distance education.

The three interactions involved here are the student-student, student-teacher, and student-content. The first two are already covered above in cooperative learning and in collaborative learning. The third interaction between the student and the content which is collaborative has been described as being aesthetic reading in transaction theory

by Rosenblatt (1994, p. 27). The process of motivation to learn is described in detail by Kawachi (2006). Briefly, the student is motivated to learn when the student compares his or her own perception of her current state with some reference goal value, when the observed gap (constituting a want or need) drives the student to act to reduce the discrepancy. The standard reference goals are generally preset socially and culturally, and the teacher should ethically make all efforts to know these in the distant students. The other factor here is that the student must also perceive there to be an opportunity to act and that there is a reasonable chance of success based on prior learning experience. The student-teacher interactions above have covered these points.

The student-content aesthetic interaction gives rise to the motivation for lifelong learning (Kawachi, 2005, 2006), which is generally recognized as being a central goal of education. The teacher or any other participant can initiate this motivation in the student. It occurs through experiencing pleasure or joy. There are only three positive affects in the affective domain. These are interest, pleasure, and joy, according to Tomkins (1984), and six negative affects (distress, fear, shame, contempt, disgust, and anger). It may be worthwhile reiterating here that ethics in interactions in distance education should carefully avoid causing these negative affects in others, and they are not discussed further here.

Barthes (1976) developed a theory of pleasure distinguishing between pleasure and joy, in which pleasure is the gratification usually previously experienced and therefore within the known world of the student. The student knows what brings pleasure and can look forward to experiencing it again by revisiting similar circumstances. Joy, on the other hand, occurs at the boundary of the student's world. When the boundary is momentarily and unexpected broken, then at that instant of ecstasy, the student experiences the joy of learning. The teacher or any other participant can bring the student to within reach of this by moving the student toward his limit and then presenting surprising new information. "The penny drops" in the student's mind, sometimes immediately, sometimes much later unexpectedly, and sometimes never. The aesthetic experience derives from this process or activity of group learning, and is addictive.

The interactions involved and the ethics involved here in the interactions to promote aesthetic motivation and lifelong learning in others are important. When carefully guiding others in this direction, one must suspend one's own desire for increasing one's own learning autonomy. Autonomy is accordingly ethically modulated by these affective factors for learning. Whether or not one is engaged in learning for oneself as a simple-minded student or is helping others to learn as a mature responsible student or teacher, nevertheless one must be careful ethically so as not to disturb others negatively, and ideally one should help others if at all possible.

FUTURE RESEARCH DIRECTIONS

Future research is warranted into optimal transactions for learning online. In particular, scaffolds should be constructed and provided to students to facilitate their cooperative learning in a group and for their collaborative learning in a group. For students new to online learning, these scaffolds can be detailed templates for them to use to support their learning, and at the same time will serve as metacognitive tools to guide their thinking and reflection. The templates will also comprise an e-learning portfolio for the students individually and as a group, and for the teachers and accrediting institution. At more advanced levels, the templates can be less detailed and more flexible.

Future research should not only focus on ways to promote ethically good practice, but should analyse online discourse to illustrate where and how unreasoned practice leads to breakdown in communication and poorer quality learning outcomes. So, three-way control studies should be undertaken into online discourse analysis of learning. Three groups are needed to detect the influence of observations and any novelty or Hawthorne effects.

How students learn online independently of others is also a worthwhile avenue to explore in future research. It is generally accepted that in conventional face-to-face education studying in a group leads to better quality learning than studying alone independently, but while hundreds of studies have demonstrated this in face-to-face education, there are none so far to date that have compared these ways of learning in an online e-learning course. This may be due to the transfer of what works best in the conventional mode into the online mode. However, the online mode now offers rich learning environments that likely support independent study. These rich environments include search engines that can pick out key phrases from blogs, wikis, stored powerpoint presentations, lecture notes, annotations by previous students, and so forth. Moreover, if learning-by-doing has validity in face-to-face conventional education, it may also have validity in online virtual reality and other technologies. Studying alone will raise many more questions of online ethics, which have hitherto not yet been considered.

CONCLUSION

This chapter has looked at what is distance education and at the three dimensions of structure, dialogue, and autonomy of transactional distance theory that can describe distance education. It has also looked at the interactions involved in distance education to achieve learning in one's own mind and to help others to learn, both in the cooperative mode and in the collaborative mode, and it has looked at the desirable good conduct that is based on reasoning which is known as ethics. All these points have defined ethics in interactions in distance education.

Some reports in the literature (for a typical example, see Conrad, 2002) have tried to uncover student thoughts and ways of learning online through teacher observations, but it is noted here that the author of this chapter has been a lifelong student within online interactivity, and this discussion draws from this long, wide and continuing learning experience. In particular, the author thanks my tutor Fred Lockwood at the British Open University, now Professor Emeritus at Manchester Metro University, and my teaching staff Stacey Rowland, Janet Gubbins and Melanie Clay at the University of West Georgia, from where the author graduated in Advanced Technologies for Distance Education in July 2007, and the fellow distance education students there, including Pam Miller, Bessie Nkonge, Diane Fulkerson, Sue Walters, Mauri Collins, and others.

REFERENCES

Barthes, R. (1976). *The pleasure of the text* (R. Miller, Trans.). London: Cape.

Boud, D. (1988). Moving toward student autonomy. In D. Boud (Ed.), *Developing student autonomy in learning* (2nd ed., pp. 17-39). London: Kogan Page.

Chen, Y-J., & Willits, F.K. (1999). Dimensions of educational transactions in a video-conferencing learning environment. *American Journal of Distance Education, 13*(1), 45-59.

Conrad, D. (2002). Deep in the hearts of learners: Insights into the nature of online community. *Journal of Distance Education, 17*(1). Retrieved April 15, 2008, from http://cade.athabascau.ca/vol17.1/conrad.html

Gibbs, G., Morgan, A., & Taylor, E. (1984). The world of the learner. In F. Marton, D. Hounsell,

& N.J. Entwistle (Eds.), *The experience of learning* (pp. 165-188). Edinburgh, Scotland: Scottish Academic Press.

Gunawardena, C.N., Lowe, C.A., & Anderson, T. (1997). Analysis of global online debate and the development of an interaction analysis model for examining social construction of knowledge in computer conferencing. *Journal of Educational Computing Research, 17*(4), 397-431.

Gunawardena, C.N., Plass, J., & Salisbury, M. (2001). Do we really need an online discussion group ? In D. Murphy, R. Walker, & G. Webb (Eds.), *Online learning and teaching with technology: Case studies, experience and practice* (pp. 36-43). London: Kogan Page.

Hillman, D.C., Willis, D.J., & Gunawardena, C.N. (1994). Learner-interface interaction in distance education: An extension of contemporary models and strategies for practitioners. *American Journal of Distance Education, 8*(2), 30-42.

Kawachi, P. (2003a). Vicarious interaction and the achieved quality of learning. *International Journal on E-learning, 2*(4), 39-45.

Kawachi, P. (2003b, November 12-14). Asia-specific scaffolding needs in grounded design e-learning: Empirical comparisons among several institutions. In *Proceedings of the 17th Annual Conference of the Asian Association of Open Universities*, Bangkok.

Kawachi, P. (2003c). Choosing the appropriate media to support the learning process. *Journal of Educational Technology, 14*(1&2), 1-18.

Kawachi, P. (2004). Course design & choice of media by applying the Theory of Transactional Distance. *Open Education Research, 2*, 16-19.

Kawachi, P. (2005). Empirical validation of a multimedia construct for learning. In S. Mishra & R. Sharma (Eds.), *Interactive multimedia in education and training* (pp. 158-183). Hershey, PA: Idea Group.

Kawachi, P. (2006). The will to learn: Tutor's role. In P.R. Ramanujam (Ed.), *Globalisation, education and open distance learning*, (pp. 197-221). New Delhi, India: Shipra.

Lewis, R. (1995). *Tutoring in open learning*. Lancaster: Framework Press.

McKinnon, J.W. (1976). The college student and formal operations. In J.W. Renner, et al. (Eds.), *Research, teaching, and learning with the Piaget Model* (pp. 110-129). Norman, OK: Oklahoma University Press.

Moore, M.G. (1990). Recent contributions to the Theory of Distance Education. *Open Learning*, *5*(3), 10-15.

Moore, M. (1993). Theory of transactional distance. In D. Keegan (Ed.), *Theoretical principles of distance education* (pp. 22-38). London: Routledge.

Perry, W.G. (1970). *Forms of intellectual and ethical development in the college years: A scheme*. New York: Holt, Rinehart and Winston.

Piaget, J. (1977). Intellectual evolution from adolescence to adulthood. In P.N. Johnson-Laird & P.C. Wason (Eds.), *Thinking: Readings in cognitive science*. Cambridge University Press.

Probst, R.E. (1987). Transactional theory in the teaching of literature. *ERIC Digest* ED 284 274. Retrieved April 15, 2008, from http://www.ed.gov/databases/ERIC_Digests/ed284274.html

Renner, J.S. (1976). Formal operational thought and its identification. In J.W. Renner, et al. (Eds.), *Research, teaching, and learning with the Piaget Model* (pp. 64-78). Norman, OK: Oklahoma University Press.

Rosenblatt, L.M. (1994). *The reader, the text, the poem: The transactional theory of the literary work*. Carbondale, IL: Southern Illinois Press. (Reprinted from 1978).

Sutton, L.A. (2001). The principle of vicarious interaction in computer-mediated communications. *International Journal of Educational Telecommunications*, *7*(3), 223-242. Retrieved April 15, 2008, from http://www.eas.asu.edu/elearn/research/suttonnew.pdf

Taylor, E. (1983). *Orientations to study: A longitudinal interview investigation of students in two human studies degree courses at Surrey University*. Doctoral thesis, Guildford, University of Surrey.

Tennant, M.C., & Pogson, P. (1995). *Learning and change in the adult years: A developmental perspective*. San Francisco: Jossey-Bass.

Tomkins, S.S. (1984). Affect theory. In K.R. Scherer & P. Ekman (Eds.), *Approaches to emotion* (pp. 163-195). Hillsdale, NJ: Erlbaum.

Vygotsky, L.S. (1978). *Mind in society: The development of higher psychological processes*. Cambridge, MA: Harvard University Press.

Wood, D., Bruner, J.S., & Ross, G. (1976). The role of tutoring in problem solving. *Journal of Child Psychology and Psychiatry*, *17*, 89-100.

Zimmer, B. (1995). The empathy templates: A way to support collaborative learning. In F. Lockwood (Ed.), *Open and distance learning today* (pp. 139-150). London: Routledge.

ADDITIONAL READING

This section offers a few selected literature references that offer different perspectives on the topic of online dialogue and interactivity based on reasoning for ethical practice.

Gorsky, P., & Caspi, A. (2005). A critical analysis of transactional distance theory. *Quarterly Review of Distance Education*, *6*(1), 1-11. Retrieved April

15, 2008, from http://telem.openu.ac.il/hp_files/pdf/Gorsky.pdf

Laurillard, D. (2002). *Rethinking university teaching: A conversational framework for the effective use of learning technologies.* London: RoutledgeFalmer.

Scardamalia, M., & Bereiter, C. (1994). Computer support for knowledge-building communities. *Journal of the Learning Sciences, 3*(3), 265-283. Retrieved April 15, 2008, from http://carbon.cudenver.edu/~bwilson/building.html

Simonson, M. (1999). Equivalency theory and distance education. *TechTrends, 43*(5), 5-8.

von Glasersfeld, E. (1995). *Radical constructivism: A way of knowing and learning.* London: RoutledgeFalmer.

Walker, K., & Hackman, M. (1992). Multiple predictors of perceived learning and satisfaction: The importance of information transfer and nonverbal immediacy in the televised course. *Distance Education, 13*(1).

Webb, N.M. (1982). Group composition, group interaction and achievement in small groups. *Journal of Educational Psychology, 74*(4), 475-484.

Chapter IV
Ethics in the Ambit of Distance Education

J. S. Dorothy
Indira Gandhi National Open University, India

Ugur Demiray
Anadolu University, Turkey

Ramesh C. Sharma
Indira Gandhi National Open University, India

Ashwini Kumar
Indira Gandhi National Open University, India

ABSTRACT

In an era when the distance teaching institution, irrespective of their type, namely single mode, dual mode, mixed mode and consortium, is involved in distance education, for the benefit of the aspirants targeted for each programme of study, which are on offer, this chapter discusses the ethics in the ambit of distance education. After citing reasons for adopting ethics in distance education, the chapter discusses about eight spheres of concern for ethics in distance education, namely Student Support Services (Administration, Admission, Eligibility Criteria/Calibre, Academic counselling and Medium of Instruction); Collaboration (Learner Support Centre, How, why they are selected); Credibility (Employability vs. Continuing Education); Duplication of Efforts (Material Production, Launch of Programmes, Course Writing); Provision of intersystem transfer (Lack for interface to aim transfer); Expertise (Academic activity and Administrative activity); Resources and Research (Who does, How it is done). Genuineness, originality, copyright/patent, Memorandum of understanding kept, and causative agent made predominant are the advantages of facilitating ethics in distance education. The disadvantages of facilitating ethics in distance education are the rules viewed as hindrances, human element given a preference over the credibility, and lack of buffer time. Distance education laid in the foundation of ethics, as viewed from the optimistic person, is that it will become more accommodative without diluting the standards. Irrespective of any comments from the critics, for any distance educator, ethics should be the signpost beyond which things should not go wrong at any cost. Ethics coupled with the scientific method of doing things will spin off the effectiveness of quality maintenance.

INTRODUCTION

The education systems globally improved during the mid-1990s, when the services were introduced and adopted information, communication and educational technologies in order to develop teaching and learning processes with an aim of providing world-class or an excellent "on-click" education on demand to the learners. With the growth of the technologies, online delivery of programmes became more popular worldwide. Format of online delivery of programmes through this was quite effective for learners placed geographically at distant places.

Distance education has become one of the most effective, economical, and productive ways of delivering instruction by the corporations, institutions, colleges and universities, when properly and timely used. Historically, distance education has continuously evolved as technology has improved. From the early 1800s to present day, educators have utilized this method of instruction to reach those unable to interact face to face due to various circumstances.

In other words, distance education and its related educational components are a media of teaching and learning that have grown significantly in the past decade. This is indicated by the amount of higher education institutions that offer courses or full degree programs via distance learning methods. According to the National Center for Education Statistics-NCES (1999), the number of degree-granting higher education institutions offering distance education courses increased from 33% in 1995 to 44% in 1997-1998. More specifically, the use of computer-based

technologies has increased from 22% in 1995 to 60% in 1997-1998 and more than 80% in 2000s. The growing dimension and ratio and the rate of increase in the delivery of distance education should be carefully examined under contemporary circumstances.

The Open and Distance Learning System (ODLS) has emerged as an alternative to the number of aspirants of education, specifically higher education that overloads the delivery system of education in the South Asian part as a conventional system. Different distance education theorists like Börje Holmberg, Charles A. Wedemeyer and Michael G. Moore have essentially identified the centrality of the learner in ODL. Otto Peters and Desmond Keegan have been concerned with organizational aspects. The emergence of ODL has thus affected the use of technology to reach mass audience, typology of distance teaching systems, emergence of post-industrial education, learner autonomy and organizational structures. The numbers in ODL have also increased many folds over a short span of 2 decades. The emergence and developments in ODL methodologies have brought certain theoretical and pragmatic approaches to the field. The numbers in ODL have also indicated many faults in applications over a short span of 2 decades. The emergence and developments in ODL methodologies have brought certain theoretical and pragmatic approaches to the field.

Distance education has been a fair option of not only the aspirants of education but also education managers/administrators in the government/private and non-government sector. The main reason for this is that education is being considered as an investment and the consumption involved for education by means of the money spent, the time utilised for studying and the efforts involved in channelising the resources are viewed in the angle of the spin off benefits reaped after the successful completion of the programme of study. The distance teaching institution, irrespective of their type, namely single mode, dual mode, mixed mode and consortium, is involved in distance education, for the benefit of the aspirants targeted for each programme of study, which are on offer.

The concept of virtual learning includes the perspective of study in a virtual medium. The virtual learning environment is seen as an environment for the teacher and learner's activities within which learning is seen as an active process in multi-informational, cooperational network environment. The concept of virtual is associated with telematics networks, as well as with flexibility in study situations, learner mobility and possible independence from time and place as it can be exemplified through the glass of modern information and communication technologies. Virtual study is often associated with open and distance learning, but especially with flexible study and learning.

The beauty of virtual learning environment technology is that it can repeat the simulation as often as the learner wants. While it is impossible for interactive videoconferencing to repeat the teaching conferences, virtual learning environment technology can do this in a WBDL environment. Winn's recent study showed that "artificial environments can help students to reify abstractions, can scaffold students to solve complex problems, and can immerse students into dynamic phenomena. When artificial environments apply to WBDL, the empowerment effect in learning can be explosive" (Winn, 2002).

As with any other new phenomenon, this online communication for education has brought up new emotional, physical and psychological issues to the agenda of education science. The teaching and learning through this new medium exposed the learning community to such experiences where the teacher and students normally do not see each other face to face. The electronic communication occurs through synchronous and asynchronous means like e-mail, discussion forums, list-serves, electronic chat, bulletin board systems, WebCT, and other Web-based communication. Thus, the virtual classroom faces issues like humanizing, role conflict, or other problems about norms, ethics, privacy and socio-psychological deficits.

By the use of speedily growing and expanding ODL the ethical issues become significant, as it is usually read in magazines and newspapers about misuse or abuse of e-mail. Electronic voyeurism is also common in online communication. Obtaining unauthorized access to someone's electronic mails, Web page, e-book, electronic materials breaking passwords, or presenting oneself with a fake identity over electronic chat is treated as unfair conduct.

WHAT IS ETHICS?

Aristotle, Socrates and Plato take the virtues to be central to a well-lived life. According to Wikepedia, ethics (via Latin *ethica* from the Ancient Greek meaning "moral philosophy," from the adjective of *ēthos* meaning "custom, habit"), a major branch of philosophy, is the study of values and customs of a person or group. It covers the analysis and employment of concepts such as right and wrong, good and evil, and responsibility. It is divided into three primary areas: *meta-ethics* (the study of the concept of ethics), *normative ethics* (the study of how to determine ethical values), and *applied ethics* (the study of the use of ethical values). According to Gearhart (2001) there are four norms to follow in one's day-to-day ethical practices for both instructors and learners in the distance education and are part of the "golden rule" for both classroom and distance course behaviors. They are honesty, keeping your word, respect for others and fairness. In short, the ethics reflect the moral character of an individual rather than the academic or physical character of an individual. Ethics talk about what people do when not noticed or unwatched and it speaks about the heart of an individual.

WHY ETHICS IN DISTANCE EDUCATION?

Distance education, aimed at inculcating education to various types of individuals aimed at various educational goals with the view of the mass approach, targeting each and every aspirants by diversification of the methods of approach used without differing in the efforts of maintaining optimum quality in the output, necessitates adoption of values for the following reasons:

1. The values governing the philosophy of distance education are at risk in proportion to the rising numbers opting to study in the distance education mode.
2. Distance education is a field where rapid growth is experienced and scope for development is enormous.
3. Distance education is a service sector with the clients being the human being whose potential is either shaped/channelised/improved during the period of association for study with a distance teaching institution.
4. Distance education necessitates collaboration, networking, partnership and linkages for its implementation and the temptation to commercialise the activities involved is very high.
5. Distance education, even though it adopts cost effective methods for production of the self-instructional materials, many times the clientele met are either very low or nil, questioning the viability of the programme and running the programme to meet the needs of a meagre percentage of the learners. The cost of launch and implementation increases the economic liabilities at the cost of the economic assets, which may or may not be experienced by the learners.
6. Distance education mainly provides avenues either to improve the current educational status or equip with an educational status, and mostly does not create avenue for career placement.

The ethical issues become significant as it is usually read in magazines and newspapers about misuse or abuse of e-mail. However, ethics is a debatable and controversial area. The university administrators, teachers and students are often faced with such issues where the commercial use of institutional resources, illegal use of facilities and invasion of privacy are reported. Sexual issues are perhaps the most common breaches of this medium. The recent reported news about Multimedia Messaging (MM) scandals in some institutions, where some people uploaded a multimedia clip over a commercial site for sale, can be counted as an example. Hacking is one of the most controversial areas. Some people realize it for remedial solutions while some others do it for destruction or for mental satisfaction.

Plagiarism is one of the most common misuses of the facilities among students. Copying assignments from other people's work or taking material from the Web is found as the easy way out for the students. Privacy of the messages is very difficult in online communications. Although encryption technologies have been developed, such as defense forces or commercial houses, educational institutions are using them insufficiently. Honesty, which is one of those rare attributes of the human characteristic perhaps, remains again a rare phenomenon in online environments.

This honesty may take the form of providing trust to the learner by the teacher, or can be exemplified as honest feedback to the researcher by the respondents for the right conclusions of research questions. One of the most significant features of the open or online distance education compared to traditional education is opening the doors of global education to the student at his desktop. What is critical to the success of this mode of education is to have ethics in place; it is a different field based on mutual trust and respect. The ethical codes that are mainly brought up by the traditional education to the distance education form a very significant base for the future of online education. The authors of this chapter will discuss how the issues of ethics affect the teaching and learning over online distance modes. Suggestions are also given on how values can be rendered and why there remain strong and urgent demands for a code of ethics that are constructed by various online universities.

SPHERES OF CONCERN FOR ETHICS IN DISTANCE EDUCATION

Under this title, we will emphasise from the point of student support services (SSS), collaboration, credibility, duplication of efforts, provision of intersystem transfer, expertise, resources and research subtitles.

Student Support Services (SSS)

The aspects of administration, admission, eligibility criteria/calibre, and academic counselling fall within the gamut of student support services.

Administration: Distance learners often learn amidst the other family, personal, social and employment commitments and the distance teaching institution is expected to serve them with the motto "Learner first." Many times, this motto is exploited by the learners by way of expecting the distance teaching institution to accept the application form very late (even after the session commences), to render personalised services, to use the personal belongings of the distance teaching institution officials like phone/mobile number for resolving official problems. The expectations of the learner may seem genuine but the line to be drawn rests again with the officials of the distance teaching institution. This leads to an unanswerable question of how the work-life balance of the distance teaching institution officials has to be maintained

and still projects the view of whether the distance teaching institution is a friend or foe.

Admission: An aspirant for a particular programme of study decides to enrol for that programme either because of his/her interest or due to the probable gain envisaged after the completion of the progamme. The distance teaching institution adopts either a closed admission norm or an open admission norm, which basically depends on its policy. In addition, the phase of admission, as evident from the various cycles of admission, also determines the time for which the admission is called for a particular programme. In other words, it can be said that there may be a lag time for the aspirants who have missed the previous cycle of admission and a hibernating period for the enrolees who have enrolled late into a programme. The state of both these cases calls for attention of what and how the distance teaching institution officials will engage these two categories of the learners. Many times, they were left to be managed by themselves.

Eligibility Criteria/Calibre: Most of the entry criteria are closed in the sense that they are based on certification obtained and not on the calibre of the person seeking the admission. This contradicts the philosophy of distance education, which talks about openness and flexibility. However, on the other hand, if everyone is made eligible to pursue a programme of study either based on the fulfilment of the certification required or through their ability to prove their potential to pursue a programme of study, this may pose a threat, the dilution of the academic standards. Thus, a dilemma exists among the distance teaching practitioners of how much a programme can be made open and how much a programme can accommodate the clientele who aspire to pursue a programme of study on offer.

Academic Counselling: Tutors to handle academic counselling are generally drawn from the academic fraternity of the host institution. Nepotism is common while choosing the tutors. This is mainly because the coordinator who heads the Learner Support Centre agrees mainly with "Team move" rather than individual academic/professional excellence. In addition, due to the prevailing unemployment many individuals who qualify to be an academic gets underemployed-thereby creating "academic drain" and thus, they are not eligible to serve as tutors. Professional ego exists due to preference clashes and is also prevalent in the academic counselling for a distance teaching institution. For example, faculty of an engineering degree college feel it below their dignity to handle classes for a certificate programme in engineering. One of the objectives of academic counselling is to optimise learner interaction. However, there are programmes which invite fewer learners and in such a case, either the learners of various learner support centres are clubbed under one or, the learners are requested to move to the nearest learner support centres of their choice. The learners of less enrolment programmes invite a new problem of ethics in distance teaching as they are exposed to the threat of isolation from other peers (who are scanty) and from the institution, besides being a potential to drop out of the programme of study.

Medium of Instruction: Even though English for distance education purposes is the main stand taken by most of the distance teaching institution, the question of usage of the regional language and dialect for effective reach of the target group remains unanswered. At times, translation of materials in the regional language and dialect needs more staff for moderation, implementation and evaluation purposes. Distance teaching institution officials need to think globally so that the theme is not left out and act locally so that the relevance of the programme on offer besides the specific target group is never missed.

Collaboration

The way by which the activities of the distance teaching institution are implemented is by means of collaboration with other educational institu-

tions. The main issue which is criticised is the Learner Support Centre.

Learner Support Centre: Many at times collaboration for Learner Support Centre are initiated by the distance teaching institution and facilitated by person specific designations. Continuity of the collaboration for Learner Support Centre suffers when there is change in the persons irrespective of the designation being perennial. Even though the memorandum of understanding between the collaborators depicts a win-win situation, most often the horse-rider approach is being adopted where the distance teaching institution is expected to serve as a horse.

How, why they are selected: Even though specific norms and guidelines exist to select a collaborator to establish a Learner Support Centre, scope or gaps exist for the element of discretion to be exerted. The person who signs the memorandum of understanding on behalf of the distance teaching institution can use the discretion to collaborate with an institution with whom liaison exist on a personal basis rather that with that which fulfils the eligibility criteria.

Credibility

The worth of the system as viewed by the academic standard of the course materials, and the degree of the student support provided culminate in the credibility of the system. The main issue viewed here is that of employability of the learners after the successful completion of the programme.

Employability vs. Continuing Education: As the case of any educational institution, the distance teaching institution paves ways for the certification of an educational qualification as it serves as a tool for continuing and lifelong education. However, it would not be apt to say that all candidates who have qualified through the distance teaching mode are employable. Employability depends on various factors. The employability of the distant learners is viewed by sceptics as the noncredibility of the distance teaching institution, which sometimes is a never ending debate.

Duplication of Efforts

Efforts replicated to do the same task either in the same institution or in two or more similar types of institutions lead to duplication of efforts, which can be manifested generally in production of materials, launch of programmes and in course writing.

Material Production: The course materials, which are generally self-instructional materials, have to be provided by the distance teaching institution to the learners who have enrolled for the programme of study. Generally, the self-instructional materials are institution-specific and are identifiable with the institution by the cover design and layout of the content in the booklet. In spite of the availability of the same type of programmes in various distance teaching institutions, each distance teaching institution prefers to produce its own materials as it represents one of its identifications and thus leads to duplication of efforts and multiplicity of the availability of resources.

Launch of Programmes: The same types of programmes are on offer by two different distance teaching institutions. In addition, the same content of the syllabi exist in two different programmes offered by the same distance teaching institution.

Course Writing: Generally, the course team approach is used to write course materials. The members of the course writing team are generally drawn through acquaintance and accessibility. However, the probability of the availability of better qualified course writers in a remote place is equally high and this aspect is often ignored.

Provision of Intersystem Transfer

The two main systems of education are the conventional educational system and the distance education system. Both systems supplement and complement each other. However, in reality, the distance education system is considered as the system for the underprivileged and those who missed their first opportunity for education. In spite of the syllabi being the same, both the systems remain as two parallel lines that never meet. The issue that inhibits the existence of the provision of intersystem transfer is mainly the lack for interface to aim transfer.

Lack for interface to aim transfer: A bridge is necessary to cross the banks on either side of a river, so also an interface is essential to ensure movement of learners from one system of education to the other. In addition, acknowledging of one's strengths and potential for excellence are necessary to arrive at mutual consensus about the possibility of the shift from one system of education to the other.

Expertise

Distance teaching institutions need expertise for academic and administrative purposes. Both these activities can be viewed as the two eyes of the individual. Generally, the personnel for these services are drawn from the conventional educational system.

Academic activity: Activities associated with academic purpose are academic counselling, evaluation of components for continuous evaluation like assignments, practical sessions, project work and term-end evaluation like evaluating answer scripts. Even though all the personnel engaged in academic activity in the conventional educational system are eligible for the academic activity in the distance teaching institution, not all are selected, as only the snowball technique is followed to generate the resource pool for all academic activities. In addition, internal academic drain, as evident by academics taking up a job other than that related to an academic activity and the preference of the personnel to be nonassociated with a distance teaching institution, still remains a problem to be solved to ensure quality of the academic staff for distance education purposes.

Administrative activity: For effective quality maintenance, administration of the activities related to pre-enrolment of a learner, learning process, placement-post certification guidance for successfully completed learners and fee payment/help desk for dropout learners are mandatory.

However, in practice, the learner at the entry stage is given a red carpet welcome, but the same cannot be said to be rendered to those who drop out of the programme.

In addition, the quantity factor as reflected by high enrolment also hinders the distance teaching institution to provide quality services to the learners on rolls and to provide placement-post certification guidance for successfully completed learners.

Resources

Resources can be either physical/financial or human resources. Ethics in distance education demand optimum utilisation of the resources. The areas which highlight the existing lacunae are the following:

1. There exists a lack of facilities to share the resources (physical/financial or human);
2. There exists a lack of facilities to lend the resources (physical/financial or human);
3. There exists a lack of system identity and preference for individual institution identity; and
4. Allocation of financial resources by the same funding agency for the same cause to two different distance teaching institutions.

Research

Research activities are important assessment indicators for the growth and development of the institution. The two significant signposts are: who does the research activities, and how is it done?

Who does: Mostly, research on distance teaching institutions are undertaken by those who are interested in the subject rather than by those who are practicing the same.

How it is done: The means by which the research activities are carried out are because of the objective of the funding agencies rather than to arrive at the need-based field research. In addition, research is done on themes which reflect quality rather than which ensures direction points for further course of action. Concurrent results are important in any type of research to prove the validity of the findings. Most often, the fluctuations in obtaining concurrent results are attributed to cultural and regional differences.

ADVANTAGES OF FACILITATING ETHICS IN DISTANCE EDUCATION

Facilitating ethics in distance education pave a way for the following advantages.

1. **Genuineness:** Integrity of the content and mode of operation in distance education pave way for the flow of genuineness in the conduct of the activities of distance education.
2. **Originality:** Ethics encourage original behaviour amidst the various players in the distance education and prevent clash of efforts and duplication of efforts for a common task.
3. **Copyright/Patent:** Ethics in distance education prevents academic theft and usage of materials without copyright/patent.
4. **Memorandum of Understanding Kept:** Distance education thrives mainly due to collaboration, networking, partnership and linkages for its implementation. Ethics enables the memorandum of understanding signed to be kept with sanctity by both the parties.

5. **Causative agent made predominant:** Ethics in distance education enables to keep the causative agent alive irrespective of the hurdles faced to meet the set objective. Many a times, the causative agent is targeted at the social upliftment and ethics make the social cause prominent among the prevalent practices.

LIMITATIONS OF FACILITATING ETHICS IN DISTANCE EDUCATION

Facilitating ethics in distance education pave a way for the following limitations.

1. **Rules viewed as hindrances:** Because ethics is viewed as what is the best that won't elicit any contradiction/confrontation, many a times the rules which are the speed breakers and regulate the steady flow are viewed as hindrances in the eyes of the spectators, which in turn make the participators of the distance teaching process, namely the learner and the administrator, to keep their fingers crossed especially when the requirement in the rule is not complied with.

2. **Human element given a preference over the credibility:** Because ethics view the importance of the human element, many a times dilution of the standards is viewed as the compromising platform to invite more learners to enrol into the programme. Because the quantity of the learners is used to depict the success of the programme, various techniques are undertaken to invite more learners, which in the long run affect the credibility of the system.

3. **Lack of buffer time:** For any activity in a distance teaching institution, time limit is set before the initiation of the activity. This time frame is to ensure the flow of chain of activities and have to be adhered to maintain smooth flow. However, due to the involvement of the human element, the last date for an activity is extended into the processing time, which prevents having a buffer time (the intentional time lag created after an activity) for an activity.

THOUGHTS ON CODES OF DISTANCE/VIRTUAL EDUCATION ENVIRONMENTS

In spite of the number of serial universal ethics code rules, some institutions and especially science institutions regulate their "Institutional Scientific Ethical Codes" or "Rules of Scientific Ethical Codes" in their bodies. They try to insert some additional rules for the reason that regional originality and society-based limitations should be given a preference.

The Brazilian Association for Distance Education, approved by the General Assembly of the Association on August 17, 2000, in Sao Paulo, dealt with "A Code of Ethics for Distance Education." The institutions affiliated with the Brazilian Association for Distance Education agree to comply with the 23 principles.

Although institutions of distance learning vary greatly as to their objectives, types of activity, resources and size, it is important to attempt to establish a set of principles applicable equally to all of them, and respected by all of them, thereby guaranteeing the orderly and qualitative development of DL in Brazil. Such principles can serve various functions: as internal policies of institutions for the task of continuous qualitative improvement; as specifications for quality standards permitting the evaluation of DL courses; and as indicators serving to protect the interests of students who are the consumers of such educational services. This code should be revised frequently because the development of new pedagogical strategies and technological advances is a permanent phenomenon, and rules and criteria can easily turn obsolete and become barriers for progress in the practice of distance learning (Details of these principles are available from http://www.friends-partners.org/GLOSAS/Global_University/Guideline/List_of_Materials.html).

Now, it is time to give brief information about the developments of distance education in Turkey. Approximately 80 years of DE experience will be summarized here. Today, almost 2.5 million people are attending the distance education programs/courses in Turkey at primary, high school and university level. Now, only Anadolu University remains one of the mega universities in the world.

FUTURE OF DISTANCE EDUCATION ON THE BASIS OF ETHICS

Distance education, laid in the foundation of ethics as viewed from the optimistic person, is that it will become more accommodative without diluting the standards. However, critics view that distance education on the basis of ethics will be a puppet in the hands of everyone who wants to have the right to know/use and review the entire process of distance education. However, for any distance educator, ethics should be the signpost beyond which things should not go wrong at any cost. Ethics, coupled with the scientific method of doing things, will spin off the effectiveness of quality maintenance.

DIRECTIONS FOR FUTURE RESEARCH

A student support service is an integral part of the distance education system where a host of resources are to be provided to assist the learners. These resources pertain to academic support, educational and career planning, psychological and emotional health and so forth. Therefore, research needs to be oriented to address ethical dimensions of academic, social, psychological,

career, preventive, and developmental issues. The future research programmes will be designed to examine the ethical dilemma of students, faculty, staff, administrators, parents, and alumni, as well as other community organizations. And also, these programs should serve by harmonicating with the marketing and media ethics dealt with cultural and social values. The authors propose the following directions for future research.

1. Experience of the learners about the student support services of the distance teaching institution, specifically in terms of administration, admission, eligibility criteria/calibre, academic counselling, and medium of instruction.

2. Case studies of misuse of the customer protection laws, marketing and media ethics rules, especially on electronic medium enforced for the service sector by the learners on the distance teaching institution.

3. Documentation of collaboration models prevalent for the Learner Support Centre of distance teaching institution.

4. Studies tracing the credibility of distance teaching institution with special reference to employability and continuing education.

5. Models for convergence and consolidation of activities of distance teaching institutions aiming to prevent duplication of efforts mainly in material production, launch of programmes, and course writing with provision of intersystem transfer.

6. Opinion of the personnel rendering expertise for academic activity and administrative activity about the distance teaching institutions.

7. Case studies of distance teaching institutions where facilities to share/lend the resources (physical/financial or human) exist with emphasis on system identity and at the same time highlighting the individual institution identity.

8. Work-life balance of employees of the distance teaching institutions.

CONCLUSION

Incredible growth of ODL and virtual learning programs on the Web environment have led to unethical practices in the growth of diploma mills. Faculties are being asked to do more and more teaching at a distance. Many are put in the fast track, often with little to no training, and ethical practices take a back seat in the rush to be prepared each semester. The suggestions are given as follows.

*   ODL and virtual learning programs faculty and administrators need to become ethical leaders in the field.
*   ODL and virtual learning programs educators must interact with others honestly, fairly, respectfully and consistently and develop policy that is ethical in practice.
*   ODL and virtual learning programs educators must interact with the ICT sector administrators honestly, fairly, respectfully and consistently and develop policy that is ethical in practice.
*   An individual ODL and virtual learning programs educator should work with administrators in close contact in order to develop policy.
*   Faculty need to consider ethical practices in course design and development and with interaction with learners.
*   In particular, faculty need to make sure that learners, especially if dealing with high school or traditional-aged learners, understand what ethical behaviour is as a learner.
*   Distance education administrators need to consider ethical practices in managing programs and developing policies and procedures.

*   It is our ethical responsibility as ODL and virtual learning programs educators to strive to reduce this digital divide.

To conclude, it can be said that ethics in distance education is important not only to launch a need-based programme, but also to implement the outcome of action research for sustainable development in the field. Besides this, ethics will inculcate more valued moral character in the officials of the distance teaching institution and will provide potential to act after getting a feel of what is wanted rather than what has been planned for action. Ethics in distance education will also help individual distance teaching institutions to arrive at a common platform and agree/accept each other as potential collaborators rather than viewing one another as competitors who must be ousted.

The authors of this chapter tried to consider how the issues of ethics affect the teaching and virtual learning over online distance modes. They also give suggestion on how values can be maintained and why there is a strong and urgent need for a code of ethics developed by various online universities. Also, Ethical Codes of Anadolu University Guide is summarized at the end of presentation.

But, this question still remains in my mind: Are distance educators and administrators following ethical practices in due course? Whether the anwser is "Yes" or "No"- are they willing to follow?-where there is a will, there is a way.

REFERENCES

Brazilian Association for Distance Education. (2000, August 17). A code of ethics for distance education. In *Proceedings of the General Assembly of the Association*, Sao Paulo, Brazil. Retrieved April 15, 2008, from http://www. friends-partners.org/GLOSAS/Global_University/Guideline/List_of_Materials.html

Cornman, J. W., Lehrer, K., & Pappas, G. S. (1982). The problem of justifying an ethical standard. *Philosophical problems and arguments: An introduction* (3rd ed.). Retrieved April 15, 2008, from http://www.ditext.com/cornman/corn6.html

Gearhart, D. (2001). Ethics in distance education: Developing ethical policies. *Journal of Distance Learning Administration, 4*(1). Retrieved April 15, 2008, from http://www.westga.edu/~distance/ojdla/spring41/gearhart41.html

Kraut, R. (2007). *Aristotle's ethics* (rev. ed.). Retrieved April 15, 2008, from http://plato.stanford.edu/entries/aristotle-ethics

National Center for Education Statistics (NCES). (1999). *Teacher quality: A report on the preparation and qualifications of public school teachers* (Tech. Rep. No. NCES 1999-080). Washington, DC: U.S. Department of Education.

Winn, W. (2002, May 23-25). What can students learn in artificial environments that they cannot learn in class? In *Paper presented at the 20th Anniversary Celebrations of the First International Symposium of the Open Education Faculty (AOF)*, Anadolu University, Eskisehir, Turkey. Retrieved April 15, 2008, from http://aof20.anadolu.edu.tr/program.htm or from http://faculty.washington.edu/billwinn/papers/turkey.pdf

ADDITIONAL READING

Balmert, M. E., & Ezzell, M. H. (2002). Leading learning by assuring distance instructional technology is an ethical enterprise. In *Proceedings of the Adult Higher Education Alliance (AHEA): Creating New Meanings in Leading Learning.* Pittsburgh, PA, (pp. 54-72). Retrieved April 16, 2008, from http://www.ahea.org/conference/proceedings.html

Belle, V. G. (2006). How cheating helps drive better instruction. Retrieved April 16, 2008, from http://www.plagiarized.com/vanb.html

Bennett, J. B. (1998). Collegial professionalism: The academy, individualism, and the common good. Phoenix, AZ: American Council on Education & Oryx Press. In D. Gearhart (Ed.), (2000). Ethics in distance education: Developing ethical policies. *Online Journal of Distance Learning Administration, 4*(1). State University of West Georgia, Distance Education Center.

Brazilian Association for Distance Education. (2000, August 17). A code of ethics for distance education. *General Assembly of the Association*, Sao Paulo, Brazil. Retrieved April 16, 2008, from http://www.friends-partners.org/GLOSAS/Global_University/Guideline/List_of_Materials.html

Carnevale, D. (1999, November 8). How to proctor from a distance. *The Chronicle of Higher Education*. Retrieved April 16, 2008, from http://www.ou.edu./archives/it-fyi/0716.html

Demiray, U., et al. (2004). *A review of the literature on the Open Education Faculty in Turkey (1982-2002)* (4th rev. ed.). E-book, Electronic ISBN 98590-2-5, Sakarya University, Turkey. Retrieved April 16, 2008, from http://www.tojet.net

Ethics Codes Guide of Anadolu University. (2002). *Anadolu University Council of Ethics Center-AUCEC.* Anadolu University Publications, Eskisehir Turkey. Retrieved April 16, 2008, from http://www.anadolu.edu.tr

Fass, R. A. (1990). Cheating and plagiarism. In W. W. May (Ed.), *Ethics and higher education.* New York: Macmillan Publishing Company and American Council on Education. In D. Gearhart. (2000). Ethics in distance education: Developing ethical policies. *Online Journal of Distance Learning Administration, 4*(1). State University of West Georgia, Distance Education Center.

Hart, M., & Friesner, T. (2004, February). Plagiarism and poor academic practice: A threat to the extension of e-learning in higher education? *Electronic Journal on E-learning, 2*(1), 89-96. Retrieved April 16, 2008, from http://www.ejel. org/volume-2/vol2-issue1/issue1-art25-hart-friesner.pdf

Hinman, L. M. (2000). *Academic integrity and the World Wide Web.* Retrieved April 16, 2008, from http://ethics.acusd.edu/presentations/cai2000/index_files/frame.htm

Hinman, L. M. (2005). Esse est indicato in Google: Ethical and political issues in search engines. *IRIE-International Review of Information Ethics, 3*(6), 25. Retrieved April 16, 2008, from http://www.i-r-i-e.net/inhalt/003/003_hinman.pdf

How do you prevent cheating in distance education? Retrieved April 16, 2008, from http://web-pt.net/wyoming/online_testing.htm

Lim, C. L., & Coalter, T. (2005). Academic integrity: An instructor's obligation. *International Journal of Teaching and Learning in Higher Education, 17*(2), 155-159. Retrieved April 16, 2008, from http://www.isetl.org/ijtlhe/pdf/IJTLHE51. pdf

McCabe, D. L., & Pavela, G. (1997). Ten principles of academic integrity. *Synthesis: Law and policy.* Retrieved April 16, 2008, from http://www.collegepubs.com/ref/10PrinAcaInteg.shtml

McCabe, D. L., & Trevino, L. K. (1993). Academic dishonesty: Honor codes and other contextual influences. *Journal of Higher Education, 64,* 522-538.

McMurtry, K. (2001). E-cheating: Combating a 21st century challenge. *The Journal Online: Technological Horizons in Education.* Retrieved April 16, 2008, from http://thejournal.com/magazine/vault/A3724.cfm

Min, R. (2003, April). Simulation and discovery learning in an age of zapping and searching: Learning models (A treatise about the educational strength and availability of digital learning tools and simulation on the World Wide Web). *Turkish Online Journal of Distance Education, 4*(2). Retrieved April 16, 2008, from http://tojde.anadolu.edu.tr/tojde10/articles/rikmin.htm

National Center for Education Statistics (NCES). (1999). *Teacher quality: A report on the preparation and qualifications of public school teachers* (Tech. Rep. No. NCES 1999-080). Washington, DC: U.S. Department of Education.

Nissenbaum, H. (1997). Accountability in a computerized society. In B. Friedman (Ed.), *Human values and the design of computer technology* (pp. 41-64). Cambridge University Press. Retrieved April 16, 2008, from http://www.cybertext.net.au/tct2002/disc_papers/organisation/russell.htm

Olt, M. R. (2002, Fall). Ethics and distance education: Strategies for minimizing academic dishonesty in online assessment. *Online Journal of Distance Learning Administration, V*(III). State University of West Georgia, Distance Education Center.

Stitt. (2000). *Not my future.* Glebe: Blake Education. *Responsibility for School Education in an Online Globalised World.* Retrieved April 16, 2008, from http://www.cybertext.net.au/tct2002/disc_papers/organisation/russell.htm

Southwest Texas State University-SWT. (2001). *Final report: The presidential task force on academic honesty.* Southwest Texas State University. Retrieved April 16, 2008, from http://uweb.txstate.edu/~sw05/FINALREPORT.htm

Taylor, B. (n.d.). *Academic integrity: A letter to my students.* Retrieved April 16, 2008, from http://www.academicintegrity.org/pdf/Letter_To_My_Students.pdf

Winn, W. (2002, May 23-25). What can students learn in artificial environments that they cannot learn in class? In *Paper presented at the 20th An-*

niversary Celebrations of the First International Symposium of the Open Education Faculty (AOF), Anadolu University, Eskisehir, Turkey. Retrieved April 16, 2008, from http://aof20.anadolu.edu.tr/program.htm or from http://faculty.washington.edu/billwinn/papers/turkey.pdf

Chapter V
Creating a Firewall Against Unethical Behaviours in Open and Distance Education Practice

Dele Braimoh
University of South Africa, South Africa

Jonathan Ohiorenuan Osiki
National University of Lesotho, Southern Africa

ABSTRACT

The current process of democratizing education has inevitably led to the explosive demands by the citizens of the different countries for unrestricted admission into the conventional tertiary institutions as full time students. Unfortunately, the universities have no absorptive capacity to meet the demands due to many perennial factors. In order to meet these enormous requirements, it therefore becomes paramount for universities to restructure, re-engineer and reform. The paradigm shift therefore necessitates the repositioning of tertiary institutions in order to effect the change from "selective learning" to "lifelong learning" and from what "we offer" to what "you need" and therefore, simultaneously develop the skills of "learning to learn," especially in their clients. Where many distance learning institutions (DLIs) have become relevant in the current dispensation is in their ability to create wider accessibility to education through the open, distance and flexible operation, which allows for learning and earning going pari-passu in meeting the needs and aspirations of their heterogeneous clientele. Paradoxically, however, the majority of the world population who are ignorant of the operation and value of distance education generally, view its products as well as its programmes, not only as useless but also as inferior when compared to those of the conventional universities. Their opaque arguments for casting aspersions on distance education institutions (DEIs) may centre on their individual doubts on the quality and massification, as well as the incidence of possible masquerading identity. Closely related to this is the general notion of whether the DEI or ODL, in any way, adhere to professional ethics or academic standards. Adherence to high academic standards, which is informed through the doggedly pursued predetermined ethics, has a predictable relationship to professional behaviour and academic integrity of the ODL, at least comparatively. Ethical principles are known indexes in organizational direction and commitments, but its lapses erode known standards in academic and research ventures, as well as the quality of community service.

INTRODUCTION

An important dimension confronting professional behaviour and academic credibility, especially in ODL today, is the challenge of multiple meanings with the concomitant dual interpretation of workplace academic standards or ethics. This chapter specifically addresses these issues with the attempt to operationalize workplace ethics generally and distance education (DE) in particular. As part of the objective, therefore, the broad spectrum of this chapter is to examine the meaning of ethics and academic standards (otherwise, professional boundaries), its role in distance education, the synthesis of the emerging ethical issues in DE, the control mechanisms required to maintain quality in distance education and its various interconnectivity in academic integrity, organizational commitments in conventional programmes and online cheating in ODL. The chapter also discusses some suggested methods for curtailing ethical abuses, and thus improving professional behaviour and academic credibility in DELs.

BACKGROUND

In education generally, but in open distance learning (ODL) in particular, the issue of ethical standards or simply ethics, especially as it defines strict professional behaviour and academic credibility, has had its debate both conjecturally and age long. Over time, the dimension of what aspect of professional behaviour or discipline should constitute the "right," or the "wrong" otherwise obnoscious practice, often attract multiple inter-

pretations the world over. Unfortunately though, despite the pace of our educational development, institutions of higher learning (IHL) still have difficulties both in the interpretation and application of institutional rules and regulations, especially when there are disciplinary crises.

The word "ethics," however, may be more appreciated within the tripod interconnectivity of "ethics," "philosophy" and "morals," which share a lot of proximity in terms of their depth of meaning and somehow, on how they are applied, especially within education. Taken from the Latin word "ethica" and from the Ancient Greek "ήθική" (φιλοσοφία), it means "moral philosophy" which is equally derived from the adjective of "ήθος ēthos" indicating either "custom," "traditions" or "habit" and which all indicate a fundamental branch of philosophy, which as well encompasses the right conduct and good life. While morals essentially connote the practice of right or good actions, the term "ethics" defines the theory of "right action" and "greater good;" but philosophy, without equivocation, gives meanings to their logics. Without doubt therefore, it is usually and often the case when such terms as "professional ethics" or "ethics of the profession" otherwise, "workplace ethics" are used to define the limits, coverage, and boundaries for members, within which organizational goals and objectives are pursued. Organizational (work or professional) ethics specifies standards that should give premium on how professional behaviour or tasks are to be facilitated while recognizing the worth, dignity, potentials and uniqueness of personnels who are the driving force within the existing socio-cultural and politico-economic contexts.

It essentially defines professional responsibilities and rights motivated and directed by known values. Professional values inform and modify principles; and are an important way (ingredients) of living out an ethical commitment (American Counselling Association (ACA), 2005). It documents and defines code of conduct (otherwise, moral responsibilities) within academics, where the organization or the institution so concerned is education. Professional behaviour in education generally, and implicates the learners and programme/course facilitators (PF/CF), whether among the teaching and the nonteaching personnels, and for whom both individual and collective responsibilities are codified to direct organizational commitments.

PROFESSIONAL BEHAVIOUR VS. ACADEMIC STANDARDS

Discussing the relevance of professional behaviour or boundaries as encapsulated in ethical behaviour equally defines the status of clientele (i.e., their responsibilities and rights) in service delivery, reception and application in education generally, and the ODL in particular. Recipients of the ODL, for instance, have rights that are made functional with the concomitant responsibilities. It is part of their rights to attend and participate in interactive lecture formats (i.e., it is the case with the centre for distance learning programme, University of Ibadan, Nigeria), to be sent lectures through correspondence, receive support (such as academic counseling, integrity/dishonesty policy information, etc.) while, it is their responsibility to undertake and submit course assignments when due. As specified in the ODL directives on the rules and regulations, it is a mandatory responsibility that learners must register within a given time frame while they must also present themselves for examinations. Where participation in examinations is to be deferred, the learners have the responsibility to inform the appropriate authority in advance. Academic competence and credibility which expectedly are the watch words for all and sundry, presuppose that learners would be independent and collaborate where and when necessary in the acquisition of relevant skills and academic competences without plagiarism.

Plagiarizing work of other people without due acknowledgement, especially in the virtual learning programme as well as in the conventional system, has a lot of ethical implications. It can lead to summary dismissal from work or studies or it could even attract demotion, a failure in course grade for a paper, and sometimes, expulsion from the programme. It equally potentially affects institutional image negatively. Using the information from academics (Distance Education Student Handbook, 2008) different perspectives on plagiarism were summarized and they include, among others, the following:

a. Copying and pasting text from online media, such as encyclopedias;

b. Copying and pasting text from any Web site;

c. Transcribing text from any printed material, such as books, magazines, encyclopedias or newspapers;

d. Simply modifying text from any of the above sources or replacing a few selected words using a thesaurus;

e. Using photographs, video or audio without permission or acknowledgment;

f. Using another student's work and claiming it as your own, even with permission (known as collusion);

g. The acquisition of work from commercial sources; and

h. Translation from one language to another is not using your own words, which fall under the guidelines for quotations, summaries and paraphrases.

In consequence, for a highly recognizable academic standards and workplace professional behaviour, both learners and PF/CF would be expected to appreciate and translate operational goals within internalized work ethics, to real positive action.

RELATED THEMES IN PURSUANCE OF ODL ACADEMIC STANDARDS

According to Fieser (2007), who discussed the field of ethics (otherwise, moral philosophy), ethical theories are categorized into three general areas: (a) metaethics; (b) normative ethics; and (c) applied ethics. While meta-ethics, with its subthemes of metaphysical and psychological issues (i.e., egoism and altruism, emotion and reason, male-female morality) talks about the origin and meaning of ethical concepts as well as the underlying mental basis of moral judgments and conduct, the normative ethics mainly concerns issues of moral standards that regulate "right and wrong conduct." Within academics, for instance, learners are prompted through effective participatory learner-teacher activities, to initiate and develop the capacity for independent and collaborative efforts to academic success rather than engaging in cheating to pass, which is punishable. The normative ethics usually operates, therefore, within the "Golden Rule" which establishes the single or set of principle (principles) against which all human actions are evaluated and judged. The assumption bothering the normative ethics gets empowered by its subtheories of: (a) virtue theories (b) duty theories or deontological or the nonconsequentialist theories (i.e., right theory, categorical imperative and prima facie vs. actual duty); and (c) the consequentialist theories summarized in ethical egoism, ethical altruism and utilitarianism. In ethical egoism, actions are considered to be morally right if the consequences of the actions are more favourable than unfavourable only to the agent performing the action. In ethical altruism, actions are considered to be morally right if the consequences of the actions are more favourable

than unfavourable to everyone except the agent. Actions are, however, morally right if the consequences of the actions are more favourable than unfavourable to everyone (utilitarianism). The third categorization of ethical theory is the applied ethics, which consists of the analysis of specific and controversial moral issues such as abortion, euthanasia, pilfering, examination malpractices, sexual abuse, and results falsification. Understanding the interconnectivity of the relatedness of the subthemes and their respective underpinnings in education has potential for mitigating abuses in workplace professional behaviour as well as academic fraud. It harnesses the opportunity for improved and sustainable individual and collective tasks commitments.

UNDERSTANDING UNETHICAL BEHAVIOUR IN GENERAL STUDIES

Over time, and globally, different methods abound to epitomize the varied sophisticated strategies that learners, whether in the conventional study stream or ODL, utilized in cheating. Without any doubt, cheating in its different forms usually erodes professional and academic credibility for which any college or university would have earned and are known. Some of the methods often adopted by learners include, among others, writing faintly, but legibly on examination slabs, handkerchiefs, thighs or palms. Ladies sometimes have written or scribbled writings tugged under their braziers and others would trade sex for improved school grades. Both men and women equally offer expensive souvenirs or gifts under similar pretext. Some programme/course facilitators (PF/CF) orchestrate some of the so tagged shielded meetings to negotiate course grades for students under agreed conditions acceptable to the parties. Cizek's (1999) study is a useful summary for understanding how some of the unethical academic-related behaviours are perpetuated. According to Cizek, these are: (a) looking at another pupil's test paper during a test, (b) dropping ones paper so that other pupils can cheat off it, (c) dropping one's paper and having another pupil pick it up, cheat from it, and re-drop the paper so the original dropper can reclaim his or her paper, (d) passing an eraser between two pupils who write test information on the eraser, (e) developing codes such as tapping the floor three times to indicate that a multiple-choice item should be answered "C," (f) looking at pupils' papers while walking up to the teacher to ask a question about the test, or (g) using cribbed notes or small pieces of paper to cheat. Cribbe notes can be hidden in many ingenious places, such as: (h) switching scratch paper, often allowed by teachers during tests, with one's own scratch paper that contains test answers, or (i) writing test information on the desktop and erasing it after the test.

The advancement and benefits arising from the effective use of technology is a notable device being utilized, especially in ODL programmes. But for several reasons, cheating-related behaviours have become prominent through e-learning. In Adkins, Kenkel and Lim's (2008) observation study, the inception of online education led to the rapid growth of dotcoms involved in the sales of prewritten and custom tailored term papers or digital paper mills. The study further revealed that paper mills such as schoolsucks.com, papertopics. com, and cheathouse.com offer recycled papers and custom tailored assignments to students at a rate of $20 to $35 (Heberling, 2002; cited in Adkins, Kenkel, & Lim, 2008). There are also paper store enterprises incorporations doing business under www.termpapers-on-file.com, who are prone to offer "the largest catalog of expertly-research model term papers at a service charge of between $9.95 for pre-existing papers and $19.95 per page for custom research. In consequence, and in writing a critique to the online paper mills activities, Anderson (2001) concluded that even though the paper mills may not outwardly endorse cheating, the message they are sending is that it is acceptable to cut corners. Using the "ringers" otherwise, experts who stand in to take test for others were equally identified as a prominent cheating source. According to Wein, at the University of Arizona campus, a flyer was circulated offering services of attending classes or lectures and taking examinations for a fee (Wein, 1994; cited in Adkins et al., 2008). While a Rutgers' survey found that half of the students utilized in the study had plagiarized work they found on the Internet (Slobogin, 2002), cell phones are used to record pictures of test questions or notes and answers to multiple choice questions through text messages to fellow classmates (Cheaters Amok, ABC, 2004).

ISSUES AND TRENDS OF ACADEMIC STANDARDS IN DISTANCE EDUCATION

Considering the controversies and the lockjam that surround the term "ethics" (otherwise, ethical standards), defining the term within education generally and the open distance learning (ODL) in particular may not be easy. In the conventional institutions, for instance, various universities' calendars specify some measures of academic standards, including rules and regulations for degree certification and the evaluation of examination results. Some of such universities' calendars define the minimum standards required for the learners' qualification to be admissible into the examination hall, while others specify conduct within examination. One of such examination rules requires, for instance, that under no circumstance should a student sitting for an examination be allowed to bring into the examination hall any material so labeled, as privileged examination aid, but that contravenes a descent conduct of the examination regulation. Added to this, particularly at the National University of Lesotho (NUL) (Rules for the Conduct of Examination,

2007), is the proviso that "no candidate shall assist, or interfere with, or obtain information from another candidate" (subsection 14). Though the same university calendar have specifications on employees' mandate (i.e., teaching and the non-teaching staff members), and as it is the case with other distance education institutions or the ODL as the case may be (University of South Africa Information Brochure, 2007, 2008; University of London External Degree Programme, 2008; University of Ibadan Centre for External Studies, 2008), several issues are easily predicated.

Foremost in the 21st century adaptation on e-learning is the problem of how the ODL management would curtail the menace of examination dishonesty and impersonation, as most examinations are conducted online at certain instances. Competing issues, such as the identification of the most adequate methods for facilitating professional behaviour and in particular academic credibility, is one of the main challenges confronting the ODL programme globally. Though some of the ODL maintain face-to-face examination format with learners (LS) following regulated and designated time frames (i.e., the case of UNISA, University of Ibadan, etc.), and most examinations are conducted through several designated centres, that does not obliterate the possibility of cheating or dishonesty. Closed to the aforementioned is the issue of how effectively ODL would ensure the loyalty of appointed designated centres' officers when the conduct of such examinations is comparable to the conventional type. The assessment of learners' coursework, and a concomitant random evaluation, has equally constituted some age-long challenge, particularly in ODL. Course assignments have been assumed to constitute the product of combined efforts rather than that of the learners alone. Using external assessors in facilitating teaching practice, counseling practicum and other related internship-prone learners' activity has often raised the question on academic credibility, especially where the students' enrolment is astronomical and coverage zones are expansive.

In the discussion on cheating via the use of technology, Olt (2002) submitted that distance does not diminish the possibility of students cheating with or without an accomplice on online assessments. Online students, rather than developing codes or passing erasers, pass private e-mails, which instructors have no means of intercepting. In some other instances, learners can download an assessment, look up the answers before actually taking it and share those answers with classmates (Olt, 2002). Rather than using cribbed notes or writing answers within the margins of the textbook or on desktop, student simply use the "verboten" sources during assessment. Olt's study reported an alarming 10-point increase from the previous survey conducted 15 years ago from *Who's Who among American High School Students,* indicating that 80% of the 3,123 students surveyed admitted to cheating on an examination (Bushweller, 1999) while in a related study another 84% of respondents said that cheating was a phenomenon in their college (Branigan, 2001). Similarly, 50% of them "did not believe that cheating was necessarily wrong," and 95% of those who had cheated "said they had never been caught" (Kleiner & Lord, 1999). The number of students reporting that they have engaged in serious cheating continues to increase (Adkins et al., 2008) while Niels' (1997) study found evidence of correlation between academic dishonesty and academic practices around the nation. The sampling of parental position on students' cheating or parents aiding and abetting dishonesty was not atypically different. In a study by McCabe (2001), it was found that out of the student respondents on cheating, and who said that copying a few sentences without citation was not wrong even though less than that number felt otherwise, 22% of the students in the study turned in assignments done by their parents. The study further found that in a poll response where 66% of students said that cheating "didn't seem like a big deal" 66% of their parents equally agreed and corroborated the assertion of their children. This is a bad omen that may taint the respectability of the quality of DE programmes if nothing drastic is done to forestall the global spread of this attitude.

PERSONAL OPINIONS IN ACADEMIC STANDARDS AND LEGAL INTERPRETATIONS

Fundamental in the strict adherence and application of standard rules and regulations, especially as it affects the ODL practice and education generally, is the challenge of double meanings arising from legal interpretation. Whether it is considered from the perspective of the employee handbook or student handbook, different codes have defined professional and academic boundaries both to the programme facilitators (PF) on one hand and the recipients of programmes (whether through the ODL or the conventional method of education) on the other. Such erstwhile rules and regulations may unequivocally specify within its proviso when and how personnels' (otherwise, students') actions can be regarded as "wrong" or "right," while simultaneously dictating sanctions. Perhaps one of the most significant challenges of the ODL through the ages is its inability in securing the protection and sanctity of the handbook regulations, at least in absolute terms. Handbook regulations and the ingrained regulations in university calendars, which have been products of flouted actions, taunt the seriousness of professional behaviour and academic credibility in the majority of the institutions of higher education (IHE) globally. Using the problem of plagiarism as the index of explanation, several interpretations abound whenever "copyright" issues are debated. In Bills' (1990) study, Statistics show that 6 out of 10 undergraduates admit to plagiarism, but on the question of what happens when those students enter law school, it then focused on the difficulty created by the lack of a uniform definition of plagiarism and differing opinions on how much "intent" matters. The discussion

further concluded when it said that plagiarism was not the same thing as copyright infringement. Such dual interpretations on the direct application of infringement rules as corrective measures, from either professional or academic abuses, are part of the constrains that confront the effective maintenance of ethical practices across many institutions.

IMPROVING ORGANIZATIONAL RESPONSIBILITY IN DISTANCE LEARNING

A critical element in this paper is how to make professional behaviour and academic credibility as the function of dividends of ethical practice in education generally, but particularly in ODL programmes. Fundamental in that regard is the utilization of the benefits or operationalisation of commitment (i.e., whether from the perspective of PF/CF or students), which serve as inducements to organizational output or service delivery. Commitment, as several studies (Meyer, Allen, & Smith, 1993; O'Relly, 1991) have confirmed, is a strong index in improving professional behaviour (otherwise, organizational performance) as well as goal attainment. Maintaining expected high academic standards with concomitant dividends, in especially output in higher education, has therefore the propensity for a strong reliance on ethical standards. Wherever the workplace ethics are unambiguously appropriated, high professional performance, which can be predictable, then becomes the product of collective behaviour.

Although Meyer et al. (1993) proposed the three model-approaches to commitment and which are affective, continuance and the normative commitments, O'Relly's proposition includes compliance, identification and internalization of organizational values (i.e., workplace ethics). In Martin and Nicholls (1987), three main pillars of commitment along with their subcategorizations were identified, and these are: (a) a sense of belongingness which ensures that the work force (otherwise, the entire student body) is (i) informed, (ii) involved and (iii) sharing in organizational success; (b) sense of excitement in job (but for the students, their academic responsibilities or professional competences and growth) reinforced by professional or academic (i) pride, (ii) trust, and (iii) accountability of results; and (c) confidence in the management which is facilitated by the attention to (i) authority (otherwise, ethical standards or workplace rules and regulations) (ii) dedication and (iii) competence. Annexing the benefits of the gains following collective organizational commitments has potency for translating ethical behaviour for good performance and professional maturity, responsibility and academic integrity.

Contributing to discussion on issues related to the mitigation of the varied challenges arising from ethical abuses, in terms of professional negligence, and in particular on the ODL and education in general, Hinman (2000), Olt (2002) and Adkins et al. (2008) have provided suggestions on the amelioration of online cheating and plagiarism. When online cheating and plagiarism (both professionally, that is, with the academics themselves, or the students), whether in the attempt to respond to examination tasks, assignment, projects and dissertation/theses writing and academic research publications, wane, professional acceptability increases just as academic credibility gets boosted while simultaneously, the direct dividends of organizational ethics then become infectious positively and functionally.

In pursuance of this paradigm, and according to Hinman (2000), the three model-approaches for minimizing online cheating should constitute (a) the virtue approach (which sought to provide necessary skills for students and academic staff members who do not want to cheat); (b) the prevention method (i.e., attempting to develop empowerment skills in the elimination or reduction of opportunities for students to cheat or simply reducing the pressure to cheat); and finally (c) the police approach (which sought to identify, catch and punish those who cheat), respectively. Other methods for improving academic integrity and professional behaviour may include developing, through concerted efforts, a rotational curriculum enabled through the allocation of original assignments and reading or providing alternative, project-based assessments where creativity is significantly the vogue, as well as difficult-to-guess multiple choice items. The importance of regulatory seminars and workshops at workable intervals, both among the PF/CF and students in the ODL, should be emphasized with a concomitant follow-up on the proviso in workplace ethics on the academic integrity/dishonesty policy. McCabe and Pavela (1997) have epitomized this in their 10-principles of academic integrity, which suggest that academic institutions should:

a. Affirm the importance of academic integrity;
b. Foster love of learning;
c. Treat students as ends in themselves;
d. Promote an environment of trust in the classroom;
e. Encourage student responsibility for academic integrity;
f. Clarify expectations for students;
g. Develop fair and relevant forms of assessment;
h. Reduce opportunities to engage in academic dishonesty;
i. Challenge academic dishonesty when it occurs; and
j. Help define and support campus-wide academic integrity standards.

CONCLUSION

Both faculty members and learners have the moral responsibility to curtail workplace professional and academic abuses. To facilitate the sustainability of adequate professional behaviour and academic credibility, all PF/CF and learners must understand, accept and utilize predetermined ethical standards to direct their daily responsibilities and be unconditionally committed to total organizational goals. It must be noted that learning is a fundamental human right. Universal access to education for all throughout life is equally an ethical priority. The efficient way of ensuring wider accessibility to education by all and sundry is through distance learning. It must be stated right from the outset that education is much more than learning, as educated citizenry will, all things being equal, contribute realistically to both national and international peace, tolerance, orderliness and respect. Education should provide each person with the creative idea to innovate and to live responsibly in relation to one another in his/her community.

Having gone this far, it is pertinent to note that the onus is on the universities the world over, whether such is a conventional or a virtual institution, not only to transfer appropriate knowledge and skills to their products but also and more importantly too to instil in them some forms of academic values such as honesty, transparency, collegiality and openness and social values, which include respect, loyalty, integrity, decency, faithfulness, civic engagement and responsibility. These are very essential components of developing a whole person to be useful both to himself or herself and to the society in which he/she lives.

Unfortunately, most distance education institutions are no longer driven by their major core business of knowledge generation, skills transfer and moral rejuvenation. Rather, they camouflage their operations under the business model paradigm, thus commercializing education and thereby treating knowledge as a commodity that is manufactured in a large quantity from an industry, with a view to increasing the profit margin. If the perception of universities in the 21st century is to create wealth at the expense of quality human capacity development, certainly there will be compromises here and there in order to stay in "business" and this will loom large on the end product which will be defective, irrelevant and unsuitable for the public's consumption.

The reason for the universities to embrace the business model of education, one would guess, stems also from the dwindling financial resource allocation to them by the state. Yet, they must strive to survive; hence, the daunting challenges of fees increase, establishment of financially self-financing academic and professional programmes and more importantly, the drive to launch full blast distance education outfits. Their full-time academic programmes are therefore packaged on DE mode and targeted at the working adults; even when such institutions have no business in dabbling to distance education because they lack the wherewithal to meaningfully and professionally engage in such an activity.

We have indicated earlier in our chapter that the problem of ethical issue is not limited to the virtual universities alone, but also affects the conventional institutions because of the changing educational landscape globally. The impact of technology on our pedagogical offering is enormous; hence, Bennett (1998) has proffered a triangular scenario for the future.

1. One possibility is that the number and size of institutions of higher education will rapidly shrink as global electronic educational opportunities grow. He notes that many campuses will become service stations through which multiple learning modules are made available to students at a distance. Price will become a greater factor in student choice.

2. A second possibility is that the telecommunications revolution will prove to have minimal impact on educational institutions. It is a fad and it will go away; however, the telecommunications revolution has already advanced too far to be reversed.

3. In the third scenario, most institutions will remain, but will find themselves playing altered roles. Most campuses now pay insufficient collegial attention to pedagogy. The

telecommunications revolution will spark renewed and revived attention to pedagogy and creative collaboration using innovative classrooms and laboratories will come about. Significant distance learning will occur, but the role will remain for the traditional residential institution. Assessment criteria will be considerably improved. The Internet provides an extension of the library and laboratory, a vehicle for rapid dissemination and critique of findings, and a forum for endlessly varied discussion groups. For faculty who have been isolated by geography or campus politics, telecommunications will rejuvenate interaction with scholars elsewhere.

Be that as it may, technology has now come to stay as an extension of human beings, and the improper use of it may render most distance education institutions impotent with their expected roles. On the other hand, technology could enhance the performance level of many distance education institutions if they are keen to put in place proper control mechanisms to monitor and standardize the quality of their programmes. Ethical consideration is a relatively new concept in education, so much that the society is endemic in the water of corruption and moral decadence that it has almost become impossible to draw the line between what is right and what is wrong in society. No matter whose horse is gored, it is pertinent for us to guarantee ethical value orientation in our education system through policy formulation, so that we can remain relevant in our national socio-economic development. In order to have further debate on how to improve the current unethical situation in our educational practices, we have given below some recommendations which may serve as signposts for addressing this menace from spreading further into all the other strata of the society.

RECOMMENDATIONS

1. **Policy Formulation:** We need to formulate policies that will set a standard pattern of behaviour and ODL operation as a model for the students in both the traditional and the virtual institutions. Such policies must not only be honoured and implemented, but also respected as a code of conduct for encouraging moral uprightness in their educational activities. These will also be similar and comparable to other professions such as medical, law and journalism to mention just a few. This will also incorporate the value orientation that sets a pace for respect and control of the use of other people's intellectual property on the Internet, for instance, and thereby develop independent learning in the learners.

2. **Misplaced Societal Value:** There must be a way by which the government can conscientize the employers of labour, both in the private and public sectors of the economy, not to lay too much emphasis on paper qualification for job employment or promotion, as the craze for such is creating criminality among the youth of African countries. Alternatively, there must be standardized tests across all disciplines for all applicants seeking employment to go through, in order to prove their mettles in whatever field they may claim to be qualified. This is because tests test knowledge, and whoever cheated the system previously in order to be awarded unmerited qualification, whether such is acquired through the conventional or virtual educational institution, will through such tests be exposed as an inadequate material.

3. **Indolent Educators:** Apathy, laziness and tardiness on the part of the lecturers should also be addressed. Inability to monitor, assess and follow up the students' work to know that whatever is submitted as an as-

signment by a student is not of the quality and standard of a particular student, based on the keen evaluation of the previous performance record of students should be a thing that could easily be detected by a curious tutor whether in a conventional or distance education institution. Maybe as a result of heavy workload, particularly in a distance education programme, where a lecturer is subjected to marking too numerous scripts and assignments may inevitably lead to frustration, especially when no form of incentive is given to them. Therefore, there is the possibility for such lecturers to merely scan through the pages of such scripts without any critical assessment of the contents. Many part-time lecturers also are in the habit of becoming "machineries" in the marking process, without any concern for quality maintenance but for the drive to make more money through the number of scripts they are able to mark, but not thoroughly. There are cases of complicity of examiners with the students on the basis of sexual gratification or monetary reward, starting even with passing some students in substandard assignments or awarding inflated marks on the examination scripts. Students have also become so sophisticated in the mode of cheating in exams. Some of them write possible answers on their palms and thighs or sit close to their friends to perpetrate their nefarious acts by either exchanging scripts in the exam halls or developing elongated necks to spy on other people's work, whether or not such is even the correct answer.

4. **Corrupt Society:** Moral decadence in terms of scandal of unbelievable magnitude is found among the top public government functionaries, private enterprises, politicians, bankers and even academics the world over. This practice has sown evil corrupt seeds in our society. Like the biblical "for-

bidden fruit" in the garden of Eden, which Eve ate and she also gave to Adam to eat, and which consequently led to their expulsion from that glorious garden, many of our college students today have also eaten, unconsciously, such forbidden fruits which have been handed over to them by some of the egocentric leaders and the "big wigs" in our societies. The youth of nowadays are therefore worse in corrupt practices, including involvement in high rates of academic fraud and crimes in different dimensions, because the word "ethics" has long been blown off from their respective dictionaries of life.

5. **Inappropriate Home Training:** Charity, they say, begins at home. Unfortunately, with the current global economic recession, which has brought about a high degree of unemployment and which has led to the practical manifestation of the Darwinian theory of the "survival of the fittest," parents have therefore abdicated their traditional roles of being "teachers" in imparting sound home training to their children. The home, which used to be the most respected potent primary agent of socialization, has collapsed almost totally, as parents have no time for their wards because they are always busy chasing after earthly treasures to the detriment of the proper upbringing of their children. There is endless matrimonial conflict leading to an upsurge of divorce and thus making the youth disillusioned about what constitutes the proper values of the society. They start with little lies, but gradually move to the level of pilfering and consequently become champions in stealing, robbery and fraud of international magnitude. Let the parents embrace the reality of the dictum which says "bend a sapling and you have bent a tree" and apply this to their process of nurturing their children, so that they will not be public nuisances when they grow up to

adulthood and thereby become a menace to the society.

RECOMMENDATION FOR FUTURE RESEARCH DIRECTIONS

a. There is need for a comparative study of conventional and distance education institutions, with possible focus on the genealogy, magnitude of practice and the implications of the violation of ethical issues which were identified in this chapter, vis-à-vis the quality of products and programmes.

b. More research effort is required on ethical issues in online educational settings with regard to the attitude, beliefs and behaviour of both the students and staff of virtual universities.

c. There must be a systematic research activity on the appropriateness or otherwise of the applications and the use of ICT for educational delivery, which is more often adopted by both the single and bi-modal tertiary institutions but with negative implication for learners' access.

REFERENCES

Academics: Distance education student handbook. (2008). Hagerstown Community College. Retrieved April 16, 2008, from http://www.hagerstowncc.edu/academics/distance/studenthandbook.php

Adkins, J., Kenkel, C., & Lim, C. L. (2008). *Deterrents to online academic dishonesty.* Retrieved April 16, 2008, from http://jwpress.com/JLHE/Issues/viii/Deterrents%20to%20Online%20Academic%20Dishonesty.pdf

American Counselling Association (ACA). (2005). *Code of ethics.* Retrieved April 16, 2008, from http://www.counseling.org

Anderson, C. (2001, Winter). Online cheating: A new twist to an old problem. *Student Affairsonline, 2.* Retrieved April 16, 2008, from http://www.studentaffairs.com/ejournal/winter_2001/plagiarism.htm

Bennett, J. B. (1998). *Collegial professionalism: The academy, individualism and the common good.* Phoenix, AZ: American Council on Education & Oryx Press.

Bills, R. D. (1990). *Plagiarism in law school: Close resemblance of the worst kind*? Retrieved April 16, 2008, from http://www.lwionline.org/publications/plagiarism/OnlineSources.html

Branigan, C. (2001). Rutgers study: Web makes student cheating easier. *E-school News Online.* Retrieved April 16, 2008, from http://www.eschoolnews.org/showstory.cfm?ArticleID=2638

Bushweller, K. (1999). Generation of cheaters. *The American School Board Journal.* Retrieved April 16, 2008, from www.asbj.com/199904/0499coverstory.html

Cheaters amok: A crisis in America's schools—how it's done and why it's happening. (2004, April 29). *ABC Primetime News.* Retrieved April 16, 2008, from http://listserv.uiuc.edu/wa.cgi?A2=indo405&L=dime-1&T=0&F=&S==&p=69

Cizek, G. (1999). *Cheating on tests: How to do it, detect it and prevent it.* Mahwah, NJ: Lawrence Erlbaum.

Fieser, J. (2007). *The Internet encyclopedia of philosophy.* Retrieved April 16, 2008, from http://www.utm.edu/`jfieser/

Heberling, M. (2002, Spring). Maintaining academic integrity in online education. *Online Journal of Distance Learning Administration, V*(1). State University of West Georgia, Distance Education Center. Retrieved April 16, 2008, from http://www.westga.edu/~distance/ojdla/spring51/heberling51.html

Hinman, L. M. (2000). *Academic integrity and the World Wide Web.* Retrieved April 16, 2008, from http://ethics.acusd.edu/presentations/cai2000/index_files/frame.htm

Holland, B. (1997, Fall). Analyzing institutional commitment to service: A model of key organizational factors. *Michigan Journal of Community Service Learning* (pp. 30-34). Retrieved April 16, 2008, from http://www.compact.org/advanced-toolkit/pdf/holland-all.pdf

Kleiner, C., & Lord, M. (1999). The cheating game: Cross-national exploration of business students' attitudes, perceptions, and tendencies toward academic dishonesty. *Journal of Education for Business. 74*(4), 38-42.

Martin, P., & Nicholls, J. (1987). *Creating a committed workforce.* Institute of Personnel Management.

McCabe, D. L. (2001). *Student cheating in American high schools.* Retrieved April 16, 2008, from http://www.academicintegrity.org/index.asp

McCabe, D. L., & Pavela, G. (1997). *Ten principles of academic integrity.* Ashville, NC: College Administration Publications. Retrieved April 16, 2008, from http://www.collegepubs.com/ref/10PrinAcaInteg.shtml

Meyer, J. P., Allen, N. J., & Smith, C. A. (1993). Commitment to organisations and occupations: Extension and test of a 3-component model. *Journal of Applied Psychology, 78,* 538-551.

National University of Lesotho (NUL). (2007). *Extract of the rules for the conduct of examination.* Morija: National University of Lesotho, NUL Public Affairs Office.

Niels, G. J. (1997). *Academic practices, school culture and cheating behaviour.* Retrieved April 16, 2008, from http://www.hawken.edu/odris/cheating/cheating.html

Olt, M. R. (2002). *Ethics and distance education: Strategies for minimizing academic dishonesty in online assessment.* Retrieved April 16, 2008, from http://www.westga.edu/`distance/ojdla/fall53/olt53.html

O'Relly, C. (1991). Corporations, culture and commitment: Motivation and social control in organisations. In R. M. Steers & L.W. Porter (Eds.), *Motivation and work behaviour* (5th ed., pp. 242-255). New York; McGraw-Hill.

Slobogin, K. (2002). Survey: Many students say cheating's OK. *CNN.com/Education.* Retrieved April 16, 2008, from httP://archivers.cnn.com/2008/fyi/teachers.ednews/04/05/highschool.cheating

University of Ibadan Center for External Studies Programme. (2007). Retrieved April 16, 2008, from http://www.ui.edu.ng/undergraduateadmission.htm

University of London External Degree Program: Our history. (2008). Retrieved April 16, 2008, from Http://www.londonexternal.ac.uk/about_us/history.shtml

University of South Africa (UNISA) information brochure. (2008). UNISA, Pretoria, South Africa. Retrieved April 16, 2008, from http://www.unisa.ac.za

Wein, E. (1994). *Cheating: Risking it all for grades.* Retrieved April 16, 2008, from http://wildcat.arizona.edu/papers/old-wildcats/fall94/December/December2,1994/03_1_m.html

ADDITIONAL READING

Campbell, E. (2003). *The ethical teacher.* Maidenhead: Open University Press.

Carr, D. (2006). *Professionalism and ethics in teaching.* London: Routledge.

Cooper, D. E. (2004). *Ethics for professionals in a multicultural world.* Upper Saddle, River, NJ: Pearson/Prentice Hall.

Hard, S., Conway, J. M., & Moran, A. C. (2006). Faculty and college student beliefs about the frequency of student academic misconduct. *Journal of Higher Education, 77*(6), 1058-1080.

Martin, M. W. (2000). *Meaningful work: Rethinking professional ethics.* Oxford: Oxford University Press.

May, W. W. (1990). *Ethics and higher education.* New York: Macmillan Publishing Company and American Council on Education.

Nash, R. J. (1996). *Real world ethics: Frameworks for educators and human service professionals.* New York: Teachers College Press.

Olt, M. R. (2002). Ethics and distance education: Strategies for minimizing academic dishonesty in online assessment. *Online Journal of Distance Learning Administration, 5*(3).

Quinn, M. J. (2005). *Ethics for the information age* (2nd ed.) Boston: Addison-Wesley.

Rowson, R. (2006). *Working ethics: How to be fair in a culturally complex world.* London: Jessica Kingsley.

Tavani, H. T. (2006). *Ethics and technology: Ethical issues in an age of information and communication technology* (2nd ed.). San Francisco: John Wiley.

Weston, A. (2007). *Creative problem-solving in ethics.* New York: Oxford University Press.

Section II
Technology–Based

Chapter VI
Ethical Concerns with Open and Distance Learning

Glenn Russell
Monash University, Australia

ABSTRACT

Some of the more important ethical concerns associated with open and distance learning are not those that may be faced by learners. Instead, the challenges faced by those that design ODL or use it in their teaching can be seen as increasingly important. These challenges include globalization, which has emphasized instrumental rather than social aims of education, and the use of cognitive rather than affective pedagogies. For ODL designers and teachers, this has resulted in a concentration on cognitive tasks and market-driven aspects of open and distance learning at the expense of the social harmony that might otherwise be achieved. The overarching ethical concern for ODL practitioners should be to implement an appropriate pedagogy that will satisfy both instrumental and social aims. While this can be achieved, in part, through the use of the pedagogies outlined in this chapter, the problem is seen as being associated with deeply interwoven social and cultural contexts. Consequently, there is a greater responsibility for all ODL practitioners to ensure that the choices that they make are ethical at all times, irrespective of the demands of any employer, institution or authority.

Meanwhile, so long as we draw breath, so long as we live among men, let us cherish humanity. Seneca, Roman Philosopher, CA 4BC-AD65 (Seneca, 2007)

PROLOGUE: ETHICAL DILEMMAS AND ODL

Increasingly, the enthusiastic adoption of Open and Distance Learning Systems (ODLS) in higher education has resulted in the increased availability of tertiary courses for students and benefits for the organizations that provide it. The concurrent emergence of theory and practice related to open and distance education (ODL) has highlighted emotional and psychological issues, and it has raised questions related to the role of virtual learning environments and pedagogies in promoting human and social needs. The future development of ODL as a mature discipline requires mutual trust between students, teachers, developers and researchers. This development is at a critical stage, because rather than anticipate ethical problems, and plan appropriate procedures to meet the challenge, it has too often been the practice for those associated with ODL to take the easiest and most pragmatic path, without adequate consideration of the long-term effects of their work on individuals and society. As Russell (2005) suggests, "It is...possible for educators to become overly preoccupied with online technologies, financial considerations, and utility at the expense of ethical and community considerations."

It is likely that the statement in the code of ethics from the Australian College of Educators that "Teachers are responsible for what they teach and for the way that they relate to students" (Haynes 1998, p. 176) probably has counterparts in similar ethical codes from other countries. It suggests that there is a continued ethical responsibility that must be faced by every individual working with ODL which cannot be excused by any characteristics of the technology itself, or

by institutional constraints. One of the problems associated with ODL has been that the long-term consequences of choices between alternatives are often unclear. Russell (2004) suggests that examples of irresponsible behaviour, including the actions of surgeons, motor vehicle manufacturers and operators of radiation equipment, are more easily identified when there is an empirically verifiable cause and effect.

In this respect, a comparison between the work of scientists and practitioners involved in ODL is instructive, in that disinterested observers can identify moral dilemmas more easily with the work of scientists. This is because the potential of a technology to result in harm is clearer when death or a physical injury is likely to result from its use. In the case of ODL designers and teachers, alleged disadvantages such as psychological effects, or long-term changes to the nature of society, are likely to be disputed.

Two examples related to scientists' approaches to moral dilemmas illustrate this point. Jungk (1958) describes the attitude of scientists who worked on the first atomic bombs. He gives the example of a brilliant mathematician at Los Alomos, whose work had contributed to the first nuclear explosions. However, his interest was in science rather than in the effects of his work on people. He did not watch the trial explosions of the bombs, and refused to look at pictures of destruction that they had caused. A second example can be found in the work of Louis Feiser (1964), whose work contributed to the development of napalm. Feiser's book describing his experiments is a well-written explanation of the scientific method used to develop napalm. However, despite discussion of incidents in his personal life (and unlike Oppenheimer, 1948), there is little evidence that he was preoccupied with the moral consequences of the technology that he was developing. Indeed, in an interview with the New York Times ("Napalm inventor discounts guilt", 1967), Feiser stated that he felt no guilt about his work, and that it was not his business to deal with political and moral questions. It is this same concept of the pure technician who is not accountable beyond his area of expertise that is criticized in Sammon's (1992) condemnation of Albert Speer as a moral failure.

While scientists' awareness of consequences and moral culpability can sometimes be criticized, as with the preceding examples, the potential for harm is clear when the technology in question is clearly related to some physical injury. ODL also requires the use of technology, but it is very different in nature; it has not been planned with the intention of causing harm, and some practitioners will overlook the possibility that ethical dilemmas may result from the adoption of distance learning unless the focus shifts to the learner. Indeed, for some writers in this field, there is a preoccupation with issues that may confront the user, such as plagiarism or online behaviour, at the expense of issues facing designers, developers and teachers. ODL usually requires a virtual learning environment (VLE) in which teachers use a range of online tools to teach students or to help them to reach their educational goals. While ODL is a convenient term to describe a range of environments, tools, and associated pedagogies, it is however, not monolithic in nature. Conceptually, it is not like a black box containing mysterious individual components.

Although there can be robust debate about the best ways to conduct ODL, it is likely that some approaches will be more effective than others in promoting student learning. In addition, as technological effects are unlikely to be limited to student learning, indirect effects can be expected, such as changes in students' ability to relate with others in society. It follows, then, that decisions to prefer one ODL technology over another is an ethical decision, because varying amounts of good or harm flow to the individual and society as a result of it. DiBiase (2000) has observed of distance education that "…professional educators have a moral obligation to students, and to society, to provide the highest quality education possible by means of the most effective means available" (p. 132). Consequently, the teacher is under an obligation to not knowingly implement any practice that will cause harm. There is a continuing responsibility for students' welfare, including that of adults, in this respect.

It is, however, difficult or even impossible to establish causal relationship between a specific ODL technique and the behaviour or attitudes of students. We can readily test cognitive outcomes and determine whether a given ODL approach has contributed to specified knowledge, but cause and effect observations based on empirical phenomena are easier to understand than their affective counterparts. For example, it would be more problematic if an ODL teacher observed that some students were intolerant of others, and linked this behaviour to teaching practices used. Nevertheless, the lack of certainty in establishing such a link does not mean that the consequences of choosing a particular pedagogy should be ignored.

As Zembylas (2005) argues, online pedagogies are about more than knowledge and its conceptual and aesthetic organisation. Specific interactions are mediated by the technology, but they are still fundamentally constructed by learners and teachers. Similarly, Meyer (2005) maintains that the Internet is the product of design choices and choices about how to use it.

Consequently, although the effects of a given ODL technology are linked to the characteristics of that technology, fundamentally, people make ethical decisions and they must accept responsibility for them. Given this observation, it is useful to note some of the ways in which ODL has been used in recent times, and for what purposes.

GLOBALIZATION AND THE GROWTH OF ENDS: MEANS INTERPRETATIONS OF ODL

The growth of globalization in recent years has been accompanied by an increased use of online technology. For Castells (1993), the transformations in the world economy represents a revolution whose core is based on information technologies. These changes have been accompanied by extensive changes in education. Torres (2002) argues that there have been changes in the kinds of goods and services that are available to people. One unwelcome change, however, is the failure to cater for noneconomic needs. Yang (2003) explains the inability of globalization to cater for what Welton (1995) describes as the "lifeworld:"

With market mechanism at its core, globalisation undermines certain basic human needs...it does not necessarily cater to non-economic needs. The need to provide for ourselves, to give, create and invent, to do things for ourselves and one another...all this is subverted by the market. (Yang, 2003, p. 272)

Kellner (2000) suggests that important consequences of these new technologies include the further colonization of education by business at the expense of politics and culture, and the undermining of democracy through the hegemonic influence of capital at the expense of other domains of life. For Streibel (1988), the technical nature of the delivery system has the capacity to shift educational interactions away from interpersonal interactions toward procedural skills and information-processing functions, while Hylnka and Belland (1991) maintain that enquiries related to educational technology seemed to be limited to enquiries about outcomes of technologically-based learning systems.

Writing in the pre-online era, Murphy and Pardeck (1985) suggest that technology advances a world view that shapes social existence, while Apple (1988) argued that computer technology embodied a form of thinking that oriented a person to approach the world in a particular way. The technical logic involved in this approach was seen as replacing critical, political and ethical understanding.

For ODL practitioners it is increasingly likely that ODL will be presented as an environment in which cognitive outcomes are emphasised at the expense of affective. If choices in ODL environments are linked to business attitudes toward issues such as social responsibility, there are some indications that ethical choices will be restricted. May (1986) describes the ways in which profit-oriented pressures can act as countervailing pressures to the ethical motivations of professional engineers, while in an article originally written in 1970, Friedman (2001) remarked that:

...there is only one social responsibility of business -to use its resources and engage in activities designed to increase its profits so long as it stays within the rules of the game, which is to say, engages in open and free competition without deception or fraud. (p. 55)

Although it is not at all certain that the majority of business people would agree with this position, the choice between alternative pedagogies in ODL are influenced by a mindset that both sees social responsibility as someone else's problem, and does not always recognise that there are choices to be made. Where a given pedagogy is seen as efficient in achieving measurable ends and is consistent with existing practices, concerns such as civic engagement, democracy and personal relationships will be marginalized. This does not mean that ODL practitioners are consciously acting in an unethical or antisocial manner; as Milojevik (2005) argues, hegemonic futures eliminate alternatives by not contesting them or making them illegal or unpopular, but by making them invisible. To extend the metaphor of the information superhighway, it is as though a driver can follow the brightly lit signs indicating the most direct route to a destination, but does not notice other signs and destinations.

It is less likely that those involved in ODL will notice that ethical choices are available to them when the predominating ethos supports corporate capitalism rather than the imperatives of society. In this respect, the observations by Aronowitz and Giroux (1993) concerning beliefs about schooling in the USA can also be applied to other areas, including ODL. Aronowitz and Giroux maintain that under the Reagan/Bush administration in the USA, the notion of schooling as a vehicle for social justice and public responsibility was "trashed for the glitter of the marketplace and the logic of the spirited entrepreneur" (p. 8). For universities, the implication of this observation in recent years in some developed countries has been that vocational aspects and profit have been considered as more important than earlier concepts of the university that involved a liberal tradition. Evans and Nation (2000) suggest that the notion of the university as a "critical community of scholars" has changed into one of the university as an educational corporation. ODL has been seen as an important means of providing an education for students and an income stream for higher education. While there is always a choice between competing pedagogies and tools in ODL, it is nevertheless likely that, in practice, choices may be restricted by prevailing expectations of the purposes of ODL and the ways in which it is used.

Summer (2000) suggests that some of the ethical problems that have been discussed in this chapter can be seen as a choice in distance education between serving the "system" or the "lifeworld." She raises the question of whether the chosen technology used in distance education enhances social learning, or whether it makes educational transactions more efficient by enhancing individualized learning. It is possible that a concurrent solution to this dilemma may be implemented which simultaneously enables ODL to be used in both areas, and the choice may not be between two polar opposites. It is important to note, however, that Summer's discussion of these issues provides an ODL context for a debate that predates online learning and has continued for more than a 100 years. Matthew Arnold (1882) cautioned against the "unfettered pursuit of the

production of wealth" at the expense of social issues, while Watt (1929) maintained that moral principles should be applied to economic activities, and Mumford (1934) explained his concerns about the tendency of capitalism to use machines rather than further social welfare, and for machines to modify the cultural forms of civilization. Collectively, the continued debate of such issues over time, despite enormous changes in society and technology, prompts a reflection about the ethical use of ODL in the near and distant future.

It seems reasonable to suggest that improvements in available ODL technology will, in turn, enable more ethical choices to be made. Arguably, there will be increases in bandwidth, and technologies such as video conferencing will become more common. A consequence of the increased use of interactive technologies could be that students' emotional and social needs could be catered for more effectively. While this scenario is initially attractive, it does not, however, meet the objection that an educator's choice of ODL technology may be driven by a complex mix of factors, of which the availability of a technology may be only one of many. Stewart and Williams (1998) remind us that social choices are inherent in the ways in which technologies are selected and implemented, and these in turn shape further change. Hence, the question of ethical choices in ODL discussed in this chapter is as much the question of globalization and related political, economic and social factors as it is of the characteristics of available technology.

THE IMPLICATIONS FOR SOCIETY OF HUMAN INTERACTION AND OPEN AND DISTANCE LEARNING

An in-depth exploration of ethical issues associated with ODL needs to establish that there are preferred alternatives to the pedagogy associated with globalisation and procedural means-ends techniques such as those discussed earlier in this chapter. It is also important that ODL developers know (or reasonably ought to know) what consequences their actions may have on society, in addition to any immediate effects on the learner. As Weckert and Adeney (1997) suggest, while experts ought to be accountable for their actions in their professional fields, to be held accountable, a person must have caused the event or knowingly allowed it to happen.

It seems clear that an ODL pedagogy which teaches a body of knowledge, but undervalues key aspects of human interaction and the impact of distance education on society must be seen as limited. Where these interactions are relevant in determining learners' emotional states, or in ascertaining what is of value to them, there are contingent links to questions of ethics.

There are indications that some pedagogies used in ODL can be considered to be more appropriate than others. This is particularly true when ODL is compared to face-to-face alternatives. While it is likely, as Russell (1999) indicates, that there is no significant difference between face-to-face and online teaching, much of this research overlooks interpersonal and affective aspects of the respective learning environments. Palmer (1995) maintains that face-to-face communication is the paradigmatic social context and medium, and it is critical for interpersonal processes. In contrast, online technologies have a reduced capacity to support affective relationships.

It is not that ODL is incapable of transmitting emotions or allowing learners to become involved in affective issues; it is, rather, that ODL practitioners do not always consider these factors when designing or using distance education. If there is a continued tendency to overlook these areas, users will look to traditional experiential contacts with other humans rather than online environments, and the notion that ODL does not cater for interaction as well as face-to-face environments will become increasingly self-fulfilling. As Nie (2001) explains, although people can convey emotion

through technologies such as e-mail, the fundamentals of our socio-emotional well-being are found in something other than computer screens. It is not surprising that some distance education texts do not have any references to issues such as ethics, emotions, or the affective domain in their index; it is not on the authors' radar.

While affective issues and the emotional aspects of education have traditionally been underrepresented in the literature, there has nevertheless been an acknowledgement of the importance of these issues. Research from the predigital era (Mehrabian, 1981) has emphasised the importance of subtle behaviours to convey feelings, and in the ability to infer attitudes from behaviours. McNess, Broadfoot and Osborn (2003) note the importance of a teacher's ability to emphasise and build relationships with the learner, while Jones and Issroff (2005) argue that for online communities to be successful, developers and designers need to pay attention to social as well as technical issues. Sunderland (2002) identifies a psychological and communications gap between instructors and learners, and suggests that it is necessary to pay attention to the affective needs of the distance learner as well as their pedagogic needs.

One of the most critical areas of difference between online and face-to-face environments is that the more traditional environments facilitate nonverbal communication. Lyons, Klunder and Tetsutai (2005) argue that an important group of learning indicators becomes more difficult because they rely at least partially on nonverbal communication, and this is atypical in most online environments.

A related but often neglected issue in this discussion is the role of emotions in ODL. Recent related research in this area include the ideas of Damasio (2000), who has argued on neurological evidence that emotions are essential to rational thinking, and Planalp(1999), who has suggested that emotions are connected to moral meaning through recognition of facial cues in face-to-face interactions. Boler(1999) has suggested that emotions have been suppressed or ignored in education, but they are nevertheless important. Because emotions give us information about what we care about and why, they shape how we treat other people and inform our moral assumptions.

Picard (1997) summarises the current position on the importance of emotions:

The latest scientific findings indicate that emotions play an essential role in rational decision making, perception, learning, and a variety of other cognitive functions. Emotions...influence the very mechanisms of rational thinking...the new scientific evidence is that too little emotion can impair decision making. (p. x)

It is also likely, as Picard and Klein (2002) argue, that the accomplishment of productivity and efficiency goals are not enough, and that the view of the user as part of a productivity equation should be replaced by one in which humans who interact with computers are seen as affective beings "motivated to action by a complex system of emotions, drives, needs and environmental conditioning in addition to cognitive factors" (p. 142).

It follows, then, that if emotions contribute to moral assumptions and the way that we treat others, then any pedagogy related to ODL should provide a role for emotions. In particular, the teacher needs to be able to recognise the emotional state of students and modify what is taught appropriately. For example, in a conventional face-to-face class, (with or without ICT), teachers have a reasonable opportunity to determine whether students are confused, satisfied, angry or distressed. In some online environments, teachers can recognise problems as they arise and modify their teaching accordingly. This process is outlined in Figure 1.

However, this situation is not true of all online environments. In some cases, the nature of the medium being used hinders teachers' recognition of students' emotions, and provides limited opportunity for feedback and interaction. Part of the problem, as Tiffin and Rajasingham (2003) suggest, is that instructional research has focused on cognitive issues:

Instructional research has been preoccupied with the cognitive aspects of instruction and with measuring standardised outcomes. We lack the research methodologies that can take into account the impact of smiles and frowns and laughter and explosions of anger. (p. 30)

Studies that compare online and face-to-face environments are often based on test scores, which themselves are based on cognitive rather than affective learning. It is appropriate to consider online environments in terms of communication theories, to see how they are related to understandings of affective issues and emotions, and to determine whether improvements in ODL technologies will enable more ethical choices between alternatives.

Figure 1. Affective steps for teachers in online environments

Affective step	Online teachers' questions
Recognition of feedback related to students' emotional state	Can the teacher obtain immediate feedback of the emotional state of the learner in this online environment? (e.g., observation of facial expressions and body language as with face-to-face interactions)
Modification of ODL practices	In what ways should online instruction be modified to enable informed and ethical practice?

COMMUNICATION THEORIES AND ONLINE AND DISTANCE EDUCATION

In simple terms, it can be argued that the increased adoption of broadband technologies will allow greater interactivity, together with an increased capacity for affective engagement. However, this solution is only partial, as it relies on a technicist approach to a complex issue, which in turn is inextricably bound up with its social, political and cultural contexts. The meaning of "technicist" used in this chapter draws on Lankshear's (1997) understanding of an amalgam of ideas in which technical purposes are privileged over social approaches. In the case of ethical concerns and ODL, this could result in the proposed solution becoming part of the problem, when other causes of restricted alternatives become invisible.

Several communication theories, including those of psychological distancing, information richness, and electronic propinquity are relevant to ODL. The greater part of these theories predate online learning, but it likely that the research is still relevant. Wellens (1986) described a *Psychological Distancing Model,* where "immediacy" was related to the number of information channels, and the reduction of telecommunication bandwidth leads to a progressive decrease in sensory modalities with the movement from face to face to videophone, telephone, and written forms of communication. The number of information channels and their bandwidth used in ODL are likely to be important in transmitting both cognitive *and* affective information.

A related theory is that of media or *information richness.* This theory argues that learning is related to the characteristics of the communications channel, and, as bandwidth becomes wider, learning becomes richer. Walther (1992), for example, saw CMC (Computer-Mediated Communication) as a lean channel while videoconferencing was seen as moderately rich. Daft and Lengel (1986) argued for the existence of a hierarchy

of information richness based on the potential information-carrying capacity of the data. They classified information mediums then available in order from highest to lowest. The application of this theory to more recent technologies, as used in ODL, suggests that face-to-face teaching or synchronous video conferencing would be seen as richer than text-based environments such as online discussion groups, and would potentially enable choices to be made that promoted an instructor's knowledge of a student's affective state.

An additional perspective is provided by the earlier work of Korzenny and Bauer (1981) in their theory of *electronic propinquity.* This theory refers to the degree to which members of an organisation experience communication satisfaction. One of the components of this theory is related to bandwidth, which was defined by these authors as the information transmission capacity of the available sensory channels for vocal and nonvocal, and verbal and nonverbal communication. Face-to face conferences involve all five channels available for communication and these were defined as having a wide bandwidth; in contrast, video conferences have only two channels (visual and auditory) available and were defined as having medium bandwidth, while audio only conferences have only one channel available and were defined as having a narrow bandwidth. The bandwidth component of this theory suggests the existence of a hierarchy, in which the reduction in the richness of information available for students is accompanied by a related reduction in the teacher's ability to discern the emotional state of students when communication channels between teacher and student become leaner. That is, when teachers attempt to assess the affective components of students' learning, an information-rich environment such as a face-to-face class or video conference will contain more cues than an information-poor environment such as text-only e-mail. When teachers are considering the best ways to use online technologies in their teaching, some pedagogies are preferred because they give the teacher more information about their students' underlying affective state. Such information is important in identifying contingent values and beliefs, and in the case of ODL practitioners, it assists them in making ethical decisions.

PRINCIPLES OF ETHICAL ODL USE

The following ethical principles of ODL use for designers and teachers can be derived from the preceding discussion, including consideration of factors such as globalization, affective issues, psychological distancing, media richness, and electronic propinquity.

Where possible, identify any commonly-held affective objectives and community norms, together with the ideals for the society of which they are related. This is a *prerequisite* to choosing individual techniques such as those in the remainder of this list. The privileging of social objectives over their more instrumental counterparts may result in an approach that is uncommon in ODL.

- The incorporation of some face-to face interaction through blended learning or experiential rather than wholly mediated distance education solutions should be helpful. The inclusion of direct human relationships will provide an increased opportunity for affective interaction and will enable students to match the relational cues derived from face-to-face contexts with available information in ODL environments.
- High bandwidth solutions including the use of desktop video conferencing and streaming video can be a useful option for an online course that relies heavily on e-mail or text-based communications.
- Consider the use of synchronous technologies, such as live chats and video conferences. Immediate feedback is valuable when teachers need to assess affective issues such

as the emotional state of their students and make ethical decisions based on the resulting information.

INDIVIDUAL RESPONSIBILITY AND ETHICAL CHOICES IN ODL

In Bertolt Brecht's play, *Life of Galileo*, Brecht (1995) uses the example of Galileo's moral dilemma to reflect on the individual responsibility and ethical decisions faced by scientists. It is relevant to a discussion of ethics and responsibility associated with ODL:

To what end are you working? Presumably for the principle that science's sole aim must be to lighten the burden of human existence.

If the scientists, brought to heel by self-interested rulers, limit themselves to piling up knowledge for knowledge's sake, then science can be crippled and your new machines will lead to nothing but new impositions.

You may in due course discover all that there is to discover, and your progress will nonetheless be nothing but a progress away from mankind. The gap between you and it may one day become so wide that your cry of triumph at some new achievement will be echoed by a universal cry of horror. – As a scientist I had a unique opportunity. In my day astronomy emerged into the marketplace. Given this situation, if one man had put up a fight it might have had tremendous repercussions. Had I stood firm the scientists would have developed something like the Hippocratic Oath, a vow to use their knowledge exclusively for mankind's benefit. As things are, the best that can be hoped for is a race of inventive dwarfs who can be hired for any purpose. (p. 100-101)

If ODL practitioners are not to be regarded in the same way as Galileo's "inventive dwarfs," they need to accept responsibility for the distance learning tools and pedagogies that they employ, including their effects on society. An ethical designer or teacher involved in ODL will consider issues relating to emotion and affect in addition to cognitive and means-ends concerns.

As ODL grows into a mature discipline, its adherents should be able to look past the constraints imposed by globalisation, and the socially constructed uses of ODL that have often been typical of its use. To revisit the metaphor of the information superhighway for a final time, the choices made by those involved in ODL should not be restricted to those roads that have been chosen by others.

FUTURE RESEARCH DIRECTIONS

Future research on this and related topics should include the notion of ethical responsibility for the pedagogies that distance educators employ. In particular, the notion that good or harm might result from the use of particular techniques or tools used in virtual learning environments has been undertheorized. This gap in the research literature (and accounts derived from current practices) often fails to consider the long-term implications of distance education practices for issues such as interpersonal relationships, harmonious communities, and civic engagement. This is especially the case when consideration is given to interactions and beliefs that extend beyond the immediate parameters of scheduled class activities.

The instructor's ability to recognise students' emotional (or affective) states in distance education is critical for ethical understanding. This is because ethical judgments are largely dependent on what people value. Research that emphasises the cognitive domain or instrumental tasks at the expense of the affective domain neglects an important area. Reliable instruments and techniques are needed to enable the identification of these affective states.

Recent research into communities of practice and sociocultural contexts suggests that informal communities allow involvement in shared enterprises. This involvement, in turn, provides understandings of community and learning that are grounded in everyday experiences as much as in the structured offerings of institutions. For distance education, the challenge is to understand the ways in which these perspectives contribute to the identity, value systems and behaviours of distance education students.

The technology used in distance education advances a view of the world that shapes social existence. A revised world view may result from this process which in turn is likely to contribute to future ways in which technology is used. There is a corresponding need for researchers to make explicit what transformations are occurring during such processes.

Finally, the nexus between globalization and technology prompts exploration of links between market forces and the nature of distance education. The characteristics of higher education, when offered in distance education mode, may show a predilection for instrumentalism that is in sharp contrast with traditional liberal concepts of education. The resulting tension may reflect an existing trend in some higher educational institutions; however, it may also be an indication that the move to online learning represents a more fundamental shift in the nature of higher education. Future research in this area could well reflect on the aims of higher education, and the role of distance education in achieving these aims.

REFERENCES

Apple, M. W. (1988). Teaching and technology: The hidden effects of computers on teachers and students. In L. E. Beyer & M. W. Apple (Eds.), *The curriculum: Problems, politics and possibilities* (pp. 289-311). Albany: State University of New York Press.

Arnold, M. (1882). *Culture and anarchy*. Retrieved April 16, 2008, from http://www.library.utoronto.ca/utel/nonfiction_u/arnoldm_ca/ca_all.html

Aronowitz, S., & Giroux, H. A. (1993). *Education still under siege*. Westport, CT: Bergin and Garvey.

Boler, M. (1999). *Feeling power: Emotions and education*. New York and London: Routledge.

Bretch, B. (1995). Life of Galileo. In J. Willett & R. Manheim (Eds.), *Bertolt Brecht collected plays: Five* (pp. 1-105) (J. Willett, Trans.). London: Methuen.

Castells, M. (1993). The informational economy and the new International Division of Labor. In M. Carnoy, M. Castells, S. S. Cohen, & F. H. Cardoso (Eds.), *The new global economy in the information age: Reflections on our changing world* (pp. 15-43). University Park, PA: Pennsylvania State University Press.

Daft, R. L., & Lengel, R. H. (1986). Organizational information requirements, media richness and structural design. *Management Science, 32*, 554-571.

Dibiase, D. (2000). Is distance education a Faustian bargain? *Journal of Geography in Higher Education, 24*(1), 130-135.

Evans, T., & Nation, D. (2000). *Changing university teaching: Reflections on creating educational technologies*. London: Kogan Page.

Feiser, L. B. (1964). *The scientific method: A personal account of unusual projects in war and peace*. New York: Reyhold.

Friedman, L. (2001). The social responsibility of business is to increase its profits. In T. L. Beauchamp & N. E. Bowie (Eds.), *Ethical theory and business* (6th ed., pp. 51-55). Upper Saddle River, NJ: Prentice Hall.

Haynes, F. (1998). *The ethical school*. London: Routledge.

Hylnka, D., & Belland, J. C. (1991). Preface. In D. Hylnka & J. C. Belland (Eds.), *Paradigms regained: The use of illuminative, semiotic and postmodern criticism as modes of enquiry in educational technology* (pp. v-ix). Englewood Cliffs, NJ: Educational Technology Publications.

Jones, A., and Issroff, K., (2005). Learning Technologies: Affective and Social Issues in Computer-Supported Collaborative Learning. *Computers and Education, 44* (4) 395-408

Jungk, R. (1958). *Brighter than a thousand suns: A personal history of the atomic scientists* (J. Cleugh, Trans.). Harmondsworth, Middlesex: Penguin.

Kellner, D. (2000). Globalization and new social movements: Lessons for critical theory and pedagogy. In N. C. Burbles & C. A. Torres (Eds.), *Globalization and education: Critical perspectives* (pp. 229-321). London: Routledge.

Kozenny, F., & Bauer, C. (1981). Testing the theory of electronic propinquity. *Communication Research, 8*(4), 479-498.

Lankshear, C. (1997). Language and the new capitalism. *International Journal of Inclusive Education, 1*(4), 309-321.

Lyons, M. J., Klunder, D., & Tetsutai, N. (2005). Supporting empathy in online learning with artificial expressions. *Educational Technology and Society, 8*(4), 22-30.

May, L. (1996). *The Socially Responsive Self: Social Theory and Professional Ethics*. Chicago and London: The University of Chicago Press.

McNess, E., Broadfoot, P., & Osborn, M. (2003). Is the effective compromising the affective? *British Educational Research Journal, 29*(2), 243-257.

Mehrabian, A. (1981). *Silent messages: Implicit communication of emotions and attitudes*. Belmont, CA: Wadsworth.

Meyer, K. A. (2005). Exploring the potential for unintended consequences in online learning. *International Journal of Instructional Technology and Distance Learning*. Retrieved April 16, 2008, from http://www.itdl.org/Journal/Sep_05/article01.htm

Mililojeck, I. (2005). *Educational futures: Dominant and contesting visions*. London and New York: Routledge.

Mumford, L. (1934). *Technics and civilisation*. New York: Harcourt, Brace & Co.

Murphy, J. W., & Pardeck, J. T. (1985). The technological world-view and the responsible use of computers in the curriculum. *Journal of Education, 167*(2), 98-108.

Napalm inventor discounts "guilt." (1967, December 27). *New York Times*, p. 8.

Nie, N. H. (2001). Sociability, interpersonal relations and the Internet: Reconciling conflicting findings. *American Behavioral Scientist, 45*(3), 420-435.

Oppeneimer, J. R. (1948). Physics in the contemporary world. *Bulletin of the Atomic Scientists, 4*(3), 65-86.

Palmer, M. T. (1995). Interpersonal communication and virtual reality: Mediating interpersonal relationships. *In F.* Biocca & M. R. Levy (Eds.), *Communication in the age of virtual reality* (pp. 277-299). Hillside, NJ: Lawrence Erlbaum.

Picard, R.W. (1997). *Affective computing*. Cambridge, MA: MIT Press.

Picard, R.W., & Klein, J. (2002). Computers that recognise and respond to user emotion: Theoretical and practical implications. *Interacting with Computers, 14*, 141-169.

Planalp, S. (1999). *Communicating emotion: Social, moral and cultural processes*. Cambridge, MA: Cambridge University Press.

Russell, T. L. (1999). *The no significant difference phenomenon: A comparative research annotated bibliography on technology for distance education*. North Carolina State University: IDECC.

Russell, G. (2004). The distancing dilemma in distance education. *International Journal of Instructional Technology and Distance Education, 2*(2). Retrieved April 16, 2008, from http://www.itdl.org/journal/Feb_04/article03.htm

Russell, G. (2005). The distancing question in online education. *Innovate, 1*(4). Retrieved April 16, 2008, from http://www.innovateonline.info/index.php?view=article&id=13

Sammons, J. L. (1992). Rebellious ethics and Albert Speer. *Professional Ethics, 1*(3-4), 77-116.

Seneca, A. L. (2007). *On anger: Seneca's essays* (Vol. 1, pp. xliii, 3-5, 111). Retrieved April 16, 2008, from http://www.stoics.com/seneca_essays_book_1.html

Stewart, J., & Williams, R. (1998). The co-evolution of society and multimedia technology. *Social Science Computer Review, 16*(3), 268-282.

Streibel, M. J. (1988). A critical analysis of three approaches to the use of computers in education. In L. E. Beyer & M. W. Apple (Eds.), *The curriculum: Problems, politics and possibilities* (pp. 259-288). Albany: State University of New York Press.

Summer, J. (2000). Serving the system: A critical history of distance education. *Open Learning, 15*(3), 267-285.

Sunderland, J. (2002). New communication practices, identity and the psychological gap: The affective function of e-mail on a distance doctoral program. *Studies in Higher Education, 27*(2), 233-246.

Tiffin, J., & Rajasingham, L. (2003). *The global virtual university*. London and New York: RoutledgeFalmer.

Torres, C. A. (2002). Globalization, education and citizenship: Solidarity versus markets? *American Educational Research Journal, 39*(2), 363-378.

Walther, J. B. (1992). Interpersonal effects in a computer-mediated interaction: A relational perspective. *Communication Research, 19*(1), 52-90.

Watt, L. (1929). *Capitalism and morality.* London: Cassell & Co.

Weckert, J., & Adeney, D. (1997). *Computer and information ethics.* Westport, CT: Greenwood Press.

Wellens, R. A. (1986). Use of a psychological distancing model to assess differences in telecommunication media. In L. A. Parker & O. H. Olgren (Eds.), *Teleconferencing and electronic communication* (pp. 347-361). Madison, WI: University of Wisconsin Extension.

Welton, M. R. (1995). Introduction. In M. R. Welton (Ed.), *In defense of the Lifeworld: Critical perspectives on adult learning* (pp. 1-10). Albany: State University of New York Press.

Yang, R. (2003). Globalization and higher education development: A critical analysis. *International Review of Education, 49*(3-4), 269-291.

Zembylas, M. (2005). Levinas and the "Inter-Face:" The ethical challenge of online education. *Educational Theory, 55*(1), 61-78.

ADDITIONAL READING

Anderson, T. (2001). The hidden curriculum in distance education. *Change, 33*(6), 28-35.

Apple, M. W. (2004). *Ideology and curriculum* (3rd ed.). New York: RoutledgeFalmer.

Ball, S. J. (1998). Big policies/small world: An introduction to international perspectives in education policy. *Comparative Education, 34*(2), 119-130.

Bates, T. (2001). International distance education: Cultural and ethical issues. *Distance Education, 22*(1), 122-136.

Blacker, D., & McKie, J. (2003). Information and communication technology. In N. Blake, P. Smeyers, R. Smith, & P. Standish (Eds.), *The Blackwell guide to the philosophy of education* (pp. 234-252). Malden, MA: Blackwell.

Bromley, H. (1997). The social chicken and the technological egg: Educational computing and the technology/society divide. *Educational Theory, 47*(1), 51-65.

Bruce, B. C. (1996). Technology as social practice. *Educational Foundations, 10*(4), 51-58.

Bruce, B. C. (1998). Speaking the unspeakable about 21st century technologies. In G. E. Hawisher & S. E. Selfe (Eds.), *Passions, pedagogies and 21st century technologies* (pp. 221-228). Logan, UT: Utah State University Press.

Burbules, N.C., & Callister, T.A., Jr. (2000). Universities in transition: The promise and the challenge of new technologies. *Teachers College Record, 102*(2), 271-293.

Burbules, N.C., & Callister, T.A., Jr. (2000). *Watch it!: The risks and promises of information technologies for education.* Boulder, CO: Westview.

Canny, J., & Paulos, E. (2000). Tele-embodiment and shattered presence: Reconstructing the body for online interaction. In K. Goldberg (Ed.), *The robot in the garden: Telepistemology in the age of the Internet* (pp. 276-294). Cambridge, MA: MIT Press.

Casey, T., & Embree, L. (1990). Introduction. In T. Casey & L. Embree (Eds.), *Lifeworld and technology: Current continental research 009* (pp. vii-xi). Washington, DC: Center for Advanced

Research in Phenomenology & University Press of America.

Connell, J. (1994). Virtual reality check: Cyberethics, consumerism and the American soul. *Media Studies Journal, 8*(1), 152-159.

Dreyfus, H. L. (2001). *On the Internet.* London: Routledge.

Goleman, D. (2005). *Emotional intelligence.* New York: Bantam.

Gunawardena, C. N., & McIsaac, M. S. (2004). Distance education. In D. H. Jonassen (Ed.), *Handbook of research on educational communications and technology* (pp. 355-395). Mahwah, NJ: Lawrence Erlbaum.

Hand, M., & Sandywell, B. (2002). E-topia as cosmopolis or citadel: On the democratizing and de-democratizing logics of the Internet, or towards a critique of the new technological fetishism. *Theory, Culture and Society, 19*(1-2), 197-225.

Hermann, A., Fox, R., & Boyd, A. (1999). Benign educational technology? *Open Learning, 14*(1), 3-8.

Keegan, D. (1996). *Foundations of distance education* (3rd ed.). London: Routledge.

Keller, C. (2005). Virtual learning environments: Three implementation perspectives. *Learning, media and technology, 30*(3), 299-311.

Kenway, J. (1996) The information superhighway and post-modernity: The social promise and the social price. *Comparative Education, 32*(2), 217-231.

Kizza, J. M. (2006). *Computer network security and cyber ethics* (2nd ed.). Jefferson, NC: McFarland & Co.

Nicol, D.J., Minty, I., & Sinclair, C. (2003). The social dimensions of online learning. *Innovations in Education and Teaching International, 40*(3), 270-280.

Lee, S., & Wolff-Michael, R. (2003). Science and the "good citizen:" Community-based scientific literacy. *Science Technology and Human Values, 28*(3), 403-424.

Leflore, D. (2000). Theory supporting design guidelines for Web-based instruction. In B. Abbey (Ed.), *Instructional and cognitive impacts of Web-based education* (pp. 102-117). Hershey, PA: Idea Group.

Mayers, T., & Swafford, K. (1998). Reading the networks of power: Rethinking "critical thinking" in computerized classrooms. In T. Todd & I. Ward (Eds.), *Literacy theory in the age of the Internet* (pp. 146-157). New York: Columbia University Press.

Nissenbaum, H., & Walker, D. (1998). Will computers dehumanize education? A grounded approach to values at risk. *Technology in Society, 20*, 237-273.

Nissenbaum, H., & Walker, D. (1998). A grounded approach to social and ethical concerns about technology and education. *Journal of Educational Computing Research, 19*(4), 411-432.

Pavlova, M. (2005). Social change: How should technology education respond? *International Journal of Technology and Design Education, 15*, 199-215.

Rickwood, P., & Goodwin, V. (1999). A worthwhile education? In A. Tait & R. Mills (Eds.), *The convergence of distance and conventional education* (pp. 110-123). London: Routledge.

Sclove, R. (2006). I'd hammer out freedom: Technology as politics and culture. In M. E. Winston & R. D. Edelbach (Eds.), *Society, ethics and technology* (3rd ed., pp. 83-91. Belmont, CA: Thomson.

Somekh, B. (2004). Taking the sociological imagination to school: An analysis of the (lack of) impact of information and communication technologies on education systems. *Technology, Pedagogy and Education, 13*(2), 163-179.

Verbeek, P.-P. (2005). *What things do: Philosophical reflections on technology, agency and design* (R. P. Crease, Trans.). University Park, PA: Pennsylvania State University Press.

Wighting, M. J. (2006). Effects of computer use on high school students' sense of community. *The Journal of Educational Research, 99*(6), 371-379.

Chapter VII
Preparing Students for Ethical Use of Technology:
A Case Study for Distance Education

Deb Gearhart
Troy University, USA

ABSTRACT

Are our students prepared to use technology ethically? This is a question of concern to this author and addressed in this chapter. Experience as the director of a distance education program with students who are ill-prepared for using technology and who use technology unethically had lead to the research for this chapter. The chapter reviews studies where ethical behaviors are reviewed. The survey responses lead to discussion on how to instill ethical use of technology for institutional distance education programs, through the use of ethical policies and procedures. The chapter concludes with a look at future research directions.

INTRODUCTION

Kidder (1995) addressed the question "why should we teach ethics in an electronic age?" by responding that we will not survive the 21st century with the ethics of the 20th century. This is becoming more evident in our teaching practices. A U. S. Department of Justice report on the ethical use of information technology in education described what the authors term "psychological distance."

When interacting with others face-to-face, the results of inappropriate and unethical behaviors are viewed immediately. When using information technology, inappropriate and unethical behavior while interacting with others can do harm. The act feels less personal because there is no immediate reaction in the exchange. The report goes on to note that traditionally moral values are learned at home and usually reinforced in school. That is not necessarily true today. Often values are not learned at home and schools are restricted in their ability to teach social values. In addition, young people are very comfortable with technology such as computer chats, instant messaging, text messaging, and so forth, where face-to-face interaction is not necessary. Our young people are becoming *psychologically distant* in their interactions with others.

As students move from school to the workplace, ethical issues for computing and information technology in education are becoming societal issues, dealing with both moral and criminal issues. Institutions of higher education need to deal with ethical issues related to computer technology. How do we teach and practice technology ethics in higher education? Here are two recommendations to be addressed in this chapter: set policy that provides a model for students to follow, and incorporate technology ethics issues in the curriculum. This chapter defines ethics and looks at how higher education, and in particular distance education, can deal with ethical issues encountered by students in using computing technology for educational purposes.

BACKGROUND

As early as 1990, informal polls showed that as many as three quarters of students on campuses today admit to some sort of academic fraud (Gearhart, 2000). Until recently research on ethics had been limited. There were two studies that demonstrated the need for a code of ethics in higher education. The first study was conducted in 1993 and a replicated study was conducted in 2001. In the first study 52.2% of education practitioners surveyed found a need for a code of ethics. When replicated in 2001, 72.8% of the education practitioners surveyed found a need for a code of ethics, demonstrating an increasing need for ethics in higher education (Brockett & Hiemstra, 2004, p. 10).

However, before dealing with educational ethics, a review of societal ethics is in order. In our society, quickly becoming a global society where information technology is concerned, the growing use of computers is becoming the norm in the workplace and in our daily lives. We are increasingly dependent on the computer.

Forester and Morrison (1994) looked at the social problems created by computers and have developed seven categories of computer-related ethical issues:

1.   Computer crimes and problems of computer security;
2.   Software theft and the question of intellectual property;
3.   The problem of hacking and the creation of viruses;
4.   Computer unreliability and key questions on software quality;
5.   Data storage and invasion of privacy;
6.   The social implications of artificial intelligence and expert systems; and
7.   The many problems associated with workplace computerization.

All seven of these issues can be considered computer crime. Computer crime generally has been defined as a criminal act that has been committed using a computer as the principal tool. It takes the form of theft of money, theft of information, or theft of goods. These issues are not only moral and ethical issues, but can be very costly. Computer crime costs companies billions of dollars every year. Also, all seven of these issues can be found in higher education and have an effect on distance education.

DEFINING ETHICS

For the purposes of this chapter, ethics is defined as a three-tier process. In the first tier, ethics is simply the study of right and wrong, of good and evil, in human conduct. The second tier involves meta-ethics, the formal study of good and bad, or right and wrong, but not the real-life instances of such behavior. The third tier examines normative ethics, the choices people make and the values behind them, where the judgments about values in a particular moral issue are addressed (Brockett & Hiemstra, 2004, pp. 5-6).

In understanding the first tier, the basic principle of right and wrong, ethics has been defined as the code or set of principles by which people live. Ethics is about what is considered to be right and what is considered to be wrong. When people make ethical judgments, they are making prescriptive or normative statements about what ought to be done, not descriptive statements about what is being done (Forester & Morrison, 1994).

To describe the second tier, look at the question: What is ethical? Webster's Collegiate Dictionary defines ethics as "the discipline dealing with what is good and bad and with moral duty and obligation." More simply, it is the study of what is right to do in a given situation; what we ought to do. Alternatively, it is sometimes described as the study of what is good and how to achieve what is good. To suggest whether an act is right or wrong we need to agree on an ethical system that is easy to understand and apply. Spafford (1997) commented that a system of ethics that considers primarily only the results of our actions would not allow us to evaluate our current activities at the time when we would need such guidance. If we are unable to discern the appropriate course of action prior to its commission, then our system of ethics is of little or no values to us. To obtain ethical guidance, we must base our actions primarily on evaluations of the actions and not on the possible results. More to the point, if we attempt to judge the morality of an ethical action based on the sum total of all future effects, we would be unable to make such a judgment, either for a specific incident or for the general class of acts. In part, this is because it is so difficult to determine the long-term effects of various actions and to discern their causes. This ethical view is very important in teaching students about ethical behaviors with using technology. It is important for students to understand that inappropriate and criminal behaviors when using technology will have a profound effect on the future.

In the third tier, we look at the normative ethics of technology which affects distance education.

Table 1. Ethical principles for students and professionals

Honor	Is the action considered beyond reproach?
Honesty	Will the action violate any explicit or implicit trust?
Bias	Are there any external considerations that may bias the action to be taken?
Professional adequacy	Is the action within the limits of capability?
Due care	Is the action to be exposed the best possible quality assurance standards?
Fairness	Are all stakeholders' views considered with regard to the action?
Consideration of social cost	Is the appropriate accountability and responsibility accepted with respect to this action?
Effective and efficient action	Is the action suitable, given the objectives set, and is it to be completed using the least expenditure of resources?

Source: Rogerson, S., & Gotterbarn, D. (1998). The ethics of software project management. UK: Centre for Computing and Social Responsibility, De Montfort University.

In 1985, Moor defined computer ethics, which included computers and associated technology, as the analysis of the nature and social impact of computer technology and the corresponding formulation and justification of policies for the ethical use of such technology. Computing technology is essentially involved in every aspect of our lives. Technology-related ethics will not be something set in stone, nor will it be acceptable to state that all technology use is done to protect the whole of society. However, basic concepts of ethical behavior should be observed when using technology, whether it be for personal use, educational use or professional use. The Association of Computing Machinery (ACM) has developed a code of ethics for their organization (Appendix A) which deals with basic philosophies of doing no harm to others to the ethics related to their organization. Codes, such as this, are a good way to define how ethics works for a particular organization or practice.

In Table 1, Rogerson and Gotterbarn (1998) provide eight ethical principles for students and professionals.

In the example of an online course, these principles can be used to analyze and inform those working on the course as to whether ethical practices are being used. By considering which of the ethical principles apply to the course, it is possible to ascertain which activities within a course are ethically charged. Attention can then be paid to the ethical issues of the course.

SUPPORTING RESEARCH

Dakota State University (DSU) has recognized the need for ethical practices in higher education and has a mission driven response to ethical issues through an information technology literacy requirement for all students.

The information technology literacy requirements at DSU are intended to provide opportunities for students to develop additional skills in academic areas related to computer technology. At DSU, the information technology literacy requirements emphasize software applications and programming. The students will: 1) be knowledgeable and competent users of computer technology, and 2) use technology appropriately to understand processes and concepts in math and science and to solve problems in those disciplines (DSU Undergraduate Catalog 2005-2006, p. 79). Incorporated in the information technology literacy requirement is the ethical use of technology and learning sound research techniques.

The Office of Institutional Effectiveness and Assessment provided information for the 2003 National Survey of Student Satisfaction (NSSE) conducted at DSU. This survey was given to freshman and seniors. Among the experimental technology questions asked in 2003 was "How often do students at your institution copy and paste information from the WWW/Internet into reports/papers without citing the source?" This question is one addressing students' ethical

Table 2. 2003 NSSE experimental technology questions: Percent of students responding "very often" or "often" (One question excerpt)

	First-year DSU Students	First-year Students Peers	Seniors at DSU	Seniors Peers
How often do students at your institution copy and paste information from the WWW/Internet into reports/papers without citing the source?	47%	27%	55%	32%

Source: DSU Office of Institutional Effectiveness and Assessment

perspectives related to technology use. Table 2 shows the DSU freshmen and senior responses in relation to their peers nationally.

The DSU student responses are of concern when compared to the national norms. With one of the DSU general education requirements being in information literacy, the ethical issues of using materials from the Web should be addressed.

The Office of Institutional Effectiveness and Assessment provided the responses to the ethics question for the graduate survey and employer survey for 2003. Tables 3 and 4 represent those results.

Demonstrated by the survey results for the graduate and employer surveys, both responded that DSU graduates/new employees could use information ethically, 91.3% cumulatively.

The same questions were asked again in the 2005 Graduate and Employer Surveys. The results were similar, showing consistency over time.

92.4% of the graduates were satisfied or very satisfied with their ability to use information ethically and 88.7% of the employers rated the graduates' ability to use information ethically as good or very good.

If the questions on the NSSE survey are an indicator of the ethical judgments of students' use of technology then responding affirmatively to the graduate survey would present a discrepancy in ethical behaviors of the students and their perceptions of their own ethical behaviors. This presents an area to be further researched on the DSU campus. Do the DSU students understand what ethical behavior is, especially ethical behavior when using technology? Are the students also prepared with ethical research practices for the Internet?

This research, and questions addressed, was presented at a symposium on campus in the spring of 2005. The concern about ethical behavior was

Table 3. 2003 graduate survey: Ability to use information ethically in your position

	Frequency	Percent	Cum Freq	Cum %
Very Satisfied	60	47.6	60	47.6
Satisfied	55	43.7	115	91.3
Neutral	10	7.9	125	99.2
Dissatisfied	1	0.8	126	100
Very Dissatisfied	0	0		
No Response	0	0		

Source: DSU Office of Institutional Effectiveness and Assessment

Table 4. 2003 employer survey: Ability to use information ethically

	Frequency	Percent	Cum Freq	Cum %
Very Good	34	49.3	34	49.3
Good	29	42.0	63	91.3
Fair	3	4.3	66	95.6
Poor	1	1.4	67	97.1
No Response	2	2.9	69	100

Source: DSU Office of Institutional Effectiveness and Assessment

Table 5. 2005 graduate survey: Ability to use information ethically in your position

	Frequency	Percent	Cum Freq	Cum %
Very Satisfied	45	42.9	45	42.9
Satisfied	52	49.5	97	92.4
Neutral	8	7.6	105	100
Dissatisfied	0	0		
Very Dissatisfied	0	0		
No Response	0	0		

Source: DSU Office of Institutional Effectiveness and Assessment

Table 6. 2005 employer survey: Ability to use information ethically

	Frequency	Percent	Cum Freq	Cum %
Very Good	37	52.1	37	52.1
Good	26	36.6	63	88.7
Fair	5	7.04	68	95.7
Poor	0	0	68	95.7
No Response	3	4.2	71	100

Source: DSU Office of Institutional Effectiveness and Assessment

recognized as an issue the campus should address. Each semester the campus conducts an academic convocation. In the fall of 2005 the theme of the convocation was ethics. The convocation was a kickoff to an online discussion for the remainder of the semester where both students and faculty participated. The campus continues to support the teaching of ethical behaviors in courses. This includes both campus and distance courses for the institutions.

Several studies conducted both in the K-12 setting and in higher education provide groundwork for the DSU study and provide data similar to that of the DSU study. Doherty and Orlofsky (2001) reported on a survey conducted with 500 students in grades 7-12. According to student response, 92% of students said having good computer skills improves the quality of people's lives "a great deal" or "somewhat," but only 40% said that knowing about computers is "extremely" or "very " important to how well they do in school (p. 45). Also, the survey reported that 56% of the students felt they learned more about computers at home and that 61% noted their home computers were better than at school. In 2001, this survey noted that schools were probably not using technology as effectively as they could. Comments from this survey support the concept that students are not acquiring technology skills in high school, and come into higher education with a lack of formal training and understanding of the concepts needed for the use of technology, except what they learn in the home. This would include the lack of the ethical use of technology. It is the job of those in higher education to instill the ethical values of using technology and it is a difficult task when bad habits are learned early on, with the secondary education system not providing the training needed. Additional research in this area, with the survey of secondary students and teachers, may find this has improved since 2001.

Spain, Engle and Thompson (2005) discuss the frustrations business professors have when teaching ethics. Some professors feel that ethics cannot be taught. Others find it a challenge to instill ethical values in students or to have students understand the issues of social responsibility leading to ethical behavior. In the study presented by Spain, Engle and Thompson (2005), the university discussed conducted an event on its campus, similar to that of the DSU convocation, an "Ethics Awareness Week" (EAW). The EAW provided an opportunity:

1. For the faculty as a whole to focus on issues of ethics and social responsibility in their respective classes;
2. For students to have exposure to and articulation of ethics and social responsibility issues; and
3. For an interesting case study that the students can relate to which stimulated debate not only on the issues of ethics and social responsibility, but also how these issues related to particular majors/courses of study (p. 9).

The results of this project demonstrated that students' learning, related to ethics, can be influenced when a wide range of interdisciplinary teaching methods are used along with the EAW and the use of a debate. The main effects of the project upon enhanced student learning and understanding of ethical and social responsibility issues resulted from:

1. Utilizing multiple pedagogical methods;
2. Presentations by faculty from a variety of disciplines; and
3. The extended length of exposure to these discussions (p.14).

A study reported by McCabe, Trevino, and Butterfield (1999) further supported the instilling of ethical behaviors in students. The study reviewed surveys completed by 2310 students at colleges with both honor code and nonhonor code environments. There are three themes that became apparent from the study:

1. Institutional/contextual factors related to academic integrity;
2. Attitudes/personal factors related to academic integrity; and
3. Institutional/contextual factors related to academic dishonesty (pp.215-216).

The first theme of the study was that in institutions with honor codes there are lower levels of academic dishonesty because the expectations are clearly spelled out in the code. Students confirmed that in their responses. Although not a question asked directly because the students in nonhonor code institutions would not have a code to respond to, academic integrity was spelled out in the open-ended responses of the students. Students in the honor code institutions commented that there was more of an effect by faculty and administrators to help prevent cheating.

There were varying attitudes toward cheating described by the students participating in the survey, the second theme. In both the honor code and nonhonor code institutions, the justifications for why students cheat ranged from family pressures, societal expectations, pressure for grades, and graduate school to laziness and apathy. Many students described "grey areas" where there were no expectations or definition of cheating, especially for assignments. The third theme of institutional factors related to academic dishonesty addressed how the students participating in the survey described the ineffectiveness of institutional policies on actual cheating within the institution and on how the pressure to report other cheating students affected students. It was clear that many of the students participating in the survey felt the institutional honor codes were ineffective and that students were uncomfortable in reporting fellow students.

Like the survey of high school students, this study, conducted prior to the DSU research, provides valuable insight to students' understanding of the issues of cheating. One student commented that society expects students to cheat; a sad statement to what higher education faces when dealing with students entering its prevue. As this chapter is dealing specifically with ethical use of technology, it becomes apparent that institutions must address policy related to the technology use on campus and for all aspects of the institution. Most policy or procedure manuals deal with technical requirements needed to support the learning experience. However, computing privilege policies are quickly addressing inappropriate behaviors and ethical issues. It has become apparent from the studies described in this section that this issue must be dealt with by the entire institution and not just in specific program areas, such as business or medical programs. When looking at the institution as a whole, distance programs are as much a part of this issue as any other area of the institution. Although distance programs are very aware of quality assurance issues within programs, the dealing of ethics for distance learners is an area which still needs to be clearly defined.

ETHICAL ISSUES RELATED TO DISTANCE EDUCATION

The E-learning Program staff at DSU has worked with faculty to deal with ethical issues in distance courses, particularly with cheating. This section of the chapter will address ethical issues related to distance course delivery and computer usage by students. Student behaviors and policy issues related to these behaviors are also discussed.

It is important to understand what leads to ethical dilemmas for students, such as cheating. As pointed out in the studies described in the pervious section, pressure for good grades, the testing environment, the lack of understanding of academic regulations, personality characteristics, and development of moral reasoning all can lead to cheating. Fass (1990) commented that many colleges and universities do not adequately spell out information on cheating in their handbooks and catalogs, which is still an issue today. Students coming from high school do not understand the issues of collegiate ethics and academic honesty. Fass recommends that the following areas should be addressed in university handbooks and be provided to both the traditional and distance student.

- Ethics of examinations
- Use of sources on papers and projects
- Writing assistance and other tutoring
- Collecting and reporting data
- Use of academic resources
- Respecting the work of others
- Computer ethics
- Giving assistance to others
- Adherence to academic regulations (pp. 173-173).

Terms that should be spelled out in policies related to computer technology include the following; however, this is not an all inclusive list.

- **Copy Protection:** A method originated by software developers to prevent a disk from being copied.
- **Copyright:** The legal right granted to an author, computer user, playwright, publisher, or distributor to exclusive publication, production, sale, or distribution of a literary, musical, dramatic, or artistic work.
- **Ethics:** A system of moral principles.
- **Freeware:** Software programs–usually written for fun by a hobbyist–offered for use free of charge.
- **Legal:** Permitted by law.

- **License:** An agreement between the vendor and the purchaser of software.
- **Piracy:** The copying or duplicating of computer software without proper authorization.
- **Public domain software:** Software available to anyone at no cost, or at a limited cost to cover the expense of the disk and the copying service.
- **Shareware:** Software available for free trial use. If users like the product, they are requested to submit a registration fee.
- **Softlifing:** The process of making illegal copies for personal use or for friends.

Review your institution's policies, both for applicability to distance education and to determine if the policies are ethically sound. It is important for a distance education program to develop a set of policies that represent the campus policy with the adaptation, if necessary, for the distance student. Create new policies when there are no current policies. Keep in mind the diverse populations encountered in distance education. Then, make the policies accessible to your distance students and keep them updated. Make sure that all campus services are provided to your distance students and again make sure they know about them.

Work with the faculty to explain how they can assist in developing an ethically sound distance learning atmosphere. Providing information to the learners, in multiple formats, is critical. Information must be addressed in the syllabi; course Web sites, assignments, examinations and projects with the deadlines; discussion boards' instructions, including "netiquette" used, and the information the instructor provides on plagiarism and cheating, instructor availability, assignment submission, learner support for technical issues and other learner support. Reinforce this, as once is not enough, especially as Web courses are "living" entities, always changing. Instructors must keep their learners informed of changes made during the course.

Work with your faculty on developing and improving e-learning policies. Faculty members work firsthand with the learners and see what works and what doesn't. The online faculty members at DSU meet regularly throughout the semester and have worked as a group to implement new policy relevant to our e-learning program.

Finally, when it comes to policy, the work is never finished, especially when related to constantly changing technology. Keeping policy ethical and current is a never ending process. Use the institutional course assessment procedure as the guide to implementing changes to the distance education program, reviewing your policies at the same time.

The following information is an example of policy or procedures that can be provided on creation of passwords for distance students to help avoid hacking. Boob (2006) provides five tips for passwords to help avoid hacking: 1) No password should be permitted that contains all or part of the user's name, ID number, or some easily guessed element; 2) Every password must use a variety of kinds of symbols and keys; 3) However, passwords should be immune to dictionary-based hacking attacks yet can be remembered by the user (e.g., 4Whippet meets this but pW4hIpt?e, does not); 4) Theoretically, changing passwords frequently is considered good security, however, users forget passwords easily and write them down, so set password change intervals at 90 days and education users on security and password creation; and finally 5) Longer is better; passwords that are 15 characters or longer are treated as essentially unhackable.

CONCLUSION

How will the ethics of distance education look in the future? Two scholars in the field of ethics have developed theories. Gorniak-Kocikowska suggests that computer technology-based ethics will evolve into an overarching, global view of ethics for the information age. The view taken by Johnson is similar. As information technology becomes commonplace and is integrated into everyday life, so does technology-based ethics become part of ordinary ethics (Bynum, 2001). In education we see the term "distance" disappearing from distance education; it is just education delivered in many formats. We will also see technology-based ethics become ethics for our society and not specifically geared to a discipline.

FUTURE RESEARCH DIRECTIONS

There are two research directions for further study of this topic. The DSU study was based on survey questions completed by students on a regular basis but with only limited information on ethics. A survey designed specifically addressing the issues related to ethical use of technology should be administered. Such a survey then could be replicated at other institutions to validate the survey and the findings. The second area of research would involve the development of ethical policy and procedures at the institutional level and a review conducted over time to ascertain if the policies or procedures made a difference in student behavior in the ethical use of technology. As an area of research, the ethical use of technology can provide a future research direction for some time.

REFERENCES

Boob, V. (2006). People, problems, and passwords. *IT Trends, 66,* 8-10.

Brockett, R. G. & Hiemstra, R. (2004). *Toward ethical practice.* Malabar, FL: Krieger Publishing Company

Bynum, T. (2001, Winter). Computer ethics: Basic concepts and historical overview. In E. N.

Zalta (Ed.), *The Stanford encyclopedia of philosophy.* Retrieved April 16, 2008, from http://plato.stanford.edu/archives/win2001/entries/ethics-computer

Doherty, K. M., & Orlofsky, G. F. (2001). Student survey says: Schools are probably not using educational technology as wisely or effectively as they could. *Education Week, 20*(35), 45-48.

DSU Undergraduate Catalog 2005-2006. Retrieved on January 20, 2005, from http://www.departments.dsu.edu/registrar/catalog/PDF/2005-06undergraduate.pdf

Fass, R. A. (1990). Cheating and plagiarism. In W. May (Ed.), *Ethics and higher education.* New York: Macmillan Publishing Company and American Council on Education.

Forester, T., & Morrison, P. (1994). *Computer ethics, cautionary tales and ethical dilemmas in computing* (2nd ed.). Cambridge, MA: The MIT Press.

Gearhart, D. (2000). Ethics in distance education: Developing ethical policies. *The Online Journal of Distance Learning Administration, 4*(1). Retrieved April 16, 2008, from Http://www.westga.edu/~distance/ojdla/spring41/gearhart41.html

Kidder, R. M. (1995). The ethics of teaching and the teaching of ethics. In E. Boschmann (Ed.), *The electronic classroom: A handbook for education in the electronic environment.* Medford, NJ: Learned Information.

McCabe, D. L., Trevino, L. K., & Butterfield, K. D. (1999). Academic integrity in honor code and non-honor code environments: A qualitative investigation. *The Journal of Higher Education, 70*(2), 211-234.

Moor, J. H. (1985). What is computer ethics? *Metaphilosophy, 16*(4), 266-275.

Rogerson, S., & Gotterbarn, D. (1998). *The ethics of software project management.* Centre for Computing and Social Responsibility, De Montfort University, UK. Retrieved April 16, 2008, from http://ccsr.cse.dmu.ac.uk/staff/Srog/teaching/sweden.htm

Spafford, E. H. (1997). Are hacker break-ins ethical? In M. D. Ermann, M. B. Williams, & M. S. Shauf (Eds.), *Computers, ethics, and society*. New York: Oxford University Press.

Spain, J. W., Engle, A. D., & Thompson, J. C. (2005). Applying multiple pedagogical methodologies in an ethics awareness week: Expectations, events, evaluation, and enhancements. *Journal of Business Ethics, 58,* 7-16.

ADDITIONAL READINGS

Allen, J., Fuller, D., & Luckett, M. (1998). Academic integrity: Behaviors, rates, and attitudes of business students toward cheating. *Journal of Marketing Education, 20*(1), 41-52.

Association for Computing Machinery (ACM). (1992). ACM proposed code of ethics and professional conduct. *Communications of the ACM, 35*(5), 94-99.

Bayles, M. D. (1981). *Professional ethics*. Belmont, CA: Wadsworth.

Blatt, M., & Kohlberg, L. (1975). The effects of classroom moral discussion on children's level of moral development. *Journal of Moral Education, 4.*

Bynum, T. W. (Ed.). (1985, October). *Computers & Ethics, 6*(4). Basil Blackwell.

Bynum, T. W., Maner, W., & Fodor, J. (Eds.). (1992). *Teaching computer ethics*. New Haven: Southern Connecticut State University, Research Center on Computing and Society.

Cizek, G. (1999). *Cheating on tests: How to do it, detect it, and prevent it*. Mahwah, NJ: Lawrence Erlbaum.

Collins, W. R., & Miller, K. W. (1992, January). Paramedic ethics for computer professionals. *Journal of Systems and Software, 17,* 23-38.

Crown, D., & Spiller, M. (1998). Learning from the literature on collegiate cheating: A review of empirical research. *Journal of Business Ethics, 17,* 683-700.

DeGeorge, R. (1990). *Business ethics* (3rd ed.). New York: Macmillan.

Dunlop, C., & Kling, R. (Eds.). (1991). *Computerization & controversy: Value conflicts & social choices*. Academic Press.

Ellenberg, J. H. (1983). Ethical guidelines for statistical practice: A historical perspective. *The American Statistician, 37*(1), 1-13.

Erdmann, M. D., Willimas, M. B., & Gutierrez, C. (1990). *Computers, ethics and society*. Oxford University Press.

Evans, E. D., Craig, D., & Mietzel, G. (1993). Adolescents' cognitions and attributions for academic cheating: A cross-national study. *The Journal of Psychology, 127*(6), 585-602.

Forester, T., & Morrison, P. (1990). *Computer ethics: Cautionary tales and ethical dilemmas in computing*. The MIT Press.

Frankel, M. S. (1989). Professional codes: Why, how, and with what impact? *Journal of Business Ethics, 8*(2 & 3), 109-116.

Franklyn-Stokes, A., & Newstead, S. E. (1995). Undergraduate cheating: Who does what and why? *Studies in Higher Education, 20*(2), 159-72.

Gotterbarn, D. (1991, Summer). Computer ethics: Responsibility regained. *National Forum,* 26-32.

Gotterbarn, D. (1992, August). Ethics and the computing professional. *Collegiate Microcomputer, 10*(3).

Gould, C. (1989). *The information Web: Ethical and social implications of computer networking.* Westview Press.

Hall, R. T., & Davis, J. U. (1975). *Moral education in theory and practice.* Prometheus Books.

Heberling, M. (2002). Maintaining academic integrity in online education. *Online Journal of Distance Learning Administration, 5*(2). Retrieved April 16, 2008, from http://www.westga.edu/%7Edistance/ojdla/spring51/spring51.html

Hinman, L. M. (2000, November 2). *Academic integrity and the World Wide Web.* Retrieved April 16, 2008, from http://ethics.acusd.edu/presentations/cai2000/index_files/frame.htm

Illinois Online Network. (2001). *Strategies to minimize cheating online.* Retrieved April 16, 2008, from http://illinois.online.uillinois.edu/pointer/IONresources/assessment /cheating.html

Johnson, D. W. (1984). *Computer ethics: A guide for the new age.* Brethren Press.

Johnson, D. G. (1985). *Computer ethics.* Prentice Hall.

Johnson, D. G. (1991). *Ethical issues in engineering.* Englewood Cliffs, NJ: Prentice Hall.

Johnson, D. G. (1993). *Computer ethics* (2nd ed.). Englewood Cliffs, NJ: Prentice Hall.

Johnson, D. G., & Snapper, J. W. (Eds.). (1985). *Ethical issues in the use of computers.* Belmont, CA: Wadsworth.

Kleiner, C., & Lord, M. (1999). The cheating game: Cross-national exploration of business students' attitudes, perceptions, and tendencies toward academic dishonesty. *Journal of Education for Business, 74*(4), 38-42.

Lambert, K., Ellen, N., & Taylor, L. (2003). Cheating ? What is it and why do it: A study in New Zealand tertiary institutions of the perceptions and justification for academic dishonesty. *Journal of American Academy of Business, 3*(1/2), 98-103.

Lee, C. (1986, March). Ethics training: Facing the tough questions. *Training,* 30-41.

Lim, V. K. G., & See, S. K. B. (2001). Attitudes toward, and intentions to report, academic cheating among students in Singapore. *Ethics and Behavior, 11*(3), 261-74.

Martin, C. D., & Martin, D. H. (1990). Comparison of ethics codes of computer professionals. *Social Science Computer Review, 9*(1), 96-108.

Martin, M. W., & Schinzinger, R. (1989). *Ethics in engineering.* McGraw-Hill.

McCabe, D. L., & Trevino, L. (1995). Cheating among business students: A challenge for business leaders and educators. *Journal of Management Education, 19*(2), 205-18.

McCabe, D. L., & Trevino, L. K. (1996). What we know about cheating in college. *Change, 28*(1), 29-33.

McMurtry, K. (2001). E-cheating: Combating a 21st century challenge. *The Journal Online: Technological Horizons in Education.* Retrieved April 16, 2008, from http://thejournal.com/magazine/vault/A3724.cfm

O'Neill, P., & Hern, R. (1991). A systems approach to ethical problems. *Ethics & Behavior, 1,* 129-143.

Parker, D. B. (1979). *Ethical conflicts in computer science and technology.* Arlington, VA: AFIPS Press.

Parker, D. B., Swope, S., & Baker, B. N. (1991). *Ethical conflicts in information and computer science, technology, and business.* QED Information Sciences.

Phillips, M. R., & Horton, V. (2000). Cybercheating: Has morality evaporated in business education? *The International Journal of Educational Management, 14*(4), 150-5.

Roberts, D. M., & Rabinowitz, W. (1992). An investigation of student perceptions of cheating in academic situations. *The Review of Higher Education, 15*(2), 179-90.

Robinett, J. (Ed.). (1989). *Computers & ethics: A sourcebook for discussions.* Polytechnic Press.

Schlaefi, A., Rest, J. R., & Thoma, S. J. (1985). Does moral education improve moral judgment? A meta-analysis of intervention studies using the defining issues test. *Review of Educational Research, 55*, 319-52.

Sivin, J. P., & Bialo, E. R. (1992). *Ethical use of information technologies in education: Important issues for America's schools.* Washington, DC: National Institute of Justice. Stevenson, J. T. (1987). *Engineering ethics: Practices and principles.* Toronto: Canadian Scholars Press.

Thompson, L. C., & Williams, P. G. (1995). But I changed three words! Plagiarism in the ESL classroom. *Clearing House, 69*(1), 27-9.

Tom, G., & Borin, N. (1988). Cheating in academe. *Journal of Education for Business, 63*(4), 153-7.

Underwood, J., & Szabo, A. (2003). Academic offences and e-learning: Individual propensities in cheating. *British Journal of Educational Technology, 34*(4), 467-77.

Valasquez, M. G. (1990). Corporate ethics: Losing it, having it, getting it. In P. Madsen & J. M. Shafritz (Eds.), *Essentials of business ethics* (pp. 228-244). Penguin Books.

Waugh, R. F., Godfrey, J. R., Evans, E. D., & Craig, D. (1995). Measuring students' perceptions about cheating in six countries. *Australian Journal of Psychology, 47*(2), 73-82.

APPENDIX A: ACM CODE OF ETHICS AND PROFESSIONAL CONDUCT

On October 16, 1992, ACM's Executive Council voted to adopt a revised Code of Ethics. The following imperatives and explanatory guidelines were proposed to supplement the code as contained in the new ACM Bylaw 17.

Commitment to ethical professional conduct is expected of every voting, associate, and student member of ACM. This code, consisting of 24 imperatives, formulated as statements of personal responsibility, identifies the elements of such a commitment.

It contains many, but not all, issues professionals are likely to face. Section 1 outlines fundamental ethical considerations, while Section 2 addresses additional, more specific considerations of professional conduct. Statements in Section 3 pertain more specifically to individuals who have a leadership role, whether in the workplace or in a volunteer capacity, for example, with organizations such as ACM. Principles involving compliance with this code are given in Section 4.

The code is supplemented by a set of guidelines, which provide explanation to assist members in dealing with the various issues contained in the code. It is expected that the guidelines will be changed more frequently than the code.

The code and its supplemented guidelines are intended to serve as a basis for ethical decision making in the conduct of professional work. Secondarily, they may serve as a basis for judging the merit of a formal complaint pertaining to violation of professional ethical standards.

It should be noted that although computing is not mentioned in the moral imperatives section, the code is concerned with how these fundamental imperatives apply to one's conduct as a computing professional. These imperatives are expressed in a general form to emphasize that ethical principles which apply to computer ethics are derived from more general ethical principles.

It is understood that some words and phrases in a code of ethics are subject to varying interpretations, and that any ethical principle may conflict with other ethical principles in specific situations. Questions related to ethical conflicts can best be answered by thoughtful consideration of fundamental principles, rather than reliance on detailed regulations.

1.   **General Moral Imperatives. As an ACM member I will...**
     *   **Contribute to society and human well-being**. This principle concerning the quality of life of all people affirms an obligation to protect fundamental human rights and to respect the diversity of all cultures. An essential aim of computing professionals is to minimize negative consequences of computing systems, including threats to health and safety. When designing or complementing systems, computing professionals must attempt to ensure that the products of their efforts will be used in socially responsible ways, will meet social needs, and will avoid harmful effects to health and welfare.

         In addition to a safe social environment, human well-being includes a safe natural environment. Therefore, computing professionals who design and develop systems must be alert to, and make others aware of, any potential damage to the local or global environment.
     *   **Avoid harm to others**. "Harm" means injury or negative consequences, such as undesirable loss of information, loss of property, property damage, or unwanted environmental impacts. This principle prohibits use of computing technology in ways that result in harm to any of the following: users, the general public, employees, and employers. Harmful actions include intentional destruction or modification of files and programs leading to serious loss of re-

sources or unnecessary expenditure of human resources such as the time and effort required to purge systems of computer viruses.

Well-intended actions, including those that accomplish assigned duties, may lead to harm unexpectedly. In such an event the responsible person or persons are obligated to undo or mitigate the negative consequences as much as possible. One way to avoid unintentional harm is to carefully consider potential impacts on all those affected by decisions made during design and implementation.

To minimize the possibility of indirectly harming others, computing professionals must minimize malfunctions by following generally accepted standards for system design and testing. Furthermore, it is often necessary to assess the social consequences of systems to project the likelihood of any serious harm to others. If systems features are misrepresented to users, coworkers, or supervisors, the individual computing professional is responsible for any resulting injury.

In the work environment the computing professional has the additional obligation to report any signs of system dangers that might result in serious personal or social damage. If one's superiors do not act to curtail or mitigate such dangers, it may be necessary to "blow the whistle" to help correct the problem or reduce the risk. However, capricious or misguided reporting of violations can, itself, be harmful. Before reporting violations, all relevant aspects of the incident must be thoroughly assessed. In particular, the assessment of risk and responsibility must be credible. It is suggested that advice be sought from other computing professionals (See principle 2.5 regarding thorough evaluations).

- **Be honest and trustworthy**. Honesty is an essential component of trust. Without trust an organization cannot function effectively. The honest computing professional will not make deliberately false or deceptive claims about a system or design, but will instead provide full disclosure of all pertinent system limitations and problems.

  A computer professional has a duty to be honest about his or her own qualifications, and about any circumstances that might lead to conflicts of interest.

  Membership in volunteer organizations such as ACM may at times place individuals in situations where their statements or actions could be interpreted as carrying the "weight" of a larger group of professionals. An ACM member will exercise care not to misinterpret ACM or positions and policies of ACM or any ACM units.

- **Be fair and take actions not to discriminate**. The values of equality, tolerance, respect for others, and the principles of equal justice govern this imperative. Discrimination on the basis of race, sex, religion, age, disability, national origin, or other such factors is an explicit violation of ACM policy and will not be tolerated.

  Inequities between different groups of people may result form the use or misuse of information and technology. In a fair society, all individuals would have equal opportunity to participate in, or benefit from, the use of computer resources regardless of race, sex, religion, age, disability, national origin, or other such similar factors. However, these ideals do not justify unauthorized use of computer resources, nor do they provide an adequate basis for violation of any other ethical imperatives of this code.

- **Honor property rights including copyrights and patents**. Violation of copyrights, patents, trade secrets and the terms of license agreements is prohibited by law in most circumstances. Even when software is not so protected, such violations are contrary to professional behavior.

Copies of software should be made only with proper authorization. Unauthorized duplication of materials must not be condoned.

- **Give proper credit for intellectual property**. Computing professionals are obligated to protect the integrity of intellectual property. Specifically, one must not take credit for other's ideas or work, even in cases where the work has not been explicitly protected, for example, by copyright or patent.

- **Respect the privacy of others**. Computing and communication technology enables the collection and exchange of personal information on a scale unprecedented in the history of civilization. Thus, there is increased potential for violating the privacy of individuals and groups. It is the responsibility of professionals to maintain the privacy and integrity of data describing individuals. This includes taking precautions to ensure the accuracy of data, as well as protecting it from unauthorized access or accidental disclosure to inappropriate individuals. Furthermore, procedures must be established to allow individuals to review their records and correct inaccuracies.

  This imperative implies that only the necessary amount of personal information be collected in a system, that retention and disposal periods for that information be clearly defined and enforced, and that personal information gathered for a specific purpose not be used for other purposes without consent of the individual(s). These principles apply to electronic communications, including electronic mail, and prohibit procedures that capture or monitor electronic user data, including messages, without the permission of users or *bona fide* authorization related to system operation and maintenance. User data observed during the normal duties of system operation and maintenance must be treated with strictest confidentiality, except in cases where it is evidence for the violation of law, organizational regulations, or this code. In these cases, the nature or contents of that information must be disclosed only to proper authorities (See 1.8).

- **Honor confidentiality**. The principle of honesty extends to issues of confidentiality of information whenever one has made an explicit promise to honor confidentiality or, implicitly, when private information not directly related to the performance of one's duties becomes available. The ethical concern is to respect all obligations of confidentiality to employers, clients, and users unless discharged from such obligations by requirements of the law or other principles of this code.

2. **More Specific Professional Responsibilities. As an ACM computing professional I will...**
   - **Strive to achieve the highest quality, effectiveness and dignity in both the process and products of professional work**. Excellence is perhaps the most important obligation of a professional. The computing professional must strive to achieve quality and to be cognizant of the serious negative consequences that may result from poor quality in a system.
   - **Acquire and maintain professional competence**. Excellence depends on individuals who take responsibility for acquiring and maintaining professional competence. A professional must participate in setting standards for appropriate levels of competence, and strive to achieve those standards. Upgrading technical knowledge and competence can be achieved in several ways: doing independent study; attending seminars, conferences, or courses; and being involved in professional organizations.

- **Know and respect existing laws pertaining to professional work**. ACM members must obey existing local, state, province, national and international laws unless there is a compelling ethical basis not to do so. Policies and procedures of the organizations in which one participates must also be obeyed. But compliance must be balanced with the recognition that sometimes existing laws and rules may be immoral or inappropriate and, therefore, must be challenged.

  Violation of a law or regulation may be ethical when that law or rule has inadequate moral basis or when it conflicts with another law judged to be more important. If one decides to violate a law or rule because it is viewed as unethical or for any other reason, one must fully accept responsibility for one's actions and for the consequences.

- **Accept and provide appropriate professional review**. Quality professional work, especially in the computing profession, depends on professional reviewing and critiquing. Whenever appropriate, individual members should seek and utilize peer review as well as provide critical review of the work of others.

- **Give comprehensive and thorough evaluations of computer systems and their impacts, including analysis of possible risks**. Computer professionals must strive to be perceptive, thorough, and objective when evaluating, recommending, and presenting system descriptions and alternatives. Computer professionals are in a position of special trust, and therefore have a special responsibility to provide objective, credible evaluations to employers, clients, users, and the public. When providing evaluations the professional must also identify any relevant conflicts of interest, as stated in imperative 1.3.

  As noted in the discussion of principle 1.2 on avoiding harm, any signs of danger from systems must be reported to those who have opportunity or responsibility to resolve them. See the guidelines for imperative 1.2 for more details concerning harm, including the reporting of professional violations.

- **Honor contracts, agreements, and assigned responsibilities**. Honoring one's commitments is a matter of integrity and honesty. For the computer professional this includes ensuring that system elements perform as intended. Also, when one contracts for work with another party, one has an obligation to keep that party properly informed about progress toward completing that work.

  A computing professional has a responsibility to request a change of assignment that he or she feels cannot be completed as defined. Only after serious consideration and with full disclosure of risks and concerns to the employer or client should one accept the assignment. The major underlying principle here is the obligation to accept personal accountability for professional work. On some occasions other ethical principles may take greater priority.

  A judgment that a specific assignment should not be performed may not be accepted. Having clearly identified one's concerns and reasons for that judgment, but failing to procure a change in that assignment, one may yet be obligated, by contract or by law, to proceed as directed. The computing professional's ethical judgment should be the final guide in deciding whether or not to proceed. Regardless of the decision, one must accept the responsibility for the consequences. However, performing assignments "against one's own judgment" does not relieve the professional of responsibility for any negative consequences.

- **Improve public understanding of computing and its consequences**. Computing professionals have a responsibility to share technical knowledge with the public by encouraging understanding of computing, including the impacts of computer systems and their limitation. This imperative implies an obligation to counter any false views related to computing.

- **Access computing and communication resources only when authorized to do so.** Theft or destruction of tangible and electronic property is prohibited by imperative 1.2 – "Avoid harm to others." Trespassing and unauthorized use of a computer or communication system is addressed by this imperative. Trespassing includes accessing communication networks and computer systems, or accounts or files associated with those systems, without explicit authorization to do so. Individuals and organizations have the right to restrict access to their systems so long as they do not violate the discrimination principle (see 1.4).

  No one should enter or use another's computing system, software, or data files without permission. One must always have appropriate approval before using system resources, including .rm57 communication ports, file space, other system peripherals, and computer time.

3. **Organizational Leadership Imperatives. As an ACM member and an organizational leader, I will…**
   - **Articulate social responsibilities of members of an organizational unit and encourage full acceptance of those responsibilities.** Because organizations of all kinds have impacts on the public, they must accept responsibilities to society. Organizational procedures and attitudes oriented toward quality and the welfare of society will reduce harm to members of the public, thereby serving public interest and fulfilling social responsibility. Therefore, organizational leaders must encourage full participation in meeting social responsibilities as well as quality performance.
   - **Manage personnel and resources to design and build information systems that enhance the quality of working life.** Organizational leaders are responsible for ensuring that computer systems enhance, not degrade, the quality of life. When implementing a computer system, organizations must consider the personal and professional development, physical safety, and human dignity of all workers. Appropriate human-computer ergonomic standards should be considered in system design and in the workplace.
   - **Acknowledge and support proper and authorized uses of an organization's computing and communications resources.** Because computer systems can become tools to harm as well as to benefit an organization, the leadership has the responsibility to clearly define appropriate and inappropriate uses of organizational computing resources. While the number and scope of such rules should be minimal, they should be fully enforced when established.
   - **Ensure that users and those who will be affected by a system have their needs clearly articulated during the assessment and design of requirements. Later the system must be validated to meet requirements.** Current system users, potential users and other persons who lives may be affected by a system must have their needs assessed and incorporated in the statement of requirements. System validation should ensure compliance with those requirements.
   - **Articulate and support policies that protect the dignity of users and others affected by a computing system.** Designing or implementing systems that deliberately or inadvertently demean individuals or groups is ethically unacceptable. Computer professionals who are in decision-making positions should verify that systems are designed and implemented to protect personal privacy and enhance personal dignity.

- **Create opportunities for members of the organization to learn the principles and limitations of computer systems**. This complements the imperative on public understanding (2.7). Educational opportunities are essential to facilitate optimal participation of all organizational members. Opportunities must be available to all members to help them improve their knowledge skills in computing, including courses that familiarize them with the consequences and limitations of particular types of systems. In particular, professionals must be made aware of the dangers of building systems around oversimplified models, the improbability of anticipating and designing for every possible operating condition, and other issues related to the complexity of this profession.

4. **Compliance with the Code. As an ACM member I will...**
   - **Uphold and promote the principles of this code**. The future of the computing profession depends on both technical and ethical excellence. Not only is it important for ACM computing professionals to adhere to the principles expressed in this code, each member should encourage and support adherence by other members.
   - **Treat violations of this code as inconsistent with membership in the ACM**. Adherence of professionals to a code of ethics is largely a voluntary matter. However, if a member does not follow this code by engaging in gross misconduct, membership in ACM may be terminated.

ACM stands for Association of Computing Machinery.

Source: Forester, T., & Morrison, P. (1994). *Computer ethics cautionary tales and ethical dilemmas in computing* (2nd ed., pp. 261-270). Cambridge, MA: The MIT Press.

Chapter VIII
Conversation Ethics for Online Learning Communities

Rocci Luppicini
University of Ottawa, Canada

ABSTRACT

There is growing recognition of the important role of conversation ethics in open and distance learning systems, particularly within online learning communities. Fostering ethical conversational practices in online learning poses a serious challenge within education. This chapter introduces key concepts and strategies to help guide online learning communities. The aim of the chapter is threefold: (1) to provide an overview of key concepts and strategies underlying conversation ethics, (2) to identify key elements of conversation ethics for online learning communities, and (3) to offer practical suggestions for leveraging online learning communities through increased attention to conversation ethics. This chapter is based on the assumption that an understanding of conversation ethics can offer instructors and learners a tool for advancing learning within online learning communities.

INTRODUCTION

Conversations are the foundation on which social interactions are built. Within this age of rapid technological change, there is growing interest in strategies for fostering meaningful conversation in online learning systems. This is particularly important in online learning systems where social interaction is fundamental, as is the case in learning communities. Framed within technoethics and studies in conversation, this article applies well-established principles of conversation ethics to online learning communities. To this end, it focuses on key strategies for guiding ethical conversations in online learning communities. Under this framework, guidelines for ethical conversation are assumed to be at the base of meaningful online collaboration and learning.

The chapter provides key insights for improving the quality of conversational exchange within online learning communities.

BACKGROUND

Challenges

The advancement of the Internet and supporting information and communication technologies (ICT) has created a number of unintended problems and challenges that deter many users from communicating online. First, the Internet has served as a conduit for criminal activity with a strong social impact (Wall, 2005). For instance, Holt and Graves (2007) conducted a qualitative analysis of advance fee fraud e-mail schemes and found a variety of writing techniques used to generate responses and information from victims. In another area, Finch (2007) explored the problem of stolen identity using the Internet. The newly created *International Journal of Cyber* Criminology is focused entirely on emerging areas of cyber-crime research, including cyber-terrorism, cyber-stalking, and online gambling. Second, the use of Internet within educational contexts has created additional challenges for online instructors and administrators such as online cheating, cyber-harassment, and cyber-bullying. Shariff and Hoff (2007) addressed the problem of cyber-bullying in schools highlighting the legal boundaries for school supervision online. Beran and Li (2005) focused on cyber-harassment issues that can arise within online educational environments. In another area, Underwood (2003) examined serious academic offenses connected to e-learning including online cheating and Internet plagiarism that can lead to student expulsion. Moreover, online learners and instructors must contend with evolving intellectual property and fair use policies governing information communication and ownership (DeGeorge, 2006). There are also communication privacy and confidentiality issues that affect online communication and information exchange (Rotenberg, 1998). This body of work raises public attention to the risks and challenges involved in communicating online. It also suggests that a framework is needed to help reduce online risk and guide communications within online learning environments.

Technoethics and Educational Technoethics

Technoethics is an interdisciplinary field concerned with all ethical aspects of technology within a society shaped by technology. It deals with human processes and practices connected to technology which are becoming embedded within social, political, and moral spheres of life. It also examines social policies and interventions occurring in response to issues generated by technology development and use. The seminal description of the field of technoethics was contributed by Mario Bunge (1977) in speaking to the field of engineering. Bunge addressed how technologists and engineers have social responsibilities dues to the immense influence their work has on society: Bunge (1979) stated "You cannot manipulate the world as if it were a chunk of clay and at the same time disclaim all responsibility for what you do or refuse to do, particularly since your skills are needed to repair whatever damages you may have done or at least to forestall future such damages" (p. 23). The field of technoethics provides theoretical grounding for dealing with ethical considerations with technology in all areas of human activity as indicated in the *Handbook of Research on Technoethics* (Luppicini & Adell, forthcoming).

Technoethics provides core grounding to work in education and educational technology. Educational technology is a goal-oriented problem-solving systems approach utilizing tools, techniques, theories, and methods from multiple knowledge domains, to: (1) design, develop, and evaluate, human and mechanical resources efficiently and effectively in order to facilitate and leverage all aspects of learning, and (2) guide change agency and transformation of educational systems and practices in order to contribute to influencing change in society (Luppicini, 2005). Technoethics challenges people working with technology to develop strategies which promote the use of technology to serve human beings in positive ways. A number of scholars within educational technology (including this author) consider ethical considerations to be central to teaching and learning. Cortés (2005) asserts that education requires an ethical framework within which to guide learning and instruction in technologically sophisticated environments. Other scholars in this area share the belief that technology and the means of communication require an ethical analysis so that they can be used suitably (Hawkridge, 1991; Nichols, 1994).

In this chapter, educational technoethics is defined as a specialized area of technoethics focused on ethical issues connected to the use of technology within education contexts. A basic framework for educational technoethics includes technical, vocational, pedagogical, and social elements.

1. **Vocational element:** Education guides students on how to cultivate technology related skills that are useful in school and the work force.
2. **Pedagogical element:** Education helps students to cultivate technology-related skills in areas where learning is leveraged through technology.
3. **Social element:** Education guides students on how to cultivate technology-related skills that contribute to learning community success and the co-construction of meaning.
4. **Technical element:** Education prepares students to deal with the use of computer technology to advance society goals.

This basic framework for educational technoethics provides useful grounding to help situate core elements of various approaches and applications in educational technology within an ethical framework. Because of growing ethical concerns over online communication discussed in a previous section, online learning communities represent one application in educational technology that aligns itself particularly well with technoethics.

CONVERSATION ETHICS IN ONLINE LEARNING COMMUNITIES

Online Learning Communities

Online learning communities (or virtual learning communities) are educational contexts where communication and technology are fundamental components. Learning communities are computer-mediated by interconnected computers. Communication characteristics of virtual learning communities include: asynchronous and synchronous communication, high interactivity, and multiway communication. Luppicini (2007) elaborated on six types of virtual learning communities.

1. **Knowledge Building Communities:** Allows members to focus on topics of interest and construct communal data bases of information.
2. **Inquiry-goal-based Communities:** Orientation among participants that requires active involvement from community members.
3. **Practice-based Communities:** Learning through lived practices of the community.
4. **Culture-based Communities:** Have a shared history, common sense of ideology, or ritualistic traditions.
5. **Socialization Communities:** Based on connecting individuals with common in-

terests or a common background for social exchange.

6. **Counseling and Development Communities:** Provides support services to individuals and nurturing individual growth.

A major challenge within online learning communities revolves around the cultivation and sustainability of successful online learning communications (Luppicini, 2006). The next section in this chapter focuses on how educational tehnoethics and conversation ethics can offer instructors and learners a tool for guiding communications within online learning communities.

The Study of Conversation and Conversation Ethics

The study of conversation is actively pursued within the social sciences and deals with conversation use and how people construct and interpret language. One important area of conversation study is rooted in Speech Act Theory (Searle, 1969) and emphasizes how utterances are interpreted in conversation. The outcome of this work gave rise to a classification scheme for a variety of language acts. Searle's (1969) Theory of Speech Acts identified five fundamental things you can do with an utterance:

1. Commit the speaker to something being the case (assertive);
2. Attempt to get the hearer to do something, such as in questioning and commanding (directive);
3. Commit the speaker to some future course of action (commissive);
4. Bring about the correspondence between the content of the speech act and reality (declarative): and
5. Express a psychological state about a state of affairs (expressive).

Under the framework, speech acts are connected to larger conversation structures and principles governing the proper use of conversation in face-to-face and online conversation. From this perspective, successful online learning communities are viewed as learning conversation systems where meaning emerges from conversation flowing freely between participants.

The study of conversation ethics is an important area of conversation study. One leading approach is rooted in Habermas' (1990) theory of discourse ethics. Habermas' discourse ethics is based on rational principles of argumentation where participants adopt the perspectives of all others in an effort to reach agreement on conditions that valid norms have to satisfy. The validity of a norm is decided intersubjectively through argumentation and depends upon mutual understanding achieved by participants. According to Habermas (1990) "Only those norms can claim to be valid that meets (or could meet) with the approval of all affected in their capacity as participants in a practical discourse" (p. 66). Related approaches to discourse and conversation ethics are offered by Horn and Carr (2000) and Jenlink (2004).

Within the context of online learning communities, conversation ethics refers to the ethical responsibility of participants within a learning community to contribute to the co-construction of understanding and the advancement of learning conversations. This requires that participants possess fundamental conversational competences underlying the co-construction of learning conversations, including cooperative conversation competencies (Grice, 1975) and rational argumentation competencies (Habermas, 1987, 1990). First, Grice's principle of cooperative conversation states, "make your conversational contribution such as is required, at the stage at which it occurs, by the accepted purpose or direction of the talk exchange in which you are engaged" (Grice, 1975, p. 26). Second, Habermas' system of validity claims conceptualizes conversational competence in terms of the truth of statements made, the rightness of norms of action, the adequacy of standards of value, the sincerity of expressions (truthfulness), and comprehensibility (Habermas, 1987, p. 51).

The concept of validity claims connects speech acts to principles of conversation ethics. Taken together, these principles provide key elements of conversation ethics. This is summarized below along with a description.

1. **Informativeness:** Enough information is provided.
2. **Truthfulness:** The information is true to the best knowledge of the participant's knowledge.
3. **Relevancy:** The information connects to the conversation.
4. **Clarity:** The information is presented clearly and orderly.
5. **Standards and Values:** The participant supports the ideas of the community of learning.

The abovementioned elements of conversation ethics depict essential conditions for creating successful learning conversations. Grice's principle of cooperative conversation and Habermas' work on discourse ethics provides a tool for gauging

conversations to ensure that learners are no more or less informative in their online contributions than is necessary, that they speak the truth, and that they are orderly and unambiguous (comprehensible). Based on an understanding of educational technoethics and the study of conversation, suggestions for building online learning communities through conversation ethics can be given.

Suggestions for Leveraging Online Learning Communities

Technoethics and conversation ethics can be combined and used by instructional designers and learners as guiding questions for leveraging conversations in online learning communities. Selected elements are provided below in Table 1.

For instance, in a recent undergraduate course, this instructor created online group activities where communication students in journalism and media studies simulated the work of an editorial committee for publishing applied to an area of real world work (vocational element). Members of the online communities participated in double blind peer, editorial committee online decision meetings, and publishing meetings to create a high quality publication. Tracking functions and comments within word processing software was used in the review process to keep track of

Table 1. A framework for leveraging conversations in online learning communities

Theoretical Framework	Elements	Guiding Questions
Educational Technoethics	Vocational element	How can instruction be designed so learners cultivate technology related skills that are useful in the work force?
	Pedagogical element	How can learners use technology to leverage learning?
	Social element	How can education help learners cultivate technology related skills that contribute to learning community success and the co-construction of meaning?
	Technical element	What strategies can be used to help prepare students use of computer technology to advance society goals?
Conversation Ethics	Informativeness	Is enough information provided?
	Truthfulness	Is the information true to the best knowledge of the participant's knowledge?
	Relevancy	Does the information connect to the conversation?
	Clarity	Is the information presented clearly and orderly?

comments (pedagogical element). The results of the review were shared within an online learning community to help advance the co-construction of meaning (social element). In making selection decisions, the merits of each piece were discussed between reviewers in an effort to provide the necessary information required (informativeness) without bias (truthfulness) on the main points of interest (relevancy) in clear jargon free language that other online community members could easily understand (clarity). The abovementioned elements and guiding questions provide a point of entry for exploring conversation ethics within online learning communities.

CONCLUSION

This chapter sketched out key concepts in techno-ethics, educational technoethics, educational technology, and conversation ethics to help guide work in online learning communities. It discussed key elements and questions that should be addressed when involved in online learning communities. There are, however, a number of limitations with the use of conversation ethics within online learning communities. First, conversation ethics relies on formal notions of conversation that are not always followed in the real world. For instance, not all participants in a community of learning will be dedicated to the pursuit of common interests. This limit is addressed by the motivation and efforts of instructors and participants to ensure that learning communities revolve around common interests. Second, promoting conversation ethics may be ineffective in situations where learning communities change membership regularly. This is a general limitation applicable to most areas of instruction and training where there are learning curves for some participants. It is partly addressed by efforts to retain learning community membership by providing high quality services and collecting regular feedback on participants' needs and interests.

FUTURE RESEARCH DIRECTIONS

Despite the breadth of work on online learning communities that exists, there is still a need to better focus attention on key areas of online learning communities. One important area of future research concerns cross-cultural communication in online learning. This is particularly salient as developing countries gradually improve their Internet capabilities and increase their use of online learning in education (See Luppicini, 2007). Building online learning communities within the global village increasingly relies on complex interactions of culture, communication, and technology. Global communication is worldwide communication across national, religious, and cultural boundaries. Sudweeks and Ess (2004) contributed an edited edition, *Cultural Attitudes Towards Technology and Communication,* which explored cross-cultural perspectives on online communication. This edited collection provided best practice on how to use ICT's within global communication system in ways which do not threaten local cultures. Future research in educational technoethics may advance the field by exploring ways to preserve local culture when implementing globally-based online learning environments. A number of useful research questions can be addressed in future work: How do instructors accommodate different cross-cultural communicative styles that satisfy guidelines for ethical conversation within online learning communities? What additional guidelines (if any) should instructors abide by when dealing with cross-cultural online learning communities? How can guidelines for ethical communication help enhance cultural experiences and learning for learners within globally-based online learning communities? These questions and others could help build on work described in this chapter by providing online communities with guidelines for ethical communications that accommodate cross-cultural differences.

A more general area of future research re-volves around the advancement of other areas of Technoethics. Now more than ever before, advances in technological growth are forcing society to re-examine how technology is viewed. This is especially salient in the pure and applied sciences where technological developments of-fer ways to surpass current human capacities. Breakthroughs in medicine, information and communication technology, transportation and industry are juxtaposed with growing needs to deal with moral and ethical dilemmas associated with new technological developments. Increased reliance on new technology creates fundamental challenges revolving around security and privacy issues, access issues to education and health care, legal issues in online fraud and theft, employer and government surveillance, policies issues in creating and implementing ethical guidelines and professional codes of conduct, along with ethical dilemmas in a number of vital areas of research and development. *The Handbook of Research on Technoethics* (Luppicini & Adell, forthcoming) provides a collection of core readings in techno-ethics in various areas including: Foundations, Environmental Technoethics, Educational Tech-noethics, Cyberethics, Computer Ethics, Health and Medical Technoethics, Engineering Ethics, and Biotech Ethics. In line with recommenda-tions from Cortés (2005), the handbook provides a promising set of new research projects aimed at optimizing a needed balance between ethical principles governing technology use and innova-tive technological practice. If successful, research in key areas of technoethics has the potential to revolutionize social practices and institutions (in-cluding distance education) relying on technology use for social benefit. Moreover, research in these areas could help ground ongoing conversations about the "wicked" problems and promises offered by technological advancement.

REFERENCES

Beran, T., & Li, Q. (2005). Cyber-harrassment: A study of a new method for an old behavior. *Journal of Educational Computing Research, 32*(3), 265-277.

Bunge, M. (1977). Towards a technoethics. *Monist, 60*, 96-107.

Cortés, P. A. (2005). Educational technology as a means to an end. *Educational Technology Review, 13*(1), 73-90.

DeGeorge, R. (2006). Information technology, globalization and ethics. *Ethics and Information Technology, 8*, 29-40.

Finch, E. (2007). The problem of stolen identity and the Internet. In Y Jewkes (Ed.), *Crime on-line* (pp. 29-43). Cullompton: Willan.

Grice, H. P. (1975). Logic and conversation. In P. Cole & J. L. Morgan (Eds.), *Syntax and semantics: Speech acts* (Vol. 3). New York: Academic Press.

Habermas, J. (1987). The theory of communica-tive action. *System and lifeworld: A critique of functionalist reason* (Vol. 2). Boston: Beacon Press.

Habermas, J. (1990). *Moral consciousness and communicative action.* Cambridge, MA: MIT Press.

Hawkridge, D. (1991). Challenging educational technology. *ETTI, 28*(2), 102-110.

Holt, T. J., & Graves, D. C. (2007). A qualitative analysis of advance fee fraud e-mail schemes. *International Journal of Cyber Criminology, 1*(1), 137-154.

Horn, R., & Carr, A. (2000). Providing systemic change for schools: Towards professional devel-opment through moral conversation. *Systems Research and Behavioral Science, 17*(3), 255-272.

Jenlink, P. (2004). Discourse ethics in the design of educational systems: Considerations for design praxis. *Systems Research and Behavioral Science, 21*(3), 237-249.

Luppicini, R. (2005). A systems definition of educational technology in society. *Educational Technology & Society, 8*(3), 103-109.

Luppicini, R. (2006). Designing online communities of learning based on conversation theory. In *Manuscript Presented at the Association for Educational Communication and Technology (AECT) Conference*, Dallas, TX.

Luppicini, R. (Ed.). (2007). *Online learning communities*. Greenwich: Information Age Publishing.

Luppicini, R., & Adell, R. (Eds.). (forthcoming). *Handbook of research on technoethics*. Hershey, PA: Idea Group.

Nichols, R. G. (1987). Toward a conscience: Negative aspect of educational technology. *Journal of Visual/Verbal Languaging, 7*(1), 121-137.

Rotenberg, M. (1998). Communications privacy: Implications for network design. In R. N. Stichler & R. Hauptman (Eds.), *Ethics, information and technology readings*. Jefferson, NC: McFarland & Company.

Searle, J. (1969). *Speech acts: An essay in the philosophy of language*. Cambridge: Cambridge University Press.

Sudweeks, F., & Ess, C. (Eds.). (2004). *Cultural attitudes towards technology and communication*. Perth: Murdoch University.

Underwood, J. (2003). Academic offenses and e-learning: Individual propensities in cheating. *British Journal of Educational Technology, 34*(4), 467-477.

Wall, D. S. (2005). The Internet as a conduit for criminal activity. In A. Pattavina (Ed.), *Information technology and the criminal justice system* (pp. 78-94), Thousand Oaks, CA: Sage.

ADDITIONAL READINGS

Allen, L., & Voss, D. (1997). *Ethics in technical communication: Shades of gray*. New York: John Wiley & Sons.

Baird, R. M., Ramsower, R., & Rosenbaum, S. E. (Eds.). (2000). *Cyberethics: Social and moral issues in the computer age*. Amherst, NY: Prometheus Books.

Capurro, R., & Christoph, P. (2002). Ethical issues of online communication research. *Ethics and Information Technology, 4*(3), 189-194.

Gearhart, D. (2000). *Ethics in distance education: Developing ethical policies*. State University of West Georgia, Distance Education Center.

Habermas, J. (1984). The theory of communicative action. *Reason and the rationalization of society* (Vol. 1). Boston: Beacon Press.

Harri-Augstein, S., & Thomas, L. (1991). *Learning conversations*. London: Routledge.

Mesthene, E. (1983). Technology and wisdom. In C. Mitcham, & R. Mackey (Eds.), *Philosophy and technology: Readings in the philosophical problem of technology*. New York: The Free Press.

Moor, J. (2005). Why we need better ethics for emerging technologies. *Ethics and Information Technology, 7*, 111-119.

Nichols, R. G. (1994). Searching for moral guidance about educational technology. *Educational Technology, 34*(2), 40-48.

Pask, G. (1975). *Conversation cognition and learning: A cybernetic theory and methodology*. Amsterdam: Elsevier.

Pask, G. (1976). *Conversation theory: Applications in education and epistemology.* Amsterdam: Elsevier.

Russell, G. (2006). Globalisation, responsibility, and virtual schools. *Australian Journal of Education, 50*(2), 140-54.

Sawyer, R. K. (2001). *Creating conversations: Improvisation in everyday discourse.* Cresskill, NJ: Hampton Press.

Scott, B. (2001). Conversation theory: A constructivist, dialogical approach to educational technology. *Cybernetics and Human Knowing, 8*(4), 25-46.

Shariff, S., & Hoff, D. L. (2007). Cyberbullying: Clarifying legal boundaries for school supervision in cyberspace. *International Journal of Cyber Criminology, 1*(1), 75-118

Spinello, R. (2003). *CyberEthics: Morality and law in cyberspace.* Sudbury, MA: Jones and Bartlett.

Tavani, H. (2007). *Ethics and technology: Ethical issues in an age of information and communication technology.* Boston: John Wiley & Sons.

Thorseth, M. (2006). Worldwide deliberation and public reason online. *Ethics and information Technology, 8,* 243-252.

Wenger, E. (1997). *Communities of practice, learning memory and identity.* Cambridge: Cambridge University Press.

Whitehead, A. N. (1949). *The aims of education and other essays.* New York: New American Library.

Yar, M. (2006). *Cybercrime and society.* London: Sage.

KEY TERMS

Cyber-Bullying: Cyber-bullying describes bullying behaviour intended to humiliate or intimidate another in online interactions.

Cyber Identity Theft: Cyber identity theft is to steal identity tokens from an individual using information and communication technologies.

Educational Technoethics: Educational technoethics is a specialized area of technoethics focused on ethical issues connected to technology within education contexts. It is constituted by technical, vocational, pedagogical, and social elements.

Educational Technology: Educational technology is a goal-oriented problem-solving systems approach utilizing tools, techniques, theories, and methods from multiple knowledge domains to: (1) design, develop, and evaluate, human and mechanical resources efficiently and effectively in order to facilitate and leverage all aspects of learning, and (2) guide change agency and transformation of educational systems and practices in order to contribute to influencing change in society (Luppicini, 2005).

Global Communication: Global communication is defined as worldwide communication across national, religious, and cultural boundaries.

Netiquette: Netiquette (or Internet etiquette) refer to normative procedures for posting messages online and maintaining a level of civility in online interactions.

Plagiarize: To plagiarize is to steal the ideas or words of someone else and pass then off as your own without acknowledging the source.

Technoethics: Technoethics is an interdisciplinary field concerned with all ethical aspects of technology within a society shaped by technology. It deals with human processes and practices connected to technology which are becoming embedded within social, political, and moral spheres of life. It also examines social policies and interventions occurring in response to issues generated by technology development and use.

Chapter IX
Ethical Conflicts in Research on Networked Education Contexts

Terry D. Anderson
Athabasca University, Canada

Heather P. Kanuka
Athabasca University, Canada

ABSTRACT

The emergent world of network-based education creates challenges for researchers who wish to further our understanding of the opportunities and limitations while acting ethically in relation with learners, educators, and educational institutions. Existing ethical guidelines and practices were developed in place bound contexts in which privacy, safety, consent, ownership, and confidentiality were exposed and protected in many different ways than that found in networked contexts. This chapter addresses these and other ethical concerns that arise when doing educational search on the net. This chapter is designed to help researchers understand the evolving ethics of research in net-mediated educational contexts. It concludes that researchers need to be prepared to innovate beyond the dictates of often dated ethical guidelines and to act as intelligent and responsible professionals.

The net changes everything - Variously attributed, Dot Com Era

Our identities have no bodies, so, unlike you, we cannot obtain order by physical coercion. We believe that from ethics, enlightened self-interest, and to commonweal, our governance will emerge.

A Declaration of the Independence of Cyberspace - John Perry Barlow, 1996

INTRODUCTION

Ebullient claims like those above give rise to a sense that the global electronic network has changed the ways in which we interact and that we need a new set of ethos and ethics to guide those activities, including research activities. The net has been instrumental in re-engineering large components of our lives, from commerce to education, and from entertainment to vocation. As both researchers and educators, we have felt these effects with resulting concern, misconception and uncertainty when our research stretches and flexes our current ethical understandings. There are many ethical dilemmas that educational researchers face when conducting studies that are based upon or make extensive use of the Internet resources, communities or conversations. These ethical dilemmas are not unique to our research in the field of education. Indeed, within the field of social sciences, clashes, conflicts and heated debates have been ongoing for over 2 decades among researchers because existing codes of practice are failing to provide appropriate and workable guidelines for Internet-based research. Upon examination of the literature on ethical issues relating to Internet-based research, we conclude that there are three main reasons for confusion and uncertainty among researchers in the field of education. These issues include participant consent, public vs. private ownership and confidentiality and anonymity. Our discussion in this chapter revolves around these issues.

The use of the Internet effects research in the field of education in two distinct ways. First, it provides a new educational context or learning environment, such as a completely virtual education institution (e.g., virtual school or university, or private training organization) or augmentation of classroom-based schooling (so called blended-learning) with network mediated activities. This new environment supports the traditional interactions between and among students, instructors and content (although they are, by definition, mediated) but it often extends these communications to span boundaries of space, time and relationship. The new environment also supports the creation

and operation of student, teacher and content agents (Anderson & Whitelock, 2004) that act autonomously on behalf of their owners while traversing the "semantic Web" (Berners-Lee, Hendler, & Lassila, 2001). The Internet is also used to create virtual learning environments (e.g., learning contexts build in SecondLife and Active Worlds) in which the physical laws of nature can be transcended.

In such novel environments, it is firstly no surprise that ethical laws and norms developed for face-to-face interaction may also be transcended or suspended. All of these contextual changes create very complicated sets of personal and impersonal interaction within an educational realm and the broader social domain. Secondly, the Internet is used to create research tools through which researchers can study, measure and observe both networked and real world activities. For example, WebCams, listening devices, Web mining tools and other forms of Web-enhanced monitoring tools and input devices, allow the researcher to continuously monitor and study real time (as well as asynchronous) activities happening anywhere on the globe. These data collecting devices may be visible and obtrusive, but they are as likely to be covertly hidden or hidden by a subject's sense of familiarity, challenging our sense of privacy and aloneness.

The application of both types of Web-enhanced research creates ethical issues and concerns, and provides opportunity for uninformed (or nefarious!) researchers to exploit or endanger unaware research subjects or participants. We write this chapter as a discussion focused on both the opportunities and the perils of Internet-based research within the field of education. We provide no simple solutions or recommendations. Rather, we write in hopes that those within the research community will benefit through an extended discussion and resulting understanding of the often hidden ethical constraints and dilemmas of Internet-based educational research. We hope that both researchers and those whose job entails funding or approval of research projects to which questions of human protection and ethical conduct are concerned will use this chapter as a platform for more informed discussion and debate related to the development of sound and workable ethical guidelines. As we delve with increasing frequency into Internet-based research, it is becoming evident that we need to be vigilant in confronting the difficult ethical issues that we are facing. At the point that we write this discussion, Internet-based research, within the field of education, continues to sit on the periphery of mainstream research and, as such, it would behoove us to step up to this challenge and act now in developing ethical practice for Internet-based research. Should we fail to increase our understanding of appropriate ethical practice related to Internet-based research, it will only be a matter of time before harm or at least wasted effort will result to both subjects and researchers. In turn, this will likely result in an increased reluctance for individuals to participate in research projects, greater institutional barriers, and less productive and effective research practice.

The purpose of this chapter is to further more practical discussion on the three most contentious issues previously identified by Kanuka and Anderson (2007). These are issues related to informed consent, ownership and confidentiality and anonymity. We begin the chapter with an overview of two competing philosophical positions that underlie the process by which ethical values, practice and constraints are adopted by research communities. In the conclusion we offer a recommendation for researchers designed to guide their ethical practice. However, we note that such positions are still evolving rapidly in networked contexts and that each action needs to be grounded in the cultural context in which they operate.

OPPOSING ETHICAL PERSPECTIVES FOR RESEARCH PRACTICE

Philosophers have noted that ethical perspectives are most often based upon one of two competing views (Thomas, 1996). The first view, referred to as the deontological perspective, asserts that codes of ethics need to be developed with clear, articulate, and explicit guidelines to which researchers must adhere. Deontological perspectives develop and evolve slowly over time and are most effective in stable research contexts. The second view, referred to as the teleological perspective, maintains that ethical behavior is determined by the consequence of an act, or the greatest social good and the least social harm. Teleological solutions can evolve rapidly as actors closely observe the results of their behavior and adjust their ethical guidelines in response to observed results.

Deontological, or rule-based solutions, are attractive in their simplicity and appeal to those who are uncomfortable dealing with situations that lack clear proscriptive guidelines. However, we generally reject the deontological perspective (rule following) and argue that researchers using the Internet today need to approach ethical research from a teleological perspective (consequentialist). The teleological view looks beyond the rule, to its immediate and long-term effect on participants as the basis for ethical action. As with all rules, ethical guidelines need to be critically reflected upon and regularly updated within the context of the research setting.

Specifically, the rule following approach offered by the deontological view is less functional within the rapidly changing and unstable technological and social culture that currently characterizes the Internet. Rapid technological and fluid social evolution, and innovation, routinely both create and resolve new ethical dilemmas in rapid succession. Moreover, as every research study and every Internet culture is unique and often transitory, the premature creation of rigid governing rules and codes of practice "would lead us to a futile exercise in perpetual rule construction" (Thomas, 1996).

Finally, we note that our view of what is ethical, and what is not, is usually acquired at an early age and shaped through our social and cultural practices and values. Specifically, customs, traditions, and culture define our ways of knowing, which in turn define our ways of expanding what we know and this is reflected in our research practices. It is these factors that influence what we perceive to be of value and how we develop personal and professional integrity. Because these principles are often unspoken, and in the case of emerging practice undocumented, we may not be aware that others do not share similar ethical principles. Thus, there is the need for mindful attention to the issue by all researchers.

THE ETHICAL CONTEXT OF THE INTERNET

If, as Benedikt (1996) argues, cyberspace "has a geography, a physics, a nature and a rule of human law" (p. 123), then obviously it is an environment that can provide insight into human behavior and nature through examination of the cultural and sociological constructs that humans create within this context. Formal education is one of the most important social functions, and one in which the ever-growing complexities of this postmodern era require us to comprehend, interpret and manage. As an evolving and important new medium for communication, the Internet has become a valuable tool for information retrieval and artifact construction and has lured both educator and educational researcher into this milieu for use as a platform for teaching, learning and research. As Marshall McLuhan (1964) has pointed out, we tend to interpret new media through our experience of older media. Thus, early educational

research on the Internet has tended to apply tools, practice and ethical concerns from a pre-Internet context to this new environment. Although it remains unclear how many of the research tools that have been developed, tested and honed in real communities have direct utility in virtual communities, it is likely that these tools will be used and modified based on our pre-Internet understanding and experience.

Moreover, it is certain that creative minds will develop new tools designed for producing and disseminating both knowledge and wisdom in an online context. Thus, the ethics of e-research is concerned both with the application and adoption of tools from the real world and the invention, refinement and calibration of a new genre of net-centric tools and practice. In particular, the Internet is an environment in which its users create social cultures that have unique communication patterns, norms, values, and interaction systems that can transform pre-Internet conceptions of self and of community (Postmas, 2007). These transformations are at the root of many of the ethical uncertainties and must be factored into any new codes of ethical behavior developed for Internet-based research. Current codes of practice in the field of education are greatly influenced by proscriptive guidelines provided by professional organizations, notably the Psychological Association's ethical principles of psychologists and code of conduct, last updated in 2003. This organization, like other professional organizations, is facing challenges evolving ethical concerns that relate to their practice as counselors and as researchers. In 1997, a statement was issued suggesting a teleological approach relating to services provided through telephone, teleconferencing or Internet and noted:

[I]n those emerging areas in which generally recognized standards for preparatory training do not yet exist, psychologists nevertheless take reasonable steps to ensure the competence of their work and to protect patients, clients, students,

research participants, and others from harm. (APA Online)

Moreover, promised to be forthcoming were ongoing guidelines and revisions of code, yet the 2003 guidelines are noticeably silent on specific guidelines for research or practice that is mediated in any format. Thus, while there has been a stated need for greater professional awareness for evolving ethical guidelines, there has yet to be a great deal of enthusiasm for venturing into relatively uncharted territory. Indeed, this evolving platform for research provides researchers with many exciting new possibilities, but is also creating many new problems with respect to ethics in the process.

For example, Peter Steiner's famous 1993 New Yorker cartoon (see http://www.unc.edu/depts/jomc/academics/dri/idog.html) illustrating a dog typing on a computer reminds us that it is still very difficult to authenticate communication or presence on the Internet. Internet-based studies have begun to reveal that some research participants have a tendency to be less inhibited when communicating online than in face-to-face (Reid, 1996), while most carefully manage their online identity through occasionally providing more mendacious or inaccurate demographic data (McKenna, 2007). Roberts (2000) noted that this occurrence is due to the ability of the Internet as a forum for communication in which we can "assume anonymous or pseudonymous online identities that obscure details such as gender, age, and demographics which may be of importance to the investigation" (see also Kendall, 1999; Jones, 1999). Reid also notes the disinhibiting effect of communicating on the Internet, as well as the allure of self-revelation. The explosion of interest in new social software sites (such as faceBook, MySpace and SecondLife) in recent years has accelerated the accurate and fantasy disclosure of personal identity.

These issues can create very interesting and often complex ethical issues for research-

ers. Notable among these are issues relating to consent, ownership and anonymity to which we now turn.

INFORMED CONSENT

Consent is a cornerstone of ethical research practice within the field of education. Except in rare cases where deception is relatively benign and integral to the research purpose, free and voluntary consent must be obtained from all participants. In limited cases when consent is not obtained before participation, it must be obtained as soon as possible after participation, usually in debriefing sessions immediately following the researcher's intervention. However, we find that this fairly simple principle can, at times, cause added complexity for Internet-based research.

For example, common practice in educational research is for a researcher to distribute consent forms to students in a classroom setting and have them immediately signed by all the participants. In an online classroom setting, this same procedure often becomes much more complicated. First, privacy legislation may prohibit institutions from providing contact information (such as e-mail addresses) to researchers that can be used to solicit participation.

Secondly, within our own practice, we have noticed reluctance by anonymous students to agree to participate, yet they very rarely refuse to participate either. That is, proportions of students just do not answer our invitation e-mails to participate. Have they, thus, refused to participate? Have they even received our request? Is it ethical to adopt "reverse marketing techniques" whereby participants inform the researcher if they do not wish to participate? And if so, must all evidence of their participation in the class be removed before any analysis of the activity takes place?

These questions have recently caused considerable argument and strain within university ethics review boards at Canadian universities.

One course of action some researchers have taken to solve this problem is to inform students that activities (postings, paths traversed on Web sites, time spent on particular resources, etc.) are being collected in a manner similar to the announcement that telephone calls are being recorded at many call centers. By implication, research participants who do not wish to partake in such investigation, like call center customers, are free to withdraw and thus their continued presence is an implied consent. Unfortunately, labeling such default participation as voluntary implies that the research participant has alternative means of obtaining the desired services.

In some educational programs, courses or individual assignments are not optional and thus the student is not really free to withdraw from the course or related learning activity. As such, researchers using such techniques for obtaining consent must insure that there are realistic and accessible options for participants who do not wish to participate.

Recently, there has been an increased interest in observing, classifying and coming to understand student behavior in a variety of Internet-based education contexts. One of the most frequently used techniques is something referred to as "data mining" (Zaiane, 2001). This technique relies on extensive analysis of Web log entries created by student requests for page delivery and other calls to an educational Web server. This technique may also make use of "cookies," small pieces of code attached to the students' browser that identify each user and their activities on a Web site. Generally, this data is considered to be "secondary," as it often is not used to identify unique activities of identifiable individuals and, as such, not in need of informed consent.

However, many researchers who are using this technique have begun to ask themselves if, under these conditions, this technique requires informed consent as it can be used to track individual behavior, and this can be matched to individual identities. And if this technique does require informed consent, does the research participant need to be made aware of all of the possible ways and uses this data can be put to use during the research process? Hearkening back to non-Internet-based research, we would generally think that students whose activities were observed by camera or by an observer sitting in the back of the classroom would have to obtain such consent. As such, using secondary data from online classrooms would also require that informed consent be obtained. Issues of informed consent also confound the practice of transcript analysis (e.g., Rourke, Anderson, Garrison, & Archer, 2000). As postsecondary institutions increase their offerings of online courses, there is a corresponding need to study the impact that Internet-based interaction is having on learning and teaching processes. Transcripts of courses gathered automatically in machine-readable format are an extremely valuable and convenient form of data for educational researchers.

However, the fluidity of many online course participants–who are often geographically dispersed–makes it difficult to not only track and identify course participants but also to communicate with them. Thus, obtaining informed consent can be an onerous challenge for education researchers. Given the critical need to investigate the impact that online courses are having on the learning process, some program administrators are requesting students who enroll in online courses to notify either their course instructor or program administrator if they do not wish to have their course transcripts used in future research. Following is an example of such a request taken from a Canadian university course Web site:

Please note that all conferences are archived, and transcripts of the conferences may later be used for research. Whenever transcripts are used for research they are redacted so that, in keeping with ethical requirements, no information is made public which can identify any participant in any way.

If you prefer, you may avoid participation in conferencing if you elect one of the options described in the course "Assignments." Also, you may request removal or revision of any posting you have made to a conference in this course. If you wish to change or remove a posting during the course, contact the course instructor. If you have questions about any of the above, please contact me or the course instructor.

Is this statement complete enough to fulfill current requirements for informed consent? In Canada, university researchers are compelled to adhere to a set of guidelines established by the three federal research-funding councils (see www.ncehr-cnerh.org/english/code_2/). A quick review of these Tri-Council recommendations for informed consent is insightful as we struggle to answer this question. These guidelines require the researcher to provide five-types of information to insure participants are informed. This includes a "comprehensible statement of the research purpose, the identity of the researcher, the expected duration and nature of participation, and a description of research procedures."

Is a broad general consent from the course participants sufficient without stating the exact purposes for which their online course transcripts will be used? In the example provided, we can see that, first, the identity of the researcher is unknown. Secondly, the purpose of the research has not been provided, nor the expected duration and nature of participation, nor a description of research procedures. In particular, a very sparse description is provided of the intended analysis process, which may expand or change as the research continues. In addition, researchers are generally expected to have their data available for examination or re-analysis by peers to insure its veracity, assuming the individual identity and privacy of the participants is protected. Finally, the use of the word "redacted" may pose an ethical problem. To save many readers the task of running to the dictionary, let us quote Oxford

dictionary's (1990) definition of redact: "to put into literary form; edit for publication." The Tri-council guidelines also state that the description of the project must be in language that is accessible and understandable to the respondents, a requirement violated for many in this instance.

While we acknowledge there are ethical problems with this kind of open consent, we also concede that we look forward to the day when very large repositories of educational conferencing transcripts can be analyzed through sophisticated quantitative techniques such as latent syntax analysis (LSA) and neural nets. However, we do not foresee how the issue of informed consent can be resolved and continue to be guided by the Tri-council guidelines. As Mann and Stewart (2000) observe "there are clear ethical considerations about using databases, as most individuals have no knowledge of where such data are stored and little power to control use of the data" (p. 42). Furthermore, the Tri-Council guidelines assert that ethics approval be obtained if the data contains information that allows identification of participants. Thus, it is possible that ethical implications can be greatly reduced if the data can be "disembodied" to the point where recognition of individuals or personal attribution of their remarks or responses can be eliminated. Work by scholarly groups such as that at the University of Toronto and Athabasca University to gather libraries of such "disembodied" data is useful and welcomed, but one should not underestimate the effort required to remove all personal identifiers from online transcripts, before they can be made available.

In the case of the examination of transcripts or photo's taken by a WebCam, it has been argued that those being studied are not research participants in the normal use of the word because they are not being asked to do anything specific by the researcher. Yet if we, again, review the Canadian Tri-Council Code of Ethical Conduct for Research Involving Humans (1994), we can see that research participants are defined as "living individuals or groups of living individuals about whom a scholar conducting research obtains;

- Data through intervention or interaction with the individual or group, or;
- Identifiable private information.

Distinguishing between active "action research" in which the researcher takes part in the conference under investigation and one on which the researcher merely examines the subsequent transcript or record, changes the nature of the "intervention or interaction" between researcher and research subject. Thus, it can be argued that a researcher analyzing the transcripts of an educational conference, without participating themselves, has not intervened in the process and thus has not placed the authors in the position of "research participants." However, it is also important to recognize that the second criterion is relevant in that transcripts can contain "private information" that has been posted to the conferencing forum. It is currently unclear if there is a sense of implied public access attached to postings on public discussion boards, especially if access is restricted to enrolled students.

Finally, issues revolving around consent become even more complex when we consider the problem of ownership of online transcripts. Based on the literature, it is not yet clear who actually owns messages posted on Internet communication forums. Cavazos and Morin (1994), for example, maintain that all Internet-based communication should be considered published written material and, as with other copyrighted material, quoting without citing the source is a violation of copyright laws.

But, as Mann and Stewart (2000) point out, there is also an implied license that mitigates absolute copyright. In particular, if copyright laws were to be followed in a literal sense in Internet-based communication, then no one could download or read a message without explicit per-

mission from the copyright owner (normally the author). However, in sending the message, Mann and Stewart (2000) argue "there is an implied license to read, or even archive, the information it contains" (p. 46). Kitchin (1998) adds to the ownership confusion by asking if perhaps the server administrator, owner of the server system, or the moderator of a discussion group might also have ownership rights.

In our own experience, we find that most students agree to participate in transcript analysis studies and only rarely do we get a definite refusal to participate. However, there are often a handful of students who do not reply to e-mail solicitations requesting their approval. Such a scenario forces researchers to either abandon the sample group or remove the postings of individuals who have not given permission. Removal of individual nonparticipating postings is possible using search and delete techniques of the analysis software, but in practice becomes problematic in that postings often contain excerpts and quotations from previous postings, any of which may have been made by nonparticipating subjects.

In addition, use of personal names is common and removing all references to nonparticipants can be very time consuming. Further, one could narrowly define removal of a nonparticipants' posting itself as an analysis process requiring permission of the participants. Finally, the removal of one or more person's postings may make understanding of the conference thread impossible and decontextualize subsequent postings.

Mann and Stewart (2000) astutely recognize that informed consent is "perhaps the key issue to be addressed anew when creating a framework for ethical online research practice" (p. 48). To complicate this issue further, Waskul and Douglass (1996) assert that if informed consent is not obtained, then a degree of deception is implied, and deceptive research is always on soft ethical grounds and generally considered to be unethical if there are any alternative ways to conduct the research. While deception invokes ethical conflicts in research in physical environments, it is complicated further in virtual environments.

Specifically, in online environments, the participants do not have outward clues to identify a researcher (e.g., taking field notes, video cameras, tape recorders, etc.). As such, in online environments where a researcher does not inform participants of his/her research role, and the participant cannot "see" the researcher, this implies a degree of deception by exploiting the ignorance of something that the participant could not possibly know about (Waskul & Douglass, 1966).

Given the ethical implications of conducting deceitful research on the one hand, and the difficulty of obtaining informed consent by some populations on the other hand, there is currently very little agreement about how to proceed with respect to obtaining informed consent in this area. Is it enough to get approval for a vague possibility of research on human subjects? Or do subjects have the right to know the specifics of the research and the specifics of how information from and about them is to be used and stored? And if so, can a researcher gain this level of specificity when they may have many types of investigation and secondary analysis in mind?

Authenticity and Consent

Unique ethical issues related to Internet-based research also occur when obtaining electronic consent and insuring its authenticity. While these issues are not unique to Internet-based research, they do tend to become more complex and, hence, more problematic when research is conducted over the Internet. For example, the process of acquiring consent usually involves signing a consent form in which the researcher outlines the relevant components of the research. In some cases, consent is implied by the completion of a survey or questionnaire.

Normally, a signature authenticates consent; however, many potential research participants do not use digital signature technologies that insure encryption and authentication. Thus, educational researchers who are collecting e-mails or Web forms, in a technical sense, do not have the legal weight of a signed consent form.

The general practice to date is that unless the researcher has reason to believe that the participant has an incentive to misrepresent him/herself, unsecured electronic consent forms are deemed to be an acceptable notice of consent, even though not all researchers agree with this practice. Mann and Stewart (2000), for example, share view that, as this practice is a relatively new way of obtaining consent, researchers must be prepared to rigorously support their decision.

This process should include citing other studies that used electronic consent, steps taken by the researcher to verify that the electronic consent form was sent by the intended participant (e.g., through the use of a code word), and identify any problems that may occur as a result of using electronic consent followed by aggressively defending how this will be overcome. To resolve the problem of verifying who actually sent the consent form, some education researchers use authentication software for both participants and themselves. Authentication software also effectively eliminates possibility of third-party interference. These services are provided at a relatively low cost through Certificate Authorities and public key infrastructure firms (e.g., see: http://www.verisign.com/). A problem with using authentication software, however, is that both the researcher and the research participant(s) must possess certain technical knowledge and skills in order to download and learn how to use the authentication add-ons, and there is currently an expense involved for this security enhancement. Besides financial considerations, insisting on secure transmission may stress technical skills and support skills of both researchers and participants and also increase the time and commitment required by both the participants and the researcher.

Researchers who obtain consent over the Internet also have to be aware of the risk of having vulnerable populations participate in their study. As discussed above, and also by Roberts (2000), potential participants may conceal demographic details, such as age. This may lead to vulnerable populations (e.g., children or persons of diminished mental capacity) being recruited and included in a study without the researcher's knowledge or parental consent. Schrum (1995) maintains that this lack of knowledge of participants alone presents a serious problem of Internet-based research. Obviously, researchers who use the Internet to obtain consent will need to acknowledge in their proposals that there are risks associated with obtaining online consent and ethics committee members need to understand the problems that can occur with this practice.

However, there are occasions when the use of the Internet is the only practical means of obtaining this consent. While attracting vulnerable participants is an ever-present possibility, the Internet also has the ability to access participants who might otherwise be unable to participate, or who traditionally may not have been able to have a voice in research projects. For a variety of reasons (e.g., geographic, disabilities, situational) researchers are sometimes not able to access specific people or populations. In certain circumstances, Internet-based research can access these populations which, in turn, provides greater inclusively. The ethical problem revolves around the following issue: Does the challenges involved in obtaining consent for certain populations and people over the Internet outweigh the possible risks of attracting unauthorized participants?

Privacy, Confidentiality, and Anonymity

Confidentiality in research refers to an agreement as to how information collected in the study will be kept secure and private (i.e., through controlled access). The terms of confidentiality are usually tailored to the needs of the participants. Privacy refers to the research participants' right to control access of others to information about themselves. Anonymity refers to the removal of any unique characteristics (e.g., names, addresses, affiliated institution) that would allow unique identification of participants. Respecting a participant's need for privacy, confidentiality or autonomy are ways a researcher respects their participants and is deemed a fundamental requirement of ethical practice among educational researchers.

This respect is shown most clearly by allowing the participants to share in the responsibility for decision making that effects them, and in particular to share knowledgeably in the decision to participate (or not) in a research project. To make decisions accurately and knowledgeably, the respondent must be informed of all the relevant details of the research, with an opportunity to refuse to participate. The general principles include competence, integrity, professional and scientific responsibility, respect for people's rights and dignity, concern for others' welfare, and social responsibility. In addition to these principles are ethical standards that include, among other things, privacy and confidentiality.

Unfortunately, it is not as straightforward or simple to uphold many of these principles when using the Internet as a research tool or communication medium during the research process. In particular, promising absolute privacy, confidentiality and anonymity may not be possible when using the Internet in the research process. Researchers need to be cognizant that other people may have access to–or may be able to access–data that is kept on an Internet server.

Hence, the same assurances for privacy, confidentiality and anonymity cannot be provided by the researcher to the research participants as compared to paper documents which are kept securely under lock and key. For example, server maintenance personnel will have access to the data that resides on the server and these individuals should be honor bound or bonded to guard the privacy of this data. More troublesome, however, is that hackers will always be a looming threat to safely securing data that resides on an Internet server.

This threat is threefold: accessing and making public the data that is collected, changing research data, or destroying data through distributed viruses. Are researchers compelled to advise participants that they cannot guarantee that the data will not be accessed and used, changed, or destroyed, by others? Or can researchers and participants assume that security standards are maintained to the equivalent of a statement that "results will be stored under lock and key in my office for a period of 12 months" as is typical language of pre-Internet research? We think researchers would be prudent to provide details of how they will attempt to provide privacy, confidentiality or anonymity.

Further, if the security of the data does become compromised, researchers will have the protection of knowing they had undertaken reasonable precautions to deal with potential security problems and avoid a great deal of embarrassment and possible legal action.

Privately-Public, Publicly-Private or Semi-Public Online Forums

Research that is being conducted in public spaces, generally, does not require the researcher to obtain consent (exceptions occur when private acts are studied in public spaces). Bulletin boards, such as newsgroups in which it is not necessary to obtain a private logon in order to post, are considered by many to be public spaces. Anyone can read newsgroup messages. Anyone can post messages to a newsgroup. In face-to-face settings, consent is not typically required of participants when research is being conducted in public spaces (as for example observing crowd behaviour at sports events).

However, applying this principle to online public spaces is difficult. King (1996) notes that

the sense of violation possible is proportional to our expectation of privacy. Most of us, for example, would not feel our privacy was being violated if we were being audio or video taped in a public space such as is done for security reasons in many transportation facilities. There would also likely be no question in the minds of ethic review committee members that voluntary and informed consent is required from each participant when data is being explicitly collected using video or audio recordings, irrespective if it is in a public space or not. With this in mind, now consider this question: How different is the researcher who "tape records" a personal conversation in a public space from the researcher who "archives text" on a public newsgroup? This is not an easy question to answer. Specifically, while permanently recording the transitory discourse that arises in a public space is not part of a normal public conversation, posting a message on a public newsgroup, which automatically creates a permanent and public record of activity, is a normal part of online conversation.

It is this difference (the permanent and public recording of online communication) that makes it difficult for researchers and ethic committee members to decide when studying electronic transcripts if this type of research requires voluntary and informed consent prior to the data collection process from those who posted the messages. Researchers have written about this ambiguity with diverse views (e.g., Mann & Stewart, 2000; Wilkins, 1991). Wilkins (1991) for example, cites opinions that public Internet forums (such as public mailing lists and Usenet groups) can be used in research if authorship is cited by reference to note, number, or name and permission from the forum owner is granted.

In describing her own experience in a public e-mail list form for breast cancer Sharf (1999) went to considerable effort to obtain written permission from those members who's posting she quoted in her research publication, while only announcing her intent (via the list) to members she did not quote directly. In contrast, a group of respected scholars from several countries in a very large scale project determined that "the issue of informed consent of authors, moderators and/or archiving institutions does not apply to a quantitative content analysis in which only publicly available text is analyzed" (Rafaeli, Sudweeks, Konstan, & Mabry, 1994).

It would seem the safest course of action would be to obtain participant consent, even when a convincing case could be made that such consent is not necessary. However, as was noted in the consent section, obtaining consent can be difficult with many inter-related complexities, as well as time and resource consuming, and in some instances, the acknowledged presence of the researcher may significantly alter the behavior under investigation (see Roberts, 2000; Turkle, 1997).

Thus, given that the Internet defies our understanding of public spaces in a physical sense, is online communication public or private? According to Waskul and Douglass (1996), it is neither public nor private. Rather, it is both and can be considered to be privately-public, publicly-private, or semi-private. As outlined in the previous section, securing access to online communication cannot be guaranteed in any absolute way; Internet server administrators and hackers may obtain access to the data.

As such, private Internet communications that occur behind passwords or firewalls can only be considered, at best, to be semi-private or privately-public. Alternatively, many e-mail lists, blogs, WIKIs and social software interest groups and newsgroups are open for the public to join, post messages, and read posted messages. However, in some instances (e.g., e-mail lists) individuals must sign-on to the group and can be removed by the list-owner. As such, some public forums are also semi-public or publicly-private. In a technical sense, there are no private spaces on the Internet, in the same way that an individual's bedroom is a private space. Because, technically, the Internet is publicly accessible (unless encryption, authen-

tication and other security services are utilized.), it has been argued that all Internet activities are equally public. However, while this conclusion does provide clarity to the public-private issue, this argument breaks down when uniformly and literally applied. Consider, for example, when using Internet forums that require a password in order to communicate, there is an implied understanding that this is a private space, even though technically it is not. Or is it? Given a general lack of deep understanding by most researchers and research subjects of the technical operation of the Internet, private and public spaces on the Internet can really only be understood in terms of metaphors.

Thus, our understanding of private space can only be used if we all agree that this metaphor can be applied to dichotomized private and public domains in terms of not only access, but also experience and perception (Waskul & Douglass, 1996). The ethical question becomes: How should we define a social sense of privacy when privacy is a matter of individual perception and experience? While few would argue over the dichotomies that occur in terms of access (either online forum are technically secured or not), agreement continues to break down with respect to applying experience and perception of the participants.

For example, unlike other public forms of communication, we can communicate in a public online forum from the privacy of our own home or workspace. Specifically, as King (1996) observes, we have the ability to interact publicly with others from the privacy of our own homes or workspace, making it possible to redefine the online communication as private and engage in private forms of communication.

In these cases, according to King, it is misleading to assume that online communication in public forms can be considered public, and not in need of obtaining consent. Waskul and Douglass (1996) concur, arguing that such a perception is intellectually barbaric and clearly unethical. Furthermore, Waskul and Douglass note that the public context of interaction does not preclude the emergence of private interactions. Awareness of this distinction is critical to the maintenance of ethical online research and public forums require informed and voluntary consent.

DISCUSSION AND CONCLUSION

As the discussion in this chapter illustrates, strict application of existing ethical guidelines for research practice may be technically impossible and could result in practices that many would consider to be unethical. This suggests the need for teleological-based modification to the deontological, rule-based ethical guidelines established for non-networked research. Moreover, there are no clear and correct research procedures in this new environment that we can all agree are ethical under all circumstances. Consensus about ethical practices disintegrates in Internet-based research when incongruency occurs between our own perceptions, values and wishes as a researcher and those of our colleagues, ethic committee members or research subjects.

The resolution of current ethical discord will only happen after there is open and honest expression of views between members of Internet communities, research participants, and the research community. Further, we must create a research environment that allows research practices to occur and evolve, yet proscribes diligent assessment of the effect and impact of the research on participants.

This secondary agenda of every Internet-based research project should be an effort to reflectively understand and documents the ethical implications of their research. In this way, we will create a responsible and evolving teleological set of ethical guidelines that will protect participants while permitting the exploration and deep understanding of this newest form of educational research. It behooves us as well to use the powerful communication and dissemination of networked tools to further this public discourse.

FURTHER RESEARCH

As time and experience evolve, so too will different degrees of acceptable practice, depending partially on the nature of the research (for example when researchers examine posting lengths versus amount of personal revelation), the types of participants (students in compulsory courses vs. those participating in nonformal educational forums) and the degree of personally identifiable material being analyzed (video transcripts vs. text chat). Further and ongoing research is required to document and track these changes. Of special interest are studies of the effect of the researcher's actions themselves, in some cases treating these as the independent variables in studies designed to empirically determine the impact of researcher behaviour related to the ethical issues discussed in this chapter. We begin the search for ethical guidelines in the more familiar physical context, but as we apply and adopt these ethical practices and constraints to online activities, the imperative (and opportunity) to engage in dialogue becomes critically important.

It is clear that sustaining ethical Internet-based research must rest not only on guiding principles outlined by external committees and authorities, but also the personal integrity of the researcher. As such it is essentially up to us, as researchers, to practice ethical behavior and to share widely the ethical underpinnings of our activities. This requires technical knowledge as well as personal integrity, self-regulation, reflection and an openness and honesty about all aspects of our work.

REFERENCES

Active Worlds. Retrieved April 22, 2008, from www.activeworlds.com

APA Online. (2003). *APA statement on services by telephone, teleconferencing, and Internet.* Retrieved April 22, 2008, from http://www.apa.org/ethics/stmnt01.html

Anderson, T., & Whitelock, D. (2004). The educational Semantic Web: Visioning and practicing the future of education. *Journal of Interactive Media in Education, 1.* Retrieved April 22, 2008, from http://www-jime.open.ac.uk/2004/1

Benedikt, M. (1996). Cyberspace: Some proposals. In M. Benedikt (Ed.), *Cyberspace: First steps* (pp. 119-224). Cambridge: MIT Press.

Berners-Lee, T., Hendler, J., & Lassila, O. (2001). The Semantic Web. *Scientific American, 284,* 34-43.

Cavazos, E. A., & Morin, G. (1994). *Cyberspace and the law: Your rights and duties in the online world.* Cambridge, MA: MIT Press.

Jones, S. (1999). *Doing Internet research: Critical issues and methods for examining the net.* London: Sage.

Kanuka, H., & Anderson, T. (2007). Ethical issues in qualitative e-learning research. *The International Journal of Qualitative Methods, 6*(2). Retrieved April 22, 2008, from http://www.ualberta.ca/~iiqm/backissues/6_2/kanuka.htm

Kendall, L. (1999). Recontextualizing "cyberspace:" Methodological consideration for on-line research. In S. Jones (Ed.), *Doing Internet research: Critical issues and methods for examining the net.* London: Sage.

King, S. (1996). Researching Internet communities: Proposed ethical guidelines for the reporting of the results. *The Information Society, 12*(2), 119-127. Retrieved April 22, 2008, from http://webpages.charter.net/stormking/eth-abs.html

Kitchin, R. (1998). *Cyberspace: The world in the wires.* New York: John Wiley.

Mann, C., & Stewart, F. (2000). *Internet communication and qualitative research. A handbook for researching online.* London: Sage.

McKenna, K. (2007). Through the Internet looking glass: Expressing and validating the true self. In A. Joinson, K. McKenna, T. Postmes, & U. Reips (Eds.), *Oxford handbook of Internet psychology.* Oxford: Oxford University Press.

McLuhan, M. (1964). *Understanding media: The extensions of man.* New York: McGraw-Hill.

Oxford concise dictionary of English. (1990). Oxford: Oxford University Press.

Postmas, T. (2007). The psychological dimensions of collective action, online. In A. Joinson, K. McKenna, T. Postmes, & U. Reips (Eds.), *Oxford handbook of Internet psychology* (pp. 165-184). Oxford: Oxford University Press.

Publication manual of the American Psychological Association (5th ed.). (2002). Washington, DC: American Psychological Association.

Rafaeli, S., Sudweeks, F., Konstan, J., & Mabry, E. (1994). *ProjectH Overview: A quantitative study of computer-mediated communication.* Retrieved April 22, 2008, from http://www.it.murdoch.edu.au/~sudweeks/papers/techrep.html

Reid, E. (1996). Informed consent in the study of on-line communities: A reflection of the effects of computer-mediated social research. *The Information Society, 12*(2), 169-174. Retrieved April 22, 2008, from http://venus.soci.niu.edu/~jthomas/ethics/tis/go.libby

Roberts, P. (2000, September 11-13). Ethical dilemmas in researching online communities: "Bottom-up" ethical wisdom for computer-mediated social research. In *Paper presented at the International Distance Education and Open Learning Conference*, Adelaide, Australia.

Rourke, L., Anderson, T., Garrison, D. R., & Archer, W. (2000). Methodological issues in the content analysis of computer conference transcripts. *International Journal of Artificial Intelligence in Education, 11*(3). Retrieved April 22, 2008, from communitiesofinquiry.com/documents/2Rourke_et_al_Content_Analysis.pdf

Schrum, L. (1995). Framing the debate: Ethical research in the information age. *Quarterly Inquiry, 1*(3), 311-326.

Secondlife. Retrieved April 22, 2008, from http://secondlife.com/

Sharf, B. (1999). Beyond netiquette: The ethics of doing naturalistic discourse research on the Internet. In S. Jones (Ed.), *Doing Internet research* (pp. 243-256). Thousand Oaks, CA: Sage.

Thomas, J. (1996). Introduction: A debate about the ethics of fair practices for collecting social science data in cyberspace. *The Information Society, 12*(2), 107-117. Retrieved April 22, 2008, from http://venus.soci.niu.edu/~jthomas/ethics/tis/go.jt

Tri-council Code of Ethical Conduct for Research Involving Humans. (1998). *Tri-council policy statement.* Retrieved April 22, 2008, from http://www.ncehr-cnerh.org/english/code_2/

Turkle, S. (1997). *Life on the screen. Identify in the age of the Internet.* New York: Touchstone.

Waskul, D., & Douglass, M. (1996). Considering the electronic participant. Some polemical observations on the ethics of on-line research. *The Information Society, 12*(2), 129-139. Retrieved April 22, 2008, from http://venus.soci.niu.edu/~jthomas/ethics/tis/go.dennis

Wilkins, H. (1991). Computer talk. *Written Communication, 8*(1), 56-78.

Zaiane, O. (2001). Web site mining for a better Web-based learning environment. In *Proceedings of the Computers and Advanced Technology in Education Conference:* Calgary: ACTA Press. Retrieved April 22, 2008, from http://www.cs.ualberta.ca/~zaiane/postscript/CATE2001.pdf

ADDITIONAL READING

Allen, C. (1996). What's wrong with the "golden rule"? Conundrums of conducting ethical research in cyberspace. *The Information Society, 12*(2). Retrieved April 22, 2008, from http: http://venus.soci.niu.edu/~jthomas/ethics/tis/go.christin

Anderson, T., & Kanuka, H. (2003). *E-research. Methods, strategies, and issues.* Allyn and Bacon.

Bakardjieva, M., & Feenberg, A. (2000). Involving the virtual subject. *Ethics and Information Technology, 2*, 233-240.

Bassett, E. H., & O'Riordan, K. (2002). Ethics of Internet research: Contesting the human subjects research model. *Ethics and Information Technology, 4*(3), 233-249.

Bruckman, A. (2002). *Ethical guidelines for research online.* Retrieved April 22, 2008, from http://www.cc.gatech.edu/~asb/ethics/

Brynum, T. W. (2001). *Computer ethics: Basic concepts and historical overview.* Retrieved April 22, 2008, from http://plato.stanford.edu/entries/ethics-computer/

Bulmer, M. (1982). The merits and demerits of covert participant observation. In M. Bulmer (Ed.), *Social research ethics* (pp. 217-251). London: Macmillan.

Cavazos, E. A., & Morin, G. (1994). *Cyberspace and the law: Your rights and duties in the online world.* Cambridge, MA: MIT Press.

Christians, C. (2000). Ethics and politics in qualitative research. In N. K. Denzin & Y. S. Lincoln (Eds.), *Handbook of qualitative research* (pp. 133-155). London: Sage.

Ess, C., & Association of Internet Researchers (AoIR) Ethics Working Committee. (2002). *Ethical decision-making and Internet research. Recommendations from the AoIR Ethics Work-*

ing Committee. Retrieved April 22, 2008, from http://www.aoir.org/reports/ethics.pdf

Fahy, P., & Spencer, B. (2004). Research experience and agreement with selected ethics principles from Canada's Tri-Council Policy Statement—ethical conduct for research involving humans. *Journal of Distance Education, 19*(2), 28-58.

Frankel, M. S., & Siang, S. (1999). *Ethical and legal aspects of human subjects research on the Internet.* Retrieved April 22, 2008, from http://www.aaas.org/spp/dspp/sfrl/projects/intres/main.htm

Glen, S. (2000). The dark side of purity or the virtues of double-mindedness? In H. Simons & R. Usher (Eds.), *Situated ethics in educational research* (pp. 12-21). New York: Routledge-Falmer.

Hawk, C. S. (2001). *Computer and Internet use on campus: Legal guide to issues on intellectual property, free speech, and privacy.* San Francisco: Jossey-Bass.

Hemmings, A. (2006). Great ethical divides: Bridging the gap between institutional review boards and researchers. *Educational Researcher, 35*(4), 12-18.

Hudson, J.M., & Bruckman, A. (2005). Using empirical data to reason about Internet research ethics. In *Proceedings of the Ninth European Conference on Computer-supported Cooperative Work.* Springer-Verlag. Retrieved April 22, 2008, from www.ecscw.uni-siegen.de/2005/paper15.pdf

Hwang, S., & Roth, W.-M. (2004). Ethics on research on learning: Dialectics of praxis and praxeology. *Forum: Qualitative Social Research, 6*(1). Retrieved April 22, 2008, from http://www.qualitative-research.net/fqs/

Jones, S. (1999). *Doing Internet research: Critical issues and methods for examining the net.* London: Sage.

Kendall, L. (1999). Recontextualizing "Cyberspace:" Methodological consideration for on-line research. In S. Jones (Ed.), *Doing Internet research: Critical issues and methods for examining the net.* London: Sage.

King, S. (1996). Researching Internet communities: Proposed ethical guidelines for the reporting of the results. *The Information Society, 12*(2), 119-127. Retrieved on April 22, 2008, from http://venus.soci.niu.edu/~jthomas/ethics/tis/go.storm

Kirsh, G. E. (1999). *Ethical dilemmas in feminist research: The politics of location, interpretation, and publication.* Albany, NY: State University of New York Press.

Kithin, H. A. (2003). The tri-council policy statement and research in cyberspace: Research ethics, the Internet, and revising a living document. *Journal of Academic Ethics, 1*(4), 397-418.

Mann, C., & Stewart, F. (2000). *Internet communication and qualitative research. A handbook for researching online.* London: Sage.

McNamee, M. (2002). Introduction: Whose ethics, which research? In M. McNamee & D. Bridges (Eds.), *The ethics of educational research* (pp. 1-21). Oxford, UK: Blackwell.

McNamee, M., & Bridges, D. (Eds.). (2002). *The ethics of educational research.* Oxford, UK: Blackwell.

Pring, R. (2002). The virtues and vices of an educational researcher. In M. McNamee & D. Bridges (Eds.), *The ethics of educational research* (pp. 111-127). Oxford, UK: Blackwell.

Pritchard, I. A. (2002). Travelers and trolls: Practitioner research and institutional review boards. *Educational Researcher, 31*(3), 3-13.

Reid, E. (1996). Informed consent in the study of on-line communities: A reflection of the effects of computer-mediated social research. *The Information Society, 12*(2), 169-174. Retrieved

on April 22, 2008, from http://venus.soci.niu.
edu/~jthomas/ethics/tis/go.libby

Roberts, P. (2000). *Ethical dilemmas in researching online communities: "Bottom-up" ethical
wisdom for computer-mediated social research.*
Retrieved on April 22, 2008, from http://www.
com.unisa.edu.au/cccc/papers/refereed/paper40/
Paper40-1.htm

Roth, W.-M. (2004). Qualitative research and
ethics. *Forum: Qualitative Social Research,
5*(2). Retrieved April 22, 2008, from http://www.
qualitative-research.net/fqs/

Rourke, L., Anderson, T., Garrison, D. R., & Archer, W. (2000). Methodological issues in the content analysis of computer conference transcripts.
*International Journal of Artificial Intelligence in
Education, 11*(3). Retrieved on April 22, 2008,
from http://http://communitiesofinquiry.com/

Schrum, L. (1997). Ethical research in the information age: Beginning the dialog. *Computer in
Human Behavior, 13*(2), 117-125.

Simons, H., & Usher, R. (Eds.). (2000). *Situated
ethics in educational research.* New York: RoutledgeFalmer.

Small, R. (2002). Codes are not enough: What
philosophy can contribute to the ethics of educational research. In M. McNamee & D. Bridges
(Eds.), *The ethics of educational research* (pp.
89-110). Oxford, UK: Blackwell.

Spinello, R. (2002). *CyberEthics: Morality and
law in cyberspace* (2nd ed.). Sudbury, MA: Jones
and Bartlett.

Stanley, B. H., Sieber, J. E., & Melton, G. B.
(Eds.). (1996). *Research ethics. A psychological
approach.* Lincoln, NE: University of Nebraska
Press.

Tickle, L. (2002). Opening windows, closing
doors: Ethical dilemmas in educational action
research. In M. McNamee & D. Bridges (Eds.),
The ethics of educational research (pp. 41-57).
Oxford, UK: Blackwell.

Turkle, S. (1997). *Life on the screen. Identity in
the age of the Internet.* New York: Touchstone.

Usher, P. (2000). Feminist approaches to a situated
ethics. In H. Simons & R. Usher (Eds.), *Situated
ethics in educational research* (pp. 22-38). New
York: RoutledgeFalmer.

Walther, J. (2002). Research ethics in Internet-
enables research: Human subjects issues and
methodological myopia. *Ethcs and information
Technology, 4*(3). Retrieved April 22, 2008, from
http://www.nyu.edu/projects/nissenbaum/eth-
ics_wal_full.html

Waskul, D., & Douglass, M. (1996). Considering the electronic participant. Some polemical
observations on the ethics of on-line research.
The Information Society, 12(2), 129-139. Retrieved April 22, 2008, from http://venus.soci.
niu.edu/~jthomas/ethics/tis/go.dennis

Chapter X
The Ethics of Designing for Multimodality:
Empowering Nontraditional Learners

Michael Sankey
University of Southern Queensland, Australia

Rod St. Hill
University of Southern Queensland, Australia

ABSTRACT

The changing nature of distance education in the higher education context is investigated in this chapter, particularly in relation to "massification" and the ethics involved in delivering technology enhanced courses to an increasingly diverse student body. Institutions may have developed policies in response to this, but it would seem that few academics have a coherent way of adhering to them. In addition, there is significant research suggesting that reliance on text-based instruction may disadvantage some students. This chapter draws on four case studies, emanating from recent research, demonstrating that higher levels of student engagement are possible when course materials are designed to cater for students with different approaches to learning. This chapter also suggests a more ethical approach to developing courses is a two-phased approach: (1) integrating a range of multimodal learning and teaching strategies; and (2) giving students the opportunity to discover their preferred approach to learning.

INTRODUCTION

This chapter investigates issues relating to the changing nature of providing higher educational course materials via **distance education**, particularly in the context of the ethics involved in delivering these courses via technology-enhanced environments. Over recent years, there has been an increasing tendency, due to the advances in learning management system (LMS) technology, to shift the delivery of course materials from printed to electronic form. However, at the same time there has also been a significant increase in the percentage of **nontraditional learners** entering universities, particularly over the last decade, many of whom are choosing to study by **distance education** (Schuetze & Slowey, 2002). These technological and societal changes affecting higher education at a global level led Professor Jim Taylor in his keynote address at the ICDE World Conference on Open and Distance Learning in February 2004 to state, "traditional approaches to learning and teaching are not capable of meeting the escalating demands of higher education" (Taylor, 2004, p. 11).

In addition to this, sociologists and pragmatic educators are increasingly noticing that people are learning to learn in different or in nontraditional ways (Oblinger & Oblinger, 2005). This realisation parallels the "**massification**" of higher education, the process whereby higher education is transformed from an elite to a mass system with a much larger proportion of the population participating (Scott, 1995). As a greater **diversity** of people enter higher education it has become clear there are different cognitive, generational, cultural and demographic needs that all need to be considered when designing instruction, particularly for those studying at a distance. For example, in any given course of study there may be students ranging in age from 17 to 70+ (Traditionalists to Millennials, Figure 1), those who only study part-time, those who have dependants or be single parents, or they could be employed part- or full-time while also studying, or they may only have English as their second language (in a western context), or come from a disadvantaged background. In many cases, this has meant students are coming to university unprepared to face the rigors of study, and with little way of knowing how to make the appropriate adjustments.

Massification of higher education has created significant ethical challenges. Indeed there is now a literature on the professionalisation of teaching in higher education (Davis, 1999; Macfarlane, 2004). It is argued that the traditional view of a university academic as a discipline expert with a strong focus on research is no longer adequate. Although academics might be professional in the sense that they are members of a professional body (e.g., in accounting, engineering, law or medicine) or are discipline experts, they must also be professional in the sense that they are cognisant of obligations to students. Students are clients and professionalism incorporates both mastery of an area of knowledge and skill (the traditional view of the university academic) *and* service from which the client derives benefit (Jarvis, 1983).

The new **diversity** *in the student body, in, inter alia, ability, social background, culture, motivation and economic status, presents significant ethical challenges for teachers. In teaching, assessing and managing students this* **diversity** *has an impact. It is no longer good enough to treat students as an immature, homogeneous group with identical educational backgrounds.* (Macfarlane, 2004, p. 11)

The need to cater for such **diversity** has never been greater; demanding new approaches to learning and teaching for the new millennium (Cameron, Shaw, & Arnott, 2002).

Many universities have equity and ethics policies designed to address some of these issues, but it would seem few academic staff at these institutions have a coherent way of adhering to these policies, due either to a lack of time, or simply not being aware of the enormity of the issues (Birch & Gardiner, 2005). At least in the Australian context adoption of technology enhanced learning has been *ad hoc* and limited and does not appear to be a coherent response to the ethical implications of **massification** (Smith, Ling, & Hill, 2006). In

Figure 1. A simplified representation of different generational classifications

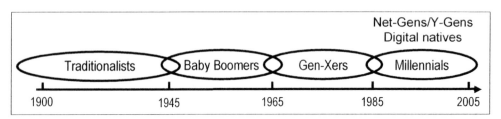

addition, there is significant research that would suggest that reliance on the more traditional text-based instructional materials supplied by many institutions may inadvertently disadvantage a significant proportion of their students (St Hill, 2000). In fact, this approach could now be considered an unethical way of approaching today's diverse student body, because it is unprofessional in the sense outlined above. If this is the case, it is incumbent upon those who design learning and teaching materials, particularly where there is no other form of instruction provided, to take into consideration changes that have occurred in the approaches students now take to study.

This chapter will report on four case studies emanating from recent research projects, conducted at the University of Southern Queensland (USQ) in Australia. These studies clearly demonstrate that higher levels of student engagement are possible when course materials can be designed to cater for students with a range of different approaches to learning and who come from a range of backgrounds. It investigates the implications of catering for a **diversity** of students, proposing that one approach to consider is **neomillennial learning**, "neo" in this context meaning "new," and "millennial" referring to the approach to learning and teaching required for the new millennium (Baird & Fisher, 2005). This should be done while acknowledging that, aligned with this issue of the ever increasing growth of **nontraditional learners** in our universities, there are still significant issues associated with these students accessing an ever increasing quantity of Internet-based learning materials. This chapter will propose that an ethical response can take the form of two phases. First, by integrating a range of multimodal learning and teaching strategies into course materials these environments can cater for a wider, more diverse range of learning approaches. Second, by giving students the opportunity to discover their preferred approach to learning these students can in turn have more confidence in their approach to study. This hypothesis will be supported with a summary of key points from the research conducted into four hybridized learning environments delivered to students from 2004 to 2006, drawing on student's comments and perceptions of these environments.

BACKGROUND AND CONTEXT INFORMATION

The University of Southern Queensland (USQ) is currently the second largest **distance education** provider in Australia (Vergnani, 2005), with 75% of its students (approximately 16,000) studying in this mode, and with almost 90 different nationalities being represented within its student body. At USQ, as with many other institutions in Australia, **distance education** course materials have traditionally been delivered via static print-based packages. However, advances in technology, especially development of the Internet, and the greater use of multimedia in education, have provided opportunities to enrich students' learning experiences.

As with many other institutions around the world USQ has responded to government policy and reduced funding by competing in the global marketplace and by widening access to new types of students (Bridge, 2006). To give some type of framework to widening access the university has been required to develop a range of policies addressing the issue of **diversity** within its student body. For example, USQ's policy on learning and teaching states specifically that the learning environment will offer choices in mode of delivery and incorporate a range of learning and teaching strategies to accommodate the diverse needs of students (USQ, 2005b). With respect to multiculturalism USQ's policy states:

As one of the leading providers of international education programs in Australia, the University will ensure that the academic programs are culturally inclusive in their content and delivery. (USQ, 2005c)

Further, USQ's Equity in Educational policy states that it is:

to be proactive in promoting and supporting fair access to higher education opportunities and ensuring that all students have the opportunity to achieve according to their own individual potential. (USQ, 2005d)

Of particular note in this policy statement are the words "ensuring that all students have the opportunity to achieve according to their own individual potential." This is an ethical statement that is consistent with the idea of professionalisation of higher education. However, if any institution is to fully embrace this ethic there are a huge range of issues that the decision makers within the institution need to consider. They would need to:

question not only what is sound from a pedagogical and andragogical point of view, but also the effectiveness and efficiency of systems through which people learn, designed in response to basic learning needs…as well as alternative and supplementary frameworks for learning. (Vissar & Suzuki, 2006, p. 236)

This is a point we will return to later in this chapter.

Many of the policies USQ has developed in recent years have been informed by the wider directions provided to the higher education sector by the Australian Federal Government. In one government report titled *"Equality, Diversity and Excellence: Advancing the National Higher Education Equity Framework"* (Postle et al., 1996), it was made clear that the higher education system in Australia was in the throes of significant change and that a future focus on flexibility was essential. For example, one of this report's recommendations that addressed the equality of access to higher education states:

*In the context of pressures for globalisation, responsiveness, public accountability and quality assurance processes, which are now shaping the sector, there is a need to focus on building a flexible system which integrates the three areas of equality, **diversity** and excellence.* (Postle et al., 1996, p. 73)

In light of these changes and corresponding policy declarations, and as a major outcome of ongoing planning processes, USQ established a new vision statement, part of which is "to become Australia's leading transnational educator" (Lovegrove, 2004). This statement is designed to provide a strong organisational focus for driving USQ forward with an emphasis on learning and teaching practices for a diverse student body. As such, two of the key strategies, articulated in the USQ Learning and Teaching Plan, are to:

- Develop a **hybrid delivery** mechanism, as a core educational resource for all courses as practicable, that accommodates different **learning styles** and opportunities; and
- Enhance the learning experience with **hybrid delivery**, without detracting from the inherent advantages of any single mode of delivery (USQ, 2005a).

Based on the above, USQ has been developing its strategy for creating course resources based on **hybrid delivery** over the last 2½ years. This delivery modal has since become known as "**Transmodal delivery**" (USQ, 2006) and has been designed to accommodate the USQ transnational vision statement mentioned above. If properly used, this has the potential of allowing USQ to provide for an increasingly diverse range of students through the provision of technology enhanced learning materials. This claim will be supported by the research findings that appear later in this chapter.

Transmodal Delivery

The term "hybrid" in the educational context embraces a range of approaches to learning and teaching that integrate a number of delivery media, mainly facilitated by the proliferation of information and communication technologies (Parsons & Ross, 2002). McDonald, McPhail, Maguire, and Millett (2004) believe that "**hybrid learning** has emerged in response to a number of global and educational changes experienced by higher education institutions… including a greater emphasis on lifelong learning, globalization, the advent of the 'Information Age' and a move to a knowledge society" (p. 287). This approach to course delivery has allowed considerable expansion of support mechanisms for both on- and off-campus students and has made them available *en masse* (Cookson, 2002). As alluded to above, this **multimodal model** was deemed necessary by USQ as a means of providing its

Figure 2. The Transmodal delivery model: Context specific support for the resource-rich learning package

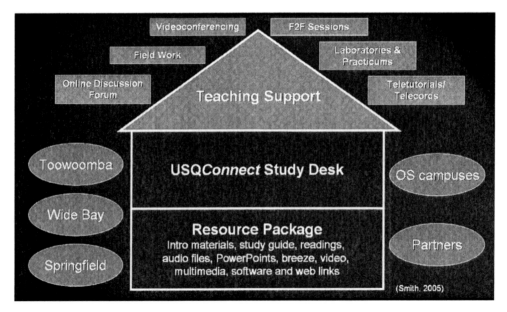

study materials in range of different contexts; across multiple campuses; for students studying at preparation level through to postgraduate; to international agents and partners; and to independent and corporate groups of students (Figure 2). However, as broadband technology is still not ubiquitous across all of these markets, particularly among many of USQ's Asian partnerships, this has made the choice of a CD-based resource the most viable option for the foreseeable future. In the context of USQ, **Transmodal delivery** is seen as the provision to students of a resource-rich multimodal learning environment, allowing students the opportunity to access their course content in a combination of ways.

This approach does not deny the perceived need (primarily among academic staff) to also provide easy access to a more traditional print-based resource, if preferred. Therefore, the CD-based approach is also used to provide students with their traditional print-based resources, in the form of PDF files (Figure 3). These printed resources are also made available for purchase if students prefer that option. More importantly, the HTML-based environment allows for significant multimedia enhancements (Figure 4) to be provided to students and, as demonstrated

later in this chapter, when given the choice, the majority of students prefer to receive this form of multimodal course materials.

However, for this to be effective as a learning and teaching strategy, learning environments need to be designed that are consistent in their approach to navigation and simultaneously able to provide students with access to significant quantities of electronic resources. This strategy in itself does not deal with the equity issue associated with increased **diversity** within the student body, but it does provide a platform to allow materials to be developed and delivered as an ethical response.

DIVERSITY AND GROWING NONTRADITIONAL STUDENT NUMBERS

Nontraditional learners have grown in prominence and are today a significant consideration when coming to design learning and teaching environment. For instance, in Australia alone, international student numbers at universities have doubled in the last 5 years to exceed 200,000 (Barrington, 2004). Schuetze and Slowey (2002) argued:

Figures 3 (left) and 4 (right). Two screen captures of the CMS1000 Transmodal environment showing the printable version of the materials and a multimedia enhancement (Breeze presentation)

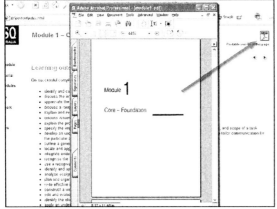
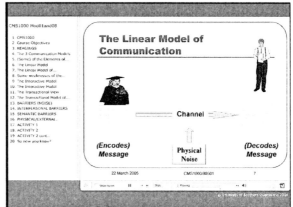

Non-traditional students in an elite higher education system were, by definition, a minority. With expansion and change in higher education some non-traditional groups have increased in number arguably to a point where the have come to form a 'new majority' in higher education. (p. 313)

This has caused a significant blurring of the boundaries in relation to how learning resources have traditionally been supplied as against how they should now be supplied to students (Bridge, 2006). These changes have caused fundamental educational questions to be asked such as "what to teach and how on earth to teach it" (Jochems, van Merrienboer, & Koper, 2004). For many universities, this has required new approaches to the delivery of course materials to be considered across the board (Kellner, 2004), and a greater flexibility in the way programs are designed and delivered (Laurillard, 2002). This situation is further highlighted when we consider the issues associated with the **learning styles** of these students. Whether we like it or not, these may not necessarily be the same as what we would normally associate with traditional higher education students (traditional learners), at least those who have succeeded at higher education and who could comfortably work within a read/write style of learning and teaching (Sarasin, 1999). Barrington (2004) believes this is increasingly becoming an issues because higher educational institutions (in the West) still privileges certain ways of knowing and focus on a narrow view of the intellect that "does not always allow for socio-cultural differences" (p. 422). The potential inequity of this situation, particularly for **nontraditional learners** wishing to fully participate in higher education, requires many of these students to have to compensate on a number of fronts. Not only are they trying to understand academic literacies and, in some cases, cultural literacies, but they may also have particular learning styles that would not traditionally be associated with success at a university level. This would suggest, as does

Askell-Williams and Lawson (2006), that there is a need to "represent more fully the **diversity** and complexity of students' cognitive models about learning" (p. 139) within contemporary university curricula. This is a particularly important ethical consideration for **nontraditional learners** for it is when "learners are placed in new situations or have to solve new types of problems that their preferred learning style has a significant influence on their experience and their learning" (Sheard & Lynch, 2003, p. 255).

In addition to the increase of **nontraditional learners** in universities, it is also known many younger students, that may have been considered "traditional," now approach learning in very different ways. For example, Oblinger and Oblinger (2005) tell us that "Net Geners" (those who have grown up with computers, usually under 25) spend so much time online, it seems reasonable to expect that they would have a strong preference for Web-based courses. Paradoxically, "the reverse is actually true" (p. 2.11) and older students (Matures and Baby Boomers) are much more likely to be satisfied with fully Web-based courses than are traditional-age students. Oblinger and Oblinger also state that:

at the same time that colleges and universities are graduating their first Net Generation learners, most campuses are experiencing an influx of non-traditional students. Three-quarters of all undergraduates are 'non-traditional', according to the National Center for Educational Statistics. (p. 2.8)

As noted above, **nontraditional learners** come to university later in life, only attend part-time, hold full- or part-time jobs, have dependants, may be single parents, or may not enter with an appropriate tertiary entrance qualifications. Importantly, as these students learn in different ways, so they may also process and represent knowledge in different ways, and as performance can be related to how they learn, it may be seen that people can learn more effectively when taught by their preferred approach to learning (Koc, 2005). Baird and Fisher (2005) believe that the key to a more just approach is to design learning materials with these new (nontraditional) learning styles in mind, creating content that allows students flexibility while also embracing the reality of the neomillennial student (p. 10). **Nontraditional learners** are "bread and butter" for USQ. Thus, the following section will investigate some of the issues that need to be considered in relation to different approaches students have to their learning.

DIFFERENT APPROACHES TO SUIT LEARNING MODALITIES

Integral to the design of the Transmodal course at USQ is the premise that students learn in different ways and that each student has a preferred **learning modality** (Sarasin, 1999). When this is considered, and materials are designed to cater to multiple sensory channels, information processing can become more effective (Kearnsley, 2000). Fundamental then to the design of the Transmodal courses are the principles of multimodal design in which "information (is) presented in multiple modes such as visual and auditory" (Chen & Fu, 2003, p. 350). This is based on research demonstrating that students prefer to learn in environments that reflect the cognitive style in which they are most comfortable (Hazari, 2004). **Transmodal delivery** makes this possible as information can be presented in ways that utilise multiple sensory channels to enhance both students' enjoyment of the learning. Chen and Fu (2003) state that, "multimodal information presentation makes people feel that it is easy to learn and they can maintain attention, which will benefit the learning process and increase the learning performance" (p. 359).

In this context, the use of images is highly important, particularly for those entering higher education straight from school, the "Net Geners." This is also true in computer-based environments where "visual displays are frequently useful for representing relationships amongst elements that are difficult to explain verbally" (Shah & Freedman, 2003, p. 317). Although visual images are proven to be an integral part of human cognition, they have tended to be marginalised and undervalued in contemporary higher education (McLoughlin & Krakowski, 2001). This is also true when utilising multimedia in learning and teaching environments to match students' different **learning modalities** (Ellis, 2004). For example, if material such as verbal texts (audio), diagrams, drawings, photographs, and videos are all regarded as texts to be read, they can be applied to the development of new inclusive curricula (Roth, 2002). It is therefore necessary to develop strategies for the **multiple representation** of a whole range of instructional concepts to cater to the **diversity** of learners we have today.

The use of **multiple representations**, particularly in computer-based learning environments is recognised as a very powerful way to facilitate understanding (Moreno, 2002). For example, when the written word fails to fully communicate a concept, a visual representation can often remedy the communication problem (Ainsworth & Van Labeke, 2002). Figure 5 presents a simple illustration of this concept. Where "Representation 1" may cater to a couple of **learning modalities**, it may not cater to others, so by including "Representation 2" the other **learning modalities** may be accommodated.

Examples of **multiple representations** include, using point-form text with video and audio in the form of mini lectures introducing each topic in a course (Figure 6), animated diagrams with voiceovers (Figure 7), video presentations (Figure 8), interactive graphs and forms, audio explanations of concepts, and still images. The type of multimodal learning approach established for **Transmodal delivery** provides a unique opportunity to bridge both generational and cul-

Figure 5. The multiple representation of a concept

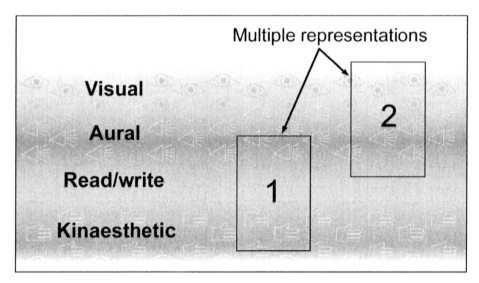

tural factors, providing the face-to-face contact requested by Baby Boomers, the independence preferred by Gen-Xers, and the interaction and sense of community for the Net Geners (Hartman, Moskal, & Dziuban, 2005). Jona (2000) asserted that this kind of learner choice represents the paradigm shift that needs to occur in higher education.

Importantly, in the examples provided above (Figures 6, 7 and 8) the multimedia element represents an additional representation of the information in another format. For example, the multimedia introductions using media enhanced PowerPoint slides, shown in Figure 6, re-represent the content that follows the presentation. Similarly, the audio content accompanying the images in Figure 7 is the same as the text in the printed version of the materials which students may read if they choose. Where a video or audio presentation is used as a primary learning object

Figure 6. Video enhanced PowerPoint presentation in ECO2000 (left) and Audio enhanced PowerPoint (Breeze) presentation in MGT2004 (right)

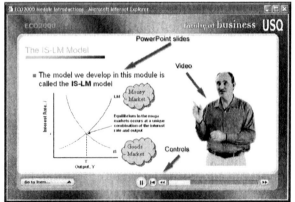 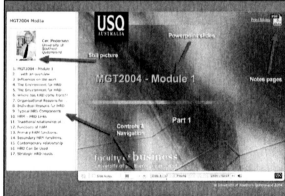

then a transcript of the content is also provided. This approach caters for a range of different learning styles. It gives students choice in how they would prefer to access course content and may be considered an ethical response to the needs **nontraditional learners**.

Facilitating Metacognition

We can try to design for all the different **learning modalities**, but there is a flip side to this coin because "many people don't even realise they are favouring one way or the other, because nothing external tells them they're any different from anyone else" (DePorter, 1992, p. 114). So, although it has been seen that there is a real need to design learning environments for a range of different **learning modalities** to aid student cognition, considering issues of students' metacognition is equally necessary. There is, therefore, a further aspect that needs to be considered, namely helping

Figures 7. Two examples of the animated and narrated diagrams used in CMS1000

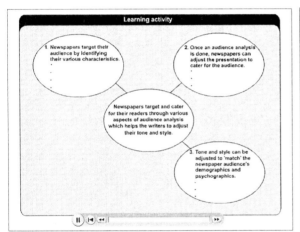 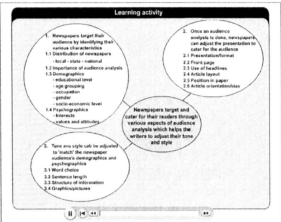

Figure 8. A video interview in CMS1000, with transcript available directly below

individual students become aware of their own preferred approach to learning.

It has been suggested that when students are aware of their individual strengths and weaknesses as learners they become more motivated to learn (Coffield, Moseley, Hall, & Ecclestone, 2004). The potential of this awareness is that students can then question their long-held beliefs or behaviours and be taught to monitor their selection and use of a range of strategies to aid their learning (Sadler-Smith, 2001). This strategy has also been shown to increase the confidence and the grades of students by helping them to make the most of the learning opportunities that match their preferred style (Coffield et al., 2004).

Typically, this is done by administering to the students some form of **learning styles** inventory. However, to be effective this should not be seen as a one off activity. Rather, it must be part of a holistic approach. The importance of this is stressed by McLoughlin (1999) who believes that "teaching students how to learn and how to monitor and manage their own learning styles is crucial to academic success" (p. 231).

In the courses used for the case studies reported in this chapter, in order to assist students' awareness of their preferred **learning modality** they were encouraged to complete a **VARK learning styles** (modal preference) inventory (Fleming, 2001) early in the semester. This is intended to help them identify the representations, within the course materials, that best suit their modal preference. Each course then supplied students with a further series of study tips based on the main four modal preferences (Visual, Aural, Read/write, and Kinaesthetic) or a combination of these preferences.

Figure 9 illustrates the results of the **VARK** learning styles survey administered to 281 students participating in the courses used as case studies in this chapter. It may be noted in this figure that although 33% of students would consider themselves to be multimodal, that is, they use all four sensory modalities, there are

significant numbers of students who have a very strong preference for using just one. For example, 17% identified themselves as being strongly Kinaesthetic, 14% Read/write, 5% Visual and 3% Aural. It is considered that those learners who have a strong preference for a particular modality, especially the K, V and A (23% of the students), are the ones that would potentially benefit the most (though certainly not exclusively) from **multiple representations** of key concepts within course materials.

Connectivity

If courses are going to utilise significant quantities of multimedia-based materials designed to accommodate the special needs of **nontraditional learners**, then these materials need to be made available electronically in both an equitable and consistent way. To facilitate this, the natural inclination for many universities, in the Western world at least, is simply to make these materials available online. And not surprisingly, it is projected that these new information and communication technologies will play an even greater role because of the potential they offer for delivering materials at a distance (Schuetze & Slowey, 2002).

Therefore, it might be argued that there is little point in USQ developing an approach to learning and teaching based on CD delivery (at least in the meantime) when the learning resources could very easily, and more cost effectively, be made available online. However, in the case of USQ where the student body is so diverse, the main reason for choosing a CD-based delivery is primary the inconsistency of Internet connections both within Australia and in the countries in which the university enrols its students. The Internet, however, still plays an important role in USQ's approach to course delivery, as all students are required to have some form of access. Each course has an online presence that enables course leaders to supplement the CD with discussion groups (synchronous or asynchronous), announcements

Figure 9. The VARK sensory modalities of 281 students, where A=Aural, K=Kinaesthetic, V=Visual, R=Read/write and a combination of these

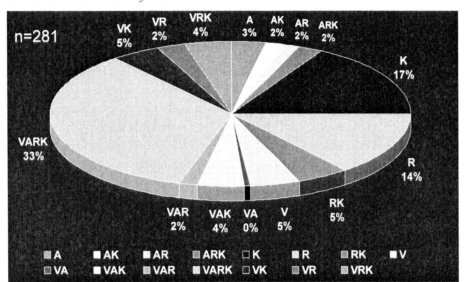

and e-mail. Therefore, **Transmodal delivery** is designed to limit the amount of time students need this access to download materials.

In a recent article by Daniel and West (2006), they suggest that students in developing countries do not usually have Internet connections at home. They go instead to Internet kiosks or cafés where access is expensive in terms of local salaries. In addition to this, given the low Internet speeds available, students are unlikely to connect for long enough to gain much information. Daniel and West also see that the central barrier to online learning is limited bandwidth due to telecommunications legislation and telecom company monopolies. Because the overwhelming majority of Internet service providers are located within OECD nations, developing nations rely too heavily on foreign Internet backbone providers for full access to networks, which in turn results in much higher connection costs for individuals and institutions. For example, the cost of monthly Internet access for individuals in developing nations may often be well over 100 times the same

cost for an individual in the United States (Daniel & West, 2006).

In China, for example, many USQ students report they can only access the Internet for the purpose of downloading PowerPoint presentations or completing online assessment during the early hours of the morning. Students from countries such as Germany (where USQ has a representative office), typically study while commuting on trains and consequently have difficulty in accessing the Internet (Sankey & St Hill, 2005). Also in Malaysia, where USQ has over 2,500 students, high speed broadband facilities are still very expensive and difficult to find, even in most educational institutions. In fact, most schools still rely on dial up technology limited to a bandwidth of 56K (Wan Mohd, 2004). In Australia, it is expected that rural and remote areas will still not have the same level of access as metropolitan areas for a considerable time (NOIE, 2004). Furthermore, USQ is a large provider of higher education to the prison system where inmates generally have no access to networked computers. Therefore, as equitable access for an increasingly diverse student body is a major consideration, USQ online delivery cannot be realistically considered *en masse* at this present time.

RESEARCHING TRANSMODAL DELIVERY

As the change to **Transmodal delivery** represented a substantial shift in the provision of course resources (previously mainly print-based), it was seen as critical to understand how the students perceived these resources. It was also important to gain a clear understanding of how effective the multimedia elements had been in aiding student understanding of the core concepts within the course. The following case studies report on four research projects conducted into **Transmodal delivery**, between 2004 and 2006.

The research model adopted for these studies was a "**Concurrent Triangulation Strategy**" (CTS) as defined by Creswell (2003). A visual representation of this model can be seen in Figure 10. This strategy allowed for the collection of both qualitative and quantitative data with a view to triangulating these data. Quantitative data was collected via online and paper-based surveys consisting of questions using a five-point Likert type scale (strongly agree/agree/no opinion/disagree/strongly disagree), and a two-point scale

(yes/no). Quantitative data was collected by using a combination of six open-ended response questions in the survey and a series of focus groups, allowing students to give a more in-depth account of their encounter with the courses. A total of 471 students participated in these studies (Table 1). Of these 356 students studied by **distance education** and 115 studied on-campus, while 335 were female and 136 male.

Punch (1998) suggests that both qualitative and quantitative methods have strengths and weaknesses and that an "over reliance on any one method is not appropriate" (p. 241). This is particularly important for this style of **mixed methods study**, where perceptions (qualitative) are being compared to responses in a quantitative survey. The qualitative measure was administered to provide students with the opportunity to give a more in-depth account of their encounter with the learning environment (Barker, Pistrang, & Elliott, 2002).

It should be noted that the investigations into these multimodal courses were far broader than can be reported here and are all the subject of individual chapters. However, as only limited data may be displayed in this chapter, a summary of the key findings related to the use of multimedia enhancements is presented. A more complete summary of these data are viewable at the URLs seen in Table 2.

Figure 10. The concurrent triangulation strategy (Adapted from Creswell, 2003)

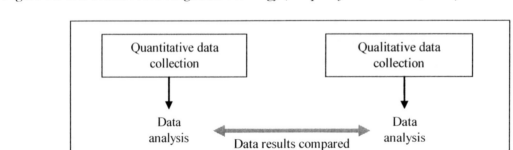

Table 1. Three multimodal courses and when each was researched

Multimodal course researched	Research performed	N =
ECO2000: *Macroeconomics for business and government*	Semester 1 2004	62
MGT2004: *People development*	Semester 2 2004	108
CMS1000: *Communication and scholarship* (external students only)	Semesters 1, 2, & 3 2005	188
CMS1000: *Communication and scholarship*	Semester 1 2006	113
Total number of students participating		471

Table 2. URLs for each research project

Course researched	Data available from
ECO2000: S1 2004	http://www.usq.edu.au/users/sankey/MDML/pages/ECO2000results.htm
MGT2004: S2 2004	http://www.usq.edu.au/users/sankey/MDML/pages/MGT2004results.htm
CMS1000: S1, 2 & 3 2005	http://www.usq.edu.au/users/sankey/CMS1000/index.htm
CMS1000: S1 2006	http://www.usq.edu.au/users/sankey/CMS1000S12006/index.htm

Figure 11. Response to the ease of navigation of materials

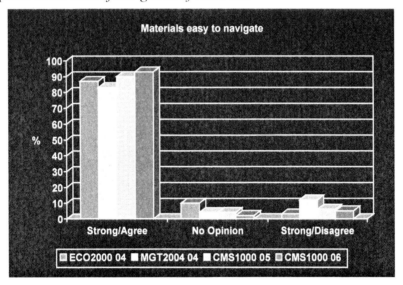

Key Findings and Discussion

As noted above, the research summarised in the following sections is from four larger studies investigating **Transmodal delivery** at USQ.

The data highlight issues related to online and CD-based environments and the use of multimedia-based enhancements that allow **multiple representations** of key concepts. In essence, the research shows that students desire to receive media-enhanced materials and that they find these materials easy to use. It also reveals to what extent students found these helpful to their learning. Finally, this section provides some preliminary evidence to suggest that this mode of delivery has met with initial success.

How Students Perceived the Transmodal Materials

In the survey students were asked to respond to the statement, *"I found the CD based materials were easy to navigate,"* between 83% and 93% of students either agreed or strongly agreed with this (Figure 11). Of those disagreeing, or offering no opinion the majority had printed most of the materials and had not bothered with the CD. This was not an undesirable outcome because these students appear to have chosen the most appropriate method for their particular approach to learning.

This was a very strong affirmative response to the ease of access of the materials and one that can be further supported by the qualitative data, of which the following two comments are examples:

The CD-based learning materials format (e.g. hyperlinking) was very helpful in helping me to locate/access related learning elements - faster/ direct access provided. Yes, I would like to see the same in other courses. (CMS1000 student)

I found them to be effective, as opposed to another course I did that only had print. Could access what I wanted easier, instead of looking through print to find what I need. (CMS1000 student)

The qualitative data also showed that students were selective in what they printed, only printing off what was necessary from the CD. This is demonstrated in the following comment: *"I feel that the CD, with the printable option was excellent. It was great to access it on the CD and then print*

the necessary documents." Further, students saw other benefits to providing the materials in this way, for example: *"The CD reduces the amount of information supplied on paper which is great for the environment and information is easier to access and find on the CD."*

In highlighting these particular points, it should not be overlooked that up to 17% of the students did not use the CD as their primary means of accessing the materials. However, it is believed the following two comments give a good initial summary as to why this was: *"I feel the CDs are an excellent resource, although I also believe that the course booklet is a viable learning material as well."* And: *"I like to have paper in front of me to read through so I can do it anywhere while looking after children etc."* The sentiments expressed by these and other students revolve around the convenience of (or lack of) access to their preferred way of accessing information.

It was also deemed important by the researchers to consider a further aspect in the CMS1000 courses (unfortunately, not explicitly examined in the first two cases), simply, did the students like the CD-based material? The data indicates between 79% and 86% of students responded in the affirmative (Figure 12). This sentiment was also confirmed by the qualitative analysis. The following comment provides a sense to why there was such a positive response:

Now that I have moved on to another subject, without a CD, I'm realising just how useful the CD was and how difficult I am finding it to learn solely from text. Thank you for the CD!!! (CMS1000 student)

Having established there was strong support for the materials students were also asked to "Please choose your ideal combination of learning materials." Figure 13 demonstrates how the students responded to this question. The majority of students (approximately 80%) chose either option 2 or 4, that is, to receive the CD and to either

Figure 12. Data indicating the level to which students liked the CD-based materials

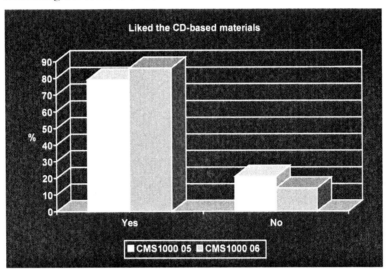

Figure 13. What students' would prefer to receive in their study package

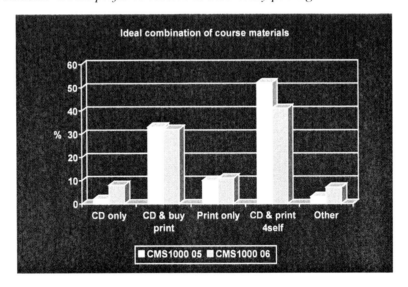

print what they required for themselves (from the CD), or purchase the printed version from the bookshop. Approximately 10% of students identified that they wanted to receive "only print materials," while about 5% preferred to receive the CD only. The remaining 5% who chose "other" wanted everything provided to them. The research team believes these data clearly support the case that the use of additional media in the CD-based environment provides sufficient advantage to the students, enough to warrant them printing for themselves, or buying, a printed version of the materials. This being the case, the following section seeks to understand what it was that students found so appealing about the use of additional media.

Multimedia Enhancements/Multiple Representations

There are two main aspects of using multimedia to provide **multiple representations** in the course materials that will be considered here, firstly, to what level did the students find these helpful to their learning and secondly, had these materials catered for their preferred approach to learning. This was based on the demonstrated assumption that each student had identified their preferred **learning modality** during their course by completing the **VARK learning styles** inventory (Fleming, 2001) and so were arguably aware of their preferred approach to learning. The **multiple representation** highlighted in these studies was animated diagrams using audio for **multiple representation** in addition to static print, and associated text and multimedia introductions using audio (or video) enhanced PowerPoint presentations.

Multimedia Animated Diagrams

In the survey students were asked to indicate the extent to which they agreed or disagreed that the multimedia had helped them understand the concepts being represented. Figure 14 represents the students' response to this. Between 86% and 64% agreed or strongly agreed with this. However, in the case of the CMS1000 courses the question was framed slightly differently to also include *"were more helpful to me than the static, print based representations."* This explains the lower level of agreement in the CMS1000 course data as they were also comparing to another form of representation. Nevertheless, this supports strongly the use of multimedia enhancements.

Strength of agreement is confirmed in the qualitative data pool where in excess of 70 students made mention of the fact that the **multiple representations** were helpful to their understanding of concepts, compared to only 10 students who did not find them helpful. The students not only found **multiple representations** helpful to their learning, but in some cases invaluable, as the following comment indicates:

Figure 14. Data showing the levels to which students agreed or disagreed that the multimedia had been helpful to them

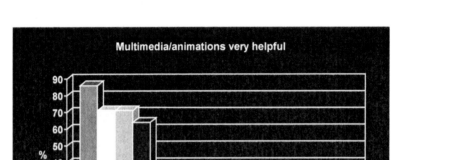

The advantages are obviously having all those different options available for the different modes of presentation. The explanation of diagrams and stuff like that are invaluable. I study a lot late at night so I'm not able to contact people. So that side of it is really good for me. (MGT2004 student)

One feature of the **multiple representations** that continued to generate the most positive comments, both from distance and on-campus students, was the use of audio within the representations. This benefit was mentioned by a substantial 45 students within the qualitative data pool. This is typified in the following comment:

... if I had trouble understanding something from the hard copy I'd go and find other means of understanding...mainly the audio...you can interpret things differently when you read it. When you get somebody explaining it to you through the audio it's like, 'oh that's what they mean by it'. You can definitely read things and they can be interpreted in a different way. (MGT2004 student)

This highlights the importance of using **multiple representations** for reinforcement. It was seen in the above comments that the audio was used to complete the picture by contextualising what had been read.

The audio feature also had the added benefit of helping external students feel less isolated. One distance student remarked of the multimedia features: *"I found them extremely helpful - made me feel more a part of the class as well."* This sentiment is expressed on at least 20 occasions in the qualitative data.

The surveys then sought to extend this understanding by asking students if multimedia features had suited their approach to learning. Students in all four courses strongly endorsed the use of the **multiple representations** in the CD-based materials. When students were asked to indicate whether they had felt that the **multiple representations** had actually catered for their approach to learning between 92% and 65% agreed they had (Figure 15).

This weight of sentiment was further highlighted in the focus groups with students reflecting:

Figure 15. Data showing the levels to which students agreed or disagreed that the multimedia had suited their approach to learning

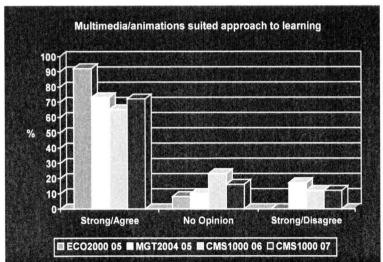

I found the biggest advantage of the CD was that it presents material in a different way. Like if you are struggling to get a concept from the written material it was presented in a different way and that sometimes makes it clearer. (MGT2004 student)

It is almost like looking at the same content from a few different angles. And the more you do that and look at it using the different media it makes for a much more dynamic and powerful learning experience. (ECO2000 student)

In these two comments lies the essence of what is seen as the advantage of supplying core information in more than one way. That is, the use of **multiple representations** can aid in making concepts clearer and in so doing enhances the opportunity for learning from the material, or in the words of one student: *"the more options the better off you are at learning what you are trying to learn."*

Multimedia Introductions

The other main **multiple representations** used in the learning environments that were very highly valued were the multimedia introductions using audio and video enhanced PowerPoint presentations (*Breeze*). When students were asked to respond to the statement, *"The multimedia introductions (using PowerPoint and audio) used for each module; assessment and course overview really helped my understanding of the course content,"* between 80% and 66% agreed this had been the case (Figure 16).

This weight of positive sentiment is confirmed by the comments made by students in the open ended questions in the survey. For example:

Sometimes reading is not enough to get it into your head and it needs to be spoken, the CD completes that need effectively. Yes. Presenting material in a variety of formats and ways facilitates and stimulated my learning. PPT (PowerPoint) with audio

Figure 16. Data showing the levels to which students perceived the multimedia introductions had been helpful to them

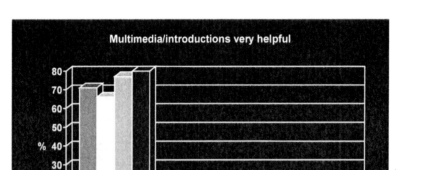

was a huge advantage in learning the material. As an external student it was great to be able to have a 'lecture' at home to reinforce what I'd been reading in the text. (CMS1000 student)

This last comment makes mention of these presentations being used to reinforce what was being read, and this was also specifically mentioned by a further 12 students in the qualitative data.

This point of reinforcement is particularly important and was further highlighted in the focus groups, with students reflecting:

...when I just read it [the materials] I don't always understand it but when you have it [see it] spoken and explained it is better. (ECO2000 student)

...It gives you a different way of learning so you can do your hard copy reading and all that type of thing, but to have it actually to listen to it reinforces what you have actually been reading as well. (MGT2004 student)

Sometimes reading is not enough to get it into your head and it needs to be spoken, the CD [with the multimedia] completes that need effectively. (CMS100 student)

These comments give a clear indication that each student used a combination of strategies to comprehend the concepts. Each mentioned reading and noted that the further representation either explained the concept better or served to reinforce it.

International students also agreed to the **multiple representation** usefulness more often than Australian students. Typical of their comments:

I think it is because some of the Indonesian students' English is not that good and they can actually repeat the audio with PowerPoint slides and they can understand better (MGT2004 student).

...You can get bored sometimes by looking at the same page but with the audio and video intro you can listen to the voice of the lecturer which helps you understand faster rather than reading the book. Sometimes the writing in the book you may not be so familiar with, you don't understand it instantly compared to that [the introductions]. (ECO2000 student)

Clearly, the additional support offered by the aural material and the ability to replay the content was considered extremely helpful in relation to understanding the concepts and aided their understanding of the English language and so was used to compliment (reinforce) their reading.

Again, the surveys then sought to extend this understanding by asking students if these multimedia introductions had suited their approach to learning. Between 72% and 56% of students believed this was the case. There were significantly less multimedia introductions used in the MGT2004 course which would serve to indicate why students did not agree as often as in the other courses.

The qualitative data again supports this weight of sentiment and serves to indicate the main areas as to why this might be the case. This sentiment may be summed up in the following comments:

I found the PowerPoint's [Breeze presentations] particularly helpful, being external students, it is hard to study without actual contact with the lecturer, but by listening to the lecturer on the PowerPoint, it made it seem a bit more real. My learning style reflects the need to listen as well as read to gain the best insight into what I am studying. (CMS1000 student)

These may seem like optional extras however I believe they enhance the learning process, by using more of the learning faculties that each person has at their disposal; a whole brain approach, including emotion and humour, which is particularly helpful for off-campus students. (CMS1000 student)

...it's great to have all the different representations to get the picture as a whole. (MGT2004 student)

I think it is absolutely imperative that you have different ways of learning so that it's not disadvan-

taging one particular group or forcing someone to learn in a way they are not comfortable with. (MGT2004 student)

Again, these comments demonstrate a strong recognition of the advantages of using multimedia enhancements to help form understanding ("get the picture as a whole"), a sentiment repeated many times by students.

Figure 17. Data showing the levels to which students agreed or disagreed that the multimedia introductions had suited their approach to learning

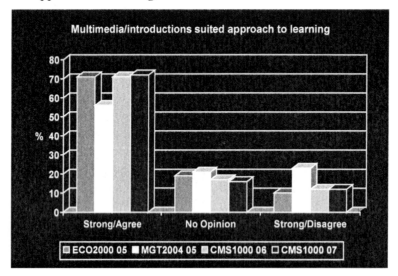

Figure 18. Comparison of final grades from the past four offers to 2004 (all students)

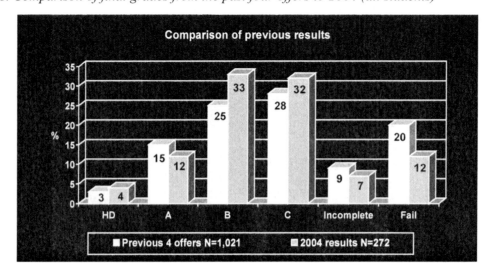

Advantages and Disadvantages

The ease of access to printed compared to electronic materials had been a concern of the research teams. The qualitative analysis clearly supports this concern and indicates that students want to retain some access to print for three main reasons:

- Portability, for example, they can read printed materials while commuting on public transport;
- Facilitating active learning, for example, using a highlight pen for important points; and
- Relief from screen fatigue by avoiding the computer at home following a work day in front of a computer.

On the other hand, students expressed their satisfaction with the CD-based materials for four main reasons:

- Use of the additional media (presentation in a variety of forms/**multiple representations**) gave them greater confidence in their learning and made the materials more dynamic/interesting/fun;
- Materials were more compact and used less paper;
- Information could be accessed quickly; and
- Navigation around the materials was easy.

This is supported by the many comments made in response to the question: *"What advantages or disadvantages did you find in having your study materials supplied to you on CD? How do you think this affected your learning of the materials?"* As the case for navigation and access have already been made above, the following two comments give a summary of the benefits in relation to the use of additional media:

I thought the CD media an excellent choice for study material. The various audio and visual presentations provided variety and a much needed reprieve from the traditional method of reading text cover to cover and it made the learning experience fun. (CMS1000 student)

The CD is a link to the university in a special way. How? Well the CD has a lecturer speaking to use. Books are good and very useful; however they can sometimes be dry and rather static. Is not any learning, especially for one's career supposed to be DYNAMIC? (CMS1000 student)

Although some students identified that their preference was to print certain segments of the materials, it was seen that the advantages of CD by way of additional media outweighed this inconvenience.

From the student's perspectives, there were clear perceived advantages of technology enhanced **multiple representations** of concepts. It is reasonable to conclude that, ethically speaking, the Transmodal pedagogy is appropriate to the needs of diverse groups of students.

Some Further Evidence of Success

Although the following data may not be considered definitive evidence (though very encouraging), the final grades attained by students in the ECO2000 and MGT2004 courses did show an improvement from the previous offers of both these courses (Figure 17). This result was true when compared with both the previous years' results and those of the previous four offers. For example, the fail rate for the previous offer of ECO2000 was 15%, with an average over the previous four offers of 14%, the fail rate fell to 8%. The same is true for MGT2004; the last offer of this course had a fail rate of 22% with an average over the previous four offers of 25%. For the offer referred to in this case study the fail rate fell to 16%. Figure 15 illustrates how the combined failure (Fail) rate fell from 20% to 12%. The retention rate also improved, with fewer students deferring (Incomplete) their assessment, down from 9% to 7%. Consequently, 10% more students attained passing grades overall. This same comparison was not possible for the CMS1000 courses, as the course had changed its assessment strategy just prior to it becoming a Transmodal course.

Clearly, this improvement would need to be demonstrated over future offers of these courses before a solid claim of significance can be made. Unfortunately, this has not been possible due to some changes that occurred in the staffing of these courses. Nevertheless, this result is extremely pleasing and is also certainly worthy of continued investigation. If it can be demonstrated conclusively that technology-enhanced **multiple representations** can improve assessment outcomes, then there are strong ethical grounds for adopting the Transmodal model generally in higher education.

Summary

There was an unmistakably strong endorsement of the multimedia enhancements in the Transmodal courses, though they clearly did not suit everyone. The use of technology, particularly the *Breeze* and multimedia enhancements, were seen to help the students' understanding of the course concepts and to help break down some of the perceived barriers to their study. Or as these two CMS1000 students said:

The different ways of learning catered for my specific needs very well and I appreciated the time taken to include all the different learning methods.

Yes. Presenting material in a variety of formats and ways facilitates and stimulated my learning. (CMS1000 student)

Overall, it can be seen that there was a strong acceptance of the use of Transmodal learning environments used in all four courses in this case study. This was demonstrated both in the survey responses and in comments made by students. In addition, students indicated that they preferred the CD-based version of the materials to the printed learning resources because they could easily access or buy a printed version if they chose. It was seen that the sentiments expressed by the majority of students relating to the CD were complementary. It is fitting that students have the last word!

I believe the study materials for this course need no improvement as they are the best I have ever experienced during my studies. (ECO2000 student)

Commendations! This material was the most superior learning package I have ever been able to use for distance education…I hope all courses at USQ adopt this form of study materials. (MGT2004 student)

There was an unmistakably strong endorsement of CD-based materials, though they clearly did not suit everyone. Having said that, those who did not use the CD were happy to either print for themselves what was required or purchase a printed version from the university bookshop. The use of technology, particularly the *Breeze* and multimedia presentations, was seen to help the students' understanding of the course concepts and to help break down some of the barriers that may make external students feel more isolated. Of some concern was that a few students did not have easy access to, or sufficient understanding of, the technology. This may require USQ to either make the access to print materials easier, or ensure clear communication of the options. Even though the results suggest the CD was successful overall and that it did serve to complement or replace the print materials, further consideration must still be given to the different **learning styles** of students. For example, print materials must be made available for students who have a read/write learning preference. The potential to make learning more interesting (and sometimes fun) for external students is clearly demonstrated in this study.

CONCLUSION

Based on the findings of the above studies, the major recommendation would be to cater for a range of different **learning modalities** by offering alternative representations of key concepts within courses. It has also been demonstrated that visual and aural representations, facilitated by the use of multimedia, can play an important role in catering for today's multiliterate, culturally diverse and dispersed student groups. This chapter has demonstrated that there are ethical reasons and pragmatic advantages for students in providing course resources designed to suit a range of different **learning modalities** and backgrounds. The findings from these research projects investigating the **Transmodal delivery** indicate that students had positive attitudes toward, and value, the multimodal course materials along with the additional multimedia components. It was seen in the feedback that higher levels of student engagement were possible when utilising imbedded multimedia elements as these were seen to cater to the students' preferred way of learning. In particular, students agreed that they enjoyed using their course CD, found it easy to use and navigate, and also agreed that the course materials had assisted their performance in the course. This was primarily achieved by providing a more complete representation of the information being presented, thereby increasing the opportunity of students to engage with their learning materials. Importantly, this was achieved while maintaining a balanced environment for more traditional learners, while at the same time integrating a range of multimedia-based enhancements for those

who learn in nontraditional ways. This chapter has argued that adopting such an approach is an appropriate ethical response to **massification** in higher education. It adequately addresses the demand for professionalisation of teaching in higher education that has arisen in response to **massification**.

It is hoped that the findings of these studies may encourage more educators to consider the adoption of a multimodal approach for the purpose of designing and delivering **distance education** courses. However, in doing so there are important issues relating to how the implementation of these new technologies can be best integrated before the full benefits to the learning community can be realised. Ultimately, what this chapter is suggesting is that, designing for multimodal learners may reduce the impact of providing course materials to a very diverse and an increasingly nontraditional student body. This new, more ethical approach for this new millennium (neomillenial) has seen USQ develop what it now calls **Transmodal delivery**.

FURTHER RESEARCH DIRECTIONS

The generalisability of the qualitative data gained by interpreting focus group interviews and open ended questions may be limited, as some issues other than those being researched were raised by the participants. However, this was somewhat offset by the process of triangulating these data with the quantitative data collected in the surveys. It was also a concern that there were not more off-campus international students participating in this aspect of the data collection, particularly those studying overseas. It is recommended that measures be taken to ensure that "the voice" of this group of students be heard in future studies of this nature.

In addition, as there were only a limited number of international students who participated in this research overall it is suggested that a greater understanding of this group be gained. This is important for USQ because of the significant proportion of international students studying either in Australia or overseas. We need to learn more about **diversity** among international students and about improvements to their access to the Internet. Nevertheless, there is sufficient evidence in this study to suggest that the CD-based mode of delivery, augmented with **multiple representations** and multimedia elements, had a noteworthy positive effect on the international students who participated. This finding needs to be supported and extended for a more comprehensive understanding of the issues related to supplying course content in this way. This is particularly true given the increasing push toward the internationalisation of the higher education market in Australia.

It might also be argued that a clearer connection between **learning styles** and multimedia enhancement needs to be demonstrated. This would require a controlled experiment which would incorporate the **learning styles** of the student and **multiple representations** of concepts using different media combinations. This type of investigation would specially seek to address what types of media specifically meet the needs of particular **learning styles**. Such research would need to be carefully designed. In particular, the participation by students must be risk-free in the sense that their learning (and assessment outcomes) must not be impaired by the research.

The final area this study would recommend for further study would be an investigation of the impost on academic staff in providing materials witch have been significantly enhanced with multimedia.

REFERENCES

Ainsworth, S., & Van Labeke, N. (2002). *Using a multi-representational design framework to develop and evaluate a dynamic simulation environment.* Paper presented at the International Workshop on Dynamic Visualizations and Learning, Tubingen, Germany.

Askell-Williams, H., & Lawson, M. J. (2006). Multi-dimensional profiling of medical students' cognitive models about learning. *Medical Education, 40*(2), 138-145.

Baird, D. E., & Fisher, M. (2005). Neomillennial user experience design strategies: Utilizing social networking media to support "always on" learning styles. *Journal of Educational Technology Systems, 34*(1), 5-32.

Barker, C., Pistrang, N., & Elliott, R. (2002). *Research methods in clinical psychology: An introduction for students and practitioners* (2ⁿᵈ ed.). West Sussex: John Wiley & Sons.

Barrington, E. (2004). Teaching to student diversity in higher education: How Multiple Intelligence Theory can help. *Teaching in Higher Education, 9*(4), 421-434.

Birch, D., & Gardiner, M. (2005, December 5-7). Students' perceptions of technology-based marketing courses. In *Paper presented at the ANZMAC 2005 Conference: Broadening the Boundaries*, Fremantle, Western Australia.

Bridge, W. (2006). Non-traditional learners in higher education. In P. Ashwin (Ed.), *Changing higher education: The development of learning and teaching* (pp. 58-68). London: RoutledgeFalmer.

Cameron, J., Shaw, G., & Arnott, A. (Eds.). (2002). *Tertiary teaching: Doing it differently, doing it better.* Darwin: NTU Press and Centre for Teaching and Learning in Diverse Educational Contexts.

Chen, G., & Fu, X. (2003). Effects of multimodal information on learning performance and judgement of learning. *Journal of Educational Computing Research, 29*(3), 349-362.

Coffield, F., Moseley, D., Hall, E., & Ecclestone, K. (2004). *Learning styles for post 16 learners: What do we know?* London: Learning and Skills Research Centre.

Cookson, P. (2002). The hybridization of higher education: Cross-national perspectives. *International Review of Research in Open and Distance Learning, 2*(2), 1-4.

Creswell, J. W. (2003). *Research design: Qualitative, quantitative, and mixed methods approaches* (2nd ed.). London: Sage.

Daniel, J., & West, P. (2006). From digital divide to digital dividend: What will it take? [Electronic Version]. *Innovate, 2.* Retrieved April 22, 2008, from http://www.innovateonline.info/index.php?view=article&id=252

Davis, M. (1999). *Ethics and the university.* London & New York: Routledge.

DePorter, B. (1992). *Quantum learning: Unleashing the genius in you.* New York: Dell.

Ellis, T. (2004). Animating to build higher cognitive understanding: A model for studying multimedia effectiveness in education. *Journal of Engineering Education, 93*(1), 59-64.

Fleming, N. D. (2001). *Teaching and learning styles: VARK strategies.* Christchurch, New Zealand: Neil D Fleming.

Hartman, J., Moskal, P., & Dziuban, C. (2005). Preparing the academy of today for the learner of tomorrow. In D. Oblinger & J. Oblinger (Eds.), *Educating the net generation* (pp. 6.1 - 6.15). Boulder, Colorado: EDUCAUSE.

Hazari, S. (2004). Applying instructional design theories to improve efficacy of technology-assisted presentations. *Journal of Instruction Delivery Systems, 18*(2), 24-33.

Jarvis, P. (1983). *Professional education.* London: Croom Helm.

Jochems, W., van Merrienboer, J., & Koper, R. (Eds.). (2004). *Integrated e-learning: Implications for pedagogy, technology and organization.* London: RoutledgeFalmer.

Jona, K. (2000). *Rethinking the design of online courses.* Paper presented at the ASCILITE 2000: Learning to choose, choosing to learn, Coffs Harbour, Australia.

Kearnsley, G. (2000). *Online education: Learning and teaching in cyber space.* Belmont, CA: Wadsworth/Thomson Learning.

Kellner, D. (2004). Technological transformation, multiple literacies, and the re-visioning of education. *E-learning, 1*(1), 9-37.

Koc, M. (2005). Individual learner differences in Web-based learning environments: From cognitive, affective and social-cultural perspectives. *Turkish Online Journal of Distance Education, 6*(4), 12-22. Retrieved April 22, 2008, http://tojde.anadolu.edu.tr

Laurillard, D. (2002). *Rethinking university teaching: A conversational framework for the effective use of learning technologies* (2nd ed.). London: RoutledgeFalmer.

Lovegrove, W. (2004, December 20). *USQ: Australia's leading transnational educator.* Retrieved April 22, 2008, from http://www.usq.edu.au/planstats/Planning/USQAustsLeadingTransEdu.htm

Macfarlane, B. (2004). *Teaching with integrity: The ethics of higher education practice.* London: RoutledgeFalmer.

McDonald, J., McPhail, J., Maguire, M., & Millett, B. (2004). A conceptual model and evaluation process for educational technology learning resources: A legal case study. *Educational Media International, 41*(4), 287-296.

McLoughlin, C. (1999). The implications of the research literature on learning styles for the design of instructional material. *Australian Journal of Educational Technology, 15*(3), 222-241.

McLoughlin, C., & Krakowski, K. (2001). *Technological tools for visual thinking: What does the research tell us?* Paper presented at the Apple University Consortium Academic and Developers Conference, James Cook University, Townsville, Queensland, Australia.

Moreno, R. (2002, June). *Who learns best with multiple representations? Cognitive theory implications for individual differences in multimedia learning.* Paper presented at the EDMEDIA 2002 Conference:, Denver, Colorado, USA.

NOIE. (2004). *Australian national broadband strategy.* Canberra, ACT: The National Office for the Information Economy. Retrieved April 22, 2008, from http://www.dcita.gov.au/ie/publications/2004/march/australian_national_broadband_strategy

Oblinger, D., & Oblinger, J. (2005). Is it age or IT: First steps toward understanding the net generation. In D. Oblinger & J. Oblinger (Eds.), *Educating the net generation* (pp. 2.1-2.20). Boulder, CO: EDUCAUSE.

Parsons, P., & Ross, D. (2002). *Planning a campus to support hybrid learning.* Retrieved April 22, 2008, from http://www.mcli.dist.maricopa.edu/ocotillo/tv/hybrid_planning.html

Postle, G., Clarke, J., Bull, D., Skuja, E., McCann, H., & Batorowicz, K. (1996). *Equity, diversity and excellence: Advancing the national higher education equity framework.* Canberra, Australia: National Board of Employment Education and Training.

Punch, K. F. (1998). *Introduction to social research: Quantitative and qualitative approaches.* London: Sage.

Roth, W. M. (2002). Reading graphs: Contributions to an integrative concept of literacy. *Journal of Curriculum Studies, 34*(1), 1-24.

Sadler-Smith, E. (2001). The relationship between learning style and cognitive style. *Personality and Individual Differences, 30*(4), 609-616.

Sankey, M., & St Hill, R. (2005, July 11-12). Multimodal design for hybrid learning materials in a second level economics course. In *Paper presented at the Eleventh Australasian Teaching Economics Conference: Innovation for Student Engagement in Economics*, University of Sydney, Australia.

Sarasin, L. C. (1999). *Learning styles perspectives: Impact in the classroom.* Madison, WI: Atwood.

Schuetze, H. G., & Slowey, M. (2002). Participation and exclusion: A comparative analysis of non-traditional students and lifelong learners in higher education. *Higher Education, 44*(3/4), 309-327.

Scott, P. (1995). *The meanings of mass higher education.* Buckingham: Society for Research into Higher Education/Open University Press.

Shah, P., & Freedman, E. G. (2003). Visuospatial cognition in electronic learning. *Journal of Educational Computing Research, 29*(3), 315-324

Sheard, J., & Lynch, J. (2003). Accommodating learner diversity in Web-based learning environments: Imperatives for future developments. *International Journal of Computer Processing of Oriental Languages, 16*(4), 243-260.

Smith, A., Ling, P., & Hill, D. (2006). The adoption of multiple modes of delivery in Australian universities. *Journal of University Teaching and Learning Practice, 3*(2), 67-81. Retrieved April 22, 2008, from http://jutlp.uow.edu.au/2006_v2003_i2002/2006_v2003_i2002.html

St Hill, R. (2000, November). Modal preference in a teaching strategy. In *Paper presented at the Effective Teaching and Learning at University*, Duchesne College, the University of Queensland.

Taylor, J. C. (2004, February). Will universities become extinct in the networked world? In *Paper presented at the ICDE World Conference on Open & Distance Learning*, Hong Kong.

USQ. (2005a). *Learning and teaching plan, goal 4: A flexible and responsive learning environment.* Retrieved April 22, 2008, from http://www.usq.edu.au/learnteach/enhancement/plan/goal4.htm

USQ. (2005b). *Policy on learning and teaching.* Retrieved April 22, 2008, from http://www.usq.edu.au/resources/75.pdf

USQ. (2005c). *Policy on multiculturalism.* Retrieved April 22, 2008, from http://www.usq.edu.au/resources/126.pdf

USQ. (2005d). *USQ equity in education policy.* Retrieved April 22, 2008, from http://www.usq.edu.au/resources/127.pdf

USQ. (2006). *Transmodal delivery.* Retrieved April 22, 2008, from http://www.usq.edu.au/dec/research/transmodal.htm

Vergnani, L. (2005, June 8). Learning to enjoy e-learning. *The Australian*, p. 31.

Vissar, J., & Suzuki, K. (2006). Designing for the world at large: A tale of two settings. In R. Reiser & J. Dempsey (Eds.), *Trends and issues in instructional design and technology* (2nd ed., pp. 234-244). NJ: Pearsons.

Wan Mohd, F. W. I. (2004). Still pictures and audio: Second class multimedia elements? *Malaysian Online Journal of Instructional Technology, 1*(1). Retrieved April 22, 2008, from http://pppjj.usm.my/mojit/articles/html/Wanfauzy.htm

ADDITIONAL READING

Ashwin, P. (Ed.). (2006). *Changing higher education: The development of learning and teaching.* London: RoutledgeFalmer.

Clark, R. C., & Mayer, R. E. (2003). *E-Learning and the science of instruction: Proven guidelines for consumers and designers of multimedia learning.* San Francisco: Jossey-Bass/Pfeiffer.

Coffield, F., Moseley, D., Hall, E., & Ecclestone, K. (2004a). *Learning styles for post 16 learners: What do we know?* London: Learning and Skills Research Centre.

Coffield, F., Moseley, D., Hall, E., & Ecclestone, K. (2004b). *Should we be using learning styles? What research has to say to practice.* London: Learning and Skills Research Centre.

Davis, M. (1999). *Ethics and the university.* London: Routledge.

Department of Education, Science and Training. (2007). *OECD thematic review of tertiary education: Country background report Australia.* Paris: Organisation for Economic Cooperation and Development. Retrieved April 22, 2008, from http://www.oecd.org/dataoecd/51/60/38759740.pdf

Jochems, W., van Merrienboer, J., & Koper, R. (Eds.). (2004). *Integrated e-learning: Implications for pedagogy, technology and organization.* London: RoutledgeFalmer.

Kress, G. (2003). *Literacy in the new media age.* London: Routledge.

Kress, G., & van Leeuwen, T. (2001). *Multimodal discourse: The modes and media of contemporary communication.* London: Arnold.

Laurillard, D. (2002). *Rethinking university teaching: A conversational framework for the effective use of learning technologies* (2nd ed.). London: RoutledgeFalmer.

Laurillard, D. (2006). E-learning in higher education. In P. Ashwin (Ed.), *Changing higher education: The development of learning and teaching* (pp. 71-84). London: RoutledgeFalmer.

Loveless, A., & Ellis, V. (Eds.). (2001). *ICT, pedagogy and the curriculum: Subject to change*. London: RoutledgeFalmer.

Macfarlane, B. (2004). *Teaching with integrity: The ethics of higher education practice*. London: RoutledgeFalmer.

Machin, D. (2007). *Introduction to multimodal analysis*. London: Hodder.

Massironi, M. (2002). *The psychology of graphic images: Seeing, drawing, communicating* (N. Bruno, Trans.). NJ: Lawrence Erlbaum.

Mayer, R. E. (2001). *Multimedia learning*. Cambridge: Cambridge University Press.

Mishra, S., & Sharma, R. C. (Eds.). (2005). *Interactive multimedia in education and training*. Hershey, PA: Ideas Group.

Oblinger, D., & Oblinger, J. (Eds.). (2005). *Educating the net generation*. Boulder, CO: EDUCAUSE.

Riding, R., & Rayner., S. (1998). *Cognitive styles and learning strategies: Understanding style differences in learning and behaviour*. London: David Fulton.

Rose, G. (2001). *Visual methodologies: An introduction to the interpretation of visual materials*. London: Sage.

Son, J. B., & O'Neill, S. (Eds.). (2005). *Enhancing learning and teaching: Pedagogy, technology and language*. Flaxton, Queensland: Post Pressed.

Sweller, J. (1999). *Instructional design in technical areas*. Melbourne: ACER Press.

Chapter XI
Why "Cultural Sensitivities" and "Localizations" in Global E-Learning?

Shalin Hai-Jew
Kansas State University, USA

ABSTRACT

This chapter examines the importance of cultural sensitivity and localization in the delivery of global e-learning. The branding, course ecology, curriculum design, instructional strategies/pedagogical approaches, multimedia builds, information handling, and direct instruction in e-learning need to fit the needs of the diverse learners. Those that offer global e-learning must consider the national, ethnic and racial backgrounds of their learners to offer customized value-added higher education. Cultural sensitivities apply to initial learner outreach and their success in the e-learning; localizations enhance the applied learning and also the transferability of the learning after the global learners graduate. Cultural sensitivities and localizations may make global e-learning more field-independent and effective because of the reliance on each learner's local resources. A "Cultural Sensitivities and Localizations Course Analysis (CSLCA)" Tool for global e-learning has been included in the appendix.

INTRODUCTION

Many engaged in higher education have been reaching across international borders to court some of the brightest minds from around the world. They are using global e-learning to reach out to the "place-bound" (those restricted to certain geographical locations) or "place free" (those who live transient lives), due in part to the high costs of studying abroad and stricter vetting of individuals by various governments. The launching of global online educational and training endeavors should consider cultural targeting and sensitivity in order to make the learning more accessible to learners and to increase student retention. E-learning has traditionally had fairly high attrition rates, even as high as 50% in some programs (Moore & Kearsley, as cited by Picciano, 2002, p. 22). Effective instruction involves motivational components that "enhance self-efficacy and perceived challenge" (Hacker & Niederhauser, 2000, p. 53).

The nature of global learning lends itself to unique challenges. Studying abroad often means a transition period of preparation, travel, resettlement, and starting the studies. In this new version, "study abroad" means going online. For e-learning, with the use of numerous online forms and easy payment options, students may find themselves enrolled at a distant university from home. People are moving from living in so-called "little boxes" to networked societies (Wellman & Hampton, 1999, p. 648). There may not be a physical change to the global learner's physical circumstances—no four-walls classrooms in a different milieu. Rather, in the "disembodied" learning of an online classroom, their bodies have not left home or the home country, but their minds have gone roaming. Mediated through the WWW and Internet, e-learning allows any number of such learners to enroll in instructor-led classes.

The disembodied aspects of e-learning also mean that instructors and facilitators will not have the benefit of informal knowledge inputs as when they make a cultural gaffe. They will not have the benefit of body language (and the classical training regarding proxemics, oculesics, kinesthetics, haptics, and others). Hailing from different time zones, they will not necessarily have the ability to resolve questions and concerns in real-time, in face-to-face venues, or to communicate their sincerity or decency as individuals. "Early work on CMC (computer-mediated communications), based on what was known as the filtered-cues position, described the medium as one bereft of *social context cues* (Sproull & Kiesler, 1986). These cues define the social nature of the situation and the status of those present and include aspects of the physical environment, body language, and paralinguistic characteristics. With such cues largely filtered out, CMC has been described as a lean medium that is relatively anonymous" (Chester & Gwynne, 1998, n.p.).

So, too, on the faculty side, there are no telltale face-to-face meetings with a group of new students or the real-time signaling and communications that go on in such lecture halls and hallway conversations. Rather, there are names and possibly a learner profile with a headshot attached. The unfolding of different learner personalities may occur over the course of the learning term, or they may never quite unfold, with the focus merely on the work and less on the individuality or personhood of the learners. The depth of personal revelations depends on the instructor facilitation, the "affordances" of the online learning space, the number of learners, the richness of the intercommunications and interactions, and possibly the particular field of study.

Cultural sensitivities involve efforts to recontextualize the online learning spaces and to surface and address cultural differences and similarities. Localization aims to add richness to the learning by considering the various "locales" of the global e-learning students and capitalizing on those resources. These endeavors to recontextualize the learning to student-local spaces may enhance the field independence of the learning, which will make the global e-learning more portable and transferable.

The objectives of this chapter are to engage the following research questions.

Research Questions

1. What is cultural sensitivity in global e-learning? What is localization in global e-learning?
2. Who may affect cultural sensitivity and localization in global e-learning?
3. What are some relevant cultural influences on global e-learning, and where do these come from?

4. Why are cultural sensitivity and localization in global e-learning relevant in terms of educational ethics?

5. What are some relevant research literature findings about cultural sensitivity and localization in global e-learning?

6. What are some helpful principles and strategies for promoting cultural sensitivity in global e-learning?

7. What are some helpful principles and strategies for promoting localization in global e-learning?

Relevance. In global e-learning, there are already a number of barriers to access (costs, technologies, language literacy, culture, gender, technological literacy, and others). Lack of cultural sensitivity in the design and delivery of e-learning should not hinder access. In a "flat earth" and "knowledge economy," access to knowledge and skills will often determine economic opportunities and livelihoods, often for generations. "The term 'learning' is now used to signal a range of political, social and economic aspirations," notes Bloomer (2001, p. 429). Given the high-stakes in global higher-education learning, efforts should be made to enhance the access of the "have-nots" to have a world of "haves." Cultural sensitivities may promote student learning, learner retention, learner dignity, fairer assessments in global online courses, and greater understandings across and between cultures. Localization in e-learning may result in more applicable hands-on learning with apprenticeships, job shadows, mentorships, and richer experiential learning through a 360-degree learning wrap. Learning may be more immersive. This approach—cultural sensitivity and localization of learning—may have implications on virtually every aspect of e-learning: branding, course ecology, curriculum design, instructional strategies/pedagogical approaches, multimedia builds, information handling, and direct instruction.

Indeed, the university instructors themselves stand to gain from the exposures they would have to real-world applications of what they teach. They may form international alliances and connections with colleagues. They may expand the global sharing of information and strategies for approaching certain tasks. They may discover new attitudes, tools, technologies, and cross-fertilization of ideas in relation to their respective fields of study and inquiry. They may become more truly cosmopolitan, less provincial.

An ideal core in academia. Academia, while it has functioned in economic realities, has always maintained an idealistic core. In academia are shared endeavors to address humankind's shared challenges. Through shared research and learning, different entities and individuals forge common professional links—even across eons of cultural and national differences. The varied trainings, diverse language effects on thinking, professional alliances, and strengths of the individual thinkers hailing from around the world make for a rich synergy that cannot be emulated through closed-world uniformity.

Sourcing. The information in this chapter comes from the extant literature, firsthand observations from over two decades in higher education in the U.S., several applied case studies in cultural sensitivities in e-learning, and insights from one university's initial endeavor to go global. This chapter is structured first with a statement of background. Then, each of the seven research questions is addressed. A final section offers insights into the future regarding cultural sensitivities and localization in e-learning.

BACKGROUND

At the intersection of global e-learning lie invisible cultural influences, which stem from many areas: the various home countries and cultures of the participants, academia, various technologies, Web 2.0 and professional realms. Cultural boundary crossing doesn't just happen when major physical distances are crossed, but rather when people of differing life influences, values, backgrounds and worldviews intermix.

The impetuses for global e-learning. Global e-learning has come to the fore for a number of reasons. First, distance learning has become a fixture in a majority of higher educational institutions in the U.S., and with the maturation of pedagogical approaches and technologies, delivering to learners abroad has been a logical next step. "It may be that consciousness of a global society, culture, and economy and global interdependence are the cornerstones of globalization (Robertson, 1992), and these—consciousness and interdependency—have saliency in knowledge-based enterprises. Institutional theory identifies organizational "fields," or institutional types, such as higher education institutions or hospitals, for example, where patterns of institutional behaviors become similar across institutions (DiMaggio & Powell, 1983). Higher education institutions, because of their cultural, social, and economic roles, are caught up in and affected by globalization" (Levin, 2001, p. 239).

Computing power has become more economical over time. So-called developed and developing countries have joined those connected to the Net and Web through the building of technology infrastructure and the infusion of lower cost and reconditioned computers. Other reasons for the spread of global e-learning relates to economic factors, in a competitive marketplace for higher education (Clegg, Hudson, & Steel, 2003, p. 41) and in a global economic superstructure of "marketplace-based dynamics" (Comor, 2001, p. 401). Some assume a technological determinism in the popularization of e-learning. They fear that technology may be driving the learning. "The key determining characteristics of globalization are taken to be demonstrated by the dynamics of technological innovation and capitalist expan-

sion, coupled with the decline of the nation state as a locus of power" (Clegg et al., 2003, p. 42). While such technologies enable online learning, attributing the popularity of online learning to technological tools seems to be an overstatement. Learners from abroad stand to benefit from "study abroad" even without the travel, relocation, overseas living costs and dormitory or host-family living experiences. Global e-learning offers another option to the former constructions of "study abroad."

Others see the need for emancipatory educational practices albeit without political meddling. "Moreover, we argue that such critique is politically vital, as the neo-liberal conception of globalization is increasingly driving policy agendas in Higher Education, as national governments compete on the basis of supply side investment in human capital" (Coffield, 1999; Schuller & Burns, 1999; Schuller, 1996, as cited by Clegg et al., 2003, p. 40).

The critical approach suggests the avoidance of a dominant ideology to frame issues: "Critical pedagogy, as an ideal type, does not suggest particular solutions; rather, it rejects the framing of 'problems' and 'solutions' in the dominant ideology. Thus in terms of e-learning it would pose the question of whether e-learning can deliver advantages to a particular group of learners in their concrete social circumstances" (Clegg et al., 2003, p. 51). And still others argue the altruism piece, of raising standards of living, through "up-skilling." The argument is that specific skills and knowledge would not be disseminated otherwise, and the access to world-class talents may not happen otherwise. Such e-learning inputs may improve the various countries' economic and social development (Bates, 1999, n.p.). The international alliances and partnerships could enrich the problem-solving and work.

Some threads of the academic literature on global e-learning posit this international exchange as part of the growth of a new world order of a global civil society, transnational learning communities made possible by connective technologies. "Through emerging forms of transnational associational life, a new political, economic, and cultural order is said to be under construction. The agents of these developments are a 'medley of boundary-eclipsing actors—social movements, interest groups, indigenous peoples, cultural groups, and global citizens'" (Pasha & Blaney, 1998: p. 418, as cited by Comor, 2001, p. 389).

Shifting self identities. Turkle suggests that global citizens would de-countrify (depayse) themselves through re-seeing, in her book *Life on the Screen.* "One leaves one's own culture to face something unfamiliar, and upon returning home it has become strange—and can be seen with fresh eyes" (Turkle, 1995, p. 218). Cyberspace is rich with opportunities for depaysement: We can experiment with how it feels to be the opposite sex or sexless, we can change our ethnicity or the color of our skin, we can develop relationships with people we would never meet face-to-face, all of which enable us to experience a different perspective from which to (re)view the self and real life constructs. This potential of cyberspace is at the heart of our teaching online. Our aim is to help students, through their work in cyberspace, experience the challenging shift in perspective that is depaysement; our aim is to encourage them to (re)see the familiar and develop a critical appreciation of the potential of technologies" (Chester & Gwynne, 1998, n.p.). Attaining the awareness of a kind of global citizenship of a shared humanity may yet be another logical outcome.

The pace of modern changes especially makes it difficult for "young people to construct a sense of self" (Bers, 2001, p. 365). Effective online environments create a sense of "mindfulness:" "Some use of the terms *self-knowledge, self-awareness,* or *self-understanding* to refer to mindfulness of one's own personality or individuality. Csikszentimihalyi and Rocheberg-Halton (1981) called it *cultivation* and described it as 'the process of investing psychic energy so that one becomes

conscious of the goals operating within oneself, among and between other persons, and in the environment' (p. 13). Gardner (1983) called it *personal intelligence* and described it as involving two forms of knowledge intimately intermingled: intrapersonal, looking inward or a sense of self-awareness, and interpersonal, looking outward at other individuals and the community" (Bers, 2001, p. 368). Such awareness involves clarity about the rights and roles as community participants (p. 369).

The high-minded rhetoric aside, other thinkers see the discontinuities of the WWW space as too inhibiting to create deep change. The "annihilation of time and space" leads to the making of "instantaneous decisions and the mounting discontinuities of experience and consciousness from one moment to the next." By its nature, this makes "the construction of transnational, progressive, and monumentalizing perspectives capable of radically reforming lifestyles and conceptual systems improbable in the coming decades" (Comor, 2001, p. 404). Mediated communications, with the resulting parasocial relationships maintained over distance, are seen as too virtual to have deep impact (Comor, 2001, p. 397). In addition, those who would interact online still live with "stubbornly local" material limits—even if their minds can conceptualize other ways of being (Tomlinson, 1996, p. 75, as cited by Comor, 2001, p. 398).

Ironically, the recruitment of international students for fully online learning often occurs through outreaches to other countries by university officials, international conferences arranged by third-party mediators, the placing of representative offices overseas, and the employment of mediating graduates and alumni. Faculty members themselves often have to use whatever open source information they may find, hearsay, and firsthand experiences with overseas students to try to understand their learners' needs. There's sometimes insufficient on-ground experience or only experiences limited to other countries or only passing acquaintance with the cultures of a particular region.

Some challenges of global e-learning. Global learning itself is fraught with ethical dilemmas, and there are few clear roadmaps. One writer looks at the economies of scale that may come from bringing in global online learners. "Should institutions in richer countries with the means to develop and deliver distance education programs into poorer countries seek to subsidize their programs at the expense of poorer countries? Is education just another commodity or service to be sold abroad? On the other hand, if students in poorer countries want to access courses from richer and perhaps more prestigious institutions from outside their own countries, and hence have the chance of better jobs and more prosperity, why should we prevent them from doing this" (Bates, 1999, n.p.)?

It is rare enough to hear of universities conducting due diligence to find out if another nation's economy will offer jobs that may support a new graduate's newly-minted career path, enabled by an expensive Western degree. Or will the new graduate be part of an exodus and "brain drain" to a developed country to work for another nation's economy? With a mix of scholarships, multinational corporation funding, teaching assistantships and research assistantships, these select individuals have been invited to study abroad in U.S. universities. Now, with global e-learning, such schools are tapping into yet another niche of elite learners and thinkers, those who do not have to leave home to participate.

"As soon as educational programs cross national borders, a number of social and cultural issues arise," observes one researcher (Bates, 1999, n.p.). Some of these may be predicted with sufficient multicultural knowledge, but many other frictions may arise as surprises.

This intellectual dominance of the West brings up questions of indigenization and homogenization. "Can we integrate disparate groups and cultures without annihilating them in the process?"

asks one researcher (Burniske, 1999, p. 131). Surely, students from other countries contribute enormously to the research work achieved in universities. They bring their culture and language as part and parcel, and those elements contribute to various new theories, practices and inventions. However, such "indigenization" may be overwhelmed by the sheer dominance of the extant intellectual global hierarchy: "What has been called the global-local dialectic (Lash & Urry, 1994) will no doubt accelerate and intensify. Locally, this likely will continue to involve various degrees of indigenization in which different cultures incorporate different elements of foreign cultures in various ways. However, given the context of structural power and the wealth, force, and knowledge resources held by some in relation to others, it appears unlikely that many such interactions will take place on anything approaching some kind of equal exchange. Arjun Appadura writes: "Globalization involves the use of a variety of instruments of homogenization (armaments, advertising techniques, language hegemonies, clothing styles and the like), which are absorbed into local political and cultural economies, only to be repatriated as heterogeneous dialogues of national sovereignty, free enterprise, fundamentalism, etc., in which the state plays an increasingly delicate role: too much openness to global flows and the nation-state is threatened with revolt—the China syndrome; too little, and the state exits the international stage, as Burma, Albania, and North Korea, in various ways, have done" (Appadurai, 1990, p. 307, as cited by Comor, 2001, p. 403).

Which countries will provide the intellectual capital to define truth, and which truths are relevant? How can something elusive like "innovation" be transferred between cultures? How may various entities respect the differing range of university degrees—some from reputable institutions and others from degree mills—and do the fact-checking in terms of checking academic credentialing? With the marketization of various online curricula, often taught by "local" in-country instructors, how may quality controls be encouraged? What then is the true essence of an institution of higher education's offering regarding global e-learning—a mixture of branding, name-instructor cachet, solid learning, and status?

How will new research information be validated or invalidated? How will power relationships be negotiated between institutions of higher education and their far-flung global learners? How will identities be authenticated and validated through the thousands of miles and across oceans? How may learning be made applicable to a range of localized learning environments? How may existing social structures not merely be replicated through global e-learning but extended to be more inclusive, and with more empowered individuals? How may the structural realities of developed countries apply to developing ones, and the learning be applied from the developed world to the developing ones? How can so-called ivory tower learning be localized and applied in useful ways in different socio-economic circumstances of citizens with various situations? How can e-learning proliferate without a sense of forced cultural assimilation and global homogenization?

Defining culture. The term "culture" is a complex and widely debated term with a wide range of definitions. Different groups and individuals apply different weights of importance to different aspects of culture.

Culture has been defined as "that complex whole which includes knowledge, belief, art, morals, law, custom, and any other capabilities and habits acquired by (a human) as a member of society" (Tylor, in Herskovits, 1967, p. 3, as cited by Joseph, et al., 2000, p. 15).

Culture exists as an invisible element in people's day-to-day lives, but it guides their thoughts, social interactions, expectations, and actions. Culture for most people becomes part of the social landscape that they're habituated to, and it often becomes invisible until it runs up against a different set of expectations. Culture may be learned or unlearned. Fluid and adaptive, culture may change (Nee & Wong, 1985, p. 287, as cited by Aldrich & Waldinger, 1990, p. 125).

Culture may be viewed as being complex and layered. "Like an onion, culture also presents many interwoven layers with characteristics specific to that layer. The outer layer of culture expresses characteristics typically encountered by tourists and travelers and includes music, language, and food. The middle layer of culture consists of norms and values, notions of right and wrong, bases of motivation, and general guidelines for accepted behavior. Finally, the core layer of culture includes naturalized assumptions about the world. Core cultural values or dimensions express those deeper rhythms of people..." (McCool, 2006, p. 337). Schein suggests that cultural differences lie at the heart of most modern contentious issues and the failure to arrive at a common shared mental model that may cut across subcultures (Schein, 1993, pp. 27-28). Indeed, collective problem solving was part of the initial idealistic impetus of Dr. Tim Berners-Lee's building of the WWW.

Exposure to different cultures may lead to critical learning moments. "As we become more reflective, we begin to realize how much our initial perceptions can be colored by expectations based on our cultural learning and our past experiences. We do not always perceive what is 'accurately' out there. What we perceive is often based on our needs, our expectations, our projections, and, most of all, our culturally learned assumptions and categories of thought. It is this process of becoming reflective that makes us realize that the first problem of listening to others is to identify the distortions and biases that filter our own cognitive processes" (Schein, 1993, p. 33).

Interest in culturally responsive teaching developed during the late 1980s and early 1990s as a result of rapidly rising diversity in U.S. classrooms and concern over the lack of success of many ethnic and racial minority students (Pewewardy & Hammer, 2003). Educators have often tried to insert culture into the education "instead of inserting education into the culture" (Pewewardy, 1993, as cited by Ladson-Billings, 1995a, p. 159). More recent publications have looked at the teaching of intercultural competence through online means and have found this to be effective in promoting interest in others' ways of life, in changing perspectives, in promoting knowledge about one's own and others' cultures for intercultural communication, and supporting knowledge about the intercultural communication process (Liaw, 2006, pp. 49-64). Schools historically contributed to the problems of learners intentionally and unintentionally by only operating according to mainstream norms (Ogbu, 1987, p. 319). Given the multiculturalism of the U.S., viewing it as a microcosm for cultural sensitivities in e-learning and localizations may be informative.

Ladson-Billings' theory of culturally relevant pedagogy suggests that instructors need to mitigate the cultural mismatch between school and home through dynamic "culturally responsive" means (Ladson-Billings, 1995b, pp. 466-467). Her research surfaced salient areas for cultural awareness and intervention:

1. "the conceptions of self and others held by culturally relevant teachers,
2. the manner in which social relations are structured by culturally relevant teachers,
3. the conceptions of knowledge held by culturally relevant teachers" (Ladson-Billings, 1995b, p. 478).

The cultural piece in education. Joseph, et al. (2000, p. 12) suggest that curricular orientations provide a "platform for awareness, analysis, and critique that allows for interpretation of a broad and perplexing field and for the encouragement of dialogue about curricular intentions and consequences." They cite Eisner's theory of three curricula that all schools teach: explicit, implicit and null. The explicit curriculum is the stated curriculum; the implicit one is the unofficial or hidden one, which may be intentional or unin-

tentional. The null curriculum refers to "what is systematically excluded, neglected, or not considered" (Eisner, 1985, as cited by Joseph, et al., 2000, pp. 3-4). Familiarity with a curriculum often renders those in that milieu unseeing; it's often not until they live in culture shock by living in another culture (termed "disequilibrium") that practitioners may notice the unique characteristics of their own. Or, individuals may be trained to conduct systematic analysis to understand their own culture (2000, p. 17). There are no pure cultures, but all are a mix of varied influences.

Hofstede's cultural dimensions model looks at issues of power distance, individualism, masculinity, uncertainty avoidance and long-term orientation to highlight differences between cultures. Power distance refers to the unequal distribution of power, prestige and wealth in a culture. Individualism looks at the degree of cultural emphasis on the individual vs. the collective. Masculinity examines the cultural focus on traditionally masculine vs. feminine traits. Uncertainty avoidance looks at the value placed on risk and ambiguity. Long-term orientation examines the focus on short-term vs. long-term forward-thinking values in a particular culture (Hai-Jew, 2007a, p. 8).

Counter viewpoints. The conceptualizations of cultural learning dispositions have critics (Bland, 1975; Stellern, Collins, Gutierrez, & Patterson, 1986; Chrisjohn & Peters, 1989). Others have found no learning benefit by culturally adapted teaching methods (Kleinfeld & Nelson, 1991, as cited by Pewewardy, 2002, pp. 22-56; Kerbo, 1981, pp. 1278-1279). Others warn of taking uncritical approaches cultural dispositions in learning, particularly those without empirical support (McCarty, Lynch, Wallace, & Benally, 1991, pp. 42-59).

Potential flashpoints in global e-learning. A range of potential flashpoints may not be fully anticipated in global e-learning. Already, the literature has mentioned challenges with faculty intellectual property rights (Noble, 1998, pp. 815-

825); the role of instructors; the nature of discourse among and between learners and the instructor; the nature of collaboration and crediting; quality control between partner organizations; and grading (their fairness and negotiability). Political differences between countries may lead to sharp disjuncture between one country's values in the handling of information and the treatment of online learners. For example, one writer observes the situation of one nation: "Politically, China's strict control over the use of the Internet is a barrier in developing online education. On one hand, the Government is highly convinced that the Internet is an important tool to modernization. On the other hand, it fears a number of 'social security' problems such as leaked State secrets and 'harmful information' from the outside world" (Ngor, 2001, p. 53). One country's concern becomes another's perception of "meddling." Whole languages and arts of diplomacy have been created to address such flashpoints at the levels of state, and similarly, such diplomacy may be necessary for global e-learning.

Moral development has been an important part of education for years. The global aspect would suggest the needs of cultural customization. An online classroom may be viewed as a "just community" microcosm of the larger global community: "Although Kohlberg is most well known for his psychological model of stages of moral development that progress from highly egocentric value judgments to reasoning about abstract universal moral principles (Kohlberg, 1976), he also contributed to the field of moral education by proposing the 'just community' model (Kohlberg, 1985). This approach proposes that the involvement in participatory democracy, social institutions, group decision-making, and self-government is critical to shaping an individual's moral development. Therefore, educational intervention should focus on both moral thinking and the moral lives of children" (Bers, 2001, p. 372). The disparate and deeply held moral underpinnings of higher education (including political structures and assumptions)) will likely be a cultural flashpoint. One academic sounds a cautionary note: "During the diffusion process, these change agents must be aware that they should respect social values and community norms because of the key roles they play in the diffusion process" (Isman, 2005, n.p.)

The potential for cultural clashes is myriad. How historical events and figures are viewed and depicted may be contentious. The definition of an ideal society, religions and religious history, the role of people in society, national and local map boundaries, and any number of issues addressed in academia may spark disagreements. Online learners engage in a surprising amount of values and philosophical debates, sometimes even in courses where these issues may not be expected. Osguthorpe, Osguthorpe, Jacob, and Davies (2003) suggest that moral principles must underlie all instructional design particularly if transformative learning is the goal. The authors call for a "conscience of craft by striving for excellence beyond that which a client may demand" (Osguthorpe et al., 2003, p. 20).

Indeed, even if the concepts of cultural sensitivities in global e-learning are accepted, the unique strategies that may be needed to create culturally sensitive e-learning spaces for global learners will likely be much debated. How the "filtered reality" of reculturated spaces may be created will require investigation and design. Testing for the efficacies of such approaches will require plenty of research attention.

WHAT IS CULTURAL SENSITIVITY IN GLOBAL E-LEARNING? WHAT IS LOCALIZATION IN GLOBAL E-LEARNING?

While the terms of "cultural sensitivity" and "localization" are straightforward on the face of it, how these may be applied involve a virtual theoretical infinity of approaches.

Cultural sensitivity. The concept of "cultural sensitivity" defines a type of approach to curriculum development and delivery that focuses on the targeted learners, their cultural milieu, and their learning needs. Here, any number of elements—from branding to interactivity design to instructor telepresence—are modified in order to ensure learner comfort, intellectual challenge, personal growth, course participation, and learning. Cultural sensitivity stands as an antithesis to the cultural neutrality approach.

A simpler *de facto* approach has involved the use of cultural neutrality. This is the concept of reducing or eradicating any contextual (read: cultural) information and leaving information at its most pristine and objective. This also involves the use of simple English that is translatable into numerous languages using online language translators (and with words which may not be provocative ones). Neutrality may work for simple multimedia messages, but for highly interactive teaching and learning over time, this becomes harder to maintain.

Approaching cultural sensitivity may be conceptualized in several ways. One is to do no cultural work on a course except in how it is taught, which relies heavily on instructor expertise. This assumes an *ad hoc* approach, and this may be the most common construct in global e-learning today. Another is to build unique cultural modules for different groups and to version out different experiences on the front-end of a course. (The concept of different cultural tracking may be highly contentious and provocative.) Another is to build cultural targeting from a neutral core of information—in a kind of repurposing or shaping of the message. A prebuilt course may be retrofitted for cultural flexibility and sensitivities. A cleaner method may be to originate contents from a cultural core from the beginning. This means in-depth analysis of the learners' cultures,

deep study of the learners, and intensive focus on localizing the contents to the targeted learners. The more monolithic the anticipated audience, the more cultural targeting may be done; however, the more diverse the anticipated learners, the more nuanced the learning will have to be and the more reliance on an objective neutral core. The point is to build curriculum and learning in a less perfunctory and more considered way.

Bates advises the development of "special programs for course developers to increase sensitivity to inter-cultural and design issues for programs being delivered internationally" (Bates, 2003, n.p.). There are additional benefits from building with an international focus early on: "Developing programs for international delivery can also enable institutions to prepare their students for an increasingly global economy and society, if courses are planned from the start with an international focus, especially if they involve contributions from or joint development with institutions in other countries" (Bates, 1999, n.p.).

Localization. The concept of "localization" addresses the issue of relating the learning to respective learners' local circumstances—their environment, economy, social milieu and cultural context—in order to magnify and strengthen their online learning experience and the applicability of their learning upon graduation. This also involves consider the learners' localized pasts and the effects of those pasts on their current and future learning. This would require a fair amount of organizational work—to identify local resources, local experts, local research facilities, and the local job market—and to form formal partnerships. Informal partnerships may also be forged. Mini-grants, professional alliances, research and publications interchanges, shared tuition, or other models may be employed to support these alliances. Or learners may be encouraged to make their own connections.

A growing emphasis on the local is affecting WWW-moderated interchanges, and possibly e-learning: "One possible avenue of interpretation in this vein might be to claim that transnational capital's challenge to national sovereignty has, in effect, forced the retreat of cultural identity to more local enclaves. Inadequately equipped to face the onslaught of investors, speculators, and other agents of global capital, nation-states become irrelevant containers for identity-construction. Instead, they become fragmented by a host of social movements seeking to articulate a more localized identity and cultural practice. In these terms, the local is often regarded as a space of resistance to both the modernist abstractions of the nation-state and the placeless globalism of transnational capital" (Rose, 1994; May, 1996, as cited by Oakes, 2000, p. 670).

The mitigations of cultural sensitivity and localization. For e-learning, several best practices ideas allude to the issues of cultural sensitivity and localization, through the frame of student-centered design. Chickering and Gamson's well-respected seven principles of good practice in undergraduate education includes learning that "respects diverse talents and ways of learning" (Mehlenbacher, Miller, Covington & Larsen, 2000, p. 169). In Lynch's (2001) summary of some course designed objectives synthesized from the works of various researchers, she includes the following, which may be viewed as a type of localization: "to emphasize application of course concepts to the students' real-world situations" (Ackerman, 1996; Carly & Palmquist, 1992; Duffy & Jonassen, 1993; Harasim, 1997; Moore & Kearsley, 1996, and Sponder, 1990, as cited by Lynch, 2001, n.p.).

Cultural issues in e-learning have not been invisible. "Cross-cultural differences have a major influence on the way instruction is shaped and the way learning takes place within any classroom" (Strother, 2003, p. 353). However, there have been differing definitions of culture, especially in online courses. There's been little in the way of meta-analyses about this issue in virtual learning.

WHO MAY AFFECT CULTURAL SENSITIVITY AND LOCALIZATION IN GLOBAL E-LEARNING?

Those who have a hand in administering, supporting, or leading global e-learning may all support these dual tracks of cultural sensitivities and localization. Subject matter experts, instructional designers, faculty, teaching assistants, global online learners and others all have a role in supporting quality in global e-learning. Often, a team of individuals may work to deliver global e-learning, in the production of digital educational materials, designing online activities, building the technological infrastructures, providing help supports, and facilitating the direct learning.

Those who work to deliver global e-learning wield a lot of power culturally. The mere action of selecting a curriculum focuses on what is important and what is not. How learning and skills are conveyed also involves power because it privileges some types of learning styles, values and attitudes and not others.

The concepts and practices of "cultural sensitivities" and "localization" potentially affect a range of practices.

- Administrator, faculty and staff cultural sensitivity trainings
- The development of course ecologies (via policies, digital artifacts, branding messages, "look-and-feel," and other elements)
- Curricular design (assignments, assessments, course e-learning path, readings, digitally-mediated experiences, pacing, and other elements)
- Designed interactivity and "social life" online
- The building of digital learning artifacts, multimedia, and ancillary materials
- Organizational branding and marketing to particular learning audiences
- Instructor and facilitator telepresence (messages, depictions, behaviors, and interactions)

- The scaffolding for informal learning
- Student information handling
- How learners interact with each other

The Cultural Sensitivities and Localizations Course Analysis (CSLCA) Tool in the appendix addresses a range of these issues in more depth at the course level.

WHAT ARE SOME RELEVANT CULTURAL INFLUENCES ON GLOBAL E-LEARNING, AND WHERE DO THESE COME FROM?

Global e-learning involves influences well beyond those of the cultures and multicultures of its various learners and instructors. There are

Figure 1. Cultural sensitivities influences on the juncture of global e-learning

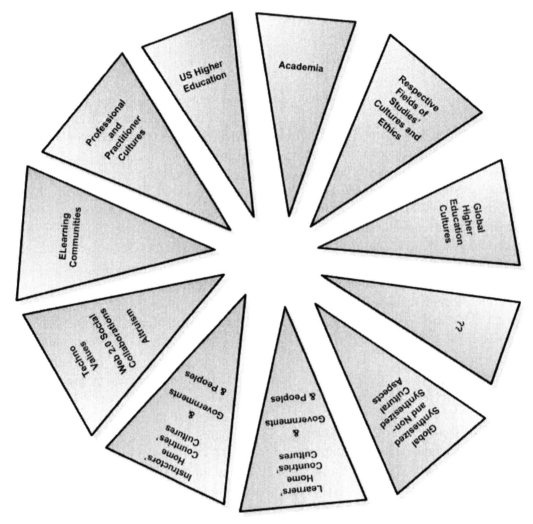

Cultural Sensitivities Influences on the Juncture in Global eLearning
(Hai-Jew, 2007)

international influences, Web 2.0, higher education/academia, technological culture, and other elements. Various learners will approach global e-learning with a variety of paradigms, described as "sets of ontological and epistemological assumptions" (Burrell & Morgan, 1979, as cited by Schultz & Hatch, 1996, p. 529).

Culture exists on both a group level and on individual levels. "As Van Maanen and Barley (1985) observed, 'while a group is necessary to invent and sustain culture, culture can be carried only by individuals'" (p. 35, as cited by Harris, 1994, p. 309).

Cultural influences come from a variety of directions in global e-learning, as may be indicated in the following figure. Thin-slicing a course, a curriculum, a program, a degree area of study, or an educational institution for its cultural influences may involve excessive complexity given the various effects and influences. However, focusing on a particular aspect for more effective learning would be critical.

One dominant aspect of e-learning has been the power of the WWW and Internet. The early onset of the popularizing of these technologies created a social layer of global elite netizens. With improved connectivity said to "connect the entire world in five steps or less" (White 1970) between peoples, there still are many who are unconnected and therefore digitally deprived (Wellman & Hampton, 1999, pp. 650-651).

With the growing popularization of the Web, questions have arisen about the impact. Are people becoming les sociable face-to-face and only comfortable online? Will the Web bring people together across cultural divides, or will it "reinforce barriers" for a "postmodern tribalism?" "To amplify, are global communications and the Internet integrative and inclusive, promoting English as a universal language and causing differences between peoples and cultures to erode? Or will these new technologies perpetuate and reinforce our separation into tribes, because immigrants effortlessly maintain thick contact

with their ethnic and cultural roots" (Aronson, 1996, p. 314)?

On a continuum, the quality of available information ranges from the accurate to the wholly untrue. The efficiency in finding relevant information in the deluge of data of the WWW is a major challenge for learners (Aronson, 1996, p. 311). One writer describes this phenomenon: "To use the language of cyberspeak, modern life is becoming 'homonized,' that is to say, increasingly brought under human control by individuals sitting at a keyboard and screen, but at the same time, to use much older language, dehumanized by an unreflective Silicon Valley about to blend with an unphilanthropic Hollywood, which put together makes 'Sillywood'" (Billington, 2001, p. 579). While intercommunications between individuals form a centerpiece of cyber culture, the collective intelligence may not have necessarily resulted in quality results. An untruth multiplied out digitally into the cyber-universe doesn't make it true.

Said another way, the proliferation of information has not meant a transmuting of that raw material into knowledge. Even the mediating influences of faculty tends to favor "the largely uncritical acceptance of information by students" instead of critical literacy (Jongsma, 1991; Mann, 1994; Fraah, 1995). "However, open web access to valuable content created by others introduces potential problems of 'authority', that is, ownership, quality control, plagiarism, and simple theft" (Wilson, 2001, p. 383). Students need to know how to access, organize and present information, not merely regurgitate information (Kuzma, 1998, p. 581).

Social informatics has been described as the "interdisciplinary study of the design, uses and consequences of information technologies that takes into account their interaction with institutional and cultural contexts" ("Learning about..." 2000, as cited by Chakrapani & Ekbia, 2004, p. 145). In such a culture, learning comes from learners' peers.

Tu and Corry (2002) summarize Online Learning Communities as having four basic components.

- Community – occurring with social interaction about common interests
- Learning – nonformal; the attainment of knowledge, skills, and attitudes through social interaction with peers
- Network – defined as a pattern of communications and relationships (Schuler, 1966)
- Technology – either a synchronous or asynchronous platform (Sumner & Dewar, 2002, n.p.)

This culture combines the technology with the human element. The foremost human-centered activities in multimedia include "content production, annotation, organization, archival, retrieval, sharing, analysis, and multimedia communication" (Jaimes, 2006, p. 12).

Language plays a central role in global e-learning and interactivity. "All higher-order functions develop out of language-based, social interaction" (Warschauer, 1997, p. 471). As such, aspects of language use in online spaces raise concerns. Global English may continue to evolve as a powerful medium for international intercommunications. "Increasingly, nonnative speakers will need to use the language daily for presentation of complex ideas, international collaboration and negotiation, and location and critical interpretation of rapidly changing information" (Warschauer, 2000, p. 511). Reading itself occurs in a cultural context. "But reading is more than a psycholinguistic act of decoding letters and words. Rather, it is a social practice that takes place in particular sociocultural contexts," notes various thinkers (de Castell & Luke, 1986; Gee, 1996). In this sense, the shift in reading from the page to the screen, and the new socioeconomic circumstances in which the shift takes place, has an even greater impact" (p. 521).

Others suggest that these new technologies may lead to linguistic collapse and linguistic homogenization. "Language, the basis of human community, as well as human communication, may be an endangered species. There were roughly six thousand languages seriously spoken on this planet at the beginning of the twentieth century. It may not be long into the twenty-first when there will probably be only about six hundred left. The erosion of linguistic and cultural diversity on the planet is far less recognized, but no less serious, than the loss of biodiversity. The new global audiovisual marketing culture is threatening to move the world with accelerating speed toward the monolinguistic pidgin English of computer programmers, air traffic controllers, and advertising sloganeers. The basic unit of human thought, the sentence, is totally eroded in chatrooms where the only punctuation tends to be 'like' and 'you know'" (Billington, 2001, p. 581).

Wherever these social technologies of Web 2.0 may be leading in terms of human interactions, learner familiarity with online learning environments has been correlated with more effective learning: information-seeking (e.g., Bromme & Stahl, 1999, 2002; Gray, 1990, 1995; Stahl, 2001; Wallace, Kupperman, Krajcik, & Soloway, 2000); online tool use (Aleven, Stahl, Schworm, Fischer, & Wallace, 2003, p. 299). This suggests that cultural insights of the learning milieu may be critical to learner performance.

Many new learners to higher education feel a distinct sense of culture shock when experiencing the values and practices assumed in academia. College itself is a ritual, a rite of passage, with high standards for becoming an insider and a complex enculturation process. Some research suggests an assimilationist model, which requires that learners integrate culturally or be rejected. Academic culture involves a rich variety of hierarchical roles, the privileging of some types of information and knowledge, a respect for research, intellectual meritocracies, tenure, and other complex elements. And this ritual is a high-risk high-reward one, because the education and sheepskin credentials serve as licenses of entry for workplaces. Higher learning offers a golden ticket to global citizenship and a voice in engaging the world's research and academic issues.

WHY ARE CULTURAL SENSITIVITY AND LOCALIZATION IN GLOBAL E-LEARNING RELEVANT IN TERMS OF EDUCATIONAL ETHICS?

Ethical dilemmas in education may be viewed through multiple paradigms but with the best interests of the students at the center. Four main ethics have been explored in educational leadership the ethic of justice, critique, care and the profession (Shapiro & Stefkovich, 2001, pp. 10-25). While there are no expeditious ways to fully explicate these approaches, cultural sensitivity and localization in global e-learning may enhance the state of learners in the following lenses.

Because cultural sensitivity makes higher education more accessible and applicable to learners' respective situations, these efforts promote "the equal sovereignty of the people" (Strike, 1991, p. 415) and respects the "social contract" implied in higher education (Shapiro & Stefkovich, 2001, p. 11). Sergiovanni's concept of "virtuous schools" suggests that educational leadership is a kind of stewardship, and educational institutions should be just and beneficent. Global e-learning should aspire to fairness, equity and justice, with an education that more closely meets the needs of its learners and respects them and supports their dignity and abilities.

The ethic of critique suggests a review of current ethics and poses a reframing of concepts such as "privilege, power, culture, language and even justice" (Shapiro & Stefkovich, 2001, p. 13). This construct views all teaching as political, potentially emancipating and focused on consciousness raising; the imperative is to empower learners through awareness of their own social class and

the inequities in the social system. This paradigm suggests that education should lead to political action for the self-betterment of the learners and the creation of a society that avoids the so-called "'isms' in society (i.e., classism, racism, sexism, heterosexism)" (p. 14). Cultural sensitivity and localization in global e-learning promote learner empowerment (and decision-making) both in the classroom and outside of the online walls into their respective communities. These approaches emphasize the power of learner voices and greater cultural awareness that may have implications on social issues.

The ethic of care focuses on issues of "loyalty, trust, and empowerment" and stems from a feminist critique (Shapiro & Stefkovich, 2001, p. 16). In this construct, nurturance of learners should be valued above achievement. "Caring, concern, and connection" (Martin, 1993, p. 144) are to be supported for the "integration of reason and emotion, self and other" (Shapiro & Stefkovich, 2001, p. 16). The concepts of cultural sensitivities and localization emphasize relationships and connections, participative leadership, and the building of e-learner loyalty and trust.

The ethic of the educational profession draws widely from a range of entities: teachers unions, institutions of higher education, a body of law and principles, and organizations built around particular academic and professional fields. There are the social ethics of the community. There are personal and individual professional codes of ethics. In some circumstances, these ethics align, and in others, they may differ widely. Professional ethics are formed through a dynamic and ever-changing process. The approaches of cultural sensitivities and localization in global e-learning may be explored and debated along numerous lines based on the various learning situations of learners. These twin considerations will most certainly manifest differently in different countries and educational situations.

A chapter titled "College Teaching and Student Moral Development" suggests that higher education may be both full of values or devoid of moral underpinnings, as in some vocational programs (McNeel, 1994, pp. 27-49). He cites Rest's Four Component Model of morality: "moral sensitivity (consciousness raising and consciousness sensitizing); moral judgment (moral imagination, ethical analysis, and moral decision making); moral motivation (values analysis, values clarification, and values criticism); and moral character (becoming a responsible agent, developing virtue, and achieving moral identity)" (p. 30). While no clear ethic of the profession is defined, these sources offer some early approaches.

WHAT ARE SOME RELEVANT RESEARCH LITERATURE FINDINGS ABOUT CULTURAL SENSITIVITY AND LOCALIZATION IN GLOBAL E-LEARNING?

An important assumption of this approach is that those engaged in higher education have a lot of formal and informal power. Instructors have the power of affecting learners' lives: their grades, their professional opportunities and alliances, their professional strategies, and their learning. "Students are more vulnerable than our researchers who may be paid and can, in any case, withhold cooperation. And we hear occasionally of instances of abuse of a teacher's authority: publishing students' work as our own; using others' ideas as our own; loading the evidence in favor of our views through selective use of data; propagandizing; breaching the confidentiality of data supplied by students. There is good reason, then, to extend our interest in professional ethics from research to teaching" (Wilson, 1982, p. 269). There are a number of ways to fail that high calling.

The research literature offers case-specific insights on global e-learning endeavors to particular and unique groups of learners. For example, one addresses fundamental Japanese cultural dimensions as high context, collectivistic and polychromic. Based on these general descriptions, the design and delivery of the online curriculum changed. Additional information was given to Japanese learners to meet their needs, too (McCool, 2006, p. 337). "Online learning environments in the US typically assume linear information structures, a reliable and proven approach toward e-learning. Linear information structures are ubiquitous in the US for many reasons but generally address writer-responsible authoring, low context communication styles, individualism and achievement, and monochromic or sequential temporal order. Each of these characteristics addresses the cultural requirements of the majority of e-learners in the US. However, when adapting or internationalizing e-learning environments for other cultures, many US assumptions fail to meet the unique demands of the target audience. Consequently, a streamlined and minimalist linear information structure excludes numerous cultural requirements for many international audiences" (McCool, 2006, p. 335).

"High context cultures tend to handle conflict in a more discrete and subtle manner and are predisposed to require learning for the sake of learning. For example, high context cultures include Japanese, Chinese, Koreans, African-American, and Native American" (Sabin & Ahern, 2002, p. S1C-11).

In another case, The Enduring Legacies Project (funded by The Lumina Foundation for Education) uses cultural sensitivities for project design, faculty training, curriculum development, and Native American teaching case studies research to create an associates curriculum for Native American learners from a number of reservations in Washington State. Teamed with WashingtonOnline (WAOL), a consortium of 34 community colleges providing distance learning, The Evergreen State College has worked closely with the tribal leaders from a number of local tribes to tailor the learning to its students who face a number of barriers: "location (being place-bound), racial prejudice, language (with many who speak

English as a second language), culture, finances, the technology divide, and learner disempowerment" (Hai-Jew, 2007a, p. 2).

This program follows an "Indian theory of education" (Hampton, 1998, p. 19, as cited by Kirkness & Barnhardt, 2001, p. 8). It enlists the support of the entire family structure and tribes to encourage learners. It trains participating faculty and staff on the on-ground cultural realities. It encourages relationship-building between all: administrators, staff, instructors, learners, and learners and their families. Firsthand and tacit knowledge are privileged along with academic formalized knowledge. Cultural awareness (including points of cultural flex and pressures) are brought to the fore for both staff and learners, in order to promote the critical thinking and growth of all. This hybrid programs brings in face-to-face meetings as well as online learning. This project enlists tribal-based study leaders as "whipman." The three main activities they would use to achieve these learning objectives would be: (1) to design and deliver a new associates of arts degree program on a number of reservations, (2) to support the redesign of courses to improve the instructional design and cultural relevance, and (3) to develop case studies about major issues facing Native Americans today. This program is not only implementing curricular changes, but it is adding to the body of knowledge about Native Americans and often by Native Americans through the Native teaching case studies, which are being housed and distributed from The Evergreen State College's Reservation Based Community Determined Program Web site.

Global E-learner profiling. So much of global e-learning seems to assume that the "other" and the "self" are one in the same. By contrast, those working in corporations have invested much into understanding the various consumer zones. "The world market is now being computer micromapped into consumer zones according to residual cultural factors (i.e., idioms, local traditions, religious affiliations, political ideologies, folk mores, tradi-

tional sexual roles, etc.), dominant cultural factors (i.e., typologies of life-styles based on consumption patterns: television ratings, musical tastes, fashions, motion picture and concert attendance, home video rentals, magazine subscriptions, home computer software selection, shopping mall participation, etc.), and emergent cultural factors (i.e., interactive and participatory video, mobile micromalls equipped with holography and super conductivity, computer interfacing with consumers, robotic services, etc.). Emergent marketing strategies must move further beyond the commodity itself and toward the commodity as image, following marketing contingencies all the way down. And here, precisely, is the task of guerrilla marketing: to go all the way with the images we create and strike where there is indecision.' Like guerrilla fighters, we must win hearts and minds'" ("guerrilla marketing" in Dirlik, 1994, p. 70, as cited by Oakes, 2000, p. 672). Some insights from learner profiling may enhance global e-learning if it is done with savvy and nuance and not taken to the extremes of stereotyping.

Along the same lines as learner profiling, more attention is being paid to how experts form their expertise in order to identify critical milestones in the learning process. "Trajectories or paths toward expertise are domain specific and must first be documented and then used within instructional contexts to promote knowledge transitions...To foster the development of expertise two goals must be achieved. The first is to determine what experts know and the second is to determine how to help novices acquire similar competencies" (Lajoie, 2003, p. 21).

The ecological fallacy risk. Some would argue that broad assertions of various peoples are necessarily stereotyping. McCool counters: "While there are always exceptions to culture, they mark only those outliers of larger discourse patterns. For example, cultures which are highly individualistic—such as the US—tend to support claims of difference and exception. Thus, dismissing cultural patterns as mere generalization may result in an individualist ethnocentricism coined an ECOLOGICAL FALLACY. The point, then, is that one may acknowledge patterns without making grandiose claims of an entire population" (McCool, 2006, p. 337).

WHAT ARE SOME HELPFUL PRINCIPLES AND STRATEGIES FOR PROMOTING CULTURAL SENSITIVITY IN GLOBAL E-LEARNING?

General strategies that promote a culturally sensitive approach to the following factors will be examined: educational organization branding, course ecology, curricular design, interactivity,

instructor presence and interactions, information handling, and the engagement of other learners and interactivity. Promoting cultural sensitivity in global e-learning may encompass a range of different strategies.

The figure below shows an ideal on a rough continuum of cultural attunements and interventions on learners in a global e-learning classroom.

This section covers some initial approaches to promoting cultural sensitivity in e-learning in global online courses. It is organized into four strategic endeavors:

1. Making cultural issues visible;
2. Promoting high interactivity for richer exchanges;
3. Empowering global e-learners; and
4. Designing a high-trust learning ecology.

Figure 2. Continuum of effects of intercultural exchanges in global e-learning classrooms

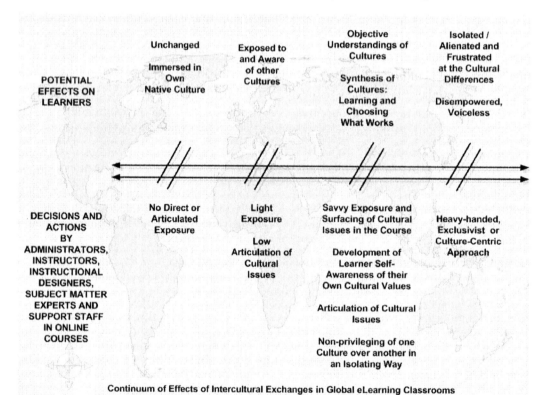

Continuum of Effects of Intercultural Exchanges in Global eLearning Classrooms
(Hai-Jew, 2007)

Making Cultural Issues Visible

"Humanity is gained as the world, in the spaces between people, is acknowledged rather than denied or pushed away" (Briggs, 1996, p. 6, as cited by Warschauer, 1998, p. 80).

"Seeing" and acknowledging cultural differences. Research in recent decades would suggest that the cultural aspect of learning cannot be separated out (Salomon & Perkins, 1998). "This theoretical shift is in reference to the view that teachers, learners, learning, and teaching are always and everywhere embedded in cultural, historical, institutional, and power-structured contexts. Although these contexts bear significantly on the ultimate shape that learning and teaching assume, learners and teachers are not mere automatons caught in a tangle of macro-level forces; instead, their individual agencies are co-constructed (Lantolf & Pavlenko, 2001, p. 148) by the interrelationships of their own desires, abilities, and histories and the particular mix of artefacts (sic), cultures, institutions, people, and situations in which they are located and in which they interact (Lantolf, 2000, as cited by Belz & Müller-Hartmann, 2003, p. 71). Culture then is co-constructed, and those within it have power to make changes.

Two researchers observe broad-based approaches to understanding culture. One is a functionalist approach that tends toward convergence or the bringing together of disparate elements into a coherent understanding of another culture. Another is an interpretivist approach that tends toward divergence, or highlighting differences by "constantly seeking more interpretations and making new associations" (Schultz & Hatch, 1996, pp. 538-539).

These authors propose a metatheoretical model for understanding different cultures through "interplay" defined as "the simultaneous recognition of both contrasts and connections between paradigms" (Schultz & Hatch, 1996, p. 530). Theirs suggests an honest respect for differences between cultural paradigms instead of either writing off any possible similarity or shading over differences. Interplay highlights the contrasts (differences) and connections (similarities) between paradigms. Multiple views may then be "held in tension" (Schultz & Hatch, 1996, p. 535). By definition, the interplay approach does not accept either the incommensurability or the integrationist approaches.

Those who would seek to understand differing cultures and their clashes may need to become comfortable with a shimmering tapestry of understandings. They may need to make peace with a "chaos theory" approach. "Derrida, Foucault, and Lyotard assumed that human experience is fragmented and discontinuous. Thus, they searched out discontinuity and difference rather than order and similarity. Because there is no pattern of sense to be found, general theories, which Lyotard and others labeled *grand narratives,* are sentimental illusions. Lyotard (1984) described the attack on the grand narrative as an argument against the modernist drive toward determinacy and consensus, whereas modernist notions of order and patterning neglect discontinuity, passion, and rupture. Similarly, in his work on deconstruction, Derrida's (1978) key concepts are *difference* and *deconstruction,* where voice is given to the silences and absences of organizational life, such as suppressed disorder in the orchestration of order or suppressed idiosyncrasy in the construction of meaning" (Derrida, 1978, 1980, as cited by Schultz & Hatch, 1996, p. 540).

The multiple layering of cultural knowledge and assumptions makes this issue more complex. "Schein explicitly described the pattern of basic assumptions as 'the deeper levels' of culture (1991, p. 252) and further emphasized the distinction between cultural surface and essence in his hierarchical three-level model of assumptions, values, and artifacts. Here, the cultural surface is *explained* by the cultural *paradigm* and cannot be decoded before the underlying essence is revealed. Schein (1992, p. 27) put it this way:

'the culture will manifest itself at the levels of observable artifacts and shared espoused values, norms, and rules of behavior...(but) to understand a group's culture, one must attempt to get at its shared basic assumptions'" (Schultz & Hatch, 1996, p. 542). While culture itself is dynamic and evolving, the study of it may require the "freezing" of it (in discreet phases) in order to analyze and compare different ones (Schultz & Hatch, 1996, pp. 542-543).

Culture and curriculum. Culture does not play an equal role in all curricula. Culture may be tangential to some subjects. It may provide a substructure to the learning for others. It may infuse the learning in yet other courses, and it may be more encompassing and broad than the subject matter being studied. It may itself be the focus of academic inquiry.

For global learners, they will not likely experience a coherent exposure to a culture but may experience it piecemeal as they move from course to course. More collaborative interactions with their peers from other countries and regions and cultures will likely enhance the opportunity for such multi- and inter-cultural understandings. If they are part of a learning cohort, they may acculturate to that particular group's sense of culture. Program or academic advisors may offer a consistent voice or view. Culture-infused curriculums may offer a coherent full-wrap experience.

Some learning has been described as the enculturation of learners into a community of practice. "Cognitive apprenticeship methods, according to John Seely Brown (1995), 'try to enculturate students into authentic practices through activity and social interaction in a way similar to that evident—and evidently successful—in craft apprenticeship.' The concept of cognitive apprenticeship is important in online learning environments because, as Geertz (1983) has shown, communities of practitioners are connected by complex socially constructed 'Webs of significance,' including beliefs and concepts and reaching beyond their apparent tasks. Understanding these Webs of

beliefs is essential to understanding their professional practices and their motivations. Therefore, if learners are to truly understand and work with other professional perspectives on international technical communication, they need to be able to work in a collaborative environment that allows them to some extent to become 'an apprentice' of the other professional groups and to understand the 'Webs of beliefs' that are important to understanding the activities of these groups. Essentially, learners need to be able to enter the culture of the professional practices they are learning" (Starke-Meyerring, 1999, pp. 16-17).

Using online networks, experts and novices come together into a shared space for collaborative learning and mutual growth. Addressing the cultural assumptions of a curriculum or a program would strengthen the learning.

Schein suggests the importance of self-awareness and then the power of dialogue for raising cultural issues. "When we operate as culture carriers and are conscious of our cultural membership, we are emotionally attached to our culturally learned categories of thought; we value them and protect them as an aspect of our group identity. One of the ways that groups, communities, organizations, or other units that develop subcultures define themselves and set their psychological boundaries is by developing a language...Using that language expresses membership and belonging, and that, in turn, provides status and identity" (Schein, 1993, p. 35).

Effective online communities may be designed. Song offers a model of online collaborative learning environments that shows that a properly-designed online environment consisting of group composition, task design, distribution of authority and evaluation practices, may enhance learner motivation (Song, 2004, p. 45).

How to foster expertise is a critical aspect of learning. "Three different approaches to fostering expertise are described here: (a) conducting basic research to explicitly define transitions in expertise; (b) developing dynamic forms of assessment that lead to learning opportunities; and (c) providing explicit exemplars or models of expertise to novices. Studies of expertise inform us that becoming an expert is a transitional process. Learning in all domains is a lifelong process that can be monitored, assessed, and scaffolded. Models of expertise can assist us in determining what to monitor, how to assess, and where to scaffold learners so that they eventually become independently proficient in their chosen fields" (Chester & Gwynne, 1998, p. 22).

Promoting High Interactivity for Richer Exchanges

High interactivity. Designing higher interactivity in online courses should offer stronger opportunities to exchange information, ask questions and receive responses, interact, and bond and learn in an online classroom. An effective environment requires both active students and instructors (Muirhead, 2000, as cited by Crisp, Thiele, Scholten, Barker, & Baron, 2003, p. 3). Open channels of communications may offer options to release tension and to address misunderstandings. This may offer opportunities to interact in the field using "insider language" specific to the area of study and practice.

Online communications may take a number of forms: one-to-one, dyadic partnerships, small groups, large groups with subgroups below; synchronous or asynchronous or blended; textual, auditory, or audio-visual; one-to-one, many-to-one, or one-to-many (micro-cast or broadcast); recorded or nonrecorded, and with other complex setups.

Getting to a stage of being able to share in-depth ideas about a field may require a time to acclimate and to create a shared sense of foundational understanding. Learners may need to be enculturated into the learning. "To communicate anything, from a simple desire to a complex message, those involved must share similar references and associations or must, at the very least, have

some preexisting familiarity with what is being conveyed. If, however, people do not share a language, cultural references, and so forth, information may be conveyed but little (if any) of it will be understood (Hall, 1959). As we are socialized, our conceptual systems become both entrenched and more complex. As we learn to mediate and interpret information in our particular cultures and relevant subcultures, we also learn to sort out what information is 'good' and what information is 'bad,' what is 'rational' and 'irrational,' 'realistic' and 'unrealistic.' As such, *all information is mediated into what we know using learned, intersubjective, and implicitly power-laden conceptual systems"* (Comor, 2001, p. 394).

The concept of symbolic interactionism also supports the formative, participatory view of meaning-making and knowledge creation. "Knowledge and meaning are created *between* rather than *within* people, whether those people are present in a strictly physical sense or symbolically present, for example in the sense of some anticipated or 'generalised' other (Mead, 1934). Knowledge-making is thus a *participatory* process in which social interaction precedes meaning-making and action. 'The whole is prior to the part, not the part to the whole; and the part is explained in terms of the whole, not the whole in terms of the part or parts'" (Mead, 1934, p. 7, as cited by Bloomer, 2001, p. 440). The critical thinking processes of learners are built up through regular instructor postings and sometimes even daily interactions (Bullen, 1998, as cited by Crisp et al., 2003, p. 3).

In addition to the timeliness element of interactions, the "immediacy" of communications is critical to support learning. "*Immediacy* refers to communication behaviors that reduce social and psychological distance between people (Mehrabian, 1971; Myers Zhong, & Guan, 1998); it includes both nonverbal and verbal behaviors. In a classroom, nonverbal immediacy behaviors are those associated with physical conduct such as eye contact, smiling, movement (or lack thereof) around the classroom, and body position (Anderson, 1979; Richmond, Gorham, & McCroskey, 1987). Verbal immediacy focuses on speaking behaviors such as including personal examples, using humor, providing and inviting feedback, and addressing and being addressed by students by name (Gorham, 1988). Both nonverbal and verbal immediacy behaviors are associated with student motivation and learning (Christophel, 1990; Menzel & Carrell, 1999; Myers et al., 1998)" (Arbaugh, 2001, p. 43).

More dialogue may enhance the learning. The development of shared mental models may take more periods of dialogue especially when cross-cultural issues are involved (Schein, 1993, p. 29). Dialogue needs to be accessible to all for effective problem-solving (p. 29), and this must be done in a situation where members feel as equal as possible (p. 31). The participants need to engage with active listening, with all communications channels activated for the highest effectiveness (p. 30).

Schein views the need to protect "face" as a stumbling block to effective communications. "In sensitivity training, the learning emphasis falls heavily on learning how to give and receive feedback, a process that is countercultural because of our need to maintain face. Therefore, it elicits high levels of emotionality and anxiety. The process promises to give us new insights, to reveal our blind sides to us, and to provide opportunity to see ourselves as others see us. For many, this is not only novel, but potentially devastating—even though it may be ultimately necessary for self-improvement. To receive feedback is to put our illusions about ourselves on the line; to give feedback is to risk offending and unleashing hostility in the receiver" (Schein, 1993, p. 30).

Not interactivity = learning. Interactivity by itself shouldn't be conflated with effective learning (Picciano, 2002, p. 23). Rather, other design elements and a confluence of factors will cumulatively build toward effective learning.

Telepresence. Interaction requires the sense of presence of the various individuals in a global classroom. Students who feel connected to others in a community and who have a digital identity or "telepresence" there have been more likely to interact and participate. In ideal online interactions, participants may experience the "illusion of nonmediation" or fail to acknowledge the technologies that are mediating the exchanges (Lombard & Ditton, as cited by Picciano, 2002, p. 24).

Various types of telepresence have been discovered in the research. "Tammelin especially establishes a relationship between telepresence and social presence as one (telepresence), leading to the other (social presence). Biocca classifies presence into three types: spatial presence, self-reflective presence and social presence. Rourke, Anderson, Garrison, and Archer with respect to online learning environments provided a community of inquiry model with three presence components: cognitive, social, and teaching…Their model supports the design of online courses as active learning environments or communities dependent on instructors and students sharing ideas, information, and opinions. What is critical here is that presence in an online course is fundamentally a social phenomenon and manifests itself through interactions among students and instructors" (Picciano, 2002, p. 24).

For instructors to be present in a way that promotes trust, they need to post through and personalized biographies. They need to respond with a sense of timeliness and immediacy. Their postings need to be personalized, not simulating the natural language of a 'bot (robot). They need to maintain respect in every interaction, and they need to give respondents a sense that the feedback loop is complete. They need to use their own original voices. They need to demonstrate knowledge and professional experience. Their interactions should feel like a shared human encounter. They should not try to be perfect but to share mistakes as well; at the same time, they have to maintain the sense of authority. Online intercommunications need to have a high mutual coherence for sensemaking.

The receptiveness of an instructor to online learners may encourage their participation. "In a review of that research, Brophy and Good (1986) summarize the findings of dozens of studies about behaviors such as allowing wait time, asking questions of varying difficulty and complexity, selecting respondents, and reacting to correct and incorrect responses" (Aleven et al., 2003, p. 287).

Mediating social conflict. Social conflict among global e-learners is assumed as a necessary part of the interactions and the learning. Disagreements are seen as necessary for social change: "A certain view of the nature of social conflict, the conditions for social reconstruction or change, and the telos of goal of human progress follow from Mead's conception of the self. According to Mead, social conflict is not combat among those stimulated by primitive impulses but is, rather, oppositional action between socially structured individual capacities that call forth social attitudes and meanings" (Simpson, 1996, p. 119).

One of the central arguments for cultural sensitivities and localizations in global e-learning involves the sense of safety in online courses. Such an ecology may be created with a combination of policies (including civility guidelines), practices, instructor modeling, designed interactivity, and culture-enriched dialogues. Building a safe online space for contentious interactions will be critical to promote learning. After all, there are not only the costs of higher learning on the line but that of social risks and risks to self-identity in the face of potential failure.

Online instructors may need to develop various cross-cultural mediation skills. They need to help learners create a sense of self-awareness of their own cultural influences and how those affect their thinking and actions. "Generating a true appreciation of the challenges of cross-cultural communication can be difficult, however.

Some students are so deeply steeped in their own cultural traditions that the elements of other cultures are viewed as amusing, disgusting, or even pathological deviations from the norm" (Myers, Buoye, McDermott, Strickler, & Ryman, 2000, p. 95). This is all the more challenging given the fact that such learning is often tangential to the main curriculum, which are not often designed with cultural awareness in mind.

Cross-cultural contacts between learners should build their own sense of sophistication in engaging in a many-cultured world. "As cross-cultural contact continues to increase and the boundaries among cultures become less and less clear, the skills needed to negotiate a culturally complicated world will continue to grow in importance" (Sleek, 1998, as cited by Myers et al., 2000, p. 95).

Encouraging appropriate help-seeking behaviors. A sense of safety affects whether learners reach out for necessary help or whether they become "invisible" in their needs. Help seeking, as a self-regulated behavior, requires learner awareness of their learning and needs; it requires strategic behavior in seeking out the specific helps that would be most effective and the source from whom they should seek the help. In integrated learning environments (ILEs), the ability to seek appropriate help is especially critical (Aleven et al., 2003, p. 278). In collaborative learning environments, social factors may affect help-seeking behaviors (p. 279).

Ironically, those who most need help tend to be the least likely to get it or to use the scaffolding resources to enhance their learning. "In sum, the studies discussed above indicate that learners with lower prior knowledge—those who need help the most—are the least likely to use help appropriately when help is under students' control. This situation presents a challenge for the designers of ILEs, especially, as we have seen, there are good reasons for placing help under student control" (Aleven et al., 2003, p. 298).

Learners may still feel alienated even if they are present, suggest some researchers. The various presences need to coalesce into a sense of inclusive community. "However, as this concept is studied, the definition is expanding and being refined to include telepresence, cognitive presence, social presence, teaching presence, and other forms of presence. The term 'community' is related to presence and refers to a group of individuals who belong to a social unit such as students in a class. In an online course, terms such as communities of inquiry, communities of learners, and knowledge-building communities have evolved" (Picciano, 2002, p. 22).

Empowering Global Learners

One major goal of higher education has been to empower learners with the appropriate knowledge and skills to go out into the world and contribute. A number of strategies may strengthen global students.

Individuals, identities and their dignity. Creating mental spaces where identities may be explored, created and solidified has been a critical part of computer-mediated communications. Research has gone into the creation of "identity construction environments" known as ICEs, technological tools to help young people explore parts of their own identities (Bers, 2001, p. 367). Here, there may be the creation of "virtual auto-topographies" or "spaces for exploring identity" (p. 392).

Some researchers see the self as naturally fractured: "The self without an identity, the schizophrenic self, is authentic because it is, precisely, not an imposed, unified self that is a creation and creature of power. The schizophrenic self is oppositional and counter-systemic because power cannot find and express itself among a cacophony of internal unorganized babbling voices" (Simpson, 1996, p. 120). Others describe stable core identities with a variety of fleeting temporal identities.

Online spaces tend to show flat affect. Sometimes, online faculty will simply let a range of learners run through their course using automations and the facilitation of teaching or research assistants. A culturally sensitive approach would suggest the need for the solicitation of humanizing information from the learners. Student backgrounds and knowledge would be important to understand for tailoring and customizing the learning. This may involve the use of posted learner profiles. Also, this would mean treating learners with a deep sense of regard and individual human dignity, especially in terms of time and energy investment. The "whole student" movement suggests the importance of building the whole person along with the learning.

"Learner centric" instructional design for distance learning focuses on student needs in an online space. A "whole student" phenomenon has emerged in terms of distance education, in which an online instructor does not merely see a text name or avatar but a whole being (Osguthorpe et al., 2003, n.p.). A holistic interactive learning model must consider learners' individual knowledge bases, affective elements and cognitive strategies (both linear and nonlinear). The affective aspect of learners is important. A much longer time horizon is needed for the reaching of affective goals such as feelings of self-esteem and an internalized commitment to integrity and moral development.

Damage may occur to a person's sense of identity without deeper considerations. "In fact, lack of acknowledgment is devastating to most human beings" (Schein, 1993, p. 28). This phenomenon may be seen with the frustrations that occur when online students are called by the wrong name, or if their concerns are ignored or dismissed.

Building learning schemas. Deep learning often requires the creation of schemas or the cognitive structures of knowledge for the respective academic fields. Schemas are critical mind maps for information acquisition and processing, sense-making, and learning (Harris, 1994, p. 309).

A cultural component affects the development of schemas. "Schemas are typically conceptualized as subjective theories derived from one's experiences about how the world operates (Markus & Zajonc 1985) that guide perception, memory, and inference" (Fiske & Taylor, 1984, as cited by Harris, 1994, p. 310). Information that conflicts with existing schemas may be ignored, recast to integrate with current schemas, change the schema or result in a new schema subcategory (Lord & Foti, 1986, as cited Harris, 1994, p. 311).

Aspects of online system design may influence help seeking. The class tone, the scaffolding, the publicizing of help resources, and other elements may promote richer help awareness and targeted help seeking. The amount of prior knowledge of the domain affects learner help-seeking behaviors and the quality of how they used the help. Those with less domain knowledge sought help more often but did not show improved learning results from that help; in contrast, those with more prior domain knowledge made fewer errors but were more likely than those with lower prior knowledge to seek help after making mistakes. One downside to those with more prior knowledge is that they often overestimated their understanding of the learning material. "As a result of such overconfidence, they may process the text less deeply" (Glenberg & Epstein, 1987; Kintsch, 1998, as cited by Aleven et al., 2003, p. 297).

This research would suggest the need for surfacing prior domain knowledge and tailoring the online learning experience to the various learners' needs. Their awareness of such tendencies regarding help seeking may enhance learner behaviors to be more constructive and less maladaptive.

Surfacing the past and priming learners. There is growing evidence that learning processes and outcomes are strongly influenced by the epistemological beliefs of learners and their teachers. Epistemological beliefs are beliefs about the nature of knowledge. Depending upon the theory, epistemological beliefs include beliefs about the structure and stability of knowledge, about sources and

justification of knowledge (e.g., Hofer, 2001), about learning and abilities (e.g., Schommer, 1990), or about the relation of knowledge and beliefs (e.g., Alexander & Dochy, 1995; Souterland, Sinatra, & Matthews, 2001). It is generally assumed that epistemological beliefs change during educational processes from more naïve views (e.g., knowledge is absolute, knowledge is an accumulation of facts) to more sophisticated beliefs (e.g., knowledge is relative and contextual, knowledge is a complex network). Further, it is widely believed that a more sophisticated belief system has positive effects on learning processes (for a critique of this view, see Elby & Hammer, 2001, as cited by Aleven et al., 2003, pp. 304-305).

The teaching of culture not only prepares learners for future cultural experiences in study and work and adds complexity to their sense of the subject matter, but there's an entertainment value (Chavez, 2002, pp. 129-130).

Power sharing in online courses. The sharing of power with learners often means greater "say" over learner assignments. The mere structure of online courses has suggested a devolution of power from a centralized instructor core to more of a shared learning environment (Strother, 2003, p. 354). That said, the control allotted by learning management system (LMS) and other e-learning technologies may also allow instructors a deep level of control that may be used in authoritarian instructor-centered ways.

Access mitigations. Global e-learning instructors should pay attention to the resource environment for the various learners. The cost of distance learning itself may be prohibitive with tuition, texts, fees, and learning resources. A major challenge may be making sure that the resources required are accessible, with possible local substitutions that may make the learning costs less burdensome. Third-party open-source freeware may be used for student assignments.

Technology mitigations. Online learning technologies may be used to enhance the learning. The identification of a portfolio as "a meaningful way to integrate language and culture in a structure that provides opportunities for students to learn about foreign culture while using other skills—reading, listening, writing and speaking" (Lee, 1997, p. 355).

"Portfolios provide students with a practical and meaningful way to gain both language and cultural knowledge, and offer many advantages to students. First, they evoke learners' interest by allowing students to focus on cultural components that interest students most. Second, the portfolio method leads them to investigate a foreign culture individually and in greater depth than they would be able to do in a normal teacher-centered classroom context. Third, selecting, planning, organizing, and producing a portfolio involves higher order cognition as well as the four basic language skills (Moore 1994. as cited by Lee, 1997, p. 358). The persistence of portfolios and the richness of the reflective learning that may be enabled with portfolios here enrich cultural conceptualizations.

Technologies should not be seen as a panacea for learning. Rather, it's their use and deployment that matter. "While studies have supported the use of technology as a method of increasing performance and student satisfaction in a course, the current project did not support this body of literature. No statistically significant relationship was found between the use of virtual learning tools and grade outcome…This lack of significance may be in part due to lack of variance in the measure and in part an insufficient operationalization (sic) of the use of that particular method" (Dietz, 2002, pp. 85-86).

Designing a High-Trust Learning Ecology

Learning involves risk-taking. Trust is a "social glue" construct that encourages learners to take risks. It is an essential part of human relations and cooperation; it has been labeled a "key enabler" and a "foundation of support for high performance

(Shaw, 1997, p. 7, as cited by Hai-Jew, 2007b, pp. 1-25).

The importance of mutual trust. The literature on global e-learning involves cautionary tales. Third-party academic matchmaker agencies have mixed reputations in terms of their efficacies (and motivations) in bringing together entities from higher education for partnerships. Others warn of years of work without payment. Quality standards between institutional partners have been an area of concern (Bates, 2003, n.p.). Various institutions of higher education have used covenants and contracts, franchise models, mediating agencies, and retainers in order to build a structural sense of trust with their various international partners.

One researcher addresses the advantages of a franchise arrangement, in mitigating financial exposure, in ensuring a supply of fee-paying students, and in shielding the institution against criticisms of differing entry requirements with in-country learners. "When students are registered and accredited through another institution, this provides a firewall regarding admissions, prior qualifications, and English language requirements for the institution developing the programs" (Bates, 1999, n.p.) Most importantly, a franchise institution "can provide cultural adaptation at both the development and delivery stage of the program. Furthermore, students who are not fluent in English can participate in their own language, through the discussion forums and the submission of assignments," writes Bates (1999, n.p.).

Trust as a cultural value may be higher in some cultural contexts. "In many Asian countries, where instructor-led training is linked to cultural issues of trust and relationship building, it is a challenge to use e-learning (often an impersonal mode of training) without modification" (Strother, 2003, p. 353). That trust still has to be built albeit through the mediated technologies.

Trust in online learning spaces, while often present as a majority assumption, is important to nurture and protect. Elements that may erode trust may include "'lack of communication with the instructor, poorly worded instructions, unclear classroom expectations, anything that confuses or shows lack of respect for the student will cause disrespect in the student,' wrote one instructor (C. Lower, Online instructor interview, April 2005, p. 5). 'Malfunctions and slow response to troubles,' wrote J.K. Erickson (Online instructor interview, April 2005, p. 3). Changes made on the 'spur of the moment' might cause learner discomfort (B. Culwell, Online instructor interview, April 2005, p. 2). Poor participation by learners early in the quarter might contribute to mistrust as well, according to one respondent" (Hai-Jew, 2007b, p. 17).

It is important not to overwhelm learners with "technological sophistication or advanced online pedagogies" (Arbaugh, 2001, p. 49). Online instructors need to lead and pace to avoid learner frustrations and burnout.

Handling of student information. Instructors handle student information that may be sensitive and private. The "indestructibility" of digital information and the low cost to their archival have brought up questions of best how to handle such data. In addition, government subpoenas for particular information have made those who provide such access hesitant to collect and store such data because anything collected may be used or misused beyond the original purpose. Some countries maintain personal dossiers and records of their citizens for life. The privacy rights lauded in the West and codified into laws like the Family Education Rights and Privacy Act (FERPA) are unheard of in other countries.

Another angle regarding student information relates to original ideas and inventions. While undergraduate students may often not surface new thinking, many in graduate studies may, particularly if there are research components in the online learning. Ethically, instructors should not use the intellectual output of students to benefit themselves or their own ambitions. Rather, such work should be supported to its full fruition in the learning environment, in publications, and someday in patents and R&D. Tracking the provenance of information may be a lot easier given the indestructibility of information online, but it would be critical to define the terms of information handling and support.

Holistic support for learning. Global e-learning students may need access to the databases at libraries and the support of professional librarians. Some will need educational and career advising. Some will need tutoring supports. Some will want help desk supports regarding various e-learning technologies. They may want to build virtual social lives with their peers from around the world; they may want to "network" and make professional connections abroad. A "whole student" build would consider these various needs and provide structures to access these online. This endeavor to create a social space will be pitted against the discontinuities of technological culture and its isolating effects.

Virtual social needs. For many of the traditional-aged global e-learners, their college years offer opportunities for connecting to their peers. Those who would design a working online learning ecology needed to build opportunities for nonacademic communications. They could plan open situations for serendipity and spontaneity, and opportunities for the online learners to meet, interact, and spark new ideas and insights. However, this should be balanced against the risks of frivolity and distractions from the actual learning. Some suggest the building of areas without instructor presence for such social needs.

A "social director" may conduct various events for global online learners. Events may include social hours, short-task group work, and digital gallery shows of student academic or professional works. This venue may feature outside guests. Synchronous and asynchronous types of interactivity may be engaged.

WHAT ARE SOME HELPFUL PRINCIPLES AND STRATEGIES FOR PROMOTING LOCALIZATION IN GLOBAL E-LEARNING?

Localization refers to endeavors to tie global e-learning to the respective unique time-place circumstances of global learners. These ties involve the use of local resources. They involve designing learning to be applicable to those spaces. This concept of localization involves some underlying premises.

First is the importance of a learner's past "habitus" ("a system of dispositions" based on past experience and learning, in a term defined by Bourdieu, 1977) in affecting the learner's expectations and skills (Brown, 1987; Jenkins, 1992) and how the learner has interacted with that habitus based on his/her personality (Harker & May, 1993; Bourdieu, 1993, pp. 76-87, as cited by Bloomer, 2001, p. 437). A major piece of the habitus may be influenced by the affordances of that learners growing up years and social context.

A second major piece to localization refers to the geographical context of the global learners. Time and place involve critical pieces of culture and influences on both group and individual levels.

"Human beings thus do not process information into what is known in necessarily 'rational' or instrumental ways. Instead, our mediating conceptual systems are shaped by lifestyles, work experiences, customs, language, mythologies—*by cultures.* In the contemporary era of globalization involving instantaneous transnational communications, however, Lipschutz believes that such personal and local biases are being increasingly 'influenced by knowledge and practices originating elsewhere' (Lipschutz with Mayer, 1996, p. 72). A continuous struggle between the global and the local is under way and this, he says, is due in part to the relevance and resilience of local cultures" (Comor, 2001, p. 395).

To one writer, this endeavor of connecting to the local may be dubbed relocalization. He writes, "Globalization is unfolding in a two-stage manner. In the first stage, global media and businesses extend their reach into new domains throughout the world. In a second stage, these same businesses and media are relocalized in order to best meet the economic and social imperatives of functioning in different regions of the world..." (Warschauer, 2000, p. 512).

Considering the students' various environments supports the concept of "whole student" learning design, in order to support the meeting of their many needs over the years of the undergraduate, graduate, and post-graduate education and beyond.

Three main endeavors in localization are as follows:

1. Connection to learner's own locale and environment: relating the learning to nearby or in-country expertise, the unique local economy, the unique job market, and other elements. The purpose of this connectivity is to emphasize the applicability of the learning. This should strengthen learners' senses of the value of their learning and show the applications to the larger environment, well beyond virtual spaces.

2. The strategic use of local resources: connecting to local libraries, labs, institutions of higher education, fieldtrip destinations, and learning communities for face-to-face interactions. This endeavor aims to magnify the learning value of the online learning. Local resources may enrich the learning and provide apprenticeship spaces in which to apply the new learning. This endeavor may be restrained by the lack of formal connections, but it's possible that short-term contractual arrangements may be created to allow the use of specific local resources. Global e-learning students themselves may

make some of the connections for their own learning.

3. Sustainable learning and professional life after graduation: connecting global learners to other co-learners for face-to-face interactions and social needs. A critical piece to higher education is to sustain the learning over time and to support a thriving professional life for graduates. Localization may support the connections that allow both to happen. It may encourage more informal learning as well.

FUTURE RESEARCH DIRECTIONS

The broad concepts of cultural sensitivity and localization in global e-learning promote the adaptivity and customization for global learners. These provide ways to mitigate the field independence of online learning for fuller learner experiences and memory retention. Indeed, a range of issues need to be considered: branding, course ecology, curriculum design, instructional strategies/pedagogical approaches, multimedia builds, information handling, and direct instruction in e-learning.

Standards for mitigations. Proper mitigations should show clear learning value, and these should be visible to the learners themselves. The design of online learning should place learners in a situated practice where cultural differences are explored and encouraged. Such issues should be overt, with critical framing around the topic. The cultural pieces may build incrementally over a student's educational career and beyond. The localization aspect should relate the online learning directly to learners' lived lives on-ground and their concerns. It should support their use of local resources. Localization should encourage the quality of learning and work after graduation.

Constant vigilance. Effective applications of cultural sensitivity and localization mean that staff members need to be constantly vigilant to the implications of real-world events. They need to maintain open channels of communications with their learners and a respect for their base of knowledge and needs. This will require no less than a cosmopolitan approach. Learner needs must be assessed and responded to, without lapsing into stereotyping or broad overgeneralizations. There must be candor about the underlying values and approaches taken. Those supporting global e-learning should be encouraged to tap a broad range of resources to understand other peoples and cultures, including less-common channels like the literature from a country (Burniske, 1999, p. 133). The design of e-learning should avoid negative learning and false correlations, and this may be done through instructor and learner awareness and uses of language to challenge such concepts.

Course cultural temperatures. Cultural temperatures in courses may stem from purposive design and conscious attitudes. Such temperatures may also evolve based on unconscious attitudes and unthinking actions. It would be safe to assert that all courses have some cultural temperature, likely viewable as positive and negative for different groups of learners and individuals. Instructors need to be aware of the cultural temperatures of their own courses and the influences of the cultural context ("doctrines, values, and practices") on their courses (Warschauer, 1998, p. 78).

Automated learning. How cultural sensitivities and localization may apply to automated learning (without instructor presence), automated tutoring, and online ecological design will require much scrutiny and research. "The ideal learning environment lies between the two poles of actual and potential development" (Alm-Lequex, 2001, p. 2).

Long-term professional supports for global e-learners. Online instructors need to strive to see global e-learners as individuals potentially deserving of graduate learning opportunities, international jobs, and other benefits that often come with abilities. Too often, online instructors forgo the "talent spotting" that happens in real-time real-space. Global e-learning needs to consider more long-term professional relationships as one option.

Course designs and redesigns. Administrators, faculty and staff may choose to pay more attention to both greater cultural sensitivity and localization endeavors in curriculum development and online instruction. Instead of merely retrofitting courses for global learners, fresh course builds may be enacted. Faculty and staff members may train on how to better reach and learn from and about their global students. Such training may engage a range of issues such as managing learner expectations; setting clear deadlines, guidelines and expectations; applying and developing empathy; designing effective interactivity; communicating effectively; designing effective instructor telepresence; creating online classroom "safety;" integrating international dimensions of the academic field; developing self-awareness of cultural attitudes; building multicultural knowledge; working to fairly assess student work across cross-cultural lines, and facilitating boundary crossings, when approaching global learners. A rich range of multicultural global competencies may be developed.

Creation of digital contents. The development of digital content should involve cultural sensitivities and localizations. Information—textual, graphical, aural and multimedia—is not value neutral. Meanings are context-dependent oftentimes, and messages may have many meanings (polysemic). Privileging some points of view over others may show arrogance, cultural imperialism or provincialism. What makes global communications even more difficult relates to the fact that culture is often assumed and invisible to the individual. While some of this exists on a surface level, it also exists in the human subconscious. Cultural, historical, geographical and mass communications literacies may enhance the creation of effective digital learning objects in global online learning.

The research in this field is rich with possibility, with focuses on the various learner groups and their unique needs. There may be general models for analyzing the embedded culture of a global e-learning course. There may be cultural "accessibility" assessments of learning experiences. There need to be clearer strategies to reach out to global e-learners to better capitalize on their local learning resources. Ideally, researchers from across countries and cultures will collaborate more to raise cultural sensitivities, and greater partnerships may promote localizations across time, miles, institutions and nations.

At heart, both cultural sensitivities and localization in global e-learning are about accommodating international learners in their various contexts and situations.

AUTHOR NOTE

A "cultural sensitivities and localizations course analysis (CSLCA)" tool is available in Appendix A. This tool covers the following arenas of a global e-learning course.

1. Course ecology
2. Curricular content
3. Planned and unplanned interactivity
4. Instructional strategies

ACKNOWLEDGMENT

Thanks to my former students from the People's Republic of China and the U.S. for all that they taught me. Many have contributed to my learning on these issues. Most recently, I would like to express gratitude to Dr. Barbara Leigh Smith, Dr. Carol Stockdale, Connie Broughton, and Dr. John Jacob Gardiner, who are global boundary-crossers, all. Thanks to R. Max, hardy traveler. The Society for Applied Learning Technology (SALT) has offered a constructive venue for much learning about e-learning these past few years. Lastly, thanks to the many talented folks at the Office of Mediated Education, K-State, who are so generous with their expertise and creativity.

REFERENCES

Aldrich, H. E., & Waldinger, R. (1990). Ethnicity and entrepreneurship. *Annual Review of Sociology, 16*, 111-135.

Aleven, V., Stahl, E., Schworm, S., Fischer, F., & Wallace, R. (2003, Autumn). Help seeking and help design in interactive learning environments. *Review of Educational Research, 73*(3), 277-320.

Alm-Lequeux, A. (2001, Spring). Using the Internet as a zone of proximal development for teaching indirect speech: A Vygotskian approach. *Die Unterrichtspraxis/Teaching German, 34*(1), 1-9.

Arbaugh, J. B. (2001). How instructor immediacy behaviors affect student satisfaction and Learning in Web-based courses. *Business Communication Quarterly, 64*, 42-54.

Aronson, J. D. (1996, April). The consequences of free trade in information flows. *International Affairs, 72*(2), 311-328.

Bates, T. (1999, September 21-23). Cultural and ethical issues in international distance education. In *Proceedings of theEngaging Partnerships Collaboration and Partnership in Distance Education: UBC/CREAD Conference,* Vancouver, Canada, (n.p.).

Belz, J. A., & Müller-Hartmann, A. (2003, Spring). Teachers as intercultural learners: Negotiating German-American telecollaboration along the institutional fault line. *The Modern Language Journal, 87*(1), 71-89.

Bers, M. U. (2001). Identity construction environments: Developing personal and moral values through the design of a virtual city. *The Journal of the Learning Sciences, 10*(2), 365-415.

Billington, J. H. (2001, December). Humanizing the information revolution. *Proceedings of the American Philosophical Society, 145*(4), 579-586.

Bloomer, M. (2001, September). Young lives, learning and transformation: Some theoretical considerations. *Oxford Review of Education, 27*(3), 429-449.

Burniske, R.W. (1999, November). Iban on the Infobahn: Can we integrate the Global Village without annihilating cultures? *The English Journal, 89*(2), 131-135.

Chakrapani, P. N., & Ekbia, H. R. (2004). Opening up technological education: The perspective from social informatics. *IEEE,* 144-147.

Chavez, M. (2002, Autumn). We say "culture" and students ask "What?": University students' definitions of foreign language culture. *Die Unterrichtspraxis/Teaching German, 35*(2), 129-140.

Chester, A., & Gwynne, G. (1998, December). Online teaching: Encouraging collaboration through anonymity. *Journal of Computer-Mediated Communication, 4*(2), n.p.

Clegg, S., Hudson, A., & Steel, J. (2003). The emperor's new clothes: Globalization and e-learning in higher education. *British Journal of Sociology of Education, 24*(1), 39-53.

Comor, E. (2001, September). The role of communication in global civil society: Forces, processes, prospects. *International Studies Quarterly, 45*(3), 389-408.

Crisp, G., Thiele, D., Scholten, I., Barker, S., & Baron, J. (2003, December 7-10). Interact, Integrate, Impact. In *Proceedings of the 20ᵗʰ Annual Conference of the Australasian Society for Computers in Learning in Tertiary Education,* Adelaide, Australia, (pp. 1-12).

Dietz, T. L. (2002, January). Predictors of success in large enrollment introductory courses: An examination of the impact of learning communities and virtual learning resources on student success in an introductory level sociology course. *Teaching Sociology, 30*(1), 80-88.

Hacker, D. J., & Niederhauser, D. S. (2000, Winter). Promoting deep and durable learning in the online classroom. *New Directions for Teaching and Learning,* (84), 53-63.

Hai-Jew, S. (2007a, January 31-February 2). Cultural sensitivities in e-learning: Designing hybridized e-learning for Native American Learners through "The Enduring Legacies Project" (case study). In *Proceedings of the Orlando New Technologies Conference: Society for Applied Learning Technologies Conference Presentation.*

Hai-Jew, S. (2007b). *Trust factor in online instructor-led college courses* (pp. 1-25). Unpublished manuscript.

Harris, S.G. (1994, August). Organizational culture and individual sensemaking: A schema-based perspective. *Organization Science,* 5(3), 309-321.

Isman, A. (2005, June). Diffusion of distance education in North Cyprus. *International Journal of Instructional Technology & Distance Learning,* 2(6). Retrieved April 22, 2008, from http://www.itdl.org/Journal/Jun_05/article06.htm

Jaimes, A. (2006). Human-centered multimedia: Culture, deployment and access. In N. Dimitrova (Ed.), *Visions and views* (pp. 12-19). IEEE Philips Research.

Joseph, P. B., Bravmann, S. L., Windschitl, M. A., Mikel, E. R., & Green, N. S. (2000). *Cultures of curriculum* (pp. 3-4, 12, 17). Mahwah, NJ: Lawrence Erlbaum.

Kerbo, H. R. (1981, June). College achievement among Native Americans: A research note. *Social Forces, 59*(4), 1275-1280.

Kirkness, V. J., & Barnhardt, R. (2001). First nations and higher education: The four R's—respect, relevance, reciprocity, responsibility. In R. Hayoe & J. Pan (Eds.), *Knowledge across cultures: A contribution to dialogue among civilizations.* Hong Kong: Comparative Education Research Centre, the University of Hong Kong.

Kuzma, L. M. (1998, September). The World Wide Web and active learning in the international relations classroom. *PS: Political Science and Politics, 31*(3), 578-584.

Ladson-Billings, G. (1995a, Summer). But that's just good teaching! The case for culturally relevant pedagogy. *Theory into Practice, 34*(3), 159-165.

Ladson-Billings, G. (1995b, Autumn). Toward a theory of culturally relevant pedagogy. *American Educational Research Journal, 32*(3), 465-491.

Lajoie, S. P. (2003, November). Transitions and trajectories for studies of expertise. *Educational Researcher, 32*(8), 21-25.

Lee, L. (1997, May). Using portfolios to develop 1.2 cultural knowledge and awareness of students in intermediate Spanish. *Hispania, 80*(2), 355-367.

Levin, J. S. (2001, September). Public policy, community colleges, and the path to globalization. *Higher Education, 42*(2), 237-262.

Liaw, M.-L. (2006, September). E-learning and the development of intercultural competence. *Language Learning & Technology, 10*(3), 49-64.

Lynch, M. M. (2001, November-December). *Effective student preparation for online learning.* The Technology Source Archives at the University of North Carolina.

McCarty, T. L., Lynch, R. H., Wallace, S., & Benally, A. (1991, March). Classroom inquiry and Navajo learning styles: A call for reassessment. *Anthropology & Education Quarterly, 22*(1), 42-59.

McCool, M. (2006, December). Adapting e-learning for Japanese audiences tutorial. *IEEE Transactions on Professional Communication, 49*(4), 335-345.

Mehlenbacher, B., Miller,C. R., Covington, D., & Larsen, J. S. (2000, June). Active and interactive learning online: A comparison of Web-based and conventional writing classes. *IEEE Transactions on Professional Communication, 43*(2), 166-184.

Myers, D. J., Buoye, A. J., McDermott, J., Strickler, D. E., & Ryman, R. G. (2000, January). Signals, symbols, and vibes: An exercise in cross-cultural interaction. *Teaching Sociology, 29*, 95-101.

Ngor, A. L. C. Y. (2001, July). The prospects for using the Internet in collaborative design education with China. *Higher Education, 42*(1), 47-60.

Noble, D. F. (1998). Digital diploma mills, Part II: The coming battle over online instruction. *Sociological Perspectives, 41*(4). The Academy under Siege (pp. 815-825).

Oakes, T. (2000, August). China's provincial identities: Reviving regionalism and reinventing "Chineseness." *The Journal of Asian Studies, 59*(3), 667-692.

Ogbu, J. U. (1987, December). Variability in minority school performance: A problem in search of an explanation. *Anthropology & Education Quarterly, 18*(4), Explaining the School Performance of Minority Students (pp. 312- 334).

Osguthorpe, R. T., Osguthorpe, R. D., Jacob, W. J., & Davies, R. (2003, March-April). The moral dimensions of instructional design. *Educational Technology,* 19-23.

Pewewardy, C. (2002). Learning styles of American Indian/Alaska Native students: A review of the literature and implications for practice. *Journal of American Indian Education, 41*(3), 22-56.

Pewewardy, C., & Hammer, P. C. (2003, December). *Culturally responsive teaching for American Indian students* (p. EDO-RC-03-10). ERIC Clearinghouse on Rural Education and Small Schools.

Picciano, A. G. (2002, July). Beyond student perceptions: Issues of interaction, presence, and performance in an online course. *Journal of Asynchronous Learning Networks (JALN), 6*(1), 21-40.

Sabin, C., & Ahern, T. C. (2002, November). Instructional design and culturally diverse learners. In *Proceedings of the 32nd ASEE/IEEE Frontiers in Education Conference,* (pp. S1C-10 to S1C-14).

Schein, E. H. (1993, April). On dialogue, culture, and organizational learning. *Reflections, 4*(4). Society for Organizational Learning (pp. 27-38).

Schultz, M., & Hatch, M. J. (1996, April). Living with multiple paradigms: The case of paradigm interplay in organizational culture studies. *The Academy of Management Review, 21*(2), 529-557.

Simpson, J. H. (1996, Summer). "The Great Reversal:" Selves, communities, and the global system. *Sociology of Religion, 57*(2), 115-125.

Starke-Meyerring, D. (1999). Developing an online learning environment for international technical communication. *Communication jazz: Improvising the new international communication culture* (pp. 13-20). IEEE.

Strother, J. B. (2003). Shaping blended learning pedagogy for East Asian learning styles. *The shape of knowledge* (pp. 353-357). IEEE.

Sumner, J., & Dewar, K. (2002). Peer-to-peer e-learning and the team effect on course completion. In *Proceedings of the International Conference on Computers in Education.*

Warschauer, M. (1997, Winter). Computer-mediated collaborative learning: Theory and practice. *The Modern Language Journal, 81*(4), 470-481.

Warschauer, M. (1998, March). Online learning in sociocultural context. *Anthropology & Education Quarterly, 29*(1), 68-88.

Warschauer, M. (2000, Autumn). The changing global economy and the future of English teaching. *TESOL Quarterly, 34*(3). TESOL in the 21st Century (pp. 511-535).

Wellman, B., & Hampton, K. (1999, November). Living networked on and offline. *Contemporary Sociology, 28*(6), 648-654.

Wilson, H. D. (2001, May). Informatics: New media and paths of data flow. *Taxon*, 50(2). Golden Jubilee, Part 4 (pp. 381-387).

APPENDIX A: CULTURAL SENSITIVITIES AND LOCALIZATIONS COURSE ANALYSIS (CSLCA) TOOL FOR GLOBAL E-LEARNING COURSES

The cultural sensitivities and localizations approaches were applied to the four following areas of an online course: course ecology, curricular content, planned and unplanned interactivity, and instructional strategies. A course ecology refers to the online and off-line spaces that comprise an e-learning experience. Curricular content refers to the (digital and other) materials used for the learning. Planned and unplanned interactivity refers to the both asynchronous and synchronous interactions: designed small group work, dialogues, team assignments, collaborations, and other interpersonal communications and work. Instructional strategies refer to the pedagogical designs underlying a course or online learning experience.

1.   Course ecology
2.   Curricular content
3.   Planned and unplanned interactivity
4.   Instructional strategies

This draft tool may be applied during a course build, during the teaching of an online course, and probably most effectively to an archived course with all the interactions (both in the archived learning management system (LMS) and the outside-course interactions like e-mails, faxes, phone conversations, and letters). A few of the questions may not apply in the different stages, but most will apply with minor changes in the verb tense.

Figure 3. A "cultural sensitivities and localizations course analysis" tool application timeline

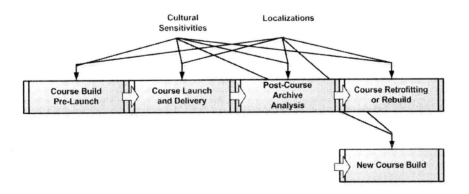

A "Cultural Sensitivities and Localizations Course Analysis" Tool Application Timeline
(Hai-Jew, 2007)

The "Cultural Sensitivities and Localizations Course Analysis (CSLCA)" Tool (for Global E-Learning)

Cultural Sensitivities

1. **Cultural Sensitivities: Course Ecology**
   - Is the courseware flexible enough for delivering the learning in a variety of ways? Instructor-led? Automated?
   - Are there ways to scaffold or structure the learning? Can the learning be linear, branched or a la carte?
   - Is automated or live tutoring (or both) available to support learners?
   - Are the tools in the learning management system (LMS) named accurately for easy use? Is there a clear logical structure? Does the LMS support the understanding of a clear e-learning path?
   - Are the supporting materials (tangibles, information, human resources, locations) required for learning widely and easily accessible during the term of the learning?
   - Are simulations repeatable? Are there explanations for simulations?
   - Are the human depictions in the simulations nonoffensive and nonstereotypical?
   - In live interactions (iTV, Net-mediated), do all learners have equal access in terms of the technologies?
   - Do the video recordings show a variety of individuals in the learning and professional environments (without omission or stereotyping)?
   - Is the online course accessible? Are there accommodations for those who may have disabilities? Are all audio and video files transcripted? Are the mitigations for accessibility at the same learning quality as those offered for others?
   - Is the sound quality in the digital contents clear and high-quality? Are the pronunciations accurate but also varied in terms of different accents?
   - Does the instructor telepresence show professional credibility, care for learners, humanity and respect for others?
   - Do digital objects and announcements anticipate learner needs?
   - Is the course tone and atmosphere welcoming? Are learner questions and interactions encouraged?
   - Does the posted information lead to a variety of digital resources for full support for learners?
   - Does the power structure in the course reflect even power distributions among learners?
   - Do the learners have power to make changes to the learning environment and their learning quality and experiences? Are they able to customize their learning?
   - Is the learning space transparent, open and accountable to the learners, in terms of administrative oversight and administrative presence?
   - Outside of online spaces, are there other aspects to the course, such as designed assignments, research, fieldtrips, observations, apprenticeships, and other types of rich learning? Is online learning enriched and value-added?
   - How strict or lenient is the course policy structure? How closely do these policies reflect the ethos of the larger organization? How closely do these policies reflect the values of the respective learners' home countries' learning organizations?

- How much follow-through occurs regarding policy stances? Are these policies applied in a fair and egalitarian way?
- How is the online course branded in terms of text, graphics, logos, interactivity, and designed online space? How is the branding perceived by learners?
- How is information handled by the instructor? Administration? Peer learners? What informational policy is used? Are intellectual property rights adhered to? How long is information kept? Under what grounds will learner information be shared with law enforcement or government agencies?
- How much power do learners have to affect this space? How much power do they have to customize their own space within the online learning LMS?
- How much flux or change occurs in this online ecology? How persistent is the online space?
- Are learners given sufficient time early in the learning term to acclimate to the LMS? The online course materials? The instructor's teaching approaches? The other learners?
- Does this learning ecology reflect underlying values and worldviews? Does it reject particular values and worldviews?
- Are certain political stances "privileged" and other stances not? Are certain "voices" privileged or validated over other voices? Are there certain voices that are not heard in this course? Or do all views have at least initial equal access before they are debated?
- How neutral or "cultured" is this online space?
- Are the technologies used in an online classroom—the third-party plug-ins, the specialized software programs, the interactivity-supports—equally available to all the learners in the course? If prices are prohibitive, are there any mitigations for costs?
- How much are the support functions of a campus made available to the global e-learners?

2. **Cultural Sensitivities: Curricular Content**
   - Does the syllabus offer insights on underlying worldviews, cultures or approaches to the particular subject or academic field?
   - How is the course e-learning path or trajectory organized? Is the pacing flexible or strictly deadline-driven/time bound? Is there sufficient room to conceptualize time differently?
   - Are course objectives clearly defined? Are they objectively measurable?
   - Are the grading strategies objective or subjective?
   - In terms of feedback, do learners get sufficient information to improve their work?
   - Are there real-world student examples of the various types of assignments from a variety of different learners, to give learners a sense of what is expected?
   - Do the assignments have clear application to the various global learners' lives?
   - Are the group projects and collaborations set up to enhance learner success?
   - Are learners of various types, locales, ages, and cultures intermingled in the interactive assignments?
   - Are there a variety of assessment strategies used? Do these accommodate various types of learners?
   - Are these assessments clearly explained to learners? Is there sufficient debriefing about the interactivity? Group dynamics? Dyadic work? Individual work?

- If learners have questions about the various assignments and assessments, are these handled in a fair and clear way?
- Are the assignments prepackaged by a publishing house or press, or are the assignments more original to the instructor(s)?
- Is the Internet used to extend the value of the learning? What sites are used as validated and usable sites? What criteria are used in the selection of such sites?
- If guests are brought into the course, what range of viewpoints do they add? What constituencies do they represent?
- How much of the online course is prepackaged, and how much of it is in play once the learning term starts? How much variance is there in terms of ranges of viewpoints?
- Does the instructor only draw from local resources, or does he/she draw from a global base of speakers and information?
- How much power do learners have in choosing topics for research projects?
- How much learning do students bring to the online class? How much do students learn from each other?
- In scenarios and role plays, how open-ended (stochastic) or close-ended/predetermined are the scenarios? How many possible options are considered? Which viewpoints are supported, and which viewpoints are not? Do the scenarios and role plays apply to the various realities of the different learners? Do the scenarios and role plays strike learners as authentic or believable or applicable?
- Are the digital learning objects (lectures, video clips, flashcards, slideshows, animated screencasts, simulations and others) well designed? Are these "boxed" premade objects or created locally? What is the quality of the digital learning objects? Does the learning of these objects apply to the various learner's respective situations?
- Is the learning exclusionary or inclusive of a variety of cultures?
- Is there cultural channeling of learners into different paths? If so, is this done fairly?
- If real-time synchronous events are scheduled, do all learners have fair access to participate in that that event?

3. **Cultural Sensitivities: Planned and Unplanned Interactivity**
   - Are learners given time to introduce themselves and to get to know each other?
   - How much interaction does the instructor have with learners as individuals off-line (via e-mail, fax, telephone, and others), as groups or teams, and as a whole class?
   - What is the quality of instructor communications? Does the instructor add substantive comments? Does the instructor show respect in how he/she treats others?
   - How much "immediacy" is in the instructor commentary? Are the comments prepackaged and rote, or are they substantive and original?
   - What sorts of planned interactivity has been designed into the e-learning?
   - How much interactivity is required of peers among themselves? How much oversight does the instructor bring to the interactivity?
   - What sorts of unplanned interactivity has been created in terms of the course "affordances"? Are there learner lounges or "cafes" where learners may interact with each other in a non-academic way?

- What sorts of outside-LMS interactions are encouraged? Do learners ever meet face-to-face?
- What sorts of asynchronous interactions are encouraged?
- What sorts of synchronous interactions are encouraged?
- Are there clearly defined times when the instructor is available for "office hours" or other types of support?
- How are student privacy rights protected? How are student intellectual property rights protected in the classroom?
- How are student talents, apprenticeships and professional development endeavors encouraged and supported?
- How many opportunities do learners have to explore and express their own backgrounds and cultural values with others in the online class?

4. **Cultural Sensitivities: Instructional Strategies**
   - What identifiable pedagogical strategies are employed in the online course? What types of learning styles are engaged, and which are not? Are more difficult hurdles raised based on cultural grounds than others?
   - How much variety is there in pedagogical strategies, in order to accommodate different learning styles?
   - How are conflicts resolved? Are disagreements handled fairly? Are individuals' reputations and "faces" protected and saved? Does the instructor also rightly handle facts in the conflict?
   - How much power do learners have in making decisions about their own learning? How much scaffolding (via information, directions and tools) is provided to support their decision-making?
   - How rich and supportive are the official feedback messages from the instructor, teaching assistants, and other online teaching facilitators?
   - What sorts of "takeaways" do learners have from their learning that will apply to their professional development and growth?

Localizations

1. **Localizations: Course Ecology**
   - What local sites on the Internet are used as learning resources?
   - Are foreign language sources used on the site?
   - What local supporting materials (tangibles, information, human resources, locations) are used for the learning?
   - What mitigations are available for localization issues?
   - What global influences does the instructor show in his/her telepresence plan?
   - How much power do learners have to localize their learning to make it applicable to their own situations?
   - Are fresh digital learning materials created by learners posted and shared in the online course?

- What outside resources beyond the LMS are accessed by the learning? Do learners have abilities to make use of the local resources in their respective communities?
- Does the instructor show awareness of possible local resources that may be used?
- Are there practical policies and mitigations regarding the use of local resources?
- Are the simulations and role plays used relevant to the respective local situations of learners, or do they come across as false or inapplicable?
- Are the localized materials created by learners treated according to the international Berne convention to respect the learners' intellectual property rights?
- Do the various localization aspects of the learners add to the richness of the learning for the entire group of learners? Do these localization contributions by learners add to the richness of future renditions of the course?

2. **Localizations: Curricular Content**
   - What globalization/localization awareness is expressed in the course syllabus?
   - Is there flexibility in the course schedule and e-learning trajectory to accommodate the various localization challenges of learners?
   - Do the course objectives show global or international awareness along with localization awareness?
   - Does the grading strategy show any valuation of the global diversity of the learners?
   - Do the assignments allow learner flexibility in using local topics or resources? Does the learning apply to a variety of local situations?
   - Do group projects and collaborations take advantage of the different local situations of the learners and yet allow for the coalescing of these diverse elements into coherent learning and cohesive learning outcomes and projects?
   - Are the assessment strategies well considered in terms of the use of local resources and local applicability of the learning?
   - Is the content packaged by a publishing or content-creation company with provincial views or global view? Or are the contents packaged originally by the instructor? And if so, do these contents reflect provincial or global views?
   - What sorts of Internet resources and sources are privileged in the curricular build? Is the instructor open to a richer variety of sites from various locales? Are foreign language sites acceptable to the instructor (with proper translations)?
   - In terms of instructor feedback, is he/she rigid about only accepting learning fitting a particular cultural framework, or is he/she flexible about a wider range of learning possibilities? What standards does he/she apply for quality learning, and are these fair and applicable standards?
   - Are there guest lecturers who are "local" to the various learners? Or are the guest lecturers only from one country?
   - Are learners allowed to base their research projects on their own locales for localized applicable findings?
   - Do the scenarios and role plays used have resonance in localized situations? Or are the examples only applicable to the instructor's local reality? Are diverse ranges of realities explored?

- Do the on-campus resources cited only offer services that apply to the institution's local situations, or do they apply to more customized and localized supports for the various learners? What is the reach of the campus in terms of international supports?
- Are learning objects local-aware and applicable to various locales? Or are they very tied in to limited or provincial (instructor-bound) situations?
- If student sample works are included, do these show a rich variety of global and localization insights? Or are these works pretty monolithic in terms of cultural influences and locale?

3. **Localizations: Planned and Unplanned Interactivity**
   - Is the planned synchronous interactivity available in the time zone of the various global learners? If there are different ways to ensure that all global learners can interact, are the qualities of the interactions fairly equal or the same?
   - Are the technologies for the planned and unplanned interactivity available to all?
   - Do all get a chance to speak, and are all ideas given fair and logical consideration?
   - Do learners from around the world have time to acclimate to the course and to ask plenty of questions? Are there resources to help mitigate their adjustment to the learning management system and various tools, curriculum, instructor and fellow learners?
   - As part of the learner introductions or profiles, are learners' backgrounds, learning ambitions, countries, cultures and other aspects supported? Are their ties to their respective communities supported?
   - Does the instructor communicate respect to the various learners and acknowledge their local conditions *and make adjustments to the learning to accommodate and support those localizations?*
   - Does the instructor avoid generalizations or stereotypes when engaging with learners? Does the instructor avoid offensive joking and other types of interactivity/communications?
   - Does the instructor set up a culture of mutual respect and civility between learners and intervene if such a culture is contravened?
   - Does the instructor design or allow outside-LMS uses of localized resources and interactivity (interviews of local experts, visits to relevant local sites, access to local librarians, and others)?
   - Is the instructor available at different times to accommodate the different time zones?
   - Does the instructor allow sufficient "quiet time" and "silences" to accommodate different communications styles of the learners, or is everything paced in an exclusivist way?
   - Is the pacing conducive to learning for those who may be using a second, third or fourth language as the main language of learning? Does the instructor show awareness that particular grammatical, syntactical and pronunciation challenges may exist but not reflect learner intelligence or capability in the subject field?
   - Does the instructor convey trust, integrity, follow-through, and care in interactions with learners from various parts of the world? Or does he/she only convey this to niche demographics? Are there wide variances between perceptions of the instructors based across cultural or national lines? (And if so, why?)

4. **Localizations: Instructional Strategies**
   - Are the instructional strategies used in an online course just appropriate to first-language speakers?

- Do the instructional strategies show global and local awarenesses?
- Do the instructional strategies show accommodation for various learning styles?
- Are the moods and tones of the course conducive to those hailing from various cultures? Or are some types of learning more privileged than others?
- Does the instructor mediate conflicts and negotiate resolutions between learners who may have cultural or other difficulties with each other? Is this achieved fairly?
- Are learners empowered in the instruction to apply the learning to their own local communities and situations?
- If an instructor is made aware of localization opportunities and challenges, does he or she respond constructively to those?
- Does the learning help highlight local resources and learning moments that apply to various learners' local situations?
- Does the instructor provide sufficient feedback during instruction to support localized/individualized/customized learning per learner?
- Does the instructor apply attention and resources to help learners localize the learning to their own communities and situations?
- Does the instructor work to connect global e-learners to global opportunities, apprenticeships, graduate school, and job opportunities (where applicable)?
- Does the instructor write letters of recommendation?
- Does the instructor work to create partnerships with local resources for the respective learners?
- Does the instructor offer pedagogical oversight (as much as possible) for localized learning (that has been prior-arranged and mutually approved)?

SUGGESTED READING LIST

Edmundson, A. (2007). *Globalized e-learning cultural challenges.* Hershey, PA: Idea Group.

Hall, B.P. (1994). *Values shift: A guide to personal and organizational transformation.* Rockport, MA: Twin Lights Publishers.

Holeton, R. (1998). *Composing cyberspace: Identity, community, and knowledge in the electronic age.* Boston: McGraw-Hill.

Joseph, P.B., Bravmann, S.L., Windschitl, M.A., Mikel, E.R., & Green, N.S. (2000). *Cultures of curriculum.* Mahwah, NJ: Lawrence Erlbaum.

McNeel, S.P. (1994). College teaching and student moral development (chap. 2). In J. R. Rest & D. Narvaez (Eds.), *Moral development in the professions: Psychology and applied ethics* (pp. 27-49). Hillsdale: Lawrence Erlbaum.

Ozmon, H.A., & Craver, S.M. (2003). *Philosophical foundations of education* (7th ed.). Upper Saddle River, NJ: Merrill Prentice Hall.

Schultz, M., & Hatch, M.J. (1996, April) Living with multiple paradigms: The case of paradigm interplay in organizational culture studies. *The Academy of Management Review, 21*(2), 529-557.

Shapiro, J.P., & Stefkovich, J.A. (2001). *Ethical leadership and decision making in education: Applying theoretical perspectives to complex dilemmas.* Mahwah, NJ: Lawrence Erlbaum.

Walker, D.F., & Soltis, J.F. (1997). *Curriculum and aims.* New York: Teachers College.

Section III
Case-Based

Chapter XII
Open to People, Open with People:
Ethical Issues in Open Learning

Ormond Simpson
Open University of the United Kingdom, UK

ABSTRACT

The increasing multiculturalism in its society has recently encouraged the study of ethical dimensions in higher education in the UK. Distance and open learning has long had such a dimension, but this chapter will argue that ethical issues need to be reviewed in the light of recent developments. Three examples in distance education are taken: the increasing use of e-learning, dropout rates, and the development of methods of predicting student success. Some evidence suggests that e-learning may harm the openness of open learning given the numbers of educationally disadvantaged potential students which it will exclude. Dropout rates in distance education appear to be markedly higher than in conventional learning, which raises ethical issues of honesty and openness, and finally the use of methods in which a student's success can be predicted raises ethical issues about if and how that information should be communicated to that student. Considerable work has gone into the development of a discourse of medical ethics in response to modern developments in medicine. But this chapter suggests that medical models are inadequate to judge ethical issues in distance and open learning and it calls for the development of a similar discourse in the ethics of distance and open learning.

INTRODUCTION

There are signs of a renewed interest in ethics in UK higher education following concerns that various changes in society mean that judgements about issues in higher education are becoming more difficult in various ways. For example, the increasing diversity of higher education in terms of ethnicity and status may mean that universities are no longer able to assume that staff and students share similar value systems. One possible sign of this increasing concern is the recent attempt at Leeds University to build the discussion of ethics into 13 disciplines in the University through its Centre for Excellence in Teaching and Learning (Lipset, A. 2005). The aim is to use a model of medical ethics and adapt it to other disciplines.

Another sign may be the recent publication of a booklet *Ethics Matters*, a joint project between the Council for Industry and Higher Education and the Institute of Business Ethics, which examines issues such as the extent to which universities can encourage free speech amid fears of extremism on campus (Shepherd, J. 2005).

Yet another sign, and one that is significant for distance learning, is the proposed appointment of a chair for a new ethics centre in the UK Open University. And perhaps this is all as it should be: if education is not itself ethically-based, then societies and institutions which depend on that education may themselves become unethically-based, with potentially disastrous consequences.

ETHICS IN OPEN AND DISTANCE LEARNING

It has indeed long been clear that open and distance learning attracts its fair share of ethical issues for practitioners. Gearhart (2001) suggests that the increasing use of information technology in distance education may actually enhance unethical behaviours because of the effects of "psychological distance"; when acts are carried out at a distance they feel less personal because the person acted on cannot be heard or seen in the exchange. Yet Visser (2001) noted that "a search of the literature including documentation on the World Wide Web reveals little explicit concern with ethical questions among the community of professionals in the area of distance education and open learning" (slide 5).

Despite Visser's comment, there have been some examinations of ethics in distance learning.

Some early work by Reed and Sork (1990) suggests that ethical dilemmas in distance learning can arise in each of six areas:

1. **Admission intake and retention of students:** For example, dealing with issues around how fair an admissions process might be;

2. **Programme and course marketing:** For example, the temptation to put the "best face" on programmes when describing them in a course catalogue, or what Simpson (2004a) calls the "recruitment vs. retention" tension;

3. **Programme and course administration:** For example, how far the institution's various regulations are fair to both students and society as a whole as the ultimate customers of qualifications awarded by the institution;

4. **Leaner/facilitator interaction:** For example, given that learning can expose the learner to difficult emotional situations, how far does the institution and its tutor have a duty to take some responsibility for the learner's emotional state and offer support?;

5. **Course development and presentation:** For example, how far should course writers develop materials that reflect diversity rather than "pre-digested material that students are in danger of soaking up uncritically" (Cole, Coats, & Lentell, 1986). This is a concern shared by Tait (1989), who is concerned about the potential of distance learning to be undemocratic; and

6. **Programme, course and learner evaluation:** For example, what are the ethical issues in ensuring that assessment is fair to all interested parties (learners, employers, and society) as a whole?

Crosling and Webb (2002) suggest that ethical issues to be addressed may also include confidentiality, care when intervening between student and tutor, and in drawing the line between work with student learning and therapeutic counseling.

ETHICAL MODELS FOR OPEN AND DISTANCE EDUCATION

Thus, there may be a range of ethical issues arising in distance education, raising the question of how such issues may be adequately addressed. Caffarella (1988) suggests that one way forward is to compile lists of learner's rights to define the ethical duties of an institution. Such rights might include:

- A clear indication of expectations of the course or programme;
- Reasonable access to the instructor and resources;
- Due process when challenging the judgements and actions of the teacher;
- Treatment with dignity and respect at all times; and
- A learning environment which is fair, safe and productive.

In writing about the UKOU "Student Charter" Simpson (1992) argues that such lists of rights also might encourage learners to be more assertive in requesting the help they need to study successfully. However, it is not clear how far such lists can be used to judge individual cases, as ethical dilemmas may often be "grounded in conflicting yet equally legitimate views of what is good or right" (Merriam & Caffarella, 1991, p. 45).

Another way forward may be to look at different types of commitments concerned in ethical reasoning. Pratt (1998) suggests that in North America there are at least three types of commitment used to guide ethical reasoning: justice, caring, and duty.

1. Commitments to justice are those where fair and impartial consideration of rights and privilege are important.
2. Commitments to caring are where the prime consideration are relationships between people, and the care of individuals.
3. Commitments to duty means meeting legal requirements; the fair treatment of learners, responsible management of instruction and so forth, which may be especially important in a climate where litigation in education is becoming more common.

However, the problem with this perspective is that different commitments may lead to different ethical judgements, as we shall see.

PARTICULAR ETHICAL ISSUES IN OPEN AND DISTANCE LEARNING

To illustrate the kind of ethical dilemmas that can arise from developments in open and distance learning, this chapter will take three examples. One is the increasing use of e-learning in distance education, raising ethical issues around accessibility; the second centres around the issues of student dropout in online open and distance learning and; relating to that, the third is the recent development of systems for predicting student success in open learning, raising ethical issues around how that information is used.

E-Learning and Accessibility

The drive toward introducing e-learning into distance education appears to be increasing. More than 70% of the articles appearing in distance education journals recently are about aspects of e-learning, and the drive to put distance learning online appears almost unstoppable. One of the largest distance education providers, the UK Open University, is intending to require its students to have computers with Internet access to be able to make full use of its facilities from 2007 onward.

Yet there are real issues about access to e-learning from educationally disadvantaged groups. In the UKOU at the time of writing, around 55% of the population have access to the Internet at home (National Statistics, 2006) and although that proportion is still growing, it is doing so recently at a slower rate than hitherto. Broadband access is increasingly necessary for effective use of the Internet and of that 55% just over half have broadband access. Thus, only 30% of the population have broadband Internet access at home. Crucially, such access is very largely concentrated among groups with high levels of education: Internet access among lower income (and therefore educationally underprivileged groups) is only one seventh that of higher income groups.

UKOU policy on Internet access is that students without home computers should have access via local libraries and government learning centres or Internet cafés. Yet it has carried out no research to assess how far this is possible. The little evidence available suggests that for many reasons–booking access, transport to centres, time availability at centres, firewalls and other technical issues–it is actually very difficult to study courses the length of OU standard undergraduate offerings without access at home (Driver, 2001).

Now the UK Open University had, as part of its original mission, an aim to be open to students without entry qualifications. Thus, it looks likely that the OU's policy decision will exclude large numbers of educationally disadvantaged students of the very kind that were included in its original mission to be open. This clearly falls into the first of Reed and Sork's (1990, op. cit.) ethical dilemmas of how to make access to higher education fair. On the face of it the policy would conflict, for different reasons, with all three of Pratt's (1998, op. cit.) commitments used to guide ethical reasoning:

- **Commitments to justice:** By further excluding the already socially excluded;
- **Commitments to care:** By closing off a possible door of social mobility to members of society who are already likely to be suffering financial and health penalties from their lack of education; and
- **Commitments to duty:** By failing to give value for tax-payers' contributions, which come largely from lower income groups who will be precisely those excluded.

Student Dropout in Online Open and Distance Learning

An often unacknowledged, yet centrally ethical issue in open learning, is its retention rates. So unacknowledged is this issue that it is very often quite difficult to find retention rates for different institutions. Institutions are also often quite secretive about their student dropout rates for marketing reasons, or do not publish distance student dropout rates separately from their full time students. But what evidence there is suggests that dropout rates in distance education are markedly higher than those in conventional higher education. For example, the UK Open University has dropout rates of around 45-50% for new students on their first course and around 65-70% to its first degree. These compare with an average of 20% dropout to a degree for full time UK universities, the range being from around 1% dropout for "Oxbridge" universities to 38% for the universities with much broader social intakes.

The reasons for the UKOU's higher dropout are often given as:

1. Its open door policy, as no previous educational qualifications are required to enter the university. This must be true to an extent as there are very clear links between dropout and previous educational qualification. Students with no previous educational

qualification drop out at more than twice the rate of students with previous degree level qualification (55% dropout as against 20% dropout).

2. The belief that many students enter the UKOU with the intention of either just studying one topic and then leaving, or with the intervention of moving on the full-time higher education once they have obtained some UKOU credits to transfer. This is also clearly true, but because the UKOU does not collect statistics on the number of students who only intended to audit courses or transfer, this belief also acts as something of an excuse for not paying attention to dropout data.

Other distance education institutions may well have higher dropout rates, but as noted earlier, it is very difficult to get reliable comparative data. For example, the Korean National Open University, a distance university very similar to the UKOU in size, apparently has dropout rates of up to 90% to a degree. This is actually lower than it looks, as despite its name the KNOU only accepts high school graduates. If the UKOU did the same, it would have dropout rates of around 55% to its degree, still higher than the highest dropout in conventional higher education in the UK. To be fair to KNOU, its higher dropout rates are very probably due to the much lower resource that it is able to devote to student support, with only around 900 staff compared with the UKOU's 4500 staff (although some of those are devoted to full time research).

What, then, are the ethical issues involved in these probably markedly higher levels of student dropout in distance education as compared with conventional higher education? The most fundamental issues it seems to me are ones of honesty and openness with potential students (i.e., the ethics of commitments to both justice and care). Because no institution publicly announces its dropout rates when recruiting new students such publicity is equivalent to inviting people to put their money into an investment without saying just how risky that investment is. This is not a fanciful analogy; the risk of investing in distance higher education in the UK is higher than the risk of putting money into wildcat oil-well drilling (Simpson, 2004b, op. cit.). In the UK a financial broker inviting such an investment without indicating that there was a considerable risk to that investment, would invite the attention of the UK Financial Services Authority. Indeed, there have been a number of cases where financial institutions have had to pay considerable compensation for "mis-selling" their products. No such compensation has yet been demanded of UK educational institutions, but there are signs that a more litigious approach to education is becoming more common as students are required to invest more up front in their education and it seems only a matter of time before the issue is tested in the courts.

Of course, no institution on its own is going to publicise its dropout rates in its recruitment material at the moment despite the strong ethical arguments for doing so. However, it is possible that they could be forced to do so by the UK Government in some way in the not very distant future, as potential students demand to know more about the very considerable investment they are having to make in their education. Some of the issues involved in making that data public are examined in the next section.

A second ethical issue is around how much effort any institution is prepared to put in to decrease its student dropout. This seems a clear example of the ethics due to commitments to care but it is too large a topic to be dealt with here: the reader is referred to the books by Simpson in the recommended reading list *"Supporting Students in Online Open and Distance Learning"* and *"Student Retention in Online Open and Distance Learning."*

PREDICTIVE METHODS IN OPEN LEARNING

As noted earlier, the UK Open University is an "open learning" institution; there are no qualifications required for entry. This is not a dead letter: some 10,000 students enter the UKOU every year without the standard entry qualification for conventional higher education in the UK. Of these students about 5,000 pass their first course, making the OU the biggest single widening participation institution in the UK. Such an open entry policy relieves the institution of moral dilemmas to do with the fairness and equal opportunities of admissions procedures, but introduces new issues to do with advice to students applying for entry as to their chances of success, which are Reed and Sork's (1990, op. cit.) first category of ethical dilemmas. These dilemmas are becoming more acute with the development of new and more accurate statistical methods of predicting that success, such as those now being used in the UKOU and elsewhere.

Along with other open entry institutions, the UKOU has always had simple algorithms which attempt to predict the chances of success of new students entering the institution. Such algorithms relied on advisers looking at student application forms and making rough pass or fail predictions largely on the basis of the student's previous educational qualifications and socio-economic status, sometimes even taking into account subjective perceptions such as the applicant's handwriting in the days when forms were completed by hand.

Recent developments have improved the accuracy of prediction enormously by using a statistical "binary logistic regression" method (Simpson, 2006). The method, developed by Woodman (1999), allows a "predicted probability of success" (pps) to be attached to every new student entering the OU derived from their known characteristics, such as previous education, age, sex, socio-economic status, ethnic category and course applied for. The calculation is derived from the previous year's students' results, and, principally because the number of students involved is very large (35,000 a year), successive evaluations have shown the predictions to be accurate for any particular group of students to within 0.5% (This of course is different from the accuracy of prediction for an individual student, which we shall return to).

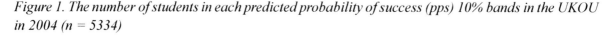

Figure 1. The number of students in each predicted probability of success (pps) 10% bands in the UKOU in 2004 (n = 5334)

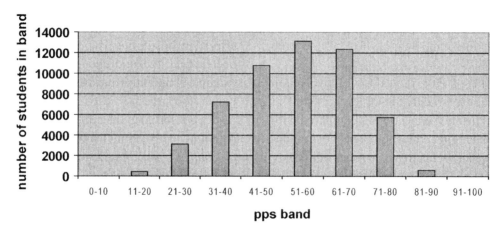

As the UKOU is an open entry institution the range of predictions is very wide. In 2004, they varied from a predicted probability of success of 83% (typically for a white, middle-aged woman, with conventional university entry qualifications, studying an arts course), to 9% (typically for a young, unemployed black man with few qualifications, studying a maths course). The distribution of probabilities between those extremes is a slightly skewed near normal curve (see Figure 1).

The use of such statistical methods to predict student success is not particularly new: logistic regression analysis has been used in the U.S. for a number of years in higher education institutions (Mager, 2003) for retention purposes and in the UK to set benchmarks in various situations. However, its use in open learning gives rise to two particular ethical issues, targeting support on students and frankness with students.

Targeting Support on Students

The main reason for developing the predicted probability of success system in the UKOU was to allow the targeting of limited resources on students most likely to need them, those with low pps's. The resource was used to make proactive phone calls to new students starting with the lowest pps's and working up the list until funding ran out (roughly half the total number of new students were contacted). The calls lasted on average about 10 minutes and the content was largely aimed at enhancing the student's integration with the institution and their motivation, using support models derived from the field of positive psychology (Simpson, 2006). Given the simplicity of the strategy it met with reasonable success, improving student retention by up to 5% against a control group with identical pps's (Simpson, 2004).

In addition, it was possible to show that in the particular financial environment of the UKOU where government grants are linked to the number of students completing a course, that the return

on the investment–the extra grant generated by increased retention divided by the cost of the call–was of the order of 450% (Simpson, 2005); that is, for every £1 invested in proactive phone calling the institution received £4.50 back in increased government grants (there were also savings on re-recruitment costs). This finding meant that it was decided that the programme should be extended in 2005 to all 33,000 new UKOU students.

However, as noted earlier, available funding only allowed about half of those students to be phoned (roughly up to a 54% pps level) and two particular concerns were expressed by OU staff:

1. Questions of which pps bands to target. Some staff argued that it was best to target the middle-band pps groups, those with (say) 40-70% predicted probability of success, the argument being that because the chances of lower groups were very small it was a waste of resources to offer them extra support. While this might seem reasonable from the institutional point of view in making the best use of limited resources, this argument was undermined when a detailed analysis of the retention figures found that with the exception of the very lowest pps groups (<15%) the increase in retention was much the same for all pps bands (the increase for the very lowest pps bands was smaller than the other bands, but this may be partly because the numbers at such low values are very small and the statistics not so reliable).

2. The ethics of offering higher levels of support to some students, especially given the arbitrariness of the cut-off point above which the extra support was not offered. This seemed less of an ethical obstacle as the UKOU had a long history of targeting support on particular groups, such as the disabled, and that targeting support on students deemed to be most likely to drop out had been going

on since the days of the "At Risk" project (Thorpe, 1988), which had used UKOU tutors to target support on students they thought likely to withdraw. Nevertheless, there was disquiet at the way that funding appeared to drive the number of students targeted. This was justified to some extent by the nature of the data. It was found that if the predictive system was used to simply predict pass or fail, then it was most accurate at the level where 56% of the students were predicted to fail. Thus, a target of the contact of 56% of students was set with at least some statistical justification (however tenuous) and attention could be turned to the attainment of this target within the resources available.

Openness with Students

The second ethical concern appears to be more serious but has not been addressed in the UKOU or elsewhere, as far as I can discover. Given that the predicted probability of success is an individual piece of data attached to an individual student, how far is it ethical to tell them what his or her predicted probability of success on their chosen course is (as distinct from telling them the average dropout rate for all students on that course or programme, as discussed earlier)? There can be no question as to a student's right to know that data, as it is held on a computer database and, as such, the UK's Data Protection Act applies (students have the right to all the data about them held on computer records unless there are very good reasons for withholding it). However, a student would have to know that the data exists in order to request it, and although the existence of the data is not secret it is not (yet) widely known.

The argument for not making the data known to students is that doing so might have adverse effects on them. A simple thought experiment would suggest that to phone a student (or worse, to write to them) and say (even among other things and

heavily caveated) that they have (for instance) only a 25% chance of passing their course, might well demoralise that student into immediate dropout. It would also be unfair. While for large groups of students the predictions are highly accurate, for individual students there is a large inaccuracy involved. The greatest of these is due to lack of input data; some students do not give full details about themselves on application forms, resulting in their pps being wrong. For example, they might not declare a particular qualification which would raise their pps. Giving a student an inaccurate piece of information would certainly be unethical, but to understand the limitations of the data would require a level of statistical expertise that most students are unlikely to possess. And of course the prediction takes no account of imponderable qualities such as motivation and resilience and personal circumstances that can make all the difference to a student's progress.

Another way to examine this ethical dilemma is to compare it with the much more serious dilemma faced by doctors when a patient asks about the success rate of the operation they are about to undergo. But the doctors' answers, however difficult, are not likely to affect the outcome for the patient, nor are they in any way a personal criticism of that patient. Thus, models drawn from medical ethics may not necessarily be helpful in considering ethical issues in education. Using Pratt's distinction (1998, op. cit.) between ethics of judgment, caring and duty, it might be argued that judgement and duty ethics would suggest that students should be told clearly when their chances of success are small, whereas caring ethics might suggest that the students self-esteem is a priority and that data should be withheld.

PREDICTING STUDENT SUCCESS — IS RESEARCH THE ANSWER?

Clearly, one way to determine what would happen if students were told up front what their chances of success were would be to undertake comparative research. For example, it might be possible to evaluate the progress of two groups of students, only one of which knew their predicted probability of success, and the other acting as a control. But another ethical issue then arises. The researcher will either have to choose a random experimental group in which case the objection of possible demoralisation is sustained for that group, or the researcher would have to ask for volunteers who are happy to be told their pps, in which case they are not a true random sample.

SELF-ASSESSMENT OF THE PROBABILITY OF SUCCESS IN CONVENTIONAL HIGHER EDUCATION

Are there ways, then, in which students could come into possession of the knowledge of their predicted probability of success but in ways to be both confidential and nonthreatening? One way might be to mediate the data through an interview with a tutor. This is the approach taken by Napier University (Johnston, 2001) which uses a questionnaire which is derived from their logistic regression analysis so that it gives reasonably reliable results. This questionnaire is completed with the help of a guidance tutor who can then help the student consider what action to take as a result. In Exhibit A, the introduction and part of the questionnaire is given as an example, together with the scoring system and Guidance Tutor Notes (Simpson, 2005, op. cit.). There were 14 questions in all.

The students complete the questionnaire by themselves and their score is then mediated by the guidance tutor. The tutor is told that students with scores up to 40 tend to progress at a rate of 35%, those with between 41-53 at a rate of 65% and those with a score of 54 or more at a rate of 90%.

Thus, the process is very open, and it is interesting that there is a clear emphasis on the ethics of the process exemplified in the first rule about the student giving informed consent to the process.

SELF ASSESSMENT OF SUCCESS IN DISTANCE AND OPEN LEARNING

Replicating this process in distance and open learning may be more difficult. While it may be possible to individually interview students in small scale systems, in mass institutions like the UKOU with 33,000 new students every year it becomes much harder. The cost of interviewing itself might be in excess of £1m pa. Are there ways, then, of providing some kind of unmediated self-assessment? It is certainly possible to provide self-assessment quizzes which are statistically-based. Exhibit B is based on the Woodman (1999, op. cit.) statistical method described earlier.

A text like this could be made available to potential students as a self-diagnostic tool by mail or over the Internet. Such students could take the test completely privately, thereby giving them feedback on their chances but hopefully in such a way as not to demoralise them unduly or publicly, or appear to be some kind of entrance exam in an open entry system.

This particular draft questionnaire has not been piloted yet so its possible effect on students and their progress is not known. The text probably needs further development to try and make it clear that the scoring, although based on proper statistical data, is only very approximate and that motivation and effort count for a very great deal in successful study. But it does represent a way forward that may be worth investigating further.

Exhibit A.

Introduction

Napier University wants all students to be successful and to enjoy and benefit from their studies. Inevitably, some people will do better than others and this is in part because of factors which are known to affect student performance in the first year of a degree programme. Based on these factors, as part of a general programme for promoting excellence, Napier has devised a short questionnaire with the following objectives:

- to make you aware of the issues that affect student performance;
- to allow you to think about how many of them apply to you, and thus your strengths and weaknesses ; and
- to point to actions you can undertake to improve things for yourself.

Each answer you give to the questions in the questionnaire is scored for its likely effect on successfully completing the first year. The higher the score, the more characteristics you exhibit which are known to contribute to student success. **It is important to remember that many students with low scores still go on to complete their first year successfully and so a low score does not mean that you will not progress to the second year.** Similarly, having a high score does not guarantee success and so it is important not be complacent. It is also important to realise that this questionnaire measures only some of the factors known to affect student success. There are lots of factors which influence progression which cannot yet be measured, including motivation, compatibility and determination.

This questionnaire should be completed in the presence of your Guidance Tutor, First Year Tutor or Programme Leader, who, if necessary, will help you devise a plan of action to help you successfully complete the year. Remember that there are lots of places within the university that can provide help and support, and academic staff want you to succeed just as much as you do.

The Napier Questionnaire

<u>Score</u>	<u>Questions</u>
	1. How old were you at the beginning of October? 18 years or less œ 19 to 23 years 24 or more years
	2. If you have "Highers" *(a Scottish educational qualification)*, how many do you have? (If you have both Highers and "A" Levels *(an English qualification)* then calculate 1 "A" Level = 2 Highers and select the nearest category below) 1-2 3 4-5 6 or more œ
	3. If you have "A" Levels (and no Highers), how many A Levels do you have? 1 2 3 4 or more
	4. What type of accommodation do you stay in? At home Napier-owned accommodation Private accommodation sharing with other students only Other
	5. If you have a job during term-time, for how many hours are you normally employed each week? None 1-10 hrs 11-15 hrs 16+hrs

continued on following page

Exhibit A. continued

Score Sheet for Questionnaire

1. Age group   Points

	Points
18 years or less	0
19 to 23 years	2
24 or more years	11

2. Number of Highers (or Highers and A Levels)

	Points
1-2	2
3	7
4-5	8
6 or more	14

3. Number of "A" Levels (no Highers)

	Points
1	2
2	7
3	8
4 or more	14

4. Accommodation   Points

	Points
At home	0
Napier	7
Private	0
Other	4

5. Hrs of employment Points

	Points
None	8
1-10 hrs	11
11-15 hrs	6
16+hrs	0

Advice to Guidance Tutors

- Students should give their informed consent before beginning the diagnostic test.
- The self-assessment is used as a focus for discussion and, where the score is low, that the outcome should be a personal plan for reducing risk linked to pointers to help sources (e.g., Student Services, Student Association, academic staff members, etc.).
- Those students with low scores are reminded that many students with low scores are still successful and that the purpose of the exercise is to both inform them where problems may exist and to encourage them to be pro-active in seeking out help. A low score does not imply that there is no hope, but merely that the hurdles are perhaps a little higher.

Exhibit B.

HOW GOOD ARE YOUR CHANCES OF PASSING?

Everyone who starts with the OU has a chance of succeeding. Of course you'll need commitment, time and energy. And a sense of humour will help!

There are also factors in your background which we know may affect your performance in your first year. This questionnaire is designed to help you:

- become aware of the factors which may affect your performance;
- to identify factors which might apply to you particularly; and
- to point to actions which you might be able to take on some of the factors to improve your chances of success.

Start with a score of 60 points. Answer each question in turn and add or subtract a point score as you go along.

	Initial Score : 60 points
1. Are you male or female? Male : Subtract 5 Female: No change	Revised Score: points
2. How old are you? Under 30 : Subtract 13 Age 30 or above : No change	Revised Score: points
3. What level is this course? Level 1: Add 23 Level 2 : Add 11 Other: No change	Revised Score: points
4. What Faculty is this course? Arts: Add 16 Social Science or Languages: Add 8 Education or Health and Social Welfare: Add 7 Maths: Add 6 Science: Subtract 3 Technology: Add 1 Other: No change	Revised Score: points
5. What is the credit rating of this course? 15pts (4 hours study per week): Subtract 23 30pts (8 hours study per week): Subtract 9 60pts (16 hours study per week): No change	Revised Score: points
6. How many courses are you taking in total this year? 1 course : Add 5 2 or more courses : No change	Revised Score: points

continued on following page

Exhibit B. continued

7. What are your current highest educational qualifications? Degree or equivalent : Add 17 School - Advanced level: Add 12 School - Ordinary level: No change None: Subtract 21 Other : No change	Revised Score: points
8. How would you classify your occupation? Working- professional occupation : Add 10 Working- other occupation : Add 5 Not working or other: No change	Revised Score: points
	Final Score : Points

How Did You Score?

- 100 or above: The outlook is very bright for you. You'll undoubtedly have your share of challenges but you should be able to get things off to a good start.
- 75 to 99: This will be a challenge you've taken on and it will be useful to see if you can increase your point score in some way. For example, do think about changing to a lower level course just for the first year; you can step up the pace later on. If you are taking more than one course, then again do think of switching to just one.
- Under 75: You'll still be able to succeed, but if you can increase your score that would really improve your chances. You may not want to change sex (!) but you could change your course, increase your current educational qualifications by taking a short course of some kind–the "Openings" courses are ideal–and so forth.

CONCLUSION AND FUTURE RESEARCH DIRECTIONS

It is likely that there are many issues in distance education which could and should be judged ethically. The two specific case studies here suggest

- Moves into e-learning by open learning institutions can be in conflict with all of the three types of ethical commitment (to justice, care and duty) unless considerable research is undertaken into issues of access to computing.
- Open entry institutions may need to find a way of informing intending students what

their chances of success are, because at least two out of three types of ethical commitment suggest that this is a requirement for an ethical open entry policy.

Some of the other issues in distance education that need to be addressed ethically might be:

1. E-learning: and in particular the overall effects of the development of e-learning in distance education, especially on the developing world. Will the current emphasis on e-learning simply increase the "digital divide" that currently exists between the developed and developing world?

2. Retention: and in particular institutional attitudes to student retention in distance education. Is it really ethical for distance education institutions to accept dropout rates of 50% of more as part of the natural order of things? There is disturbing evidence in the UK that students dropping out of full time higher education have higher levels of depression, unemployment and physical ill-health than either graduates or young people who never went to university. We do not know the effects of dropping out of distance education, given that (for example) every year the UKOU produces more dropout students than successful ones, there is surely an urgent need for ethical research here.

3. Focusing support on vulnerable students (as outlined previously in this article). In effect this is what is called "Affirmative action" in the U.S., which continues to be controversial there. Given limited resource to support students, what are the ethical issues involved in targeting that resource on particular groups of students?

4. Students who raise moral issues. Like many other open learning institutions, the UKOU has a number of students in prisons; more than 1,400 in 2006. Some of those students are in prison for particularly abhorrent crimes and on occasion it has been known for tutors to refuse to meet them when they learn of those crimes. What are the ethical issues in such situations?

All these case studies and examples suggest that, at the moment, the ethics of distance education are in a relatively undeveloped condition. The field of medical ethics is in a much more advanced state of maturity, although the systems developed for medical ethics are not necessarily appropriate for education generally or for distance education in particular. Yet it may be as important

that decisions in distance education are taken in as ethical a manner as those in medicine. It is therefore urgent that distance education institutions begin to study how ethics can be applied to their decision-making in a rapidly changing and challenging world.

REFERENCES

Caffarella, R. S. (1988). Ethical dilemmas in the teaching of adults. In R.G. Brockett (Ed.), *Ethical issues in adult education* (pp. 103-117). New York: Teachers College Press.

Cole, S., Coates, M., & Lentell, H. (1986). Towards good teaching by correspondence. *Open Learning, 11*(1), 16-22.

Crosling, G., & Webb, G. (2002). Introducing student learning support. In G. Crosling & G. Webb (Eds.), *Supporting student learning: Case studies experience and practice from higher education.* London: Kogan Page.

Driver, A. (2001). *Access to IT.* Report to the UK Open University Learning and Teaching Innovation Committee.

Gearhart, D. (2001). Ethics in distance education: Developing ethical policies. *Online Journal of Distance Learning Administration, 4*(1). Retrieved April 22, 2008, from http://www.westga.edu/~distance/ojdla/spring41/gearhart41.html

Johnston, V. (2001). Retention. In *Paper presented at the "Holistic Student Support" Conference*, University of Central Lancashire, Preston, UK.

Lipset, A. (2005, September 30). Pioneers set ethics at heart of courses. *Times Higher Education Supplement*, p. 56.

Mager, J. (2003). Personalization and customization. In *Paper presented at the Noel-Levitz National Student Retention Conference*, San Diego, CA.

Merriam, S.B., & Caffarella, R.S. (1991). *Learning in adulthood: A comprehensive guide.* San Francisco: Jossey-Bass.

National Statistics. (2006). Retrieved April 22, 2008, from http://www.statistics.gov.uk/StatBase/ssdataset.asp?vlnk=6936&Pos=1&ColRank=1&Rank=272

Pratt, D. (1998). Ethical reasoning in teaching adults. In M. Galbraith (Ed.), *Adult learning methods: A guide for effective instruction* (chap. 6). Malabar: Krieger.

Reed, D., & Sork, T.J. (1990). Ethical considerations in distance education. *American Journal of Distance Education, 4*(2), 30-43.

Shepherd, J. (2005, October 7). Guide steers campuses through moral mazes. *Times Higher Education Supplement*, p. 6.

Simpson, O. (1992). Specifying support services in the OU—the so-called "student charter." *Open Learning, 7*(2), 57-59.

Simpson, O. (2004a). Student retention and the course choice process—the UK open university experience. *Journal of Access Policy and Practice, 2*(1), 44-58.

Simpson, O. (2004b). The impact on retention of interventions to support distance students. *Open Learning, 19*(1), 79-95.

Simpson, O. (2005). The costs and benefits of student retention for students, institutions and governments. *Studies in Learning Evaluation Innovation and Development (Australia), 2*(3), 34-43. Retrieved April 22, 2008, from http://sleid.cqu.edu.au/viewissue.php?id=8

Simpson, O. (2006). Predicting student progress. *Open Learning, 21*(2), 125-138.

Tait, A. (1989). The politics of open learning. *Adult Education, 61*(4), 308-313.

Thorpe, M. (1988). *Evaluating open and distance learning.* Harlow, UK: Longman.

Visser, J. (2001). Ethics in distance education and open learning. In *Proceedings of the Presidential Session at the International Council for Distance Education Conference, Dusseldorf.* Retrieved April 22, 2008, from http://www.learndev.org/ppt/ICDE-2001/

Woodman, R. (1999). *Investigation of factors that influence student retention and success rate on open university courses in the East Anglia region.* Unpublished masters dissertation, submitted to Sheffield Hallam University, UK.

ADDITIONAL READING

Books

McGivney, V. (1996). *Staying or leaving the course.* Leicester, UK: National Institute of Adult Continuing Education.

Moxley, D., Najor-Durack, A., & Dumbrigue, C. (2001). *Keeping students in higher education—successful practices and strategies for retention.* London: Kogan Page.

Simpson, O. (2002). *Supporting students in online, open and distance learning* (p. 168). London: RoutledgeFalmer. ISBN 0 749437405.

Simpson, O. (2003). *Student retention in online, open and distance learning* (p. 168). London: RoutledgeFalmer. ISBN 0 7494 3999 8.

Tinto, V. (1997). *Leaving college: Rethinking the causes and cures of student attrition* (2nd ed.). Chicago, IL: University of Chicago Press.

Yorke, M. (1999). *Leaving early.* London: RoutledgeFalmer.

Book Chapters

Simpson, O. (2004). Social exclusion and online learning. *Global perspectives on e-learning—rhetoric and reality* (pp. 89-100). Sage. ISBN 1412904897.

Simpson, O. (2004). Doing it hard. In G. Crosling & G. Webb (Eds.), *Supporting student learning: Case studies, experience and practice from higher education* (pp. 34-40). Kogan Page. ISBN 0 7494 3535 6.

Simpson, O. (2006). Rescuing the personal tutor. In Thomas & Hixenbaugh (Eds.), *Perspectives on personal tutoring in mass higher education.* Trentham Books. ISBN-10:1-85856-385-2.

Simpson, O. (2007). Cost benefits of student retention policies and practices. In Bramble & Panda (Eds.), *Economics of distance and online learning.* Lawrence Erlbaum.

Articles

Asbee, S., Woodall, S., & Simpson, O. (1999). Student mentoring in distance education. *Journal of Access and Credit Studies, 2*(2), 220-232. ISSN 1462-0367.

Bean, J., & Eaton Bogdan, S. (2001). The psychology underlying successful student retention. *Journal of College Student Retention, 3*(1), 73-89.

Case, P., & Elliot, B. (1997). Attrition and retention in distance learning programs, problems, strategies, and solutions. *Open Praxis*, (1), 30-33.

Clutterbuck, D. (1995). Managing customer defection. *Customer Service Management,* (7).

Gaskell, A. Gibbons, S., & Simpson, O. (1990). Taking off and bailing out. *Open Learning, 3*(2), 49.

Hawksley, R., & Owen, J. (2002). *Going the distance: Are there common factors in high performance distance learning?* National Extension College, Cambridge and UK Learning and Skills Development Agency, London. Retrieved April 22, 2008, from www.LSDA.org.uk

Jackson, S. F. (2001). Online distance education and undergraduate student retention and recruitment. In *Proceedings of the Third Annual WebCT Users Conference "Transforming the Educational Experience,"* Vancouver.

Johnston, V. (2001). By accident or design? *Exchange, 1,* 9-11. Open University Milton Keynes.

Johnston, V., & Simpson, O. (2006). Retention-eering higher education in the UK: Attitudinal barriers to addressing student retention in universities. *Widening Participation and Lifelong Learning, 8*(3).

Martinez, P. (2001). *Improving student retention and achievement—what we do know and what we need to find out.* UK Learning and Skills Development Agency, London. Retrieved April 22, 2008, from www.lsda.org.uk

Martinez, P., & Maynard, J. (2002). *Improving colleges: Why courses improve or decline over time.* UK Learning and Skills Agency, London. Retrieved April 22, 2008, form www.lsda.org.uk

Martinez, P., & Mendey, F. (1998). *9000 voices: Students' persistence and dropout in further education.* UK Learning and Skills Agency, London. Retrieved April 22, 2008, from www.lsda.org.uk

Mclinden, M. *Retention: A practitioners guide to developing and implementing pre-entry induction and ongoing retention tactics.* Anglia Polytechnic University: Four Counties Group of Higher Education Institutions.

Rekkedal, T. (1982). The drop out problem and what to do about it. In J. Daniel, M. Stroud, &

J. Thompson (Ed.), *Learning at a distance—a world perspective.*

Shin, N., & Kim, J. (1999). An exploration of learner progress and drop out in the Korean National Open University. *Distance Education, 20*(1), 81-95.

Simpson, O. (2005). Web-based learning: Are we becoming obsessed? *Distance Learning, 26*(1), 153-157. ISSN 0158-7919.

Simpson, O. (2006). This door is alarmed. *Journal of Access, Policy and Practice, 3*(2).

Woodley, A. (1987). Understanding adult student dropout. In M. Thorpe & D. Grugeon (Eds.), *Open learning for adults.* Harlow, Essex: Longman.

Woodley, A., De Lange, P., & Tanewski, G. (2001). Student progress in distance education: Kember's model revisited. *Open Learning, 16*(2), 113-131.

Woodley, A., & Parlett, M. (1983). Student dropout. *Teaching at a Distance, 24,* 2-23.

Zajkowski, M. (1997). Price and persistence in distance education. *Open Learning, 12*(1), 12- 23.

Chapter XIII
An American Perspective of Ethical Misconduct in ODLS:
Who's to Blame?

Chi Lo Lim
Northwest Missouri State University, USA

ABSTRACT

Open and distance learning systems (ODLS) brought about immeasurable advancement in the delivery of education. Albeit all the benefits ODLS offers, there are some issues that need to be addressed. One of the most prevalent issues is the problem of persistent academic dishonesty. Much research effort has been devoted to explain why students commit acts of dishonesty, but there is limited research done on why faculty members do not take on a stronger position against it. This chapter offers cases of ODLS misconducts at an American University, the process that faculty members took to document academic dishonesty, the appeals process used by students, and the consequences of dishonesty. This chapter provides insights from faculty faced with dishonesty. It also addresses what administrators should do to support their faculty in curbing dishonesty in their institutions.

INTRODUCTION

Higher education is experiencing a new growth through technological advancements. In the 21st century workforce, a college degree has become a competitive advantage. Globalization demands an educated workforce. Many American employers today are requiring their employees to seek further education in the forms of certifications or college degrees. The majority of American employers are also offering some form of tuition reimbursement as an incentive to encourage more of their employees to return to schools. The constraints of limited time and family demands have made open and distance learning systems (ODLS) very popular and appealing to fulltime workers. The growth of open and distance learning systems has created a new educational delivery mode that offers a formidable means to fulfil the needs of fulltime employees seeking further education. ODLS offers students the flexibility to further their education with less restriction to time and location. Although these benefits are indisputable, researchers have also found problems, including an increasing problem of dishonesty in academia, that can partially be due to the availability of electronic resources.

This chapter focuses on the growing problem of dishonesty in higher education in the United States. It provides an extensive literature review on factors that contribute to the epidemic of dishonesty. This chapter also sheds light from the perspective of faculty in regards to administrators' support or lack thereof. The objectives of this chapter are to present actual cases of ODLS dishonesty, and explore why students cheat, and what administrators and faculty should do to curtail the epidemic of dishonesty in higher education.

BACKGROUND

Cheating on campus is not a new phenomenon, nor is it limited to higher education. Evidence of cheating in U.S. schools was reported by the Centre for Academic Integrity at Duke University and the Rutgers' Management Education Centre to have increased in the last 10 years and 75% of all college students confessed to cheating at least once (Bushweller, 1999; Kleiner & Lord, 1999; Niels, 1997; Olt, 2002; Slobogin, 2002). McCabe indicated a 200% increase in cheating since the early 1960s (as cited in Carroll, 2002). Koch found that 20-30% of undergraduate students cheat regularly (Koch, 2002). According to McCabe, "... these results indicate that dishonesty appears to not carry the stigma that it used to" (as cited in Koch, 2002). Kleiner and Lord (1999) concur and found that 50% of those who had never been

caught cheating also believe that there is nothing wrong with cheating.

The advancement of technology created a new venue for educational institutions to offer new delivery formats to accommodate the needs of an increasing number of people returning to schools. Although there are many advantages of electronically delivered education, there are also the unfortunate and unforeseen problems of dishonesty due to availability, ease of obtaining material illegally, and companies aggressively enticing students to cut corners. Heberling (2002) documented the availability of papers and custom-tailored assignments available to students for purchase from digital paper mills such as Schoolsucks.com, PaperTopics.com, and Cheathouse.com. Academic dishonesty through technology was also reported in a survey conducted at Rutgers, which found that 50% of their students plagiarized Internet resources they used (Slobogin, 2002).

Kenkel (2004) found that students who took online classes are more likely to obtain unauthorized help than those who take classes in the classroom. Numerous studies reported the use of "ringers," or people who are paid to take classes for others (Maramark & Maline, 1993; Wein, 1994). Obviously, in an online environment, the use of "ringers" to complete courses for students becomes a very challenging problem, as technological advancement in identifying course-takers is not yet at the stage where we can monitor it consistently or systematically. Faculty members are concerned with this issue and many have reservations about online or distance education because they consider the use of "ringers" among the most serious forms of academic dishonesty (Nuss, 1984).

CASES OF ODLS MISCONDUCT

The cases of ODLS misconduct discussed in this chapter took place in a midsize public university in the United States. The grading system at the university is as follows: "A" superior, "B" above average, "C" average, "D" below average, and "F" failure. The university has a clearly written academic honesty policy in place, which applies to all courses offered by the institution. Furthermore, faculty members are encouraged to copy the policy onto their individual course syllabi. The academic honesty policy requires that when misconduct is discovered, documented, and verified, the faculty member needs to notify the student and the administrators in writing and submit a grade of "F" for the course. In addition, the university also has a clear appeal process, which allows students to appeal a case if they feel that the charge was biased or unfair. The appeal process consists of two levels, one within the department that the student has declared a major in and a second level with the university-wide appeals committee. Any student charged with academic misconduct has 10 business days to file an appeal in writing.

ODLS Misconduct: Case 1

The first case of ODLS misconduct happened in a traditional class over a 4-month period, where the students have to read a book of their choice and critically analyze the book as part of the requirement to fulfil the course. The student (Dick) was not performing well in class and needed his book critique to be well written to achieve at least a "C" for the course. Dick met with the faculty and requested the faculty to grade his critique as early as possible so that if he needed to retake the course, he could do so before he left the country for Christmas break. The faculty agreed and, upon reading the first few paragraphs, was dumbstruck with conflicting statements in Dick's critique. There were obvious contradictions in Dick's paper on his perspectives about the book. The faculty did a preliminary search and phrases in Dick's paper immediately surfaced. She thoroughly searched the Internet for the rest of Dick's paper and found a total of 11 instances of plagiarism.

The telltale signs of ODLS misconduct were obvious because there was no logical flow between many of the statements in the critique. Dick did not even take the time to rephrase statements he lifted from Internet sources. Apparently, Dick was in too much of a hurry, and did not even bother to read what he was cutting and pasting to his paper. The faculty spent the next 3 days documenting the ODLS misconduct and requested the assistance of a librarian to independently verify the information. Once the librarian verified the misconduct, the faculty informed her superiors. Dick was immediately notified that he would be receiving an "F" for the course due to academic dishonesty. Dick did not appeal the case and retook the course.

ODLS Misconduct: Case 2

The second case involved a student (Rick) who was repeating a course to complete his graduate degree. This particular course was offered exclusively online during a summer session that lasted 8 weeks. Rick was doing acceptable work until the submission of the final term project, which was an in-depth analysis of an industry selected by the student. When the faculty started reading Rick's paper, there were numerous transition problems that made the reading extremely challenging. There were some specifically problematic sentences that neither seemed to flow properly nor did the sentences seem to correlate to each other. The faculty used a search engine and uncovered multiple incidents of plagiarism. A university librarian was requested to confirm the findings and she verified seven instances of plagiarism in the first four pages of the term project.

The faculty contacted her superiors about the ODLS misconduct and a formal written charge was filed. The faculty contacted Rick through electronic mail and informed him of the findings and that the consequence of his actions is an immediate "F" for the course and he need not take the final exam. Rick immediately communicated with the faculty professing ignorance and pleaded for an opportunity to rectify the situation. Because the course was offered exclusively online, Rick was in another state and made arrangements to come back on campus to meet with the faculty. Rick was able to find the faculty's home address and called her home phone and requested to meet with the faculty in her home on a Saturday. Meeting with a concerned student at a critical time is definitely not protocol and potentially dangerous as the faculty was uncertain what state of mind the student was in. On the other hand, the faculty fully understood the importance of completing the course for Rick, as it was his last course and he had a position lined up that required the completion of the graduate degree. The faculty refused to meet with Rick in her home and arranged with him to meet in her office the following Monday.

The faculty received a phone call from her superior asking the details of the case and whether or not there was any possibility that it was a case of misunderstanding and miscommunication. Apparently, Rick informed the faculty's superiors that he had made a terrible mistake of submitting a draft instead of the final version of his term project. Rick was able to convince the faculty's superiors that he made a mistake and in turn the faculty's superior requested that the faculty afford Rick the benefit of the doubt. The faculty complied with the request and upon reading the first few pages of the "final" version, areas of concerns again became apparent. The faculty asked a librarian to assist in checking the problem areas and after 2 days of reading and extensive search on the Internet, the faculty and the librarian both found multiple areas of plagiarism.

The faculty contacted her superior and made arrangement to have a meeting with Rick in the superior's office. Rick was asked numerous questions about his explanation for the draft and the final version of his term project. There was time differential that Rick could not account for

between the "draft" and the final versions of his paper. He had made the mistake of trying to cover up his mistake by changing the clock on his computer to reflect that his "final" version was indeed the right version. However, in his haste he did not change the time on the computer and it showed that his "final" version was completed 2 days before his draft. The second term project that Rick submitted had 45 instances of plagiarism from multiple articles he copied off from the Internet in his 11-page paper. The librarian printed all the material and colour-coded all the areas of plagiarism.

In the last few minutes of the meeting, the faculty confronted Rick about the problem with the time differential of the papers; Rick was unable to provide any explanation and was completely dumbfounded. In addition, when the faculty asked Rick about the areas of plagiarism, his immediate response was that he had been doing research papers by cutting and pasting articles he found online and that no one had ever told him it was unacceptable. Rick further professes that online material is easily accessible, and he would change a word here and there to ensure that the sentences fit together. The final result of this case of academic misconduct was an "F" for the course after two levels of appeal. Rick retook the course a year later and completed his program.

ODLS Misconduct: Case 3

The third case of ODLS misconduct took place in a blended course that was offered in a summer session over a 4-week period. The class met online for the 1st, 3rd, and 4th weeks, but met on campus during the 2nd week for seminars and expert speakers. The student (Jane) was doing well in the class and was among the top 10% after all the required tests and other assignments. As part of the requirement for the course, Jane had to do an in-depth analysis on the evolution of quality in an industry of her choice. When the faculty was reading the paper, she was surprised to read a familiar passage. The faculty felt strongly that she had read the passage previously and reviewed some of the material she had collected for class readings. After a brief search, she found the familiar passage from a document that she had shared with the class. Another area of concern was the use of British English in the paper; that prompted an uneasy feeling but knowing Jane's background, it was highly probable that she was accustomed to writing in British English. Further reading of the paper showed transition problems and lack of correlation between thoughts shared in the paper.

The faculty suspected that Jane had plagiarized but due to the lack of citations in the content of the paper, the faculty contacted Jane and afforded her an opportunity to complete the citations. Jane immediately offered to do another paper if the faculty was unhappy with the first paper she submitted. Furthermore, Jane asked the faculty for a delay of grade if she thought that she might receive a grade lower than a "B" in order to have more time to improve her performance in class. The faculty was surprised at the request and informed Jane that the only opportunity she had at that point in time was to submit the rest of the citations in the paper. Jane professed that all the sources she used were in the reference page she included at the end of the paper. After a number of e-mail exchanges and an ultimatum, Jane finally submitted a version of her paper with citations in the body of the paper.

The revised version of the paper was disappointing. Not only did Jane provide improper citations in the body of the paper; she also made changes to the reference page. After further analysis of the citations Jane provided, the faculty found that she placed superficial citations at inappropriate locations in the paper and also provided numerous incorrect and incomplete citations. The reference page was revised to include more citations than the original submission and some

had been deleted, which apparently were never used in the paper.

The faculty spent the next 10 days reading the paper and documenting areas of plagiarism. After the faculty completed the search, she asked a librarian to independently verify the areas of plagiarism and the result was 64 instances of ODLS misconduct in Jane's 30-page paper. The faculty followed the university's policy and filed a report to her superior as well as informing Jane of the finding. Jane never appealed the case and received an "F" for the course.

WHY DO STUDENTS CHEAT?

Academic dishonesty is not a new problem to education, but in recent years, it appears that this problem has continued to increase. Numerous researchers offer strategies to curtail academic dishonesty, but the fact of the matter is that unethical behaviours in academia seems to be increasing exponentially. Some rationalize that technology contributes to the ease for students to retrieve information without giving proper credit. Others indicate that students should not be faulted if they were not clearly taught what constitutes academic dishonesty.

Donald McCabe, Professor of Organization Management at Rutgers University and founding president of the Centre of Academic Integrity based at Duke University had done extensive research into cheating in higher education. In his 15 years of research in the area, McCabe found the two most common reasons why faculty members may choose to ignore academic dishonesty were sympathy for students and the tedious procedures required to document dishonesty incidents (McCabe, 2001). In an earlier study of 200 faculty members, McCabe and Trevino found that 40% of those surveyed had never enforced their institution's academic policy, while 54% seldom did and only 6% indicated that they did enforce the policy (McCabe & Trevino, 1993). The trend of faculty not wanting to report academic misconduct is alarming. Numerous researchers concur, with their own studies finding that faculty members predominantly choose to confront student offenders themselves rather than subject these students to university authorities (Jendrek, 1989; McCabe, 1993; Nuss, 1984; Singhal, 1982; Wright & Kelly, 1974). Other researchers found that 79% of their faculty respondents reported that they had observed cheating, but only 9% of the same respondents actually took action against the student offenders (Graham, Monday, O'Brien, & Steffen, 1994).

USA Today reported that students and professors who suspected cheating would not likely take action if existing academic policy is seldom enforced ("Cheating thrives on campus as officials turn their heads", 2001). McCabe found a third of the 1,000 faculty members he interviewed from 21 campuses admitted that they observed cheating in their classes but chose not to take any action (as cited in Koch, 2002). It was also reported that students were discouraged with how some of their faculty members dismissed obvious cheating and with how others punished cheating without implementing their institutional policy (McCabe, 2005). Other factors that contributed to the lack of action from faculty members include fear of lawsuits, time, institutional policy, and so forth (Koch, 2002). Online cheating had been perceived as more rampant and easier than in the traditional classroom setting. Many believed that the distance and lack of face-to-face interaction between the students and the faculty made it less threatening for students to cheat (George & Carlson, 1999; James, 2002). Students admitted that they would be more likely to cheat in an online class than in traditional classrooms; however, when informed that surveillance would be used, the percentage dropped from 42% to 14% (Chapman, Davis, Toy, & Wright, 2004). Ironically, those who choose to teach their courses online tend to believe that

cheating is not a major problem (Kaczmarczyk, 2001).

SOLUTIONS AND RECOMMENDATIONS ACADEMIC INTEGRITY: INSTITUTIONAL RESPONSIBILITY

Institutions of higher education are charged with the duty of educating and preparing youths for a better future. As they complete their academic training, they should be able to contribute positively to the society. Instilling integrity is vital to the stability in the new world under the leadership of future generations. The Centre for Academic Integrity defined academic integrity as "a commitment even in the face of adversity, to five fundamental values: honesty, respect, trust, fairness, and responsibility" (1999, p. 4). It requires all the constituents at educational institutions to actively work toward an honest environment where these five values can be introduced and instilled in our future leaders.

Most institutions of higher education have established some form of policy to discourage academic misconduct and to establish a level of academic integrity. Policies to deter dishonesty are written to provide guidance to all constituents, including faculty members and students. Research found that academic policies are written to guide members on how they are expected to behave within the institution (Kilbler, 1993; McCabe & Pavela, 2000; Olt, 2002; Taylor, 2001). Integrity guidelines are there to lay down the ground rules for a good working relationship for all concerned. Faculty members are held responsible for implementing their institutional policy when faced with an academic infraction. To successfully achieve the goal of any institution to uphold a high level of integrity, all members must abide by the set rules. However, the deterioration in academic integrity raises concerns about whether integrity policies actually help prevent misconduct. It appears that policies that should uphold integrity are not functioning as they were meant to. In fact, the contrary can be said with the emergence of honour codes in many schools of higher education in the United States. There is evidence to show that schools with honour codes have less misconduct than those without (McCabe, 1993). The creation of honour codes does help deter dishonesty, but the continuous increase of incidents of dishonesty in higher education indicates that honour codes alone are insufficient.

Research found that faculty members are reluctant to implement institutional policy, because the process of documenting academic misconduct is time-consuming, tedious, and emotionally exhausting (McCabe, 1993). McCabe found that, more often than not, faculty members usually experience personal struggle because it appears that they are on trial instead of the student offenders and have to prove that they have done the right thing (1993). Furthermore, confirmation of faculty members' inaction was reported in a study of research universities where 57.2% of the faculty members professed concern about dishonesty, but only 53% of these faculty members will actually charge a student (Wajda-Johnston, Handal, Brawer, & Fabricatore, 2001). Faculty members showed strong reluctance to carry out institutional policies on academic dishonesty, partly because of a lack of trust, but also because of a felt need to assert their authority in their classrooms (Simon, Carr, McCullough, Morgan, Oleson, & Ressel, 2003). McCabe (1993) concurred with his findings that 25% of faculty members reported dissatisfaction with implementing institutional policies.

There appears to be a lack of communication between administrators and faculty members about how institutional policy would work when actually implemented. Institutional policies are established to help constituents focus on their institutional goals, but they require that all members of the institution understand and believe that they are fair and just for all concerned.

Academic Integrity: Faculty Responsibility

Faculty have a very important role in instilling academic integrity in their students. According to the American College Personnel Association, faculty members are responsible for making sure that their students understand the importance of ethical issues (ACPA, 2002, Section 2.9). Furthermore, the American Association of University Professors Statement of Ethics clearly indicated that faculty members must cultivate honest academic conduct (AAUP, 1987).

In an extensive study, McCabe (1995) found that students in general wanted their administrators and faculty members to take a strong stand against unethical behaviour. In fact, the same sentiment had been reported by another researcher, who found that students expect their faculty members to take the lead in nurturing and guiding them to become more responsible members of society (Boyer, 1987). Furthermore, Boyer posits that "If high standards of conduct are expected of students, colleges must have impeccable integrity themselves" (Boyer, 1987). McCabe states that student-offenders confessed that they dislike cheating and would prefer to be honest if they would not be in a position of disadvantage (McCabe, 2001). McCabe challenges the educational industry to deter academic misconduct by teaching students to take responsibility and be held accountable for their actions (McCabe, 2005).

Researchers found that students have a higher tendency to cheat if they believe that their peers are cheating (Chapman et al., 2004; McCabe & Trevino, 1993). It appears that faculty members' active involvement in deterring academic misconduct might help lessen dishonesty in academe. Numerous researchers indicated that students' inclination to behave inappropriately decreased when they perceived that their faculty members were serious about honesty and would enforce institutional policies on academic misconduct (Hall, 1996; Jendrek, 1989; Lim & Coalter, 2006;

Wajda-Johnston et al., 2001). Olt (2002) and Dirks (1998) found that online faculty members do not appear to be enthusiastic about actually discussing integrity with their students and that a majority of them do not even have an academic honesty policy in their syllabus. Communication and interaction between faculty members and students could build trust, which helps deter dishonesty (Chapman et al., 2004; George & Carlson, 1999; Graham, Cagiltay, Lim, Craner, & Duffy, 2001). Faculty should actively participate in discouraging dishonesty and instilling integrity in the classroom (McCabe & Pavela, 2000; McMurtry, 2001; Rowe, 2004; Sims, 1993).

CONCLUSION

The cases of ODLS misconduct discussed in this chapter show a problem area that needs the attention of all the constituents of higher education. From the cases, the actions of the students confirm the research that students believe their faculty would not take action against cases of ODLS misconduct. Furthermore, it showed that documenting suspected cases of ODLS misconduct can be a very tedious and emotionally exhausting endeavour for faculty members who choose to follow institutional protocol. Finally, the judicial procedure set by institutions can appear to be one-sided where faculty members have to prove their charge time and again.

In the technologically advanced world that we live in, the ease and accessibility of ODLS enable innovative ways of delivering education. This allows many learners the opportunity to fulfil their educational goals. Inadvertently, it also creates opportunities for unscrupulous paper-mill entrepreneurs who make ODLS misconduct available to those who are willing to pay and not learn. On the other hand, the availability of technology also provides educators a new tool to stop ODLS misconduct.

Who then should we blame for ODLS misconduct and academic dishonesty? In order to maintain an environment of true learning, all the constituents of ODLS need to take up the challenge. The temptation of cut-and-paste is too great and with increasing demands in the 21st century, it is not difficult to see why some might be tempted. Administrators must provide their students and faculty with a clear policy of institutional ethical expectations. In order for faculty members to nurture their students to become ethical and responsible citizens of society, they need to pursue all suspected cases of ODLS misconduct even in the face of possible hardships. As for students, they need to be aware that the 21st century society demands its members be socially responsible members where unethical behaviour is not tolerated. If all the constituents of higher education can come to the consensus that we all have a responsibility to create a better society for the future, we can certainly curtail any misconduct that is taking place in the open and distance learning systems.

FUTURE RESEARCH DIRECTIONS

Open and distance learning systems will continue to benefit from technological advancements. Unfortunately, misconduct and unethical behaviour will likewise be present. Based on the cases included in this chapter, it is imperative that all the constituents of higher education join forces to put a stop to any temptations and opportunities that would appeal to unscrupulous participants. Future research into ethics in open and distance learning systems should focus on an in-depth study of existing policies on integrity and their utilization in the new technology-based society. An in-depth analysis of existing policy can discover any possible oversight. Policies are established to set rules and guidelines but are only good if they appropriately reflect the needs of all the constituents.

A second area for future research is to identify the most prevalent acts of misconduct in open and distance learning systems and the factors that contribute to these actions. Obviously, the types of misconduct vary between the modes of delivery and in the open and distance learning system, the ease of "cut and paste" and an abundance of Internet sources make it all too appealing and tempting to cheat. A study that identifies the most prevalent acts of misconduct can provide researchers with a foundation to curtail specific actions.

A third area for future research is to identify factors that discourage faculty from pursuing unethical behaviour in open and distance learning systems. Technological advancement may present more opportunities for misconduct but by the same token, it also makes it easier to detect these acts of misconduct. It is interesting to see that previous research indicated a lack of interest from online faculty to actively explain or include integrity policies in their syllabi (Dirks, 1998; Olt, 2002). A study that identifies the factors can clarify what needs to be done for faculty to take on an active role in instilling ethical behaviour in their classrooms.

Finally, research should focus on the correlation between unethical conduct and its impact on society. The business world has a rude awakening in the aftermath of scandalous unethical cases such as Enron, Tyco, Anderson, and others. The 21st century business world demands ethical conduct and a study in this area could serve as a guide for would-be cheaters that unethical conduct will no longer be tolerated.

REFERENCES

AAUP. (1987). *Statement of professional ethics.* American Association of University Professors. Retrieved April 22, 2008, from http://www.aaup.org/AAUP/pubsresearch/policydocs/statementon-professionalethics.htm

ACPA. (2002). *Statement of ethical principles and standards.* American College Personnel Association. Retrieved April 22, 2008, from http://www.myacpa.org/au/au_ethical.cfm

Bushweller, K. (1999, April). Generation of cheaters. *The American School Board Journal, 186,* 24-32.

Boyer, E. L. (1987). *College: The undergraduate experience in America.* New York: Harper & Row.

Carroll, D. (2002, February 8). Cheating in classrooms reflects a growing culture of dishonesty, some say. *Kansas City Star,* p.1.

Center for Academic Integrity (CAI). (1999, October). *The fundamental values of academic integrity.* Retrieved April 22, 2008, from http://www.academicintegrity.org/fundamental_values_project/pdf/FVProject.pdf

Chapman, K., Davis, R., Toy, D., & Wright, L. (2004). Academic integrity in the business school environment: I'll get by with a little help from my friends. *Journal of Marketing Education, 26,* 236-249.

Cheating thrives on campus, as officials turn their heads. (2001, May 21). *USA Today,* p. 13A.

Dirks, M. (1998, May). How is assessment being done in distance learning? In *Paper presented at the Northern Arizona University Web.95 Conference.*

George, J., & Carlson, J. (1999, January). Group support systems and deceptive communication. In *Proceedings of the 32nd Hawaii International Conference on Systems Sciences,* (p. 1038).

Graham, C., Cagiltay, K., Lim, B., Craner, J., & Duffy, T. M. (2001). *Seven principles of effective teaching: A practical lens for evaluation online courses.* Assessment. Retrieved April 22, 2008, from http://technologysource.org/?view=article&id=274

Graham, M. A., Monday, J., O'Brien, K., & Steffen, S. (1994). Cheating at small colleges: An examination of student and faculty attitudes and behaviors. *Journal of College Student Development, 35*, 255-260.

Hall, T. L. (1996). Honor among students: Academic integrity and student cultures. Doctoral dissertation, Indiana University. *Dissertation Abstracts International, 57*, 2960A.

Heberling, M. (2002). Maintaining academic integrity in on-line education. *Online Journal of Distance Learning Administration, 5.* Retrieved April 22, 2008, from http://www.westga.edu/%7Edistance/ojdla/spring51/spring51.html

James, M. (2002). *Are you ethical? The truth isn't exactly clear: Politics, circumstances, excuses can blur what is right.* Retrieved April 22, 2008, from http://abcnews.go.com/US/story?id=89985&page=1

Jendrek, M. P. (1989). Faculty reactions to academic dishonesty. *Journal of College Student Development, 30,* 401-406.

Kaczmarczyk, L. (2001). Accreditation and student assessment in distance education: Why we all need to pay attention. In *Proceedings of the 6th Annual SIGCSE Conference on Innovation and Technology in Computer Science Education,* Canterbury, UK, (pp. 113-116).

Kibler, W. L. (1993). A framework for addressing academic dishonesty from a student development perspective. *NASPA Journal, 31,* 8-18.

Kenkel, C. (2004). Balancing online course deadlines with the need to remain flexible. *Campus Technology, 18,* 34-36.

Kleiner, C., & Lord, M. (1999, November 2). The cheating game: Everyone's doing it, from grade school to graduate school. *U.S. News & World Report,* pp. 55-66.

Koch, K. (2000). Cheating in schools. *CQ Researcher, 10,* 745-768.

Lim, C. L., & Coalter, T. (2006). Academic integrity: A faculty's obligation. *International Journal of Teaching and Learning in Higher Education, 17,* 155-159. Retrieved April 22, 2008, from http://www.isetl.org/ijtlhe/pdf/IJTLHE51.pdf

Maramark, S., & Maline, M. B. (1993). Academic dishonesty among college students. *Issues in education* (pp. 1-14). U.S. Department of Education.

McCabe, D. L. (1993). Faculty responses to academic dishonesty: The influence of student honor codes. *Research in Higher Education, 34,* 647-658.

McCabe, D. L. (2001). Cheating: Why students do it and how we can help them stop. *American Educator.* Retrieved April 22, 2008, from http://www.aft.org/pubs-reports/american_educator/winter2001/Cheating.html

McCabe, D. L. (2005). It takes a village: Academic dishonesty and educational opportunity. *Liberal Education, Summer/Fall,* 26-31.

McCabe, D. L., & Pavela, G. (2000). *Ten principles of academic integrity.* Ashville, NC: College Administration Publications. Retrieved April 22, 2008, from http://www.collegepubs.com/ref/10PrinAcaInteg.shtml

McCabe, D. L., & Trevino, L. K. (1993). Academic dishonesty: Honor codes and other contextual influences. *Journal of Higher Education, 64,* 522-538.

McMurtry, K. (2001). E-cheating: Combating a 21st century challenge. *The Journal Online: Technological Horizons in Education.* Retrieved April 22, 2008, from http://thejournal.com/magazine/vault/A3724.cfm

Niels, G. J. (1997). Academic practices, school culture and cheating behavior. *Student Development, 43,* 374-85.

Nuss, E. M. (1984). Academic integrity: Comparing faculty and student attitudes. *Improving College and University Teaching, 32,* 140-144.

Olt, M. (2002, Fall). Ethics and distance education: Strategies for minimizing academic dishonesty in online assessment. *Online Journal of Distance Learning Administration, V*(III).

Rowe, N. (2004, Summer). Cheating in online student assessment: Beyond plagiarism. *Online Journal of Distance Learning Administration, VII*(II). Retrieved April 22, 2008, from http://www.westga.edu/~distance/ojdla/articles/summer2004/rowe72.pdf

Simon, C. A., Carr, J. R., McCullough, S. M., Morgan, S. J., Oleson, T., & Ressel, M. (2003). The other side of academic dishonesty: The relationship between faculty skepticism, gender, and strategies for managing student academic dishonesty cases. *Assessment & Evaluation in Higher Education, 28,* 193-207.

Sims, R. L. (1993, March-April). The relationship between academic dishonesty and unethical business practices. *Journal of Education for Business, 68,* 207-211.

Singhal, A. (1982). Factors in students' dishonesty. *Psychological Reports, 51,* 775-780.

Slobogin, K. (2002). *Survey: Many students say cheating's ok.* CNN.com/Education. Retrieved April 22, 2008, from http://archives.cnn.com/2002/fyi/teachers.ednews/04/05/highschool.cheating

Taylor, B. (2001). *Academic integrity: A letter to my students.* Retrieved April 22, 2008, from http://www.grinnell.edu/academic/writinglab/faculty_resources/letter_to_my_students.pdf

Wajda-Johnston, V. A., Handal, P. J., Brawer, P. A., & Fabricatore, A. N. (2001). Academic dishonesty at the graduate level. *Ethics & Behavior, 11,* 287-305.

Wein, E. (1994, December 2). *Cheating: Risking it all for grades.* Retrieved on April 22, 2008, from http://wc.arizona.edu/~wildcat/papers/old-wildcats/fall94/December/December2,1994/03_1_m.html

Wright, J. C., & Kelly, R. (1974). Cheating: Student/Faculty views and responsibilities. *Improving College University Teaching, 22,* 31-34.

ADDITIONAL READING

Ackerman, T. (2003, October). Colleges' war against cheats goes high-tech: Computers used to fight rising Internet plagiarism. *University of Houston.* Retrieved April 22, 2008, from http://www.uh.edu/ednews/2003/hc/200310/20031006cheat.html

Adkins, J., Kenkel, C., & Lim, C. L. (2005). Deterrents to online academic dishonesty. *The Journal of Learning in Higher Education, 1,* 17-22. Retrieved April 22, 2008, from http://jwpress.com/JLHE/JLHE.htm

Bowers, W. J. (1964). *Student dishonesty and its control in college.* New York: Bureau of Applied Social Research, Columbia University.

Brennan, L. L., & Johnson, V. E. (2004). *Social, ethical and policy implications of information technology.* Hershey, PA: Information Science.

Brown, B. S. (1995). The academic ethics of graduate business students: A survey. *Journal of Education for Business, 70,* 151-157.

Brown, V. J., & Howell, M. E. (2001). The efficacy of policy statements on plagiarism: Do they change students' views? *Research in Higher Education, 42,* 103-118.

Buchanan, E. (2004). Ethical considerations for the information professions. In R. Spinello and H. Tavani (Eds.), *Readings in cyberethics* (2nd ed.). Jones and Bartlett.

Cizek, G. J. (1999). *Cheating on tests: How to do it, detect it, and prevent it.* Mahwah, NJ: Lawrence Erlbaum.

Clos, K. (2002). When academic dishonesty happens on your campus. *National Institute for Staff and Organizational Development* (Vol. XXIV, No. 26). ISOD Innovation Abstracts. College of Education, The University of Texas at Austin.

Conradson, S., & Hernansez-Ramos, P. (2004). Computers, the Internet, and cheating among secondary school students: Some implications for educators. *Practical Assessment, Research and Evaluation, 9*(9). Retrieved April 22, 2008, from http://pareonline.net/getvn.asp?v=9&n=9

Cromwell, S. (2000, January 24). What can we do to curb student cheating? *Education World.* Retrieved April 22, 2008, from http://www.education-world.com/a_admin/admin144.shtml

Darbyshire, P., & Burgess, S. (2006). Strategies for dealing with plagiarism and the Web in higher education. *Journal of Business Systems, Governance and Ethics, 1,* 27-39. Retrieved April 22, 2008, from http://www.jbsge.vu.edu.au/issues/vol01no4/Darbyshire-Burgess.pdf

Davis, M. (2004, Spring). Five kinds of ethics across the curriculum: An introduction to four experiments with one kind, *Teaching Ethics, 4,* 1-14.

Decoo, W. (2002). *Crisis on campus: Confronting academic misconduct.* Cambridge, MA: MIT Press.

Eplion, D., & Keefe, T. (2005). On-line exams: Strategies to detect cheating and minimize its impact. Retrieved April 22, 2008, from http://www.mtsu.edu/~itconf/proceed05/dEplion.pdf

Ercegovac, Z., & Richardson, J. (2004). Academic dishonesty, plagiarism included, in the digital age: A literature review. *College & Research Libraries, 65,* 301-318.

Foster, A. L. (2002). Plagiarism-detection tool creates legal quandary. The *Chronicle of Higher Education, 48,* A37-38.

Fussell, J. A. (2005, May 15). Cheaters use new array of gadgets to get that "A." *The Kansas City Star,* p. A1.

Gehring, D. D. (1998). When institutions and their faculty address issues of academic dishonesty: Realities and myths. *Academic Integrity Matters,* 77-92.

Gleason, D. H. (2001). Subsumption ethics. In R. Spinello & H. Tavani (Eds.), *Readings in cyberethics* (pp. 557-571). Subdury, MA: Jones and Barlett.

Gorry, G. A. (2003, May 23). Steal this MP3 file. *The Chronicle of Higher Education,* p. B20.

Gross, J. (2003, November 26). Exposing the cheat sheet, with the students' aid. *The New York Times.* Retrieved April 22, 2008, from http://www.softwaresecure.com/pdf/CheatingWaterBottle_112603_.pdf

Harris, R. A. (2001). *The plagiarism handbook: Strategies for preventing, detecting, and dealing with plagiarism.* Los Angeles, CA: Pyrczak.

Harris, R. (2004). Anti-plagiarism strategies for research papers. *VirtualSalt. Retrieved April 22, 2008, from* http://www.virtualsalt.com/antiplag.htm

Hendershott, A., Drinan, P. F., & Cross, M. (2000). Toward enhancing a culture of academic integrity, *The NASPA Journal, 37,* 587-598.

Jocoy, C., & DiBiase, D. (2006, June). Plagiarism by adult learners online: A case study in detection and remediation. *International Review of*

Research in Open and Distance Learning, 7. Retrieved April 22, 2008, from www.irrodl.org/index.php/irrodl/article/downloadSuppFile/242/21

Kelley, K. B., & Bonner, K. (2005). Digital text, distance education and academic dishonesty: Faculty and administrator perceptions and responses. *Journal of Asynchronous Learning Networks, 9.*

Keying in: The Newsletter of the National Business Education Association. (2004, January). *Employers value communication and interpersonal abilities, 14, 3-6.*

Kumar, A. (2003, August 31). High-tech sleuthing catches college cheats. *St. Petersburg Times.* Retrieved April 22, 2008, from http://www.sptimes.com/2003/08/31/State/High_tech_sleuthing_c.shtml

Lathrop, A., & Foss, K. (2000). *Student cheating and plagiarism in the Internet era: A wake-up call.* Englewood, CO: Libraries Unlimited.

Layton, T. G. (2000). Digital learning: Why tomorrow's schools must learn to let go of the past. *American School Board Journal.* Retrieved April 22, 2008, from http://www.electronic-school.com/2000/09/0900f1.html

Macleod, D. (2005, February 10). Universities urged to root out student cheats. *Education-Guardian.co.uk.* Retrieved April 22, 2008, from http://education.guardian.co.uk/students/work/story/0,12734,1410054,00.html

McCabe, D. L., & Pavela, G. (2005). Honor codes for a new generation. *Inside Higher Education.* Retrieved April 22, 2008, from http://www.insidehighered.com/views/new_honor_codes_for_a_new_generation

McCabe, D. L., Trevino, L. K., & Butterfield, K. (1996). The influences of collegiate and corporate codes of conduct on ethics-related behavior in the workplace. *Business Ethics Quarterly, 6,* 441-460.

McCabe, D. L., Trevino, L. K., & Butterfield, K. (2001, July). Cheating in academic institutions: A decade of research. *Ethics & Behavior, 11,* 219-233.

Morgan, B. L., & Korschgen, A. J. (2001). The ethics of faculty behavior: Students' and professors' views. *College Student Journal.* Retrieved April 22, 2008, from http://www.findarticles.com/cf_0/m0FCR/3_35/80744654/print.jhtml

Quinn, M. J. (2005). *Ethics for the information age* (2nd ed.). Boston: Addison-Wesley.

Reynolds, G. (2006). *Ethics in information technology* (2nd ed.). Boston: Thomson Course Technology.

Shaw, T. (2003). Making IT work for learning: Technology and the test. *Multimedia Schools 10,* 38-39. Retrieved April 22, 2008, from http://www.infotoday.com/mmschools/may03/shaw.shtml

Spinello, R. (2003). *Case studies in information technology ethics* (2nd ed.). Upper Saddle River, NJ: Prentice Hall.

Spinello, R. A., & Tavani, H. T. (2004). *Readings in cyberethics* (2nd ed.). Sudbury, NJ: Jones and Bartlett.

Sterngold, A. (2004). Confronting plagiarism: How conventional teaching invites cybercheating. *Change, 36,* 16-21.

Straw, J. (2000). Keep your eyes off the screen: Online cheating and what we can do about it. *Academic Exchange Quarterly, 4,* 21-25.

Szabo, A., & Underwood, J. (2004). Cybercheats: Is information and communication technology fuelling academic dishonesty? *Active Learning in Higher Education, 5,* 180-199.

Underwood, J., & Szabo, A. (2003). Academic offences and e-learning: Individual propensities in cheating. *British Journal of Educational Technology, 34,* 467-477.

Whitley, B. E., Jr., & Keith-Spiegel, P. (2001). *Academic dishonesty: An educator's guide*. Mahwah, NJ: Lawrence Erlbaum.

Chapter XIV
Ethics Review Concerns of Canada's Distance Researchers

Patrick J. Fahy
Athabasca University, Canada

ABSTRACT

Ethics review of research involving humans is intended to protect human dignity by balancing harms and benefits. The foci and methods used in reviews vary nationally, but tend, as in Canada, to address core principles including free and informed consent, privacy and confidentiality, inclusiveness and fairness, and the rights of dependent subjects. Under examination in relation to the policy that governs research ethics in Canada, the Tri-Council Policy Statement (TCPS, 2005), these principles admit numerous exceptions, a fact that, as shown by a study reported here, is better understood by those actually engaged in research than those who are not. The implications of these findings, and the specific priorities of non-Canadian researchers (especially those in developing nations), are described and discussed.

BACKGROUND

The global increase in online and distance programming has resulted in widespread interest on the part of researchers in exploring and analyzing distance learning processes and outcomes (Bucharest Declaration, 2004; Mishra, 1998; *Tri-council Policy Statement* [TCPS], 2005). At the same time, granting agencies almost globally have increased their scrutiny of the ethics of research involving humans, especially in universities and other centres where public funding is typically used by researchers.

While distance practitioners internationally appear almost universally to support research standards (Gordon & Sork, 2001), in the view of some the effect of increased scrutiny by some ethics review has sometimes been deleterious, constraining unnecessarily the scope of inquiry, inhibiting or limiting innovative or unconventional methods, lengthening and complicating the process of gaining research approvals, whether externally funded or not, and, in some particularly unfortunate cases, resulting in the outright cancellation of projects ("Complexity of the IRB process," 2005; Rourke, Anderson, Garrison, & Archer, 2001; Savulescu, Chalmers, & Blunt, 1996). The impact on distance researchers has been particularly severe, as distance research almost always involves human subjects, and often entails the collection and analysis of personal data.

In Canada, the *Tri-council Policy Statement: Ethical Conduct for Research Involving Humans* (TCPS, 2005) is the federal government's statement on research ethics principles applicable to institutions receiving federal funding (Medical Research Council of Canada, 2005). The TCPS articulates the standards that Research Ethics Boards (REBs), responsible for applying the TCPS institutionally, must enforce. The purpose of the TCPS is to assure ethical treatment of human research subjects in Canada. While there is no debate about the worth of this objective, there have been several conflicts since the appearance of the TCPS in 1998 over how this goal might best be achieved. Specifically, there is lively debate about whether the current policy guarantees appropriate freedom for researchers, especially those in the social sciences and humanities, whose work is typically minimal- or no-risk.

The nature of core ethical principles contained in the TCPS, their interpretations, their similarities to and differences from global standards and concerns, and some of the implications of these for distance research are discussed in the following.

IDENTIFYING CORE ETHICAL PRINCIPLES

The objections of social sciences and humanities researchers to aspects of the Canada's TCPS, and to some practices of REBs in implementing it, do not question the importance of ethical treatment of subjects. There are two issues: how

distance research, as a form of social science inquiry, may adhere to high ethical standards, given the special circumstances under which that research is often conducted; and how the approval process for distance research might be revised–made "proportionate" –to the low levels of risk that usually accompany these proposals (TCPS, 2005, p. 1.7).

The debate about core ethical principles and proportionate review of proposals is not new. Globally, ethics in human subjects' research has been the subject of increasingly heated debate for some time, in North America even appearing in the popular press. Beck and Kaufman (1994) some time ago identified various ethical "pitfalls" that could entrap researchers; in 2002, Begley (2002) described, in *The Wall Street Journal*, a growing "rift" between researchers and ethicists; more recently, others (Dohy, 2004; Elliott & Lemmens, 2005; Lemonick & Goldstein, 2002; Munro, 2004) have publicly raised questions about doubtful practices such as paid ethics review in clinical trials, while bloggers have debated the impartiality of online product reviews (Lasica, 2005).

To create a common ethics framework for researchers and those responsible for reviewing and approving research proposals, policies such as the TCPS present principles that researchers must respect and REBs enforce. Key principles contained in the TCPS include:

- Respect for human dignity
- Free and informed consent
- Privacy and confidentiality
- Inclusiveness and justice
- Balancing of harms and benefits
- The status of "subjects" in clinical and nonclinical research
- The role and composition of REBs

Human dignity. Interest in this principle arises chiefly from the emergence of programs of systematic, industry-funded medical research (Evans & Jakupec, 1996, p. 72), and from egregious violations of basic ethical principles, such as the Tuskegee syphilis study (Centers for Disease Control and Prevention, 2005), and the Willowbrook hepatitis studies (University of Utah, 2005). The underlying ethical principle is that respect for persons requires they not be used solely as means to ends, and that "the multiple and interdependent interests of the person" (including the right to effective treatment or therapy) be protected in any research studies (TCPS, 2005, p. i.5). Most ethics policies hold that the rights of subjects should always take precedence over the advancement of knowledge (TCPS, 2005, p. 74). Under this principle, special protection is provided heteronomous (dependent) groups or persons (those not capable of exercising fully freedom of choice, or of protecting their own interests independently). This includes cross-cultural or power-authority situations, where subjects (e.g., patients, inmates, students, minors, clients, etc.) might be the victims, even inadvertently, of coercion (TCPS, 2005, p. 2.4; Rigano, 2001).

Human dignity is respected when researchers obtain and maintain the free and informed consent of subjects throughout their research involvement. However, there are many exceptions to this surprisingly complex principle.

Free and informed consent. Also spoken of as the "cornerstone" of ethical research (McNamee, 2001; O'Connor, 2002; Vujakovic & Bullard, 2001), the TCPS calls informed consent "the heart of ethical research involving humans" (TCPS, 2005, p. 2.1). Despite its primacy, however, there are a wide variety of situations in which the TCPS recognizes that informed consent can either be waived completely, obtained after the fact, or suspended (TCPS, 2005, p. 2.1):

1.   The research is minimal risk.
2.   The waiver is unlikely to adversely affect the rights and welfare of the subjects.
3.   The research could not practicably be carried out without it.

4.   Subjects will be provided with additional information after participation, "whenever possible and appropriate."
5.   A therapeutic intervention is not involved (normally covered by point 1).

In situations where full informed consent cannot be obtained under one or more of the above exemptions, the TCPS suggests that subjects be debriefed after participation, when "feasible." Where subjects object to participation for any reason after the debriefing, they may be given the opportunity to remove themselves and their data from the study (TCPS, 2005, p. 2.3). However, the researcher need not grant requests for removal of data if doing so might "colour the responses of the [other] subjects and thus invalidate the research" (TCPS, 2005, pp. 2.2-2.3).

This exception is important, as it recognizes the legitimate rights of the majority to participate in research, even over the objections of some (Under this principle, the barrier encountered by Rourke, Anderson, Garrison, and Archer (2001), where one objecting member of a group caused an entire sponsored research project to be cancelled, might have been surmounted.) The TCPS states this right to participate clearly:

*In cases where a subject expresses concerns about a study, the researcher may give the subject the option of removing his or her data from the project. **This approach should be used only when the elimination of the subject's data will not compromise the validity of the research design, and hence diminish the ethical value of participation by other subjects**.* (TCPS, 2005, p. 2.3; emphasis added)

The following shows that the rights of the minority are confined to personal refusal to participate:

Nothing in this Policy should be interpreted to mean that research subjects have the right to veto a project, though they do, of course, have the right to refuse to cooperate with the researcher(s). (TCPS, 2005, p. 1.2; emphasis added)

Several other exemptions to the principle of informed consent are acknowledged by the TCPS, giving researchers the right to deal *without their cooperation* with certain individuals and organizations:

1. **Public bodies and corporations**, including governments, political parties, authoritarian organizations, and criminal groups (TCPS, 2005, p. 2.2).
2. **Private organizations**. These may decline to participate, deny access to private records, and attempt to set limits on the participation of members or employees, but they are not permitted to limit or veto research about their own activities, and their participation or consent for research are not needed (TCPS, 2005, p. 2.2).
3. **Public figures**. "Certain types of research … may legitimately have a negative effect on public figures .…" (TCPS, 2005, p. 1.6), including all "public" persons, artists and performers (and their works), politicians, and business leaders (TCPS, 2005, p. i.9).
4. **Subjects of naturalistic observation**. If subjects are not identified, and events are not staged, the TCPS suggests these studies be regarded as minimal risk; if the participants expect visibility (i.e., at a political rally), consent may be assumed (pp. 2.4-2.5).
5. **Students in classroom and course evaluations**. "Nothing in this Section [Article 2.4] should be interpreted as meaning that normal classroom assessments of course work require REB approval" (TCPS, 2005, p. 2.6).
6. **Those involved in quality assurance and performance reviews**. "Quality assurance studies, performance reviews or testing within normal educational requirements

should also not be subject to REB approval" (TCPS, 2005, p. 1.1).

Privacy and confidentiality. This is truly a cornerstone principle, arguably more central than any other in research with human subjects. Evans and Jakupec (1996) state that anonymity addresses many ethical issues in research. The TCPS observes that "in many cultures, privacy and confidentiality are considered fundamental to human dignity" (TCPS, 2005, p. i.5); further, "privacy is a fundamental value, perceived by many as essential for the protection and promotion of human dignity" (TCPS, 2005, p. 3.1). Gordon and Sork (2001) found that confidentiality was the most sensitive ethical issue among adult education practitioners, especially any sharing of information regarded as private.

While the TCPS calls privacy "a fundamental value" (TCPS, 2005, p. 3.1), it is not absolute. Issues affecting the public good (e.g., public health and safety, and, increasingly, security preservation and crime prevention) may ethically require disclosure of some personal information. Further, use of information already in the public domain, even of identifiable nonpublic persons, is permitted (TCPS, 2005, p. 3.2), as is information under subpoena. Exemptions to the privacy principle suggest that it is not the collection of personal data per se that is problematic in evaluating risks, it is subsequent use (Population, Inc., 2001; "The logic of privacy," 2007).

It can be argued that postings to public listservs or blogs, and information in non-password-protected Web sites, are not protected by privacy or confidentiality provisions of the Policy. Even password-protected postings, if used under "secondary use of data" provisions, may be accessed: "If it is impossible to identify individuals whose records exist within a database, then researchers should be allowed access to that database" (TCPS, 2005, p. 3.5).

Justice and inclusiveness. This principle is intended to assure that no group bears an unfair burden, or enjoys disproportionately the benefits, of research. Respecting this principle requires development of a sound research methodology (to assure an efficient experience for those participating), anonymity, and protection of private information in any published reports.

The principle of justice and inclusiveness ethically extends to researchers themselves. Social science and humanities researchers in Canada have asserted their "traditional mandate to gather information about and critically analyze all aspects of society," which some feel is "threatened by a narrowing of permissible topics and approaches" due to concern for "non-ethics criteria such as liability management and other forms of 'ethics drift'" (van den Hoonaard, 2004, p. 12). Studying traditionally sensitive topics and exploring the margins of society require that social scientists be permitted access to salient research methods and approaches, even over the objections of those who might be discomfited by their inquiries or findings. This argument asserts that society's "right to know" is accompanied by a "right to find out," shared by practitioners of disciplines that systematically study human behavior. Academic freedom in the social sciences demands, this argument concludes, that these special and traditional rights of inquiry be safeguarded.

Balancing harms and benefits. Ethical review is intended to assure that any potential harms are compensated for by the prospective benefits of research. O'Connor (2002) argues that no research is completely harmless. Others claim that perceptions of ethical soundness depend upon one's point of view (Pendlebury & Enslin, 2001), sometimes to the disadvantage of developing countries which are trying to "keep up," often simply through "mimicry" of the West (Leach & Oakland, 2007; Yang, 2001). The TCPS holds that a balanced assessment of the potential harms and possible benefits of research, employing multiple points of view and without privileging any particular disciplinary or moral perspective, is required (TCPS, 2005, p. i.2; Small, 2001). As

a consequence, as noted earlier, some ethical approaches and forms of research, while having the clear potential for negative effects on identifiable persons, institutions, or organizations, are ethically permissible because an assessment of social benefit vs. individual harm favors the former, despite the latter (TCPS, 2005, p. i.9).

Key points in the assessment of harms and benefits include the following: 1) the TCPS does not require that research be free of all risk, only of *unnecessary* risks; 2) all the risks potentially present in the research do not have to be known or addressed before research can be commenced (indeed, identifying and assessing risks to humans is often a central purpose of research) (TCPS, 2005, p. i.6); 3) acceptance of obvious and suspected risks may be justified, if subjects consent and the potential benefits outweigh them; and 4) in cases where risks are known, the researcher's responsibility is to assure participants accept the possibility of harm initially, and continue to do so throughout their involvement.

Clinical and nonclinical research. Those who work in predominantly minimal-risk (nonclinical) research situations have argued with increasing vigor that the only research that warrants stringent REB review is that which exceeds minimal risk. The difficulty seen by social scientists is that they are subject to default assumptions about risk, applicable to biomedical situations but often grossly inappropriate in most humanities and social sciences contexts. It is suggested that REBs should be required to specify the "identifiable harms" in any research to which they object (van den Hoonaard, 2004, p. 6), rather than placing the onus on researchers to prove no harms exist or might arise (Proving the impossibility of any phenomenon, it is argued, is logically impossible.)

The stance of social science and humanities researchers in Canada has hardened in the face of what they regard as a "one size fits all" mentality of the TCPS and its developers. One description of changes needed to address problems with the current ethics policy reads in part:

... [the] next version [of the TCPS must] acknowledge and respond to the diversity in research perspectives, reassert a commitment to principles of academic freedom, and ensure adequate protection for human participants. Doing so will require bold initiatives ... to create an effective counterbalance to the biomedical/experimental hegemony that currently dominates the TCPS and that ... threatens the diversity of the social sciences and humanities and their ability to carry out their traditional social and cultural mandate. (van den Hoonaard, 2004, p. 10)

In addition to the historical examples of abuse in experimental biomedical research mentioned earlier, Canadian researchers' concerns about ethics in clinical trials have more recently been piqued, and focused, by the highly public case of University of Toronto researcher Dr. Nancy Olivieri. Dr. Olivieri claimed the right to inform her subject (also her patients) at the Hospital for Sick Children of potentially serious side-effects of an experimental drug treatment. When she did so over the objections of the drug's owner, in the view of the Canadian Association of University Teachers (CAUT), her university and her employer failed to support her promptly or adequately in the ensuing public and legal brouhaha. While the details of the dispute are murky (for some patients the treatment appeared effective, and was continued), the fundamental ethical issue, not always clear in the press, was the researcher's duty to advise her subjects that the experimental conditions had changed, and that data were now in hand indicating the treatment might have potentially more serious risks than had been known when the subjects agreed to participate (Thompson, Baird, & Downie, 2002). Researchers in the social sciences and humanities insist that this sort of imbroglio is vanishingly less likely to arise in their fields.

The role and composition of REBs. Another perceived irritant for distance researchers in Canada arises from the composition and structure of the ethics board (REBs) that enforce the policy. According to the TCPS, REBs should consist of at least five persons, academics and nonacademics, two of whom having "broad expertise" in the types of research the board will be reviewing. There is no requirement that members be researchers or, in the case of disciplines such as distance education, that they even be familiar with the field.

REBs have a great deal of autonomy in their workings and decision-making processes. This autonomy, when coupled with a lack of experience with or knowledge of research practices, may cause problems social science researchers regard as predictable (van den Hoonaard, 2004).

VIEWS OF CANADIAN RESEARCHERS: NEEDED CHANGES TO RESEARCH POLICY AND PRACTICES

In response to the problems described above, and based on numerous and persistent complaints about the treatment that social science and humanities researchers encountered under the TCPS, the Social Sciences and Humanities Research Ethics Special Working Committee (van den Hoonaard, 2004) produced a list of specific recommendations, some, as discussed later, with international applicability. These include:

- Greater clarity over the distinction between "minimal risk" and "identifiable harm."
- Respect for the rights of researchers, especially those engaged in research of minimal or lower risk (Costley and Gibbs's (2006) international perspective, and their concept of the "ethics of care," suggests that researchers have differing obligations as a result of their specific context, particularly their relation to the people and objects under study).
- A more nuanced understanding of fundamental principles such as informed consent,

confidentiality, and anonymity (Gardner's (2005) view of the importance of intercultural perceptions and conceptions apply here).

- Respect for standard practices in different disciplines.
- Acknowledgement of the needs and rights of student researchers (Husu (2004) speaks of the need for "reference points," to help novices and practitioners translate abstract theories into useful principles in specific situations).
- Overall, a need to acknowledge the greater variety of research methods as found in the social sciences and humanities (pp. 5-6).

Such requests both confirm a problem in regard to ethics review in Canada, and lay out what may be required in the way of change to the existing process. The views of researchers are critical, because, as the TCPS points out:

*... ethical principles must operate neither in the abstract, nor in isolation from one another. Ethical principles are sometimes criticized as being applied in formulaic ways. To avoid this, **they should be applied in the context of the nature of the research and of the ethical norms and practices of the relevant research discipline**. Good ethical reasoning requires thought, insight and sensitivity to context...* (TCPS, 2005, p. i.9; emphasis supplied)

Mugridge and Kaufman (1986) have previously applied the concept of *context* to training, arguing that distance researchers should learn within the community in which they subsequently intend to work. They believe an apprenticeship in the community of intended practice, even online, would ensure standards were learned effectively. The following section describes a study intended to determine whether this has occurred in Canada.

Survey of Distance Practitioners Regarding The TCPS

In 2003, a study was conducted of the views of Canadian distance educators about principles contained in the TCPS (Fahy & Spencer, 2004). The purpose of the study (nothing similar to which had been previously conducted) was to determine the views of distance practitioners, scholars, and students, with varying research backgrounds (including, by their own assessment, none), concerning selected ethical principles found in the TCPS. Volunteers were recruited by invitations posted on the Web sites of three Canadian distance education organizations: the Alberta Distance Education and Training Association (ADETA), the Canadian Association for Distance Education (CADE), and Athabasca University's Centre for Distance Education. A further group of "researchers," who had published papers within the recent past in the CADE *Journal of Distance Education* (*JDE*), were personally invited to participate.

In the analysis, the views of respondents were examined on two criteria: self-described research experience (from "none" to "high"), and a record of recent research publication (published and not published). The research questions were:

1. To what degree does self-assessed research experience (including none) affect agreement with selected ethical principles?
2. To what degree do the views of published researchers differ from those of other distance education practitioners?

The survey instrument was a questionnaire consisting of 31 statements about ethics in research, reflecting principles which experience had shown produced problems of interpretation (the authors had both been members of their institutional REB, and Research Ethics Appeal Board (REAB)). Eighteen of the statements used in the questionnaire were consistent with principles found in the TCPS, while 13 were contrary to, or asserted positions not found in, the TCPS. Participants were asked to rate their agreement with the items using a 7-point Likert-type scale.

Of the 172 usable returns received, 68% were from women; over 97% of respondents held at least one degree (18% held doctorates), and 15% assessed their research experience as "high" (23% "moderate"). Twenty-four percent rated their ethics experience as "none," and 50% rated it "low." Only 11% had experience serving on an REB. Forty-eight percent of the respondents rated their familiarity with the TCPS as "none," while 5% rated it "high."

A major finding of the study was that, when faced with pronouncements that purported to reflect ethical positions, the subjects with the most research experience were more likely to agree with statements consistent with the TCPS, and to disagree with statements inconsistent with the policy. Further, experienced researchers (those who had published) were less likely to agree with categorical statements containing the terms "never," "always," and "must" (rare in the TCPS, where "... because principles are designed to guide ethical reflection and conduct, they admit flexibility and exceptions;" TCPS, 2005, p. i.9).

The conclusions of the study included several observations potentially applicable to international problems in ethics review of distance research. First, it was apparent that those who were not active researchers (those without recent publications) were much less likely to have familiarity with the ethics adjudication process, or with the TCPS: 27% of this group rated their experience judging the ethics of research proposals as "none," and 54% rated it "low." Further, 50% of the nonresearchers admitted "no" familiarity with the TCPS, and a further 37% claimed only "low" levels of experience; 97% of this group reported "no" direct REB experience.

It was also clear that nonresearchers tended to be more dogmatic (were "more royalist than the king") in relation to ethical principles: they were prepared to place more restrictions on researchers than were actually required by the TCPS. On the following items, all of which in fact *are consistent* with the TCPS, nonresearchers expressed *less agreement* than researchers:

- Ethics review should incorporate flexibility in the implementation of common principles.
- In assessing a research proposal, the ethical review process should consider the nature of the research and the ethical norms and practices of the relevant research discipline.
- The principle of proportionate review permits research which exposes human subjects to minimal risk or less to receive only minimal review.
- Subjects do not have the right to veto a project.
- The requirement for informed consent may be waived, under some circumstances.

Some statements that were *not consistent* with the TCPS received more support from nonresearchers than from researchers (to the detriment of research flexibility and freedom of inquiry generally):

- In ethical research, human subjects are never subjected to risks of harm.
- The ethical review process has as one of its aims the purpose of blocking research which does not include collaboration with the research subjects.
- Written consent to participate must be obtained for research to be fully ethical.
- Corporations must approve of the participation of their employees in research conducted by outsiders involving the corporation.
- Research must not be conducted in circumstances where subjects do not know they are being observed, or otherwise cannot give their free and informed consent.

Finally, nonresearchers were more likely to regard the TCPS as the ultimate arbiter of ethical issues: they were more likely to agree that "the TCPS may be regarded by researchers as a source of definitive answers to contentious ethical questions they may face in their research." This role is explicitly rejected by the TCPS (2005, p. i.3).

Research Experience and REBs

The survey findings suggest why problems arise between researchers and REBs, and changes that might reduce conflict and improve the quality of ethics reviews, in the eyes of social scientists. The survey indicates that *the group with best under-standing of the TCPS are published researchers*, especially those with REB experience. In the TCPS's own terms, the more research-experienced individuals best understood distance education's "ethical norms and practices" (p. i.9).

It is not clear that the experts' views are adequately represented, let alone deferred to, on most REBs, however. The problem is engrained in their composition. The TCPS legislates that REBs must comprise members, "at least two [with] broad expertise in the methods of the areas of research that are covered by the REB," "one member . . . knowledgeable in ethics," "one member . . . knowledgeable in the relevant law" (suggested, but not required, for nonbiomedical research), and "at least one member who has no affiliation with the institution but is recruited from the community served by the institution" (p. 1.3). The objective is to "ensure the expertise, multidisciplinarity and independence essential to competent research ethics review by REBs" (p. i.3), and to avoid "the imposing [of] one disciplinary perspective on others" (p. i.2).

Problems may arise if the expert members of the REB are outnumbered by nonexperts. The potential for this problem is recognized by the TCPS: "The majority of members of an REB should have both the training and the expertise to make sound judgments on the ethics of research proposals involving human subjects" (p. 1.3). To achieve this objective, the TCPS declares, REBs must assure staff possess "both the training and the expertise to make sound judgments on the ethics of research proposals involving human subjects" (p. 1.3). The policy says nothing about how such balance is to be achieved, however. Based upon the findings of the survey, the answer is that the majority of REB members must be experienced researchers, actively working and publishing in the discipline being assessed.

REBs acknowledging researcher expertise will abide by the following principles:

1. **Experienced researchers sit on REBs, and their judgments are respected.** The survey demonstrated that distance education practitioners who are not active researchers are much more likely to admit they do not have knowledge of the field of ethics, nor of the TCPS; yet, they may be appointed to the REB under current eligibility criteria. It is a strange logic that holds that ignorance or naiveté are qualifications for REB membership. REB members make highly technical judgments, requiring understanding both of the TCPS and of the ethical norms and research practices of various disciplines. These decisions cannot be wisely made by unprepared individuals.

   The importance of specialized competence is becoming clearer as appreciation for the differences between distance and other forms of research increases (Anderson & Kanuka, 2003). Evans and Jakupec (1996) argue for the importance of context in evaluating research proposals. The TCPS (2005, p. i.2) itself acknowledges that "sound ethical reasoning" requires scrutiny of contexts, especially of specialized disciplines. The survey indicates that experienced researchers are more capable of appreciating aspects of context, and of the nuances in differences among disciplines.

2. **The norms and practices of different disciplines are respected.** This key notion from the TCPS (2005, p. i.9) attempts to assure that "alien" ethical standards are not inflicted on researchers (Owen, Robert, Burgess, Golfman, & Sykes, 2001). Researchers have complained of policy misinterpretations, and other abuses, from adjudicators not attuned to the expectations of specific disciplines (Gibbs & Gambrill, 2002). Active researchers are more likely, the survey showed, to accept the need to respect unique needs and traditions within disciplines.

3. **The value of anonymity, and subjects' freedom to volunteer, is acknowledged.** Subjects have the right to participate in research, even when reviewers may regard participation as risky, unworthy, unattractive, or unwise. The ethical issues concern whether consent is informed and truly voluntary, and whether the degree of anonymity provided is as promised. Anonymity and confidentiality are versatile tools. The TCPS (2005) states, in the context of a discussion of confidentiality, "If the data being stored are truly anonymous, the research project will need only minimal REB scrutiny" (p. 3.2); in a discussion of secondary use of data, the policy reads, "This issue [secondary use of data] becomes of concern *only* when data can be linked to individuals...." (p. 3.4). "As a general rule," the TCPS summarizes, "the best protection of the confidentiality of personal information and records will be achieved through anonymity" (p. 3.2).

4. **Freedom of inquiry is preserved**. If the activities of authoritarian REBs inhibit free and open inquiry to too great an extent, only innocuous research will be approved. There is no ethical requirement that research be toothless, bland, void of embarrassing findings, or unchallenging, however (Furedi, 2002). Questions of academic freedom, the balance between society's right to know and personal privacy, and the issue of the public interest over the welfare of individuals (including their privacy), arise here. Without diminishing the importance of any of these complex issues, it is sufficient to point out that a chilling of the research climate in Canada by overzealous REBs, "threaten[ing] free inquiry for no ethical gain" (van den Hoonaard, 2004, p. 10), has not improved the protection of subjects in fields such as the humanities and social sciences, where there has been no evidence of serious ethical risks.

5. **Attention is focused on biomedical and clinical research.** Especially where evidence exists that standards are inadequate or enforcement lax in the protection of subjects or the integrity of results, ethical review should be stringent. Nonexperimental and qualitative approaches should be distinguished from experimental ones, and proportionate review should reflect the potential for identified harms. REBs and ethics policymakers should recognize that it is the biomedical disciplines that are presently "under siege" (Nurse, 2006) for ethical violations. These disciplines need more stringent review mechanisms to recover their credibility and public confidence; research in the social sciences and humanities, including distance education, should not be punished for the transgressions of other disciplines.

The uniqueness of distance research. Distance practitioners globally argue that distance research is different in important ways from traditional forms, and thus has different requirements for ethical review. Some types of research may be easier to perform at a distance, both because different tools and approaches are used, and because the interpersonal dynamics between researcher and subject vary at a distance.

The tools that the global distance education and training community commonly uses for interaction also make new forms of effective contact with research subjects possible. Online surveys, participatory and collaborative research models (including culturally and geographically dispersed subjects, and longitudinal studies), iterative projects, and scrutiny of system-generated data are all easier to employ in a distance context than they may be in more traditional research traditions, because technology is involved. In addition to facilitating access and participation (for some participants, though admittedly not for all), the marginal cost of adding additional subjects to technology-based distance research projects may be much less than in traditional face-to-face situations (Kraut, Olson, Banaji, & Bruckman, 2004).

It is also often easier to create and analyze online social networks at a distance, and to capture and scrutinize their interactions. Protections for participants are based upon the greater voluntariness of participation (there is less social pressure online to join a group), the ease with which individuals may withdraw, or refuse to answer or participate (continued "consent" is easier to assure), and the overall anonymity of the medium. At the same time, the presence (and even the participation) of the observer/researcher may be less obtrusive.

Analysis of the results of online interaction may also take advantage of the media and modes of communication employed. Transcripts of the text of online interactions can be assessed using the increasingly sophisticated analytic tools and procedures developed in the past decade for this purpose (Anderson, Rourke, Garrison, & Archer, 2001; Fahy, 2004, 2005; Fahy, Crawford, & Ally, 2001; Garrison, Anderson, & Archer, 2000, 2001; Garrison, Cleveland-Innes, Koole, & Koppelman, 2005; Herring, 1996; Rourke et al., 1999). While the transcript

analysis process is not without difficulties (Fahy, 2001; Rourke et al., 2001), results suggest that analysis of interaction patterns in online communities is ethically accepted, and profitable in terms of insights into social patterns (Fahy, 2002, 2003).

Not unexpectedly, there are also hazards in online research. Fraud and misrepresentation are easier to perpetrate online: identities cannot be readily confirmed; pseudonyms, alter egos, and false identities are common; fraudulent or even malicious research participation can occur; and, even assuming the best will and most conscientious moderator, unintentional misunderstandings may arise.

Furthermore, the media used may themselves be foreign to some participants, or may prove unreliable, uneconomical, or too complex for some of the intended audience. It is also possible for unprincipled researchers to obtain information surreptitiously, or to violate confidentiality or privacy agreements ("administrator access" gives broad powers to the unscrupulous). Credentials or expertise may be misstated, and the contributions of individuals to group products may be misidentified. All of these dangers exist in face-to-face research, too, but they are sometimes exacerbated, and more difficult to detect, in online situations, especially when conducted internationally. Their existence makes commitment to ethical behavior by distance practitioners and researchers all the more vital.

Canada Compared with Other Countries on Research Ethics

The concerns of Canada's distance researchers can be compared, with similarities and differences as follows, in relation to researchers internationally.

Similarities

- The conviction that integrity in inquiry is one of the foundations of higher education (Bucharest Declaration, 2004; Lane, 2004; Mishra, 1998).
- The conviction that students of research must become "critically competent ... professional communicators" as part of their research training (Savage, 2001).
- Concern for the rights of dependent persons in research situations (Iacono, 2006).
- Desire for clear principles for researchers and practitioners (Crosta, 2004).
- Awareness of the impact of the World Wide Web, and technology generally, on research and researchers (Karmakar, 2002).

Differences

International researchers seem more concerned that:

- "Nontraditional" students (those in cross-cultural learning situations) are being forced to learn and adopt Western research methods and values (Leach & Oakland, 2007; Robinson-Pant, 2005);
- New, rapidly evolving technologies, combined with a variety of pre-existing unresolved issues, increase economic and organizational stresses on adopting cultures and organizations (Chozos, Lytras, & Pouloudi, 2002);
- Harmonious integration of forces for internationalization vs. localization (Yang, 2001), and a cross-cultural perspective on research ethics (Robinson-Pant, 2005; Sikes, 2006), have been slow to occur; and
- There is considerable variation in the attention paid to instruction regarding ethics in different learning environments (Lysaght, Rosenberger, & Kerridge, 2006).

CONCLUSION

Implications of Findings

Canada's distance researchers believe that ethical inquiry is not necessarily harmed, and indeed may sometimes be facilitated, by psychological, geographical, temporal, and other distances existing between researchers and online subjects. Used properly, some distances may even encourage desirable attributes of research, such as candor, reflection, thoughtfulness, and objectivity. At the same time, it is clear that online researchers everywhere need to be exceptionally skilled communicators, designers of materials, interpreters of their data, and masters of methodology, to overcome the difficulties distance may present to those unfamiliar with its character. Researchers must also be highly flexible, and capable of creating and employing hybrid instruments and approaches, because, in the event of problems or questions, the timely intervention of the researcher is unlikely or impossible.

Recent examination of the behaviors and beliefs of distance practitioners suggest that ethical concerns are not common in the field. Most distance educators do not appear to be concerned about the ethical value of their practices, including their research. By their own admission, most nonpublishing practitioners are not well-informed about the policies under which distance research must be conducted. Nonresearchers freely admit that they do not understand, or have much cause to use, Canada's research policy.

On the other hand, it appears that experienced (published) distance researchers internationally are relatively well-informed about the requirements of ethical research. Like their colleagues in the humanities and social sciences generally, they tend to believe that they are better judges of the ethics of their research than REBs, and they often object to being treated as if their research posed the same risks as found in biomedical and clinical-experimental situations. They believe that their research should be regarded differently from studies that have been publicly associated with actual harms or malfeasance.

The eventual disposition of these ethics review issues in Canada will be determined in part by the reactions of policymakers to the advice of distance researchers about where vigilance is needed. It is clear that, presently, distance researchers generally do not perceive the same problems, actual or potential, that policymakers have anticipated in development of the TCPS, and in this, Canadian researchers resemble their international colleagues. Active researchers generally believe ethics review should recognize local realities, just as it recognizes other obvious disciplinary differences in methods and procedures. In Canada, our research has shown that distance researchers believe the traditions within which they operate already embody effective standards, including their tools, relationships with subjects (Bogdan & Bilken, 1992), data handling and analysis, reporting processes and methods, design and development, and, most importantly, protection of subjects. Likewise, the literature suggests, researchers worldwide tend to view ethics as a supplement, rather than an addition, to the provisions they already make to safeguard the integrity of their work. The two are in harmony except, as noted earlier, for the priorities developing nations have for creating a distinct, non-Western research culture, an objective, it might be argued, that is not primarily ethical at all. Issues related to "internationalization" and "localization" (Yang, 2001) arise from these priorities.

On another level, however, the concerns of both groups are similar: Both address the need for researchers to have sufficient independence and autonomy to conduct their research without unnecessary encumbrances. Whether barriers are raised unintentionally by existing paradigms and hegemonies, or intentionally by overreaching or poorly trained ethics boards and review processes, the effects are the same: needed, important research may be stymied, and researchers may be muzzled (Taber, 2002).

Future Research

Based on the above findings and analysis, the following directions for future research are suggested.

1. Social science and humanities researchers have complained that they are threatened with the same restraints as their biomedical colleagues, despite the fact that recent urgent research ethics-related scandals have concerned the latter group almost solely (Elliott, 2008). It will be important to determine whether this pattern persists in the future, and whether the restraints imposed by national ethics policies constrain ethical violations among those currently most prone to them.

2. The research reported here suggests that experienced researchers make better judges of the ethical value of proposed research. It also recommends that research experience be a consideration in the composition of REBs and IRBs. Researchers must monitor the behavior and efficacy of research review boards who follow this advice, to determine whether they do indeed produce better assessments of the ethical issues in proposals, and thereby facilitate improved relations with researchers.

3. An overall concern is the freedom of researchers to inquire with minimal hindrance. Future research must determine whether the freedom researchers currently enjoy changes, and, if the freedom to do research is constrained, what the costs and benefits are, to society and to individuals.

4. Finally, distance researchers believe they have advantages over their colleagues who do face-to-face inquiries, because the "strategic" use of the impersonality distance imposes can produce greater candor, more objectivity, and increased social presence (Walther, 1996). Whether these effects can

actually be detected in their work remains to be determined, and would be a potentially important area of inquiry.

REFERENCES

Anderson, T., & Kanuka, H. (2003). *E-research: Methods, strategies, and issues.* Boston: Allyn and Bacon.

Anderson, T., Rourke, L., Garrison, D.R., & Archer, W. (2001). Assessing teaching presence in a computer conferencing context. *Journal of Asynchronous Learning Networks, 5*(2), 1-17.

Beck, M., & Kaufman, G. (1994). Scientific methodology and ethics in university education. *Journal of Chemical Education, 94*(11), 922-924.

Begley, S. (2002, November 1). Review boards pose threat to social scientists' work. *The Wall Street Journal Online.* Retrieved April 23, 2008, from http://online.wsj.com/public/article_print/0,,SB1036101057183429471,00.html

Bogdan, R., & Biklen, S. (1992). *Qualitative research for education* (2nd ed.). Toronto, Canada: Allyn and Bacon.

Bucharest Declaration. (2004). The Bucharest Declaration concerning ethical values and principles for higher education in the Europe region. *Higher Education in Europe, 29*(4), 503-507.

Centers for Disease Control and Prevention (CDC). (2005). *The Tuskegee timeline.* Retrieved April 23, 2008, from: http://www.cdc.gov/nchstp/od/tuskegee/time.htm

Chozos, P., Lytras, M., & Pouloudi, N. (2002, October 15-19). Ethical issues in the learning: Insights from the application of stakeholder analysis in three e-learning cases. In *Proceedings of the E-learn 2002 World Conference on E-learning in Corporate, Government, Health Care, and Higher Education.* Association for the Advancement of Computing in Education. ERIC Documents: ED 479443.

Complexity of the IRB process: Some of the things you wanted to know about IRBs but were afraid to ask. (2005). *American Journal of Evaluation, 26*(3), 353-361.

Costley, C., & Gibbs, P. (2006). Researching others: Care as an ethic for practitioner researchers. *Studies in Higher Education, 31*(1), 89-98.

Crosta, L. (2004). Beyond the use of new technologies and adult distance courses: An ethical approach. *International Journal on E-Learning, 3*(1), 48-60.

Dohy, L. (2004, February 29). Clear policy needed for medical research trials. *The Edmonton Journal*, p. E10.

Elliott, C. (2008, January 7). Guinea-pigging. *The New Yorker*, pp. 36-41.

Elliott, C., & Lemmens, T. (2005, December 13). Ethics for sale. *Slate.* Retrieved April 23, 2008, from http://www.slatetv.net/id/2132187/

Evans, T., & Jakupec, V. (1996). Research ethics in open and distance education: Context, principles and issues. *Distance Education, 17*(1), 72-94.

Fahy, P. J. (2001). Addressing some common problems in transcript analysis. *The International Review of Research in Open and Distance Learning, 1*(2). Retrieved April 23, 2008, from http://www.irrodl.org/content/v1.2/research.html#Fahy

Fahy, P. J. (2002). Epistolary and expository interaction patterns in a computer conference transcript. *Journal of Distance Education, 17*(1), 20-35.

Fahy, P. J. (2003). Indicators of support in online interaction. *International Review of Research in Open and Distance Learning, 4*(1). Retrieved April 23, 2008, from http://www.irrodl.org/content/v4.1/fahy.html

Fahy, P. J. (2004, November 22-24). Use of the Bales model for analysis of small group communications in the analysis of interaction in computer-based asynchronous conferences. In M. Boumedine & S. Ranka (Eds.), *Proceedings of the IASTED International Conference on Knowledge Sharing and Collaborative Engineering*, St. Thomas, U.S. Virgin Islands. Calgary: ACTA Press.

Fahy, P. J. (2005, March). Two methods for assessing critical thinking in computer-mediated communications (CMC) transcripts. *International Journal of Instructional Technology and Distance Learning.* Retrieved April 23, 2008, from http://www.itdl.org/Journal/Mar_05/article02.htm

Fahy, P. J., Crawford, G., & Ally, M. (2001). Patterns of interaction in a computer conference transcript. *International Review of Research in Open and Distance Learning, 2*(1). Retrieved April 23, 2008, from http://www.irrodl.org/content/v2.1/fahy.html

Fahy, P. J., & Spencer, B. (2004). Research experience and agreement with selected ethics principles from Canada's Tri-Council Policy Statement–Ethical Conduct for Research Involving Humans. *Journal of Distance Education, 19*(2), 28-58.

Furedi, F. (2002, January 11). Don't rock the research boat. *The Times Higher Education Supplement* (pp. 20-21). Retrieved April 22, 2008, from: http://www.thes.co.uk/

Gardner, V. (2005). Uncontested terrains: A personal journey through image, (national) identity and ethics. *Research in Drama Education, 10*(2), 175-188.

Garrison, R., Anderson, T., & Archer, W. (2000). Critical inquiry in a text-based environment: Computer conferencing in higher education. *Internet and Higher Education, 2*(2), 87-105.

Garrison, D. R., Anderson, T., & Archer, W. (2001). Critical thinking, cognitive presence, and computer conferencing in distance education. *The American Journal of Distance Education, 15*(1), 7-23.

Garrison, D.R., Cleveland-Innes, M., Koole, M., & Kappelman. (2005). Revisiting methodological issues in transcript analysis: Negotiated coding and reliability. *Internet and Higher Education, 9*(2006), 1-8. Retrieved April 23, 2008, from http://www.elsevier.com/wps/find/journaldescription.cws_home/620187/description#description

Gibbs, L., & Gambrill, E. (2002). Evidence-based practice: Counterarguments to objections. *Research on Social Work Practice, 12*(3), 452-476.

Gordon, W., & Sork, T. (2001). Ethical issues and codes of ethics: Views of adult education practitioners in Canada and the United States. *Adult Education Quarterly, 51*(3), 202-218.

Herring, S. C. (1996). Two variants of an electronic message schema. In S.C. Herring (Ed.), *Computer-mediated communication* (pp. 81-106). Philadelphia, PA: John Benjamins.

Husu, J. (2004). A multifocal approach to study pedagogical ethics in school settings. *Scandinavian Journal of Educational Research, 48*(2), 123-140.

Iacono, T. (2006). Further comments on the researched, researchers and ethics committees: A response. *Journal of Intellectual and Developmental Disability, 31*(3), 189-191.

Karmakar, N.L. (2002, June 24-29). Online privacy, security and ethical dilemma: A recent study. In *Proceedings of the 14th ED-MEDIA 2002 World Conference on Multimedia, Hypermedia and Telecommunications,* Denver. Association for the Advancement of Computing in Education. ERIC Documents: ED477037.

Kraut, R., Olson, J., Banaji, M., Bruckman, A., Cohen, J., & Couper, M. (2004). Psychological research online: Report of Board of Scientific Affaires' Advisory Group on the conduct of research on the Internet. *American Psychologist, 59*(2), 105-177.

Lane, J. F. (2004, March 3-7). Competencies and training needs of financial aid administrators. In *Proceedings of the Academy of Human Resource Development (AHRD) International Research Conference*, Austin, TX (Vol. 1-2, pp. 190-197). ERIC Documents: ED491481.

Lasica, J.D. (2005). The cost of ethics: Influence peddling in the blogosphere. *AUSC Annenberg Online Journalism Review. Downloaded* April 23, 2008, from http://www.ojr.org/ojr/stories/050217lasica/

Leach, M.M. & Oakland, T. (2007). Ethics standards impacting test development and use: A brief review of 31 ethics codes impacting practices in 35 countries. *International Journal of testing, 7*(1), 71-88.

Lemonick, M.D. & Goldstein, A. (2002). At your own risk. *Time Magazine, 159*(16), 40-49.

Lysaght, T., Rosenberger, P.J., & Kerridge, I. (2006). Australian undergraduate biotechnology student attitudes towards the teaching of ethics. *International Journal of Science Education, 28*(10), 1225-1239.

McNamee, M. (2001). Introduction: Whose ethics, which research? *Journal of Philosophy of Education, 35*(3), 309-327.

Medical Research Council of Canada. (2005). *Tri-council policy statement [TCPS]: Ethical conduct for research involving humans.* Ottawa: Government of Canada. Retrieved April 23, 2008, from http://www.pre.ethics.gc.ca/english/policystatement/policystatement.cfm

Mishra, S. (1998). Distance education research: A review of its structure, methodological issues and priority areas. *Indian Journal of Open Learning, 7*(3), 267-282.

Mugridge, I., & Kaufman, D. (1986). *Distance education in Canada.* London: Croom Helm.

Munro, M. (2004, February 27). Alberta's ethics board has the toughest requirements in the country. *The Edmonton Journal,* pp. A1, A13.

Nurse, P. (2006, January 13). U.S. biomedical research under siege. *Cell, 124,* 9-12. Retrieved April 23, 2008, from http://www.cell.com/content/article/fulltext?uid=PIIS0092867405014613

O'Connor, T. (2002). Research ethics. Retrieved April 23, 2008, from http://faculty.ncwc.edu/toconnor/308/308lect10.htm

Owen, M., Robert, L., Burgess, J., Golfman, N., & Sykes, S. (2001). *Report to the Social Sciences and Humanities Research Council of Canada, Implementation of the Tri-Council Policy Statement on Ethics in Human Research (TCPS) (Humanities Project).* Unpublished paper, Humanities and Social Sciences Federation of Canada.

Pendlebury, S., & Enslin, P. (2001). Representation, identification and trust: Towards and ethics of educational research. *Journal of Philosophy of Education, 35*(3), 361-370.

Population, Inc. (2001, April). *Technology Review, 104*(3), 51-55.

Rigano, D. (2001). Researcher-participant positioning in classroom research. *International Journal of Qualitative Studies in Education, 16*(6), 741-755.

Robinson-Pant, A. (2005). *Cross-cultural perspectives in educational research. Conducting educational research.* Columbus, OH: Open University press.

Rourke, L., Anderson, T., Garrison, R., & Archer, W. (1999). Assessing social presence in asynchronous text-based computer conferencing. *Journal of Distance Education, 14*(2), 50-71.

Rourke, L., Anderson, T., Garrison, D.R., & Archer, W. (2001). Methodological issues in the content analysis of computer conference transcripts. *International Journal of International Journal of Artificial Intelligence in Education, 12,* 8-22. Retrieved April 23, 2008, from http://cbl. leeds.ac.uk/ijaied/

Savage, G.J. (2001). International technical communication programs and global ethics. In *Proceedings of the 28th Annual Conference, Council for Programs in Technical and Scientific Communication: Managing Change and Growth in Technical and Scientific Communication,* Pittsburgh, PA, (pp. 84-85).

Savulescu, J., Chalmers, I., & Blunt, J. (1996). *Are research ethics committees behaving unethically? Some suggestions for improving accountability and performance.* Retrieved April 23, 2008, from http://www.bmj.com/cgi/content/full/313/7069/1390?ijkey=uMbVZJcQJvX3E

Sikes, P. (2006). On dodgy ground? Problematics and ethics in educational research. *International Journal of Research and Method in Education, 29*(1), 105-117.

Small, R. (2001). Codes are not enough: What philosophy can contribute to the ethics of educational research. *Journal of Philosophy of Education, 35*(3), 387-406

Taber, K. (2002). "Intense, but it's all worth it in the end:" The co-learner's experience of the research process. *British Educational Research Journal, 28*(3), 435-457.

TCPS. (2005). *Tri-council policy statement [TCPS]: Ethical conduct for research involving humans.* See Medical Research Council of Canada.

The logic of privacy. (2007, January 6). *The Economist, 382*(8510), 65-66.

Thompson, J., Baird, P., & Downie, J. (2002). *Report of the committee of inquiry on the case involving Dr. Nancy Olivieri, the Hospital for Sick Children, the University of Toronto, and Apotex Inc.* Downloaded April 23, 2008, from http://www.caut.ca/en/issues/academicfreedom/olivieriinquiryreport.pdf

University of Utah. (2005). *Willowbrook Hepatitis studies.* Retrieved April 23, 2008, from http://www.hum.utah.edu/~bbenham/Research%20Ethics%20Website/INTMDcs_Willowbrook.htm

Van den Hoonaard, W. (2004). *Giving voice to the spectrum.* Report of the Social Sciences and Humanities Research Ethics Special Working Committee to the Interagency Advisory Panel on Research Ethics. Ottawa, Canada: Author.

Vujakovic, P., & Bullard, J. (2001). The ethics minefield: Issues of responsibility in learning and research. *Journal of Geography in Higher Education, 25*(2), 275-283.

Walther, J.B. (1996). Computer-mediated communication: Impersonal, interpersonal and hyperpersonal interaction. *Communication Research, 23*(1), 3-43.

Yang, S. (2001, March 14-17). Dilemmas of education reform in Taiwan: Internationalization or localization? In *Paper presented at the Annual Meeting of the Comparative and International Education Society,* Washington DC. ERIC Documents: ED 453137.

ADDITIONAL READING

The following is a selective listing of studies and opinion useful to understanding the issues of ethical review of research in education and distance education, in Canada and globally. (The reader should also consider readings in the "references.")

Baser, S. (2006). Ethics and power in community-campus partnerships for research. *Action Research, 4*(1), 9 -21.

Bryon-miller, M., & Greenwood, D. (2006). A re-examination of the relationship between action research and human subjects review processes. *Action Research, 4*(1), 117-128.

Clarkeburn, H.M., Downie, J.R., Gray, C., & Matthew, R. G. S. Measuring ethical development in life sciences students: A study using Perry's developmental model. *Studies in Higher Education, 28*(4), 443-456.

Colvin, J., & Lanigan, J. (2005). Ethical issues and best practice considerations for Internet research. *Journal of Family and Consumer Sciences, 97*(3), 34-39.

Detardo-bora, K.A. (2004). Action research in a world of positivist-oriented review boards. *Action Research, 2*(3), 237-253.

Ethical standards and procedures for research with human beings. World Health Organization (WHO). Retrieved April 23, 2008, from http://www.who.int/ethics/research/en/

Ford, R.C., & Richardson, W.D. (1994). Ethical decision-making: A review of the empirical literature. *Journal of Business Ethics, 13*(3), 205-221.

Herring, S.C. (2002). Computer-mediated communication on the Internet. *Annual Review of Information Science and Technology (ARIST), 36,* 109-168.

History of ethics and ethical review of human research in Australia. Retrieved April 23, 2008, from http://www.nhmrc.gov.au/ethics/human/ahec/history/

Humbarger, M., & DeVaney, S.A. (2005). Ethical values in the classroom: How college students responded. *Journal of Family and Consumer Sciences, 97*(3), 40-47.

Hutchings, P. (2003). Competing goods: Ethical issues in the scholarship of teaching and learning. *Change, 35*(5), 26-33.

Jeffers, B.R. (2002). Continuing education in research ethics for the clinical nurse. *Journal of Continuing Education in Nursing, 33*(6), 265-269.

Lysaght, T., Rosenberger, P.J., & Kerridge, I. (2006). Australian undergraduate biotechnology student attitudes towards the teaching of ethics. *International Journal of Science Education, 28*(10), 1225-1239.

MacFarlane, B. (2002). Dealing with Dave's dilemmas: Exploring the ethics of pedagogic practice. *Teaching in Higher Education, 7*(2), 167-178.

McKee, H. (2003). Changing the process of institutional review board compliance. *College Composition and Communication, 54*(3), 488-493.

Medical Research Council of Canada. (2005). *Tri-council policy statement [TCPS]: Ethical conduct for research involving humans.* Ottawa: Government of Canada. Retrieved April 23, 2008, from http://www.pre.ethics.gc.ca/english/policystatement/policystatement.cfm

New Zealand health and disability ethics committees. Retrieved April 23, 2008, from http://www.newhealth.govt.nz/ethicscommittees/

Nind, M., Shereen, B., Sheehy, K., Collins, J., & Hall, K. (2004). Methodological challenges in researching inclusive school cultures. *Educational Review, 56*(3), 259-270.

Olivier, S. (2002). Ethics review of research projects involving human subjects. *Quest, 54*(3), 196-204.

Pritchard, I.A. (2002). Travelers and trolls: Practitioner research and institutional review boards. *Educational Researcher, 31*(3), 3-3.

Research ethics review. *The Journal of the Association of Research Ethics Committees.* Retrieved April 23, 2008, from http://www.research-ethics-review.com/

Revised ethical guidelines for educational research (2004). *British Educational Research Association.* Retrieved April 23, 2008, from http://www.bera. ac.uk/publications/guides.php

Savulescu, J., Chalmers, I., & Blunt, J. (1996). *Are research ethics committees behaving unethically? Some suggestions for improving accountability and performance.* Retrieved April 23, 2008, from http://www.bmj.com/cgi/content/full/313/7069/ 1390?ijkey=uMbVZJcQJvX3E

Swaner, L.E. (2005). Educating for personal and social responsibility: A review of the literature. *Liberal Education, 91*(3), 14-21.

The logic of privacy. (2007, January 6). *The Economist, 382*(8510), 65-66.

Tilley, S.A., Killins, J., & Van Oosten, D. (2005). Connections and tensions between university and school districts: Research review boards and school-based research. *Alberta Journal of Educational Research, 51*(3), 277-293.

Zheng, L., & Hui, S. (2005). Survey of professional ethics of teachers in institutions of higher education: Case study of an institution in central China. *Chinese Education & Society, 38*(5), 88-99.

Chapter XV
Market Forces in Higher Education:
Cheating and the Student-Centred Learning Paradigm

Judy Nagy
Deakin University, Australia

ABSTRACT

This chapter discusses the globalisation of education and the challenges and opportunities arising from technologies that can impact cheating behaviours in higher education students. The chapter, commencing by contextualising cheating, discusses the endemic nature of cheating and presents various reasons for and factors that may encourage students to engage in cheating. To illustrate the potential for favourable outcomes when the particular needs of a student cohort are recognised, the chapter then considers a case study that proactively changed assessment strategies in postgraduate education to forestall cheating. The positive outcomes are then used to support a proposition to offer students more than one learning pathway as a means of recognising that student populations have become increasingly diverse with a corresponding need for diversity in teaching paradigms.

INTRODUCTION

The current environment of higher education in Australia is a complex mix of competing ideologies and constraints placing pressures on academics and supporting infrastructures. As successive governments have responded to economic ratio-nalism and reduced funding to higher education, universities have been forced to compete with one another both within state and country boundaries and also internationally (Milliken & Colohan, 2004), changing the landscape of higher education. In essence, universities have been propelled into the uncomfortable position of responding to the market and becoming "enterprise universities" (Marginson & Considine, 2000). Two important factors have contributed to this changed landscape. The first is international students that have made education Australia's third largest service export, earning $5.8 billion (Business Review Weekly, November 16-22, 2006, p.19). The second is technologies that have developed to facilitate online education and assessments for both teaching within institutions and for distance learning.

The impact of these two variables has meant that where student cohorts were once homogenous and captive to domestic constraints and expectations, cohorts have become multicultural, dispersed and subject to a plethora of constraints and expectations. While this new demographic has had many consequences, the impact of relevance here is the epidemic in cheating behaviors. The reasons for cheating, the means available (opportunity) to cheat and the frequency of cheating, has spread like a virus across the global education market (Hutton, 2006; Kennedy, 2004). Cheating appears to be endemic across many cultures and pedagogies (Magnus, Polterovich, Danilov, & Satvvateev, 2002) with business students being credited as the most likely to engage in cheating behaviors (Chapman & Lupton, 2004; Karassavidou & Glaveli, 2006; McCabe & Trevino, 1995; Phillips & Horton, 2000). McCabe, Butterfield and Trevino (2006) have also extended research findings to the postgraduate environment with consistent results. This chapter will examine a case study from a postgraduate unit within a business faculty to illustrate the strategies employed to combat cheating behaviors as part of subject design. The implications of strategies employed are then considered from a competitive markets viewpoint, to consider whether there is justification for the composition of student cohorts to be explicitly targeted and catered for by course design. How this perspective fits with a student-centred learning paradigm will also be considered.

BACKGROUND: GLOBAL CHEATING BEHAVIOUR

The contribution of technologies to education processes has been immense, with students and faculty each learning to adapt to an environment of continuous change and opportunities. Technologies have enabled greater access, richness and multimodality to suit individual learning styles, with students being empowered in ways that were previously not possible. However, this freedom has met with challenges as the diffusion of best practice pedagogies clashes with culturally grounded values, attitudes toward honesty and pressures to succeed as access to education becomes more open. Chapman and Lupton (2004) point out that:

while it is difficult for an instructor to manage academic dishonesty when the student and faculty are from the same country, the task becomes exponentially difficult when students and faculty have significantly different cultural backgrounds. Education, just like business, is now a global product. (Chapman & Lupton, 2004, pp. 426-7)

With business studies being the most popular course of study for international students, not only are students traveling to acquire an education but business schools are under increasing pressure from accrediting agencies to give their students and faculty international opportunities. With many partnership programs negotiated between U.S., UK, European and Australian institutions in emerging economies, faculty are indeed becoming more familiar with cultural diversity in student cohorts.

Chapman and Lupton (2004) have pointed out that there have been many studies in the U.S. which have addressed the subject of cheating, while in Asian countries research evidence about cheating behavior is more problematic. However, they site evidence from the Shanghai Star (2002) which makes the claim that "(i)n China, Hong Kong, South Korea, and Taiwan, cheating on the computerized Graduate Records Exam (GRE) and the Test of English as a Foreign Language (TOEFL) has become so problematic that the exams have been suspended by the Educational Testing Service (ETS)" (Chapman & Lupton, 2004, p. 425). This suggests that cheating behaviors are widespread even though academic research concerning cheating in these countries is elusive. Chapman and Lupton (2004) also note that it is difficult to draw comparisons between attitudes toward cheating between cultural groups unless survey instruments are identical. Despite this conceptual difficulty, they refer to a number of surveys that variously indicate the following:

- Comparing U.S. to Hong Kong students, Chapman and Lupton (2004) conclude, "(o)verall, it appears that American business students are more likely to engage in academic dishonesty that Hong Kong business students …(perhaps because) … American students appear to have a more liberal interpretation of what is or is not academic dishonesty and additionally appeared more inclined to admit to the behaviors being assessed" (Chapman & Lupton, 2004, p. 432).
- There is "a relationship between cheating, country, and grade vs learning oriented attitudes" (Davis, Noble, Zak, & Dreyer, 1994, p. 427) when comparing Australian and American university students, with U.S. students being more grade focused.
- When comparing Japanese and U.S. students, the Japanese had higher cheating tendencies with a greater propensity to rationalize behaviors (Diekhoff, LaBeff, Shinohara, & Yasukawa,1999).
- When comparing Polish with American students the Polish students admitted to higher

frequencies of cheating (Lupton, Chapman, & Weiss, 2000).

In another study by Magnus et al. (2002), it was confirmed, by surveying students in Russia, the Netherlands, Israel and the U.S., that "students have a different attitude towards cheating depending on where they live" (p. 134). These studies contribute to the conclusions of Chapman and Lupton (2004) who suggest that no matter where an educator is in the world "it is imperative, even prudent, to consider the different academic integrity norms utilized by your foreign students and faculty" (p. 434).

CHEATING: ACADEMIC DISHONESTY

While studies concerning academic integrity are not new, as they have been reported since the 1940s (Phillips & Horton, 2000), the innovations in cheating behaviors arise from the ways in which technologies have facilitated and enabled different modes of cheating. The "newest nemesis in the academic marketplace – the Internet" (p. 150) provides the ultimate capitalist tool for supplying educational assistance for profit, perhaps at the expense of ethics, morality and experiential learning. The rising popularity of Internet sites for purchasing assessment tasks suggests that the acquisition of lifelong learning skills for the benefit of the knowledge economy has been circumvented with money being the only limitation. In the past, finding such assistance may have been a deterrent to engaging in this form of dishonesty. However, now opportunity is simple and impersonal with the familiar capitalist rules of supply and demand governing the process.

Hard, Conway and Moran (2006) define academic misconduct by reference to their university's code of conduct. The code reads as follows:

providing or receiving assistance in a manner not authorised by the instructor in the creation of work to be submitted for academic evaluation including papers, projects and examinations (cheating); and presenting, as one's own, the ideas or words of another person or persons for academic evaluation without proper acknowledgment (plagiarism). (Hard, Conway & Moran, 2006, p. 1059)

Plagiarism can be characterized as unintentional due to ignorance or lack of understanding or as deliberate. Universities all, to a greater or lesser extent, provide students with information about what constitutes plagiarism. And yet, instances of plagiarism are prolific. The rise in instances and methods of cheating supports a premise of intent. However, plagiarism represents only one facet of cheating. Students have become more adept at using a variety of techniques to enhance perceptions of performance, some of which have been significantly enabled by online technologies (Stoney & McMahon, 2004). In the past, deliberate cheating took the form of looking at another's exam paper, or trying to take into an exam reference material or copying portions (or the whole) of another's assessment task. While the Internet may have made plagiarism easier to execute, the avenues now available to allow others to do a student's work have grown significantly. Online technologies, in essence "cybercheating" (or cyber-pseudepigraphy as described by Page, 2004), can be harnessed to circumvent a variety of different assessment regimes and also as a means of communication to gain advantage (Stoney & McMahon, 2004; Phillips & Horton, 2000). Examples include allowing someone other than the enrolled student to:

- Feign engagement in assessable online group discussion;
- Construct database or Web-based data for information technology-based courses of study;

- Access technologies and complete randomly generated case studies;
- Provide a completed assessment task as an economic transaction over the Internet (these may be individual rather than replicated; however, they are still the work of another).

Students can also gain advantage by speedy communication of information in test environments where resource constraints do not allow simultaneous testing across all campuses and cohorts, or even within test environments. In online testing environments, evidence has shown that e-mail communication software can be surreptitiously open while students were engaged in completion of the test, ostensibly to request some form of assistance. In many circumstances, just who is sitting behind the keyboard completing the task and who has acquired the skills and knowledge gained during assessments is questionable. This is a particular problem in the provision of distance education.

Just as technologies have enabled cheating, so technologies have also been harnessed to find cheats. Software tools, such as *CopyCatch* or *Turnitin,* used by many universities can detect plagiarism but not whether the enrolled student actually completed the work submitted. In Australia, 30 universities use such software to detect students who cut and paste from the Internet. It is not unusual for international students to have a less than adequate command of spoken English, a perception supported by poor demonstrated literacy in student e-mail or intranet correspondence, and for them to display exceptional standards of English competency in assessment tasks. It is acknowledged that native English speaking students also have the same opportunities without language barriers arousing suspicion; however, the pressures on international students to perform can be more significant. Zobel and Hamilton (2002), confirm that international students were "a clear majority identified as plagiarists by software" (p. 24). This was also supported by the chair of Academic Board at Deakin University, who claimed that there was a strong cultural factor in inadvertent plagiarism (*The Age* 12/11/06).

Why Cheat?

The issues contributing to the cheating epidemic can be categorized as a combination of traditional factors and more recent developments in the education market. The influence of the commercialization of the education process on attitudes to learning and the perception of value attached to learning have changed. Learning now competes with part-time work and is often the means to an end rather than an end in itself. How the means are achieved can be less important than just receiving the credential. This is true more so in the postgraduate environment where family, work and other pressures impinge upon time for study. McCabe et al. (2006) and Ghoshal (2005) suggest that the propensity to cheat in business students may be influenced by the free market philosophies which form the foundation of many units of study within business faculties. Such philosophies are suggested to be amoral, distancing students from a sense of moral responsibility for cheating and may be a factor in the willingness to "play" the odds of being caught.

While the temptation to cheat has always existed, the opportunities to execute cheating using an indirect technology medium may offer avenues which are perceived as somehow less risky. Phillips and Horton (2000), together with Stoney and McMahon (2004), confirm that "simple opportunity" plays a role in cheating behavior. Simon (2005) agrees that

when students have little to lose and much to gain by cheating, some will invariably choose to do so ... The little that students stand to lose by cheating appears to be further diminished by

remoteness. When they never see their teachers or administrators, when everyone else involved is reduced to text messages at the other end of an Internet connection, there appears to be less concern about loss of face. (p. 500)

For distance learning students, remoteness and a sense of disconnection from the core learning environment can also contribute to a lack of affinity with behaviors that are characterized as cheating. This is particularly true when the online environment directs students to multiple further sites where cheating and plagiarism are detailed, requiring multiple "clicks" to drill down through Intranet sites and requiring detailed reading of material. When such self-information materials compete for scarce learning time, students are unlikely to utilize such resources well. Some of the more traditional factors contributing to the propensity to cheat were noted by Kennedy (2004) as including:

- not fully understanding university culture;
- inappropriate study skills:
  ○ poor time management
  ○ inadequate assignment preparation and writing skills
  ○ inadequate examination and test preparation skills
  ○ assignment tasks not clearly understood;
- no control over submission dates of assignments that coincide/clash;
- poor quality teaching by lecturers; and
- life issues (family, work, health) (Kennedy, 2004, p. 2).

To this list can be added reasons which are more prevalent among international students for whom the decision to study in Australia can involve significant financial sacrifices by family and involve lifestyle as well as learning challenges. Additional reasons for cheating (Zobel & Hamilton, 2002; Hinton, 2004) may include:

- an inability to adapt to western style learning;
- slow adaptation or inability to cope with Australian cultural diversities and differences including religious isolation and in some instances being unchaperoned;
- poor English comprehension skills in subject contexts;
- poor technological and computer skills; and
- fear of failure and consequent:
  - ○ financial hardship
  - ○ loss of face either personal or by the family
  - ○ inability to extend visas and complete the course of learning.

Hamilton, Hinton, and Hawkins (2003) suggest that the rising volume of international students seeking an Australian education requires that the needs of this group of students be addressed. In particular, they identify that international students are not a homogenous group with the individual student having to "come to terms with not only the teaching style of an Australian academic but also a diversity of learning approaches among classmates" (p. 55).

The factors noted can individually or in combination contribute to student cheating behaviors. However, the temptation and motivation for cheating is also impacted by perceptions about faculty and student attitudes in general toward cheating, opportunity, the risks of being caught and the penalties imposed. Hard et al. (2006) suggest "that expectations and beliefs about peers' behavior influence individual behavioral choices …and that overestimating the frequency that one's peers engage in a behaviour can lead to increases in that behavior" (p. 1059). Their research also suggests that "faculty beliefs about the frequency of student academic misconduct were positively related to two important behaviors: prevention effort and efforts to challenge students suspected of misconduct" (Hard et al., 2006, p. 1075). This suggests that an active presence with regard to the policing of academic misconduct, the pursuit of those suspected of such behavior and making it known (rather than trying to keep quiet for sake of reputation) and meaningful penalties, can contribute to less academic misconduct. This is supported by Hutton (2006) who suggests that "peer and instructor influences, and administrative policies and institutional characteristics, appear to be more important than individual student characteristics" (p. 173) in influencing cheating behaviors (see also McCabe et al., 2006).

The Evolution of the Learning Environment

"Cybercheating" has been significantly enabled and has emerged as a consequence of the evolution of higher education under an economic rationalist agenda. The online revolution requires increasingly sophisticated technologies to administer student records, student access regimes, unit-specific material and research tools available through libraries. For the providers of distance education, technologies have allowed a greater connection with students in addition to the resource materials mailed to students. The ability to have greater communication with the teachers and other online learning tools are important measures for enriching the learning experience, reducing isolation and creating a greater sense of connection to a learning community. While these tools have facilitated access to education without the need to be on-site when engaged in the learning process, they increasingly require that academics be responsive, progressive and technology literate. These pressures challenge time management, which must be balanced within an environment of increasing class sizes, computer resource limitations and the need to maintain academic integrity. The complicated and time consuming disciplinary processes can also mean that the reporting of student cheating can be viewed as a burden on academics with a reluctance to pursue cheating behavior by students (Gallant & Drinan, 2006). A perception of a soft approach toward international students by discipline committees to safeguard income streams has also been speculative commentary among academics in general.

Enabling of Cheating

The harnessing of technologies for learning has also fostered a corresponding innovation in assessment methods to generate efficiencies with more transparent tools and assessment criteria. This desire for greater transparency is in accord with the "market" perspective supporting a standardized (Marginson & Considine, 2000, p. 177), nondiscriminatory approach to education which can meet professional requirements and is offered to all qualifying students on the same basis (Parker, 2005). There are now many assessment processes within business studies which take advantage of online technologies to either mediate or deliver a particular task. For example, databases of randomly generated multiple choice questions can be made available to students for testing. Marginson and Considine (2000, p. 60) provide evidence that student-staff ratios in business studies are significantly higher than in other academic areas which can mean that resource issues generate a less than desirable environment for testing. For example, if all students in one cohort cannot have access to computers in a controlled environment for testing at one time, then opportunities for "cybercheating" emerge.

Consequences for Learning Styles

The paradigm shift from academic-centred to student-centred learning discussed by Gallie and Joubert (2004) presumes to a significant extent that the majority of students have the requisite underlying skills to deal with challenges faced. The new paradigm requires that students are generally self-motivated to move through unit materials and initiate contact with academics. This style of learning supports a critical appraisal approach with emphasis on open debate rather than acceptance of the role of the academic as an expert. The importance of interaction in forms of flexible, online and distance education is well established (Wilson & Stacey, 2004, p. 33). Evidence suggests that international students from Asian countries are more likely to take information uncritically and not question authority figures. This approach is at odds with the student centred learning paradigm (Hamilton et al., 2003) and may contribute to learning environment alienation, giving rise to reasons for cheating.

Anecdotal evidence also suggests that certain cultural groups have varying competencies in self-mediated study and computer literacy. Learning styles that provide basic data to be rote learnt requires little need for students to access technologies and seek information. A consequence of these variables is that students that lack confidence in using computers, mine the same basic unit data for assessments, thereby increasing the propensity for plagiarism.

Student Centred Learning as the Means to Lifelong Learning

Garrison and Anderson (2003) suggest that "the value-add in a 'knowledge based future' will be a learning environment that develops and encourages the ability to think and learn both independently and collaboratively ... with the motivation to continue learning throughout their lives" (p. 20). "If one accepts the premise that learning is enhanced through discovery, the Internet sets the stage of individualized growth" (Corder & Ruby, 1996, p. 31). The use of the Web-based learning allows for intelligent, flexible learning with facilitators and students searching, navigating and exploiting multimodal pathways.

This pedagogical approach would seem to best facilitate the needs of a knowledge economy. However, the knowledge and skills that students bring to a course will necessarily impact how they deal with new knowledge being taught. To presume that all have the same foundation skills and are thus able to equally conceptualise and utilize technologies to accomplish assessment tasks and graduate outcomes is naïve (Laurillard, 1993). Knowledge-based economies are dependant on learning outcomes that are derived from a continuum of learning experiences. Where this continuum presumes a standardized core of skills, the environment of global education is challenged.

Chapman and Lupton (2004) claim that cheating behaviors undermine learning outcomes by misrepresenting "what a student may actually have learned and can use after graduation. Academic dishonesty violates the foundations of the pedagogical process by undermining educator's attempts to motivate students to be life-long learners … cheating is a violation of trust, which is necessary to cultivate an active intellectual learning environment" (pp. 433-434). The utilization of best practice pedagogies in the form of student centred learning in these circumstances can be questioned.

As a means of combating the epidemic in cheating, the outcomes of a case study that applied a pragmatic approach to maintaining academic integrity and created a discord with a student centred learning paradigm, is discussed. The discord is considered as a rational approach to ensuring course quality by combining online learning with invigilated individual assessments.

A CASE STUDY OF STRATEGIES TO REDUCE CHEATING AND IMPROVE OUTCOMES

This case study represents a reflective analysis of changes that were initiated as a consequence of increasingly poor student outcomes for one subject in a postgraduate business program. The case study is not part of a carefully constructed program of analysis for which justification of strategies can be supported by reference to best-practice techniques. Rather, the strategies adopted reflect the outcomes of a number of meetings between academics, teaching and learning development staff and student support experts sharing a concern for deteriorating student performance. The existence of an imminent window of opportunity to initiate change in assessment methods for the forthcoming semester provided limited opportunity for a more systematic and considered approach to the issues highlighted. It is acknowledged that longer timeframes and other strategies may have yielded more pedagogically defensible methods.

Discussions with colleagues from other institutions suggest that the following scenario would not be uncommon for postgraduate education in a number of higher education institutions in Australia. For a postgraduate core unit in business studies, international students represented approximately 80-90% of the student cohort. Students enrolled did not necessarily hold an undergraduate degree related to the course of study being undertaken and generally demonstrated an inadequate level of English proficiency with respect to business terminologies. Incidences of reported and penalized plagiarism together with suspicion that many students did not prepare the assessment that was submitted increased substantially from semester 2/2003. Unit statistics also showed that although student outcomes for progressive assessments were satisfactory, there was a high incidence of poor exam results, particularly for those that did well in progressive tasks. The assessment regime became the focus of attention as there had been no significant change to unit content or staffing over the period of review.

Table 1.

	2/ 2003	1/ 2004	2/ 2004	1/ 2005
Number of students on campus	134	149	185	206
Number via distance learning mode	31	40	31	43
Total students enrolled	**165**	**189**	**216**	**249**
Staff-student ratio	1:41	1:47	1.43	1:41.5
Failure rate (%)	22	28.5	43.5	23.5
International students–on Campus (%)	70	75	85	85 +
Average mark for progressive tasks (/35)	26.3	24	26.7	21.8
Average exam mark (100%)	49.6	48	45.8	53.9

Unit Statistics

While the percentage of students who are designated as international cannot be conclusively determined as a consequence of pathways of entry into particular university courses, the trend supports rising enrolments for international students across the whole Australian university sector. During the period of review, it was generally perceived that students were not meeting the required standard for success. The content of the unit is subject to accreditation requirements with a professional body and thus, while content could not be significantly changed in the short term, the way in which the subject was communicated and assessed was able to be reviewed.

Additional complications arose as a consequence of the unique blend of distance learning mode students within the same learning environment as other students enrolled in this unit of study. All students were treated equally using the same study material, the same assessment tasks and the same online discussion areas with all

resources used on campus made available online. In this respect, as advocated by Clarke, Butler, Schmidt-Hansen, and Somerville (2004) "an established equivalent full-time course provides the gold standard" (p. 7) for distance learning to ensure the quality, accreditation and recognition of credentials. Accordingly, any variation to the assessment regime had to be suitable for both on and off campus as much as possible. In the case study, no attempts were made to unravel and discover whether findings were more or less applicable to distance learning students, however certain issues emerged that challenged the practical application of an equity model.

Cultural Awareness

During 2003 and 2004 awareness of cultural learning modes which impeded students' ability to generate positive outcomes within the case study institution began to occur. Discussions with individual students, within seminar groups, among academic staff in teaching and learning forums and as part of student centred learning resource groups provided insights into differing learning approaches. These following comments are not empirically justifiable; however, discussion with numerous students and with many other academic colleagues, suggest that these issues are not unusual. While insights may help to explain poor outcomes to some degree, they are also recognized as part of a larger group of issues.

In certain international cultures, the level of tuition fees paid to a tertiary institution provides an indication of the level of effort that is required to obtain a degree. The more that is paid, the lower is the effort required to attain an outcome. One student (subsequently confirmed by many others) commented that "in our country we do not work at all during the semester, then study like crazy for three weeks at the end and so long as we get 35% on the exam, we pass." This suggested one possible reason why encouraging students to complete progressive assessment tasks by motivating them early, produced very poor responses. The unfamiliarity of studying in a progressive manner also meant that some students did not appreciate that weekly topics required some preparation before class delivery and for this to be followed up with problem solving in their own time. Such poor appreciation of study requirements initially suggested that many students had become so far behind in just 4 weeks that they were unable to recover sufficiently to pass the unit. While this may have been a contributing factor, there was, however, overwhelming evidence that many did exceptionally well in progressive assessment tasks and then produced very poor exam outcomes with many questions on the exam not being attempted at all. Such evidence suggests that progressive assessment tasks were either poorly retained by a large group of students, or that results obtained were not entirely a product of the students' own efforts.

Other evidence of learning styles at odds with a student centred approach emerged from the use of online learning environments. Students complained that when using the Intranet discussion areas that staff (who had been instructed to engage students and promote discussion) were "evasive and did not get to the point and provide the answer wasting people's time." These cultural groups wanted all materials to be provided and not to have to engage in discussion or group learning which would challenge their comprehension skills and perhaps embarrass by evident poor written or verbal skills. Not engaging in more broad-based learning techniques meant that, where theoretical concepts were applied to new situations and case studies, students were unable to make the link between the theory and practical applications. The perception by students that exam questions should be written the same way as they had been the year before with perhaps only the numbers changing was symptomatic of this approach.

Assessment Tasks

Without addressing the merits or otherwise of particular forms of assessment in an accredited postgraduate environment, the following assessment tasks are discussed as a means of identifying the forms of assessment that existed within the case study unit and how and why they were changed. During 2003/4 the university was in the process of changing from one intranet-based learning platform to another with the online environment generally characterized as a repository for stored material and for limited communication between students and academic staff.

For semesters 2/2003, 1/2004 and 2/2004 the assessment tasks in this unit were:

1. 10% essay;
2. 5% computer-based randomly generated case study in an uncontrolled environment;
3. 20% assignment based on application of theory to a case study with calculated outcomes and an analytical component; and
4. 65% closed book exam with a hurdle requirement that students must pass the exam.

Task one was required to be submitted in approximately week 4 of a 13-week semester, with many international students enrolling late and not yet having access to or being familiar with university infrastructures. Students in the majority of cases had only recently arrived and this was their first course of study in Australia. The task was submitted in hardcopy form, precluding the application of software such as *Turnitin* to detect plagiarism. However, the task was still the subject of many allegations and subsequent penalization of plagiarism. Various issues that became apparent were:

- Students were found to have copied from one another with only formatting type changes;

- One had taken another's copy from a shared printer and submitted it as their own;
- Level of English comprehension and grammar were far in excess of perceived student abilities; and
- Whole paragraphs from the text were constantly identified.

Task two required students to apply knowledge gained in seminars to a randomly generated computer-based case study, and to submit this case study for assessment. The task was essentially self-assessing so that where students did not attain full marks, they could attempt another exercise as often as they wished until the knowledge level increased and the final best effort was submitted. Most students were able to attain full marks for this assessment. Subsequent student efforts using these basic concepts cast significant doubt over the abilities demonstrated in assessments submitted. It became very clear in the exam that knowledge assumed, based on this task, was not held.

Task three was also submitted in hardcopy form with many calculations being identical, making it difficult to assess the presence of plagiarism. However, where calculations were consistently incorrect and written analysis demonstrated the same spelling errors on more than one submission, cheating was reported. Also worthy of note, were the observations of a sessional staff member in the student cafeteria. Having been warmly greeted by a past student, it was observed that the student was "checking" (in effect preparing) many assignments for students in what looked like a small business operation. This task was worth 20% of the assessment in the unit and exam outcomes for questions relating to this topic cast significant doubt that knowledge demonstrated in submissions was held by students. Distance learning students posted their completed assessments for tasks one, two and three to the university and these were subjected to the same scrutiny and marking processes as all other students. All students were treated equally with markers not being aware of the mode of enrollment.

Task four was a traditional exam with a section containing multiple choice questions and then a number of theoretical and practical problems. It was evident in the statistical analysis that many students did not attempt whole questions for which they had attained high marks in progressive assessments. Students were also found to have performed badly on the multiple choice section and in theory responses which supported a perception of selective underlying knowledge. Despite repeated written and verbal instruction advising students that a passing grade was necessary on the exam, students believed that if they did well in internal assessments they could still pass the unit. Many failing students found it difficult to accept that marks were not cumulative and that the exam represented a significant hurdle which they were required to individually attain. Distance students were examined using the same exam paper as domestic students with the exam scheduled as the same time by arrangement with other reputable educational providers in the country where distance learning students were domiciled.

Much soul searching and analytical review of student outcomes was conducted after the failure rate for students almost doubled over 2003/04. It is important to note that at no stage was any pressure applied from any quarter to change or gild results. The poor outcomes and cheating behaviors were also being experienced in other units with the faculty administrative system being burdened with rising incidences of reported and penalized cheating. It was noted, however, that at this time period the university had been successful in recruiting large numbers of international students from geographical areas previously underrepresented in previous cohorts. An analysis of the assessments tasks as set determined that they were appropriate in relation to the content of the unit, and that the assessment tasks and the criteria used to grade them were considered to be reasonable. However, students were achieving significantly poorer outcomes in a unit which had changed little in staffing, unit content and assessment regimes. In essence, the task of assessment review became to identify how the needs of predominantly international students in terms of competencies and learning styles could be addressed to reduce the incidence of cheating and to enhance learning (Hamilton et al., 2003). It was perceived that the most significant challenge was to encourage students to complete their own tasks so that knowledge was self-sustaining, providing students with the best opportunity to achieve a successful outcome.

Changed Assessment Regime: Semester 2/2004

Online technologies and infrastructure had developed over 2003/04 to allow consideration of new methods of assessment which would foster a more conducive learning environment for international students. We could not hope to find solutions to all issues raised; however, there was sufficient motivation by education development personnel and academic staff to initiate change and to ensure the means to assess the impact of change was available. Wilson and Stacey (2004) point out that being a "competent, confident online academic is a new and different role" facing many academics particularly if they are not from a technology background. With support, staff adapted to this new role with evidence of significant positive results.

Assessments Eliminated

The essay in task one submitted in week 4 was not considered to be a useful measure of learning. Students were still arriving in week 3. They were not significantly familiar with learning modes, where resources were available and multicultural assimilation had not yet been resolved. Requir-

ing electronic lodgment and applying plagiarism software to a task set so early in the semester were not considered to solve the underlying issues of personal effort and students who were not prepared. This task was eliminated.

The random case study on computer software was also removed as subsequent efforts in the exam for related questions provided strong support for questioning the authenticity of assessment submissions. A student had also suggested that the task was a waste of time as he was aware of a person who knew how to operate the software and was completing multiple case studies registering in the name of various students for a fee.

Having eliminated the first two assessment tasks, and with significant doubts about the learning outcomes facilitated by assessment task three, all progressive assessments could thus be reconfigured and changed to reflect what was considered to be most supportive of individual student learning. The types of tasks selected to assess student learning were those that could be implemented within the short time frame available. It was understood that other alternatives may be equally or better able to achieve the desired results and the process of review would be continuous. The tasks to be used for assessment were determined by consensus between academics, student support specialists and teaching and learning development staff. The exam and percentage of assessment attributed to progressive vs. external (exam-based) portions of assessment in the unit were published data that could not be changed in the short term. As a consequence, the value of the exam and structure of the exam paper remained unchanged.

The New Assessment Regime

The new assessment tasks introduced were as follows:

1.   15% for a test-based case study using computer software in a controlled environment;

2.	20% for a short answer and multiple choice test using controlled release infrastructure technologies in a controlled environment; and

3.	65% for a closed book exam.

Task one involved the use of a commonly used brand of proprietary business software applied to a particular case study in week 8 of a 13-week academic period in a controlled environment. All students were required to purchase the software and had the option of using the software on their own computers or making use of computers on-campus. With additional funding made available to allow effective implementation, students were provided with dedicated tutorial support to become proficient in software usage. The tutorials were scheduled to ensure an appropriate basic level of knowledge has been constructed before the tutorial work consolidated their learning in a practical manner. Computer-based tutorials commenced in week 4 and concluded prior to the assessment task. Distance learning students were provided with the same tutorial program to work through with staff consciously providing more detailed support online for this task. All students were required to register for a particular limited number of test sessions that were controlled and invigilated by staff. Because resource constraints did not allow for all students to be tested at one time, there were three versions of the test which were randomly assigned to registered test sessions. The test files were released to students only at the registered time for a 1-hour window of opportunity and were electronically submitted at the end of the test session. The need to register for a timed selective release of test file data was applied to both on-campus and distance students with a "practice test" given to trial the electronic upload function. While there were many teething problems associated with access to software, willingness of students to apply themselves to a task they deemed too difficult in the initial stages, and the need to develop a contingency plan for

students that did not successfully submit the task, the average outcome for the completed task by students was a grade of 75%.

For assessment task one, opportunities to cheat in terms of plagiarism were not present. Opportunities to "cybercheat" existed only for those with strong information technology competencies where the test operating environment may have been circumvented. Because the test was run in a controlled small group environment with the necessity for registration and checking of student identification, students were compelled to personally attend and complete the assessment task. It was recognized that those students leaving the controlled environment could verbally pass on information to students in another session and evidence of this appeared in the form of prepared pertinent notes brought into a later session which were confiscated. It was interesting to note that students on campus were resorting to more traditional forms of cheating rather than "cybercheating." We recognized that perceptions of equity between on campus and distance students for this task were questionable as a consequence of not being able to verify who actually sat behind the keyboard at any remote location. However, we rationalised that for the minority of students possibly affected, for any one student to find an accomplice knowledgeable in the particular brand of software, to be available at exactly the right time, with the ability to complete and upload the task in the required manner, was statistically low.

Assessment task two was a short answer and multiple choice test timed and designed to provide an early warning mechanism to students in week 10 about their level of knowledge in preparation for the exam. In seminar groups, random exercises to ascertain the level of ability to write an appropriate response to theory questions, or to attain an adequate result in demonstrated multiple choice questions, indicated a poor level of student preparedness. A database of questions for both short theory and multiple choice questions was constructed which, via controlled release to individual students in registered session times, produced randomly generated questions for every student. Assessing in a controlled environment again compelled students to attend the test in person. As the time for this assessment task approached there was flurry of activity among some students with an observed concern for "catching up." For this task the rationalization process we employed to consider equity between on and distance learning students was not as strong. We were not able to discern who sat at the remote keyboard nor were we able to control whether students used material to assist with answering questions (In subsequent periods the second of these anomalies was rectified by making the test "open book"). Outcomes were published in week 12 with an average mark of 55%. It was interesting to note that many students were not confident about their achievement in this test, with subsequent published outcomes confirming this perception. The test also acted to dispel a level of overconfidence by a distinct group that had an optimistic view of their abilities. However, the early warning mechanism allowed sufficient time for students to address knowledge short-comings before the final exam.

For assessment task two, again opportunities to cheat in terms of plagiarism were not present. Opportunities to "cybercheat" existed only for those with strong information technology competencies. Distance education students (as noted above) were not so constrained. It was observed that one on campus student surreptitiously had a form of e-mail communication software open while completing the test, ostensibly to request answers from another person. Also, a number of issues associated with the integrity of the testing environment have been noted for resolution as part of further development.

The final exam was, in content and format, similar to that of past years. Results in semester 1/2005 showed a significant improvement in student outcomes with the failure rate being dramatically reduced. While we were very en-

thusiastic about this result, the reasons for such outcomes are to a significant degree speculative. Statistical analysis of student performance showed that while progressive assessment marks were less than during 2003/04, students performed significantly better in the exam. The impact of the need for personal completion of assessment tasks with limited opportunities for cheating is suggested as a substantial contributing factor to the improvement in results. In addition, the ability for students to get some feedback concerning demonstrated test outcomes allowed for a "wake up" call before the final exam.

Other factors which undoubtedly contributed to the improved outcomes were a concerted presence on the unit's intranet site, specific computer-based tutorial support and a team of administrative and academic staff coordinating infrastructure technologies to ensure that unforeseen issues were quickly resolved. The use of progressive technologies seemed initially to make students uncomfortable; however, independently conducted student evaluations in semesters 2/2004 and 1/2005 provided strong student endorsement of the practical application and usefulness of online technologies. Students who considered the unit was "well taught," were prepared to "recommend" the unit to others and considered it "very useful to their future." Ratings for these criteria averaged four on a five point scale.

CONCLUSION

Cheating represents a global problem for those engaged in the provision of education. Distance and online learning environments have, in many ways, been enriched by the usage of technologies to connect learners and teachers and, at the same time, they have also been challenged by the opportunities these same technologies provide. Attitudes to learning and the perception of the value attached to learning in a knowledge economy have raised the perception of a need for engagement with a learning paradigm. However, conflicting and competing priorities and cultural tensions associated with academic honesty suggests that a standardized approach to achieving, and the processes of learning, will not adequately address the needs of a diverse learning populace.

In the swing of the pendulum away from academic-centred learning to student-centred learning, it is acknowledged that the above case study involves a movement away from a perception of student-centred learning. This alone should not be cause for condemnation of the strategies adopted to improve unit outcomes. There is a place for flexibility in higher education, although it is acknowledged that comments from the minority group of domestic students were less than supportive of "being treated like under-graduates or school kids." The rising incidence of cheating in progressive assessment tasks was the catalyst for questioning the efficacy of applying a standardized model of learning based on best practice student-centred models to a heterogeneous student body. As part of a strategy to meet marketplace needs (and reduce cheating behavior) there may be a place for deliberately designing subject assessment strategies to better fit the learning styles of the "customer" in postgraduate education cohorts.

International (and other) students are faced with a myriad of reasons which may induce them to engage in conduct that is deemed to be cheating. However, the case study above suggests that while academics have little influence on the reasons for cheating, there is much that can be done to limit opportunity, a factor that Phillips and Horton (2000) and Stoney and McMahon (2004) confirm as being of significant relevance to cheating behaviors. Gallant and Drinan (2006) on the other hand, suggest that "the student cheating problem is an adaptive challenge (one that requires learning and changes in attitudes, behaviors, or values) rather than a technical problem (one that can be solved in routine ways)" (p. 839). I acknowledge that the case study adopted a technical solution to solve an immediate crisis, an intolerable failure

rate. While the university in this case study is proactive in its approach to limiting opportunities for cheating, detection and penalization of those found to be cheating, it would be difficult to convince the quality control monitors (both professional and within the university) that the current attitudes and values of the global student population can be accepted as trustworthy in the short term.[1]

FUTURE RESEARCH DIRECTIONS

It would be useful to explore the possibility of proactively offering students a choice in the style of learning within their chosen studies. Where sufficient volume exists to offer multiple streams of study, students could choose between a student-centred learning experience and alternatively an academic-centred learning experience. This recognizes that students accumulate, by virtue of all previous years of education, diverse styles of learning along the continuum from student to academic-centred learning. While it is not possible for students to be offered all possible permutations, a style that is less alien may diminish the likelihood of engaging in cheating behaviors. Commencing from a perspective that there are at least two clearly delineated styles of learning, the provision of choice, which is a hallmark of competitive markets, allows students to select a style of learning that has assessments and pedagogies specifically targeted toward a more explicit expectation of the learning experience.

New "corporate universities," in particular, are responding to the market and offering students what they wish to learn. There has been a proliferation of courses with increasing specializations providing students with a myriad of choice in the subjects which can be combined to make up an award. Extending choice to the style of learning particularly for international students may contribute a better transition from previous learning experiences to higher education (Demiray, Nagy,

& Yilmaz, 2007). Explicit streaming potentially allows choice for both academics and students recognizing that, like students, academics may have a preference for a particular teaching style. Not all academics have the willingness or ability to engage with students using increasingly more prevalent online and social software-based learning environments. Academic choice combined with student choice of learning style may contribute to a far more positive learning experience and for a shared view of expectations of that experience (Nagy & McDonald, 2007). However, the acceptance and explicit recognition of student diversity alone presents the academy with significant challenges in relation to the current uniform approach to teaching and learning, something that is likely to have significant implications for university processes.

It is acknowledged that the links between more familiar learning styles and cheating behaviors is speculative, and that further research is required to provide evidence that the streaming of students can be beneficial. However, as a deliberate marketing strategy, a university may find that student choice of course combined with choice in the style of learning provides a market advantage in an already competitive higher education market. It remains to seen how competition in higher education will continue to develop and whether flexibility for students will include the addition of choice between alternative learning styles. The conflict between the marketing appeal of more choice for students and the marketing appeal of economies of scale using a standardized teaching and learning approach is a domain that higher education can explore.

REFERENCES

Business Review Weekly, 16-22 November 2006, pp 19.

Chapman, K. J., & Lupton, R. A. (2004). Academic dishonesty in a global educational market: A comparison of Hong Kong and American university business students. *The International Journal of Educational Management, 12*(7), 425- 435.

Clarke, M., Butler, C., Schmidt-Hansen, P., & Somerville, M. (2004). Quality assurance for distance learning: A case study at Brunel University. *British Journal of Educational Technology, 35*(1), 5-11.

Corder, S., & Ruby, R., Jr. (1996. Using the Internet and the World Wide Web: The international connection. *Business Education Forum*, 31-32.

Davis, S. F., Noble, L. M., Zak, E. N., & Dreyer, K. K. (1994). A comparison of cheating and learning/grade orientation in American and Australian college students. *College Student Journal, 28*, 353-356.

Demiray, U., Nagy, J., & Yilmaz, R. A. (2007). Strategies for the marketing of higher education—with comparative contextual references between Australia and Turkey. *Turkish Online Journal of Distance Education, 8*(2), Article 14.

Diekhoff, G. M., LaBeff, E. E., Shinohara, K., & Yasukawa, H. (1999). College cheating in Japan and the United States. *Research in Higher Education, 40*(13), 343-345.

Gallant, P. B., & Drinan, P. (2006). Organisational theory and student cheating: Explanation, responses, and strategies. *Journal of Higher Education*, 839-861.

Gallie, K., & Joubert, D. (2004). Paradigm shift: From traditional to on-line education. *Studies in Learning, Evaluation Innovation and Development, 1*(1), 32-36.

Garrison, D. R., & Anderson, T. (2003). *E-learning in the 21st Century.* London: Routledge-Falmer.

Ghoshal, S. (2005). Bad management theories are destroying good management practice. *Academy of Management Learning and Education, 4*(1), 75-91.

Hamilton, D., Hinton, D. T. L. S., & Hawkins, K. (2003). International students at Australian universities—plagiarism and culture. In *Paper presented at the Academic Integrity Conference*, University of South Australia, Adelaide.

Hard, S. F., Conway, J. M., & Moran, A. C. (2006). Faculty and college student beliefs about the frequency of student academic misconduct. *The Journal of Higher Education, 77*(6), 1058-1080.

Hinton, D. T. L. S. (2004). Plagiarism: Learning from our challenges. *Studies in Learning, Evaluation Innovation and Development, 1*(1), 37-46.

Hutton, P. A. (2006). Understanding cheating and what educators can do about it. *College Teaching,* 171-177.

Karassavidou, E., & Glaveli, N. (2006). Towards the ethical or the unethical side? An explorative research of Greek business students' attitudes. *International Journal of Management Education, 20*(5), 348-364.

Kennedy, I. (2004). An assessment strategy to help forestall plagiarism problems. *Studies in Learning, Evaluation Innovation and Development, 1*(2), 1-8.

Laurillard, D. (1993). *Rethinking university teaching.* London: Routledge.

Lupton, R. A., Chapman, K., & Weiss, J. (2000). American and Slovakian university business students' attitudes, perceptions and tendencies towards academic cheating. *Journal of Education for Business, 75*(4), 231-241.

Magnus, J. R., Polterovich, V. M, Danilov, D. L., & Satvvateev, A. V. (2002). Tolerance of cheating: An analysis across countries. *Journal of Economic Education,* 125-135.

Marginson, S., & Considine, M. (2000). *The enterprise university. Power, governance and reinvention in Australia.* Cambridge, UK: Cambridge University Press.

McCabe, D. L., Butterfield, K. D., & Trevino, L. K. (2006). Academic dishonesty in graduate business programs: Prevalence, causes, and proposed action. *Academy of Management Learning & Education, 5*(2), 294-305.

McCabe, D. L., & Trevino, L. K. (1995). Cheating among business students: A challenge for business leaders and educators. *Journal of Management Education, 19*(2), 205-218.

Milliken, J., & Colohan, G. (2004). Quality or control? Management in higher education. *Journal of Higher Education Policy and Management, 26*(3), 381-391.

Nagy, J., & McDonald, J. (2007, December). *New policies for learning flexibility: Negotiated choices for both academics and students.* In *Proceedings of the Ascilite Conference: Providing Choices for Learners and Learning,* Singapore.

Page, J. S. (2004). Cyber-pseudepigraphy: A new challenge for higher education policy and management. *Journal of Higher Education Policy and Management, 26*(1), 429-433.

Parker, L. D. (2005). Corporate governance crisis down under: Post-Enron accounting education and research inertia. *European Accounting Review, 14*(2), 383-394.

Phillips, M. R., & Horton, V. (2000). Cybercheating: Has morality evaporated in business education? *International Journal of Educational Management, 14*(4), 150-155.

Simon, (2005). Assessment in online courses: Some questions and a novel technique. *Research & Development in Higher Education, 28,* 500-506.

Stoney, S., & McMahon, M. (2004, December). Bulletproof assessment, war stories, and tactics: Avoiding cybercheating. In R. Atkinson, C. McBeath, D. Jonas-Dwyer, & R. Phillips (Eds.), *Beyond the comfort zone: Proceedings of the 21st ASCILITE Conference,* (pp. 881-886). Perth. Retrieved April 23, 2008, from http://www.ascilite.org.au/conferences/perth04/procs/stoney.html

Wilson, G., & Stacey, E. (2004). Online interaction impacts learning: Teaching the teachers to teach online. *Australasian Journal of Educational Technology, 20*(1), 33-48.

Zobel, J., & Hamilton, M. (2002). Managing student plagiarism in large academic departments. *Australian Universities Review, 45*(2), 23-30.

ADDITIONAL READING

Berg, G. A. (2005). Reform higher education with capitalism? Doing good and making money at the for-profit universities. *Change*, 28-34.

Blass, E. (2005). The rise and rise of the corporate university. *Journal of European Industrial Training, 29*(1), 58-74.

De Freitas, S. (2005). Does e-learning policy drive change in higher education? A case study relating models of organisational change to e-learning implementation. *Journal of Higher Education Policy and Management, 27*(1), 81-95.

Demiray, U., Nagy, J., & Yilmaz, A. (2007). Strategies for the marketing of higher education–with comparative contextual references between Australia and Turkey. *The Turkish Online Journal of Distance Education, 8*(2), Article 14.

Department of Education, Science and Training (DEST). (2007). *Higher education report 2005.* Australian Government.

Dutton, W. H., Cheong, P. H., & Park, N. (2004). An ecology of constraints on e-learning in higher education: The case of a virtual learning environment. *Prometheus, 22*(2), 131-149.

Gabbott, M., Mavondo, F., & Tsarenko, Y. (2002). International student satisfaction: Role of re-sources and capabilities. *Academic Exchange*, 170-176.

Galbraith, K. (2003). Towards quality private education in Central and Eastern Europe. *Higher Education in Europe, XXVIII*(4), 539-558.

Hartley, D. (2007). Personalisation: The emerging "revised" code of education? *Oxford Review of Education*, iFirst article, 1-14.

Koehne, N. (2005). (Re)construction: Ways international students talk about their identity. *Australian Journal of Education, 49*(1), 140-119.

Levy, D. C. (2006). The unanticipated explosion: Private higher education's global surge. *Comparative Education Review, 50*(2), 217-240.

Lynch, R., & Baines, P. (2004). Strategy development in UK higher education: Towards resource-based competitive advantages. *Journal of Higher Education Policy and Management, 26*(2), 171-187.

Montgomery, L. M., & Canaan, J. E. (2004). Conceptualizing higher education students as social actors in a globalizing world: A special issue. *International Journal of Qualitative Studies in Education, 17*(6), 739-748.

Redding, P. (2005). The evolving interpretations of customers in higher education: Empowering the elusive. *International Journal of Consumer Studies, 29*(5), 409-417.

Rolfe, H. (2003). University strategy in an age of uncertainty: The effect of higher education funding on old and new universities. *Higher Education Quarterly, 57*(1), 24-47.

Shumur, W. (2004). Global pressures, local reactions: Higher education and neo-liberal economic policies. *International Journal of Qualitative Studies in Education, 17*(6), 823-839.

Washburn, J. H., & Petroshius, S. M. (2004). A collaborative effort at marketing the university:

Detailing a student-centred approach. *Journal of Education for Business*, 35-40.

Watkins, M. (2007). Thwarting desire: Discursive constraint and pedagogical practice. *International Journal of Qualitative Studies in Education, 20*(3), 301-318.

ENDNOTE

[1] This chapter is developed from a paper published in *Studies in Learning, Evaluation, Innovation and Development,* Nagy, J. (2006). Adapting to market conditions: plagiarism, cheating and strategies for cohort customization, 3(2), 37-47.

Chapter XVI
Using Real Case Studies to Teach Ethics Collaboratively to Library Media Teachers

Lesley Farmer
California State University, Long Beach, USA

ABSTRACT

Case studies provide an authentic way to teach ethical behavior through critical analysis and decision-making because it reveals nuanced factors in complex situations and stimulates productive discussion. Case studies also address the affective domain of learning. The creation and choice of case studies is key for optimum learning, and can reflect both the instructor's and students' knowledge base. Case studies are used successfully in distance education as students share their perspectives and respond to their peers' comments. As a result of this approach, students support each other as they come to a deeper, co-constructed understanding of ethical behavior, and they link coursework and professional lives. The instructor reviews the writing to determine the degree of understanding and internalization of ethical concepts/applications, and to identify areas that need further instruction.

INTRODUCTION

As professionals, librarians are expected to behave ethically. Learning what ethical issues are encountered in school librarianship, and knowing how to address them, constitutes a core knowledge set. Case studies provide a grounded theory means to investigate authentic situations in order to ascertain ethical ways to deal with them.

BACKGROUND

Ethics in School Librarianship

The library profession encounters ethical issues daily: providing accurate information, observing intellectual property rights, dealing with privacy issues, maintaining confidential relationship with clientele. The autumn 1991 theme of *Library*

Trends was "Ethics and the Dissemination of Information." With the advent of the Internet, ethical questions abound. Because school libraries have a *loco parentis* status, they are more apt than other library settings to deal with ethical dilemmas (Hannabuss, 1996).

The American Library Association began talking about an ethical code in the early twentieth century, with the first code being adopted in 1938 (Rubin, 2000). Their core operational definition of ethics posits an "essential set of core values which define, inform, and guide our professional practice" (ALA, 2004). This Code of Ethics, which was most recently revised in 1995, provides a framework to guide ethical decision-making. It includes statements about excellence in service, intellectual property and freedom, collegiality, conflict of interest, and professional growth.

The Information Ethics Special Interest Group (SIG) of the Association of Library and Information Science Education (ALISE) developed a position on information ethics in library and information science education. Building on the premises of the UNESCO University Declaration of Human Rights, the SIG asserts that it is their responsibility to discuss information ethics critically. They further state that information ethics should inform teaching, research, scholarship, and service, particularly as they instruct preservice librarians. Focusing on library and information science curriculum, the SIG states that students should be able to:

- Identify professional ethical conflicts;
- Reflect ethically;
- Link ethical theories and concepts to daily practice; and
- Internalize a sense of ethical responsibility (Association of Library and Information Science Educators, 2006).

While the SIG encourages offering a separate course in professional ethics, a strong case may be made that ethical considerations be integrated, and explicitly addressed throughout the curriculum. In this manner, students realize that each function within librarianship involves ethical decision-making.

In their set of information literacy standards (1998), the American Association of School Librarians (AASL) explicitly address ethical behavior, stating that "the student who contributes positively to the learning community and to society is information literacy and practices ethical behavior in regard to information and information technology" (p. 6). In K-12 school settings, which serve as *loco parentis,* the legal and ethical responsibilities of the library media teacher (LMT) surpass the comparable work of librarians in other settings. Dealing with minors adds another layer of legal issues, and implies an additional need to model ethical behavior so children will experience and integrate such values. For instance, LMTs need to make sure that students do not access pornographic Web sites. For that reason, school libraries need to provide telecommunications filters if they wish to accept federal funding. On a more pro-active level, LMTs try to teach students how to be socially responsible in terms of information literacy (AASL & AECT, 1998).

Bloom's Affective Domain and the Development of Ethical Practice

Professional ethical behavior focuses on individuals and organizational behavior, as much as it does on the specific issue at hand. Policies created by the LMT's school or district reflect the ethical values of decision-makers, be it in response to plagiarism or facility use. Because the library program should support the organization, LMTs need to support the associated policies. Library profession policies and ethical codes also exist, some of which concern matters that might be encountered at school, such as access to information and selection policies. When the policies of those two entities conflict or when no policy exists relative to a problematic situation—or when confronted with an ethical situation that is foreign to their experience—LMTs may have to decide for themselves how to act ethically. Therefore, as librarianship educators aim to help preservice LMTs develop ethical stances and practice their craft ethically, they need to attend to the affective nature of value acceptance (Simpson, 2003).

Bloom's 1973 affective domain taxonomy (Krathwohl, Bloom, & Bertram, 1973) can serve as a critical lens to examine how preservice library media teachers (LMT) become ethically competent. This chapter examines how using case studies can facilitate professional ethical behavior. Furthermore, technology-infused instruction and learning can enhance the affective domain. Bloom's taxonomy of the affective domain posits five stages:

1. **Receiving:** Getting and holding one's attention relative to professional ethical issues;
2. **Responding:** Active participation and satisfaction in learning about professional ethics;
3. **Valuing:** Commitment to the underlying value of professional ethics;
4. **Organization:** Integration of possibly conflicting values to support professional ethics; and
5. **Value Complex:** Pervasive and consistent incorporation of professional ethics.

Typically, each stage needs to be addressed before the next stage can occur.

To establish a professional ethical baseline, instructors can have students identify how they act ethically presently, and what they wanted to accomplish that could be facilitated through professional ethics. By valuing the present level of professional ethical comfort and willingness to risk change and learn, instructors help preservice LMTs feel more relaxed and open to developing a professional ethic. Students should also feel that they can control their learning focus and pacing.

At the initial stages of *awareness and receiving,* instructors can present case studies that demonstrate the benefits of ethical decision-making. At this point, instructors can work with preservice LMTs to identify issues in *site ethics,* particularly in terms of K-12 student behavior and impact. Perhaps clearer communication with parents is needed. Maybe K-12 students have a hard time understanding an ethical concept, or LMTs do not how to teach it to students. How might ethics provide a solution? By sharing a simple case study focusing on a challenged book and showing a grievance procedure along with a selection policy and challenge form, instructors can provide a nonthreatening tool that preservice LMTs can use immediately to address an ethical issue.

This focus on processes can help preservice LMTs advance to the next stage in Bloom's affective domain: *responding.* Because preservice LMTs are motivated to engage in activities that reduce plagiarism to improve K-12 student learning, they can use an associated case study to brainstorm ways to teach ways to respect intellectual property. For instance, LMTs may mention using organizational resources such as graphic organizers and Cornell notetaking. They also appreciate articles written by other LMTs who learned how to leverage a learning tool to help K-12 students avoid plagiarism.

By this point, preservice LMTs begin to *value* professional ethics (Bloom's third stage within the affective domain), and seek ways to incorporate professional ethics in their library program. To insure that LMTs control their application of ethics, instructors can have preservice LMTs share their own case studies, which may be based on real-life experiences or created to test hypothetical situations. Using telecommunications, they can easily share their case studies with their course colleagues. It should be noted that most preservice LMTs start with ethical case studies that help in their own practice; afterwards, they feel more relaxed about using ethics as a learning tool with their K-12 students. They also value developing a concrete *product* as a means to demonstrate authentic results. Throughout the process, the emphasis should be on close transfer of learning, not generic ethical practice but issue-specific applications. Of course, instructors have to show that they have dealt with ethnical issues in order to gain credibility with their preservice LMTs.

These efforts lead to the next stage in Bloom's taxonomy: *organization.* It also signals readiness for collaboration. Case studies can address program-wide ethical review and interventions. Typical projects might include technology selection policies, donation policies, plagiarism-proof learning activities design, and research handbooks, all of which foster consistent teaching and assessment.

Particularly if preservice LMTs work in the same school district, such collaborative effort facilitates the top stage in Bloom's taxonomy: *value complex.* Case studies may investigate initiatives to develop an ethics curriculum or create a district policies and procedures manual that would weave in professional ethics. Preservice LMTs might seek outside consulting and funding to sustain their efforts, demonstrating their long-term commitment to professional ethics.

Externalization of Ethical Knowledge

Arnseth and Ludvigen (2006) suggest that "social interaction with artifacts in an organized setting becomes the site where these processes are made available for study" (p. 171). The interaction between the intellectual discourse and the external setting relative to case studies lead to authentic meaning and the source for relevant action. Each student brings his or her own experiences and values to library courses. As all students are exposed to new information, they make their implicit knowledge explicit. In sharing and reviewing their peers' reflections, they combine and refine the explicit knowledge, and then internalize it in order to improve their ethical values and ensuring behaviors. Indeed, Yi (2006) asserts that in

online learning environments, "sharing one's own experience is the most effective way people use when sharing their tacit knowledge with others" (p. 670).

Interactive and collaborative discussion leads to co-construction of knowledge where the whole is greater than the sum of its parts; no one person could have created the ultimate insight or solution. "Each participant takes up another's contribution and does something further with it" (Suthers, 2005, p. 667). Yukawa (2006) asserted that narrative analysis "accommodates both individual and group learning and provides a means to ascertain the roles of affect and relationship building" (p. 205).

MAIN THRUST OF THE CHAPTER

Using Case Studies to Study Ethics

A case study is basically a story or narrative that illustrates a phenomenon or concept. Critical features that further define a case study include:

- **Boundedness:** The critical elements are self-contained within the situation;
- **particularity:** The focus is specific and consists of a unique combination of elements;
- **descriptiveness:** The study provides a thick dataset of grounded reality; and
- **heuristics:** The study lends itself to reveal "rules" or reasons (Merriam, 1998).

Merriam (1998) further categorizes case studies according to function or intent:

- **Description:** They provide basic information about a topic that has not been well researched; this type of case study often focuses on innovative practices;
- **Interpretation:** Information is analyzed to generalize a situation or to develop a conceptual framework; and

• **Evaluation:** The underlying issues can be deduced by applying existing theory to the grounded experience.

For the purposes of explaining ethics within the field of school librarianship, a case study sets up a situation that presents an ethical dilemma or conflict of values, which the student needs to resolve.

Case studies constitute an important aspect of library education as they provide a reality check for theories and concepts taught in the classroom; they provide contextualized situations that can bridge abstract theory and daily practice (Bridges, 1992; Mostert & Sudzine, 1996). Case studies offer an authentic way to teach critical analysis and decision-making because they reveal nuanced factors in complex situations and they stimulate productive discussion incorporating multiple perspectives. Students are likely to engage in case studies because they are concrete and typically include some affective elements. They may be approached intuitively, and so can engage the novice learner in a constructivist learning model to make meaning (Gerring, 2007). Allen (1994) noted that case-based teaching not only reinforces course concepts, but the in-depth discussion leads to higher levels of reflective critical thinking. Library educator Hannabuss (1996) asserts:

Case studies can incorporate elements of research, as students work on legal, organizational or political issues which require more factual evidence, concentrate key ideas into achievable learning tasks and objectives for students or groups of students, and enable students to develop skills in presenting not just information but reasoned arguments too. (p. 30)

Case studies provide positive experiences for student learning, but this methodology also has limitations. Indeed, some academians consider case studies nonrigorous, nonsystematic, and nonscientific (Gerring, 2007). For example, while case studies provide rich data sets, those data are usually context-dependent for accurate interpretation; overgeneralization of the solutions can lead to misleading perceptions. In a different vein, because analysis usually requires insightful writing, assessment might evaluate writing expertise more than content analysis. Moreover, if students lack academic knowledge or professional experience, they are less likely to interpret the data accurately (Mostert & Sudzine, 1996).

Other common practical problems need to be addressed when using case studies. For example, optimal discussion occurs with groups of 12 to 15 members, so large classes need to be subdivided; online discussion groups should be even smaller in number in order to keep track of discussion threads. Case study discussion can be very time-consuming, particularly if deep analysis is to be gained. Participation may be uneven, so the instructor or facilitator needs to make sure that everyone contributes to the discussion (Mostert & Sudzine, 1996).

Choosing and Creating Case Studies

Faculty effort to identify or create appropriate case studies can be time-intensive, particularly because case studies are usually incorporated *after* concepts are introduced; the case is chosen to exemplify the concept (Bridges, 1992). One of the tasks in using case studies for teaching professional ethical behavior is to select the more effective ones, based on the intended outcome and taking into account the prior experiences of preservice LMT. As with any other potential resource selection in support of teaching and learning, instructors need to develop and apply appropriate evaluation criteria:

• Includes ethical elements;
• includes context for making ethical decisions;
• poses an ethical conflict; and
• offers multiple perspectives or interpretations (Gerring, 2007).

Instructors may locate suitable ethics-based case studies from the professional literature, ask their professional peers for applicable true stories, create their own case studies, or ask preservice LMTs to tell their stories. Each option has its advantages and disadvantages. Probably the most valid action is to locate "vetted" case studies in the literature; these may exhibit real-life situations or may be artificially constructed to make a point about ethics. It should be noted that the quantity and quality of published appropriate case studies varies according to the specific ethical dilemma under investigation. For that reason, instructors may want to construct their own scenarios in order to insure that the points they want to make will be covered in the scenario. In the process of creating a scenario, however, instructors need to make sure that the situation is based on facts and is credible. Getting real-life stories from peers can provide authentic factors, but may jeopardize confidentiality; instructors should ask for a written version of the story and obtain written permission to share it (Mostert & Sudzine, 1996). Yin (2003) notes the importance of using theory as a basis for choosing case studies in terms of research design, defining the critical issues, addressing rival theories, and legitimately generalizing to other cases.

Having students locate or share their own stories or case studies provides an authentic link between classroom practice and real-life applications. Some preservice LMTs serve as library staff, and others work in school setting with easy access to library programs. Other preservice LMTs may intern at libraries or volunteer in a service learning capacity. The American Association for Higher Education (1997) defines service learning as:

a method under which students learn and develop through thoughtfully organized service that: is conducted in and meets the needs of a community and is coordinated with an institution of higher education, and with the community; helps foster civic responsibility; is integrated into and en-

hances the academic curriculum of the students enrolled; and includes structured time for students to reflect on the service experience.

Service learning is especially useful in distant and remote library education because it motivates students and facilitates a community of practice (Mellon & Kester, 2004).

One of the benefits of student-chosen case studies is a sense of ownership. Preservice LMTs are more likely to choose a case study that has personal meaning for them, be it an issue that that have confronted or an issue that they want to explore in a safe learning environment. The choice of case study can also constitute an opportunity for assessment because instructors can determine if the case study is relevant to the topic at hand. As with instructors, preservice LMTs have to deal with authenticity and ethical considerations of sharing when locating or creating case studies. Usually, information shared within a class for instruction and research is not held to the same legal standard as public information, but students should model ethical behaviors even in this selection and sharing process.

Typically, instructors would provide case studies at the beginning of a library preparation program and individual course, but by the end of the time frame, instructors might want to have students locate or create their own case studies as a way to apply prior knowledge and demonstrate authentic performance. To involve students from the start, instructors might consider asking students to describe an ethically critical event that they experienced, stating its significance and detailing their response to the issue. This *narrative* can be analyzed in terms of the aforementioned criteria for possible modification into a formal case study.

Reflection Using Case Studies

A key factor in using case studies is critical reflection. While providing a relevant case study constitutes a necessary condition for learning, student response constitutes the act of learning itself. Dewey (1933) defined reflection as the "active, persistent, and careful consideration of any belief or supposed form of knowledge in the light of the grounds that support it and the further conclusions to which it tends" (p. 9). He asserted that, while thinking was natural, active reflection was a learned skill. Boud, Koeugh, and Walker (1985) pointed out that reflection also includes affective activities "in order to lead to new understandings and appreciations" (p. 19). Spalding and Wilson (2002) further contended that reflection should begin with uncertainty or doubt, with the idea that critical analysis will shed light on the problem and help result it. Ethics, too, demands conscious learning, so the partnership of reflection and ethics constitutes a sound combination.

Valli (1997) positives four types of reflection:

- **Reflecting in/on action:** Thinking about one's own performance in context of a setting or situation;
- **deliberative:** Thinking about a range of librarianship concerns (e.g., students, curriculum, organization, strategies);
- **personalistic:** Thinking about personal growth and relationships; and
- **critical:** Social, moral, and political dimensions of librarianship.

All of these modes contribute to a better understanding of ethics because both cognitive and affective domains need to be addressed in ethical attitude and behavior. Nevertheless, students need to transcend the personal to see the broader theory and implications so they can make ethical decisions about currently unknown situations. Additionally, they need to provide credible evidence to support their stances, and thus build their knowledge base, as well as draw upon affective perspectives.

To help students benefit from case studies, instructors need to structure the learning experience. Here are some valid approaches.

- Have students develop decision-making flowcharts, identifying and tracing the consequences of alternative solutions.
- Have students use a problem-solving model: identify the problem, identify the underlying ethical issues, identify the stakeholders, identify alternative solutions and their possible conflicts, decide on a solution, evaluate its effectiveness.
- Identify an ethical premise. Locate a case study or identify a real-life situation that illustrates the conflict. Identify the underlying reasons for the conflict and their impact. Choose a solution, and trace its ethical ramifications.

Instructors also need to follow up after students reflect upon a case study. According to Spalding and Wilson (2002), timely and specific feedback is a necessary component of reflection because it provides a reality check on students' perceptions, and helps instructors see what additional information and interventions are needed in order to insure student learning and application. Reflections are evaluated in terms of: 1) demonstrated knowledge of ethical principles; and 2) ability to apply ethics appropriately to specific settings. During a course, the reflective process itself should improve, due to added content and feedback. As students self-monitor their reflections and applications of knowledge, they can increase their understanding, improve their responses, and act more ethically.

Co-reflection increases both the intellectual and the affective integration of ethical behavior. Yukawa (2006) points out that "a core element appears to be living experience within a shared world, and a core recognition is the opacity of interior life and social life, which presents obvious barriers to the attainment of intersubjective understanding" (p. 207). At the minimum, whereby students individually create or react to a case study in a shared learning space (e.g., open online discussion board), intersubjective understanding and co-constructed knowledge tacitly occurs. By introducing active peer reflection, instructors enable students to share understanding and perceptions explicitly so that relationships can increase. In effect, a triangulation of grounded feedback is established, which provides more valid assessment. Students also appreciate peer observations because it offers an opportunity to interact with others, fostering a sense of belonging and facilitating a sustainable social *and* professional network. By couching reflection in an online environment, distance constraints are virtually eliminated so students can continue their professional relationships wherever they go.

Ethics and Distance Education

One of the benefits of case study is that the core elements–content and analysis–are space-neutral. Students may engage in examination and discussion both face-to-face and remotely, in real time or asynchronously. Indeed, case studies can bring distance learners together, offering a common text for multiple interpretations. Lavargnino, Bowker, Heidorn, and Basi (2001) detailed the incorporation of social informatics (i.e., study of socially-constructed information) in a distance library education program, asserting that case studies underlined the importance of storytelling to learning and simulated real-life processes. Distance education also provides more equitable discourse in that English language learners, low-verbal learners, and more contemplative learners can respond to the case study "prompt" after they have had time to comprehend and reflect on the underlying issues (Tait & Mills, 1999). Researching online discursive activity focused on case studies, the author (Farmer, 2004a, 2004b) noted the following benefits related to the affective domain:

- Increased frequency and quality of out-of-class, student-to-student dialogue (e.g., collaboration on assignments and projects; peer review of work, etc.) via e-mail, online "chat" and discussion group facilities;
- Increased opportunity for faculty-student communication through individual and group e-mail;
- Ability of instructors to evaluate efficiently the quality of student work by means of online quizzes and exams and to monitor student effort and engagement with the subject matter on a more frequent and regular through the use of online discussion groups;
- Mutual reinforcement of out-of-class and in-class student interaction; and
- Increased student confidence in their ability to apply concepts.

Examples of Ethics-based Case Studies

The California State University Long Beach (CSULB) Library Media Teacher program prepares LMTs to work in K-12 school library settings. Throughout the program, these preservice LMTs incorporate service learning and case studies to "flesh out" theory and contextualize it within their daily practice. Ethics-base case studies, provided by both instructors and classmates, facilitate a community of practice, melding the experiences of face-to-face and distance education participants.

The course ELIB 520 Information Literacy and Reference Services provide additional opportunities for candidates to design learning activities that meld information literacy and ethics. This project is done after candidates have read case studies about youth-serving librarians and student information-seeking behaviors in various library settings according to predetermined topics. One of the main ethical concepts is the assurance that all students will have equitable access to information resources and services. Students develop a case study at an at-risk population (e.g., unwed mothers, English language learners, reluctant readers), identify barriers to information, discuss the basis and implication in inequity, and offer library based-solutions; peers respond by suggesting another solution based on a reading. The learning activities are assessed in terms of analysis of the population, ethical decision-making, and quality of response (both distance and face-to-face students pair up). As a result of analyzing case study reflections, instructors can modify or add ethics-based case studies to provide knowledge that preservice LMTs need to use appropriate resources, such as practices to insure privacy and confidentiality. An example case study follows.

My Reference Services Overview examined xxx School, a K-3 site in the xxx Unified School District currently serving approximately 572 K-3 students and a staff of 50. xxx is a community of 31, 415 as of the 2000 U.S. Census figures, which indicate 27.8%, are Hispanic or Latino with 28.3% indicating that language other than English is spoken at home. 37.2% of the population is children under the age of 18. Families at the poverty level measure 25.4% using the 1999 figures used in the 2000 Census. The school is located nearest the eastern boundary of the community adjacent to xxx College in an area of low to moderate income. 2002-03 Academic Performance Index (API) Growth Report indicates that 43% of K-3 students participating in the STAR reporting (287 second and third graders) are eligible for Free or Reduced Price Lunch Programs. The key feature of access, both physical and intellectual, is one of the concerns for the marginalized group of poverty level children and families. Access at the school currently consists of a scheduled weekly opportunity for K-3 students with their classes. Some limited extra time for collaboration is available. The Library Media Tech is a part time position of M-F for twenty hours per week. The classrooms are not equipped with reference materials beyond dictionaries. The Library Media Center has dictionaries in various formats, atlases, encyclopedias in English and Spanish, CD-ROMs, almanacs and other basic "ready reference" resources. Last year an online database was available for curricular support. Students from families struggling at the poverty level will not have these resources in their homes. Given a choice of putting food on the table or buying computers or books is ridiculous to even consider. These K-3 students additionally will need greater "access" to the public library or school library. The funding levels have affected the public library available hours of operation in this community. Students in this group require access to additional print, reference, and computer resources. The Library Media Center is adjacent to a computer lab equipped with 22 networked student workstations using Accelerated Reader/STAR software, Kid Pix, Typing, Storybook Weaver, Math Workshop and other software. Again, classes are on a fixed schedule as well. The Library Media Center itself includes three computer workstations for OPAC searching, word processing or CD-ROM reference use. How will these identified K-3 students become "effective users of ideas and information" given a narrow access of opportunity? As Library Media Teachers we are challenged to help all students succeed. Both the Library Media Center goals and plans in conjunction with the site's technology plans need to reflect inclusion for the entire community. Possible solutions include:

- *The Library Media Center should try to be available before school, during lunch and after school.*
- *Technology access could be available for K-3 students and families to use these resources.*
- *The Library Media Center staff hours should be increased and professional certificated personnel in place.*

- *Design change to create a reference area "welcoming" K-3 students and staff to the area for research.*
- *Additional materials have been purchased with a cart for teachers to use in the classroom.*
- *Access to the library collection with a Web portal and resources connecting the K-3 students from the public library resources is encouraged.*
- *Increase public relations with the public library promoting literacy connections, summer reading, schedule, invite personnel to literacy night, and share library card sign-up info.*
- *Seek funding to initiate "after school" opportunities with K-3 students and their families in the LMC and using technology and training in their use.*
- *Older computers may be available to loan with some application software.*
- *Research free or reduced Internet possibility.*

  Response: Dr. Farmer's Digital Inclusion, Teens, and Your Library states, "Libraries constitute an effective and efficient means for all people to have access to information technology." One of the goals of the school library media center is providing information access and delivery. ALA's Information Power: Building Partnerships for Learning goal for the School Library Media Specialist is "To work collaboratively with the learning community to develop and implement policies and practices that
  - ○ *Make resources, facilities, and professional assistance available at the time of learning need through such mechanisms as flexible scheduling, extended service hours, and after-hours technological access."*
  - ○ *...Encourage the widest possible use of program resources and services by*

making them available throughout the school and through remote access as well as in the library media center."

The Library Media Center Management course (ELIB 550) requires preservice LMTs to analyze critical incidents they face, either as classroom teachers or as beginning LMTS, incorporating ethical issues. Each student posts his/her event on the online course management discussion forum, and must reply online to a peer's case study with the intent of providing another solution or give another insight. The instructor performed a content analysis of these incidents in order to predict likely ethical issues; as a result, she expanded discussion about communicating with administrators, and increased the use of case studies (Farmer, 2004a). The following is a sample student case study analysis.

Problem: Someone was using the library's main computer to go to Internet pornography sites and had bookmarked them as well. Action: I notified the principal of the situation. I told all adults who I came into contact with at the school that someone had bookmarked pornography sites on my computer. The principal contacted all groups that used the library after hours to find out if anyone ever touched the computers. The answer in all cases was, "No." The school district sent over the computer technician to install a firewall on all of the computers in the library. Outcome: I announced once again to any adult who would listen at the school that a firewall had been installed on all of the computers. My suspicions were correct. The parent volunteer, a father, who I suspected had been doing this, stopped volunteering in the library. Problem solved. Discussion: I believe in intellectual freedom, however when it comes to pornography, that is inappropriate for an elementary school. Pornography has nothing whatsoever to do with the elementary school curriculum. It is my job to make sure that the students are exposed to a safe environment in which they can learn how to use a library and find the materials that are needed for school work and pleasure reading. The parent had no right using the computer for his own personal satisfaction and potentially giving the children easy access to pornography sites. Probably the reason why the father did this at the school was that he did not want it traced to his own computer at home. The public library has an antipornography policy. Therefore, the only available place to do this was at his children's little school library.

Peer response: How sad that a parent set such a negative model for children. It seems that if would be a good idea to interview and screen all volunteers. What kind of policies and procedures are set at the school to minimize that possibility?

The Library Media Technologies course (ELIB 570) requires preservice LMTs to assess a school library in terms of its technology resources and use (according to the state's technology planning guide), and to develop a technology plan for its effective incorporation. In the process, they examine ethical issues that arise in technology incorporation: software piracy, filtering, privacy, copyright infringement. Each student poses an ethical scenario, posting it online, and a peer has to solve the issue using relevant documentation. The student-created case studies usually reflect issues that students encounter in their professional lives, or address problems that they fear they will have to address in their new role as a librarian. Thus, case studies provide a means to expand preservice LMTs' encounter with unethical situations–and their ramifications–in a safe environment. In this manner, they can decide how to design preventative measures to forestall potential ethical disasters. A typical case study follows.

AUP Scenario: Ms. Levin originally went through all of her classes and cleared their Acceptable Use Policy (AUP) for the Internet. She has used the library for Internet research several times during the fall semester. Now in February, Ms. Levin brings her classes in for the first time in the spring semester. The LMT notices there are some new faces in her classes, and approaches Ms. Levin to ask if all of the students have their AUPs signed. She responds by saying she assumes so but has not checked the new students. What does the LMT do?

Response: First – Make sure you know what the AUP policy is for your school and what the consequences are. You need to know whether a signature is required on a form or if K-12 students just need to be aware of the policy. If some students have had them signed at the beginning of the year, it is likely that the policy says they are required to be signed before using the Internet. In order to protect herself and her school, the LMT should stop the class from using the computers at once and have the teacher go get the signed AUPs to determine who does and does not have them. In the meantime, the LMT can teach a lesson on preparing to do research on the Internet, making sure that students have developed good questions and have sought out print resources for their work as well. Once the teacher returns with the AUPs, they should be checked against the students present. Students without an AUP should be given a blank one and told what needs to be done with them. The LMT should then hold a discussion with all the students, helping them to understand why this is being done and what the legal ramifications are (A teachable moment!). Afterwards, students who have a signed AUP can be allowed to use the computers while the other students continue their work using other resources that are not covered by the AUP. If the teacher pleads lack of time or that the students should be able to use the system "just this once," the LMT should point out to her (privately) that she is putting herself, the LMT and the school at risk by not enforcing a school/district policy. The key here is to know what is in the AUP. Content is not standard for these and enforceability and consequences may vary depending on the language. As a rule, it's a good idea to be consistent in enforcing the policy in order to ensure that the policy holds water. Assuming that the policy addresses things like slander, defamation of character and posting of inappropriate information/comments, consistent enforcement is critical to the ability to use the policy as a defense in a lawsuit against the district. It is also critical to being able to enforce the policy as a safeguard against plagiarism, hacking and other inappropriate or illegal uses of the Internet. The LBUSD Policy Regarding Student Use of the Internet, for instance, specifically prohibits a number of illegal and inappropriate uses of the Internet and clearly states that the student is releasing the district from liability by signing the agreement. It also says that the student agrees that if they violate the agreement, they will be subject to the same rules and guidelines that are in place for other campus infractions. In addition, it states that parents have the right to determine whether their children should have access to the Internet. Because of these conditions in the AUP, if the teacher or LMT allow students to access the Internet without a signed agreement, they put the school and the district at risk from the consequences of illegal behavior by students, from the actions of parents who did not agree to allow their students access and from the consequences of students who use the system inappropriately. When policies are not consistently enforced, they do not convey the protection that they intend. Assuming that the agreement requires a parent's signature, by failing to have an AUP-signed form, the school also creates a situation that may cause a problem with enforcement of the Children's Online Privacy Protection Act (COPPA). If the school or district has determined that they will require consent from the parents to allow access, not having this on file for some students puts the school in the position of acting in the absence of the parents in some cases and not in others. This opens up the potential for a violation of the COPPA laws. In addition, if the school is bound by the Children's Internet Protection Act (CIPA),

not enforcing the AUP could result in a loss of funding to the school due to failure to comply with the act (ALA, 2005).

Sources:
LBUSD Library Procedures Manual
Guidelines for developing a library privacy policy. (2005). Chicago: American Library Association. www.ala.org/oif/iftoolkits/privacy/guidelines/ Accessed Feb. 19, 2006.
Cromwell, S. (2003). Getting started on the Internet: Developing an acceptable use policy. www. education-world.com/ Accessed Feb. 20, 2006.

CONCLUSION

This case study approach to professional ethics incorporation into school library programs through preservice instruction mirrors the complexity of changing and maturing attitudes as posited in Bloom's Affective Domain. Researching online reflective activity focused on case studies, the author (Farmer, 2004a, 2004b) noted the following benefits related to the affective domain:

- Increased frequency and quality of out-of-class, student-to-student discussion (e.g., collaboration on assignments and projects; peer review of work, etc.) via e-mail, online "chat" and discussion group facilities;
- Increased opportunity for faculty-student communication through individual and group telecommunications;
- Ability of instructors to evaluate efficiently the quality of student work by monitoring student effort and engagement in the ethics subject matter on a more frequent and regular through the use of online discussion groups;
- Mutual reinforcement of out-of-class and in-class student interaction; and
- Increased student confidence in their ability to apply ethical concepts.

FUTURE RESEARCH DIRECTIONS

The use of case studies provides a rich venue for future research. Particularly with increased digital communication, the sources of case studies about ethical dilemmas and the opportunities for discussing them are likely to expand exponentially. A beginning list of issues that warrant further study follow.

- How does complexity of ethical dilemmas in case studies impact decision-making? To what extent does the complexity of the case study impact the ease with which decisions are made? To what extent can ethical case studies be parsed by contributing factors? To what degree does one factor impact another; is this impact a sequential event, or does the holistic issue drive the decision-making?
- How do demographics impact ethical decision-making as seen in case studies, and the discussion of those case studies? For example, what influence do age, gender, race, ethnicity, socio-economic status, health status, locale have on ethical decisions?
- How does the format of delivery of ethical case studies impact decision-making? How would discussion and decision-making differ if the case study were re-enacted on video or captured "live" on video? Do imagery/visual features impact how students respond to case studies?
- How does the format of discussion of ethical case studies impact decision-making? Do face-to-face students respond differently from distance learners? What impact does individual vs. collaborative discussion of ethical case studies have on decision-making?
- How does the setting of the ethical case study impact decision-making (i.e., public library vs. academic library)? What differences in decision-making occur when students are examining case studies in a different type of library (e.g., preservice school librarians studying a case study about an ethical dilemma in a special library) vs. studying a case study in their intended library setting?
- What instructional practices in the use of case studies effectively scaffold students from one level of ethical decision-making to the next (e.g., choice of case study, critical thinking components, type of discussion, group discussion arrangement, etc.)

In short, the research agenda even for such a specific approach to ethical decision-making and instruction can occupy several individuals for a lifetime.

REFERENCES

Allen, B. P. (1994). Case-based reasoning: Business applications. *Communications of the ACM, 37*(3), 40-42.

American Association for Higher Education. (1997). *Series on service-learning in the disciplines.* Washington, DC: American Association for Higher Education.

American Association of School Librarians and Association of Educational Communications and Technology. (1998). *Information literacy standards for student learning: Standards and indicators.* Chicago, IL: American Library Association.

American Library Association. (2004). *Core values task force II final report.* Chicago, IL: American Library Association.

Arnseth, H., & Ludvigen, S. (2006). Approaching institutional context: Systematic versus dialogic research in CSCL. *Computer-supported Collaborative Learning, 1*, 167-183.

Association of Library and Information Science Education. (2006, October 20). *Information Ethics Special Interest Group: Position statement on information ethics in LIS education.* Message posted to JESSE mailing list.

Boud, D., Keogh, R., & Walker, D. (Eds.). (1985). *Reflection: Turning experiences into learning.* London: RoutledgeFalmer.

Bridges, E. (1992). Problem-based learning: Background and rationale. In E. M. Bridges (Ed.), *Problem-based learning for administrators.* Eugene, OR: ERIC.

Dewey, J. (1933). *How we think: A restatement of the relation of reflective thinking to the educative process.* New York: D. C. Heath and Company.

Farmer, L. (2004a). Narrative inquiry as assessment tool: A case study. *Journal of Education for Library & Information Science, 45*(4), 340-355.

Farmer, L. (2004b). Foundations of information: A course case study in metacognition. *Journal of Education for Library & Information Science, 45*(3), 180-188.

Gerring, J. (2007). *Case study research: Principles and practices.* New York: Cambridge University Press.

Hannabuss, S. (1996). Teaching library and information ethics. *Library Management, 17*(2), 24-35.

Krathwohl, D. R., Bloom, B. S., & Bertram, B. M. (1973). *Taxonomy of educational objectives, the classification of educational goals. Handbook II: Affective domain.* New York: David McKay.

Lavagnino, M., Bowker, G., Heidorn, P., & Basi, M. (1998). Incorporating social informatics into the curriculum for library and information science professionals. *Libri: International Journal of Libraries and Information Services, 48(*1), 13-25.

Mellon, C., & Kester, D. (2004). Online library education papers: Implications for rural students.

Journal of Education for Library & Information Science, 45(3), 210-220.

Merriam, S. (1998). *Qualitative research and case study applications in education.* San Francisco: Jossey-Bass.

Mostert, M., & Sudzine, M. (1996, February). Undergraduate case method teaching: Pedagogical assumptions vs. the real world. In *Paper presented by the Annual Meeting of the Association of Teacher Education*, St. Louis.

Rubin, R. (2000). *Foundations of library and information science.* New York: Neal-Schuman.

Simpson, C. (Ed.). (2003). *Ethics in school librarianship: A reader.* Worthington, OH: Linworth.

Spalding, E., & Wilson, A. (2002). Demystifying reflection, *Teachers College Record, 104*(7), 1393-1421.

Suthers, D. (2005, January). Collaborative knowledge building through shared representations. In *Proceedings of the 38ᵗʰ Hawaii International Conference on the System Sciences,* Wakaloa.

Tait, A., & Mills, R. (1999). *The convergence of distance and conventional education: Patterns of flexibility for the individual learner.* New York: Routledge.

Valli, E. (1997). Listening to other voices: A description of teacher reflection in the United States. *Peabody Journal of Education, 72*(1), 67-88.

Yakuwa, J. (2006). Co-reflection in online learning: Collaborative critical thinking as narrative. *Computer-Supported Collaborative Learning. 1,* 203-228.

Yi, J. (2006). Externalization of tacit knowledge in online environments. *Information Journal on E-learning. 5*(4), 663-674.

Yin, R. (2003). *Applications of case study research* (2ⁿᵈ ed.). Thousand Oaks, CA: Sage.

ADDITIONAL READING

Alfino, M., & Pierce, L. (1997). *Information ethics for librarians.* Jefferson, NC: McFarland.

American Association of Law Libraries. (1999). *Ethical principles.* Chicago, IL. Retrieved April 23, 2008, from http://www.aallnet.org/about/policy_ethics.asp

American Library Association. (1995). Code of ethics. Chicago, IL. Retrieved April 23, 2008, from http://www.ala.org/ala/oif/statementspols/codeofethics/codeethics.htm

Ball, K., & Oppenheim, C. (2005). Attitudes of UK librarians and librarianship students to ethical issues. *International Review of Information Ethics, 3,* 54-61.

Bier, M., Sherblom, S., & Gallo, M. (1996). Ethical issues in a study of Internet use: Uncertainty, responsibility, and the spirit of research relationships. *Ethics and Behavior, 6*(2), 141-151.

Bodi, S. (1998). Ethics and information technology: Some principles to guide students. *Journal of Academic Librarianship, 24*(6), 459-463.

Buchanan, E. (2004). Ethics in library and information science: What are we teaching? *Journal of Information Ethics, 13*(1), 51-60.

Carbo, T., & Almagno, S. (2001). Information ethics: The duty, privilege and challenge of educating information professionals. *Library Trends, 49*(3), 510-518.

Doyle, T. (2002). A critical discussion of "The ethical presuppositions behind the Library Bill of Rights." *Library Quarterly, 72*(3), 275-293.

Fallis, D. (2007). Information ethics for 21st century library professionals. *Library Hi Tech, 25*(1).

Froehlich, T. (2005). A brief history of information ethics. *Computer Society of India Communications, 28*(12), 11-13.

Garoogian, R. (1991). Librarian/patron confidentiality: An ethical challenge. *Library Trends, 40*(2), 216-233.

Gorman, M. (2000). *Our enduring values: Librarianship in the 21st century.* Chicago, IL: American Library Association.

Hauptman, P. (2002). *Ethics and librarianship.* Jefferson, NC: McFarland.

Lancaster, F. (Ed.). (1991). *Ethics and the librarian.* Urbana-Champaign, IL: University of Illinois, Graduate School of Library and Information Science.

Mathiesen, K. (2004). What is information ethics? *Computers and Society, 32*(8). Retrieved April 23, 2008, from http://www.computersandsociety.org

Maufefette-Leenders, L., & Erskine, J. (1999). *Learning with cases.* Ontario, CA: University of Western Ontario.

McDonald, F. (1993). *Censorship and intellectual freedom: A survey of school librarians' attitudes and moral reasoning.* Metuchen, NJ: Scarecrow Press.

Moran, G. (2001). Ethics, strengths and values: A review article. *Journal of Librarianship and Information Science, 33*(2), 98-101.

Oppenheim, C., & Pollecutt, N. (2000). Professional associations and ethical issues in LIS. *Journal of Librarianship and Information Science, 32*(4), 187-203.

Schmidt, K. (Ed.). (1999). *Understanding the business of library acquisitions.* Chicago, IL: American Library Association.

Spinello, R. (1997). *Case studies in information and computer ethics.* Upper Saddle River, NJ: Prentice Hall.

United States Congress, Senate Committee on Governmental Affairs. (2001). *Office of Govern-*

ment Ethics Authorization Act of 2001: Report of the Committee on Governmental Affairs. Washington, DC: Government Printing Office.

Wengert, R. (2001). Some ethical aspects of being an information professional. *Library Trends, 49*(3), 486-509.

Woodward, D. (1990). A framework for deciding issues in ethics. *Library Trends, 39*(1-2), 8-17.

Yasuoka, K. (2004). The case study of the information ethics education by the Media Center. *Online Kensaku, 25*(3-4), 159-166.

KEY TERMS

Affective Domain: Emotional aspects of learning.

Case Study: Story or narrative that illustrates a phenomenon or concept; it typically self-contains the focused critical elements and lends itself to heuristics.

Collaboration: Cooperative efforts between two or more parties in which the results require interdependence.

Constructivist Learning: A student-centric model of learning that encourages self-initiated inquiry and meaning-making.

Ethical Code: A framework to guide ethical decision-making; it typically includes statements about excellence in service, intellectual property and freedom, collegiality, conflict of interest, and professional growth.

Information Ethics: Ethics related to the information profession and information literacy.

Information Literacy: The ability to locate, evaluate, use, communicate, and manage information.

Librarianship Education: Formal academic education (usually at the post-graduate level) that prepares librarians and other information professionals.

Library Media Teacher: A professional/licensed librarian who works in an elementary or secondary school setting.

Reflection: Thoughtful and self-analytical written response.

Chapter XVII
Preparing Faculty to Integrate Ethics into Online Facilitation

Tina J. Parscal
Regis University, USA

Peter Bemski
Regis University, USA

ABSTRACT

This qualitative case study was designed to determine the extent to which a framework for exploring ethical principles for online facilitation is integrated into an online training course for faculty preparing to teach online. Specifically, this study examined the extent to which the principles of ethical teaching are addressed in an asynchronous faculty training course where participants complete learning activities designed to promote comprehension, application, and synthesis of ethical principles for teaching. Content analysis was performed on archived discussion forum transcripts from 18 randomly selected faculty members over a 12-month period. This chapter summarizes the ethical themes that emerged through content analysis.

INTRODUCTION

While training courses for new online faculty have become more common, they often address only the technical aspects of online teaching, which are certainly important but not sufficient. To properly prepare faculty to address student learning online a discussion of the ethics involved must be included in their preparation.

Recent perspectives on the importance of ethics in teaching are exemplified by Paulo Freire in Pedagogy of Freedom: Ethics, Democracy, and Civic Courage (1998), to the effect that unless ethical principals are a part of a teacher's approach, education will be no more than content. Other examples of this increased focus of the importance of ethics in teaching include The National Education Association (n.d.) publication of a brief code of ethics statement for primary and secondary educators that focuses on teachers' commitment to students and the profession and Murray, Gillese, Lennon, Mercer, and Robinson's (1996) set of nine basic ethical principles intended to define the professional responsibilities of university professors in their role as teachers.

Concurrently, there is a rise in the number of education programs offered online. Research indicates that online learning requires a shift in the role for educators, moving from the central role of distributing information to a role of facilitator (Harasim, Hiltz, Teles, & Turoff, 1996; Kearsley, 2000; Knowlton, 2000; Palloff & Pratt, 1999). The convergence of this heightened awareness of ethical professional practice for educators and the new roles for educators teaching online has led to the need for online educators to consider ethical principles to guide our practice in the virtual environment. Educators in such areas as nursing (Fulton & Kellinger, 2004), engineering (Chachra, 2005), and information technology (Gearhart, 2001) have called for the inclusion of ethical principles within their distance learning curriculum.

In alignment with the university's mission and consistent with these trends, Bemski and Parscal introduced a focus on ethics into the online Teaching Online Preparation Course (TOP) in 2004. "People welcome the conversation about ethics" (Lorenzetti, 2006, p. 8). Modeling and exploring ethical principles within the online learning environment have been identified by faculty among best practices for online learning (Parscal, 2007).

Participants in the TOP course complete learning activities designed to promote comprehension, application, and ultimately, synthesis of ethical principles. A qualitative study using content analysis examined the success of this approach. The results inform the importance of the topic as well as the success of this approach and lead the authors to believe that introducing ethics as part of an online teacher preparation course increases the likelihood that teachers will integrate ethical principals into their applied pedagogical activities in the online classroom.

BACKGROUND

The comprehension, application, and synthesis framework for teaching ethical principles for online facilitation was added to the online Teaching Online Preparation (TOP) course for online faculty at a private western, Jesuit university in the United States. The TOP course is a 2-week, asynchronous online course that is facilitated by one of the researchers. The TOP course utilizes the cognitive apprenticeship framework which underscores the importance of modeling strategies and reflection (Collins, Brown, & Newman, 1989). The course is offered every 8 weeks and is preceded by an assessment process to screen potential candidates. In the assessment course, participants are asked to read the mission of the university and write an essay that addresses their perspective on the ethical principles put forward in the university mission.

Candidates who move on to the TOP course are introduced to the Society for Teaching and Learning in Higher Education's nine principles for ethical teaching. They are asked to reflect and consider these principles beginning at the cognitive level of comprehension and working their way to analysis and synthesis. Figure 1 outlines the learning activities used to present and reinforce learning about ethical principles for online facilitation.

In the first week of the TOP course, participants are asked to read the principles and reflect on them as they relate to teaching online. In the

Figure 1. Cognitive levels for learning activities that support ethical principles for online facilitation

Cognitive Level	Learning Activity That Support Ethical Principles
Comprehension	Each participant is asked to read the principles and reflect on them as they relate to teaching online. In the discussion forum, participants discuss how each of these principles applies to online learning; how they may need to be adjusted for online teaching, and whether online teaching requires additional principles.
Application	In pairs, participants are asked to use the principles of ethical teaching in university online courses as the foundation for practicing strategies for initiating discussion questions and providing formative feedback.
Analysis and synthesis	Each participant is asked to initiate, manage, and close a forum discussion thread related to building online communities and the ethical principles of teaching in the online environment. All participants engage in reflective discourse on topics posed by their colleagues related to ethical principles of teaching and learning online.

discussion forum, they are asked to discuss how each of these principles applies to online learning. They are also asked to comment on how these principles may need to be adjusted to be appropriate for online teachers and if any additional principles need to be developed specifically for online teachers.

The discussion of the ethical principles is followed by an application activity in which participants are matched into pairs and assigned one or two of the ethical principles. For each assigned ethical principle, the participants are asked to craft two engaging discussion questions that support two different cognitive levels of learning. Then, each of the participants is asked to provide feedback to their partner's questions. This activity is scaffolded with resources on writing robust discussion levels, writing learning assignments that support particular cognitive levels, and strategies for providing formative feedback.

In the second week of the course, participants are asked to deepen their understanding of ethical principles by facilitating their own discussion thread related to ethical teaching. In addition to facilitating their own threads, each participant is asked to reflectively contribute to the threads launched by their colleagues.

Ethical topics such as plagiarism, intellectual property, academic freedom, etiquette, privacy, and tolerance for diverse cultures and perspectives as they relate to online teaching and learning are also presented and discussed throughout the course.

RESEARCH METHODS

In order to examine the extent to which principles of ethical teaching are addressed in the course for online faculty, content analysis took the place of archived discussion transcripts from randomly selected participants. The textual content from the compiled forum transcripts was segmented, open coded using QSR International's Nivo7, and analyzed to identify and describe themes. Coding was performed by the researchers. The ethical principles introduced in the course were used for categorization as well other items that arose from the data.

Participants

The population of this study consisted of 18 faculty members who participated in the TOP course in 2005 and 2006. Transcripts of online discussions from three faculty participants were randomly selected from among the participants in six sections of the TOP course over a period of 1 year. Participants included 11 females and 7 males.

Data Analysis

Compiled messages from the discussion forums were retrieved from course archives. The data from the surveys and self-evaluations were imported into NVivo7 for analysis by two researchers. Initial coding focused on the STLHE's nine ethical principles of teaching and additional ethical principles for teaching online as identified by participants. Those dominate themes were segmented and coded for topical subnodes. Cognitive levels of consideration of ethical issues were also examined.

FINDINGS

Nine Ethical Principles

In a message board assignment requiring the discussion of the STLHE's nine ethical principles of teaching, participants described each of the nine principles and how they relate to online learning. Participants also identified ethical principles that were not included in STLHE's nine ethical principles, but should be added.

Participants discussed the nine ethical principles within the forum discussions of the TOP course. Instances of discussion related to: (1) content competence; (2) pedagogical competence; (3) dealing with sensitive topics; (4) student development (5) dual relationships with students; (6) confidentiality; (7) respect for colleagues; (8) valid assessments of students; and (9) respect for institutions. For each of these principles, several themes emerged from the participants.

Content competence for online facilitators was a topic of much discussion in all sections of the training. Participants most frequently mentioned the importance of teachers to remain current in the research and best practices within

their respective disciplines. However, some participants argued that online facilitators have the advantage of asynchronicity and are not "put on the spot" like a classroom teacher. For online facilitators "there is always additional time to respond giving you a chance to research before responding. On ground [traditional classroom], you don't always have that luxury. You might attempt a response to a question without being fully prepared." Other participants argued that online teachers need to have a deeper level of expertise than their classroom counterparts because of the importance of the ability for online facilitators to accurately and succinctly communication content information in written form as much of the online discussions occurs in writing. Further, along with the advantage of asynchronicity for reflection and composition of feedback and responses comes the responsibility of being very familiar with the trusted sources within one's discipline and the ability to direct students to online or library resources germane to the inquiry.

Utilizing varied instructional strategies that are appropriate for online learning was the most commonly mentioned items for the ethical principles of **pedagogical competence**. Facilitators in both online and classroom settings should consider the learning objectives of the course, the affordances of the technology and media, and the learning styles of the students. One participant stated, "I consider it essential for facilitators to use a variety of instructional methods. The reason for this is that research has shown that there are a variety of learning styles that students have."

Effective communication strategies were also frequently identified as a component of pedagogical competence. One participant stated that "knowledge of techniques of communication and knowledge about the student are an ethical obligation [for] the facilitator." Timeliness and accuracy of communication in the online environment was also reported to be important as indicated in the following quote.

The instructor also does not have the advantage of being able to look into the eyes of the class as a gauge whether or not the instructions for an assignment make sense. If they don't, the instructor can immediately adjust. In the virtual environment, the instructor is slower to respond oftentimes and the process is more dependent on the instructor getting it right the first time.

Given that the participants in this study were preparing to teach adult students, there was also much discussion about the "need to substitute pedagogical (traditional, teacher-directed) competency with andragogical (facilitated, self-directed) competency."

Participants expressed that setting clear expectations for privacy, confidentiality, mutual respect and caring was a crucial first step in **dealing with sensitive topics** online. Through communication strategies, online facilitators can set the tone and ground rules for mutual respect and a climate of caring. As one participant noted:

Especially in an online environment, the teacher should insist that students discuss course material that might be controversial in respectful and polite manner. Written words on the message board can easily be misconstrued or misinterpreted, especially when the writer is using sarcasm or humor. Therefore, students should be encouraged to forego both while on the message board.

Given the lack of nonverbal cues and because emotion is more difficult to convey online, the online environment "demands an additional degree of awareness on the part of the facilitator to spot potential issues, either between students or between student and professor, and the best means of communication for dealing with problems."

Student development was considered to involve student intellectual development, but also fostering the development of the student as a whole person. Several references were made to the Jesuit commitment to *cura personalis* such

as the following excerpt in which the participant align cura personalis to several of the ethical principles.

We as instructors must allow the characteristics of Jesuit education, especially cura personalis, to inform all that we do online. Cura personalis means that we respect and appreciate each person in our online course as an individual, with a unique and precious set of talents, gifts, hopes, and dreams. How can we not build community if we treat people this way? If we encourage this ethic on the message board, we will most assuredly build community. If we embrace this ethic, of course we will respect our colleagues. If we embrace this ethic, of course we will avoid favoritism in the classroom. If we embrace this ethic, of course we will be honest and forthright in assessing student work.

Participants also discussed the importance of cultivating life-long learning as part of the educational experience of students online and in the classroom.

Participants observed the parallels between student development and the ethical principle of **dual relationships with students**. Facilitators, whether online or in the classroom, breach the trust between student and educator and ultimately violate the student as a whole person when entering into dual relationships with students.

In the classroom and online, **confidentiality** is paramount in the student-teacher relationship. Participants referred to United States privacy laws related to student information. They also discussed the permanence of the course transcripts that exist in online learning as well as the importance of providing summative feedback to students privately rather than in the public discussion forum.

Participants discussed the importance of collegiality in their discussion on **respect for colleagues**. This included discussions on academic freedom and the importance of never critiquing a colleague's instructional strategies or teaching to a student.

The ethical principle related to the **valid assessment of students** in the online environment often produced rich discussions on the nature of assessing and evaluating student work. These discussions were dominated by a conversation related to plagiarism. While some participants assumed a policing stature on the topic, others addressed it from an ethical standpoint, as evidenced in this quote.

While I believe we should be on the look out for aspects of plagiarism, we must not forget our role as educators. If we can instill morals and ethics through our teaching and correctly assess that our students are indeed learning; plagiarism will be less wide-spread. Prevention is always better than cure.

Participants also invested much time discussing the importance of aligning assessments with learning objectives as the training introduced Bloom's (1956) taxonomy of educational objectives.

The mission and standards of the university was a dominate theme in the discussion related to **respect for the institution**. Participants discussed ways in which online facilitators should support the goals and objectives of the university. The following excerpt illustrated that commitment.

Jesuits use the term "Magis" which literally translated from Latin means the "more," the "greater," the "better." The discussion specifically states this doesn't mean working more hours etc.... but instead it speaks to our hopes and aspirations that our students will find the "the Magis" in the curriculum and their experiences at Regis University. That whatever the reasons they decided to attend Regis University, they will find "more" in challenging reflections on ethics, spirituality, justice and service. After reviewing the Ethical Principles I believe the "more" is implied in Ethical Principle number nine Respect for Institution.

Additional Principles

Participants also identified several missing or additional principles of ethical teaching. Participants recognized the **respect for the student** was not explicitly stated as one of the ethical principles for teaching. One participant commented that he found the absence of respect for the student surprising particularly in the adult learning environment. "A university teacher should respect the expertise and opinions that the students bring to the learning environment."

Class management was identified as a recommended additional ethical principle.

A facilitator is aware of the unique dynamics of online facilitation and creates an environment conducive to learning and creativity, an environment free of communication challenges or content blocks. A facilitator helps students understand the unique online dynamics and leads them by example.... [Joe] offered that we may extend this thinking to "teaching environment," where the facilitator is also responsible for creating an environment conducive for the student learning. This could include being available, checking in regularly, doing things to create dialogue, and so forth.

Timely feedback to students was also noted as a missing ethical principle and this was observed to be critical in online learning. Other principles mentioned at least once included netiquette technology acumen and respect for diversity.

Cognitive Levels

Participants primarily demonstrated comprehension in their discussion related to the description of the ethical principles. However, there were some instances of synthesis when participants drew parallels among the ethical principles, for example, respect for colleagues and respect for institution or confidentiality and sensitive topics. Participants also demonstrated application through discussion on how these ethical principles have surfaced in their teaching or professional experiences.

In the activity in which participants are asked to craft discussion questions and provide feedback to their assigned colleague, most participants demonstrated both comprehension and application. For example, a participant posted the following discussion question written for the evaluation cognitive level and related to the ethical principle of respect for colleagues.

Based upon your experience with online adult learners, what changes or revisions to Bloom's taxonomy might you suggest? Please examine the due process provisions in the University of Virginia's Honor System, and suggest ways in which its provisions might be incorporated in the Regis' policy with regard to plagiarism? What policy recommendation would you make so as to ensure that grade inflation does not begin to undermine the validity and value of a degree from Regis University?

By aligning the reading about crafting online discussion questions and cognitive levels, participants proposed discussion questions for peer review. In this activity, participants applied their learning about ethical principles as well as pedagogical skills. Participants were also asked to evaluate the quality of their peers' questions and practice writing feedback in response to their colleagues' submission. This is another way in which participants applied their learning related to the ethical principles.

When it occurred, synthesis primarily occurred when participants facilitated their own discussion threads. This involved weaving together multiple ethical principles for teaching or synthesizing ethical principles with other lessons in the training course.

DISCUSSION

The exploration of ethical principles was intentionally a central component of the TOP course and participants were engaged in ethical thinking at various cognitive levels throughout the training. Sims and Felton (2006) suggested six learning environment features that support and promote learning about ethics. These include: (a) fostering reciprocity among students and the faculty member; (b) making the learning experiential; (c) emphasizing the personal application of ethical thinking; (d) providing individualized and self-directed; (e) promoting collaborative and cooperative learning; and (f) providing learners opportunities for testing hypotheses. Many of these strategies were utilized in the online TOP course. Faculty reported that the activities related to the ethical principles of teaching online could be made more engaging and experiential. Parscal (2007) recommended that using a simulation could make this exploring ethical principles of teaching at a distance more engaging and experiential.

Through collaborative online interaction, participants explored and discussed the role of ethics in teaching and learning in the online environment. However, there was little discussion about the ethical uses of technology and in fact, there seemed to be an underlying assumption on the behalf of the participants that distance learning tools and technology are ethically neutral. Sale (1995) contends that "Technologies are never neutral and some are hurtful." He goes on to argue that they are culturally loaded as well as dependent upon the user for ethical nature. Sussman (1997) contended that technology is not produced accidentally nor created for the common good. Stoll (1995) questions the systemic implications of the every increasing use of technology and the contribution that does or does not make to our quality of life. Sumner (2000) argued that distance learning technologies serve the dominant paradigm and distance educators must make "value choices" to serve the status quo or work toward the common good because both options are open to distance and online educators. By engaging in dialogue regarding ethical considerations in online learning, faculty may begin to consider these value choices. By becoming reflective practitioners, which involves techniques utilized in the TOP course, faculty members can "refute the idea that distance education is just a set of value-free techniques" (Atthill, 2001, p. 87). However, additional activities would need to be added to the TOP course to prompt faculty to reflect on the underlying assumptions about technology and ethics. Indiana Wesleyan University utilizes team-based learning to help students and faculty become what they term as "World Changers" (Gaide, 2004). Chachra (2005, p. 461) suggested that conducting ongoing discussions of ethical issues, through such medium as asynchronous discussion forums, may work toward "correcting the misapprehension… that technical knowledge is intrinsically value-neutral."

There are cases online that encourage ethical analysis, yet few pose questions of ethics. Those involving plagiarism, a subject familiar to most of us, are readily available and lend themselves to this. Rather than create new cases, it is our suggestion that one take any of these cases and include in the analysis questions such as:

- What might the professor have done initially to avoid this situation?
- Are there cultural biases at play here?
- Is all plagiarism created equal?
- Does our institution address this issue well?
- Will my solution help prevent this issue in the future?
- Will my solution lead to student growth?

Indeed, any case will profit from first asking what ethical perspectives might be present and then asking how to frame questions about them.

FUTURE RESEARCH DIRECTIONS

This study described the extent to which faculty addressed the principles of ethical teaching within a faculty training course. Future study is needed to examine the extent to which faculty who were introduced to the ethical principles of teaching apply these principles to their teaching practice within their respective disciplines and in various learning environments (classroom, online, and blended or hybrid learning). There is also a need to examine the impact of such integration of ethical principles has on student learning and program outcomes.

The increasing popularity of virtual worlds such as Second Life will also require research into the ethical considerations of using such tools for teaching and learning. For example, to what extent do synchronous virtual worlds require the reexamination of ethical behavior within education and distance learning in particular?

Additional research is also needed to address the deeper integration of social networking and Web 2.0 technologies within distance learning. Do the deeper integration of social networking software and other Web 2.0 technologies into distance education amplify the importance of preparing faculty to engage in conversations about ethics and values in teaching and learning specifically those involving the definition of scholarship and the definition of valid academic work?

These are a few future directions for research in the examination of ethical principles in distance learning. By inviting new faculty into a conversation about ethical principles of teaching in online and distance learning environments may foster research within these areas of faculty development and scholarship.

CONCLUSION

One might assume that as a Jesuit university, Regis is more likely to attract faculty candidates predisposed to embrace the discussion of ethical principles. Certainly, those in the TOP course have done so. However, the authors' experience, gained through discussion with colleagues as well as through presenting on this topic in a variety of settings, suggests that faculties elsewhere are also likely to embrace it. The fact that proposals by the authors to present on this topic are most often accepted further leads one to believe that the need to include ethics in the discussion of online learning is widely accepted.

While participants felt that these principles are relevant in both classroom and online settings, there was consistent recognition of the distinct nature of online learning and the ways in which it plays a part in many of the principles mentioned. These include the advantage of a more measured asynchronous response, the importance of technological facility, and the need for clarity in postings. Because of the dynamic and rapid changes that will undoubtedly take place in the technology available to universities and faculty, it becomes important to monitor, on an ongoing basis, the changes in the online experience for students. Design and implementation of straightforward, nonthreatening, informative and concise approaches to going about this will be an ongoing challenge.

If we believe that education is in part an effort to help students to become all that they can be, ethical principles can and should be built into online courses, and must also be modeled and proactively made a part of the course by faculty. The integration of social networking software and Web 2.0 technologies does not only have the potential to change the way in which we offer distance and online courses, it also shapes the dialogue on ethics in online and distance learning. Within Web 2.0, faculty and learners become co-creators of e-learning and thus, our concept of "scholarship" may be redefined. As the origin and aggregation of distance and online course content shift, so must the conversation about ethics in this

domain. Privacy, intellectual property, academic integrity, and all of the STLHE's nine principles for ethical teaching will need to be considered vis-à-vis Web 2.0. Therefore, it is imperative to invite educators into this dialogue now while these trends are emerging.

For future study, the authors suggest an examination of the degree to which ethical development takes place in online courses taught by faculty who have taken part in the faculty training. Another rich approach would involve self-reflection on the part of faculty and structured opportunities to revisit the topic. This should both deepen it and broaden the research presented in this chapter. The effectiveness of a multimedia ethical dilemma presented in a simulation could be evaluated as well as the role of social networking software in the consideration of ethics.

This study indicates that the study and reflection of ethical teaching practices is not only relevant to teaching in all modalities, but is also embraced by faculty committed to honing their teaching and learning skills. It is the authors' belief that intentionally engaging faculty in a discussion of ethical principles in an orientation process such as this one both deepens their awareness of the principles and increases the likelihood that they will apply them. In teaching online, a tension is occasionally seen between professionalism and ethics. It is our belief that the former does not exist without the latter. Appropriate teacher orientation includes attention to both together.

REFERENCES

Atthill, C. (2001). Notes and comments: Towards ethical distance education. *Open Learning, 16*(1), 85-87.

Bloom, B. S. (1956). *Taxonomy of educational objectives: Handbook I: The cognitive domain.* New York: David McKay.

Chachra, D. (2005). Beyond course-based engineering ethics instruction: Commentary on "topics and cases for online education in engineering." *Science and Engineering Ethics, 11*(3), 459-461.

Collins, A., Brown, J. S., & Newman, S. (1989). Cognitive apprenticeship: Teaching the crafts of reading, writing, and mathematics. In L. B. Resnick (Ed.), *Knowing, learning, and instruction: Essays in honor of Robert Glaser* (pp. 453-494). Hillsdale, NJ: Lawrence Erlbaum.

Freire, P. (1998). *Pedagogy of freedom: Ethics, democracy and civic courage.* Lanham, MD: Rowman and Littlefield.

Fulton, J., & Kellinger, K. (2004). An ethics framework for nursing education on the Internet. *Nursing Education Perspectives, 25*(2), 62-66.

Gaide, S. (2004, June 15). Teaching ethical business practice online. *Distance Education Report, 8*(12), 8.

Gearhart, D. (2001). Ethics in distance education: Developing ethical policies. *The Online Journal of Distance Learning Administration, 4*(1). Retrieved April 23, 2008, from http://www.westga.edu/~distance/ojdla/spring41/gearhart41.html

Harasim, L., Hiltz, R. S., Teles, L., & Turoff, M. (1996). *Learning networks.* Cambridge, MA: The MIT Press.

Kearsley, G. (2000). *Online education: Learning and teaching in cyberspace.* Belmont, CA: Wadsworth/Thomson Learning.

Knowlton, D. S. (2000). A theoretical framework for the online classroom: A defense and delineation of a student-centered pedagogy. In R.E. Weiss, D.S. Knowlton, & B.W. Speck (Eds.), *Principles of effective teaching in the online classroom* (pp. 5-14). San Francisco: Jossey-Bass.

Lorenzetti, J. P. (2006, November 15). Integrating ethics into online faculty development: Hints from Regis University. *Distance Education Report, 10*(22), 5, 8.

Murray, H., Gillese, E., Lennon, M., Mercer, P., & Robinson, M. (1996). *Ethical principles in university teaching.* North York, Ontario: Society for Teaching and Learning in Higher Education. Retrieved April 23, 2008, from http://www.umanitoba.ca/uts/documents/ethical.pdf

National Education Association. (n.d.) *Code of ethical of the education profession.* Retrieved April 23, 2008, from http://www.nea.org/code.html

Palloff, R. M., & Pratt, K. (1999). *Building learning communication in cyberspace: Effective strategies for the online classroom.* San Francisco: Jossey-Bass.

Parscal, T. J. (2007). *Using the cognitive apprenticeship framework to teach asynchronous facilitation skills for faculty teaching in an online accelerated adult learning setting.* Doctoral dissertation, Capella University, MN. Retrieved April 23, 2008, from ProQuest Digital Dissertations database. (Publication No. AAT 3264302)

Sale, K. (1995). *Rebels against the future.* Reading, MA: Addison-Wesley.

Sims, R. R., & Felton, E. L., Jr. (2006). Designing and delivering business ethics teaching and learning. *Journal of Business Ethics, 63*, 297-312.

Stoll, C. (1995). *Silicon snake oil.* New York: Anchor Books Doubleday.

Sumner, J. (2000). Serving the system: a critical history of distance education. *Open Learning 15*(3), 267-285.

Sussman, G. (1997). *Communication, technology, and politics in the Information Age.* Newbury Park, CA: Sage.

ADDITIONAL READING

Boschmann, E. (1996). *The electronic classroom: A handbook for education in the electronic environment.* Medford, NJ: Learned Information.

Carr, D. (2000). *Professionalism and ethics in teaching.* New York: Routledge Taylor and Francis Group.

Gearhart, D. (2001). Ethics in distance education: Developing ethical policies. *The Online Journal of Distance Learning Administration, 4*(1). Retrieved April 23, 2008, from http://www.westga.edu/~distance/ojdla/spring41/gearhart41.html

Keith-Spiegel, P., Whitley, Jr., B., Balogh, D., Perkins, D., & Wittig, A. (2002). *The ethics of teaching: A casebook.* Mahwah, NJ: Lawrence Erlbaum.

Sale, K. (1995). *Rebels against the future.* Reading, MA: Addison-Wesley.

Speck, B.W. (2002). The academy, online classes, and the breach in ethics. *New Directions for Teaching and Learning, 2000*(84), 73-81.

Stoll, C. (1995). *Silicon snake oil.* New York: Anchor Books Doubleday.

Strike, K., Ternasky, P., & Lance, E. (1993). *Ethics for professionals in education: Perspectives for preparation and practice.* New York: Teachers College Press.

Zemblyas, M., & Vrasidas, C. (2005). Levinas and the "inter-face:" The ethical challenge of online education. *Educational Theory, 55*(1), 61-78.

Chapter XVIII
Computer Ethics:
Scenes from a Computer Education Department in Turkey

Yavuz Akbulut
Anadolu University, Turkey

H. Ferhan Odabaşi
Anadolu University, Turkey

Abdullah Kuzu
Anadolu University, Turkey

ABSTRACT

This chapter focuses on academic work on computer ethics conducted at a computer education department in Turkey. The chapter starts with the conceptual framework of computer ethics followed by the colleagues at the department, and mentions some scale development and administration papers. Along with research conducted at the department, applications of these researches in departments' courses are summarized. Then, implications of ethical practices for distance education are provided. Changes in the computing science along with those in distance education are considered to require distance education professionals to update their concepts and practices regarding integrity. Finally, future research directions, opportunities, and additional ideas regarding mentioned research and coursework are presented.

INTRODUCTION

When computer ethics is mentioned in Turkey, it is regarded double wise, that is, either the legal side of computer use or a list of unethical behaviors occurring to one's mind are regarded. This chapter therefore focuses on a different area, academic work on computer ethics. Because ethics is a rather esoteric subject, computer professionals usually find it difficult to study, so they choose to deal with the practical ethics mainly. However, starting from 1998, Turkey found a new platform for computer ethics studies. In 1998, the Turkish Higher Education Council opened new departments in education faculties of the universities in Turkey. These new departments are named Computer Education and Instructional Technology (CEIT). The basic aim of these departments is to equip students with up-to-date knowledge about computer and other information technologies, required for K-12 teachers. The departments combining the pedagogical knowledge with computer skills became unique standpoints for fields like computer ethics. In this chapter, we present academic work on computer ethics realized by one of these departments, Anadolu University, CEIT Department. When doing so, we prefer to classify the work as research and course work. Finally, implications of ethical endeavors for distance education practices are provided.

RESEARCH

The CEIT department at Anadolu University started working on conceptual framework of computer ethics at the very beginning of the 2000s. Odabasi and Can (2002) discussed the application of ethics to computer teaching, and suggested specifications for a scale after studying with 37 undergraduate students enrolled in the BTO 408 Computer and Internet Safety course. The study classified ethical principles, firstly those involving ethical demeanors that should be demonstrated by students as well as those involving responsibilities regarding computer and laboratory use. The study finalized with the recommendation that there should be robust scales to measure unethical computer using behaviors of Turkish undergraduate students.

Fortunately, Namlu and Odabasi (2007) developed the items further, generated new items

addressing several aspects of computer ethics, referred to expert opinions and produced the final version of the scale after administering it to 216 undergraduate students of computer technology. In the study, a robust factor analysis was conducted and unethical computer using behaviors of undergraduate students were classified under five categories, as intellectual property, social impact, safety and quality, net integrity and information integrity. Items in the first category, intellectual property, referred to the fact that information, unlike tangible property, was found hard to safeguard and hard to keep to one's self (Mason, 1986). Using unlicensed software, using crack programs, providing access to licensed software without authorization, copying and selling licensed software CDs, and distributing software licenses were instances of the first factor. The second factor of the scale, social impact, involved those items which were either socially chaotic or happened in social environments. Disturbing people in the virtual environments and using computers as means of blackmail are instances of the second factor. The third factor, safety and quality, involved items that were inclined to affect safety as well as influenced the quality of job that was carried out. Sample behaviors involve deliberately damaging the hardware of public computers, deliberately sending virus e-mails, accessing other peoples' personal computers and hacking through Internet. Items within the fourth dimension (i.e., net integrity) involved items that were corruptive for the integrity of the net, such as sending advertisement and chain mails for financial purposes. The last dimension, information integrity, involved behaviors such as misuse of information or things that disturb accessing information. Sample behaviors include plagiarizing other's software through small changes in the interface or using someone else's software as one's own by getting hold of the necessary codes. The study ended with the suggestion that unethical computer using behaviors should be studied under the light of several independent variables that might affect unethical computer using behaviors of undergraduate students.

Bearing Namlu and Odabasi's (2007) suggestion in mind, Uysal (2006) scrutinized the views of teacher candidates in his MA thesis study. He administered the scale to 559 undergraduate students. He found out that students reported to be extremely ethical with regard to five factors mentioned by Namlu and Odabasi (2007). However, students' means was somewhat at an undesired level in terms of intellectual property and net integrity. An interesting finding was that males reported to demonstrate unethical computer using behaviors significantly more than females in terms of all factors at a probability value of .01 or below. Besides, he found significant differences among different departments in terms of information integrity. More specifically, graduates of the CEIT departments seemed to be at a worse situation in comparison to other departments in terms of information integrity. This finding might reveal that the more students use computers, the more unethical behaviors they are likely to demonstrate. The finding also suggests that there should be a higher emphasis on courses involving computer ethics in CEIT departments.

Previous studies revealed that unethical behaviors might vary with regard to gender (Underwood & Szabo, 2003) and program of study (McCabe & Trevino, 1997; Roberts, Anderson, & Yanish, 1997). Thus, findings of Uysal (2006) were expected. Underwood and Szabo (2003) further suggested an interrelationship among gender, frequency of Internet use, and maturity of students. Maturity of students was not a plausible variable for undergraduate students who had participated in the Uysal (2006) study. However, department, gender and PC experience were all applicable. Akbulut, Uysal, Odabasi, and Kuzu (2008b) scrutinized the dataset of Uysal (2006) and investigated whether gender, program of study and PC experience have an impact on ethical judgments of undergraduate students. The study also checked the relationships among these independent variables through conducting a three-way ANOVA. The results indicated no significant differences among different programs of study and between high and low experienced PC users. The analysis showed significant differences between males and females. A significant interaction between the program of study and gender was found, that is, females' unethical computer behaviors were consistent across different fields while males' behaviors varied according to the field of study. This finding was interpreted in accordance with the gender socialization and occupational socialization theories that were tested in Mason and Mudrack's (1996) study. More specifically, gender socialization theory maintains that women are more likely to obey the rules of the society in order to socialize and accommodate the environment. On the other hand, occupational socialization theory claims that individuals behave in accordance with their occupation regardless of their gender. Findings supported gender socialization theory. However, the occupational socialization theory and gender socialization theory seemed to interact when the target gender is males.

With the increasing use of Internet and distance education practices in Turkey, the scope of computer ethics started to extend. Thus, the CEIT department started to scrutinize the conceptual framework of electronic misconduct, which involves the type of academic misdemeanors conducted in e-environments. The department focused on several aspects of e-misconduct. For instance, Birinci and Odabasi (2006) referred to the types and reasons of misdemeanors that occur in academic life. The study also made a special reference to Internet and made clear that academic dishonesty is made easier through e-environments. Odabasi et al. (2007) contributed to the ethics through a conceptual paper which focused on academic misconduct getting easier with Internet. Following this conceptual paper, Akbulut, Sendag, Birinci, Kilicer, Sahin, and Odabasi (2008a) prepared specifications for a scale to measure academic dishonesty instances in open and distance education practices. While defining ethics, the unique context of Turkey was also taken into account. More specifically, definitions of unethical conducts were made through referring to scientific authorities in Turkey, including Anadolu University Scientific Ethics Guide (BEK, 2003) and The Scientific and Technological Research Council of Turkey (TUBITAK, 2006). The guide released by Anadolu University focused particularly on academic misdemeanors conducted in academic settings. The guide classified these misdemeanors in accordance with the context of unethical behavior. More specifically, unethical behaviors related to participant selection and sampling, research methodology and data analysis, publication and presentation, addressing contributing authors, acknowledging resources, editorship in peer-reviewed journals, article review process, committee memberships and advisory duties in dissertations were mentioned in the guide. The guide provided by TUBITAK (2006) also advises practitioners on different aspects of ethics. Based on these two guides, instances of academic misdemeanors realized through Internet were classified under the titles of fabrication, falsification, finagling, plagiarism, duplication, least publishable units, neglecting support and misusing credit.

Three hundred and forty nine education faculty students from the faculty of education were administered two Likert-Scale questionnaires developed by the researchers, one focusing on the instances of academic misdemeanors while the other focusing on the reasons of electronic misconduct. Results of two factor analyses on two questionnaires classified types of misdemeanors under the titles of fraudulence, plagiarism, falsification, delinquency and unauthorized help, while the reasons for misdemeanors were classified under the titles of individual reasons, institutional policies and peer pressure.

Aside from the above studies Sendag and Odabasi (2006) scrutinized on Internet and children, and provided suggestions to develop cyber-awareness for kids. Kilicer and Odabasi (2006) discussed why and how to teach ethics in terms of accuracy, property, accessibility and privacy (i.e., PAPA) in the field of computer teacher education. Uysal and Odabasi (2006) further developed the ways of teaching computer ethics to students through scrutinizing on different teaching and learning methods. Finally, another research team at the CEIT department translated Moor's (1985) classic paper "What is computer ethics." These studies constituted the conceptual framework for offering computer ethics courses at the department.

COURSE WORK

The department has been offering BTO 408 Computers and Internet Safety for 7 years. The course aims at equipping students with skills to detect harmful software, and set up and implement necessary programs to prevent network fraudulence. Besides, the course also involves legal arrangements regarding computer use and Internet use, along with social and ethical issues regarding computers.

Within the framework of the project called Open Distance Inter-University Synergies between Europe, Africa and Middle East (ODISEAME), the department has offered an online computer ethics course which involved trends and issues in computer ethics. The aim of the ODISEAME project has been to establish a network of Euro-Mediterranean higher education institutions that will cooperate in generating and disseminating contents for educational purposes. ODISEAME has particularly tried to improve higher education in partner countries by offering Web-based lessons corresponding to the higher education study programs. The course offered by the CEIT department has primarily dealt with ethical foundations as a starting point. It explains why ethical issues are important for computer professionals. Life in cyber space and different ethical behavior models in the cyber world are also investigated with regard to privacy, accuracy, property and accessibility. Students and teachers from different countries took part in the project and several students have been offered the course starting from August 2005. All the relevant material such as readings, links, questions or related bibliography have been delivered online, that is, no hard copies have been available to students. Two practitioners of Web-based training who are also instructors at Anadolu University have moderated the course so far. The course was first piloted with the senior students of the department. Then, assessment of the units was realized through student and expert views. The first group to take the course consisted of eight graduate students who attended online classes between August 22, 2005, and October 2, 2005. Based on their suggestions, further modifications on the course content and methodology have been made.

Within the scope of the masters course named BTO509 Online Learning and Teaching Technologies, contents of the ODISEAME course were revised, and adapted for up-to-date Web-based training practices. Eleven doctorate students at the department contributed to this process by following the course books of Horton (2000) and Jochems, van Merrienboer, and Koper (2004). The unit will be ready by the end of the 2007 spring semester to be used in open and distance learning practices. Finally, the department aims to offer an online masters degree program in computer education and instructional technologies in which computer ethics will be one of the required courses. Most of the theoretical and practical details have been considered and a comprehensive proposal has been submitted to the Scientific and Technological Research Council of Turkey (TUBITAK), yet bureaucratic procedures to initiate the program continue.

IMPLICATIONS FOR DISTANCE EDUCATION

The impact of technology on both conventional classrooms and distance learning environments is considered to be enormous (Gearhart, 2001). Bennett (1998) suggests three scenarios for the future of teaching-learning endeavors. In the first scenario, it is maintained that the size of higher education institutions will shrink as global electronic educational opportunities increase. Campuses will be just service stations where several learning modules are made available to students at a distance. In the second scenario, it is claimed that the telecommunication revolution will have minimal influence on educational institutions. The third scenario suggests that higher education institutions will remain, but they will have altered educational roles involving higher emphasis on pedagogy and collaboration using innovative classrooms and laboratories. This scenario also suggests that significant amount of distance education will be realized but the conventional roles of residential institutions will continue. Gearhart (2001) believes that the third scenario is the most realistic one, while the first two seem unrealistic. However, we believe that the first scenario maintaining that all education might be realized at a distance is a realistic one as well. In Turkey, the Open Education Faculty of Anadolu University provides undergraduate degree distance education to approximately one third of all undergraduate students. Thus, it is crucial to update institutional policies in accordance with the diverse population we work with. In this respect, research conducted by the department on computer ethics and e-misconduct might be helpful.

It is more difficult for distance education students to deal with unethical behaviors than it is for conventional students. This is a double-sided problem. The first side involves practitioners' responsibility to provide equal and rich opportunities for distance education students. Here, we would like to adapt The Code of Ethics presented by the Association for Educational Communications and Technology (AECT, 2005) to emphasize our responsibilities. The first principle of the first section states that professionals should encourage independent action in an individual's pursuit of learning and should provide open access to knowledge regardless of delivery medium or varying points of view of the knowledge. That means all learners should be provided with equal opportunities. Principle 7 states that in fulfilling obligations to the individual, professionals should provide current and sound professional practices in the appropriate use of technology in education. Principle 3 requires that in fulfilling obligations to the individual, the professionals should guarantee to each individual the opportunity to participate in any appropriate program. These two principles suggest that students be provided with learning materials suited to their needs. Moreover, students with special needs should be accommodated appropriately (Hall, 2007). If applied to distance education settings, all these principles place a crucial responsibility on practitioners in distance education, because it is harder to manage the teaching-learning endeavors in distance education practices. The second side of the problem involves students in demonstrating appropriate ethical behaviors in distance learning environments. Such delicate requirements can only be met with the help of practitioners who are equipped with necessary skills to demonstrate sound ethical demeanors in distance education. Graduates of the CEIT departments are employed as computer instructors and material developers in distance education environments as well. Thus, ethical endeavors of the department carries utmost importance for sustaining ethical standards in distance education practices.

One of the critical threats to sustaining academic integrity in distance education is the challenge to administer assessment appropriately. During online assessment, instructors are not able to ascertain who is actually taking the test. In addition, instructors cannot control unauthorized use of additional resources. Finally, unauthorized collaboration of students cannot be prevented. Anadolu University administers conventional tests three times a year as a precaution. Olt (2002) proposes several strategies to minimize academic dishonesty in online assessment such as acknowledging disadvantages of unethical behaviors, taking necessary time to design effective online assessments, assigning original project-based assessments and providing students with a sound academic integrity policy. All precautions suggested in the literature require distance education institutions to employ professional staff who can understand and apply ethical endeavors properly. Thus, the CEIT department has a crucial role in training these professionals.

CONCLUSION

Distance education and open learning are likely to change the learning landscape forever. Computer science, which has a crucial place in distance education, is a rapidly changing field as well. These changes require distance education professionals to update their concepts and practices regarding integrity. No doubt that distance education practices have provided several advantages to individuals such as providing education to those who do not have the chance to come to traditional classrooms. Besides, the way students access to information sources, the way they are instructed and the way they are assessed have all improved. However, application of ethics in traditional face-to-face learning might not be applicable to open and distance learning environments. Individuals might have the inclination to demonstrate unethical demeanors because they do not have to threaten their faces in distance education environments. As indicated by a comprehensive and recent study, undergraduate students' inclination to demonstrate unethical behaviors increase over the years (McCabe, 2005). Therefore, necessary precautions should be taken through following grounded policies and instructional processes.

FUTURE RESEARCH DIRECTIONS

The current paper summarizes research and coursework on computers and academic integrity realized at a CEIT department in Turkey. Department members aim to administer the developed scales to a larger population so that they will be able to see whether their hypotheses regarding computer ethics and electronic misconduct hold true. Besides, new courses and course contents are being offered each year to equip students with a thorough understanding of computer ethics. With the advent of an online MA degree on computer education and instructional technologies, the department will be able to share its experience with students around the world, and receive feedback from other practitioners in the field.

Surveys mentioned in the current study could be further validated and administered at several universities in order to investigate the organizational climate of Turkish universities in terms of computer and Internet ethics. The current study mostly focuses on unethical computer or Internet using behaviors of undergraduate students. The items covered in current surveys might not be applicable to graduate students, academicians and staff at other organizations. Developing new items through expert opinion and conducting the surveys at multiple universities and organizations can give further insights about the ethical practices observed at different contexts.

It is important to differentiate between what is ethical and what is legal in the academic context. While deciding what ethical or unethical behavior is, people rely mostly on their personal judgments (Kreie & Cronan, 2000). Besides, it has been indicated that disapproval of cheating among peers is an important variable to prevent cheating (Bowers, 1964). However, these personal restraining mechanisms might not be sufficient to prevent unethical demeanors, that is, official precautions and well-developed sanctions might be necessary to prevent unethical behaviors. McCabe and Trevino (1993) underlined the importance of official precautions to prevent cheating. More specifically, 29% of students enrolling in schools with honor codes reported to have conducted academic misdemeanors while 53% of students enrolling in schools without honor code reported to conduct such behaviors. Thus, development of well-prepared honor codes like the one proposed by AECT (2005) is an important step in determining the ethical standards. Moreover, because different organizations and fields might involve different types of academic misdemeanors, studies particularly focusing on ethical standards in distance education are necessary for our field.

Finally, studies mentioned here mostly carry the characteristics of cross-sectional studies where data are collected at one shot. Besides, we have not examined the efficiency of our coursework on computer ethics on preventing unethical behaviors yet. In this respect, longitudinal studies, which explore the effectiveness of different precautions on preventing electronic misconduct, carry utmost importance.

REFERENCES

AECT. (2005). *Code of ethics*. Bloomington, IN. Retrieved April 23, 2008, from http://www.aect.org/About/Ethics.asp

Akbulut, Y., Sendag, S., Birinci, G., Kilicer, K., Sahin, M.C., & Odabasi, H. F. (2008a). Exploring the types and reasons of internet triggered academic dishonesty among Turkish undergraduate students. *Computers and Education*. Retrieved April 23, 2008, from http://dx.doi.org/10.1016/j.compedu.2007.06.003

Akbulut, Y., Uysal, O., Odabasi, H. F., & Kuzu, A. (2008b). Influence of gender, program of study and

PC experience on unethical computer using behaviors of Turkish undergraduate students. *Computers and Education*. Retrieved April 23, 2008, from http://dx.doi.org/10.1016/j.compedu.2007.06.004

BEK. (2003). *Bilim Etigi Kilavuzu (Scientific ethics guide)*. Anadolu University: Eskisehir. Retrieved April 23, 2008, from http://www.anadolu.edu.tr/tr/bilimsel/bek.pdf

Birinci, G., & Odabasi, H. F. (2006, April 19-21). Akademik calismalarda Internet kullanimi: Etik bunun neresinde? (Use of Internet for academic endeavors: Where does ethics lie?). In *Proceedings of the 6th International Educational Technology Conference*, (pp. 289-295). Famagusta, Turkish Republic of Northern Cyprus.

Bowers, W. J. (1964). *Student dishonesty and its control in college*. New York: Bureau of Applied Social Research, Columbia University.

Gearhart, G. (2001, Spring). Ethics in distance education: Developing ethical policies. *Online Journal of Distance Learning Administration, 4*(1).

Hall, L. D. (2007). Professional ethics: Scenarios and principles. *TechTrends, 51*(1), 15-16.

Horton, W. (2000). *Designing Web-based training*. New York: John Wiley & Sons.

Jochems, W., van Merrienboer, J., & Koper, R. (2004). *Integrated e-learning: Implications for pedagogy, technology and organization*. London: Routledge Falmer.

Kilicer, K., & Odabasi, H. F. (2006, April 19-21). Bilgisayar ogretmenligi: Etik bunun neresinde? (Computer education: Where does ethics lie?). In *Proceedings of the 6th International Educational Technology Conference*, (pp. 1124-1129). Famagusta, Turkish Republic of Northern Cyprus.

Kreie, J., & Cronan, T. P. (2000). Making ethical decisions. *Communications of the ACM, 43*(12), 66-71.

Mason, R. (1986). Four ethical issues of the information age. *MIS Quarterly, 10*(1), 5-11.

Mason, E. S., & Mudrack, P. E. (1996). Gender and ethical orientation: A test of gender and occupational socialization theories. *Journal of Business Ethics, 15*, 599-604.

McCabe, D. L. (2005). *CAI research*. Retrieved April 23, 2008, from http://www.academicintegrity.org/cai_research.asp

McCabe, D. L., & Trevino, L. K. (1993). Academic dishonesty: Honor codes and other contextual influences. *Journal of Higher Education, 64*(5), 552-538.

McCabe, D. L., & Trevino, L. K. (1997). Individual and contextual influences on academic dishonesty: A multi-campus investigation. *Research in Higher Education, 38*, 379-396.

Moor, J. H. (1985). What is computer ethics? *Metaphilosophy, 16*(4), 266-275. (Turkish translation available online at http://home.anadolu.edu.tr/~fodabasi/doc/ty11.swf)

Namlu, A. G., & Odabasi, F. (2007). Unethical computer using behavior scale: A study of reliability and validity on Turkish university students. *Computers and Education, 48*, 205-215.

Odabasi, H. F., Birinci, G., Kilicer, K., Sahin, M. C., Akbulut, Y., & Sendag, S. (2007). Bilgi iletisim teknolojileri ve Internet'le kolaylasan akademik usulsuzluk (Academic dishonesty: Getting easier with Internet and ICT). *Anadolu Universitesi Sosyal Bilimler Dergisi*.

Odabasi, H. F., & Can, V. (2002, October 23-26). Bilgisayar ve ogretim teknolojileri ogretmenligi dorduncu sinif ogrencilerinin bilgisayar ogretmenligi meslegi etik ilkelerine yonelik olcut gelistirme cabalari (Endeavors to develop a computer education ethics scale for senior students of computer education departments). *XI Egitim Bilimleri Kongresi* (pp. 64-69). *Nicosia, Turkish Republic of Northern Cyprus*.

ODISEAME. (2005). *Open distance inter-university synergies between Europe, Africa and Middle East*. Retrieved April 23, 2008, from http://proyectos.cedetel.es/General-web/ponLocale.jsp?idProyecto=328&nombreClave=ODISEAME

Olt, M. R. (2002, Fall). Ethics and distance education: Strategies for minimizing academic dishonesty in online assessment. *Online Journal of Distance Learning Administration, 5*(3).

Roberts, P., Anderson, J., & Yanish, P. (1997). Academic misconduct: Where do we start? In *Paper presented at the Annual Conference of the Northern Rocky Mountain Educational Research Association*, Jackson, WY.

Sendag, S., & Odabasi, H. F. (2006, April 19-21). Internet ve cocuk: Etik bunun neresinde?(Internet and the child: Where does ethics lie?). In *Proceedings of the 6th International Educational Technology Conference*, (pp. 1508-1515). Famagusta, Turkish Republic of Northern Cyprus.

TUBITAK. (2006). Bilimsel dergilere gonderilen makalelerde dikkat edilmesi gereken noktalar (Matters to consider in articles being sent to scientific journals). *Council of Research and Publication Ethics*. Retrieved April 23, 2008, from http://journals.tubitak.gov.tr/genel/brosur.pdf

Underwood, J., & Szabo, A. (2003). Academic offences and e-learning: Individual propensities in cheating. *British Journal of Educational Technology, 34*(4), 467-477.

Uysal, O. (2006). *Ogretmen adaylarinin bilgisayar etigine iliskin gorusleri (Views of teacher trainees on computer ethics)*. Doctoral dissertation, Anadolu University Graduate School of Educational Sciences, Eskisehir, Turkey.

Uysal, O., & Odabasi, H. F. (2006, April 19-21). Bilgisayar etigi ogretiminde kullanilan yontemler (Methods used in teaching computer ethics). In *Proceedings of the 6th International Educational Technology Conference*, (pp. 1639-1652). Famagusta, Turkish Republic of Northern Cyprus.

ADDITIONAL READING

Adam, A. (2000, December). Gender and computer ethics. *Computers and Society*, 17-24.

Austin, M. J., & Brown, L. D. (1999). Internet plagiarism: Developing strategies to curb student academic dishonesty. *The Internet and Higher Education, 2*(1), 21-33.

Baase, S. (2003). *A gift of fire: Social, legal, and ethical issues for computers and the Internet* (2nd ed.). Upper Saddle River, NJ: Pearson Education.

Bear, G. G. (1990). Knowledge of computer ethics: Its relationship to computer attitude and socio moral reasoning. *Journal of Educational Computing Research, 6*, 77-87.

Bennett, J. B. (1998). *Collegial professionalism the academy, indiviualism, and the common good*. Phoenix: American Council on Education & Oryx Press.

Bowyer, K. (1996). *Ethics and computing: Living responsibly in a computerized world*. IEEE Computer Society Press.

Bynum, T. W., & Rogerson, S. (2004). *Computer ethics and professional responsibility*. Malden, USA: Blackwell.

Carey, S. F. (2003). Combating plagiarism. *Phi Delta Kappa Fastbacks, 514*, 7-32.

Crown, D. F., & Spiller, M. S. (1998). Learning from the literature on collegiate cheating: A review of empirical research. *Journal of Business Ethics, 17*, 683-700.

DeVoss, D., & Rosati, A. (2002). It wasn't me, was it? Plagiarism and the Web. *Computers and Composition, 19*, 191-203.

Ercegovac, Z., & Richardson, J. V. (2004). Academic dishonesty, plagiarism included, in the digital age: A literature review. *College & Research Libraries, 65*(4), 301-318.

Ermann, M. D., Williams, M. B., & Shauf, M. S. (Eds.). (1997). *Computers, ethics, and society.* New York: Oxford University Press.

Gattiker, U. E., & Kelley, H. (1999). Morality and computers: Attitudes and differences in moral judgments. *Information Systems Research, 10,* 233-254.

Hughes, J. C., & McCabe, D. (2006). *Academic misconduct major problem in Canada, study finds.* University of Guelph, Communications and Public Affairs. Retrieved April 23, 2008, from http://www.uoguelph.ca/mediarel/2006/09/academic_miscon.html

Kibler, W. L. (1993). Academic dishonesty: A student development dilemma. *NASPA Journal 30,* 252-267.

Langford, D. (1995). *Practical computer ethics.* Cambridge: McGraw-Hill.

Marshall, S., & Garry, M. (2005, December 4-7). How well do students really understand plagiarism? In H. Goss (Ed.), *Proceedings of the 22nd Annual Conference of the Australasian Society for Computers in Learning in Tertiary Education (ASCILITE),* (pp. 457-467). Brisbane, Australia.

Mason, E. S., & Mudrack, P. E. (1996). Gender and ethical orientation: A test of gender and occupational socialization theories. *Journal of Business Ethics, 15,* 599-604.

Mercuri, R. (1998). In search of academic integrity. *Communications of the ACM, 40*(5), 136.

Park, C. (2003). In other (people's) words: Plagiarism by university students—literature and lessons. *Assessment and Evaluation in Higher Education, 28*(5), 471-488.

Ross, K. A. (2005). Academic dishonesty and the Internet. *Communications of the ACM, 48*(10).

Ward, D. A., & Beck, W. L. (1990). Gender and dishonesty. *The Journal of Social Psychology, 130,* 333-339.

Warnken, P. (2004). Academic original sin: Plagiarism, the Internet, and librarians. *The Journal of Academic Librarianship, 30*(3), 237-242.

Whitaker, E. E. (1993). A pedagogy to address plagiarism. *College Teaching, 42,* 161-164.

Woodbury, M. C. (2003). *Computer and information ethics.* IL, USA: Stipes.

Chapter XIX
Ethical Practice and Online Learning—A Contradiction?
A Case Study

Donna Harper
Liverpool Hope University, UK

Petra Luck
Liverpool Hope University, UK

ABSTRACT

The aim of this chapter is to investigate ethical issues such as individual integrity and rights affecting online students who are Early Years Managers, leading a range of child care and education settings. This study has as its focus the student experience and explores student attitude from the perspective of participants who are transferring knowledge and skills on a day-to-day basis in an ethically and socially responsible Early Years sector via online learning. This type of learning has been characterised by distance and perceived reduced empathy. The research adopts a case study approach and proposes that Pelz's (2004) "three principles of effective online pedagogy" perspective could be used to explore the tension and ethical issues experienced by online and distance learners. Questionnaires were used and semi structured interviews conducted to collect data. Analysis of the data found no significant ethical concerns in terms of individual integrity and rights perceived by the students. The contributions of an effective pedagogical approach and the students' professional context to the positive findings are highlighted.

INTRODUCTION

Much of the discussion and research around ethics and on online learning has been restricted to the following key areas: learning and teaching strategies, plagiarism, intellectual property and copyright issues. Luck and Norton (2002) pointed to the long standing argument that, as the distance between people increases, the possibility for genuine empathy decreases. This study analyses ethical dimensions of relationships online. It is acknowledged that the nature of human dignity forms the basis of our consideration of individual rights. Human beings are considered worthy of respect and should always be treated with dignity and respect. This research poses the question:

How are the students' integrity and rights affected by online learning?

As the ethical dimension and the distance factor is a much unexplored area, this chapter then addresses a further question:

What ethical issues are identified by online students themselves?

This study has as its focus the student experience. These students are managers in the ethically and socially responsible Early Years sector. Yet their vehicle for learning has been characterised by its distance and perceived reduced empathy.

Therefore, this chapter sets out the background to the study, providing the theoretical and the professional contexts in which students are engaged, and gives some information about the online course studied. An outline of the methodology is followed by presentation and discussion of results arising from the study. Finally, conclusions are drawn and implications of the findings suggested.

BACKGROUND TO THE STUDY

Theoretical Context

In the Early Years sector, those who work with young children face many daily decisions that have moral and ethical implications. Child carers acknowledge responsibility to provide the best possible programmes of care and education for children and to conduct themselves with honesty and integrity. They have a specialized expertise in early childhood development and education. As professionals they acknowledge a collective obligation to advocate the best interests of children within early childhood programs and, in the larger community serve as a voice for young children everywhere. This ethics of care can be seen as fundamentally relational, not individual-agent-based in the way of virtue ethics, and the ethics of care is more indirect than character education. This posits the image of a "relational self," a moral agent who is embedded in concrete relationships with others and who acquires a moral identity through interactive patterns of behaviour, perceptions and interpretations (Addelson, 1991). In this way, work in the Early Years Sector can be identified as a "high-touch" ethical environment.

Child care practitioners work with one of society's most vulnerable groups: young children. The quality of the relations among young children and their caregivers has a substantial, long-term influence on children's lives. The nature of the relationship and the potential that exists to do harm require the child care practitioners to abide by the highest standards of ethical practice.

These ethical parameters influence the professional identity of this sample studied. Given this heightened ethical awareness of the student sample, it would appear even more pertinent to investigate the relationships (tutor-student and student- student) online. Hence, this study explores the experiences by students from Northern Ireland and England on Early Years Management programmes, examining the potential tension between learning in a sector which professionally promotes an ethical and socially responsive approach in behaviour while undertaking an online study programme, which can be characterised by distance and reduced empathy.

Lawhead et al. (1997) suggest that a majority of the ethical issues surrounding Web-based distance learning have existed in some guise in traditional learning and also in non e-based distance learning. Student integrity has been a concern of the teaching profession since the inception of formal education.

Lawhead et al. (1997) grouped ethical issues into Web-based distance learning into five sections:

1. Institutional, societal and global
    Issues are raised such as changes in recruitment and enrolment practices to questions around the volume of resources dedicated to it and amount of regulation it is subjected to. The degree of competition and lack of traditional territorial borders give rise to consideration of issues such as community vs. remote institutions for learning.

2. Equivalence of product (or quality)
    …. a distance learner who is granted a degree should be as broadly educated and should have the same level of mastery in a field of specialization as a student who earned a degree in a traditional setting. To promote distance learning and to provide anything less is unethical. (Lawhead et al., 1997, p. 30)

3. Student integrity, confidentiality, and security
    Issues due to a lack of physical contact such as the decrease in the ability for the teacher to gauge student integrity using interpersonal cues are raised. The concerns over the ability to provide security and confidentiality of student work stored in the institutions' Virtual Learning Environment (VLE) are made. The World Wide Web and opportunities to commit plagiarism are raised by Lawhead et al. (1997).

4. Intellectual property, copyright, and ownership
    Academic integrity of copyright and intellectual property, an issue for both teachers (appropriation of a student's work without their permission/recognition is unethical) and students, are pointed out by Lawhead et al. (1997).

5. Effect on the teaching profession
    Lawhead et al. (1997, p. 30) highlight the ethical concern of the "*status of the college professor*" and ask what professional qualifications are required to design and deliver such distance courses.

The above five points are valuable and contribute to the discussion of ethical issues and online distance learning. However, as there exists a plethora of literature with regard to learning and teaching strategies online, plagiarism and copyright issues, the focus of this study centres on point (3) of Lawhead et al.'s (1997) main ethical concerns, that of student integrity, confidentiality, and security, and then expands upon this to include rights. The study is framed from the point of view of the student online distance learning experience in terms of integrity and rights.

Crane and Matten (2007, p. 100) define natural rights as "*certain basic important, unalienable entitlements that should be respected and protected in every single action.*" If it is accepted that a person is entitled to rights, this means then that another person has a duty to respect these rights. It is now acknowledged that the term "human rights" has generally replaced the term "natural rights." These human rights are based on generally agreed principles about the nature of human dignity, which are manifested globally in the United Nations Declaration of Human Rights (1948). These underpin an accepted agreement on how human beings should be treated. In the context of this study, we are looking at the student experience of distance online learning and the student right to privacy, not to be discriminated against and the right to respect. Therefore, to investigate the ethical dimensions of the "tutor-student" and "student-student" online relationships seem particularly pertinent, given the ethical nature of the work undertaken by students in this sector.

De George (2006) points to privacy as a relative term which can mean different things to different societies. In relation to computers, De George suggests that there are two types of privacy, which he terms information privacy and electronic privacy. Information privacy is a term which refers to individuals' right to keep information about themselves private. Another concern that De George (2006) raises is the Big Brother syndrome, where computers are known to assemble and store large amounts of information about us all, and we are never too sure who has access to this. In addition to these concerns, in an online distance learning environment, could a tutor's monitoring role of a student, tracing their every move (or lack of it) electronically, be construed as "Big Brother" by the student?

The issue of student work and data is linked to information privacy. De George (2006, p. 495) suggests that "*computer access is much easier to compromise and more difficult to control than physical access.*" De George (2006) discusses electronic privacy in terms of use of e-mails and Internet use. In the context of this study, although electronic privacy can also refer to e-mail privacy issues, it appertains to the nature of information available on the VLE. What do students feel about security offered by the institution, about the privacy of their personal information and the academic integrity of their work in online distance learning? Further to this question, do students feel there is an invasion of their privacy due to the openness and recorded transcripts on the virtual learning environment (VLE)?

Bullying is normally understood to mean the abuse or humiliation of a person. Fisher and Lovell (2006) ask the question at what point does assertion in negotiation become aggression and therefore bullying? Bullying can be seen as morally wrong (doing harm). The student's right to respect and dignity would preclude another student's right to bully them. In the context of this study and the

high level of group work, could the distance factor of the tutor contribute to an online environment where student bullying could occur?

In essence, this study explores ethical issues experienced by Early Years Managers online with its focus on the student experience in terms of rights and integrity.

Underpinning these issues above are the relationships of tutor-student and student-student. Therefore, to explore the ethical dimensions of these online relationships seems particularly pertinent given the questions posed in the research.

PROFESSIONAL CONTEXT

Early Years education and care is an employment sector characterised by "low tech/high touch" (Donohue, 2002). Practitioners tend to have little involvement with high tech equipment in the workplace as much of their practice is "high touch" concerned with managing relationships with children, parents and colleagues (Luck & Norton, 2005). Yet, the Centre for Early Years Management and Leadership at a University in the Northwest of England has been offering online degree programmes since 2002. Furthermore, a European Union funded European Enhancement of Early Years Management Skills (EEEYMS) project proposed to educate education and care managers through online delivery methods.

The practitioners, who comprise the learning community in the case study explored in this chapter, are in positions of management in the Early Years sector and are undertaking one of the following programmes: The Foundation Degree Management of Childcare Provision, the BA Early Years Management or the Certificate in European Early Years Management, which are all delivered online. The latter is a programme that is part of the above mentioned EEEYMS project. These programmes aim to give students the opportunity to share best management practice through collaboration with other colleagues from other European countries, gaining a knowledge and understanding of current theories, models and research relating to key aspects of their practice.

In the UK, the market for these programmes has grown as a result of government initiatives since the 1997 introduction of a National Childcare Strategy. For example, the Children's Workforce Development Council (CWDC) in the UK recognises the need to increase levels of training and development across the whole of the children's workforce, recruit and retain highly qualified staff and provide opportunities for more people to receive on-the-job training to equip them for their role and offer career progression opportunities seeking "graduate level managers (Level 6) and leaders" (CWDC, 2006).

Early Years care and education in the UK has continued to expand: The 2002 Comprehensive Spending Review announced a doubling of funding in a range of resources for child care, rising to £1.5 billion by 2005-2006 to fund the development of children's centres which will support the creation of 250,000 new child care places (Daycare Trust, 2003). The UK economy depends on working parents; in the UK in 2002 almost 90% of men with dependent children were in employment and 65% of women in employment had dependent children (Daycare Trust, 2003). Furthermore, the government is encouraging Early Years education and care providers to offer extended day care and a total of £24m is being made available to enable the conversion of playgroups to full day care for the period 2003-2006.

In the European context, there has also been a rapid increase of Child Care and Early Years educational provision, due to the increasing participation of women, particularly mothers of children below compulsory school age, in the workforce. This is documented in the Organisation for Economic Co-operation and Development report (OECD, 2001) on Early Years care and education provision in 13 OECD countries. In Finland, 12% of 1-3 year olds now attend family day care centres with another 12% in child care

centres. 54% of the 3-6-age range attends centres on a full time basis and a further 12% on a part time basis. It is similar in France, Norway, Netherlands and Belgium, and is higher in Italy. Significant child carer recruitment targets have been set in all European countries and this will require a considerable amount of training provision, much of which will need to be distance leaning-orientated. Due to the nature of this employment sector it is evident from OECD research that the current provision for training and development of child care staff is only of a pedagogic or vocational nature, with no specific training and development opportunities in child care management. They are, however, expected to perform these management roles, "In countries with complex funding streams, staff are expected to be social entrepreneurs to juggle various funding sources, compete for scarce resources and grants" (OECD, 2001, p. 91). The EEEYMS project has undertaken an assessment of management education for senior practitioners and managers in the Early Years sector and identified a need for such training in a number of countries.

In setting up online Early Years Management programmes, staff at the university have argued that the use of e-learning or online learning can support teaching and learning strategies which will encourage a deep approach to learning provided that the teacher utilises the technology to support the pedagogy rather than vice versa. Ramsey (2003) warns that some teachers link the use of VLEs with a distancing effect between teachers and students but suggests that the reverse is in fact the case; "that a use of VLEs can mean resource enriched, although significantly re-formed, learning relations."

According to Russell (2005), when students use online communication, distancing is likely to occur and argues that *"distancing has yet unexplored consequences in on-line learning."* Face-to-face communication, the standard of the traditional classroom, is the "paradigmatic social context and medium" and it is critical for interpersonal processes (Palmer, 1995, p. 282). In contrast, online technologies have a reduced capacity to support affective relationships. Following these arguments, collaborative online learning should be beset by problems.

However, the learning and teaching activities on the degree programmes are designed to provide flexible ways of working with a view to encouraging high levels of engagement with the programme, thereby promoting high retention and achievement rates.

A valuable feature of the e-learning strategy is that it seeks to increase flexibility of learning for the student in so far as it removes the need for travel, and students will be able to access the programme via the Internet, from home or their workplace. The asynchronous nature of computer-mediated communication means that students can participate in activities at convenient times for themselves, to fit in with work commitments and aspects of family life.

Innovative methods in teaching and learning such as Problem Based Learning (PBL) are used that are particularly suited to the work-based nature of the programmes as well as online learning. Considerable attention is given to ensure that students feel part of a community of learning.

PBL has been chosen as it serves to satisfy all these factors; it promotes self-directed, independent learning, assists in the development of transferable skills and requires students to work in small groups which enhance peer support. The role of the tutor is a facilitator, a role often adopted in online programmes, which entirely supports the mode of problem-based learning.

METHODOLOGY

The ethical issues arising from students' online learning experiences are examined. This experience is underpinned by the pedagogical approach of the subject/institution. It seems logical then to explore ethical issues experienced by the student

by using a pedagogical framework. Pelz's (2004) framework, which attempts to identify best practice in online learning, is used to examine the ethical issues as perceived by students.

This study proposes that Pelz's (2004) "three principles of effective on-line pedagogy" perspective could be used to explore the tension and ethical issues experienced by online learning with its characteristic "distance factor" and the managers from the Early Years sector characterised by "high touch/low tech." The purpose of this chapter is not to enter the theoretical debate with regard to effective pedagogy, but to explain the use of the theoretical framework adopted for this study, Pelz's (2004) "three principles of effective on-line pedagogy."

Pelz established the following three principles for effective online pedagogy:

1. Let the students do most of the work
    *   In moving from "sage on the stage" to "guide on the side," strategies are suggested for putting students in charge of their own work
2. Interactivity is the heart and soul of effective asynchronous learning
    *   It is suggested that online interaction requires reading and writing, but goes beyond discussion. Students can interact in a variety of ways: student-student, student-tutor, student-text, student-Internet, students-assessments (PBL).
3. Strive for presence
    *   Pelz (2004, p. 41) points to recent research (Garrison, Anderson, & Archer, 2000) which suggests that "discussion responses that add value to a discussion" are found in one or more of the following three categories:
        ◦   Social Presence
        ◦   Cognitive Presence
        ◦   Teaching Presence

As Pelz's framework has a strong emphasis on relational elements in online learning, it lends itself as a model and location for the exploration of the ethical issues in this study. Pelz's model thus provides a framework for analysis that constructs a holistic view of the students experience, by exploring experiences of online methods used (principles i and ii) and the more deeper issues of students experience as a "person" within this process (principle iii).

Within current literature with regards to ethics and online learning, there is limited research which examines the tension between learning in a sector which fosters ethical and socially responsive behaviour such as the Early Years and online study. Consequently, it is necessary to undertake an exploratory empirical study to gain information which will provide some insight into this situation.

A case study approach is adopted for this study, as Yin (2003) acknowledges that the case study approach can be used in organizational and management studies to help appreciate the complexity of the organizational phenomena, which in this study is in the field of organisational learning by the Early Years managers using online delivery of the study programme.

A sample of 60 students from Northern Ireland and England was used to explore the effects of online learning.

The findings are discussed in relation to Pelz's (2004) framework, and ethical issues are identified and examined. Furthermore, this study questions whether the findings might apply to education and training in other professional sectors that have a strong value base as a core to their professional identity.

In framing the questionnaires and semi structured interviews for the case study, the rights and integrity of individuals and their relationships were considered in terms of privacy, group pressure, tutor related issues, empathy and the extent of tutor control.

Questionnaires, consisting of 11 closed- and 1 open-ended question, and semi structured interviews were devised using the concept of Pelz's three principles underpinned by a focus on the ethical issues identified. This questionnaire was piloted using colleagues with particular research and sector expertise.

The semi structured interviews were designed with open-ended questions and used as a method to obtain richer data concerning students' experiences and allowed respondents to relate freely their thoughts and feelings. These semi structured interviews were conducted via e-mail and followed up by phone interviews.

RESULTS

The e-mailed questionnaires to 60 participants were completed by 39 respondents; this constitutes a return rate of 65%. Of the 39 returned questionnaires, 35 respondents answered all 12 questions.

The analysis suggests that there were no major concerns around the areas questioned, with the smallest minority identifying privacy or not forming strong relationships with their group members as concerns. In fact, in terms of privacy, only 15% of respondents felt that there is less privacy online than in a classroom and a further 15% stated that they felt under pressure to give private details to group members online.

Only 13% of respondents were concerned that their progress and contributions online were visible to all and 21% agreed that they had regretted online disclosures later on. 24% of respondents felt that an online tutor is not as caring as a face to face tutor, whereas only 20% felt under constant scrutiny by tutors online.

65% of respondents stated that they had developed close relationships with group members online, while only 16% disagreed.

These responses suggest that there are no major concerns in the areas of privacy, group relations and tutor-related issues and relationships.

The analysis does suggest, however, that there was a significant minority expressing concerns about the process of group work, as Figure 1 shows.

A minority of students expressed concerns about the process of learning online to be impersonal. This is illustrated in Figure 2.

A further significant minority agreed that it is difficult studying Early Years Management online, while working in a people-centred and high touch profession (Figure 3).

A number of respondents also found theoretical concepts difficult to grasp online (Figure 4).

To allow for further exploration of the four areas where a significant minority of respondents expressed some concerns, semi structured e-mailed interviews were conducted involving

Figure 1.38 respondents answered this question, of which: 53% disagree to strongly disagree; 22% neither disagree nor agree; 25% agree to strongly agree

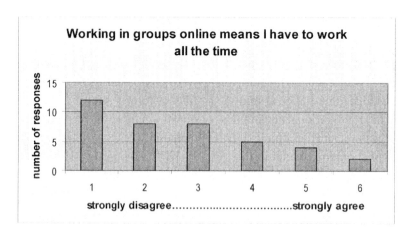

Figure 2.36 respondents answered this question, of which: 53% disagree to strongly disagree; 22% neither disagree nor agree; 25% agree to strongly agree

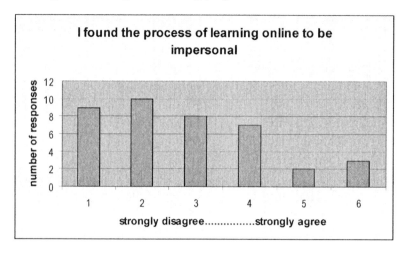

two students randomly chosen. Responses to the e-mailed semi structured interview questions were used to trigger more illuminating questions and probes in the follow-up telephone interviews. In this manner, the mixed method approach was used to triangulate findings.

The following case studies illustrate the experiences of the respondents. In both case studies the respondents expressed very little concern over the issues of privacy, group pressures, distancing factors, tutor issues and relationships. Both respondents, however, acknowledged their positive experience of a blended approach used in their online delivery, such as *"the usefulness of initial study days"* where you could put a *"face to an identity number"* and an occasional *"warm phone conversation"* with tutors or peers can prevent any feelings of isolation. Furthermore, both respon-

Figure 3. 37 respondents answered this question, of which: 54% disagree to strongly disagree; 19% neither disagree nor agree; 27% agree to strongly agree

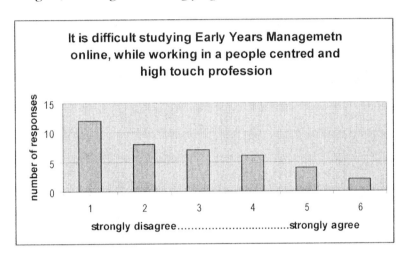

Figure 4. 36 respondents answered, of which: 38% disagree to strongly disagree; 34% neither disagree nor agree; 28% agree to strongly agree

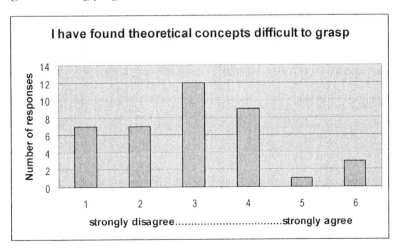

dents highly valued their group experience in the learning process, pointing out that *"group work was of great value,"* with support and feedback obtained *"from fellow professionals,"* not just students, and that working in a group *"has been essential to combat any feelings of isolation."*

CASE STUDY - X

X is an existing third year online student in the North West of England studying for a BA in Early Years Management. X qualified for a National Nursery Examination Board UK (NNEB) in 1988, and then undertook an Advanced Diploma in Childcare and Education. X wanted to progress in the field, to improve management skills, obtain more qualifications and meet other professionals. Hence, the decision was made to undertake a BA degree. X works part time (3 days a week) as part of the Senior Management team in a private nursery, which is a registered charity. X opted to study online because of the flexibility of the mode of study and as a mechanism of improving IT skills. X studies and uses the PC mainly at home or in the local university library, rather than at work. X has no concerns with regard to privacy, but points out that use of identity numbers and passwords *"enables me to keep my work safe"* and feels that the *"university is a safe and secure website."* X feels that far from being impersonal, online learning has enabled X to *"acquire some fantastic friends and build up relationships with some great professionals."* X does acknowledge that learning online is a skill, but once learned had *"proven to be enjoyable."* X does point to the usefulness of initial study days, where you could put a *"face to an identity number."* X feels that supportive tutors come across as more caring online *"If you have their support and guidance it makes you feel like they care and have your best interest at heart."* X found the experience with group work of great value, with support and

feedback obtained *"from fellow professionals,"* not just students. Rather than feel that theoretical concepts were difficult to grasp online, X finds that the flexible nature of learning and clarity of the written word actually assists in the learning process.

X sees no contradiction in working in a "high touch/low tech" profession and learning online: In fact, the opposite was found, as *"this way of learning has developed my skills of using my IT. In my workplace I am now able to apply my new skills. Nowadays, it is an important aspect of any role to use IT and progress with the times."*

CASE STUDY - Y

Y is a Nursery Manager and owner from the South of England. She has been an online student on a Foundation degree programme for Early Years managers for the last 2 years. Y decided to enrol as an online student as it allowed her to combine work and family commitments with study. Learning online reduces travel time and allows her to study from the *"comfort of my own home."* She uses both her PC in work and at home, making the most of short breaks at work to contribute to online discussions or e-mail, but tends to research and produce assignments at home in the evenings. While Y acknowledges that privacy can be an issue in online learning, the use of passwords and encryption in a secure VLE allays such worries. Y has not experienced any concerns about online learning being too impersonal, but advocates a blended approach where an occasional *"warm phone conversation"* with tutors or peers can prevent any feelings of isolation. She particularly values the online group work and feels that learning from others is vital to meeting her objectives. Rather than feeling pressured by her group, she thinks that her peers are all mature students who have realistic expectations of each other and sometimes don't make enough demands. Y feels that working in a group has been essential to combat any feelings of isolation.

In terms of a possible contradiction between working in a high touch/ low tech sector and studying in a high tech/low touch mode, Y states that "*I don't think so, because one has to go with the times and make efforts to learn new things and be knowledgeable on-line or offline, because if you are not willing to learn new things how can we in childcare progress and teach children new things?*"

DISCUSSION

In relation to Pelz's first principle:

1.   Let students do most the work:

In line with this principle, Problem Based Learning (PBL) is used as a vehicle for student centred learning, with students in charge of their own work.

With regard to lack of privacy and academic integrity with this mode of delivery, only a small minority expressed concern over their work being visible and being a member of a group.

It is even more positive that so many (65%) felt that they had formed close relationships with members in their groups. This perception of being a member of a close-knit community of learners also relates to Pelz's second principle of effective online pedagogy:

2.   Interactivity is the heart and soul of effective asynchronous learning.

Students comment both on the variety of interactions and the warmth of some of these such as acquiring "*some fantastic friends and build up relationships with some great professionals.*" This supports Pelz's notion that successful online interaction goes beyond discussion.

However, the research undertaken has been most fruitful with regard to Pelz's third principle. It is in this principle that this research attempts to draw out the ethical student concerns, in terms of integrity and rights. However, far from expressing infringements of these rights, students overwhelmingly feel valued and respected. This can be demonstrated through the research findings for all three aspects of principle three, where positive relationships between "tutor-student" and "student-student" engendered feeling valued and respected.

3.   Strive for presence
    i.   social presence

For example, in the case study, Y suggests that working in a group has been "*essential to combat any feelings of isolation*" and X "*valued feedback from fellow professionals.*" The majority of students (65%) indicated that they "*formed close relationships with group members*" and a further 66% "*had not regretted any disclosures on-line,*" demonstrating the students' view of each other as real people with whom they can form bonds and also points to the students feeling comfortable with one another.

These findings contradict Russell (2005), that distancing is likely to occur in online learning and supports Ramsey's assertion (2003) that online learning can resource enriched learning relations.

    ii.   cognitive presence

The cognitive presence as advocated by Pelz as an enabler to construct and confirm meaning between tutors and students was recognised in different ways throughout from the questionnaire and case study results.

While there was a significant minority (28%) that pointed to having difficulties constructing theoretical meaning online, it is worth noting that the remaining respondents (72%) had no major concern. In addition, in the case study, X highlights *"the flexible nature of learning and the clarity of the written word"* as assisting in this learning process and thereby demonstrates positive construction of meaning online.

iii.   teaching presence

According to Pelz, the tutor's role is the facilitation and direction of the above two principles, and this in turn aids the achievement of worthwhile learning outcomes. Although a significant minority (25%) found the learning process to be impersonal, the remaining (75%) disagreed, and statements in the case study such as *"supportive tutors come across more supportive on-line"* and *"it makes you feel like they care"* vindicate the crucial role of the tutor as facilitator in the PBL process. The tutors within this PBL process referred to by the respondents are most likely to possess a *"humanistic view of people ...tend to be more student directed in their teaching, and think of themselves as catalysts in the learning process"* (Caffarella, 1988, cited in Imel, 1991).

In relation to the issue of rights in terms of privacy and academic integrity and security (Lawhead et al., 1997), the responses received in this research appear to indicate that students perceive those two rights have been met in their online learning experiences.

* privacy

With regard to the first of these rights, in terms of privacy, only 15% of respondents felt there was less privacy online than in a class room and only 13% were concerned about the visibility of their online contributions. On the contrary, respondents perceive that a strong social presence allowed them to be real people (see Pelz's social presence above).

* academic integrity and security

Only 15% of respondents felt under pressure to give their private details, and 20% felt under scrutiny from their online tutor (Big brother effect). Supporting this general lack of concern in the case study, X suggests that *"using identity numbers and passwords enables me to keep my work safe"* and her experiences of working with tutors who *"have your best interests at heart."*

CONCLUSION

In relation to the question posed in this study, regarding students' individual integrity and rights, no major ethical concerns emerged. It is interesting to note that the findings suggest there was no contradiction between working in their professional context (an ethical environment) and studying online.

Students, far from worrying about their privacy being invaded, welcomed the opportunity to share and learn from their colleagues, facilitated by a strong social presence. Furthermore, students perceived the online learning environment as being safe and fair.

What did emerge from the research was the importance of the role of the student context with its focus on relationships. It could be argued that this particular pedagogical approach experienced by the research respondents, helped foster positive relationships online. Flexibility of online learning and opportunity of networking across groups allowed learners to bridge that distance factor, enhanced possibly by the shared professional context of the respondents. The research suggests that PBL online, embracing a facilitative approach which is student centred, provides an environment where positive relationships can flourish.

Following the discussion of the research undertaken in this chapter, the questions remain. Could this mode of learning be successfully replicated for education and training of other professional groups? While the study looked at the experiences of professional, mature students, might online learning for other student groups pose ethical dilemmas, and if so in what way?

FUTURE RESEARCH DIRECTIONS

This chapter addressed two research questions: How are students' individual integrity and rights affected by online learning and what ethical issues are identified by online students themselves? The students participating in this research worked in Early Years Care and Education and completed online management programmes in the UK. This research found no major ethical concerns in online study to the questions posed, and furthermore, participants expressed no contradiction between working in their professional context (an ethical environment) and studying online.

Further research, however, should investigate the differing professional contexts of other employment groups, such as health and social care staff and their involvement in online learning. These are employment groups that have strong vocational and ethical dimensions to their practice. While PBL is already prevalent in UK medical schools, there is scope for research to investigate the suitability of online delivery to this target group rather than the traditional face to face mode.

The arrival of Web 2.0 brings an emphasis on users creating and uploading content. This may pose new ethical challenges for higher education. There is a generation of new students entering higher education who have functioned in a digital environment all their lives, and with increasing knowledge transfer on the Internet, this will likely pose new ethical challenges.

While the research in this chapter has involved professional working mature students, there is scope to investigate the emerging experiences of this new net generation, which constitutes the majority of fulltime students in higher education.

REFERENCES

Addelson, K.P. (1991). *Impure thoughts: Essays on philosophy, feminism and ethics.* Philadelphia, PA: Temple University Press.

Caffarella, R.S. (1988). Ethical dilemmas in the teaching of adults. In R. G. Brockett (Ed.), *Ethical issues in adult education.* New York: Teachers College Press.

Children's Workforce Development Council. (2006). *Developing the early years workforce.* Retrieved April 23, 2008, from http://www.cwd-council.org.uk/projects/earlyyears.htm

Crane, A., & Matten, D. (2007). *Business ethics* (2nd ed.). Oxford.

Daycare Trust. (2003). *Towards universal childcare: Analysing childcare in 2003.* London: Daycare Trust.

De George, R.T. (2006). *Business ethics* (6th ed.). Prentice Hall.

Donohue, C. (2002). It's a small world: Taking your first steps into on-line teaching and learning. *Childcare Information Exchange, 9*(20-25).

Fisher, C., & Lovell, A. (2006). *Business ethics and values* (2nd ed.). Harlow: Prentice Hall.

Garrison, D.R, Anderson, T., & Archer, W. (2000). Critical inquiry in a text-based environment: Computer conferencing in higher education. *The Internet and Higher Education, 2*(2-3), 1-19.

Imel, S. (1991). Ethical practice in adult education. *ERIC Clearinghouse on Adult Career and Vocational Education.* Columbus, OH. Retrieved April 23, 2008, from http://www.ericdigests.org/1992-5/adult.htm

Lawhead, B.P., Alpert, E., Bland, C.G., Caerswell, L., Cizmar, D., DeWitt, J., et al. (1997). The Web and distance learning: What is appropriate and what is not. In *Proceedings of the ITiCSE'97*

Working Group on the Web and Distance Learning Working Group Reports: SIGCSE/SIGUE ITiCSE'97.

Luck, P., & Norton, B. (2005). Collaborative management education—an on-line community in Europe? *International Journal of Web Based Communities, 3*(22-31).

OECD. (2001). *Starting strong—early childhood education and care.* Paris: OECD Publications.

Palmer, M.T. (1995). Interpersonal communication and virtual reality: Mediating interpersonal relationships. In F. Biocca & M.R. Levy (Eds.), *Communication in the age of virtual reality* (pp. 277-299). Hillside, NJ: Lawrence Erlbaum.

Pelz, B. (2004, June). (My) three principles of effective on-line pedagogy. *JALN, 8*(3).

Ramsey, C. (2003). Using virtual learning environments to facilitate new learning relationships. *The International Journal of Management Education, 3*(2), 31-51.

Russell, G. (2005). The distancing question in on-line education. *Innovate, 1*(4). Retrieved April 23, 2008, from http://www.innovateon-line.info/index.php?view=article&id=13

Yin, R.K. (2003). *Case study research design and methods* (3rd ed.). London: Sage.

ADDITIONAL READING

Academic Texts

Figueiredo, A.D., & Afonso, A.P. (2006). *Managing learning in Virtual settings—the role of context.* London: Information Science.

Lockwood, A., & Gooley, A. (2001). *Innovation in open & distance learning.* London: Kogan Page.

McEwan, T. (2001). *Managing values and beliefs in organisations.* Harlow: Prentice Hall.

Palloff, R., & Pratt, K. (2003). *The virtual student—a profile and guide to working with online learners.* San Francisco: Jossey-Bass.

Savin-Baden, M., & Wilkie, K. (2006). *Problem-based learning online.* Maidenhead: Open University Press.

Stephenson, J. (2001). *Teaching & learning online—pedagogies for new technologies.* London: Kogan Page.

Journal Articles

Beer, M., Green, S., Armitt, G., & van Bruggen, J. (2002). The provision of education and training for health care professionals through the medium of the internet. *Campus-Wide Information Systems, 19*(4), 135-144.

Dobos, J. (1996). Collaborative learning: Effects of students expectations and communication apprehension on student motivation. *Communication Education, 45*(2), 15-29.

Donohue, C. (2002). It's a small world: Taking your first steps into online teaching and learning. *Childcare Information Exchange, 9*, 20-24.

Donohue, C., & Clark, D. (2004, November). Learning online: The places you'll go! *Child Care Information Exchange*, 49-54. Retrieved April 23, 2008, from www.childcareexchange.com

Donohue, C., Fox, S., & LaBonte, M. (2004, July). E-learning: What out students can teach us. *Child Care Information Exchange*, 79-82. Retrieved April 23, 2008, from www.childcare-exchange.com

Donohue, C., & Neugebauer, R. (2004, May). Innovations in e-learning: New promise for professional development. *Young Children*, 22-25.

Retrieved April 23, 2008, from www.journal.naeyc.org/btj/

Honey, P. (2001). E-learning: A performance appraisal and some suggestions for improvement. *The Learning Organization, 8*(5).

Kerbs, R. W. (2005). Social and ethical considerations in virtual worlds. *The Electronic Library, 53*(5), 539-546.

Luck, P., & Norton, B. (2004, December). Problem based management education—better online. *European Journal of Open and Distance Learning.*

Luck, P., & Owens, T. (2002). Problem-based learning on-line for nursery management. *Journal of Problem-Based Learning, 1*(1).

Sharma, P., & Maleyeff, J. (2003). Internet education: Potential problems and solutions. *International Journal of Educational Management, 17*(1), 19-25.

Stefkovich, J.A., & O'Brien, G.M. (2004). Best interests of the student: An ethical model. *Journal of Educational Administration, 42*(2), 197-214.

Walker, T., & Donohue, C. (2004, July). Decoding technology: E-tools for teacher education & professional development. *Child Care Information Exchange.* Retrieved April 23, 2008, from www.childcareexchange.com

Williams, P., Nicholas, D., & Gunter, B. (2005). E-learning: What the literature tells us about distance education: An overview. *Aslib Proceedings, 57*(2), 109-122.

Chapter XX
Bilingual Plagiarism in the Academic World

Carmel McNaught
The Chinese University of Hong Kong, Hong Kong

David M. Kennedy
The University of Hong Kong, Hong Kong

ABSTRACT

This chapter is an essay about a new ethical problem that has become apparent to us in recent years. Bilingual plagiarism is the act of passing off the work of others (in particular, the writing of others) as one's own and disguising the plagiarism by intentionally translating the work into another language without giving due attribution to the original author. In an increasingly connected and multilingual world where access to vast amounts of text is relatively easy, bilingual plagiarism may well be an increasing phenomenon. It is undoubtedly difficult to detect. In the chapter we analyze the drivers facilitating, and mitigating against, this new (?) phenomenon. We offer an old-fashioned solution, that of reinforcing the values on which the modern university is founded.

AN UNSEEN PHENOMENON?

The motivation for this chapter developed after both authors repeatedly found their material plagiarized on various Web sites. Both authors are visual in their work. Our papers often have diagrams to describe research plans and resulting models. The first author's (Carmel) first experi- ence of bilingual plagiarism was when she found a diagram from a report written for the Australian government which is openly available online in a conference paper written in Spanish. Carmel does not read Spanish and would not otherwise know if text had been lifted and reused without due acknowledgement. The second author (David) had a similar experience when he found that a colleague had plagiarized his work in Chinese. The only form of detection was, again, the diagrams, because David does not read Chinese.

We have heard suggestions that plagiarism is a great form of flattery but we prefer attribution and citation. Soon after these irritating, but not really major, events David was coordinating the reviewing for a conference. He received a request from an academic in China for 50 full papers to review. We had become sensitized to the issue of bilingual plagiarism and felt a little suspicious. Neither of us know any academic who has time to review 50 papers in a matter of a few weeks. The request was politely declined.

Now, undoubtedly these three experiences of actual and potential bilingual plagiarism are not an accurate reflection of the normal practices of most academics. However, for two academics to have these experiences in the same year was an alert that bilingual plagiarism may be a problem that we need to consider. Also, if some academic teachers behave this way, then it is not unreasonable to assume that we have some students behaving in a similar fashion.

THE MULTILINGUAL INTERNET

The world is increasingly globalized. One of the consequences of globalization is that information flow across linguistic and cultural boundaries is increasing. The statistics (Year 2004) in Table 1 show that, while English may currently dominate, this may not be a long-term phenomenon. Un-

doubtedly, a 2008 snapshot would show marked changes.

In China, the information infrastructure has made significant progress. Yan and Liu (2006) reported a survey covering citation analysis and investigation into academic Web sites over the period 1998 to 2002. Their data showed that the environment of scholarly communication and the information behaviour of scholars have changed dramatically in mainland China with the Internet now playing an increasingly important role in scholarly communication. The situation in China is particularly fluid as is expected in any rapidly expanding situation.

DEFINING BILINGUAL PLAGIARISM

Plagiarism is the act of passing off the work of others (in particular, the writing of others) as one's own. Plagiarism involves an intentional act of using the work of others. It is more than an editorial slip of forgetting a citation. No doubt "sloppy" editing does occur and should be seen as such, regrettable but not necessarily unethical. Plagiarism is unethical. Scholars have an obligation to be meticulous in their use of source material, and any significant deviation from rigorous attention to the ethical use of other work should be seen as plagiarism. Our motivation for this article began with incidents of plagiarism involving university academic staff who might be expected to know about, and rigorously adhere to, established norms of academic publication. Such acts of plagiarism

Table 1. Global Internet statistics by language (adapted from Global Reach, 2004)

Language	Internet access (M)	Percentage of population online	Population online (est. in M)	Total population (M)
English	287.5	35.8	280	508
Non-English	516.7	64.2	680	5,822
European languages (non-English)	276	37.9	328	1,218
All Asian languages	240.6	33.0	263	N/A

are undoubtedly, in our view, unethical. Is the situation as clear-cut with students who are studying in a multilingual situation?

Both authors are long-term academics. We believe that universities constitute a global community with some shared principles of respect for knowledge and respect for the rights of academics who develop knowledge to gain credit for their work. Many universities have "honesty" Web sites (see e.g., "Honesty in academic work: A guide for students and teachers" at http://www.cuhk.edu.hk/policy/academichonesty/). We believe that we need to induct our students into these rigorous standards of academic ethics. While students may not come to the university with an ingrained sense of respecting intellectual property, and this may be more common in societies where collective values are emphasized, one of the aims of university education is to explore and articulate the norms of scholarly discourse that are accepted in the majority of our international universities. There is evidence (Kember, Ma, R. & McNaught, C., et al. 2006) that academics world-wide share common educational values and principles and there is a set of accepted academic norms that we should share with our students.

We recognize that there are different cultural interpretations to ownership of knowledge. Students from Middle Eastern, Asian and African cultures may need more support in negotiating the norms of Western scholarly discourse (Sweda, 2004; Zobel & Hamilton, 2002). Recent interviews with international students from Asia who are currently studying in Australia (Devlin & Gray, 2007) demonstrate how complex the pressures on these students are. They may come from an experiential background that downplays individual ownership of knowledge; they face language challenges in living and studying in Australia and the consequences of failure are very severe. It is incumbent on our universities to provide support for students to gain the skills and conceptual frameworks they need to work in the globalized world of the 21st century. Accept-

ing plagiarism on the grounds that students are struggling is an abrogation of our responsibility to assist our students in their journey of growth and understanding.

The thrust of this chapter is that the issues of plagiarism that are the concern of every major university (distance or face-to-face) are both more serious in a bilingual (or indeed multilingual) context and more challenging to detect. We define bilingual plagiarism as the act of passing off the work of others (in particular, the writing of others) as one's own and disguising the plagiarism by intentionally translating the work into another language without giving due attribution to the original author(s).

DRIVERS FOR AND AGAINST BILINGUAL PLAGIARISM

The model presented in Table 2 has four major dimensions. These are language competence, personal advancement, institutional advancement and ease of detection. These four dimensions have evolved from our discussions with colleagues at several universities in Hong Kong, other countries in Asia, Australia and South Africa. In all these countries there are a significant number of academic staff and students for whom English is a second (or third) language. Most of our examples will be taken from Hong Kong as this is where we both work.

1. Language Competence

It is undoubtedly harder to write in a language other than one's first language. For example, in a comprehensive study of first year university students' English proficiency in Hong Kong, Littlewood and Liu (1996) found that the students lacked an adequate command of grammar, vocabulary, speaking, writing, listening, and reading. Although both students and teachers acknowledged writing as most important to academic success,

Table 2. Drivers for and against bilingual plagiarism

Drivers for bilingual plagiarism		Drivers against bilingual plagiarism
1. Language competence		
Challenges in writing in English as a second or third language	←→	Pride in bilingual capacity
2. Personal advancement		
Pressure to publish for personal career (teachers). Pressure to complete written assignments (students)	←→	The notion of scholarship and demonstration of excellence through sustained writing (teachers). Designing assessment tasks which require personal reflection (students)
3. Institutional advancement		
Pressure to publish for institutional rankings	←→	Institutional reputation for scholarship and also for integrity
4. Ease of detection		
Difficulty of detection	←→	Evolution of better detection strategies

writing (along with speaking) was the lowest rated and least confident skill. There are dual "temptations" about bilingual plagiarism. If you can read Chinese and know that your peers or teachers cannot, there is a strong temptation to directly translate a Chinese article into English and use the ideas as original ones. This could be true for both teachers and students. Conversely, if you have an article written in English, then a direct translation into Chinese can be republished in a rapidly increasing number of Chinese journals. This converse situation is likely to be used by teachers, rather than students.

We have no evidence that flagrant bilingual plagiarism exists. We have our own anecdotes and the testimony of a number of Chinese colleagues who have admitted that they have detected a small number of such cases. So what are the key drivers acting against bilingual plagiarism from a linguistic perspective?

We believe that one of the key features of globalization is a fluency in language use and a pride in the ability to operate across linguistic boundaries. We have witnessed how rapidly language demands can change. When we came to Hong Kong 6 years ago, Cantonese and English were the main languages and relatively little

Pǔtōnghuà was spoken. Pǔtōnghuà is the official term for Standard Mandarin and translates as "common speech." In the short time of our sojourn here, the situation has changed and many of our graduates expect to need to be relatively fluent in English and Pǔtōnghuà as well as their home language of Cantonese. While Cantonese and Pǔtōnghuà share a common written form, they are very distinct languages and, in Hong Kong, English is often spoken in conversations between local (Hong Kong) and mainland Chinese. So, the linguistic landscape of Hong Kong is complex and evolving and one can detect unmistakable pride in being able to attain bilingual or trilingual capabilities. This pride in being able to function well in a multilingual context mitigates against bilingual plagiarism.

2. Personal Advancement

A defined set of research publications is one measure used by the many government agencies as an indicator of the research performance of universities. The authors have first-hand experience of the national systems that exist in Australia, New Zealand, the United Kingdom and Hong Kong. The publication types that are eligible usually comprise commercially published books and book chapters, and peer-reviewed articles in journals and conference proceedings.

This emphasis on numbers of research publications can be seen as a driver toward bilingual plagiarism, especially considering the fact that detection is so difficult. The concept of "insistent individualism" was coined by Bennett (2003). He explored what he saw as a growing acceptance on the part of academics that building their own careers should be their first priority, and that success in terms of reputation, academic kudos and personal publicity was the raison d'etre of academic life. If an academic takes only a self-seeking approach, then a degree of dissatisfaction and cynicism may well develop. Further, the bar for advancement is constantly being raised and the number of publications expected of any academic is increasing. Pressure to produce publications and an attitude of cynicism about the value of academic work can make bilingual plagiarism tempting for an academic who has the linguistic skills to act this way. A fuller description of the phenomenon of insistent individualism is given in McNaught (2007).

So, the pressures on students for whom English is not their first language to perform well in written assignments, and the pressures on all academics to publish, feed the unethical practices of bilingual plagiarism. Detection is very challenging and so strategies for prevention are essential.

For academic staff, the strategy of mentoring about the process of academic writing can be helpful. Building one's curriculum vitae (CV) requires a number of papers in the one area. When one reads an academic CV one looks for evidence of a progressive development of ideas and evidence. In most academic disciplines, this demonstration of evidence is through writing. This is true for all areas of scholarship. The model of the four Boyer (1990) scholarships is an excellent one to show the breadth of scholarly discourse that any academic can choose to focus on in building a strong academic CV. The four scholarships are the scholarship of discovery—traditional disciplined-based research; the scholarship of integration—connections across disciplines and contexts; the scholarship of application—professional and community-oriented research; and the scholarship of teaching—where the principles of scholarly inquiry are applied to planning and implementing teaching. In any of these areas sustained writing is needed for any academic to lay claims to being an expert. Using bilingual plagiarism as a strategy to get a "quick" paper does not do much for the long-term development of a CV. Mentoring young academics about the need for sustained scholarship is an important strategy to mitigate against bilingual plagiarism.

For students, we consider that it is important to ensure that assessments are designed so that direct plagiarism is difficult. If students are asked to provide informed personal opinions as part of an essay or project report, this section at least cannot be plagiarized. Designing assessment tasks that have a personal component is important for the development of students' ability to apply and critique the abstract theories they learn about. This type of assessment is thus educationally sound and this style of assessment mitigates against the temptation to plagiarize.

3. Institutional Advancement

"League tables" of universities abound. Many are produced by newspapers (e.g., the Times Higher Education Supplement and Newsweek). Some disciplines such as Business seem to be more focused on these rankings and the market in Master of Business Administration (MBA) degrees seems particularly sensitive (Walker, 2007).

Within all universities the latest rankings are always examined with attention and, whether one approves of this type of comparison or not, there is no doubt that they are important. It is interesting that we are frequently asked about the standing of various Australian universities (we have worked in five Australian universities) by Hong Kong students who want to check if such and such a ranking is really accurate. So, there is a mixture of adherence to and distrust of these university rankings. Certainly the diversity of criteria is bewildering and better criteria of comparison are needed. Several commentators in this area (e.g., Marginson, 2007) believe that the Shanghai Jiao Tong University indicators (Shanghai Jiao Tong University Institute of Higher Education, 2006) enable a "purpose-based and disaggregated comparison" which should be encouraged for the "improvement of the global higher education sector" (Marginson, 2007).

As academic output in terms of number of publications feature in these rankings, this could be construed as a driver toward bilingual plagiarism. The culture of most universities rewards high academic output and reward statements are often phrased as "making a significant contribution to the discipline and to the university community" or words to that effect.

However, universities do not welcome publications obtained by any strategy and the need to preserve a reputation for institutional integrity has a high priority. The consequences of plagiarism are very serious for a university if any of its staff are found guilty and the matter becomes public knowledge. We do not know of any cases of high-profile bilingual plagiarism and so can only provide an example of plagiarism in the English language to show how problematic this can be for a university and the guilty party. David Robinson was a prominent British sociologist in the 1970s. Eventually, he moved to Australia and become Vice-Chancellor of Monash University, a large multicampus university considered to be one of Australia's elite universities (a member of the Group of Eight; http://www.go8.edu.au/). This was his third Vice-Chancellorship. He was also a member of the Hong Kong University Grants Committee and held other prestigious international positions. In 2002, substantial plagiarism from the 1970s and 1980s came to light. David Robinson resigned in disgrace. Peele (2002) provides a readable account of the saga. However, he left Monash University with the task of re-establishing its reputation as a highly reputable institution. The damage done in Asia was significant as the university was considered to have lost considerable "face," and this disquiet had financial implications for a university that has a very large number of international students from Asia. Newspaper headlines such as "Campuses galore, but was it academe?" (Miller, 2002) continued to embarrass Monash for some time.

Incidents such as the "Robinson affair" act as a strong institutional driver against bilingual plagiarism, as no university wishes to experience anything similar.

4. Ease of Detection

At present bilingual plagiarism is very difficult to detect. Most search engines and plagiarism detectors work only with Roman scripts and do not handle Chinese characters (or other non-Roman written languages). The Chinese University of Hong Kong (CUHK) is a bilingual university and so some assignments are submitted in Chinese (though most are in English). But no matter what the language of the assignment, the growing Chinese influence on the Internet means that Chinese students and teachers have access to a vast bank of material that could be translated and reused without due attribution. Computer scientists at CUHK have developed a plagiarism detection system, CUPIDE (Chinese University Plagiarism IDentification Engine; http://cupide. cse.cuhk.edu.hk/). This system can handle double-byte characters and thus can handle English and Chinese texts. While this is a bilingual system, it obviously does not compare translated texts. It can only match English with English and Chinese with Chinese.

Google's Babelfish is a primitive automatic translator that attempts a word by word translation.

For simple statements this can be helpful, but it does not have the level of discernment to negotiate multiple possible nuances and interpretations that occur in normal translations. The development of sensitive translation and comparison engines that do context- and content-sensitive semantic translations is likely to occur eventually. Such engines would take a substantial piece of text in one language and translate it into a form with similar meaning in another language. There are complex linguistic and technical challenges in this arena. A sufficiently sophisticated system might provide several concurrent translations that can be compared with the text that is being checked. However, all this is for the future and the timeline for such engines to be widely available is likely to be a long one. What can be done in the near future that is possible?

A PARTIAL SOLUTION FOR THE FUTURE: EMPHASIZING THE COMMUNITY OF SCHOLARS

The framework produced by Bennett (2003) is one where "conversation" is the "essential metaphor" (chapter 5) for university life. Conversation implies active and open engagement between all members of the university, both teachers and students. In Bennett's model, institutional leaders need to foster a conversational community at all levels of the organization. Our universities need to be more vigilant about plagiarism of all forms, including the bilingual variety. One way to do this is to strenuously emphasize values of integrity and scholarship, and to nurture those values in new cohorts of academics and students. Universities have a tremendously important potential role in the 21st century and we must not abrogate that potential or that responsibility. The health of the academy is the only true cure.

REFERENCES

Bennett, J. B. (2003). *Academic life: Hospitality, ethics, and spirituality.* Bolton, MA: Anker.

Boyer, E. L. (1990). *Scholarship reconsidered. Priorities of the professoriate.* Princeton, NJ: The Carnegie Foundation for the Advancement of Teaching.

Devlin, M., & Gray, K. (2007). In their own words: A qualitative study of the reasons Australian university students plagiarize. *Higher Education Research & Development, 26*(2), 181-198.

Global Reach. (2004). *Global Internet statistics (by Language).* Retrieved April 23, 2008, from http://www.glreach.com/globstats/index.php3

Kember, D., Ma, R., & McNaught, C., et al. (2006). *Excellent university teaching.* Hong Kong: Chinese University Press.

Littlewood, W., & Liu, N. F. (1996). *Hong Kong students and their English.* Hong Kong: Hong Kong University/ Macmillan.

Marginson, S. (2007, March 7-9). Global university rankings: Where to from here? In *Paper presented at the Asia-Pacific Association for International Education, National University of Singapore.* Retrieved April 23, 2008, from http://www.cshe.unimelb.edu.au/people/staff_pages/Marginson/APAIE_090307_Marginson.pdf

McNaught, C. (2007). Individual and institutional responses to staff plagiarism. In M. Quigley (Ed.), *Encyclopedia of information ethics and security* (pp. 342-347). Hershey, PA: Idea Group Reference.

Miller, C. (2002, July 20). Campuses galore, but was it academe? *The Age* (Melbourne).

Peele, S. (2002). *The continuing significance of David Robinson's plagiarism career.* Retrieved April 23, 2008, from http://www.peele.net/debate/robinson.html

Shanghai Jiao Tong University Institute of Higher Education, SJTUIHE. (2006). *Academic ranking of world universities.* Retrieved April 3, 2008, from http://ed.sjtu.edu.cn/ranking.htm

Sweda, J. E. (2004). *When is plagiarism not cheating*? Retrieved April 23, 2008, from http://www.library.cmu.edu/ethics8.html

Yan, J., & Liu, Z. (2006). Development of, and trends in, scholarly communication in China. In H. S. Ching, P. W. T. Poon, & C. McNaught (Eds.), *E-learning and digital publishing* (pp. 195-219). Dordrecht: Springer-Verlag.

Walker, P. (2007). *The vexed issue of MBA league tables.* CNN World Business. Retrieved April 23, 2008, from http://edition.cnn.com/2007/BUSINESS/04/10/execed.news/

Zobel, J., & Hamilton, M. (2002). Managing student plagiarism in large academic departments. *Australian Universities Review, 45*(2), 23-30.

ADDITIONAL READING

There does not appear to be an existing literature base on bilingual plagiarism. Readers who wish to explore plagiarism in general are referred to a bibliography by Stoeger (2006). This bibliography describes 28 articles on staff plagiarism and 39 on student plagiarism. The site also contains a number of additional links to other useful compilations on the topic of plagiarism.

Stoeger, S. (2006). *Plagiarism.* Retrieved April 23, 2008, from http://www.web-miner.com/plagiarism

Chapter XXI
Ethical Practices and Implications in Distance Education:
Lessons Learned

Ramesh C. Sharma
Indira Gandhi National Open University, India

Ugur Demiray
Anadolu University, Turkey

ABSTRACT

The changing dimensions of distance education methodologies, new roles of distance teachers, and learners and use of modern communication technologies have necessitated putting ethics on the top of agenda of educational administrators, thinkers and practitioners. This chapter highlights major outcomes emerged from the research, theory, practice and discussion on different themes of distance education by various authors in their respective chapters. This chapter also highlights various themes entangled in this book.

INTRODUCTION

The Open and Distance Learning System (ODLS) has emerged as an alternate benefiting a number of aspirants of education, specifically higher education. The numbers in ODL has also increased many fold over a short span of 4 decades. The emergence and developments in ODL methodologies have brought certain theoretical and pragmatic approaches to the field. As with any other new phenomenon, this mode of education has brought a new set of emotional, physical and psychological issues. The teaching and learning through this new medium exposed the learning community to such experiences where the teacher and students normally do not see face to face with each other. The virtual classroom faces issues, including humanizing, roles, norms, ethics, privacy and socio-psychological.

The ethical issues become significant, and we keep reading about misuse of Internet and e-mail. Electronic voyeurism is also common in online communication. Plagiarism is one of the most common misuses of the Internet facilities among students. Copying assignments from others' work or taking material from the Web is seen as the easy way out for the students. Privacy of the messages is very difficult in online communications. The most striking feature besides traditional education of the open distance education and especially online distance education is to open its doors of global education to the student at his desktop. What is critical to the success of this mode of education is to have ethics in place; it is a different field which is based on mutual trust and respect. This trust, respect and honesty may be in the form of providing conviction to the learner by the teacher or vice-versa, or an honest feedback to the researcher by the respondents for the right conclusions of research questions. These ethical concerns, which are carried on from the traditional education to the distance education, thus form a very significant base for the future of online education.

Even though ethics is a relative term, it absolutely depends on each and every individual who comprises the group initially, and later the society at large. Moral science classes, which we have undergone in school, reminds of what ethics is even now. In an era where achievement and progress are in the priority list by any means, reaching the top/goal with the optimum ethics is like leaving footsteps to follow.

This book, Ethical Practices and Implications in Distance Education, has covered topics such as student support services, international

distance education partnerships, organizational culture of the partners and leadership patterns in the partner institutions in the distance education field, the rise in academic cheating, multiculturalism as the causative factor, unethical computer using behaviors, academic dishonesty and theft, research ethics, interactions involved in teaching and learning at a distance, students' individual integrity and rights, ethical concerns of ODL practitioners and so forth.

MAJOR OUTCOMES

The objective of this book was to provide a bunch of case studies on implementation of the ethics aspect in different contexts of open and distance learning viz. nonformal education, school education, college and universities, industry and corporate world, social development, vocational education, the health sector, the agricultural sector and lifelong learning and further education. The purpose of this book was to showcase the ethical practices for all those involved in the production of materials, copying, licensing and implementation of ethical perspectives in ODLS.

- One of the most significant developments to the education and training sectors has been the growth of online programs, virtual institutions, corporate universities, and for-profit providers of instructional software. Whatever the impact of instructional technology has on the education and training sector, the supreme position of the teacher cannot be put to question. Therefore, the acts and behaviour of teachers must be guided by ethical and moral values. If adequate safeguards are not put in place, increasing use of technology in the distance education, especially, may cultivate unethical behaviour.
- Prevalence of strong emphasis on ethical dilemmas both at in the philosophical and

the practical realm for those who enter into distance education partnerships so as to ensure promotion of the "right" values and fostering of ethical behavior.

- Emotions play an important role to the psychological development of individual. Emotions are related to moral values as well. Therefore, ODL pedagogy must create enough room for recognition of the emotional state of the learners and take appropriate measures to transform the same when needed.

- The prominent rise in academic cheating in the era of globalisation of education. Availability of technologies to the higher education students cited as the causative factor for rendering challenges and opportunities for exhibiting cheating behaviours.

- The learners must not be blamed if they are not properly guided about what is academic dishonesty.

- Cheating has been reported to be rampant in the educational institutions. ODL also is not immune to this "phenomenon." Often the urge to have good grades, examination stress, personality traits, difficulty in understanding the content well and so forth are some of the reasons students resort to cheating. Therefore, ODL institutions need to prominently highlight the policies related to cheating in their profiles, manuals or handbooks.

- The research, theory and practice should be focused to have optimum ethics in the field of distance education. There is a need for formulation of models by practitioners to judge ethical issues in distance and open learning instead of adapting from the medical fields.

- Foundations in ethics, environmental technoethics, educational technoethics, cyberethics, computer ethics, Internet search ethics, Web research ethics, health and medi-

cal technoethics, engineering ethics, and biotech ethics are the areas which are being taken seriously by the ODL functionaries.

- Prevalence of the unethical computer using behaviors prevalent in undergraduate students. Emphasis on the prevention of unethical behavior in all forms because computer science has a crucial place in distance education.

- What the administrators should do to support their faculty in curbing dishonesty in their institutions and the fact that academic integrity is both the responsibility of the institution and the faculty.

- The way of how ethics-based case studies assist practice and pave way to improve the day-to-day life. As suggested by one of our authors about the potential use of case studies, especially with the increased use of digital communication with a specific approach to ethical decision-making and instruction.

- Among the well-informed experienced (published) internationally known distance researchers, nonpublishing practitioners and nonresearchers, the nonpublishing researchers are not well-informed about the policies under which distance research must be conducted.

- Academic theft under the head of translation to facilitate reach to the potential group is bilingual plagiarism (The plagiarized work in the different language could be identified by the original authors themselves incidentally by the presence of graphics).

- Learners need to be properly oriented to the concepts and their implications like copy protection, license agreements, shareware use, freeware programs, softlifting, copyright issues, computer ethics, use of academic resources, examination ethics, citation ethics and a respect toward work of others.

- One's own learner autonomy is reduced both to facilitate others and oneself to learn in both cooperative group learning and in collaborative group learning in distance education.
- Optimum social interaction exists when students prefer the opportunity to share and learn from their colleagues and when there is no contradiction between working in their professional context (an ethical environment) and studying online.
- Concentrating on cognitive tasks and market-driven aspects of open and distance learning at the expense of the social harmony instead of implementing an appropriate pedagogy which satisfies both aims, remains a challenge for ODL designers and teachers, that is, pedagogy should be seen in association with the deep rooted social and cultural contexts.
- The ethical principles for online facilitation can be integrated into an online training course for ODL practitioners.
- The ways computing technology is intended for educational purposes are misused by the learners and that too during the study process besides the importance of institutional/contextual/attitudes/personal factors related to academic integrity/ academic need to be examined closely.
- The network-enabled education is both the means and an institution.
- A two-phased ethical approach can act as an effective model to develop courses, which highlights integration of multimodal learning/teaching strategies and availability of opportunity for the students to discover their preferred approach to learning and the way to "Massification" and delivering technology-enhanced courses to an increasingly diverse student body.
- The fact that the subject matter experts, instructional designers, faculty, teaching assistants, global online learners and others

affect cultural sensitivity and localization in global e-learning is very much relevant in terms of educational ethics.

THEMES ENTANGLED IN THE BOOK

- Causative factors for academic cheating
- Need for standards
- Things to be known by researchers
- Importance of ethics in distance education
- Integrity in the individuals of the academic fraternity in all forms
- Maintenance of ethics is both the institutional and faculty responsibility
- Individual integrity amounts to all
- Sharing and learning
- Effect of globalisation on distance teaching/learning
- Globalization emphasizes instrumental aims (instead of social aims) of education and hence is a challenge for the ODL practitioner
- Increased attention to conversation ethics optimizes social interactions
- Multimodal learning/teaching strategies
- Cultural sensitivity in global e-learning

CONCLUSION

To conclude, every reader of this book would agree that even though human beings live in social groups, they have to depend on each other for mutual benefit and sustenance. Ultimately, every drop counts in the group and the individual moral values reflect highly the group morale and a little fraction of poison is sure to damage the entire slot. Distance education is no exception for this.

This volume will be one of the main source books for people interested in ethics for open and distance learning/online learning or e-learning, especially those who would like to know what has worked and what has not worked. As different sectors of education and training is covered, the book will be of interest to teachers, students, and administrators in educational institutions, human resource managers in the industry, and professionals involved with the social development sectors.

Compilation of References

Aaron, R. M. (1992). Student academic dishonesty: Are collegiate institutions addressing the issue? *NASPA Journal, 29*(2), 107-113.

AAUP. (1987). *Statement of professional ethics.* American Association of University Professors. Retrieved April 22, 2008, from http://www.aaup.org/AAUP/pubsresearch/policydocs/statementonprofessionalethics.htm

Academics: Distance education student handbook. (2008). Hagerstown Community College. Retrieved April 16, 2008, from http://www.hagerstownccc.edu/academics/distance/studenthandbook.php

Ackerman, T. (2003, October). Colleges' war against cheats goes high-tech: Computers used to fight rising Internet plagiarism. *University of Houston.* Retrieved April 22, 2008, from http://www.uh.edu/ednews/2003/hc/200310/20031006cheat.html

ACPA. (2002). *Statement of ethical principles and standards.* American College Personnel Association. Retrieved April 22, 2008, from http://www.myacpa.org/au/au_ethical.cfm

Active Worlds. Retrieved April 22, 2008, from www.activeworlds.com

Adam, A. (2000, December). Gender and computer ethics. *Computers and Society*, 17-24.

Addelson, K.P. (1991). *Impure thoughts: Essays on philosophy, feminism and ethics.* Philadelphia, PA: Temple University Press.

Adkins, J., Kenkel, C., & Lim, C. L. (2005). Deterrents to online academic dishonesty. *The Journal of Learning in Higher Education, 1*, 17-22. Retrieved April 22, 2008, from http://jwpress.com/JLHE/JLHE.htm

Adkins, J., Kenkel, C., & Lim, C. L. (2008). *Deterrents to online academic dishonesty.* Retrieved April 16, 2008, from http://jwpress.com/JLHE/Issues/viii/Deterrents%20to%20Online%20Academic%20Dishonesty.pdf

AECT. (2005). *Code of ethics.* Bloomington, IN. Retrieved April 23, 2008, from http://www.aect.org/About/Ethics.asp

Akbulut, Y., Sendag, S., Birinci, G., Kilicer, K., Sahin, M.C., & Odabasi, H. F. (in press-a). Exploring the types and reasons of internet triggered academic dishonesty among Turkish undergraduate students. *Computers and Education.* Retrieved April 23, 2008, from http://dx.doi.org/10.1016/j.compedu.2007.06.003

Akbulut, Y., Uysal, O., Odabasi, H. F., & Kuzu, A. (in press-b). Influence of gender, program of study and PC experience on unethical computer using behaviors of Turkish undergraduate students. *Computers and Education.* Retrieved April 23, 2008, from http://dx.doi.org/10.1016/j.compedu.2007.06.004

Aldrich, H. E., & Waldinger, R. (1990). Ethnicity and entrepreneurship. *Annual Review of Sociology, 16,* 111-135.

Aleven, V., Stahl, E., Schworm, S., Fischer, F., & Wallace, R. (2003, Autumn). Help seeking and help design in interactive learning environments. *Review of Educational Research, 73*(3), 277-320.

Alfino, M., & Pierce, L. (1997), *Information ethics for librarians.* Jefferson, NC: McFarland.

Allen, B. P. (1994). Case-based reasoning: Business applications. *Communications of the ACM, 37*(3), 40-42.

Allen, C. (1996). What's wrong with the "golden rule"? Conundrums of conducting ethical research in cyberspace. *The Information Society, 12*(2). Retrieved April 22, 2008, from http: http://venus.soci.niu.edu/~jthomas/ethics/tis/go.christin

Allen, J., Fuller, D., & Luckett, M. (1998). Academic integrity: Behaviors, rates, and attitudes of business students toward cheating. *Journal of Marketing Education, 20*(1), 41-52.

Allen, L., & Voss, D. (1997). *Ethics in technical communication: Shades of gray.* New York: John Wiley & Sons.

Alm-Lequeux, A. (2001, Spring). Using the Internet as a zone of proximal development for teaching indirect speech: A Vygotskian approach. *Die Unterrichtspraxis/Teaching German, 34*(1), 1-9.

American Association for Higher Education. (1997). *Series on service-learning in the disciplines.* Washington, DC: American Association for Higher Education.

American Association of Law Libraries. (1999). *Ethical principles.* Chicago, IL. Retrieved April 23, 2008, from http://www.aallnet.org/about/policy_ethics.asp

American Association of School Librarians and Association of Educational Communications and Technology. (1998). *Information literacy standards for student learning: Standards and indicators.* Chicago, IL: American Library Association.

American Counselling Association (ACA). (2005). *Code of ethics.* Retrieved April 16, 2008, from http://www.counseling.org

American Library Association. (1995). Code of ethics. Chicago, IL. Retrieved April 23, 2008, from http://www.ala.org/ala/oif/statementspols/codeofethics/codeethics.htm

American Library Association. (2004). *Core values task force II final report.* Chicago, IL: American Library Association.

Anderson, C. (2001, Winter). Online cheating: A new twist to an old problem. *Student Affairsonline, 2.* Retrieved April 16, 2008, from http://www.studentaffairs.com/ejournal/winter_2001/plagiarism.htm

Anderson, T. (2001). The hidden curriculum in distance education. *Change, 33*(6), 28-35.

Anderson, T. D., & Garrison, D. R. (1998). Learning in a networked world: New roles and responsibilities. In C. C. Gibson (Ed.), *Distance learners in higher education* (pp. 97-112). Madison, WI: Atwood.

Anderson, T., & Kanuka, H. (2003). *E-research. Methods, strategies, and issues.* Allyn and Bacon.

Anderson, T., & Whitelock, D. (2004). The educational Semantic Web: Visioning and practicing the future of education. *Journal of Interactive Media in Education, 1.* Retrieved April 22, 2008, from http://www-jime.open.ac.uk/2004/1

Anderson, T., Rourke, L., Garrison, D.R., & Archer, W. (2001). Assessing teaching presence in a computer conferencing context. *Journal of Asynchronous Learning Networks, 5*(2), 1-17.

Angeles, P. A. (1992). *Dictionary of philosophy* (2nd ed.). New York: Harper Collins.

AOIR. (2001). *Ethics working committee—a preliminary report.* Retreived April 15, 2008, from http://aoir.org/reports/ethics.html

APA Online. (2003). *APA statement on services by telephone, teleconferencing, and Internet.* Retrieved April 22, 2008, from http://www.apa.org/ethics/stmnt01.html

Apple, M. W. (1988). Teaching and technology: The hidden effects of computers on teachers and students. In L. E. Beyer & M. W. Apple (Eds.), *The curriculum: Problems, politics and possibilities* (pp. 289-311). Albany: State University of New York Press.

Apple, M. W. (2004). *Ideology and curriculum* (3rd ed.). New York: RoutledgeFalmer.

Arbaugh, J. B. (2001). How instructor immediacy behaviors affect student satisfaction and Learning in

Web-based courses. *Business Communication Quarterly, 64,* 42-54.

Arnold, M. (1882). *Culture and anarchy.* Retrieved April 16, 2008, from http://www.library.utoronto.ca/utel/non-fiction_u/arnoldm_ca/ca_all.html

Arnseth, H., & Ludvigen, S. (2006). Approaching institutional context: Systematic versus dialogic research in CSCL. *Computer-supported Collaborative Learning, 1,* 167-183.

Aronowitz, S., & Giroux, H. A. (1993). *Education still under siege.* Westport, CT: Bergin and Garvey.

Aronson, J. D. (1996, April). The consequences of free trade in information flows. *International Affairs, 72*(2), 311-328.

Asbee, S., Woodall, S., & Simpson, O. (1999). Student mentoring in distance education. *Journal of Access and Credit Studies, 2*(2), 220-232. ISSN 1462-0367.

Ashwin, P. (Ed.). (2006). *Changing higher education: The development of learning and teaching.* London: RoutledgeFalmer.

Ashworth, P., & Bannister, P. (1997). Guilty in whose eyes? University students' perceptions of cheating and plagiarism in academic work and assessment. *Studies in Higher Education, 22*(2), 187-203.

Askell-Williams, H., & Lawson, M. J. (2006). Multi-dimensional profiling of medical students' cognitive models about learning. *Medical Education, 40*(2), 138-145.

Association for Computing Machinery (ACM). (1992). ACM proposed code of ethics and professional conduct. *Communications of the ACM, 35*(5), 94-99.

Association of Library and Information Science Education. (2006, October 20). *Information Ethics Special Interest Group: Position statement on information ethics in LIS education.* Message posted to JESSE mailing list.

Atthill, C. (2001). Notes and comments: Towards ethical distance education. *Open Learning, 16*(1), 85-87.

Austin, M. J., & Brown, L. D. (1999). Internet plagiarism: Developing strategies to curb student academic dishonesty. *The Internet and Higher Education, 2*(1), 21-33.

Baase, S. (2003). *A gift of fire: Social, legal, and ethical issues for computers and the Internet* (2nd ed.). Upper Saddle River, NJ: Pearson Education.

Baggaley, J., & Spencer, B. (2005). The mind of a plagiarist. *Learning, Media and Technology, 30*(1), 55-62.

Baird, D. E., & Fisher, M. (2005). Neomillennial user experience design strategies: Utilizing social networking media to support "always on" learning styles. *Journal of Educational Technology Systems, 34*(1), 5-32.

Baird, R. M., Ramsower, R., & Rosenbaum, S. E. (Eds.). (2000). *Cyberethics: Social and moral issues in the computer age.* Amherst, NY: Prometheus Books.

Bakardjieva, M., & Feenberg, A. (2000). Involving the virtual subject. *Ethics and Information Technology, 2,* 233-240.

Ball, K., & Oppenheim, C. (2005). Attitudes of UK librarians and librarianship students to ethical issues. *International Review of Information Ethics, 3,* 54-61.

Ball, S. J. (1998). Big policies/small world: An introduction to international perspectives in education policy. *Comparative Education, 34*(2), 119-130.

Balmert, M. E., & Ezzell, M. H. (2002). Leading learning by assuring distance instructional technology is an ethical enterprise. In *Proceedings of the Adult Higher Education Alliance (AHEA): Creating New Meanings in Leading Learning.* Pittsburgh, PA, (pp. 54-72). Retrieved April 16, 2008, from http://www.ahea.org/conference/proceedings.htm

Barker, C., Pistrang, N., & Elliott, R. (2002). *Research methods in clinical psychology: An introduction for students and practitioners* (2nd ed.). West Sussex: John Wiley & Sons.

Barnes, J. (1979). *Who should know what? Social science, privacy and ethics.* Harmondsworth: Penguin.

Barrington, E. (2004). Teaching to student diversity in higher education: How Multiple Intelligence Theory can help. *Teaching in Higher Education, 9*(4), 421-434.

Barthes, R. (1976). *The pleasure of the text* (R. Miller, Trans.). London: Cape.

Baser, S. (2006). Ethics and power in community-campus partnerships for research. *Action Research, 4*(1), 9 -21.

Bassett, E. H., & O'Riordan, K. (2002). Ethics of Internet research: Contesting the human subjects research model. *Ethics and Information Technology, 4*(3), 233-249.

Bates, T. (1999, September 21-23). Cultural and ethical issues in international distance education. In *Proceedings of the Engaging Partnerships Collaboration and Partnership in Distance Education: UBC/CREAD Conference,* Vancouver, Canada, (n.p.).

Bates, T. (2001). International distance education: Cultural and ethical issues. *Distance Education, 22*(1), 122-136.

Bayles, M. D. (1981). *Professional ethics.* Belmont, CA: Wadsworth.

Bean, J., & Eaton Bogdan, S. (2001). The psychology underlying successful student retention. *Journal of College Student Retention, 3*(1), 73-89.

Bear, G. G. (1990). Knowledge of computer ethics: Its relationship to computer attitude and socio moral reasoning. *Journal of Educational Computing Research, 6*, 77-87.

Beck, L. G., & Murphy, J. (1994). *Ethics in educational leadership programs: An expanding role.* Thousand Oaks, CA: Corwin Press.

Beck, M., & Kaufman, G. (1994). Scientific methodology and ethics in university education. *Journal of Chemical Education, 94*(11), 922-924.

Beer, M., Green, S., Armitt, G., & van Bruggen, J. (2002). The provision of education and training for health care professionals through the medium of the internet. *Campus-Wide Information Systems, 19*(4), 135-144.

Begley, S. (2002, November 1). Review boards pose threat to social scientists' work. *The Wall Street Journal Online.* Retrieved April 23, 2008, from http://online.wsj.com/public/article_print/0,,SB1036101057183429471,00.html

BEK. (2003). *Bilim Etigi Kilavuzu (Scientific ethics guide).* Anadolu University: Eskisehir. Retrieved April 23, 2008, from http://www.anadolu.edu.tr/tr/bilimsel/bek.pdf

Bell, F., & Adam, A. (2004). Information systems ethics. In B. Kaplan, D. Truex, D. Wastell, T. Wood-Harper, & J. DeGross (Eds.), *Information systems research. Relevant theory and informed practice* (pp. 159-174). Boston: Kluwer.

Belle, V. G. (2006). How cheating helps drive better instruction. Retrieved April 16, 2008, from http://www.plagiarized.com/vanb.html

Belz, J. A., & Müller-Hartmann, A. (2003, Spring). Teachers as intercultural learners: Negotiating German-American telecollaboration along the institutional fault line. *The Modern Language Journal, 87*(1), 71-89.

Benedikt, M. (1991). Cyberspace: Some proposals. In M. Benedikt (Ed.), *Cyberspace: First steps* (pp. 119-224). Cambridge, MA: MIT Press.

Bennett, J. B. (1998). Collegial professionalism: The academy, individualism, and the common good. Phoenix, AZ: American Council on Education & Oryx Press. In D. Gearhart (Ed.), (2000). Ethics in distance education: Developing ethical policies. *Online Journal of Distance Learning Administration, 4*(1). State University of West Georgia, Distance Education Center.

Bennett, J. B. (2003). *Academic life: Hospitality, ethics, and spirituality.* Bolton, MA: Anker.

Beran, T., & Li, Q. (2005). Cyber-harrassment: A study of a new method for an old behavior. *Journal of Educational Computing Research, 32*(3), 265-277.

Berg, G. A. (2005). Reform higher education with capitalism? Doing good and making money at the for-profit universities. *Change*, 28-34.

Berners-Lee, T., Hendler, J., & Lassila, O. (2001). The Semantic Web. *Scientific American, 284,* 34-43.

Bers, M. U. (2001). Identity construction environments: Developing personal and moral values through the design of a virtual city. *The Journal of the Learning Sciences, 10*(2), 365-415.

Bier, M., Sherblom, S., & Gallo, M. (1996). Ethical issues in a study of Internet use: Uncertainty, responsibility, and the spirit of research relationships. *Ethics and Behavior, 6*(2), 141-151.

Billington, J. H. (2001, December). Humanizing the information revolution. *Proceedings of the American Philosophical Society, 145*(4), 579-586.

Bills, R. D. (1990). *Plagiarism in law school: Close resemblance of the worst kind?* Retrieved April 16, 2008, from http://www.lwionline.org/publications/plagiarism/OnlineSources.html

Birch, D., & Gardiner, M. (2005, December 5-7). Students' perceptions of technology-based marketing courses. In *Paper presented at the ANZMAC 2005 Conference: Broadening the Boundaries,* Fremantle, Western Australia.

Birinci, G., & Odabasi, H. F. (2006, April 19-21). Akademik calismalarda Internet kullanimi: Etik bunun neresinde? (Use of Internet for academic endeavors: Where does ethics lie?). In *Proceedings of the 6th International Educational Technology Conference,* (pp. 289-295). Famagusta, Turkish Republic of Northern Cyprus.

Blacker, D., & McKie, J. (2003). Information and communication technology. In N. Blake, P. Smeyers, R. Smith, & P. Standish (Eds.), *The Blackwell guide to the philosophy of education* (pp. 234-252). Malden, MA: Blackwell.

Blass, E. (2005). The rise and rise of the corporate university. *Journal of European Industrial Training, 29*(1), 58-74.

Blatt, M., & Kohlberg, L. (1975). The effects of classroom moral discussion on children's level of moral development. *Journal of Moral Education, 4.*

Bloom, B. S. (1956). *Taxonomy of educational objectives: Handbook 1: The cognitive domain.* New York: David McKay.

Bloomer, M. (2001, September). Young lives, learning and transformation: Some theoretical considerations. *Oxford Review of Education, 27*(3), 429-449.

Bodi, S. (1998). Ethics and information technology: Some principles to guide students. *Journal of Academic Librarianship, 24*(6), 459-463.

Bogdan, R., & Biklen, S. (1992). *Qualitative research for education* (2nd ed.). Toronto, Canada: Allyn and Bacon.

Boler, M. (1999). *Feeling power: Emotions and education.* New York and London: Routledge.

Boob, V. (2006). People, problems, and passwords. *IT Trends, 66,* 8-10.

Born, A. D. (2003). How to reduce plagiarism. *Journal of Information Systems Education, 14*(3), 223.

Boschmann, E. (1996). *The electronic classroom: A handbook for education in the electronic environment.* Medford, NJ: Learned Information.

Boud, D. (1988). Moving toward student autonomy. In D. Boud (Ed.), *Developing student autonomy in learning* (2nd ed., pp. 17-39). London: Kogan Page.

Boud, D., Keogh, R., & Walker, D. (Eds.). (1985). *Reflection: Turning experiences into learning.* London: RoutledgeFalmer.

Bowers, W. J. (1964). *Student dishonesty and its control in college.* New York: Bureau of Applied Social Research, Columbia University.

Bowyer, K. (1996). *Ethics and computing: Living responsibly in a computerized world.* IEEE Computer Society Press.

Boyer, E. L. (1987). *College: The undergraduate experience in America.* New York: Harper & Row.

Boyer, E. L. (1990). *Scholarship reconsidered. Priorities of the professoriate*. Princeton, NJ: The Carnegie Foundation for the Advancement of Teaching.

Branigan, C. (2001). Rutgers study: Web makes student cheating easier. *E-school News Online*. Retrieved April 16, 2008, from http://www.eschoolnews.org/showstory.cfm?ArticleID=2638

Brazilian Association for Distance Education. (2000, August 17). A code of ethics for distance education. In *Proceedings of the General Assembly of the Association*, Sao Paulo, Brazil. Retrieved April 15, 2008, from http://www.friends-partners.org/GLOSAS/Global_University/Guideline/List_of_Materials.html

Brennan, L. L., & Johnson, V. E. (2004). *Social, ethical and policy implications of information technology*. Hershey, PA: Information Science.

Bretch, B. (1995). Life of Galileo. In J. Willett & R. Manheim (Eds.), *Bertolt Brecht collected plays: Five* (pp. 1-105) (J. Willett, Trans.). London: Methuen.

Bridge, W. (2006). Non-traditional learners in higher education. In P. Ashwin (Ed.), *Changing higher education: The development of learning and teaching* (pp. 58-68). London: RoutledgeFalmer.

Bridges, E. (1992). Problem-based learning: Background and rationale. In E. M. Bridges (Ed.), *Problem-based learning for administrators*. Eugene, OR: ERIC.

Bromley, H. (1997). The social chicken and the technological egg: Educational computing and the technology/society divide. *Educational Theory, 47*(1), 51-65.

Brown, B. S. (1995). The academic ethics of graduate business students: A survey. *Journal of Education for Business, 70*, 151-157.

Brown, V. J., & Howell, M. E. (2001). The efficacy of policy statements on plagiarism: Do they change students' views? *Research in Higher Education, 42*, 103-118.

Bruce, B. C. (1996). Technology as social practice. *Educational Foundations, 10*(4), 51-58.

Bruce, B. C. (1998). Speaking the unspeakable about 21st century technologies. In G. E. Hawisher & S. E. Selfe (Eds.), *Passions, pedagogies and 21st century technologies* (pp. 221-228). Logan, UT: Utah State University Press.

Bruckman, A. (2002). *Ethical guidelines for research online*. Retrieved April 22, 2008, from http://www.cc.gatech.edu/~asb/ethics/

Brynum, T. W. (2001). *Computer ethics: Basic concepts and historical overview*. Retrieved April 22, 2008, from http://plato.stanford.edu/entries/ethics-computer/

Bryon-miller, M., & Greenwood, D. (2006). A re-examination of the relationship between action research and human subjects review processes. *Action Research, 4*(1), 117-128.

Buchanan, E. (2004). Ethical considerations for the information professions. In R. Spinello and H. Tavani (Eds.), *Readings in cyberethics* (2nd ed.). Jones and Bartlett.

Buchanan, E. (2004). Ethics in library and information science: What are we teaching? *Journal of Information Ethics, 13*(1), 51-60.

Bucharest Declaration. (2004). The Bucharest Declaration concerning ethical values and principles for higher education in the Europe region. *Higher Education in Europe, 29*(4), 503-507.

Bull, J., Collins, C., Coughlin, E., & Sharp, D. (2001). *Technical review of plagiarism detection software report*. Retrieved April 15, 2008, from http://www.jiscpas.ac.uk/images/bin/luton.pdf#search=%22technical%20review%20of%20plagiarism%20detection%20software%20report%22

Bulmer, M. (1982). The merits and demerits of covert participant observation. In M. Bulmer (Ed.), *Social research ethics* (pp. 217-251). London: Macmillan.

Bunge, M. (1977). Towards a technoethics. *Monist, 60*, 96-107.

Burbules, N. C., & Callister, T. A., Jr. (2000). Universities in transition: The promise and the challenge of new technologies. *Teachers College Record, 102*(2), 271-293.

Burbules, N.C., & Callister, T.A., Jr. (2000). *Watch it!: The risks and promises of information technologies for education.* Boulder, CO: Westview.

Burgess, R. G. (1984). *In the field: An introduction to field research.* London: Routledge.

Burniske, R.W. (1999, November). Iban on the Infobahn: Can we integrate the Global Village without annihilating cultures? *The English Journal, 89*(2), 131-135.

Bushweller, K. (1999). Generation of cheaters. *The American School Board Journal.* Retrieved April 16, 2008, from www.asbj.com/199904/0499coverstory.html

Bynum, T. (2001, Winter). Computer ethics: Basic concepts and historical overview. In E. N. Zalta (Ed.), *The Stanford encyclopedia of philosophy.* Retrieved April 16, 2008, from http://plato.stanford.edu/archives/win2001/entries/ethics-computer

Bynum, T. W. (Ed.). (1985, October). *Computers & Ethics, 6*(4). Basil Blackwell.

Bynum, T. W., & Rogerson, S. (2004). *Computer ethics and professional responsibility.* Malden, USA: Blackwell.

Bynum, T. W., Maner, W., & Fodor, J. (Eds.). (1992). *Teaching computer ethics.* New Haven: Southern Connecticut State University, Research Center on Computing and Society.

Caffarella, R. S. (1988). Ethical dilemmas in the teaching of adults. In R.G. Brockett (Ed.), *Ethical issues in adult education* (pp. 103-117). New York: Teachers College Press.

Cameron, J., Shaw, G., & Arnott, A. (Eds.). (2002). *Tertiary teaching: Doing it differently, doing it better.* Darwin: NTU Press and Centre for Teaching and Learning in Diverse Educational Contexts.

Campbell, E. (2003). *The ethical teacher.* Maidenhead: Open University Press.

Campbell, M. A. (2005). Cyber bullying: An old problem in a new guise? *Australian Journal of Guidance and Counselling, 15*(1), 68-76.

Canny, J., & Paulos, E. (2000).Tele-embodiment and shattered presence: Reconstructing the body for online interaction. In K. Goldberg (Ed.), *The robot in the garden: Telepistemology in the age of the Internet* (pp. 276-294). Cambridge, MA: MIT Press.

Capurro, R. (2000). Ethical challenges of the information society in the 21st century. *The International Information & Library Review, 32*(3/4), 257-276.

Capurro, R. (2005). Privacy: An intercultural perspective. *Ethics and Information Technology, 7*(1), 37-47.

Capurro, R., & Christoph, P. (2002). Ethical issues of online communication research. *Ethics and Information Technology, 4*(3), 189-194.

Capurro, R., & Pingel, C. (2002). Ethical issues of online communication research. *Ethics and Information Technology, 4*(3), 189-194.

Carbo, T., & Almagno, S. (2001). Information ethics: The duty, privilege and challenge of educating information professionals. *Library Trends, 49*(3), 510-518.

Carey, S. F. (2003). Combating plagiarism. *Phi Delta Kappa Fastbacks, 514*, 7-32.

Carnevale, D. (1999, November 8). How to proctor from a distance. *The Chronicle of Higher Education.* Retrieved April 16, 2008, from http://www.ou.edu./archives/it-fyi/0716.html

Carr, D. (2000). *Professionalism and ethics in teaching.* New York: Routledge Taylor and Francis Group.

Carroll, D. (2002, February 8). Cheating in classrooms reflects a growing culture of dishonesty, some say. *Kansas City Star*, p.1.

Case, P., & Elliot, B. (1997). Attrition and retention in distance learning programs, problems, strategies, and solutions. *Open Praxis*, (1), 30-33.

Casey, T., & Embree, L. (1990). Introduction. In T. Casey & L. Embree (Eds.), *Lifeworld and technology: Current continental research 009* (pp. vii-xi). Washington, DC: Center for Advanced Research in Phenomenology & University Press of America.

Castells, M. (1993). The informational economy and the new International Division of Labor. In M. Carnoy, M. Castells, S. S. Cohen, & F. H. Cardoso (Eds.), *The new global economy in the information age: Reflections on our changing world* (pp. 15-43). University Park, PA: Pennsylvania State University Press.

Cavalier, R. (Ed.). (2005). *The Internet and our moral lives.* Albany, NY: State University of New York Press.

Cavazos, E. A., & Morin, G. (1994). *Cyberspace and the law: Your rights and duties in the online world.* Cambridge, MA: MIT Press.

Center for Academic Integrity (CAI). (1999, October). *The fundamental values of academic integrity.* Retrieved April 22, 2008, from http://www.academicintegrity.org/fundamental_values_project/pdf/FVProject.pdf

Centers for Disease Control and Prevention (CDC). (2005). *The Tuskegee timeline.* Retrieved April 23, 2008, from: http://www.cdc.gov/nchstp/od/tuskegee/time.htm

Chachra, D. (2005). Beyond course-based engineering ethics instruction: Commentary on "topics and cases for online education in engineering." *Science and Engineering Ethics, 11*(3), 459-461.

Chakrapani, P. N., & Ekbia, H. R. (2004). Opening up technological education: The perspective from social informatics. *IEEE,* 144-147.

Chapman, K. J., & Lupton, R. A. (2004). Academic dishonesty in a global educational market: A comparison of Hong Kong and American university business students. *The International Journal of Educational Management, 12*(7), 425- 435.

Chapman, K., Davis, R., Toy, D., & Wright, L. (2004). Academic integrity in the business school environment: I'll get by with a little help from my friends. *Journal of Marketing Education, 26,* 236-249.

Chavez, M. (2002, Autumn). We say "culture" and students ask "What?": University students' definitions of foreign language culture. *Die Unterrichtspraxis/Teaching German, 35*(2), 129-140.

Cheaters amok: A crisis in America's schools—how it's done and why it's happening. (2004, April 29). *ABC Primetime News.* Retrieved April 16, 2008, from http://listserv.uiuc.edu/wa.cgi?A2=indo405 &L=dime-1&T=0&F=&S==&p=69

Cheating thrives on campus, as officials turn their heads. (2001, May 21). *USA Today,* p. 13A.

Chen, Y-J., & Willits, F.K. (1999). Dimensions of educational transactions in a video-conferencing learning environment. *American Journal of Distance Education, 13*(1), 45-59.

Chester, A., & Gwynne, G. (1998, December). Online teaching: Encouraging collaboration through anonymity. *Journal of Computer-Mediated Communication, 4*(2), n.p.

Children's Workforce Development Council. (2006). *Developing the early years workforce.* Retrieved April 23, 2008, from http://www.cwdcouncil.org.uk/projects/earlyyears.htm

Chozos, P., Lytras, M., & Pouloudi, N. (2002, October 15-19). Ethical issues in the learning: Insights from the application of stakeholder analysis in three e-learning cases. In *Proceedings of the E-learn 2002 World Conference on E-learning in Corporate, Government, Health Care, and Higher Education.* Association for the Advancement of Computing in Education. ERIC Documents: ED 479443.

Christians, C. (2000). Ethics and politics in qualitative research. In N. K. Denzin & Y. S. Lincoln (Eds.), *Handbook of qualitative research* (pp. 133-155). London: Sage.

Cizek, G. (1999). *Cheating on tests: How to do it, detect it and prevent it.* Mahwah, NJ: Lawrence Erlbaum.

Clark, R. C., & Mayer, R. E. (2003). *E-Learning and the science of instruction: Proven guidelines for consumers and designers of multimedia learning.* San Francisco: Jossey-Bass/Pfeiffer.

Clarke, M., Butler, C., Schmidt-Hansen, P., & Somerville, M. (2004). Quality assurance for distance learning: A case study at Brunel University. *British Journal of Educational Technology, 35*(1), 5-11.

Clarkeburn, H.M., Downie, J.R., Gray, C., & Matthew, R. G. S. Measuring ethical development in life sciences students: A study using Perry's developmental model. *Studies in Higher Education, 28*(4), 443-456.

Clegg, S., Hudson, A., & Steel, J. (2003). The emperor's new clothes: Globalization and e-learning in higher education. *British Journal of Sociology of Education, 24*(1), 39-53.

Clos, K. (2002). When academic dishonesty happens on your campus. *National Institute for Staff and Organizational Development* (Vol. XXIV, No. 26). ISOD Innovation Abstracts. College of Education, The University of Texas at Austin.

Clutterbuck, D. (1995). Managing customer defection. *Customer Service Management,* (7).

Coffield, F., Moseley, D., Hall, E., & Ecclestone, K. (2004). *Learning styles for post 16 learners: What do we know?* London: Learning and Skills Research Centre.

Coffield, F., Moseley, D., Hall, E., & Ecclestone, K. (2004). *Should we be using learning styles? What research has to say to practice.* London: Learning and Skills Research Centre.

Cole, S., Coates, M., & Lentell, H. (1986). Towards good teaching by correspondence. *Open Learning, 11*(1), 16-22.

Collins, A., Brown, J. S., & Newman, S. (1989). Cognitive apprenticeship: Teaching the crafts of reading, writing, and mathematics. In L. B. Resnick (Ed.), *Knowing, learning, and instruction: Essays in honor of Robert Glaser* (pp. 453-494). Hillsdale, NJ: Lawrence Erlbaum.

Collins, W. R., & Miller, K. W. (1992, January). Paramedic ethics for computer professionals. *Journal of Systems and Software, 17*, 23-38.

Colvin, J., & Lanigan, J. (2005). Ethical issues and best practice considerations for Internet research. *Journal of Family and Consumer Sciences, 97*(3), 34-39.

Comor, E. (2001, September). The role of communication in global civil society: Forces, processes, prospects. *International Studies Quarterly, 45*(3), 389-408.

Complexity of the IRB process: Some of the things you wanted to know about IRBs but were afraid to ask. (2005). *American Journal of Evaluation, 26*(3), 353-361.

Connell, J. (1994). Virtual reality check: Cyberethics, consumerism and the American soul. *Media Studies Journal, 8*(1), 152-159.

Conrad, D. (2002). Deep in the hearts of learners: Insights into the nature of online community. *Journal of Distance Education, 17*(1). Retrieved April 15, 2008, from http://cade.athabascau.ca/vol17.1/conrad.html

Conradson, S., & Hernansez-Ramos, P. (2004). Computers, the Internet, and cheating among secondary school students: Some implications for educators. *Practical Assessment, Research and Evaluation, 9*(9). Retrieved April 22, 2008, from http://pareonline.net/getvn.asp?v=9&n=9

Cookson, P. (2002). The hybridization of higher education: Cross-national perspectives. *International Review of Research in Open and Distance Learning, 2*(2), 1-4.

Cooper, D. E. (2004). *Ethics for professionals in a multicultural world.* Upper Saddle, River, NJ: Pearson/Prentice Hall.

Corder, S., & Ruby, R., Jr. (1996. Using the Internet and the World Wide Web: The international connection. *Business Education Forum,* 31-32.

Cornman, J. W., Lehrer, K., & Pappas, G. S. (1982). The problem of justifying an ethical standard. *Philosophical problems and arguments: An introduction* (3rd ed.). Retrieved April 15, 2008, from http://www.ditext.com/cornman/corn6.html

Cortés, P. A. (2005). Educational technology as a means to an end. *Educational Technology Review, 13*(1), 73-90.

Costley, C., & Gibbs, P. (2006). Researching others: Care as an ethic for practitioner researchers. *Studies in Higher Education, 31*(1), 89-98.

Council of Writing Program Administrators. (2003). Defining and avoiding plagiarism: The WPA statement on best practices. Retrieved April 15, 2008, from http://www.wpacouncil.org/positions/WPAplagiarism.pdf

Crane, A., & Matten, D. (2007). *Business ethics* (2nd ed.). Oxford.

Creswell, J. W. (2003). *Research design: Qualitative, quantitative, and mixed methods approaches* (2nd ed.). London: Sage.

Crisp, G., Thiele, D., Scholten, I., Barker, S., & Baron, J. (2003, December 7-10). Interact, Integrate, Impact. In *Proceedings of the 20th Annual Conference of the Australasian Society for Computers in Learning in Tertiary Education*, Adelaide, Australia, (pp. 1-12).

Cromwell, S. (2000, January 24). What can we do to curb student cheating? *Education World.* Retrieved April 22, 2008, from http://www.education-world.com/a_admin/admin144.shtml

Crosling, G., & Webb, G. (2002). Introducing student learning support. In G. Crosling & G. Webb (Eds.), *Supporting student learning: Case studies experience and practice from higher education.* London: Kogan Page.

Crosta, L. (2004). Beyond the use of new technologies and adult distance courses: An ethical approach. *International Journal on E-Learning, 3*(1), 48-60.

Crown, D. F., & Spiller, M. S. (1998). Learning from the literature on collegiate cheating: A review of empirical research. *Journal of Business Ethics, 17*, 683-700.

Daft, R. L., & Lengel, R. H. (1986). Organizational information requirements, media richness and structural design. *Management Science, 32*, 554-571.

Daniel, J., & West, P. (2006). From digital divide to digital dividend: What will it take? [Electronic Version]. *Innovate, 2.* Retrieved April 22, 2008, from http://www.innovateonline.info/index.php?view=article&id=252

Darbyshire, P., & Burgess, S. (2006). Strategies for dealing with plagiarism and the Web in higher education. *Journal of Business Systems, Governance and Ethics, 1*, 27-39. Retrieved April 22, 2008, from http://www.jbsge.vu.edu.au/issues/vol01no4/Darbyshire-Burgess.pdf

Davis, M. (1999). *Ethics and the university.* London & New York: Routledge.

Davis, M. (2004, Spring). Five kinds of ethics across the curriculum: An introduction to four experiments with one kind, *Teaching Ethics, 4*, 1-14.

Davis, S. F., Noble, L. M., Zak, E. N., & Dreyer, K. K. (1994). A comparison of cheating and learning/grade orientation in American and Australian college students. *College Student Journal, 28*, 353-356.

Daycare Trust. (2003). *Towards universal childcare: Analysing childcare in 2003.* London: Daycare Trust.

De Freitas, S. (2005). Does e-learning policy drive change in higher education? A case study relating models of organisational change to e-learning implementation. *Journal of Higher Education Policy and Management, 27*(1), 81-95.

De George, R.T. (2006). *Business ethics* (6th ed.). Prentice Hall.

Decoo, W. (2002). *Crisis on campus: Confronting academic misconduct.* Cambridge, MA: MIT Press.

DeGeorge, R. (1990). *Business ethics* (3rd ed.). New York: Macmillan.

DeGeorge, R. (2006). Information technology, globalization and ethics. *Ethics and Information Technology, 8*, 29-40.

Demiray, U., et al. (2004). *A review of the literature on the Open Education Faculty in Turkey (1982-2002)* (4th rev. ed.). E-book, Electronic ISBN 98590-2-5, Sakarya University, Turkey. Retrieved April 16, 2008, from http://www.tojet.net

Demiray, U., Nagy, J., & Yilmaz, A. (2007). Strategies for the marketing of higher education–with comparative contextual references between Australia and Turkey. *The Turkish Online Journal of Distance Education, 8*(2), Article 14.

Department of Education, Science and Training (DEST). (2007). *Higher education report 2005.* Australian Government.

Department of Education, Science and Training. (2007). *OECD thematic review of tertiary education: Country background report Australia.* Paris: Organisation for Economic Cooperation and Development. Retrieved April 22, 2008, from http://www.oecd.org/dataoecd/51/60/38759740.pdf

DePorter, B. (1992). *Quantum learning: Unleashing the genius in you.* New York: Dell.

Detardo-bora, K.A. (2004). Action research in a world of positivist-oriented review boards. *Action Research, 2*(3), 237-253.

Devlin, M., & Gray, K. (2007). In their own words: A qualitative study of the reasons Australian university students plagiarize. *Higher Education Research & Development, 26*(2), 181-198.

DeVoss, D., & Rosati, A. (2002). It wasn't me, was it? Plagiarism and the Web. *Computers and Composition, 19*, 191-203.

Dewey, J. (1933). *How we think: A restatement of the relation of reflective thinking to the educative process.* New York: D. C. Heath and Company.

Dibiase, D. (2000). Is distance education a Faustian bargain? *Journal of Geography in Higher Education, 24*(1), 130-135.

Diekhoff, G. M., LaBeff, E. E., Shinohara, K., & Yasukawa, H. (1999). College cheating in Japan and the United States. *Research in Higher Education, 40*(13), 343-345.

Dietz, T. L. (2002, January). Predictors of success in large enrollment introductory courses: An examination of the impact of learning communities and virtual learning resources on student success in an introductory level sociology course. *Teaching Sociology, 30*(1), 80-88.

Dirks, M. (1998, May). How is assessment being done in distance learning? In *Paper presented at the Northern Arizona University Web.95 Conference.*

Dobos, J. (1996). Collaborative learning: Effects of students expectations and communication apprehension on student motivation. *Communication Education, 45*(2), 15-29.

Doherty, K. M., & Orlofsky, G. F. (2001). Student survey says: Schools are probably not using educational technology as wisely or effectively as they could. *Education Week, 20*(35), 45-48.

Dohy, L. (2004, February 29). Clear policy needed for medical research trials. *The Edmonton Journal*, p. E10.

Donohue, C. (2002). It's a small world: Taking your first steps into online teaching and learning. *Childcare Information Exchange, 9*, 20-24.

Donohue, C., & Clark, D. (2004, November). Learning online: The places you'll go! *Child Care Information Exchange*, 49-54. Retrieved April 23, 2008, from www.childcareexchange.com

Donohue, C., & Neugebauer, R. (2004, May). Innovations in e-learning: New promise for professional development. *Young Children*, 22-25. Retrieved April 23, 2008, from www.journal.naeyc.org/btj/

Donohue, C., Fox, S., & LaBonte, M. (2004, July). E-learning: What out students can teach us. *Child Care Information Exchange*, 79-82. Retrieved April 23, 2008, from www.childcareexchange.com

Douglas, J. (1976). *Investigative social research: Individual and team research.* London: Sage.

Doyle, T. (2002). A critical discussion of "The ethical presuppositions behind the Library Bill of Rights." *Library Quarterly, 72*(3), 275-293.

Dreyfus, H. L. (2001). *On the Internet.* London: Routledge.

Driver, A. (2001). *Access to IT.* Report to the UK Open University Learning and Teaching Innovation Committee.

Dunlop, C., & Kling, R. (Eds.). (1991). *Computerization & controversy: Value conflicts & social choices.* Academic Press.

Dutton, W. H., Cheong, P. H., & Park, N. (2004). An ecology of constraints on e-learning in higher education: The case of a virtual learning environment. *Prometheus, 22*(2), 131-149.

Edmundson, A. (2007). *Globalized e-learning cultural challenges.* Hershey, PA: Idea Group.

Ellenberg, J. H. (1983). Ethical guidelines for statistical practice: A historical perspective. *The American Statistician, 37*(1), 1-13.

Elliott, C. (2008, January 7). Guinea-pigging. *The New Yorker*, pp. 36-41.

Elliott, C., & Lemmens, T. (2005, December 13). Ethics for sale. *Slate.* Retrieved April 23, 2008, from http://www.slatetv.net/id/2132187/

Eplion, D., & Keefe, T. (2005). On-line exams: Strategies to detect cheating and minimize its impact. Retrieved April 22, 2008, from http://www.mtsu.edu/~itconf/proceed05/dEplion.pdf

Ercegovac, Z., & Richardson, J. V. (2004). Academic dishonesty, plagiarism included, in the digital age: A literature review. *College & Research Libraries, 65*(4), 301-318.

Erdmann, M. D., Willimas, M. B., & Gutierrez, C. (1990). *Computers, ethics and society.* Oxford University Press.

Ermann, M. D., Williams, M. B., & Shauf, M. S. (Eds.). (1997). *Computers, ethics, and society.* New York: Oxford University Press.

Ess, C., & Association of Internet Researchers (AoIR) Ethics Working Committee. (2002). *Ethical decision-making and Internet research. Recommendations from the AoIR Ethics Working Committee.* Retrieved April 22, 2008, from http://www.aoir.org/reports/ethics.pdf

Ethical standards and procedures for research with human beings. World Health Organization (WHO). Retrieved April 23, 2008, from http://www.who.int/ethics/research/en/

Ethics Codes Guide of Anadolu University. (2002). *Anadolu University Council of Ethics Center-AUCEC.* Anadolu University Publications, Eskisehir Turkey. Retrieved April 16, 2008, from http://www.anadolu.edu.tr

Evans, E. D., Craig, D., & Mietzel, G. (1993). Adolescents' cognitions and attributions for academic cheating: A cross-national study. *The Journal of Psychology, 127*(6), 585-602.

Evans, T., & Jakupec, V. (1996). Research ethics in open and distance education: Context, principles and issues. *Distance Education, 17*(1), 72-94.

Evans, T., & Nation, D. (2000). *Changing university teaching: Reflections on creating educational technologies.* London: Kogan Page.

Fahy, P. J. (2001). Addressing some common problems in transcript analysis. *The International Review of Research in Open and Distance Learning, 1*(2). Retrieved April 23, 2008, from http://www.irrodl.org/content/v1.2/research.html#Fahy

Fahy, P. J. (2002). Epistolary and expository interaction patterns in a computer conference transcript. *Journal of Distance Education, 17*(1), 20-35.

Fahy, P. J. (2003). Indicators of support in online interaction. *International Review of Research in Open and Distance Learning, 4*(1). Retrieved April 23, 2008, from http://www.irrodl.org/content/v4.1/fahy.html

Fahy, P. J. (2004, November 22-24). Use of the Bales model for analysis of small group communications in the analysis of interaction in computer-based asynchronous conferences. In M. Boumedine & S. Ranka (Eds.), *Proceedings of the IASTED International Conference on*

Knowledge Sharing and Collaborative Engineering, St. Thomas, U.S. Virgin Islands. Calgary: ACTA Press.

Fahy, P. J. (2005, March). Two methods for assessing critical thinking in computer-mediated communications (CMC) transcripts. *International Journal of Instructional Technology and Distance Learning*. Retrieved April 23, 2008, from http://www.itdl.org/Journal/Mar_05/article02.htm

Fahy, P. J., & Spencer, B. (2004). Research experience and agreement with selected ethics principles from Canada's Tri-Council Policy Statement–Ethical Conduct for Research Involving Humans. *Journal of Distance Education, 19*(2), 28-58.

Fahy, P. J., Crawford, G., & Ally, M. (2001). Patterns of interaction in a computer conference transcript. *International Review of Research in Open and Distance Learning, 2*(1). Retrieved April 23, 2008, from http://www.irrodl.org/content/v2.1/fahy.html

Fallis, D. (2007). Information ethics for 21st century library professionals. *Library Hi Tech*, 25(1).

Farmer, L. (2004). Narrative inquiry as assessment tool: A case study. *Journal of Education for Library & Information Science, 45*(4), 340-355.

Farmer, L. (2004). Foundations of information: A course case study in metacognition. *Journal of Education for Library & Information Science, 45*(3), 180-188.

Fass, R. A. (1990). Cheating and plagiarism. In W. W. May (Ed.), *Ethics and higher education*. New York: Macmillan Publishing Company and American Council on Education. In D. Gearhart. (2000). Ethics in distance education: Developing ethical policies. *Online Journal of Distance Learning Administration, 4*(1). State University of West Georgia, Distance Education Center.

Feiser, L. B. (1964). *The scientific method: A personal account of unusual projects in war and peace*. New York: Reyhold.

Fieser, J. (2007). *The Internet encyclopedia of philosophy*. Retrieved April 16, 2008, from http://www.utm.edu/`jfieser/

Figueiredo, A.D., & Afonso, A.P. (2006). *Managing learning in Virtual settings—the role of context*. London: Information Science.

Finch, E. (2007). The problem of stolen identity and the Internet. In Y Jewkes (Ed.), *Crime on-line* (pp. 29-43). Cullompton: Willan.

Fisher, C., & Lovell, A. (2006). *Business ethics and values* (2nd ed.). Harlow: Prentice Hall.

Floridi, L. (2000). *Information ethics: On the philosophical foundation of computer ethics*. Retrieved April 15, 2008, from http://www.wolfson.ox.ac.uk/~floridi/ie.htm

Ford, R.C., & Richardson, W.D. (1994). Ethical decision-making: A review of the empirical literature. *Journal of Business Ethics, 13*(3), 205-221.

Forester, T., & Morrison, P. (1994). *Computer ethics cautionary tales and ethical dilemmas in computing* (2nd ed., pp. 261-270). Cambridge, MA: The MIT Press.

Foster, A. L. (2002). Plagiarism-detection tool creates legal quandary. The *Chronicle of Higher Education, 48*, A37-38.

Frankel, M. S. (1989). Professional codes: Why, how, and with what impact? *Journal of Business Ethics, 8*(2 & 3), 109-116.

Frankel, M. S., & Siang, S. (1999). *Ethical and legal aspects of human subjects research on the Internet*. Retrieved April 22, 2008, from http://www.aaas.org/spp/dspp/sfrl/projects/intres/main.htm

Frankfort-Nachmias, C., & Nachmias, D. (1996). *Research methods in the social sciences* (5th ed.). New York: St Martin's Press.

Franklyn-Stokes, A., & Newstead, S. E. (1995). Undergraduate cheating: Who does what and why? *Studies in Higher Education, 20*(2), 159-72.

Freire, P. (1998). *Pedagogy of freedom: Ethics, democracy and civic courage*. Lanham, MD: Rowman and Littlefield.

Friedman, L. (2001). The social responsibility of business is to increase its profits. In T. L. Beauchamp & N. E. Bowie (Eds.), *Ethical theory and business* (6th ed., pp. 51-55). Upper Saddle River, NJ: Prentice Hall.

Froehlich, T. (2005). A brief history of information ethics. *Computer Society of India Communications, 28*(12), 11-13.

Fulton, J., & Kellinger, K. (2004). An ethics framework for nursing education on the Internet. *Nursing Education Perspectives, 25*(2), 62-66.

Furedi, F. (2002, January 11). Don't rock the research boat. *The Times Higher Education Supplement* (pp. 20-21). Retrieved April 22, 2008, from: http://www.thes.co.uk/

Fussell, J. A. (2005, May 15). Cheaters use new array of gadgets to get that "A." *The Kansas City Star,* p. A1.

Gabbott, M., Mavondo, F., & Tsarenko, Y. (2002). International student satisfaction: Role of resources and capabilities. *Academic Exchange,* 170-176.

Gaide, S. (2004, June 15). Teaching ethical business practice online. *Distance Education Report, 8*(12), 8.

Galbraith, K. (2003). Towards quality private education in Central and Eastern Europe. *Higher Education in Europe, XXVIII*(4), 539-558.

Gallant, P. B., & Drinan, P. (2006). Organisational theory and student cheating: Explanation, responses, and strategies. *Journal of Higher Education,* 839-861.

Gallie, K., & Joubert, D. (2004). Paradigm shift: From traditional to on-line education. *Studies in Learning, Evaluation Innovation and Development, 1*(1), 32-36.

Galus, P. (2002). Detecting and preventing plagiarism. *The Science Teacher, 69*(8), 35-37.

Gardner, V. (2005). Uncontested terrains: A personal journey through image, (national) identity and ethics. *Research in Drama Education, 10*(2), 175-188.

Garoogian, R. (1991). Librarian/patron confidentiality: An ethical challenge. *Library Trends, 40*(2), 216-233.

Garrard, D. J. (2002). *A question of ethics.* Retrieved April 15, 2008, from http://www.watton.org/ethics/subject/ethics/index.html

Garrison, D. R., & Anderson, T. (2003). *E-learning in the 21st Century.* London: Routledge-Falmer.

Garrison, D. R., Anderson, T., & Archer, W. (2001). Critical thinking, cognitive presence, and computer conferencing in distance education. *The American Journal of Distance Education, 15*(1), 7-23.

Garrison, D.R, Anderson, T., & Archer, W. (2000). Critical inquiry in a text-based environment: Computer conferencing in higher education. *The Internet and Higher Education, 2*(2-3), 1-19.

Garrison, D.R., Cleveland-Innes, M., Koole, M., & Kappelman. (2005). Revisiting methodological issues in transcript analysis: Negotiated coding and reliability. *Internet and Higher Education, 9*(2006), 1-8. Retrieved April 23, 2008, from http://www.elsevier.com/wps/find/journaldescription.cws_home/620187/description#description

Garrison, R., Anderson, T., & Archer, W. (2000). Critical inquiry in a text-based environment: Computer conferencing in higher education. *Internet and Higher Education, 2*(2), 87-105.

Gaskell, A. Gibbons, S., & Simpson, O. (1990). Taking off and bailing out. *Open Learning, 3*(2), 49.

Gaskell, G., Thompson P. B., & Allum, N. (2002). Worlds apart? Public opinion in Europe and the USA. In M. W. Bauer & G. Gaskell (Eds.), *Biotechnology: The making of a global controversy* (pp. 351-375). UK: Cambridge University Press.

Gattiker, U. E., & Kelley, H. (1999). Morality and computers: Attitudes and differences in moral judgments. *Information Systems Research, 10,* 233-254.

Gearhart, D. (2000). Ethics in distance education: Developing ethical policies. *The Online Journal of Distance Learning Administration, 4*(1). Retrieved April 16, 2008, from Http://www.westga.edu/~distance/ojdla/spring41/gearhart41.html

Gearhart, D. (2001). Ethics in distance education: Developing ethical policies. *Journal of Distance Learning Administration, 4*(1). Retrieved April 15, 2008, from http://www.westga.edu/~distance/ojdla/spring41/gearhart41.html

Gehring, D. D. (1998). When institutions and their faculty address issues of academic dishonesty: Realities and myths. *Academic Integrity Matters,* 77-92.

George, J., & Carlson, J. (1999, January). Group support systems and deceptive communication. In *Proceedings of the 32nd Hawaii International Conference on Systems Sciences,* (p. 1038).

Gerring, J. (2007). *Case study research: Principles and practices.* New York: Cambridge University Press.

Ghoshal, S. (2005). Bad management theories are destroying good management practice. *Academy of Management Learning and Education, 4*(1), 75-91.

Gibbs, G., Morgan, A., & Taylor, E. (1984). The world of the learner. In F. Marton, D. Hounsell, & N.J. Entwistle (Eds.), *The experience of learning* (pp. 165-188). Edinburgh, Scotland: Scottish Academic Press.

Gibbs, L., & Gambrill, E. (2002). Evidence-based practice: Counterarguments to objections. *Research on Social Work Practice, 12*(3), 452-476.

Gibelman, M., Gelman, S. R., & Fast, J. (1999). The downside of cyberspace: Cheating made easy. *Journal of Social Work Education, 35*(3), 67-76.

Gitanjali, B. (2004). Academic dishonesty in Indian medical colleges. *Journal of Postgraduate Medicine, 50*(4), 281-284.

Gladieux, L.E., & Swail, W.S. (1999). *The virtual university and educational opportunities.* Washington, DC: The College Board.

Gleason, D. H. (2001). Subsumption ethics. In R. Spinello & H. Tavani (Eds.), *Readings in cyberethics* (pp. 557-571). Subdury, MA: Jones and Barlett.

Glen, S. (2000). The dark side of purity or the virtues of double-mindedness? In H. Simons & R. Usher (Eds.), *Situated ethics in educational research* (pp. 12-21). New York: RoutledgeFalmer.

Global Reach. (2004). *Global Internet statistics (by Language).* Retrieved April 23, 2008, from http://www.glreach.com/globstats/index.php3

Goleman, D. (2005). *Emotional intelligence.* New York: Bantam.

Gordon, W., & Sork, T. (2001). Ethical issues and codes of ethics: Views of adult education practitioners in Canada and the United States. *Adult Education Quarterly, 51*(3), 202-218.

Gorman, M. (2000). *Our enduring values: Librarianship in the 21st century.* Chicago, IL: American Library Association.

Gorry, G. A. (2003, May 23). Steal this MP3 file. *The Chronicle of Higher Education,* p. B20.

Gorsky, P., & Caspi, A. (2005). A critical analysis of transactional distance theory. *Quarterly Review of Distance Education, 6*(1), 1-11. Retrieved April 15, 2008, from http://telem.openu.ac.il/hp_files/pdf/Gorsky.pdf

Gotterbarn, D. (1991, Summer). Computer ethics: Responsibility regained. *National Forum,* 26-32.

Gotterbarn, D. (1992, August). Ethics and the computing professional. *Collegiate Microcomputer, 10*(3).

Gould, C. (1989). *The information Web: Ethical and social implications of computer networking.* Westview Press.

Gourley, B. (2007). Foreword. *Open Learning, 22*(2), 105.

Graham, C., Cagiltay, K., Lim, B., Craner, J., & Duffy, T. M. (2001). *Seven principles of effective teaching: A practical lens for evaluation online courses.* Assessment. Retrieved April 22, 2008, from http://technologysource.org/?view=article&id=274

Graham, M. A., Monday, J., O'Brien, K., & Steffen, S. (1994). Cheating at small colleges: An examination of student and faculty attitudes and behaviors. *Journal of College Student Development, 35,* 255-260.

Grice, H. P. (1975). Logic and conversation. In P. Cole & J. L. Morgan (Eds.), *Syntax and semantics: Speech acts* (Vol. 3). New York: Academic Press.

Gross, J. (2003, November 26). Exposing the cheat sheet, with the students' aid. *The New York Times*. Retrieved April 22, 2008, from http://www.softwaresecure.com/pdf/CheatingWaterBottle_112603_.pdf

Gunasekara, C. (2004). The third role of Australian universities in human capital formation. *Journal of Higher Education Policy and Management, 26*(3), 331-343.

Gunawardena, C. N., & McIsaac, M. S. (2004). Distance education. In D. H. Jonassen (Ed.), *Handbook of research on educational communications and technology* (pp. 355-395). Mahwah, NJ: Lawrence Erlbaum.

Gunawardena, C.N., Lowe, C.A., & Anderson, T. (1997). Analysis of global online debate and the development of an interaction analysis model for examining social construction of knowledge in computer conferencing. *Journal of Educational Computing Research, 17*(4), 397-431.

Gunawardena, C.N., Plass, J., & Salisbury, M. (2001). Do we really need an online discussion group ? In D. Murphy, R. Walker, & G. Webb (Eds.), *Online learning and teaching with technology: Case studies, experience and practice* (pp. 36-43). London: Kogan Page.

Habermas, J. (1984). The theory of communicative action. *Reason and the rationalization of society* (Vol. 1). Boston: Beacon Press.

Habermas, J. (1987). The theory of communicative action. *System and lifeworld: A critique of functionalist reason* (Vol. 2). Boston: Beacon Press.

Habermas, J. (1990). *Moral consciousness and communicative action.* Cambridge, MA: MIT Press.

Hacker, D. J., & Niederhauser, D. S. (2000, Winter). Promoting deep and durable learning in the online classroom. *New Directions for Teaching and Learning,* (84), 53-63.

Hai-Jew, S. (2007, January 31-February 2). Cultural sensitivities in e-learning: Designing hybridized e-learning

for Native American Learners through "The Enduring Legacies Project" (case study). In *Proceedings of the Orlando New Technologies Conference: Society for Applied Learning Technologies Conference Presentation.*

Hai-Jew, S. (2007). *Trust factor in online instructor-led college courses* (pp. 1-25). Unpublished manuscript.

Hall, B.P. (1994). *Values shift: A guide to personal and organizational transformation.* Rockport, MA: Twin Lights Publishers.

Hall, L. D. (2007). Professional ethics: Scenarios and principles. *TechTrends, 51*(1), 15-16.

Hall, R. T., & Davis, J. U. (1975). *Moral education in theory and practice.* Prometheus Books.

Hall, T. L. (1996). Honor among students: Academic integrity and student cultures. Doctoral dissertation, Indiana University. *Dissertation Abstracts International, 57*, 2960A.

Hamilton, D., Hinton, D. T. L. S., & Hawkins, K. (2003). International students at Australian universities—plagiarism and culture. In *Paper presented at the Academic Integrity Conference*, University of South Australia, Adelaide.

Hand, M., & Sandywell, B. (2002). E-topia as cosmopolis or citadel: On the democratizing and de-democratizing logics of the Internet, or towards a critique of the new technological fetishism. *Theory, Culture and Society, 19*(1-2), 197-225.

Hannabuss, S. (1996). Teaching library and information ethics. *Library Management, 17*(2), 24-35.

Harasim, L., Hiltz, R. S., Teles, L., & Turoff, M. (1996). *Learning networks.* Cambridge, MA: The MIT Press.

Hard, S., Conway, J. M., & Moran, A. C. (2006). Faculty and college student beliefs about the frequency of student academic misconduct. *Journal of Higher Education, 77*(6), 1058-1080.

Harri-Augstein, S., & Thomas, L. (1991). *Learning conversations.* London: Routledge.

Harris, R. (2004). Anti-plagiarism strategies for research papers. *VirtualSalt. Retrieved April 22, 2008, from* http://www.virtualsalt.com/antiplag.htm

Harris, R. A. (2001). *The plagiarism handbook: Strategies for preventing, detecting and dealing with plagiarism.* Los Angeles, CA: Pyrczak.

Harris, S.G. (1994, August). Organizational culture and individual sensemaking: A schema-based perspective. *Organization Science, 5*(3), 309-321.

Hart, M., & Friesner, T. (2004, February). Plagiarism and poor academic practice: A threat to the extension of e-learning in higher education? *Electronic Journal on E-learning, 2*(1), 89-96. Retrieved April 16, 2008, from http://www.ejel.org/volume-2/vol2-issue1/issue1-art25-hart-friesner.pdf

Hartley, D. (2007). Personalisation: The emerging "revised" code of education? *Oxford Review of Education,* iFirst article, 1-14.

Hauptman, P. (2002). *Ethics and librarianship.* Jefferson, NC: McFarland.

Hawk, C. S. (2001). *Computer and Internet use on campus: Legal guide to issues on intellectual property, free speech, and privacy.* San Francisco: Jossey-Bass.

Hawkridge, D. (1991). Challenging educational technology. *ETTI, 28*(2), 102-110.

Hawksley, R., & Owen, J. (2002). *Going the distance: Are there common factors in high performance distance learning?* National Extension College, Cambridge and UK Learning and Skills Development Agency, London. Retrieved April 22, 2008, from www.LSDA.org.uk

Haynes, F. (1998). *The ethical school.* London: Routledge.

Heberling, M. (2002). Maintaining academic integrity in online education. *Online Journal of Distance Learning Administration, 5*(1). Retrieved April 15, 2008, from http://www.westga.edu/~distance/ojdla/spring51/heberling51.html

Hemmings, A. (2006). Great ethical divides: Bridging the gap between institutional review boards and researchers. *Educational Researcher, 35*(4), 12-18.

Hendershott, A., Drinan, P. F., & Cross, M. (2000). Toward enhancing a culture of academic integrity, *The NASPA Journal, 37,* 587-598.

Hermann, A., Fox, R., & Boyd, A. (1999). Benign educational technology? *Open Learning, 14*(1), 3-8.

Herring, S. C. (1996). Two variants of an electronic message schema. In S.C. Herring (Ed.), *Computer-mediated communication* (pp. 81-106). Philadelphia, PA: John Benjamins.

Herring, S.C. (2002). Computer-mediated communication on the Internet. *Annual Review of Information Science and Technology (ARIST), 36,* 109-168.

Hillman, D.C., Willis, D.J., & Gunawardena, C.N. (1994). Learner-interface interaction in distance education: An extension of contemporary models and strategies for practitioners. *American Journal of Distance Education, 8*(2), 30-42.

Hinman, L. M. (2000). *Academic integrity and the World Wide Web.* Retrieved April 16, 2008, from http://ethics.acusd.edu/presentations/cai2000/index_files/frame.htm

Hinman, L. M. (2005). Esse est indicato in Google: Ethical and political issues in search engines. *IRIE-International Review of Information Ethics, 3*(6), 25. Retrieved April 16, 2008, from http://www.i-r-i-e.net/inhalt/003/003_hinman.pdf

Hinton, D. T. L. S. (2004). Plagiarism: Learning from our challenges. *Studies in Learning, Evaluation Innovation and Development, 1*(1), 37-46.

History of ethics and ethical review of human research in Australia. Retrieved April 23, 2008, from http://www.nhmrc.gov.au/ethics/human/ahec/history/

Holeton, R. (1998). *Composing cyberspace: Identity, community, and knowledge in the electronic age.* Boston: McGraw-Hill.

Holland, B. (1997, Fall). Analyzing institutional commitment to service: A model of key organizational factors. *Michigan Journal of Community Service Learning* (pp. 30-34). Retrieved April 16, 2008, from http://www.compact.org/advancedtoolkit/pdf/holland-all.pdf

Holt, T. J., & Graves, D. C. (2007). A qualitative analysis of advance fee fraud e-mail schemes. *International Journal of Cyber Criminology, 1*(1), 137-154.

Honey, P. (2001). E-learning: A performance appraisal and some suggestions for improvement. *The Learning Organization, 8*(5).

Horn, R., & Carr, A. (2000). Providing systemic change for schools: Towards professional development through moral conversation. *Systems Research and Behavioral Science, 17*(3), 255-272.

Horton, W. (2000). *Designing Web-based training.* New York: John Wiley & Sons.

How do you prevent cheating in distance education? Retrieved April 16, 2008, from http://web-pt.net/wyoming/online_testing.htm

Hudson, J.M., & Bruckman, A. (2005). Using empirical data to reason about Internet research ethics. In *Proceedings of the Ninth European Conference on Computer-supported Cooperative Work.* Springer-Verlag. Retrieved April 22, 2008, from www.ecscw.uni-siegen.de/2005/paper15.pdf

Hughes, J. C., & McCabe, D. (2006). *Academic misconduct major problem in Canada, study finds.* University of Guelph, Communications and Public Affairs. Retrieved April 23, 2008, from http://www.uoguelph.ca/mediarel/2006/09/academic_miscon.html

Humbarger, M., & DeVaney, S.A. (2005). Ethical values in the classroom: How college students responded. *Journal of Family and Consumer Sciences, 97*(3), 40-47.

Husu, J. (2004). A multifocal approach to study pedagogical ethics in school settings. *Scandinavian Journal of Educational Research, 48*(2), 123-140.

Hutchings, P. (2003). Competing goods: Ethical issues in the scholarship of teaching and learning. *Change, 35*(5), 26-33.

Hutton, P. A. (2006). Understanding cheating and what educators can do about it. *College Teaching,* 171-177.

Hwang, S., & Roth, W.-M. (2004). Ethics on research on learning: Dialectics of praxis and praxeology. *Forum: Qualitative Social Research, 6*(1). Retrieved April 22, 2008, from http://www.qualitative-research.net/fqs/

Hylnka, D., & Belland, J. C. (1991). Preface. In D. Hylnka & J. C. Belland (Eds.), *Paradigms regained: The use of illuminative, semiotic and postmodern criticism as modes of enquiry in educational technology* (pp. v-ix). Englewood Cliffs, NJ: Educational Technology Publications.

Iacono, T. (2006). Further comments on the researched, researchers and ethics committees: A response. *Journal of Intellectual and Developmental Disability, 31*(3), 189-191.

Illinois Online Network. (2001). *Strategies to minimize cheating online.* Retrieved April 16, 2008, from http://illinois.online.uillinois.edu/pointer/IONresources/assessment /cheating.html

Imel, S. (1991). Ethical practice in adult education. *ERIC Clearinghouse on Adult Career and Vocational Education.* Columbus, OH. Retrieved April 23, 2008, from http://www.ericdigests.org/1992-5/adult.htm

Isman, A. (2005, June). Diffusion of distance education in North Cyprus. *International Journal of Instructional Technology & Distance Learning, 2*(6). Retrieved April 22, 2008, from http://www.itdl.org/Journal/Jun_05/article06.htm

Jackson, S. F. (2001). Online distance education and undergraduate student retention and recruitment. In *Proceedings of the Third Annual WebCT Users Conference "Transforming the Educational Experience,"* Vancouver.

Jaimes, A. (2006). Human-centered multimedia: Culture, deployment and access. In N. Dimitrova (Ed.), *Visions and views* (pp. 12-19). IEEE Philips Research.

James, M. (2002). *Are you ethical? The truth isn't exactly clear: Politics, circumstances, excuses can blur what is right.* Retrieved April 22, 2008, from http://abcnews.go.com/US/story?id=89985&page=1

Jarvis, P. (1983). *Professional education.* London: Croom Helm.

Jeffers, B.R. (2002). Continuing education in research ethics for the clinical nurse. *Journal of Continuing Education in Nursing, 33*(6), 265-269.

Jendrek, M. P. (1989). Faculty reactions to academic dishonesty. *Journal of College Student Development, 30,* 401-406.

Jenlink, P. (2004). Discourse ethics in the design of educational systems: Considerations for design praxis. *Systems Research and Behavioral Science, 21*(3), 237-249.

Jochems, W., van Merrienboer, J., & Koper, R. (Eds.). (2004). *Integrated e-learning: Implications for pedagogy, technology and organization.* London: RoutledgeFalmer.

Jocoy, C., & DiBiase, D. (2006, June). Plagiarism by adult learners online: A case study in detection and remediation. *International Review of Research in Open and Distance Learning, 7.* Retrieved April 22, 2008, from www.irrodl.org/index.php/irrodl/article/downloadSuppFile/242/21

Johnson, D. (2001). *Computer ethics* (3rd ed.). Upper Saddle River, NJ: Prentice Hall.

Johnson, D. G. (1985). *Computer ethics.* Prentice Hall.

Johnson, D. G. (1991). *Ethical issues in engineering.* Englewood Cliffs, NJ: Prentice Hall.

Johnson, D. G. (1993). *Computer ethics* (2nd ed.). Englewood Cliffs, NJ: Prentice Hall.

Johnson, D. G., & Snapper, J. W. (Eds.). (1985). *Ethical issues in the use of computers.* Belmont, CA: Wadsworth.

Johnson, D. W. (1984). *Computer ethics: A guide for the new age.* Brethren Press.

Johnston, V. (2001). By accident or design? *Exchange, 1,* 9-11. Open University Milton Keynes.

Johnston, V. (2001). Retention. In *Paper presented at the "Holistic Student Support" Conference,* University of Central Lancashire, Preston, UK.

Johnston, V., & Simpson, O. (2006). Retentioneering higher education in the UK: Attitudinal barriers to addressing student retention in universities. *Widening Participation and Lifelong Learning, 8*(3).

Jones, D. (2004). The conceptualisation of e-learning: Lessons and implications. *Studies in Learning, Evaluation Innovation and Development, 1*(1), 47-55.

Jones, S. (1999). *Doing Internet research: Critical issues and methods for examining the net.* London: Sage.

Joseph, P. B., Bravmann, S. L., Windschitl, M. A., Mikel, E. R., & Green, N. S. (2000). *Cultures of curriculum* (pp. 3-4, 12, 17). Mahwah, NJ: Lawrence Erlbaum.

Jungk, R. (1958). *Brighter than a thousand suns: A personal history of the atomic scientists* (J. Cleugh, Trans.). Harmondsworth, Middlesex: Penguin.

Kaczmarczyk, L. (2001). Accreditation and student assessment in distance education: Why we all need to pay attention. In *Proceedings of the 6th Annual SIGCSE Conference on Innovation and Technology in Computer Science Education,* Canterbury, UK, (pp. 113-116).

Kanuka, H., & Anderson, T. (2007). Ethical issues in qualitative e-learning research. *The International Journal of Qualitative Methods, 6*(2). Retrieved April 22, 2008, from http://www.ualberta.ca/~iiqm/backissues/6_2/kanuka.htm

Karassavidou, E., & Glaveli, N. (2006). Towards the ethical or the unethical side? An explorative research of Greek business students' attitudes. *International Journal of Management Education, 20*(5), 348-364.

Karmakar, N.L. (2002, June 24-29). Online privacy, security and ethical dilemma: A recent study. In *Pro-*

ceedings of the 14ᵗʰ ED-MEDIA 2002 World Conference on Multimedia, Hypermedia and Telecommunications, Denver. Association for the Advancement of Computing in Education. ERIC Documents: ED477037.

Katz, J. (1972). *Experimentation with human beings.* New York: Sage.

Kawachi, P. (2003). Vicarious interaction and the achieved quality of learning. *International Journal on E-learning, 2*(4), 39-45.

Kawachi, P. (2003, November 12-14). Asia-specific scaffolding needs in grounded design e-learning: Empirical comparisons among several institutions. In *Proceedings of the 17ᵗʰ Annual Conference of the Asian Association of Open Universities*, Bangkok.

Kawachi, P. (2003). Choosing the appropriate media to support the learning process. *Journal of Educational Technology, 14*(1&2), 1-18.

Kawachi, P. (2004). Course design & choice of media by applying the Theory of Transactional Distance. *Open Education Research, 2*, 16-19.

Kawachi, P. (2005). Empirical validation of a multimedia construct for learning. In S. Mishra & R. Sharma (Eds.), *Interactive multimedia in education and training* (pp. 158-183). Hershey, PA: Idea Group.

Kawachi, P. (2006). The will to learn: Tutor's role. In P.R. Ramanujam (Ed.), *Globalisation, education and open distance learning,* (pp. 197-221). New Delhi, India: Shipra.

Kearsley, G. (2000). *Online education: Learning and teaching in cyberspace.* Belmont, CA: Wadsworth/ Thomson Learning.

Keegan, D. (1996). *Foundations of distance education* (3ʳᵈ ed.). London: Routledge.

Keith-Spiegel, P., Whitley, Jr., B., Balogh, D., Perkins, D., & Wittig, A. (2002). *The ethics of teaching: A casebook.* Mahwah, NJ: Lawrence Erlbaum.

Keller, C. (2005). Virtual learning environments: Three implementation perspectives. *Learning, media and technology, 30*(3), 299-311.

Kelley, K. B., & Bonner, K. (2005). Digital text, distance education and academic dishonesty: Faculty and administrator perceptions and responses. *Journal of Asynchronous Learning Networks, 9.*

Kellner, D. (2000). Globalization and new social movements: Lessons for critical theory and pedagogy. In N. C. Burbles & C. A. Torres (Eds.), *Globalization and education: Critical perspectives* (pp. 229-321). London: Routledge.

Kellner, D. (2004). Technological transformation, multiple literacies, and the re-visioning of education. *E-learning, 1*(1), 9-37.

Kelly, P., & Mills, R. (2007). The ethical dimensions of learner support. *Open Learning, 22*(2), 149-157.

Kember, D., Ma, R., & McNaught, C. (2006). *Excellent university teaching.* Hong Kong: Chinese University Press.

Kendall, L. (1999). Recontextualizing "Cyberspace:" Methodological consideration for on-line research. In S. Jones (Ed.), *Doing Internet research: Critical issues and methods for examining the net.* London: Sage.

Kenkel, C. (2004). Balancing online course deadlines with the need to remain flexible. *Campus Technology, 18,* 34-36.

Kennedy, I. (2004). An assessment strategy to help forestall plagiarism problems. *Studies in Learning, Evaluation Innovation and Development, 1*(2), 1-8.

Kenway, J. (1996) The information superhighway and post-modernity: The social promise and the social price. *Comparative Education, 32*(2), 217-231.

Kerbo, H. R. (1981, June). College achievement among Native Americans: A research note. *Social Forces, 59*(4), 1275-1280.

Kerbs, R. W. (2005). Social and ethical considerations in virtual worlds. *The Electronic Library, 53*(5), 539-546.

Keying in: The Newsletter of the National Business Education Association. (2004, January). *Employers value communication and interpersonal abilities, 14, 3-6.*

Kibler, W. L. (1993). A framework for addressing academic dishonesty from a student development perspective. *NASPA Journal, 31,* 8-18.

Kibler, W. L. (1993). Academic dishonesty: A student development dilemma. *NASPA Journal 30,* 252-267.

Kidder, R. (1995). *How good people make tough choices.* New York: Fireside.

Kidder, R. M. (1995). The ethics of teaching and the teaching of ethics. In E. Boschmann (Ed.), *The electronic classroom: A handbook for education in the electronic environment.* Medford, NJ: Learned Information.

Kilicer, K., & Odabasi, H. F. (2006, April 19-21). Bilgisayar ogretmenligi: Etik bunun neresinde? (Computer education: Where does ethics lie?). In *Proceedings of the 6th International Educational Technology Conference,* (pp. 1124-1129). Famagusta, Turkish Republic of Northern Cyprus.

King, S. (1996). Researching Internet communities: Proposed ethical guidelines for the reporting of the results. *The Information Society, 12*(2), 119-127. Retrieved on April 22, 2008, from http://venus.soci.niu.edu/~jthomas/ethics/tis/go.storm

Kirby, P. C., Pardise, L. V., & Protti, R. (1990, April). The ethical reasoning of school administrators: The principled principal. In *Paper presented at the Annual Meeting of the American Educational Research Association,* Boston. ED 320 253.

Kirkness, V. J., & Barnhardt, R. (2001). First nations and higher education: The four R's—respect, relevance, reciprocity, responsibility. In R. Hayoe & J. Pan (Eds.), *Knowledge across cultures: A contribution to dialogue among civilizations.* Hong Kong: Comparative Education Research Centre, the University of Hong Kong.

Kirsh, G. E. (1999). *Ethical dilemmas in feminist research: The politics of location, interpretation, and publication.* Albany, NY: State University of New York Press.

Kitchin, R. (1998). *Cyberspace: The world in the wires.* New York: John Wiley.

Kithin, H. A. (2003). The tri-council policy statement and research in cyberspace: Research ethics, the Internet, and revising a living document. *Journal of Academic Ethics, 1*(4), 397-418.

Kizza, J. M. (2006). *Computer network security and cyber ethics* (2nd ed.). Jefferson, NC: McFarland & Co.

Kleiner, C., & Lord, M. (1999). The cheating game: Cross-national exploration of business students' attitudes, perceptions, and tendencies toward academic dishonesty. *Journal of Education for Business. 74*(4), 38-42.

Kleiner, C., & Lord, M. (1999, November 2). The cheating game: Everyone's doing it, from grade school to graduate school. *U.S. News & World Report,* pp. 55-66.

Knowlton, D. S. (2000). A theoretical framework for the online classroom: A defense and delineation of a student-centered pedagogy. In R.E. Weiss, D.S. Knowlton, & B.W. Speck (Eds.), *Principles of effective teaching in the online classroom* (pp. 5-14). San Francisco: Jossey-Bass.

Koc, M. (2005). Individual learner differences in Web-based learning environments: From cognitive, affective and social-cultural perspectives. *Turkish Online Journal of Distance Education, 6*(4), 12-22. Retrieved April 22, 2008, http://tojde.anadolu.edu.tr

Koch, K. (2000). Cheating in schools. *CQ Researcher, 10,* 745-768.

Koehne, N. (2005). (Re)construction: Ways international students talk about their identity. *Australian Journal of Education, 49*(1), 140-119.

Kozenny, F., & Bauer, C. (1981). Testing the theory of electronic propinquity. *Communication Research, 8*(4), 479-498.

Krathwohl, D. R., Bloom, B. S., & Bertram, B. M. (1973). *Taxonomy of educational objectives, the classification of educational goals. Handbook II: Affective domain.* New York: David McKay.

Kraut, R. (2007). *Aristotle's ethics* (rev. ed.). Retrieved April 15, 2008, from http://plato.stanford.edu/entries/aristotle-ethics

Kraut, R., Olson, J., Banaji, M., Bruckman, A., Cohen, J., & Couper, M. (2004). Psychological research online: Report of Board of Scientific Affaires' Advisory Group on the conduct of research on the Internet. *American Psychologist, 59*(2), 105-177.

Kreie, J., & Cronan, T. P. (2000). Making ethical decisions. *Communications of the ACM, 43*(12), 66-71.

Kress, G. (2003). *Literacy in the new media age.* London: Routledge.

Kress, G., & van Leeuwen, T. (2001). *Multimodal discourse: The modes and media of contemporary communication.* London: Arnold.

Kumar, A. (2003, August 31). High-tech sleuthing catches college cheats. *St. Petersburg Times.* Retrieved April 22, 2008, from http://www.sptimes.com/2003/08/31/State/High_tech_sleuthing_c.shtml

Kuzma, L. M. (1998, September). The World Wide Web and active learning in the international relations classroom. *PS: Political Science and Politics, 31*(3), 578-584.

Ladson-Billings, G. (1995, Summer). But that's just good teaching! The case for culturally relevant pedagogy. *Theory into Practice, 34*(3), 159-165.

Ladson-Billings, G. (1995, Autumn). Toward a theory of culturally relevant pedagogy. *American Educational Research Journal, 32*(3), 465-491.

Lajoie, S. P. (2003, November). Transitions and trajectories for studies of expertise. *Educational Researcher, 32*(8), 21-25.

Lambert, K., Ellen, N., & Taylor, L. (2003). Cheating ? What is it and why do it: A study in New Zealand tertiary institutions of the perceptions and justification for academic dishonesty. *Journal of American Academy of Business, 3*(1/2), 98-103.

Lancaster, F. (Ed.). (1991). *Ethics and the librarian.* Urbana-Champaign, IL: University of Illinois, Graduate School of Library and Information Science.

Lane, J. F. (2004, March 3-7). Competencies and training needs of financial aid administrators. In *Proceedings of the Academy of Human Resource Development (AHRD) International Research Conference*, Austin, TX (Vol. 1-2, pp. 190-197). ERIC Documents: ED491481.

Langford, D. (1995). *Practical computer ethics.* Cambridge: McGraw-Hill.

Lankshear, C. (1997). Language and the new capitalism. *International Journal of Inclusive Education, 1*(4), 309-321.

Lasica, J.D. (2005). The cost of ethics: Influence peddling in the blogosphere. *AUSC Annenberg Online Journalism Review. Downloaded* April 23, 2008, from http://www.ojr.org/ojr/stories/050217lasica/

Lathrop, A., & Foss, K. (2000). *Student cheating and plagiarism in the Internet era: A wake-up call.* Englewood, CO: Libraries Unlimited.

Laurillard, D. (1993). *Rethinking university teaching.* London: Routledge.

Laurillard, D. (2002). *Rethinking university teaching: A conversational framework for the effective use of learning technologies* (2nd ed.). London: RoutledgeFalmer.

Laurillard, D. (2006). E-learning in higher education. In P. Ashwin (Ed.), *Changing higher education: The development of learning and teaching* (pp. 71-84). London: RoutledgeFalmer.

Lavagnino, M., Bowker, G., Heidorn, P., & Basi, M. (1998). Incorporating social informatics into the curriculum for library and information science professionals. *Libri: International Journal of Libraries and Information Services, 48*(1), 13-25.

Lawhead, B.P., Alpert, E., Bland, C.G., Caerswell, L., Cizmar, D., DeWitt, J., et al. (1997). The Web and distance learning: What is appropriate and what is not. In *Proceedings of the ITiCSE'97 Working Group on the Web and Distance Learning Working Group Reports: SIGCSE/SIGUE ITiCSE'97.*

Layton, T. G. (2000). Digital learning: Why tomorrow's schools must learn to let go of the past. *American School Board Journal.* Retrieved April 22, 2008, from http://www.electronic-school.com/2000/09/0900f1.html

Leach, M.M. & Oakland, T. (2007). Ethics standards impacting test development and use: A brief review of 31 ethics codes impacting practices in 35 countries. *International Journal of testing, 7*(1), 71-88.

Lee, C. (1986, March). Ethics training: Facing the tough questions. *Training*, 30-41.

Lee, L. (1997, May). Using portfolios to develop 1.2 cultural knowledge and awareness of students in intermediate Spanish. *Hispania, 80*(2), 355-367.

Lee, S., & Wolff-Michael, R. (2003). Science and the "good citizen:" Community-based scientific literacy. *Science Technology and Human Values, 28*(3), 403-424.

Leflore, D. (2000). Theory supporting design guidelines for Web-based instruction. In B. Abbey (Ed.), *Instructional and cognitive impacts of Web-based education* (pp. 102-117). Hershey, PA: Idea Group.

Lemonick, M.D. & Goldstein, A. (2002). At your own risk. *Time Magazine, 159*(16), 40-49.

Levin, J. S. (2001, September). Public policy, community colleges, and the path to globalization. *Higher Education, 42*(2), 237-262.

Levy, D. C. (2006). The unanticipated explosion: Private higher education's global surge. *Comparative Education Review, 50*(2), 217-240.

Lewis, R. (1995). *Tutoring in open learning.* Lancaster: Framework Press.

Liaw, M.-L. (2006, September). E-learning and the development of intercultural competence. *Language Learning & Technology, 10*(3), 49-64.

Lim, C. L., & Coalter, T. (2005). Academic integrity: An instructor's obligation. *International Journal of Teaching and Learning in Higher Education, 17*(2), 155-159. Retrieved April 16, 2008, from http://www.isetl.org/ijtlhe/pdf/IJTLHE51.pdf

Lim, V. K. G., & See, S. K. B. (2001). Attitudes toward, and intentions to report, academic cheating among students in Singapore. *Ethics and Behavior, 11*(3), 261-74.

Lipset, A. (2005, September 30). Pioneers set ethics at heart of courses. *Times Higher Education Supplement,* p. 56.

Littlewood, W., & Liu, N. F. (1996). *Hong Kong students and their English.* Hong Kong: Hong Kong University/Macmillan.

Lockwood, A., & Gooley, A. (2001). *Innovation in open & distance learning.* London: Kogan Page.

Lorenzetti, J. P. (2006, November 15). Integrating ethics into online faculty development: Hints from Regis University. *Distance Education Report, 10*(22), 5, 8.

Lovegrove, W. (2004, December 20). *USQ: Australia's leading transnational educator.* Retrieved April 22, 2008, from http://www.usq.edu.au/planstats/Planning/USQAustsLeadingTransEdu.htm

Loveless, A., & Ellis, V. (Eds.). (2001). *ICT, pedagogy and the curriculum: Subject to change.* London: RoutledgeFalmer.

Luck, P., & Norton, B. (2004, December). Problem based management education—better online. *European Journal of Open and Distance Learning.*

Luck, P., & Norton, B. (2005). Collaborative management education—an on-line community in Europe? *International Journal of Web Based Communities, 3*(22-31).

Luck, P., & Owens, T. (2002). Problem-based learning on-line for nursery management. *Journal of Problem-Based Learning, 1*(1).

Luppicini, R. (2005). A systems definition of educational technology in society. *Educational Technology & Society, 8*(3), 103-109.

Luppicini, R. (2006). Designing online communities of learning based on conversation theory. In *Manuscript Presented at the Association for Educational Communication and Technology (AECT) Conference*, Dallas, TX.

Luppicini, R. (Ed.). (2007). *Online learning communities*. Greenwich: Information Age Publishing.

Luppicini, R., & Adell, R. (Eds.). (forthcoming). *Handbook of research on technoethics*. Hershey, PA: Idea Group.

Lupton, R. A., Chapman, K., & Weiss, J. (2000). American and Slovakian university business students' attitudes, perceptions and tendencies towards academic cheating. *Journal of Education for Business, 75*(4), 231-241.

Lynch, M. M. (2001, November-December). *Effective student preparation for online learning*. The Technology Source Archives at the University of North Carolina.

Lynch, R., & Baines, P. (2004). Strategy development in UK higher education: Towards resource-based competitive advantages. *Journal of Higher Education Policy and Management, 26*(2), 171-187.

Lyons, M. J., Klunder, D., & Tetsutai, N. (2005). Supporting empathy in online learning with artificial expressions. *Educational Technology and Society, 8*(4), 22-30.

Lysaght, T., Rosenberger, P.J., & Kerridge, I. (2006). Australian undergraduate biotechnology student attitudes towards the teaching of ethics. *International Journal of Science Education, 28*(10), 1225-1239.

MacFarlane, B. (2002). Dealing with Dave's dilemmas: Exploring the ethics of pedagogic practice. *Teaching in Higher Education, 7*(2), 167-178.

Macfarlane, B. (2004). *Teaching with integrity. The ethics of higher education practice*. London: RoutledgeFalmer.

Machin, D. (2007). *Introduction to multimodal analysis*. London: Hodder.

MacKay, E., & O'Neill, P. (1992). What creates the dilemma in ethical dilemmas? Examples from psychological practice. *Ethics & Behavior, 2*, 227-244.

Macleod, D. (2005, February 10). Universities urged to root out student cheats. *EducationGuardian.co.uk*. Retrieved April 22, 2008, from http://education.guardian.co.uk/students/work/story/0,12734,1410054,00.html

Mager, J. (2003). Personalization and customization. In *Paper presented at the Noel-Levitz National Student Retention Conference*, San Diego, CA.

Magnus, J. R., Polterovich, V. M, Danilov, D. L., & Satvvateev, A. V. (2002). Tolerance of cheating: An analysis across countries. *Journal of Economic Education*, 125-135.

Mann, C., & Stewart, F. (2000). *Internet communication and qualitative research. A handbook for researching online*. London: Sage.

Maramark, S., & Maline, M. B. (1993). Academic dishonesty among college students. *Issues in education* (pp. 1-14). U.S. Department of Education.

Marginson, S. (2007, March 7-9). Global university rankings: Where to from here? In *Paper presented at the Asia-Pacific Association for International Education, National University of Singapore*. Retrieved April 23, 2008, from http://www.cshe.unimelb.edu.au/people/staff_pages/Marginson/APAIE_090307_Marginson.pdf

Marginson, S., & Considine, M. (2000). *The enterprise university. Power, governance and reinvention in Australia*. Cambridge, UK: Cambridge University Press.

Marshall, S., & Garry, M. (2005, December 4-7). How well do students really understand plagiarism? In H. Goss (Ed.), *Proceedings of the 22nd Annual Conference of the Australasian Society for Computers in Learning in Tertiary Education (ASCILITE)*, (pp. 457-467). Brisbane, Australia.

Martin, C. D., & Martin, D. H. (1990). Comparison of ethics codes of computer professionals. *Social Science Computer Review, 9*(1), 96-108.

Martin, D. F. (2005). Plagiarism and technology: A tool for coping with plagiarism. *Journal of Education for Business, 80*(3), 149-153.

Martin, M. W. (2000). *Meaningful work: Rethinking professional ethics.* Oxford: Oxford University Press.

Martin, M. W., & Schinzinger, R. (1989). *Ethics in engineering.* McGraw-Hill.

Martin, P., & Nicholls, J. (1987). *Creating a committed workforce.* Institute of Personnel Management.

Martinez, P. (2001). *Improving student retention and achievement—what we do know and what we need to find out.* UK Learning and Skills Development Agency, London. Retrieved April 22, 2008, from www.lsda.org.uk

Martinez, P., & Maynard, J. (2002). *Improving colleges: Why courses improve or decline over time.* UK Learning and Skills Agency, London. Retrieved April 22, 2008, form www.lsda.org.uk

Martinez, P., & Mendey, F. (1998). *9000 voices: Students' persistence and dropout in further education.* UK Learning and Skills Agency, London. Retrieved April 22, 2008, from www.lsda.org.uk

Mason, E. S., & Mudrack, P. E. (1996). Gender and ethical orientation: A test of gender and occupational socialization theories. *Journal of Business Ethics, 15,* 599-604.

Mason, R. (1986). Four ethical issues of the information age. *MIS Quarterly, 10*(1), 5-11.

Massironi, M. (2002). *The psychology of graphic images: Seeing, drawing, communicating* (N. Bruno, Trans.). NJ: Lawrence Erlbaum.

Mathiesen, K. (2004). What is information ethics? *Computers and Society, 32*(8). Retrieved April 23, 2008, from http://www.computersandsociety.org

Maufefette-Leenders, L., & Erskine, J. (1999). *Learning with cases.* Ontario, CA: University of Western Ontario.

Mauthner, M., Birch, M., Jessop, J., & Miller, T. (Eds.). (2002). *Ethics in qualitative research.* London: Sage.

May, W. W. (1990). *Ethics and higher education.* New York: Macmillan Publishing Company and American Council on Education.

Mayer, R. E. (2001). *Multimedia learning.* Cambridge: Cambridge University Press.

Mayers, T., & Swafford, K. (1998). Reading the networks of power: Rethinking "critical thinking" in computerized classrooms. In T. Todd & I. Ward (Eds.), *Literacy theory in the age of the Internet* (pp. 146-157). New York: Columbia University Press.

McCabe, D. L. (1993). Faculty responses to academic dishonesty: The influence of student honor codes. *Research in Higher Education, 34,* 647-658.

McCabe, D. L. (2001). Cheating: Why students do it and how we can help them stop. *American Educator.* Retrieved April 22, 2008, from http://www.aft.org/pubs-reports/american_educator/winter2001/Cheating.html

McCabe, D. L. (2001). *Student cheating in American high schools.* Retrieved April 16, 2008, from http://www.academicintegrity.org/index.asp

McCabe, D. L. (2005). *CAI research.* Retrieved April 23, 2008, from http://www.academicintegrity.org/cai_research.asp

McCabe, D. L. (2005). It takes a village: Academic dishonesty and educational opportunity. *Liberal Education, Summer/Fall,* 26-31.

McCabe, D. L., & Pavela, G. (1997). *Ten principles of academic integrity.* Ashville, NC: College Administration Publications. Retrieved April 16, 2008, from http://www.collegepubs.com/ref/10PrinAcaInteg.shtml

McCabe, D. L., & Pavela, G. (2000). *Ten principles of academic integrity.* Ashville, NC: College Administration

Publications. Retrieved April 22, 2008, from http://www.collegepubs.com/ref/10PrinAcaInteg.shtml

McCabe, D. L., & Pavela, G. (2005). Honor codes for a new generation. *Inside Higher Education*. Retrieved April 22, 2008, from http://www.insidehighered.com/views/new_honor_codes_for_a_new_generation

McCabe, D. L., & Trevino, L. (1995). Cheating among business students: A challenge for business leaders and educators. *Journal of Management Education, 19*(2), 205-18.

McCabe, D. L., & Trevino, L. K. (1993). Academic dishonesty: Honor codes and other contextual influences. *Journal of Higher Education, 64,* 522-538.

McCabe, D. L., & Trevino, L. K. (1995). Cheating among business students: A challenge for business leaders and educators. *Journal of Management Education, 19*(2), 205-218.

McCabe, D. L., & Trevino, L. K. (1996). What we know about cheating in college. *Change, 28*(1), 29-33.

McCabe, D. L., & Trevino, L. K. (1997). Individual and contextual influences on academic dishonesty: A multi-campus investigation. *Research in Higher Education, 38,* 379-396.

McCabe, D. L., Butterfield, K. D., & Trevino, L. K. (2006). Academic dishonesty in graduate business programs: Prevalence, causes, and proposed action. *Academy of Management Learning & Education, 5*(2), 294-305.

McCabe, D. L., Trevino, L. K., & Butterfield, K. (1996). The influences of collegiate and corporate codes of conduct on ethics-related behavior in the workplace. *Business Ethics Quarterly, 6,* 441-460.

McCabe, D. L., Trevino, L. K., & Butterfield, K. (2001, July). Cheating in academic institutions: A decade of research. *Ethics & Behavior, 11,* 219-233.

McCabe, D. L., Trevino, L. K., & Butterfield, K. D. (1999). Academic integrity in honor code and non-honor code environments: A qualitative investigation. *The Journal of Higher Education, 70*(2), 211-234.

McCabe, D. L., Treviño, L. K., & Butterfield, K. D. (2001). Cheating in academic institutions: A decade of research. *Ethics & Behavior, 11*(3), 219-232.

McCarty, T. L., Lynch, R. H., Wallace, S., & Benally, A. (1991, March). Classroom inquiry and Navajo learning styles: A call for reassessment. *Anthropology & Education Quarterly, 22*(1), 42-59.

McCool, M. (2006, December). Adapting e-learning for Japanese audiences tutorial. *IEEE Transactions on Professional Communication, 49*(4), 335-345.

McDonald, F. (1993). *Censorship and intellectual freedom: A survey of school librarians' attitudes and moral reasoning.* Metuchen, NJ: Scarecrow Press.

McDonald, J., McPhail, J., Maguire, M., & Millett, B. (2004). A conceptual model and evaluation process for educational technology learning resources: A legal case study. *Educational Media International, 41*(4), 287-296.

McEwan, T. (2001). *Managing values and beliefs in organisations.* Harlow: Prentice Hall.

McGivney, V. (1996). *Staying or leaving the course.* Leicester, UK: National Institute of Adult Continuing Education.

McKee, H. (2003). Changing the process of institutional review board compliance. *College Composition and Communication, 54*(3), 488-493.

McKenna, K. (2007). Through the Internet looking glass: Expressing and validating the true self. In A. Joinson, K. McKenna, T. Postmes, & U. Reips (Eds.), *Oxford handbook of Internet psychology.* Oxford: Oxford University Press.

McKinnon, J.W. (1976). The college student and formal operations. In J.W. Renner, et al. (Eds.), *Research, teaching, and learning with the Piaget Model* (pp. 110-129). Norman, OK: Oklahoma University Press.

Mclinden, M. *Retention: A practitioners guide to developing and implementing pre-entry induction and ongoing retention tactics.* Anglia Polytechnic University: Four Counties Group of Higher Education Institutions.

McLoughlin, C. (1999). The implications of the research literature on learning styles for the design of instructional material. *Australian Journal of Educational Technology, 15*(3), 222-241.

McLuhan, M. (1964). *Understanding media: The extensions of man.* New York: McGraw-Hill.

McMurtry, K. (2001). E-cheating: Combating a 21st century challenge. *The Journal Online: Technological Horizons in Education.* Retrieved April 16, 2008, from http://thejournal.com/magazine/vault/A3724.cfm

McNamee, M. (2001). Introduction: Whose ethics, which research? *Journal of Philosophy of Education, 35*(3), 309-327.

McNamee, M. (2002). Introduction: Whose ethics, which research? In M. McNamee & D. Bridges (Eds.), *The ethics of educational research* (pp. 1-21). Oxford, UK: Blackwell.

McNamee, M., & Bridges, D. (Eds.). (2002). *The ethics of educational research.* Oxford, UK: Blackwell.

McNaught, C. (2007). Individual and institutional responses to staff plagiarism. In M. Quigley (Ed.), *Encyclopedia of information ethics and security* (pp. 342-347). Hershey, PA: Idea Group Reference.

McNeel, S.P. (1994). College teaching and student moral development (chap. 2). In J. R. Rest & D. Narvaez (Eds.), *Moral development in the professions: Psychology and applied ethics* (pp. 27-49). Hillsdale: Lawrence Erlbaum.

McNess, E., Broadfoot, P., & Osborn, M. (2003). Is the effective compromising the affective? *British Educational Research Journal, 29*(2), 243-257.

Medical Research Council of Canada. (2005). *Tri-council policy statement [TCPS]: Ethical conduct for research involving humans.* Ottawa: Government of Canada. Retrieved April 23, 2008, from http://www.pre.ethics.gc.ca/english/policystatement/policystatement.cfm

Mehlenbacher, B., Miller, C. R., Covington, D., & Larsen, J. S. (2000, June). Active and interactive learning online: A comparison of Web-based and conventional writing classes. *IEEE Transactions on Professional Communication, 43*(2), 166-184.

Mehrabian, A. (1981). *Silent messages: Implicit communication of emotions and attitudes.* Belmont, CA: Wadsworth.

Mellon, C., & Kester, D. (2004). Online library education papers: Implications for rural students. *Journal of Education for Library & Information Science, 45*(3), 210-220.

Mercuri, R. (1998). In search of academic integrity. *Communications of the ACM, 40*(5), 136.

Merriam, S. (1998). *Qualitative research and case study applications in education.* San Francisco: Jossey-Bass.

Merriam, S.B., & Caffarella, R.S. (1991). *Learning in adulthood: A comprehensive guide.* San Francisco: Jossey-Bass.

Mesthene, E. (1983). Technology and wisdom. In C. Mitcham, & R. Mackey (Eds.), *Philosophy and technology: Readings in the philosophical problem of technology.* New York: The Free Press.

Meyer, J. P., Allen, N. J., & Smith, C. A. (1993). Commitment to organisations and occupations: Extension and test of a 3-component model. *Journal of Applied Psychology, 78*, 538-551.

Meyer, K. A. (2005). Exploring the potential for unintended consequences in online learning. *International Journal of Instructional Technology and Distance Learning.* Retrieved April 16, 2008, from http://www.itdl.org/Journal/Sep_05/article01.htm

Meyer, L. (1996). *The socially responsive self: Social theory and professional ethics.* Chicago and London: The University of Chicago Press.

Mililojeck, I. (2005). *Educational futures: Dominant and contesting visions.* London and New York: Routledge.

Miller, C. (2002, July 20). Campuses galore, but was it academe? *The Age* (Melbourne).

Milliken, J., & Colohan, G. (2004). Quality or control? Management in higher education. *Journal of Higher Education Policy and Management, 26*(3), 381-391.

Min, R. (2003, April). Simulation and discovery learning in an age of zapping and searching: Learning models (A treatise about the educational strength and availability of digital learning tools and simulation on the World Wide Web). *Turkish Online Journal of Distance Education, 4*(2). Retrieved April 16, 2008, from http://tojde.anadolu.edu.tr/tojde10/articles/rikmin.htm

Mishra, S. (1998). Distance education research: A review of its structure, methodological issues and priority areas. *Indian Journal of Open Learning, 7*(3), 267-282.

Mishra, S., & Sharma, R. C. (Eds.). (2005). *Interactive multimedia in education and training.* Hershey, PA: Ideas Group.

Montgomery, L. M., & Canaan, J. E. (2004). Conceptualizing higher education students as social actors in a globalizing world: A special issue. *International Journal of Qualitative Studies in Education, 17*(6), 739-748.

Moor, J. (2005). Why we need better ethics for emerging technologies. *Ethics and Information Technology, 7,* 111-119.

Moor, J. H. (1985). What is computer ethics? *Metaphilosophy, 16*(4), 266-275. (Turkish translation available online at http://home.anadolu.edu.tr/~fodabasi/doc/ty11.swf)

Moore, M. (1993). Theory of transactional distance. In D. Keegan (Ed.), *Theoretical principles of distance education* (pp. 22-38). London: Routledge.

Moore, M.G. (1990). Recent contributions to the Theory of Distance Education. *Open Learning, 5*(3), 10-15.

Moran, G. (2001). Ethics, strengths and values: A review article. *Journal of Librarianship and Information Science, 33*(2), 98-101.

Morgan, B. L., & Korschgen, A. J. (2001). The ethics of faculty behavior: Students' and professors' views. *College Student Journal.* Retrieved April 22, 2008, from http://www.findarticles.com/cf_0/m0FCR/3_35/80744654/print.jhtml

Mostert, M., & Sudzine, M. (1996, February). Undergraduate case method teaching: Pedagogical assumptions vs. the real world. In *Paper presented by the Annual Meeting of the Association of Teacher Education,* St. Louis.

Moxley, D., Najor-Durack, A., & Dumbrigue, C. (2001). *Keeping students in higher education—successful practices and strategies for retention.* London: Kogan Page.

Mugridge, I., & Kaufman, D. (1986). *Distance education in Canada.* London: Croom Helm.

Mumford, L. (1934). *Technics and civilisation.* New York: Harcourt, Brace & Co.

Munro, M. (2004, February 27). Alberta's ethics board has the toughest requirements in the country. *The Edmonton Journal,* pp. A1, A13.

Murphy, J. W., & Pardeck, J. T. (1985). The technological world-view and the responsible use of computers in the curriculum. *Journal of Education, 167*(2), 98-108.

Murray, H., Gillese, E., Lennon, M., Mercer, P., & Robinson, M. (1996). *Ethical principles in university teaching.* North York, Ontario: Society for Teaching and Learning in Higher Education. Retrieved April 23, 2008, from http://www.umanitoba.ca/uts/documents/ethical.pdf

Myers, D. J., Buoye, A. J., McDermott, J., Strickler, D. E., & Ryman, R. G. (2000, January). Signals, symbols, and vibes: An exercise in cross-cultural interaction. *Teaching Sociology, 29,* 95-101.

Nagy, J., & McDonald, J. (2007, December). *New policies for learning flexibility: Negotiated choices for both academics and students.* In *Proceedings of the Ascilite Conference: Providing Choices for Learners and Learning,* Singapore.

Namlu, A. G., & Odabasi, F. (2007). Unethical computer using behavior scale: A study of reliability and validity on Turkish university students. *Computers and Education, 48,* 205-215.

Napalm inventor discounts "guilt." (1967, December 27). *New York Times,* p. 8.

Nash, R. J. (1996). *Real world ethics: Frameworks for educators and human service professionals.* New York: Teachers College Press.

National Center for Education Statistics (NCES). (1999). *Teacher quality: A report on the preparation and qualifications of public school teachers* (Tech. Rep. No. NCES 1999-080). Washington, DC: U.S. Department of Education.

National Education Association. (n.d.) *Code of ethical of the education profession.* Retrieved April 23, 2008, from http://www.nea.org/code.html

National Statistics. (2006). Retrieved April 22, 2008, from http://www.statistics.gov.uk/StatBase/ssdataset.asp?vlnk=6936&Pos=1&ColRank=1&Rank=272

National University of Lesotho (NUL). (2007). *Extract of the rules for the conduct of examination.* Morija: National University of Lesotho, NUL Public Affairs Office.

Needham, G., & Johnson, K. (2007). Ethical issues in providing library services to distance learners. *Open Learning, 22*(2), 117-128.

New Zealand health and disability ethics committees. Retrieved April 23, 2008, from http://www.newhealth.govt.nz/ethicscommittees/

Ngor, A. L. C. Y. (2001, July). The prospects for using the Internet in collaborative design education with China. *Higher Education, 42*(1), 47-60.

Nichols, R. G. (1987). Toward a conscience: Negative aspect of educational technology. *Journal of Visual/Verbal Languaging, 7*(1), 121-137.

Nichols, R. G. (1994). Searching for moral guidance about educational technology. *Educational Technology, 34*(2), 40-48.

Nicol, D.J., Minty, I., & Sinclair, C. (2003). The social dimensions of online learning. *Innovations in Education and Teaching International, 40*(3), 270-280.

Nie, N. H. (2001). Sociability, interpersonal relations and the Internet: Reconciling conflicting findings. *American Behavioral Scientist, 45*(3), 420-435.

Niels, G. J. (1997). Academic practices, school culture and cheating behavior. *Student Development, 43*, 374-85.

Nind, M., Shereen, B., Sheehy, K., Collins, J., & Hall, K. (2004). Methodological challenges in researching inclusive school cultures. *Educational Review, 56*(3), 259-270.

Nissenbaum, H. (1997). Accountability in a computerized society. In B. Friedman (Ed.), *Human values and the design of computer technology* (pp. 41-64). Cambridge University Press. Retrieved April 16, 2008, from http://www.cybertext.net.au/tct2002/disc_papers/organisation/russell.htm

Nissenbaum, H., & Walker, D. (1998). A grounded approach to social and ethical concerns about technology and education. *Journal of Educational Computing Research, 19*(4), 411-432.

Nissenbaum, H., & Walker, D. (1998). Will computers dehumanize education? A grounded approach to values at risk. *Technology in Society, 20*, 237-273.

Noble, D. F. (1998). Digital diploma mills, Part II: The coming battle over online instruction. *Sociological Perspectives, 41*(4). The Academy under Siege (pp. 815-825).

NOIE. (2004). *Australian national broadband strategy.* Canberra, ACT: The National Office for the Information Economy. Retrieved April 22, 2008, from http://www.dcita.gov.au/ie/publications/2004/march/australian_national_broadband_strategy

Nurse, P. (2006, January 13). U.S. biomedical research under siege. *Cell, 124*, 9-12. Retrieved April 23, 2008, from http://www.cell.com/content/article/fulltext?uid=PIIS0092867405014613

Nuss, E. M. (1984). Academic integrity: Comparing faculty and student attitudes. *Improving College and University Teaching, 32*, 140-144.

O'Connor, T. (2002). Research ethics. Retrieved April 23, 2008, from http://faculty.ncwc.edu/toconnor/308/308lect10.htm

O'Neill, P. (1998). Communities, collectivities, and the ethics of research. *Canadian Journal of Community Mental health, 17*, 67-78.

O'Neill, P. (1999). Ethical issues in working with communities in crisis. In R. Gist & B. Lubin (Eds.), *Response to disaster: Psychosocial, community, and ecological approaches*. Philadelphia, PA: Taylor & Francis.

O'Neill, P. (2002). Good intentions and awkward outcomes: Ethical issues for qualitative researchers. In W. C. van den Hoonaard (Ed.), *Good intentions and awkward outcomes: Issues for qualitative researchers*. Canada: University of Toronto Press.

O'Neill, P., & Hern, R. (1991). A systems approach to ethical problems. *Ethics & Behavior, 1*, 129-143.

O'Relly, C. (1991). Corporations, culture and commitment: Motivation and social control in organisations. In R. M. Steers & L.W. Porter (Eds.), *Motivation and work behaviour* (5th ed., pp. 242-255). New York; McGraw-Hill.

Oakes, T. (2000, August). China's provincial identities: Reviving regionalism and reinventing "Chineseness." *The Journal of Asian Studies, 59*(3), 667-692.

Oates, B. J. (2006, 2007). *Researching information systems and computing*. New Delhi: Sage.

Oblinger, D., & Oblinger, J. (2005). Is it age or IT: First steps toward understanding the net generation. In D. Oblinger & J. Oblinger (Eds.), *Educating the net generation* (pp. 2.1-2.20). Boulder, CO: EDUCAUSE.

Oblinger, D., & Oblinger, J. (Eds.). (2005). *Educating the net generation*. Boulder, CO: EDUCAUSE.

Odabasi, H. F., & Can, V. (2002, October 23-26). Bilgisayar ve ogretim teknolojileri ogretmenligi dorduncu sinif ogrencilerinin bilgisayar ogretmenligi meslegi etik ilkelerine yonelik olcut gelistirme cabalari (Endeavors to develop a computer education ethics scale for senior students of computer education departments). *XI Egitim Bilimleri Kongresi* (pp. 64-69). Nicosia, Turkish Republic of Northern Cyprus.

Odabasi, H. F., Birinci, G., Kilicer, K., Sahin, M. C., Akbulut, Y., & Sendag, S. (2007). Bilgi iletisim teknolojileri ve Internet'le kolaylasan akademik usulsuzluk (Academic dishonesty: Getting easier with Internet and ICT). *Anadolu Universitesi Sosyal Bilimler Dergisi.*

ODISEAME. (2005). *Open distance inter-university synergies between Europe, Africa and Middle East*. Retrieved April 23, 2008, from http://proyectos.cedetel. es/General-web/ponLocale.jsp?idProyecto=328&nombr eClave=ODISEAME

OECD. (2001). *Starting strong—early childhood education and care*. Paris: OECD Publications.

Ogbu, J. U. (1987, December). Variability in minority school performance: A problem in search of an explanation. *Anthropology & Education Quarterly, 18*(4), Explaining the School Performance of Minority Students (pp. 312- 334).

Oliver, P. (2003). *The student's guide to research ethics*. Maidenhead: Open University Press.

Olivier, S. (2002). Ethics review of research projects involving human subjects. *Quest, 54*(3), 196-204.

Olt, M. R. (2002). Ethics and distance education: Strategies for minimizing academic dishonesty in online assessment. *Online Journal of Distance Learning Administration, (5)*, 3. Retrieved April 15, 2008, from http://www. westga.edu/~distance/ojdla/fall53/olt53.html

Oppeneimer, J. R. (1948). Physics in the contemporary world. *Bulletin of the Atomic Scientists, 4*(3), 65-86.

Oppenheim, C., & Pollecutt, N. (2000). Professional associations and ethical issues in LIS. *Journal of Librarianship and Information Science, 32*(4), 187-203.

Osguthorpe, R. T., Osguthorpe, R. D., Jacob, W. J., & Davies, R. (2003, March-April). The moral dimensions of instructional design. *Educational Technology*, 19-23.

Owen, M., Robert, L., Burgess, J., Golfman, N., & Sykes, S. (2001). *Report to the Social Sciences and Humanities Research Council of Canada, Implementation of the Tri-Council Policy Statement on Ethics in Human Research*

(TCPS) (Humanities Project). Unpublished paper, Humanities and Social Sciences Federation of Canada.

Oxford concise dictionary of English. (1990). Oxford: Oxford University Press.

Ozmon, H.A., & Craver, S.M. (2003). *Philosophical foundations of education* (7th ed.). Upper Saddle River, NJ: Merrill Prentice Hall.

Page, J. S. (2004). Cyber-pseudepigraphy: A new challenge for higher education policy and management. *Journal of Higher Education Policy and Management, 26*(1), 429-433.

Palloff, R. M., & Pratt, K. (1999). *Building learning communication in cyberspace: Effective strategies for the online classroom.* San Francisco: Jossey-Bass.

Palloff, R., & Pratt, K. (2003). *The virtual student—a profile and guide to working with online learners.* San Francisco: Jossey-Bass.

Palmer, M. T. (1995). Interpersonal communication and virtual reality: Mediating interpersonal relationships. *In F.* Biocca & M. R. Levy (Eds.), *Communication in the age of virtual reality* (pp. 277-299). Hillside, NJ: Lawrence Erlbaum.

Park, C. (2003). In other (people's) words: Plagiarism by university students—literature and lessons. *Assessment & Evaluation in Higher Education, 28*(5), 471-488.

Parker, D. B. (1979). *Ethical conflicts in computer science and technology.* Arlington, VA: AFIPS Press.

Parker, D. B., Swope, S., & Baker, B. N. (1991). *Ethical conflicts in information and computer science, technology, and business.* QED Information Sciences.

Parker, L. D. (2005). Corporate governance crisis down under: Post-Enron accounting education and research inertia. *European Accounting Review, 14*(2), 383-394.

Parscal, T. J. (2007). *Using the cognitive apprenticeship framework to teach asynchronous facilitation skills for faculty teaching in an online accelerated adult learning setting.* Doctoral dissertation, Capella University, MN.

Retrieved April 23, 2008, from ProQuest Digital Dissertations database. (Publication No. AAT 3264302)

Parsons, P., & Ross, D. (2002). *Planning a campus to support hybrid learning.* Retrieved April 22, 2008, from http://www.mcli.dist.maricopa.edu/ocotillo/tv/hybrid_planning.html

Pask, G. (1975). *Conversation cognition and learning: A cybernetic theory and methodology.* Amsterdam: Elsevier.

Pask, G. (1976). *Conversation theory: Applications in education and epistemology.* Amsterdam: Elsevier.

Pavlova, M. (2005). Social change: How should technology education respond? *International Journal of Technology and Design Education, 15*, 199-215.

Peele, S. (2002). *The continuing significance of David Robinson's plagiarism career.* Retrieved April 23, 2008, from http://www.peele.net/debate/robinson.html

Pelz, B. (2004, June). (My) three principles of effective on-line pedagogy. *JALN, 8*(3).

Pendlebury, S., & Enslin, P. (2001). Representation, identification and trust: Towards and ethics of educational research. *Journal of Philosophy of Education, 35*(3), 361-370.

Perry, W.G. (1970). *Forms of intellectual and ethical development in the college years: A scheme.* New York: Holt, Rinehart and Winston.

Peters, R. S. (1966). *Ethics and education.* London: George Allen and Unwin.

Pewewardy, C. (2002). Learning styles of American Indian/Alaska Native students: A review of the literature and implications for practice. *Journal of American Indian Education, 41*(3), 22-56.

Pewewardy, C., & Hammer, P. C. (2003, December). *Culturally responsive teaching for American Indian students* (p. EDO-RC-03-10). ERIC Clearinghouse on Rural Education and Small Schools.

Phillips, M. R., & Horton, V. (2000). Cybercheating: Has morality evaporated in business education? *International Journal of Educational Management, 14*(4), 150-155.

Piaget, J. (1977). Intellectual evolution from adolescence to adulthood. In P.N. Johnson-Laird & P.C. Wason (Eds.), *Thinking: Readings in cognitive science.* Cambridge University Press.

Picard, R.W. (1997). *Affective computing.* Cambridge, MA: MIT Press.

Picard, R.W., & Klein, J. (2002). Computers that recognise and respond to user emotion: Theoretical and practical implications. *Interacting with Computers, 14,* 141-169.

Picciano, A. G. (2002, July). Beyond student perceptions: Issues of interaction, presence, and performance in an online course. *Journal of Asynchronous Learning Networks (JALN), 6*(1), 21-40.

Planalp, S. (1999). *Communicating emotion: Social, moral and cultural processes.* Cambridge, MA: Cambridge University Press.

Population, Inc. (2001, April). *Technology Review, 104*(3), 51-55.

Postle, G., Clarke, J., Bull, D., Skuja, E., McCann, H., & Batorowicz, K. (1996). *Equity, diversity and excellence: Advancing the national higher education equity framework.* Canberra, Australia: National Board of Employment Education and Training.

Postmas, T. (2007). The psychological dimensions of collective action, online. In A. Joinson, K. McKenna, T. Postmes, & U. Reips (Eds.), *Oxford handbook of Internet psychology* (pp. 165-184). Oxford: Oxford University Press.

Pratt, D. (1998). Ethical reasoning in teaching adults. In M. Galbraith (Ed.), *Adult learning methods: A guide for effective instruction* (chap. 6). Malabar: Krieger.

Pring, R. (2002). The virtues and vices of an educational researcher. In M. McNamee & D. Bridges (Eds.), *The ethics of educational research* (pp. 111-127). Oxford, UK: Blackwell.

Pritchard, I. A. (2002). Travelers and trolls: Practitioner research and institutional review boards. *Educational Researcher, 31*(3), 3-13.

Probst, R.E. (1987). Transactional theory in the teaching of literature. *ERIC Digest* ED 284 274. Retrieved April 15, 2008, from http://www.ed.gov/databases/ERIC_Digests/ed284274.html

Publication manual of the American Psychological Association (5th ed.). (2002). Washington, DC: American Psychological Association.

Punch, K. F. (1998). *Introduction to social research: Quantitative and qualitative approaches.* London: Sage.

Punch. M. (1998). Politics and ethics in qualitative research. In N. Denzin & Y. Lincoln (Eds.), *The landscape of qualitative research: Theories and issues* (pp. 156-184). London: Sage.

Quinn, M. J. (2005). *Ethics for the information age* (2nd ed.) Boston: Addison-Wesley.

Radoykov, B. (Ed.). (2007). *Ethical implications of emerging technologies: A survey.* Paris: UNESCO, Information Society Division, Communication and Information Sector.

Rafaeli, S., Sudweeks, F., Konstan, J., & Mabry, E. (1994). *ProjectH Overview: A quantitative study of computer-mediated communication.* Retrieved April 22, 2008, from http://www.it.murdoch.edu.au/~sudweeks/papers/techrep.html

Ramsey, C. (2003). Using virtual learning environments to facilitate new learning relationships. *The International Journal of Management Education, 3*(2), 31-51.

Redding, P. (2005). The evolving interpretations of customers in higher education: Empowering the elusive. *International Journal of Consumer Studies, 29*(5), 409-417.

Reed, D., & Sork, T.J. (1990). Ethical considerations in distance education. *American Journal of Distance Education, 4*(2), 30-43.

Reid, E. (1996). Informed consent in the study of on-line communities: A reflection of the effects of computer-mediated social research. *The Information Society, 12*(2), 169-174. Retrieved on April 22, 2008, from http://venus.soci.niu.edu/~jthomas/ethics/tis/go.libby

Rekkedal, T. (1982). The drop out problem and what to do about it. In J. Daniel, M. Stroud, & J. Thompson (Ed.), *Learning at a distance—a world perspective.*

Renner, J.S. (1976). Formal operational thought and its identification. In J.W. Renner, et al. (Eds.), *Research, teaching, and learning with the Piaget Model* (pp. 64-78). Norman, OK: Oklahoma University Press.

Research ethics review. *The Journal of the Association of Research Ethics Committees.* Retrieved April 23, 2008, from http://www.research-ethics-review.com/

Revised ethical guidelines for educational research (2004). *British Educational Research Association.* Retrieved April 23, 2008, from http://www.bera.ac.uk/publications/guides.php

Reynolds, G. (2006). *Ethics in information technology* (2nd ed.). Boston: Thomson Course Technology.

Rickwood, P., & Goodwin, V. (1999). A worthwhile education? In A. Tait & R. Mills (Eds.), *The convergence of distance and conventional education* (pp. 110-123). London: Routledge.

Riding, R., & Rayner., S. (1998). *Cognitive styles and learning strategies: Understanding style differences in learning and behaviour.* London: David Fulton.

Rigano, D. (2001). Researcher-participant positioning in classroom research. *International Journal of Qualitative Studies in Education, 16*(6), 741-755.

Roberts, D. M., & Rabinowitz, W. (1992). An investigation of student perceptions of cheating in academic situations. *The Review of Higher Education, 15*(2), 179-90.

Roberts, P. (2000). *Ethical dilemmas in researching online communities: "Bottom-up" ethical wisdom for computer-mediated social research.* Retrieved on April 22, 2008, from http://www.com.unisa.edu.au/cccc/papers/refereed/paper40/Paper40-1.htm

Roberts, P., Anderson, J., & Yanish, P. (1997). Academic misconduct: Where do we start? In *Paper presented at the Annual Conference of the Northern Rocky Mountain Educational Research Association*, Jackson, WY.

Robinett, J. (Ed.). (1989). *Computers & ethics: A sourcebook for discussions.* Polytechnic Press.

Robinson-Pant, A. (2005). *Cross-cultural perspectives in educational research. Conducting educational research.* Columbus, OH: Open University press.

Rogerson, S., & Gotterbarn, D. (1998). *The ethics of software project management.* Centre for Computing and Social Responsibility, De Montfort University, UK. Retrieved April 16, 2008, from http://ccsr.cse.dmu.ac.uk/staff/Srog/teaching/sweden.htm

Rolfe, H. (2003). University strategy in an age of uncertainty: The effect of higher education funding on old and new universities. *Higher Education Quarterly, 57*(1), 24-47.

Rose, G. (2001). *Visual methodologies: An introduction to the interpretation of visual materials.* London: Sage.

Rosenblatt, L.M. (1994). *The reader, the text, the poem: The transactional theory of the literary work.* Carbondale, IL: Southern Illinois Press. (Reprinted from 1978).

Ross, K. A. (2005). Academic dishonesty and the Internet. *Communications of the ACM, 48*(10).

Rotenberg, M. (1998). Communications privacy: Implications for network design. In R. N. Stichler & R. Hauptman (Eds.), *Ethics, information and technology readings.* Jefferson, NC: McFarland & Company.

Roth, W.-M. (2004). Qualitative research and ethics. *Forum: Qualitative Social Research, 5*(2). Retrieved April 22, 2008, from http://www.qualitative-research.net/fqs/

Rourke, L., Anderson, T., Garrison, D. R., & Archer, W. (2000). Methodological issues in the content analysis of computer conference transcripts. *International Journal of Artificial Intelligence in Education, 11*(3). Retrieved on April 22, 2008, from http://http://communitiesofinquiry.com/

Rourke, L., Anderson, T., Garrison, R., & Archer, W. (1999). Assessing social presence in asynchronous text-based computer conferencing. *Journal of Distance Education, 14*(2), 50-71.

Rowe, N. (2004, Summer). Cheating in online student assessment: Beyond plagiarism. *Online Journal of Distance Learning Administration, VII*(II). Retrieved April 22, 2008, from http://www.westga.edu/~distance/ojdla/articles/summer2004/rowe72.pdf

Rowson, R. (2006). *Working ethics: How to be fair in a culturally complex world.* London: Jessica Kingsley.

Rubin, R. (2000). *Foundations of library and information science.* New York: Neal-Schuman.

Russell, G. (2004). The distancing dilemma in distance education. *International Journal of Instructional Technology and Distance Education, 2*(2). Retrieved April 16, 2008, from http://www.itdl.org/journal/Feb_04/article03.htm

Russell, G. (2005). The distancing question in online education. *Innovate, 1*(4). Retrieved April 16, 2008, from http://www.innovateonline.info/index.php?view=article&id=13

Russell, G. (2006). Globalisation, responsibility, and virtual schools. *Australian Journal of Education, 50*(2), 140-54.

Russell, T. L. (1999). *The no significant difference phenomenon: A comparative research annotated bibliography on technology for distance education.* North Carolina State University: IDECC.

Ryen, A. (2004). Ethical issues. In C. Seale, G. Gobo, J. F. Gubrium, & D. Silverman (Eds.), *Qualitative research practice* (pp. 230-247). London: Sage.

Sabin, C., & Ahern, T. C. (2002, November). Instructional design and culturally diverse learners. In *Proceedings of the 32nd ASEE/IEEE Frontiers in Education Conference,* (pp. S1C-10 to S1C-14).

Sadler-Smith, E. (2001). The relationship between learning style and cognitive style. *Personality and Individual Differences, 30*(4), 609-616.

Sale, K. (1995). *Rebels against the future.* Reading, MA: Addison-Wesley.

Sammons, J. L. (1992). Rebellious ethics and Albert Speer. *Professional Ethics, 1*(3-4), 77-116.

Sankey, M., & St Hill, R. (2005, July 11-12). Multimodal design for hybrid learning materials in a second level economics course. In *Paper presented at the Eleventh Australasian Teaching Economics Conference: Innovation for Student Engagement in Economics,* University of Sydney, Australia.

Sarasin, L. C. (1999). *Learning styles perspectives: Impact in the classroom.* Madison, WI: Atwood.

Savage, G. J. (2001). International technical communication programs and global ethics. In *Proceedings of the 28th Annual Conference, Council for Programs in Technical and Scientific Communication: Managing Change and Growth in Technical and Scientific Communication,* Pittsburgh, PA, (pp. 84-85).

Savin-Baden, M., & Wilkie, K. (2006). *Problem-based learning online.* Maidenhead: Open University Press.

Savulescu, J., Chalmers, I., & Blunt, J. (1996). *Are research ethics committees behaving unethically? Some suggestions for improving accountability and performance.* Retrieved April 23, 2008, from http://www.bmj.com/cgi/content/full/313/7069/1390?ijkey=uMbVZJcQJvX3E

Sawyer, R. K. (2001). *Creating conversations: Improvisation in everyday discourse.* Cresskill, NJ: Hampton Press.

Scardamalia, M., & Bereiter, C. (1994). Computer support for knowledge-building communities. *Journal of the Learning Sciences, 3*(3), 265-283. Retrieved April 15, 2008, from http://carbon.cudenver.edu/~bwilson/building.html

Schein, E. H. (1993, April). On dialogue, culture, and organizational learning. *Reflections, 4*(4). Society for Organizational Learning (pp. 27-38).

Schlaefi, A., Rest, J. R., & Thoma, S. J. (1985). Does moral education improve moral judgment? A meta-analysis of intervention studies using the defining issues test. *Review of Educational Research, 55,* 319-52.

Schmidt, K. (Ed.). (1999). *Understanding the business of library acquisitions.* Chicago, IL: American Library Association.

Schrum, L. (1995). Framing the debate: Ethical research in the information age. *Quarterly Inquiry, 1*(3), 311-326.

Schrum, L. (1997). Ethical research in the information age: Beginning the dialog. *Computer in Human Behavior, 13*(2), 117-125.

Schuetze, H. G., & Slowey, M. (2002). Participation and exclusion: A comparative analysis of non-traditional students and lifelong learners in higher education. *Higher Education, 44*(3/4), 309-327.

Schultz, M., & Hatch, M. J. (1996, April). Living with multiple paradigms: The case of paradigm interplay in organizational culture studies. *The Academy of Management Review, 21*(2), 529-557.

Sclove, R. (2006). I'd hammer out freedom: Technology as politics and culture. In M. E. Winston & R. D. Edelbach (Eds.), *Society, ethics and technology* (3rd ed., pp. 83-91. Belmont, CA: Thomson.

Scott, B. (2001). Conversation theory: A constructivist, dialogical approach to educational technology. *Cybernetics and Human Knowing, 8*(4), 25-46.

Scott, P. (1995). *The meanings of mass higher education.* Buckingham: Society for Research into Higher Education/Open University Press.

Searle, J. (1969). *Speech acts: An essay in the philosophy of language.* Cambridge: Cambridge University Press.

Secondlife. Retrieved April 22, 2008, from http://secondlife.com/

Seitz, J., & O'Neill, P. (1996). Ethical decision making and the code of ethics of the Canadian Psychological Association. *Canadian Psychology, 37,* 23-30.

Sendag, S., & Odabasi, H. F. (2006, April 19-21). Internet ve cocuk: Etik bunun neresinde?(Internet and the child: Where does ethics lie?). In *Proceedings of the 6th International Educational Technology Conference,* (pp. 1508-1515). Famagusta, Turkish Republic of Northern Cyprus.

Seneca, A. L. (2007). *On anger: Seneca's essays* (Vol. 1, pp. xliii, 3-5, 111). Retrieved April 16, 2008, from http://www.stoics.com/seneca_essays_book_1.html

Sergiovanni, T. (1992). *Moral leadership—getting the most of school improvement.* San Francisco: Jossey-Bass.

Shanghai Jiao Tong University Institute of Higher Education, SJTUIHE. (2006). *Academic ranking of world universities.* Retrieved April 3, 2008, from http://ed.sjtu.edu.cn/ranking.htm

Shapiro, J.P., & Stefkovich, J.A. (2001). *Ethical leadership and decision making in education: Applying theoretical perspectives to complex dilemmas.* Mahwah, NJ: Lawrence Erlbaum.

Sharf, B. (1999). Beyond netiquette: The ethics of doing naturalistic discourse research on the Internet. In S. Jones (Ed.), *Doing Internet research* (pp. 243-256). Thousand Oaks, CA: Sage.

Sharma, P., & Maleyeff, J. (2003). Internet education: Potential problems and solutions. *International Journal of Educational Management, 17*(1), 19-25.

Shaw, T. (2003). Making IT work for learning: Technology and the test. *Multimedia Schools 10,* 38-39. Retrieved April 22, 2008, from http://www.infotoday.com/mmschools/may03/shaw.shtml

Sheard, J., & Lynch, J. (2003). Accommodating learner diversity in Web-based learning environments: Imperatives for future developments. *International Journal of Computer Processing of Oriental Languages, 16*(4), 243-260.

Shepherd, J. (2005, October 7). Guide steers campuses through moral mazes. *Times Higher Education Supplement,* p. 6.

Shin, N., & Kim, J. (1999). An exploration of learner progress and drop out in the Korean National Open University. *Distance Education, 20*(1), 81-95.

Shumur, W. (2004). Global pressures, local reactions: Higher education and neo-liberal economic policies. *International Journal of Qualitative Studies in Education, 17*(6), 823-839.

Sichel, B. A. (1993). Ethics committees and teacher ethics. In K. Strike & P. L. Ternasky (Eds.), *Ethics for professionals in education: Perspectives for preparation and practice* (pp. 162-75). New York: Teachers College Press.

Sikes, P. (2006). On dodgy ground? Problematics and ethics in educational research. *International Journal of Research and Method in Education, 29*(1), 105-117.

Simon, (2005). Assessment in online courses: Some questions and a novel technique. *Research & Development in Higher Education, 28*, 500-506.

Simon, C. A., Carr, J. R., McCullough, S. M., Morgan, S. J., Oleson, T., & Ressel, M. (2003). The other side of academic dishonesty: The relationship between faculty skepticism, gender, and strategies for managing student academic dishonesty cases. *Assessment & Evaluation in Higher Education, 28*, 193-207.

Simons, H., & Usher, R. (Eds.). (2000). *Situated ethics in educational research*. New York: RoutledgeFalmer.

Simonson, M. (1999). Equivalency theory and distance education. *TechTrends, 43*(5), 5-8.

Simpson, C. (Ed.). (2003). *Ethics in school librarianship: A reader*. Worthington, OH: Linworth.

Simpson, J. H. (1996, Summer). "The Great Reversal:" Selves, communities, and the global system. *Sociology of Religion, 57*(2), 115-125.

Simpson, O. (1992). Specifying support services in the OU—the so-called "student charter." *Open Learning, 7*(2), 57-59.

Simpson, O. (2002). *Supporting students in online, open and distance learning* (p. 168). London: RoutledgeFalmer. ISBN 0 749437405.

Simpson, O. (2003). *Student retention in online, open and distance learning* (p. 168). London: RoutledgeFalmer. ISBN 0 7494 3999 8.

Simpson, O. (2004). Doing it hard. In G. Crosling & G. Webb (Eds.), *Supporting student learning: Case studies, experience and practice from higher education* (pp. 34-40). Kogan Page. ISBN 0 7494 3535 6.

Simpson, O. (2004). Social exclusion and online learning. *Global perspectives on e-learning—rhetoric and reality* (pp. 89-100). Sage. ISBN 1412904897.

Simpson, O. (2004). Student retention and the course choice process—the UK open university experience. *Journal of Access Policy and Practice, 2*(1), 44-58.

Simpson, O. (2004). The impact on retention of interventions to support distance students. *Open Learning, 19*(1), 79-95.

Simpson, O. (2005). The costs and benefits of student retention for students, institutions and governments. *Studies in Learning Evaluation Innovation and Development (Australia), 2*(3), 34-43. Retrieved April 22, 2008, from http://sleid.cqu.edu.au/viewissue.php?id=8

Simpson, O. (2005). Web-based learning: Are we becoming obsessed? *Distance Learning, 26*(1), 153-157. ISSN 0158-7919.

Simpson, O. (2006). Predicting student progress. *Open Learning, 21*(2), 125-138.

Simpson, O. (2006). Rescuing the personal tutor. In Thomas & Hixenbaugh (Eds.), *Perspectives on personal tutoring in mass higher education*. Trentham Books. ISBN-10:1-85856-385-2.

Simpson, O. (2006). This door is alarmed. *Journal of Access, Policy and Practice, 3*(2).

Simpson, O. (2007). Cost benefits of student retention policies and practices. In Bramble & Panda (Eds.), *Economics of distance and online learning*. Lawrence Erlbaum.

Sims, R. L. (1993, March-April). The relationship between academic dishonesty and unethical business practices. *Journal of Education for Business, 68,* 207-211.

Sims, R. R., & Felton, E. L., Jr. (2006). Designing and delivering business ethics teaching and learning. *Journal of Business Ethics, 63,* 297-312.

Singhal, A. (1982). Factors in students' dishonesty. *Psychological Reports, 51,* 775-780.

Sivin, J. P., & Bialo, E. R. (1992). *Ethical use of information technologies in education: Important issues for America's schools.* Washington, DC: National Institute of Justice.

Slobogin, K. (2002). *Survey: Many students say cheating's ok.* CNN.com/Education. Retrieved April 22, 2008, from http://archives.cnn.com/2002/fyi/teachers.ednews/04/05/highschool.cheating

Small, R. (2002). Codes are not enough: What philosophy can contribute to the ethics of educational research. In M. McNamee & D. Bridges (Eds.), *The ethics of educational research* (pp. 89-110). Oxford, UK: Blackwell.

Smith, A., Ling, P., & Hill, D. (2006). The adoption of multiple modes of delivery in Australian universities. *Journal of University Teaching and Learning Practice, 3*(2), 67-81. Retrieved April 22, 2008, from http://jutlp.uow.edu.au/2006_v2003_i2002/2006_v2003_i2002.html

Somekh, B. (2004). Taking the sociological imagination to school: An analysis of the (lack of) impact of information and communication technologies on education systems. *Technology, Pedagogy and Education, 13*(2), 163-179.

Son, J. B., & O'Neill, S. (Eds.). (2005). *Enhancing learning and teaching: Pedagogy, technology and language.* Flaxton, Queensland: Post Pressed.

Southwest Texas State University-SWT. (2001). *Final report: The presidential task force on academic honesty.* Southwest Texas State University. Retrieved April 16, 2008, from http://uweb.txstate.edu/~sw05/FINALRE-PORT.htm

Spafford, E. H. (1997). Are hacker break-ins ethical? In M. D. Ermann, M. B. Williams, & M. S. Shauf (Eds.), *Computers, ethics, and society.* New York: Oxford University Press.

Spain, J. W., Engle, A. D., & Thompson, J. C. (2005). Applying multiple pedagogical methodologies in an ethics awareness week: Expectations, events, evaluation, and enhancements. *Journal of Business Ethics, 58,* 7-16.

Spalding, E., & Wilson, A. (2002). Demystifying reflection, *Teachers College Record, 104*(7), 1393-1421.

Speck, B.W. (2002). The academy, online classes, and the breach in ethics. *New Directions for Teaching and Learning, 2000***(84), 73-81.**

Spinello, R. (1997). *Case studies in information and computer ethics.* Upper Saddle River, NJ: Prentice Hall.

Spinello, R. (2002). *CyberEthics: Morality and law in cyberspace* (2nd ed.). Sudbury, MA: Jones and Bartlett.

Spinello, R. (2003). *Case studies in information technology ethics* (2nd ed.). Upper Saddle River, NJ: Prentice Hall.

Spinello, R. (2003). *CyberEthics: Morality and law in cyberspace.* Sudbury, MA: Jones and Bartlett.

Spinello, R. A., & Tavani, H. T. (2004). *Readings in cyberethics* (2nd ed.). Sudbury, NJ: Jones and Bartlett.

St Hill, R. (2000, November). Modal preference in a teaching strategy. In *Paper presented at the Effective Teaching and Learning at University,* Duchesne College, the University of Queensland.

Stanley, B. H., Sieber, J. E., & Melton, G. B. (Eds.). (1996). *Research ethics. A psychological approach.* Lincoln, NE: University of Nebraska Press.

Starke-Meyerring, D. (1999). Developing an online learning environment for international technical communication. *Communication jazz: Improvising the new international communication culture* (pp. 13-20). IEEE.

Starratt, R. J. (1991). Building an ethical school: A theory for practice in educational leadership. *Educational Administration Quarterly, 27*(2), 185-202.

Starratt, R. J. (2004). *Ethical leadership.* San Francisco: Jossey-Bass.

Stefkovich, J.A., & O'Brien, G.M. (2004). Best interests of the student: An ethical model. *Journal of Educational Administration, 42*(2), 197-214.

Stephenson, J. (2001). *Teaching & learning online—pedagogies for new technologies.* London: Kogan Page.

Sterngold, A. (2004). Confronting plagiarism: How conventional teaching invites cybercheating. *Change, 36,* 16-21.

Stevenson, J. T. (1987). *Engineering ethics: Practices and principles.* Toronto: Canadian Scholars Press.

Stewart, J., & Williams, R. (1998). The co-evolution of society and multimedia technology. *Social Science Computer Review, 16*(3), 268-282.

Stitt. (2000). *Not my future.* Glebe: Blake Education. *Responsibility for School Education in an Online Globalised World.* Retrieved April 16, 2008, from http://www.cybertext.net.au/tct2002/disc_papers/organisation/russell.htm

Stoeger, S. (2006). *Plagiarism.* Retrieved April 23, 2008, from http://www.web-miner.com/plagiarism

Stoll, C. (1995). *Silicon snake oil.* New York: Anchor Books Doubleday.

Stoney, S., & McMahon, M. (2004, December). Bulletproof assessment, war stories, and tactics: Avoiding cybercheating. In R. Atkinson, C. McBeath, D. Jonas-Dwyer, & R. Phillips (Eds.), *Beyond the comfort zone: Proceedings of the 21st ASCILITE Conference,* (pp. 881-886). Perth. Retrieved April 23, 2008, from http://www.ascilite.org.au/conferences/perth04/procs/stoney.html

Straw, J. (2000). Keep your eyes off the screen: Online cheating and what we can do about it. *Academic Exchange Quarterly, 4,* 21-25.

Streibel, M. J. (1988). A critical analysis of three approaches to the use of computers in education. In L. E. Beyer & M. W. Apple (Eds.), *The curriculum: Problems,* *politics and possibilities* (pp. 259-288). Albany: State University of New York Press.

Strike, K., Ternasky, P., & Lance, E. (1993). *Ethics for professionals in education: Perspectives for preparation and practice.* New York: Teachers College Press.

Strother, J. B. (2003). Shaping blended learning pedagogy for East Asian learning styles. *The shape of knowledge* (pp. 353-357). IEEE.

Sudweeks, F., & Ess, C. (Eds.). (2004). *Cultural attitudes towards technology and communication.* Perth: Murdoch University.

Summer, J. (2000). Serving the system: A critical history of distance education. *Open Learning, 15*(3), 267-285.

Sumner, J., & Dewar, K. (2002). Peer-to-peer e-learning and the team effect on course completion. In *Proceedings of the International Conference on Computers in Education.*

Sunderland, J. (2002). New communication practices, identity and the psychological gap: The affective function of e-mail on a distance doctoral program. *Studies in Higher Education, 27*(2), 233-246.

Suthers, D. (2005, January). Collaborative knowledge building through shared representations. In *Proceedings of the 38th Hawaii International Conference on the System Sciences,* Wakaloa.

Sutton, L.A. (2001). The principle of vicarious interaction in computer-mediated communications. *International Journal of Educational Telecommunications, 7*(3), 223-242. Retrieved April 15, 2008, from http://www.eas.asu.edu/elearn/research/suttonnew.pdf

Swaner, L.E. (2005). Educating for personal and social responsibility: A review of the literature. *Liberal Education, 91*(3), 14-21.

Sweda, J. E. (2004). *When is plagiarism not cheating?* Retrieved April 23, 2008, from http://www.library.cmu.edu/ethics8.html

Sweller, J. (1999). *Instructional design in technical areas.* Melbourne: ACER Press.

Szabo, A., & Underwood, J. (2004). Cybercheats: Is information and communication technology fuelling academic dishonesty? *Active Learning in Higher Education, 5,* 180-199.

Taber, K. (2002). "Intense, but it's all worth it in the end:" The co-learner's experience of the research process. *British Educational Research Journal, 28*(3), 435-457.

Tait, A, & Mills, R. (1999). *The convergence of distance and conventional education: Patterns of flexibility for the individual learner.* New York: Routledge.

Tait, A. (1989). The politics of open learning. *Adult Education, 61*(4), 308-313.

Tavani, H. (2007). *Ethics and technology: Ethical issues in an age of information and communication technology.* Boston: John Wiley & Sons.

Tavani, H. T. (2003). *Ethics in an age of information and communication technology.* Chichester: Wiley.

Tavani, H. T. (2004). *Ethics and technology: Ethical issues in an age of information and communication technology.* Hoboken, NJ: John Wiley and Sons.

Tavani, H. T. (2006). *Ethics and technology: Ethical issues in an age of information and communication technology* (2nd ed.). San Francisco: John Wiley.

Taylor, B. (2001). *Academic integrity: A letter to my students.* Retrieved April 22, 2008, from http://www.grinnell.edu/academic/writinglab/faculty_resources/letter_to_my_students.pdf

Taylor, E. (1983). *Orientations to study: A longitudinal interview investigation of students in two human studies degree courses at Surrey University.* Doctoral thesis, Guildford, University of Surrey.

Taylor, J. C. (2004, February). Will universities become extinct in the networked world? In *Paper presented at the ICDE World Conference on Open & Distance Learning,* Hong Kong.

TCPS. (2005). *Tri-council policy statement [TCPS]: Ethical conduct for research involving humans.* See Medical Research Council of Canada.

Tennant, M.C., & Pogson, P. (1995). *Learning and change in the adult years: A developmental perspective.* San Francisco: Jossey-Bass.

The logic of privacy. (2007, January 6). *The Economist, 382*(8510), 65-66.

Thomas, J. (1996). When cyber research goes awry: The ethics of the Rimm "Cyberporn" study. *The Information Society, 12*(2), 189-198. Retrieved April 22, 2008, from http://venus.soci.niu.edu/~jthomas/ethics/tis/go.jt

Thomas, J. (1996). Introduction: A debate about the ethics of fair practices for collecting social science data in cyberspace. *The Information Society, 12*(2), 107-117. Retrieved April 22, 2008, from http://venus.soci.niu.edu/~jthomas/ethics/tis/go.jt

Thompson, J., Baird, P., & Downie, J. (2002). *Report of the committee of inquiry on the case involving Dr. Nancy Olivieri, the Hospital for Sick Children, the University of Toronto, and Apotex Inc.* Downloaded April 23, 2008, from http://www.caut.ca/en/issues/academicfreedom/olivieriinquiryreport.pdf

Thompson, L. C., & Williams, P. G. (1995). But I changed three words! Plagiarism in the ESL classroom. *Clearing House, 69*(1), 27-9.

Thompson, P. B. (2007). *Food biotechnology in ethical perspective* (2nd ed.). Dordrecht, NL: Springer-Verlag.

Thorpe, M. (1988). *Evaluating open and distance learning.* Harlow, UK: Longman.

Thorseth, M. (2006). Worldwide deliberation and public reason online. *Ethics and information Technology, 8,* 243-252.

Tickle, L. (2002). Opening windows, closing doors: Ethical dilemmas in educational action research. In M. McNamee & D. Bridges (Eds.), *The ethics of educational research* (pp. 41-57). Oxford, UK: Blackwell.

Tiffin, J., & Rajasingham, L. (2003). *The global virtual university.* London and New York: RoutledgeFalmer.

Tilley, S.A., Killins, J., & Van Oosten, D. (2005). Connections and tensions between university and school districts: Research review boards and school-based research. *Alberta Journal of Educational Research, 51*(3), 277-293.

Tinto, V. (1997). *Leaving college: Rethinking the causes and cures of student attrition* (2nd ed.). Chicago, IL: University of Chicago Press.

Tom, G., & Borin, N. (1988). Cheating in academe. *Journal of Education for Business, 63*(4), 153-7.

Tomkins, S.S. (1984). Affect theory. In K.R. Scherer & P. Ekman (Eds.), *Approaches to emotion* (pp. 163-195). Hillsdale, NJ: Erlbaum.

Torres, C. A. (2002). Globalization, education and citizenship: Solidarity versus markets? *American Educational Research Journal, 39*(2), 363-378.

Trevino, L. K., Hartman, L. P., & Brown, M. (2000). Moral person and moral manager: How executives develop a reputation for ethical leadership. *California Management Review, 42*(4), 128-142.

Tri-council Code of Ethical Conduct for Research Involving Humans. (1998). *Tri-council policy statement.* Retrieved April 22, 2008, from http://www.ncehr-cnerh.org/english/code_2/

TUBITAK. (2006). Bilimsel dergilere gonderilen makalelerde dikkat edilmesi gereken noktalar (Matters to consider in articles being sent to scientific journals). *Council of Research and Publication Ethics.* Retrieved April 23, 2008, from http://journals.tubitak.gov.tr/genel/brosur.pdf

Turkle, S. (1997). *Life on the screen. Identify in the age of the Internet.* New York: Touchstone.

Underwood, J. (2003). Academic offenses and e-learning: Individual propensities in cheating. *British Journal of Educational Technology, 34*(4), 467-477.

Underwood, J., & Szabo, A. (2003). Academic offences and e-learning: Individual propensities in cheating. *British Journal of Educational Technology, 34*(4), 467-77.

United States Congress, Senate Committee on Governmental Affaris. (2001). *Office of Government Ethics*

Authorization Act of 2001: Report of the Committee on Governmental Affairs. Washington, DC: Government Printing Office.

University of Ibadan Center for External Studies Programme. (2007). Retrieved April 16, 2008, from http://www.ui.edu.ng/undergraduateadmission.htm

University of London External Degree Program: Our history. (2008). Retrieved April 16, 2008, from Http://www.londonexternal.ac.uk/about_us/history.shtml

University of South Africa (UNISA) information brochure. (2008). UNISA, Pretoria, South Africa. Retrieved April 16, 2008, from http://www.unisa.ac.za

University of Utah. (2005). *Willowbrook Hepatitis studies.* Retrieved April 23, 2008, from http://www.hum.utah.edu/~bbenham/Research%20Ethics%20Website/INTM-Dcs_Willowbrook.htm

Usher, P. (2000). Feminist approaches to a situated ethics. In H. Simons & R. Usher (Eds.), *Situated ethics in educational research* (pp. 22-38). New York: RoutledgeFalmer.

USQ. (2005). *Learning and teaching plan, goal 4: A flexible and responsive learning environment.* Retrieved April 22, 2008, from http://www.usq.edu.au/learnteach/enhancement/plan/goal4.htm

USQ. (2005). *Policy on learning and teaching.* Retrieved April 22, 2008, from http://www.usq.edu.au/resources/75.pdf

USQ. (2005). *Policy on multiculturalism.* Retrieved April 22, 2008, from http://www.usq.edu.au/resources/126.pdf

USQ. (2005). *USQ equity in education policy.* Retrieved April 22, 2008, from http://www.usq.edu.au/resources/127.pdf

USQ. (2006). *Transmodal delivery.* Retrieved April 22, 2008, from http://www.usq.edu.au/dec/research/transmodal.htm

Uysal, O. (2006). *Ogretmen adaylarinin bilgisayar etigine iliskin gorusleri (Views of teacher trainees on computer ethics).* Doctoral dissertation, Anadolu University Graduate School of Educational Sciences, Eskisehir, Turkey.

Uysal, O., & Odabasi, H. F. (2006, April 19-21). Bilgisayar etigi ogretiminde kullanilan yontemler (Methods used in teaching computer ethics). In *Proceedings of the 6th International Educational Technology Conference,* (pp. 1639-1652). Famagusta, Turkish Republic of Northern Cyprus.

Valasquez, M. G. (1990). Corporate ethics: Losing it, having it, getting it. In P. Madsen & J. M. Shafritz (Eds.), *Essentials of business ethics* (pp. 228-244). Penguin Books.

Valli, E. (1997). Listening to other voices: A description of teacher reflection in the United States. *Peabody Journal of Education, 72*(1), 67-88.

Van den Hoonaard, W. (2004). *Giving voice to the spectrum.* Report of the Social Sciences and Humanities Research Ethics Special Working Committee to the Interagency Advisory Panel on Research Ethics. Ottawa, Canada: Author.

Verbeek, P.-P. (2005). *What things do: Philosophical reflections on technology, agency and design* (R. P. Crease, Trans.). University Park, PA: Pennsylvania State University Press.

Vergnani, L. (2005, June 8). Learning to enjoy e-learning. *The Australian,* p. 31.

Vissar, J., & Suzuki, K. (2006). Designing for the world at large: A tale of two settings. In R. Reiser & J. Dempsey (Eds.), *Trends and issues in instructional design and technology* (2nd ed., pp. 234-244). NJ: Pearsons.

Visser, J. (2001). Ethics in distance education and open learning. In *Proceedings of the Presidential Session at the International Council for Distance Education Conference, Dusseldorf.* Retrieved April 22, 2008, from http://www.learndev.org/ppt/ICDE-2001/

von Glasersfeld, E. (1995). *Radical constructivism: A way of knowing and learning.* London: RoutledgeFalmer.

Vujakovic, P., & Bullard, J. (2001). The ethics minefield: Issues of responsibility in learning and research. *Journal of Geography in Higher Education, 25*(2), 275-283.

Vygotsky, L.S. (1978). *Mind in society: The development of higher psychological processes.* Cambridge, MA: Harvard University Press.

Wajda-Johnston, V. A., Handal, P. J., Brawer, P. A., & Fabricatore, A. N. (2001). Academic dishonesty at the graduate level. *Ethics & Behavior, 11,* 287-305.

Walker, D.F., & Soltis, J.F. (1997). *Curriculum and aims.* New York: Teachers College.

Walker, K., & Hackman, M. (1992). Multiple predictors of perceived learning and satisfaction: The importance of information transfer and nonverbal immediacy in the televised course. *Distance Education, 13*(1).

Walker, P. (2007). *The vexed issue of MBA league tables.* CNN World Business. Retrieved April 23, 2008, from http://edition.cnn.com/2007/BUSINESS/04/10/execed.news/

Walker, T., & Donohue, C. (2004, July). Decoding technology: E-tools for teacher education & professional development. *Child Care Information Exchange.* Retrieved April 23, 2008, from www.childcareexchange.com

Wall, D. S. (2005). The Internet as a conduit for criminal activity. In A. Pattavina (Ed.), *Information technology and the criminal justice system* (pp. 78-94), Thousand Oaks, CA: Sage.

Walther, J. (2002). Research ethics in Internet-enables research: Human subjects issues and methodological myopia. *Ethcs and information Technology, 4*(3). Retrieved April 22, 2008, from http://www.nyu.edu/projects/nissenbaum/ethics_wal_full.html

Walther, J. B. (1992). Interpersonal effects in a computer-mediated interaction: A relational perspective. *Communication Research, 19*(1), 52-90.

Walther, J.B. (1996). Computer-mediated communication: Impersonal, interpersonal and hyperpersonal interaction. *Communication Research, 23*(1), 3-43.

Wan Mohd, F. W. I. (2004). Still pictures and audio: Second class multimedia elements? *Malaysian Online Journal of Instructional Technology, 1*(1). Retrieved April 22, 2008, from http://pppjj.usm.my/mojit/articles/html/Wanfauzy.htm

Ward, D. A., & Beck, W. L. (1990). Gender and dishonesty. *The Journal of Social Psychology, 130,* 333-339.

Warnken, P. (2004). Academic original sin: Plagiarism, the Internet, and librarians. *The Journal of Academic Librarianship, 30*(3), 237-242.

Warschauer, M. (1997, Winter). Computer-mediated collaborative learning: Theory and practice. *The Modern Language Journal, 81*(4), 470-481.

Warschauer, M. (1998, March). Online learning in sociocultural context. *Anthropology & Education Quarterly, 29*(1), 68-88.

Warschauer, M. (2000, Autumn). The changing global economy and the future of English teaching. *TESOL Quarterly, 34*(3). TESOL in the 21st Century (pp. 511-535).

Washburn, J. H., & Petroshius, S. M. (2004). A collaborative effort at marketing the university: Detailing a student-centred approach. *Journal of Education for Business,* 35-40.

Waskul, D., & Douglass, M. (1996). Considering the electronic participant. Some polemical observations on the ethics of on-line research. *The Information Society, 12*(2), 129-139. Retrieved April 22, 2008, from http://venus.soci.niu.edu/~jthomas/ethics/tis/go.dennis

Watkins, M. (2007). Thwarting desire: Discursive constraint and pedagogical practice. *International Journal of Qualitative Studies in Education, 20*(3), 301-318.

Watson, D. (2006). The university and civic engagement. *Ad-lib: Journal for Continuing Liberal Adult Education, 31,* 2-6. University of Cambridge Institute of Continuing Education, Cambridge.

Watt, L. (1929). *Capitalism and morality.* London: Cassell & Co.

Waugh, R. F., Godfrey, J. R., Evans, E. D., & Craig, D. (1995). Measuring students' perceptions about cheating in six countries. *Australian Journal of Psychology, 47*(2), 73-82.

Webb, N.M. (1982). Group composition, group interaction and achievement in small groups. *Journal of Educational Psychology, 74*(4), 475-484.

Weckert, J., & Adeney, D. (1997). *Computer and information ethics.* Westport, CT: Greenwood Press.

Wein, E. (1994). *Cheating: Risking it all for grades.* Retrieved April 16, 2008, from http://wildcat.arizona.edu/papers/old-wildcats/fall94/December/December2,1994/03_1_m.html

Wellens, R. A. (1986). Use of a psychological distancing model to assess differences in telecommunication media. In L. A. Parker & O. H. Olgren (Eds.), *Teleconferencing and electronic communication* (pp. 347-361). Madison, WI: University of Wisconsin Extension.

Wellman, B., & Hampton, K. (1999, November). Living networked on and offline. *Contemporary Sociology, 28*(6), 648-654.

Welton, M. R. (1995). Introduction. In M. R. Welton (Ed.), *In defense of the Lifeworld: Critical perspectives on adult learning* (pp. 1-10). Albany: State University of New York Press.

Wenger, E. (1997). *Communities of practice, learning memory and identity.* Cambridge: Cambridge University Press.

Wengert, R. (2001). Some ethical aspects of being an information professional. *Library Trends, 49*(3), 486-509.

Weston, A. (2007). *Creative problem-solving in ethics.* New York: Oxford University Press.

Whitaker, E. E. (1993). A pedagogy to address plagiarism. *College Teaching, 42,* 161-164.

Whitehead, A. N. (1949). *The aims of education and other essays.* New York: New American Library.

Whitley, B. E. (1998). Factors associated with cheating among college students: A review. *Research in Higher Education, 39*(3), 235-274.

Whitley, B. E., Jr., & Keith-Spiegel, P. (2001). *Academic dishonesty: An educator's guide.* Mahwah, NJ: Lawrence Erlbaum.

Wighting, M. J. (2006). Effects of computer use on high school students' sense of community. *The Journal of Educational Research, 99*(6), 371-379.

Wilcox, J.R., & Ebbs, S.L. (1992). The leadership compass: Values and ethics in higher education. *ASHE-ERIC Higher Education Report* (No. 1). Washington, DC: George Washington University.

Wilkins, H. (1991). Computer talk. *Written Communication, 8*(1), 56-78.

Williams, P., Nicholas, D., & Gunter, B. (2005). E-learning: What the literature tells us about distance education: An overview. *Aslib Proceedings, 57*(2), 109-122.

Wilson, G., & Stacey, E. (2004). Online interaction impacts learning: Teaching the teachers to teach online. *Australasian Journal of Educational Technology, 20*(1), 33-48.

Wilson, H. D. (2001, May). Informatics: New media and paths of data flow. *Taxon, 50*(2). Golden Jubilee, Part 4 (pp. 381-387).

Winn, W. (2002, May 23-25). What can students learn in artificial environments that they cannot learn in class? In *Paper presented at the 20ᵗʰ Anniversary Celebrations of the First International Symposium of the Open Education Faculty (AOF),* Anadolu University, Eskisehir, Turkey. Retrieved April 15, 2008, from http://aof20.anadolu.edu.tr/program.htm or from http://faculty.washington.edu/billwinn/papers/turkey.pdf

Wood, D., Bruner, J.S., & Ross, G. (1976). The role of tutoring in problem solving. *Journal of Child Psychology and Psychiatry, 17*, 89-100.

Woodbury, M. C. (2003). *Computer and information ethics.* IL, USA: Stipes.

Woodley, A. (1987). Understanding adult student dropout. In M. Thorpe & D. Grugeon (Eds.), *Open learning for adults.* Harlow, Essex: Longman.

Woodley, A., & Parlett, M. (1983). Student drop-out. *Teaching at a Distance, 24*, 2-23.

Woodley, A., De Lange, P., & Tanewski, G. (2001). Student progress in distance education: Kember's model revisited. *Open Learning, 16*(2), 113-131.

Woodman, R. (1999). *Investigation of factors that influence student retention and success rate on open university courses in the East Anglia region.* Unpublished masters dissertation, submitted to Sheffield Hallam University, UK.

Woodward, D. (1990). A framework for deciding issues in ethics. *Library Trends, 39*(1-2), 8-17.

Wright, J. C., & Kelly, R. (1974). Cheating: Student/Faculty views and responsibilities. *Improving College University Teaching, 22*, 31-34.

Yakuwa, J. (2006). Co-reflection in online learning: Collaborative critical thinking as narrative. *Computer-Supported Collaborative Learning. 1*, 203-228.

Yan, J., & Liu, Z. (2006). Development of, and trends in, scholarly communication in China. In H. S. Ching, P. W. T. Poon, & C. McNaught (Eds.), *E-learning and digital publishing* (pp. 195-219). Dordrecht: Springer-Verlag.

Yang, R. (2003). Globalization and higher education development: A critical analysis. *International Review of Education, 49*(3-4), 269-291.

Yang, S. (2001, March 14-17). Dilemmas of education reform in Taiwan: Internationalization or localization? In *Paper presented at the Annual Meeting of the Comparative and International Education Society*, Washington DC. ERIC Documents: ED 453137.

Yar, M. (2006). *Cybercrime and society.* London: Sage.

Yasuoka, K. (2004). The case study of the information ethics education by the Media Center. *Online Kensaku, 25*(3-4), 159-166.

Yi, J. (2006). Externalization of tacit knowledge in online environments. *Information Journal on E-learning. 5*(4), 663-674.

Yin, R. (2003). *Applications of case study research* (2nd ed). Thousand Oaks, CA: Sage.

Yin, R.K. (2003). *Case study research design and methods* (3rd ed.). London: Sage.

Yorke, M. (1999). *Leaving early.* London: Routledge-Falmer.

Zaiane, O. (2001). Web site mining for a better Web-based learning environment. In *Proceedings of the Computers and Advanced Technology in Education Conference.* Calgary: ACTA Press. Retrieved April 22, 2008, from http://www.cs.ualberta.ca/~zaiane/postscript/CATE2001.pdf

Zajkowski, M. (1997). Price and persistence in distance education. *Open Learning, 12*(1), 12- 23.

Zemblyas, M., & Vrasidas, C. (2005). Levinas and the "inter-face:" The ethical challenge of online education. *Educational Theory, 55*(1), 61-78.

Zheng, L., & Hui, S. (2005). Survey of professional ethics of teachers in institutions of higher education: Case study of an institution in central China. *Chinese Education & Society, 38*(5), 88-99.

Zimmer, B. (1995). The empathy templates: A way to support collaborative learning. In F. Lockwood (Ed.), *Open and distance learning today* (pp. 139-150). London: Routledge.

Zobel, J., & Hamilton, M. (2002). Managing student plagiarism in large academic departments. *Australian Universities Review, 45*(2), 23-30.

About the Contributors

Ugur Demiray holds the BA in the area of media studies at Anadolu University, faculty of communication sciences, Department of Cinema and Television, Eskisehir-Turkey, and also the PhD at Anadolu University, Social Sciences Graduate Institution, Department of Educational Communication Eskisehir-Turkey. He is currently working for Anadolu University. His research has dealt with distance education application at Anadolu University, Ministry of Education and by other universities in Turkey. He is interested in changing ethical behaviors around the world by inserting technological developments to the educational field, especially to the distance education applications, for 3 years. His interest also lies toward the profile of DE students, and the relationship of graduates and the job market. He has extensive experience publishing an e-journal on distance education internationally under the patronage of Anadolu University for 9 years, named, *TOJDE-Turkish Online Journal for Distance Education. The Turkish Online Journal of Distance Education (TOJDE)* is a peer-reviewed quarterly e-journal. International in scope, this scholarly e-journal publishes refereed articles focusing on the issues and challenges of providing theory, research and information services to global learners in any kind of distance education or open learning applications. *TOJDE* particularly strives to meet the continuing education needs of practitioners and educators by providing a forum for the discussion of extended learning strategies, policies and practices, and trends in information technology as they impact the delivery of student support services for distance learners and faculties. He is also an editor, consultant editor reviewer and book reviewer for more than 10 journals which deal with distance education, educational technology and on education fields around the world, such as *Quarterly Review of Distance Education (QRDE)*, editor, *Association for Educational Communication and Technology, Information Age Publishing*, Miami, USA; *The Turkish Online Journal of Educational Technology (TOJET)*, editor, Sakarya Universitesi, Turkey; Universite ve Toplum, Editor, Ankara, Turkey; *Open Education-The Journal for Open and Distance Education and Educational Technology*, editor, *Hellenic Network of Open and Distance Education*, Greece; Sınırsız Öğrenme Dergisi [*Journal of Learning Witout Frontiers*], Turkey; The *e-Journal of Instructional Science and Technology (e-JIST)*, editor, University of Southern Queensland; *Studies in Learning, Evaluation, Innovation and Development*, Central Queensland University, Australia; *The International Journal of Education and Development Using Information and Communication Technology (IJEDICT)*, The University of the West Indies, West Indies; *Malaysian Online Journal of Instructional Technology (MOJIT)*, editor, Malaysian Educational Technology Association (META), Malaysia; Anadolu Üniversitesi Sosyal Bilimler Dergisi [*Anadolu University Journal of Social Sciences*], Anadolu University; *EGITIM ARASTIRMALARI DERGISI (Eurasian Journal of Educational Research, EJER)*, Turkey; *Education and Progress eJournal-EPeJ*, associate editor, http://www.hamdan-edu.com, Syria; *Educational Research and Reviews*, associate editor, http://www.academicjournals.org/ERR; Ilorin *Jour-*

nal of Education, University of Ilorin, Conusulting Editor, http://www.ijeunilorin.net/editorial_board.php. In addition, he has responsibilities on Advisory, the Scientific Board and Referee on conferences, symposiums and panels. He has co-authored and individually contributed chapters in some Turkish and international books as well.

Ramesh Sharma holds a PhD in education in the area of educational technology and is currently working as Regional Director in Indira Gandhi National Open University (IGNOU). He has been a teacher trainer and taught Educational Technology, Educational Research and Statistics, Educational Measurement and Evaluation, Special Education, Psychodynamics of Mental Health Courses for the B.Ed. and M.Ed. programmes. He has conducted many human development training programmes for the in- and pre-service teachers. He had established a Centre of ICT in the college he was working. He is a member of many committees on the implementation of technology in the open university. His areas of specialization include staff development, online learning, student support services in open and distance learning, and teacher education. He is a member of the Advisory Group meeting on Human Resources Development for the United Nations Conference on Trade and Development (UNCTAD). He is the Co-editor of the *Asian Journal of Distance Education*, ISSN 1347-9008, (www.ASIANJDE.org). In addition to this, he is/has been on the Editorial Advisory Board of Distance Education, International Review of Research in Open and Distance Learning, and the Turkish Online Journal of Distance Education Technologies (IJDET-published by IGI Global). He has co-authored one book on distance education research. IGI-Global has published his books Interactive Multimedia in Education and Training and Cases on Global E-learning Practices: Successes and Pitfalls (Co-editor Dr. Sanjaya Mishra). He is also on the Advisory Board Member and author for the Encyclopedia of Distance Learning (http://www.idea-group.com/encyclopedia/details.asp?ID=4500&v=editorialBoard).

* * *

Yavuz Akbulut is an instructor and PhD candidate at the Department of Computer Education and Instructional Technologies at Anadolu University. Prior to his joining Anadolu University, he worked at Boğaziçi University (Istanbul, Turkey) as a research and teaching assistant, at Marmara University (Istanbul, Turkey) as a part-time lecturer, and at Old Dominion University (Virginia, USA) as a graduate research assistant. He has an MA in English language education with emphasis on the use of computers in second language teaching. He has been teaching undergraduate courses, including Statistic Applications in Computer, Applications of Instructional Technology and New Learning Systems in Organizations. He conducts research on ICT integration at tertiary education, cyber-plagiarism, academic obsolescence and computer assisted language learning.

Terry Anderson is professor and Canada Research Chair in Distance Education at Athabasca University, Canada's Open University. He has published widely in the area of distance education and educational technology and has co-authored or edited five books and numerous papers. Terry is active in provincial, national, and international distance education associations and a regular presenter at professional conferences. He teaches educational technology courses in Athabasca's Masters of Distance Education program. Terry is also the director of CIDER, the Canadian Institute for Distance Education Research (cider.athabascau.ca) and the editor of the International Review of Research on Distance and Open Learning (IRRODL, www.irrodl.org). The complete text of his most recent edited book, The Theory and Practice of Online Learning, is available as an Open Access resource at cde. athabascau.ca/online_book. More information is available on his Web site at http://cider.athabascau. ca/Members/terrya.

Michael F. Beaudoin, EdD is professor of education at the University of New England, (Maine, USA), where he was previously founding dean of a new college. He is recognized for designing and directing innovative projects, including several successful distance education programs. He has held senior administrative positions and faculty appointments at several institutions in the U.S. and abroad, and has been a visiting scholar at institutions in Germany and China, and a Fulbright scholar in Ghana. With over 75 publications and presentations, including two books, he has written extensively in the field of distance education and related areas, presents frequently at conferences, and serves as an evaluator and consultant for distance education programs and courses.

Peter Bemski is currently working as the assistant dean, graduate programs, College for Professional Studies, Regis University. He has, since 1999, worked closely with the dean, program chairs and faculty on the design and delivery of faculty orientation, faculty assessment, professional development, new program development, and curriculum updates. He also works with strategic partners such as ITESO University, analyzes program budgets and data on issues such as student retention; conducts outcome assessment, and participates in university governance by service on numerous academic and administrative committees. In the past few years, Dr. Bemski has presented both nationally and internationally on a variety of topics, including leadership, ethics in teaching and organizational identity. Dr. Bemski has excellent intercultural skills, including extensive for-profit and non-profit administrative experience and speaks Portuguese, Spanish and French. Immediately before coming to Regis University, Dr. Bemski was a consultant working on such international projects as the E900 Center in Qingdao, China, and an Action English Center in Kissimmee, Florida, which involved Brazilian private party ownership. Prior to that, Dr. Bemski was the President of English Pathways, a wholly owned subsidiary of Teikyo University, Center Director for ESL Denver, and Associate Director of Centro de Cultura Anglo-Americana in Rio de Janeiro, Brazil. He earned his PhD in education leadership and innovation at the University of Colorado at Denver, MA in English literature at Boston College at Massachusetts, and BA in English literature at the University of Colorado at Boulder.

Dele Braimoh is a professor and UNESCO Chair of Open and Distance Learning at the University of South Africa (UNISA) where he heads a new Institute for Open & Distance Learning. He was, for 15 years, a professor of adult and distance education at the National University of Lesotho, where he was the founding coordinator of the part-time BEd degree in adult education and the MEd programme in adult and distance education, both of which are now being offered on a distance learning mode. He was also for about 2 years with the University of Zululand, South Africa, as professor and deputy project leader for a cooperatives programme, a new academic cum professional development initiative as a collaborative venture between the KwaZulu Natal Provincial Government and the University of Zululand. A well travelled scholar, professor Braimoh holds a PhD in adult education and belongs to many reputable professional associations world wide. His special research interest areas include: adult, distance and continuing education, higher education policy and management, community education and rural development, research design and methodology, including development communication.

J. S. Dorothy is currently working as an assistant regional director in the regional Centre of the Indira Gandhi National Open University at Chennai. She had also worked in the same capacity at the Regional Centre at Jaipur and Bangalore. After completing the master of science and master of philosophy in food and nutrition, she had also completed the master of arts in public administration and distance education. Her special areas of interest in research include student support services and management and quality control in dual mode institution.

Patrick J. Fahy is a professor in the Centre for Distance Education, Athabasca University, Canada, where he has worked for over 11 years. His research interests include interaction analysis, and the problems experienced by students and professional researchers in conducting research in online learning contexts. He has served two terms as chairman of his university's Research Ethics Board (REB), and is currently a member of the Research Ethics Appeal Board, Athabasca University.

Lesley Farmer, professor at California State University, Long Beach, coordinates the Library Media Teacher program. She earned her MS in library science at the University of North Carolina Chapel Hill, and received her doctorate in adult education from Temple University. Dr. Farmer has worked as a teacher-librarian in K-12 school settings (independent single-sex and public co-ed) as well as in public, special and academic libraries. A frequent presenter and writer for the profession, Dr. Farmer's most recent books include *Librarians, Literacy and the Promotion of Gender Equity* (McFarland, 2005) and *Digital Inclusion, Teens, and Your Library* (Libraries Unlimited, 2005). Her research interests include information literacy, collaboration, and educational technology.

Deb Gearhart recently became the director of E-Campus for Troy University. Previously, Deb served as the founding director of E-Education Services at Dakota State University in Madison, South Dakota, and was there for the 11 years. Before joining Dakota State, she spent 10 years with the Department of Distance Education at Penn State. Deb is an associate professor for educational technology at Dakota State University, teaching at both the undergraduate and graduate levels. She has co-authored at textbook entitled *Designing and Developing Web-Based Instruction*. Dr. Gearhart has a BA in sociology from Indian University of Pennsylvania. She earned a MEd in adult education with a distance education emphasis and an MPA in public administration, both from Penn State. Deb completed her PhD program in education, with a certificate in distance education, from Capella University.

Shalin Hai-Jew has been teaching in e-learning since the late 1990s through WashingtonOnline (WAOL). She has BAs in English and psychology, and an MA in English from the University of Washington (Seattle); she has a doctorate in educational leadership/public administration from Seattle University, where she was a Morford Scholar. Her doctoral dissertation (2005) is about the role of trust in online instructor-led learning. She works as an instructional designer for Kansas State University and writes as Eruditio Loginquitas for the Instructional Design Open Studio (IDOS) blog, which she founded in February 2006. She lived and worked in the People's Republic of China from 1988-1990 and 1992-1994, with the latter 2 years in the United Nations Development Programme (UNDP) as a UN volunteer. She taught at Jiangxi Normal University (Nanchang, Jiangxi Province) and Northeast Agriculture University (Harbin, Heilongjiang Province) while there.

Donna Harper is a senior lecturer at Liverpool Hope University. Her research interests are in areas related to business ethics and corporate social responsibility (CSR) with a particular interest in CSR and small and medium sized organizations. Donna Harper is a member of the Christ College–Liverpool Hope University Institute of Business, Management and Leadership. Donna is also a fellow of the Higher Education Academy in the UK.

Rod St Hill is a professor and the foundation Dean of Students at the University of Southern Queensland (USQ). He has previously been associate dean (academic) and dean, faculty of business at USQ. An economist by training, he has taught and published in the areas of development economics and macroeconomics. In recent years, he has focused on learning and teaching in economics and has published a number of papers in this area. Rod has a particular interest in the design of distance education learning resources that cater for a diversity of student learning modalities.

Heather Kanuka is a Canada research chair (e-learning) and associate professor at Athabasca University's Centre for Distance Education. Her areas of research focus include educational technology, philosophy of technology and technological determinism. Her current research focuses on the impact of the Internet in higher education settings and on extending the understanding of changes that occur in learning experiences as a result of using Internet technology as a communication medium. Prior to her appointment at Athabasca University, Dr. Kanuka was associate director of the Learning Commons, University of Alberta. The Learning Commons provides services to the university community for faculty development in teaching and learning, distance delivery and multimedia and video production. Dr. Kanuka's research on e-learning has focused the need for Canadian administrators and policy makers to monitor closely transformations resulting from advances in Internet technologies in order to better understand the technological drivers of change and possible ensuing consequences on the learning process, with a particular focus on issues relating to the reshaping of institutional barriers, learner support, and transformations of teaching practices within the Canadian context. Higher education in Canada is moving into a third decade of profound changes in how courses and programs are designed and delivered resulting from the increased integration of Internet communication technologies into the learning process. Many new possibilities have become apparent, but also many new challenges. Dr Kanuka's research has revealed that existing and emerging Internet technologies are having intense, immediate, and disruptive transformations on Canadian higher education institutions, and nowhere is the impact felt more than on the academic staff who teach with Internet communication technologies.

Paul Kawachi, professor, has been teaching at universities in Japan for more than 25 years. He holds a doctorate in education, three master's degrees and several teaching diplomas with distinction. He is a fellow of the British Institute of English Language Teaching, and a fellow of the Asian Society of Open and Distance Education. He has recently graduated (July 2007) in advanced technologies for education from the University of West Georgia, with Grade A distinctions in all modules. Earlier, he graduated from the UK Open University, Institute of Educational Technology, with a master's in open and distance education, and won the Gold Medal for his research from the Asian Association of Open Universities. He is editor of the *Asian Journal of Distance Education*, and on the editorial board of many others. He is a founding member of the International Society for the Scholarship of Teaching and Learning, and elected Board Director of International Professors for volunteer teaching in developing countries.

He is Director of a TOEIC regional open programme. His research interests are in third-generation instructional design (ID3) and how this facilitates lifelong learning (3L), English language teaching with internationally accredited licenses to teach other teachers at all levels either face-to-face or online, teacher professional development, cognitive learning theories (especially lifelong learning and adult learning theories), educational psychology, and learning technologies (especially when applied across cultures). Contact: kawachi@open-ed.net. He does international consultancy on curriculum design and e-learning, most recently through agents for the Government of Pakistan, and for Saudi Arabia, as well as for Blackboard.com. He is widely published in books and leading international journals.

David M. Kennedy has nearly 3 decades of teaching experience. His responsibilities in the faculty of education at the University of Hong Kong (HKU) involve teaching about using information and communication technologies (ICTs) for learning, and researching (design, development and evaluation) e-learning and m-learning environments, including Web 2.0 applications. He has presented invited seminars and workshops in Hong Kong, the UK, Finland, Canada, Australia, South Africa and Mauritius. He is on the editorial boards of the Journal of Multimedia and Hypermedia and the International Journal of Teaching and Learning in Higher Education (IJTLHE). Further details may be found at http://www. cite.hku.hk/people/dkennedy/DMK/dmk0.html.

Ashwini Kumar is presently working as deputy director at the Vranasi Regional Center (Uttar Pradesh) of Indira Gandhi National Open University. His doctoral work is based on an exhaustive survey on status, effectiveness, suitability, and impact of electronic media in distance education from the perspective of learners and functionaries, namely faculties, counselors and coordinators of open universities in India. Besides, he has several research papers and book chapters to his credit. He also had a distinguished academic career and received many scholarships at national level during his studies.

Abdullah Kuzu is a faculty member and the deputy head of the Department of Computer Education and Instructional Technologies at Anadolu University. He has an MA in German language education and a PhD in educational technology. He has offered several courses at the undergraduate level, including Information and Communication Technologies in Teacher Education, Authoring Languages, Internet Applications in Education, and Database Applications in Internet Environment. He offers graduate courses including Research Problems in Instructional Technologies, Statistical Methods in Education, Multimedia Design and Implementation, and Distance Education Theory and Applications. He has supervised several dissertations, published in both national and international, peer-reviewed periodicals, supervised and actively took part in national and international research projects, and prepared educational software. He mostly conducts action research on several aspects of instructional technology, including Web-based training, mobile learning, multimedia learning, and computer ethics.

Chi Lo Lim is an associate professor of management in Northwest Missouri State University. She received her DBA in strategic management from Alliant International University (Formerly United States International University). She has published in the *Southwestern Business Administration Journal, International Journal of Learning* and *Teaching in Higher Education, Journal of Business* and *Leadership: Research, Practice and Teaching*, and *Journal of Learning in Higher Education*. Her current research interests include distance education, team effectiveness, academic integrity, and corporate governance.

Petra Luck is the award director of the online BA Early Years Management at Liverpool Hope University. Research interests are gender and professionalisation in the Early Years sector, gender and management and online learning. Petra Luck is a fellow of the Higher Education Academy in the UK, member of the European Distance and E-learning network (EDEN) and member of the British Academy of Management (BAM). Petra Luck has also project-managed a European funded initiative aimed at improving work-based learning in the Early Years sector through the use of online technology.

Rocci Luppicini, PhD, is a replacement professor in the Department of Communication at the University of Ottawa in Canada. He has published in a number of areas including virtual learning communities and practice (*Quarterly Review of Distance Education*), research methodology on online instruction (*Journal of Distance Education*), issues in higher education, instructional design (*Canadian Journal of Learning and Technology*), and design research (*International Journal of Technology and Design Education*). His most recent book is an edited volume entitled *Online Learning Communities in Education* (Information Age Publishing, 2007).

Carmel McNaught is director and professor of learning enhancement in the Centre for Learning Enhancement and Research (CLEAR) at The Chinese University of Hong Kong. Carmel has had several decades experience in teaching and research in higher education in universities in Australasia and Southern Africa, working in the discipline areas of chemistry, science education, second language learning, e-learning, and higher education curriculum and policy matters. Current research interests include evaluation of innovation in higher education, strategies for embedding learning support into the curriculum, and understanding the broader implementation of the use of technology in higher education. Further details at http://www.cuhk.edu.hk/clear/staff/staff7.htm.

Judy Nagy is a graduate of Melbourne University, completing her PhD at the University of Wollongong, and is currently working at Deakin University's postgraduate Business School. Judy commenced her career in industry with 10 years business experience, initially at Pricewaterhouse, followed by a period in a major Australian company. She has experience in auditing, management accounting, financial accounting and government auditing. Her primary research interests are shared between comparative business issues between government and the commercial sectors, and the scholarship of teaching, with a particular interest in online learning.

H. Ferhan Odabasi is a faculty member and the head of the Department of Computer Education and Instructional Technologies at Anadolu University, Turkey. She has an MA in English language education and a PhD in educational technology. She has offered several undergraduate courses on English language education, and both undergraduate and graduate courses on educational technology. She has supervised several PhD dissertations, published in both national and international peer-reviewed periodicals, supervised and actively took part in national and international research projects, and prepared educational software. She developed "Hypervocab" with Steve Neufeld, and received the European Academic Software Award: Best Software in the Field of Language. She conducts research on missionary-parental awareness on Internet and visionary-professional development of higher education educators, with a particular emphasis on computer ethics and academic obsolescence.

Osiki Jonathan Ohiorenuan holds BEd, MEd and doctorate degrees in education and education guidance and counseling (i.e., educational/counseling/clinical psychology), University of Ibadan, Nigeria. Widely traveled, he has had quite a number of published articles to his credit; and presently, awaits the announcement for his associate professor (2006) position. He has held various positions, some of which include the director of the Counselling Unity, and deputy dean, both of the faculty of education, University of Ibadan Nigeria, and a member of the University of Ibadan Senate. He is presently employed at the National University of Lesotho, Southern Africa, where he facilitates the Clinical Pastoral Care and Counselling Programme. His research interest is in the development, validation and application of psychotherapeutic packages for assessing human psychopathology and for improving professional behaviour and academic performance in education and the distance learning programme. The main focus of his research centers on the clinical and overall assessment of the multifactor affecting learners' potentials in the achievement of sustainable standard of academic performance with consistent improved school grades. Over the years, different psychological packages (i.e., the Multi-diagnostic Academic Performance Inventory for Students-MAPIS, the Academic Achievers' Selectory for African Subjects-AASAS; Proto-type Practicum Case report Guide (PPCRG); among others, that have been identified, developed, validated and applied in ameliorating the difficult academic condition of learners while simultaneously, boosting outcome in educational settings. Precisely, the research effort is directed at ascertaining how counseling psychotherapeutic strategies can be used to assess and foster effective study behavioural patterns among learners, improve their school grades and ultimately, enhance academic achievement.

Tina Parscal is the assistant director of distance education in Regis University's School for Professional Studies. In this capacity, she designs, directs, and facilitates training and professional development for online faculty and faculty teaching with technology. Dr. Parscal also teaches graduate courses in education and technology. She has consulted internationally in distance learning, online instructional design, and online facilitation. She has published in the areas of online teaching and learning and is currently researching cognitive apprenticeship strategies for faculty development. Prior to her work with Regis University, Dr. Parscal served as the academic dean of a small, private online university. She earned her PhD in education at Capella University, master of social sciences at the University of Colorado at Denver, and BA in psychology and sociology at Regis College.

Glenn Russell spent nearly 20 years teaching in country and suburban schools in Victoria, Australia, before joining Griffith University, Queensland, where he received his doctorate in 1998. He has developed an international reputation in virtual schooling, cyberspace, educational uses of hypertext, and ethics in distance education. Since 1999, he has been part of the faculty of education at Monash University, in Victoria, Australia, where he teaches undergraduate and graduate classes in ICTE. His current research involves ethical uses of information and communications technology in school and university education, educational futures in globalized environments, and responsibilities in online schools. He is particularly interested in ways that schooling may change in response to new uses of information and computer technologies in education (ICTE). He is one of the joint authors of *Finger, Russell, Jamieson-Proctor, and Russell* (2007), *Transforming Learning with ICTs—make IT Happen!*, and *French's Forest: Pearsons Australia*.

Michael Sankey is a senior lecturer in the Learning and Teaching Support Unit at the University of Southern Queensland (USQ). He specialises in the areas of e-learning pedagogies, multimodal and Web design, visual and multiliteracies. His research focuses on the multiple representation of concepts when utilising multimedia technologies, and how the use of hybridized electronic environments can enhance learning opportunities for students, particularly for those studying at a distance. With a background in art and design, he is passionate about the ways in which aesthetically-enhanced learning environments can better transmit concepts to students of all backgrounds.

Ormond Simpson is senior lecturer in institutional research, UK Open University, having previously worked in the OU's student support area. Before the OU, he worked in universities in Africa, the U.S. and in the UK. His interests are in distance student support and retention, and he has written two books, *Supporting Students in Online Open and Distance Learning* and *Student Retention in Online Open and Distance Learning*, both with Taylor and Francis. He has also written more than 30 journal articles and has recently been a consultant on student support in the Gambia, New Zealand, Korea, China, and Papua New Guinea.

Alan Tait is pro-vice chancellor for curriculum and awards at the Open University, UK, and was formerly dean of the faculty of education and language studies. He is professor of distance education and development and has a long record of professional practice, publication and the support of professional development in distance and e-learning. He is editor in chief of the *European Journal of Distance and E-Learning (EURODL)*, and co-director of the Cambridge International Conference on Open and Distance Learning. He has worked widely in developing countries for international organisations such as UNESCO, the European Commission and the Commonwealth of Learning, and is currently president of the European Distance and E-learning Network (EDEN).

Index